# Nations and States

*Hugh Seton-Watson*

# Nations and States

An Enquiry into the Origins of Nations
and the Politics of Nationalism

*Westview Press*
*Boulder, Colorado*

*Copyright © 1977 by Hugh Seton-Watson*

*Published in 1977 in the United States of America by*
  *Westview Press, Inc.*
  *1898 Flatiron Court*
  *Boulder, Colorado 80301*
  *Frederick A. Praeger, Publisher and Editorial Director*

Library of Congress Cataloging in Publication Data

Seton-Watson, Hugh.
  Nations and states.

  Includes bibliographical references.
  1. Nationalism—History.  I. Title.
D32.S47          320.5'4          77-4237
ISBN 0-89158-227-4

Printed and bound in the United States of America

# M.H.S-W.

dilectissimae
laborum et gaudiorum
participi

Ganz vergessener Völker Müdigkeiten
Kann ich nicht abtun von meinen Lidern
Noch weghalten von der erschrockenen Seele
Stummes Niederfallen ferner Sterne

# Contents

# Preface

This book is the result not only of a few years of intensive study and writing, but of a large part of a lifetime spent trying to understand this force of nationalism which has continued to shake the world in which I have lived. I must therefore begin with a bit of autobiography.

I was made aware at a very early age of the existence of nations. My first national symbol was King Robert and the spider. Starting my formal education in a French school, I imbued some of the mythology of Vercingétorix, St. Louis and the Chevalier Bayard, before making the acquaintance at my first English school of King Alfred and his cakes. My father was considerably involved in the emergence of new states in Central Europe, and not only the names but some of the actors in those events became familiar household figures. The text-books from which I learnt modern European History had been written by men who both hoped and believed, in the age of Wilsonian liberalism, that the liberty of the citizen and the liberty of the nation were inseparable.

In my penultimate year at school Adolf Hitler became Chancellor of the country which he was to rename the Third Reich. Immediately after leaving school I had my first direct experience of the Third Reich and of the Germans as people. In the following years I visited countries to the south and east of Germany, and the more I saw the less it seemed to me that the claims of nationalists and the rights of individuals could easily be reconciled. Believing that nationalism, which provided the hard core of the fascist movements which pullulated in those lands in those times, was a menace to both liberty and peace, I put my faith in internationalism, and looked for a better future to socialism. No wiser nor more foolish than thousands of my compatriots, though worried by the Ribbentrop-Molotov treaty, I admired Soviet Russia both as the ally which bore the main burden of fighting after 1941, and as a socialist state. It was the news from 'liberated' Eastern Europe after 1944, and personal observation of the implications of 'liberation' on the spot in 1946 and 1947, which destroyed these illusions, which were no less remote from reality than had been the Wilsonian illusions which preceded them. In the last thirty years a multitude of crimes have been committed in the name of socialism by

*xi*

persons whom the historical pioneers of socialism would have been loth to recognise as their disciples.

As I have gone on studying nationalism, and travelled from time to time in Europe, the Muslim world and North America, with occasional shorter journeys still further afield, it has become ever clearer to me, both that injustices and conflicts between classes and between nations remain bitter realities, and that so far neither nationalists nor socialists—nor indeed any one else—have found answers to them. Nations exist; conflicts between nations exist; nationalists in power often do violence to the human rights of their subjects; and attempts to abolish national loyalties, even when ostensibly pursued in the name of higher human solidarity, do not achieve their object, but do increase the sum total of explosive human hatred in the world.

All this has convinced me that merely to inveigh against nationalism does little to help the human race. It now seems to me more desirable to spare denunciations and rather to seek understanding and compassion for the longings and the frailties alike of human individuals and of nations.

Nationalism has been a pressing and dangerous force throughout my lifetime; but it has had its roots in historical processes going far back into the past. To study nationalism, one must be interested in politics, sociology and history. The impression which I had already as an undergraduate, that it is impossible to draw a clear line of demarcation between 'social' and 'national' or between 'national' and 'international' problems, and that past and present are quite inextricably bound up with each other, has been strengthened by almost everything that I have learnt or seen in the intervening years. When social scientists stress the need to compare phenomena which may have points of similarity; and when historians insist on the absolute uniqueness of every historical event; I find myself agreeing with both. The either-or-ism which dogmatically rejects all comparison, or which dismisses uniqueness as unimportant, seems to me the mark of the barbarian; and barbarians are to be found within all academic 'disciplines'. Both the comparable and the unique exist: the searcher after truth must struggle always to keep them in balance, knowing that he will never be entirely successful. If this were generally accepted, we could be spared a great deal of *odium academicum*.

I have not sought in this work to elaborate any general theory of nationalism. I have learnt much from modern pioneers in this field, such as Anthony Smith and Karl Deutsch;[1] but I have not tried to follow their paths. I have also not sought either to analyse nationalism as a doctrine, or to collect samples of nationalist rhetoric. My concern is rather with the formation of nations, the activities of nationalist movements, and the ways in which these have influenced and been influenced by the emergence, creation and dissolution of states. In this field too there is already a large literature; and I owe more than I can ever acknowledge to my many predecessors, among whom the two outstanding seem to me Hans Kohn and Eugen Lemberg. I do not think however that I am treading precisely in the footsteps of any of them. I have tried to do something much less than to create a general theory, namely to juxtapose and to compare examples from different periods and different parts of the world.

Nationalist movements have been an outstanding feature of the international landscape in my time, and seem likely so to remain for many years yet. They are a world-wide phenomenon. My aim has been to contribute to understanding them—that is, both to explain the phenomenon to my contemporaries who are dimly aware that they are affected by it, and to provide some material and some guidance to those who intend to explore the phenomenon in depth. In this book a number of historical examples are presented, some covering a few decades and others reaching back over centuries. The facts contained in my brief case histories are easily discoverable elsewhere, but they have not all been set side by side previously in one book. It is my purpose to enable, and indeed persuade, persons who are familiar with some or many of these cases to look at others with which they are not familiar. The facts have been selected because it has seemed to me that they are the most significant from the point of view of the processes with which I am concerned: formation of national consciousness, movements for national independence, movements for national unity and formation of nations through action by the state. Each section of each chapter is concerned with one or more of these processes in relation to the nation or state under consideration. No single section is, or was intended to be, a summary of the history of any nation or of any state. Any other person than myself would have included much that I have left out, and left out much that I have put in. But one has to make one's own choice.

Profoundly convinced as I am that modern nationalist movements are a world-wide phenomenon, I have felt that I cannot shirk the obligation to look at movements all over the world. This means that I cannot confine myself to nations whose countries, languages and cultures are familiar to me. My own experience as a reader of other people's books has been that the method of the symposium, in which individual experts on particular aspects of a problem, or on particular regions of the world, contribute separate chapters, is seldom successful; and that the view of a single mind, even if incomplete and distorted, can sometimes have the virtue of unity. It is my hope that my efforts may contribute something to the understanding of the phenomena of nations, states and nationalist movements, and that they may stimulate others whose personal combinations of experience and knowledge are different from mine, to try their hand in turn at an overall one-mind view, and so correct and improve on my work, and thus provoke others in turn to correct and improve on theirs.

Though this book is long, I have tried not to make it wordy. I have sought to marshall my arguments, facts and hypotheses without embellishment. The reader may find my narrative bald, though I must hope not unconvincing. I can assure him or her that the underlying emotion is not cold. I have been mindful throughout my labours of the men and women, the lands, artefacts and cultures which have deeply affected my sight and thought, whether or not this becomes apparent in my words. Scenes and conversations, crowds and solitudes, the cruel fate of friends and the survival of others, ancient ruins in four continents, medieval cities in three and mountains and forests in five, jostle together in my memory, and lie beneath my drab prose, perhaps occasionally inserting a tongue of flame through a crack in its flat surface. To express all these emotions, to give thanks for all that I have seen, heard, learnt, forgotten or retained, is beyond my powers. Something of the resultant mood is contained within the lines from Hugo von Hofmannsthal which I have presumed to quote on another page.

I have read enough history to know that the interplay of personalities, institutions, ideas, impersonal forces and mere chance is exceedingly complex and infinitely variable, and this has caused me to distrust allegedly comprehensive and scientific theories. I am also painfully aware that history, still more than the natural sciences, needs and gets constant revision. It is hard enough to keep up with these revisions even in one's own specialised field: to do so on the scale of time and space with which this book is concerned, would surpass the ability even of a genius. Most of my readers will therefore have little difficulty in finding out-of-date interpretations in these pages. Even so, a little scepticism is in order about 'revolutionary' discoveries in historiography: often, when some years have passed since such historic break-throughs, the historical landscape, beheld from a certain distance, looks remarkably similar to that depicted by out-of-date predecessors. And is there a 'correct' distance for a view of history, any more than for a view of a city—Paris from the level of those hopeful fishermen on the banks of the Seine, or of the *bouquinistes* above them, or the tower of Notre Dame, or the steps of the Sacré Coeur, or an overflying jet at 30,000 feet?

My sources have been various. First is the printed word—historical documents and interpretative works, imaginative literature and periodical press. I have listed in the bibliography some of those works which have been most useful to me, and in which readers may find a wealth of further information should they wish it. A second source has been conversation, spread over at least forty years and nearly as many lands. Individual conversations may provide a smaller quantity of information than massive answers to distributed questionnaires, but they leave more vivid memories, and with luck and persistence can fairly often be checked against each other or against documents. A third source has been such travel as has come my way, in peace and in war, including countries in which I knew no indigenous people and could not read the newspapers. To see with one's own eyes not only buildings and paintings but also—perhaps still more— landscapes, can be no less conducive to understanding than to read books.

Conversion into Latin script of the names of persons or places in non-Latin languages always presents insuperable difficulties, and it is probably impossible to satisfy all specialists. Some names have acquired an English spelling which, though inaccurate, is widely accepted: in such cases it is this spelling which I have used. In most cases of East European languages I have adopted the accents or cedillas in use in their countries, but some exceptions have been made where special difficulties arose. The greatest difficulty has been with Arab and Chinese names. To use all the diacritical marks of orientalists seemed to me, rightly or wrongly, unsuitable for a book which claims no place in specialised orientalist literature. The *ad hoc* compromises between specialist usage, popular spelling and common sense to which I have resorted are of course open to valid objections. I hope however that the persons and places will be recognisable, and ask indulgence of the reader in view of the formidable complexity of the task.

I am most grateful to the Rockefeller Foundation for the weeks which I was able to spend at the Villa Serbelloni in Bellagio, in September 1971, when I embarked on the actual writing of the book, and to Mr. and Mrs. William Olson for ensuring such perfect conditions for the beginning of the enterprise. My gratitude is equally due to the Council of the School of Slavonic and East European Studies for study leave during the autumn term of 1975.

My friends Stephen Clissold and Peter Lyon read the whole of the text; and their comments, based on long experience and deep knowledge, were of great help to me. Many colleagues have been generous with their time, and both students and other audiences over the years have both stimulated and encouraged me. I remember with special affection my colleagues and students at Indiana University and the University of Washington. I should also like to express my appreciation to my publishers, and my personal gratitude to Antony Forster and Frederick Praeger for their support and confidence at a time when these were sorely needed.

Of my two greatest debts, one is to my father, most of whose active life was involved in these problems, and who aroused, sustained and deepened my interest in them; the other is noted on another page.

# 1  Nations and Nationalism

The object of this book is to examine the processes by which nations have been formed, the types of political movements which have sought to achieve what has been considered to be the national purpose, and the ways in which such movements have influenced and been influenced by the internal policies of states and the relations of states with each other.

The distinction between states and nations is fundamental to my whole theme. States can exist without a nation, or with several nations, among their subjects; and a nation can be coterminous with the population of one state, or be included together with other nations within one state, or be divided between several states. There were states long before there were nations, and there are some nations that are much older than most states which exist today. The belief that every state is a nation, or that all sovereign states are national states, has done much to obfuscate human understanding of political realities. A state is a legal and political organisation, with the power to require obedience and loyalty from its citizens. A nation is a community of people, whose members are bound together by a sense of solidarity, a common culture, a national consciousness. Yet in the common usage of English and of other modern languages these two distinct relationships are frequently confused.

In the United States the expression 'throughout the nation' simply means 'throughout the country'. In the main European languages the words 'international relations' and their equivalent are used to denote the relations between states. The organisation set up at the end of the Second World War with the hope of preventing war and promoting peace between states was called 'United Nations', and its predecessor had been called 'League of Nations'. But membership of both these organisations was confined in fact to governments of states. It was assumed in the age of President Wilson that states would embody nations; that the people of every state would form a nation; and that eventually, in the golden age of self-determination which was dawning, every nation would have its state. There were of course in 1918 many such states: the expression 'nation-state' in such cases reflected a reality. There were, however, many others, some of which became members of the League of Nations, of which this was not true. The rhetoric of Wilson was still used in the age of Roosevelt (a founding father of the United Nations, though he did not live to see it function). Many of the original members, and many who later joined it, were nation-states, but many of each category were not. The United Nations in fact has proved to be little more than a meeting place for representatives of Disunited States. The frequently heard cliché that 'we live in an age of nation-states' is at most a half-truth. What is arguably true is that we live in an age of sovereign states. Many people believe that state sovereignty is a major cause of international tension, and a potential cause of future wars; and that steps should be taken to diminish it. It is also often asserted that 'the age of the nation-state is coming to an end'. The truth is less simple; the problems of sovereignty and of nationalism, of states and of nations, are not the same. There have been times when the existence of state sovereignty has been a cause of war, and others when the aspirations of nations have led to war. There have been examples in recent times of diminution of state sovereignty, and it is quite possible that there will be a growing trend in this direction. But the disappearance of state sovereignties has not caused the disappearance of nations, any more than the creation of new state sovereignties has sufficed to create new nations. Whether nations *can* be destroyed is a subject for dispute.

Even more confusion commonly attaches to the word 'nationalism'. It is often used to denote any form of collective selfishness or aggressiveness of which the writer or speaker disapproves. It has become a pejorative term, used in contrast to the respectable word 'patriotism'. In fact, 'I am a patriot: you are a nationalist'.

Governments are often said to have 'nationalist' policies if they pursue their own interests at the expense of other governments. 'Economic nationalism' is the pursuit of the supposed economic interests of the people of one country, without regard for those of other peoples in other countries. Yet selfish regard for their own interests has been a feature of the policies of countless governments throughout history, long before nationalism or nations were heard of. Another misuse of the words 'national' and 'nationalism' relates to the collectivist policies of the governments of states. In the course of the last half-century governments, whether as a result of military or financial pressures or of the ideological convictions of their politicians, have intervened more and more in the economic activities and private lives of their citizens, have mobilised more and more their persons and their possessions. This trend was described in the French language by the useful word *étatisme*, which has no satisfactory equivalent in English. Seizure of property or of business enterprises by the state (*étatisation*) has been misleadingly rendered in English as 'nationalisation', and this word has also passed into French and other languages. It is misleading because the seized properties are in reality placed at the disposal not of the nation but of a dominant bureaucratic caste.

This book is concerned with nations and states, and only to a lesser extent with nationalism. Nevertheless the word and the phenomenon of 'nationalism' will frequently occur in the following pages, and it is necessary at the outset at least to give some indication of what I mean by it. As I see it, the word 'nationalism' has two basic meanings. It would greatly improve the clarity of individual and public thinking if the word could be shorn of all accretion, and confined to these two. One of these meanings is a doctrine about the character, interests, rights and duties of nations. The second meaning is an organised political movement, designed to further the alleged aims and interests of nations.

The two most generally sought aims of such movements have been independence (the creation of a sovereign state in which the nation is dominant), and national unity (the incorporation within the frontiers of this state of all groups which are considered, by themselves, or by those who claim to speak for them, to belong to the nation). In the case of many, though not of all, nations there has been a further task for nationalists: to build a nation within an independent state, by extending down to the population as a whole the belief in the existence of the nation, which, before independence was won, was held only by a minority.

I shall be concerned in this book overwhelmingly with the movements. I shall not rigidly limit discussion of movements to the pursuit of the three aims of independence, unity and nation-building, but they will occupy most of my attention. With the doctrine, or ideology, this book is hardly concerned at all. There are already many good books, both old and new, on this subject. As a doctrine, it is not very interesting, being essentially a variant of eighteenth century doctrines of popular sovereignty, with half-digested chunks of socialism added to the broth in the course of time. It has inspired immense outputs of rhetoric, and each brand has its own peculiarities, some of which must be admitted to be picturesque, though literary distinction and beauty are qualities which I should hesitate to attribute to them. The preparation of an anthology of nationalist rhetoric has not been part of the task which I have undertaken; but such anthologies exist, some with penetrating commentaries,[1] and readers whose main interest lies in that field would do well to study them.

All that has been said above assumes the use of the word 'nation', and this is much more difficult to explain. Many attempts have been made to define nations, and none have been successful. The most widely known without doubt is that of the late Joseph Stalin, whose work *Marxism and the National Question*, based on an article which he wrote at the request of Lenin in 1913, was later diffused in scores of languages in scores of millions of copies. All that Stalin could say was that a nation must have four characteristics: a common language, a common territory, a common economic life and a common mental make-up. No group which did not possess all four was entitled to be considered a nation. The fourth of these characteristics is of course vague. One may indeed strongly argue that vagueness is inherent in the phenomenon itself. But that is not an argument used by Stalin; on the contrary, he seems to have believed, and it was certainly claimed on his behalf by his disciples, that his four points provided a fully scientific definition. Stalin mentioned neither religion nor historical tradition. The truth is that Stalin's article was written not as a piece of social-political analysis, but as a polemic—arising out of the conditions of 1913, against the Jewish socialist movement, the *Bund*—intended to prove that the Jews were not a nation.[2]

Most definitions have in fact been designed to prove that, in contrast to the community to which the definer belonged, some other group was not entitled to be called a nation. The distinction between 'cultural nation' (a community united by language or religion or historical mythology or other cultural bonds) and 'political nation' (a community which in addition to cultural bonds also possesses a legal state structure) has at times been useful, but it too has often been misused for the purpose noted above.

In nineteenth century Central Europe a distinction was made between 'nations' and 'nationalities', the former being the superior category. 'My community is a nation: yours is a nationality'. Whole theories were based on this distinction, the purpose of which was to deny the status of nation to others. In later chapters I shall discuss the distinction at greater length. Apart from the sense mentioned, the word 'nationality' has, in the English language (more frequently in its British than in its American variant), the meaning of 'state citizenship' (*Staatsangehörigkeit* is the more precise German term). When I have occasion, in the following pages, to refer to this legal category, I shall use the unambiguous word 'citizenship'. There is, however, a third sense in which 'nationality' can be used: as a neutral and abstract word, meaning the quality of belonging to a nation. This is at times a useful concept, and it is the only sense in which I shall use it, without quotation marks, in the following pages.

Another distinction seems at first sight to have much to commend it: the distinction between 'nation' and 'tribe'. The word 'tribe' has usually been applied to comparatively small groups of people, with a rather low level of culture. Such were the tribes which the Romans met in Gaul and Germany (there was no Gaulish or Germanic 'nation'), or the groups, following various leaders, who spoke various Baltic or Slavonic or Turkic languages, and came into conflict with the Holy Roman, Byzantine and Abbasid empires. Other examples can be found among the various land invaders of India and China. The Scottish clans, and the septs into which they were divided, might also be considered to be 'tribes'; and something of the same sort could be found also in Ireland. In the nineteenth century European explorers, and the European administrators who followed in their steps, made frequent use of the word 'tribe' for African peoples. Most of these communities, scattered across the globe and the centuries, shared a fierce loyalty both to their chiefs and to fellow-members of the community. The difficulty is to decide at what point 'tribal consciousness' becomes 'national consciousness'. Those who use the word 'tribe' of others are usually convinced that they themselves belong to a higher culture and are looking at persons of a lower culture. Such was certainly the view of Romans and Chinese, and in modern times of European colonial officials. Yet arbitrary differentiation between 'nation' and 'tribe' closely resembles the differentiation between 'nation' and 'nationality' discussed above, and amounts to no more than that between 'my group' and 'your group'. In the independent new states of Africa, 'tribalism' has become a blanket term to cover, and to condemn, any sort of movement for autonomy, let alone separate statehood. Nevertheless, great differences in cultural level have existed, do exist, and are recognisable. Should one say that in 1900 the Yorubas were a nation, and the Dinkas a tribe? How can differences in the level of culture be measured, and who is an impartial judge? Because there are no clear answers to these questions, one has to be very cautious in the use of the words 'nation' and 'tribe'; yet the difference does exist, just as the difference in the spectrum between blue and green exists, though the colours merge in the human eye which beholds the rainbow.

Thus I am driven to the conclusion that no 'scientific definition' of a nation can be devised; yet the phenomenon has existed and exists. All that I can find to say is that a nation exists when a significant number of people in a community consider themselves to form a nation, or behave as if they formed one. It is not necessary that the whole of the population should so feel, or so behave, and it is not possible to lay down dogmatically a minimum percentage of a population which must be so affected. When a significant group holds this belief, it possesses 'national consciousness'. Common sense suggests that if this group is exceedingly small (let us say, less than one percent of the population), and does not possess great skill in propaganda, or a strong disciplined army to maintain it until it has been able to spread national consciousness down into much broader strata of the population, then the nationally conscious elite will not succeed in creating a nation, and is unlikely to be able to indefinitely remain in power on the basis of a fictitious nation.

It is hoped that these introductory remarks have served to indicate the nature of my subject; and that this will become clearer in the course of later chapters.

The doctrine of nationalism dates from the age of the French Revolution, but nations existed before the doctrine was formulated. Once the doctrine had been formulated, it was used as a justification for creating nationalist movements, and then sovereign states to encompass the lands in which it was claimed that nations lived.

The French revolutionaries, and their disciples outside France, zealously spread oversimplified versions of some of the ideas of the eighteenth century Enlightenment. In the revolutionary era a man who had a little education, setting him above the majority, felt himself both qualified and morally bound to translate his principles into political action. Government must now be based, not on the accidents of history and privilege, on institutions and hierarchies which had grown up in the past, but on rational principles, worked out in programmes and blueprints. Nationalism as a doctrine was derived from the eighteenth century notion of popular sovereignty. In France, when the hated old regime had been overthrown, power belonged to the nation, or to those who claimed to speak for it. It was obvious who were the French nation: France was populated by Frenchmen, and Frenchmen were not to be found outside France, though there were some thousands of people of French speech on the borders of Switzerland and Belgium. Beyond the Rhine and the Alps things were not so clear. The enemy, the old regime, was easily identifiable, but it was not obvious what should be the units in which popular sovereignty should be exercised. The answer increasingly given by the local converts to the new ideas was the German nation, or the Italian nation—not just the people of Hesse-Kassel or of Lucca.

Nationalist doctrine, as it developed in the Napoleonic era, had also another source, the cult of individuality, both personal and cultural. The German philosophers Fichte and Herder stressed the importance of language as the basis of nationality. Herder emphasised the divine diversity of the family of nations, the unique quality of each culture. His enthusiasm was by no means confined to the Germans: in a famous chapter on 'the Slavs' he idealised their moral and cultural qualities. Herder's ideas spread to the few educated persons among the smaller and more backward peoples of Central and Eastern Europe. Each group in turn felt more strongly that the community with which it identified itself was, or ought to be made into, a nation.

I shall make no attempt to summarise the ideas of the founding fathers of nationalist doctrine, or to trace their philosophic origins. This has been done by many writers, and perhaps best of all in a recent short master-piece.[3] It is, however, important to distinguish between two categories of nations, which we will call the old and the new. The old are those which had acquired national identity or national consciousness before the formulation of the doctrine of nationalism. The new are those for whom two processes developed simultaneously: the formation of national consciousness and the creation of nationalist movements. Both processes were the work of small educated political elites.

The old nations of Europe in 1789 were the English, Scots, French, Dutch, Castilians and Portuguese in the west; the Danes and Swedes in the north; and the Hungarians, Poles and Russians in the east. Of these, all but three lived in states ruled by persons of their nationality, and therefore needed no national independence movement; though this of course does not mean that these peoples did not suffer from various degrees of political or social oppression, and so, in the opinion of radicals and revolutionaries, 'needed' liberation. The three exceptions were the Scots, who since 1707 had shared a single state with the English and the Welsh, while preserving important institutions of their own; and the Hungarians and Poles, who were simply subjected to foreign rule. The Hungarians had at one time been divided between three states (the Habsburg Monarchy, the Ottoman empire and the **principality of Transylvania**), but at the end of the eighteenth century were all subject to the Habsburg Monarchy; whereas the Poles had been divided since 1795 between the kingdom of Prussia, the Russian empire and the Habsburg Monarchy. Thus, though Poles and Hungarians had a continuous national consciousness going back for several centuries, the continuity of the Polish and Hungarian sovereign states had been broken.

There were also at this time other communities in which there was, in the educated class, undoubted awareness of a cultural community and a long history, but in which the formation of national consciousness even in the elite was incomplete. Such were the Germans and Italians; perhaps also the Irish, Catalans and Norwegians.

In the rest of Europe there was little sign of national consciousness. In these lands, new nations were formed in the course of the following century, and this process was then extended, by educated elites influenced by European ideas, into the Muslim lands, southern and eastern Asia and sub-Saharan Africa. Nations of European origin also emerged in the colonies of settlement in America, South Africa and Australia.

The distinction between old and new nations seems more relevant than that between 'historical' and 'unhistorical', which came into use in Central Europe in the late nineteenth century. All nations have a history. Some of the communities in which, in 1789, national consciousness did not exist, or was still weak, had had long and brilliant histories—not only the Italians and Germans, but the Greeks and Bohemians and Serbs. However, continuity had been broken by conquest. The basic difference, then, is between old continuous nations and new nations; and it is of some importance for our theme.

The process of formation of national identity and national consciousness among the old nations was slow and obscure. It was a spontaneous process, not willed by any one, though there were great events which in certain cases clearly accelerated it.

In medieval Europe the word *natio* was in legal use, but it did not mean the same thing as the modern 'nation'. Many medieval universities attracted many students from other lands beside their own. These were placed in *nationes*, named after the territories from which the largest number of each originated, but including also persons from other countries.[4]

In Transylvania in the fifteenth century there were three *nationes* recognised by law, who were represented in the Transylvanian Diet: Hungarian, Székély and Saxon.[5] The Hungarian *natio* was confined to persons of noble status, but not to those of Hungarian speech. The Székély and Saxons, in contrast to the Hungarians, had no serfs in their community, and the whole population was to some extent represented.

Though the word *natio* thus varied in meaning, it and its derivatives in modern languages essentially comprised restricted categories. Separate words existed to describe the whole population: *populus*, *peuple*, *people*, *popolo* and *pueblo*. In the lands further east, however, as the ideas of the Enlightenment began to spread, this distinction became blurred. *Volk* in German, and *narod* in the Slav languages, soon came to combine the meanings of *natio* and *populus*, and such adaptations as *Nation* and *natsiya* were little used.[6]

In the case of those which I have called the 'old nations' a process took place of which it is difficult to pinpoint the stages, but of which the result is unmistakable. For example, in 1200 neither a French nor an English nation existed, but in 1600 both were important realities. At the first of these quite arbitrarily chosen dates, the countries now known as France and England were ruled by monarchs and noblemen who spoke the same language, had much the same outlook, and fought wars against each other because of conflicting claims to the territory, or joined each other in fighting the Muslims in the Crusades. Their subjects were mostly serfs, who had no part in public affairs, spoke in both countries a variety of languages, and were bound by duties toward their feudal superiors and the church. At the second date these traditional obligations had not disappeared, but the differences between the peoples of the two countries had enormously increased, while within both countries there was a much stronger and wider sense of community. Englishmen and Frenchmen recognised themselves as such; accepted obligations to the sovereign; and admitted the claim of the sovereign on their loyalty at least in part because the sovereign symbolised the community as a whole, stood for France, or for England. There were of course exceptions to this statement. There were still regions and social strata which had hardly been affected, yet the trend was unquestionable. During the intervening centuries larger sections of the population had been drawn upwards into public life, and the awareness of forming a community had spread downwards into the population. This was largely a matter of economic and social development, of growing trade, specialised manufactures, the rise of cities and the enrichment of merchants. Schools and learning began to flourish (though formal education still only affected a small minority), and the French and English languages became fixed by a growing literature, both religious and secular. This was, to use a modern term, a growth of communication, albeit restricted in scope. In this process geography, economics, language, religion, and the power of the state all played their part. The last was, on balance, the most important, for it was the growth of the monarchical power—of its military, fiscal and bureaucratic controls—which determined the boundaries within which the sense of community should develop.


In the case of the new nations the process is easier to grasp, for it took place over a much shorter period and is well documented. The leaders of national movements since the French Revolution have been by definition articulate persons, and their propaganda among their own populations, designed to implant in them a national consciousness and a desire for political action, though largely conducted by word of mouth, was also put in writing at the time. The growth of new modern means of communication still further accelerated the process in the twentieth century in comparison with the nineteenth. In the case of the new nations of nineteenth and early twentieth century Europe, the main factor in the creation of national consciousness was language. In the formation of the overseas nations of European origin, economic and geographical causes were the most important. In colonial Africa, state boundaries arbitrarily fixed by imperial governments largely determined the units within which the attempt was made to create modern nations. In India and China the attempt to build modern national movements was superimposed on ancient civilisations to which the European categories of nationality had only limited relevance.

A fundamental feature of all these movements is that the nationalist elites were only able to mobilise support from peasants, merchants, artisans or factory workers because many persons in these various classes were discontented with political and social conditions. One may plausibly argue that the foundations of their discontent were economic. Nevertheless the discontent was directed by the nationalist elites into nationalist movements rather than towards economic change. Where this happened, one may say that the masses accepted nationalist rather than social revolutionary leadership. As this book is concerned with nationalist movements, attention will be concentrated inevitably on the activities, political aims and social composition of the nationalist elites rather than on the nature of their followers' economic grievances. Without the discontents there would have been no movements; but without the nationalist elites the movements would not have been nationalist.

I shall be obliged from time to time to mention widely divergent religious and secular cultures, economic problems, forms of government, foreign policies and diplomatic and military events; but these are essentially peripheral to my subject. The peripheral subjects are of vast importance in themselves, but they are not my theme.

In the process of formation of national consciousness, and in movements for national independence and unity, there has been in each case a different combination of certain constantly recurring forces: state power, religion, language, social discontents and economic pressures. Where political and social power are concentrated in a group who differ in both religion and language from the majority of the population among whom they dwell, and an educated elite is emerging from that population, then the optimum conditions are given for the rapid growth of a nationalist movement. Where several small elites of different languages are emerging within the same state, or where the population shares either the religion or the language of its rulers but not both, a more complex situation arises, and the tasks of nationalist leaders are more difficult.

My first intention was to make a rough typology of nationalist movements by grouping cases according to the relative importance, in the formation of national consciousness among their people, of the main forces listed above, in particular of the state, religion and language. Thus, one can say without much hesitation that the French nation grew up together with the French monarchy; that religion played a decisive role in the making of the Irish nation; and that Slovak and Ukrainian national consciousnesses were based on language. However, I found so many cases in which it was impossible to give a definite priority to one factor over the others, that I decided instead to arrange my material according to conventional regional divisions. This does not mean that comparison of the operation of these main forces is neglected: on the contrary, these factors are constantly emphasised, and similarities or differences are pointed out, though I have also assumed that my readers are capable of discovering patterns for themselves.

Each case has been taken historically. I feel no need to apologise for the element of chronological narrative which this must imply. A serious student of nationalist movements can no more ignore their past than a doctor can ignore the medical history of his patients. I have tried to pick those moments in time which seem to me to have been decisive for the formation of national consciousness, and for the struggles for independence and unity. In the case of 'new' nations these processes are well documented, and the task—not always easy or simple in practice though obvious in principle—is to make the essential landmarks and trends stand out from the chronological detail. In the case of 'old' nations the task is much more difficult, for the historical record from which one must select or discard is much longer and richer, and leads back to ancient cultures whose essence could not be briefly expounded in a work of this kind, even if *per impossibile* there existed in this world a person capable of grasping the essence of all these cultures. A second formidable difficulty is that, during the stages of their history in which the national identity and self-consciousness of these 'old' nations were formed, the concepts of 'national consciousness' and the modern concept of 'nation' did not exist. The leaders had no idea that they were engaged in forming nations. This is the basic difference between the 'old' nations and the post-1789 'new' nations: in the case of the latter, the leaders knew perfectly well what it was that they were trying to do—which does not, of course, mean that what they achieved in fact was what they had set out to achieve.

There is an inherent and inescapable anachronism in the application to the past of the 'old' nations of the categories derived from the history of the 'new'. Yet this has to be done, and aspects of the earlier cultures and institutions, and events from medieval or even ancient times which seem relevant to the formation of national consciousness, have to be mentioned. It may seem odd to the reader that within a few pages I refer to the examination system of the Sung dynasty, the T'aiping Rebellion and Mao Tse-tung; or to the replacement of Pictish by Irish Gaelic in Scotland, the fall into disuse of literary Lowland Scots after the court of James VI adopted southern English, and the discovery of oil off the North Sea coast of Scotland. Yet further reflection may induce the reader to share my conviction that juxtaposition of this sort cannot be avoided.

I have given a good deal of space to the growth and the reform of languages. I have had to rely on the work of historians of language, but have been able to supplement this by my own knowledge of spoken and written languages, amateurish and non-technical though this may be. Just because history of language is usually in our time kept so rigidly apart from conventional political, economic and social history, it has seemed to me desirable to bring it together with these, even at the cost of less expertise.

Three chapters are concerned with Europe: the second with the continuous nations, the third with movements for national unity, and the fourth with 'new' nations arising within multinational states. It has sometimes been difficult to decide in which category to place certain cases. The Poles could have been treated as an old continuous nation, or the Serbs and Croats as new nations arising within the Ottoman and Habsburg empires.

However, the aspect of the Polish case which seemed to me of greatest interest for the theme of this book was the movement to reunite a nation already divided between three empires; and of the Serbian and Croatian cases the movement to create a common Yugoslav state and nation, and the obstacles which it encountered.

The fifth, sixth, seventh and eighth chapters are concerned with movements for independence by the peoples of colonial empires, the consequent emergence of new states, the attempts to create new nations within them, and the one case where all such efforts have been suppressed—the Soviet Russian empire. The regions in which these problems are considered in turn are the lands of European settlement overseas, the western part of the Muslim world, East Asia and Africa. The subject of the ninth chapter is the relationship between racialism (white, black and red) and nationalist movements in the Americas and South Africa. The tenth chapter considers diaspora nations, that is, nations which have a large number of their members scattered in communities over great distances. The most obvious case is the Jews, but overseas Chinese and Indians are two others.

The role of different social classes in national movements, and especially in the leadership of these movements, is of great interest and importance. The eleventh chapter is devoted to this subject. The twelfth chapter is concerned with the relationship of other major political movements, based on ideologies, to nationalism, and the extent to which they have influenced each other. No attempt is made at philosophical analysis, or model-building, nor is any systematic summary of these ideologies given: all these things can easily be found in an abundant (though contradictory, and not always intelligible) literature. My concern is to show not whether the ideas are valid, or logically coherent, but whether and how they have influenced each other, and whether and to what extent those who profess one ideology have in practice followed another. This has of course made it necessary from time to time to discuss some of the ideas; but my concern has been with liberal, socialist, fascist and communist movements as political realities and historical case-studies (from which some tentative generalisations can be risked), rather than with abstract propositions.

Nationalist doctrines will no more stand up to critical analysis than any other ideologies, yet this has not prevented them from capturing men's minds. Nationalism has been responsible for floods of rhetoric and for the debasement of human language. Nationalists have shown ignorant contempt for institutions, customs and beliefs which had proved their worth for centuries, and have replaced them with fragile structures and empty slogans. Extreme nationalism has been a crude substitute religion, replacing withered faith by fanatical hatreds. Too often its leaders have been frustrated social misfits and self-important semi-intellectuals. At its worst, extreme nationalism has led to massacres and forcible expulsions of millions of mainly innocent people.

Nevertheless, the nation is something which has been formed, at least in many lands, by long historical processes, which it is foolish, as well as arrogant, to despise. In the years after 1789 the problem of finding a unit for the exercise of popular sovereignty was a real problem, and the nation, based usually on language, was the only answer which could have been given at that time. The intolerance and the illusions of nationalism are part of the intolerance and the illusions of democracy. If the doctrine of nationalism can be torn to pieces by analysis, so can the doctrine of popular sovereignty. It is arguable, and it certainly cannot be irrefutably disproved, that men were happier under the great despotic empires or the petty feudal sovereignties than under modern mass democracies or nation states, even though these more primitive regimes lacked television sets and computers. Yet this is useless wisdom in a world which has become divided into mass societies, in which sovereign states have become firmly rooted, and in which there is no prospect of a return to the past.

# 2 Europe: The Old Continuous Nations

## From empire to sovereign state

The long process by which in Europe sovereign states arose and nations were formed has its origins in the collapse of the Roman Empire, the attempts to revive an imperial power, the slow decay of the revival, and the still slower withering away of its mythology.

History, of course, does not begin with the Roman empire, nor was the empire simply the heir to the Roman republic or to the Italian tribes from which its founders sprang. Everyone knows that first Hellas and then Christianity contributed to the legacy of Rome; but Rome's Hellenistic heritage contained a Persian element, itself derived no doubt in part from Egypt and Sumer. The Roman emperor was less remote from the Great King, the King of Kings, the *Shahinshah*, than from the philosopher-king of Plato; Roman government owed something to Xerxes as well as to Themistocles.

The barbarians beyond the *limes* regarded the empire with admiration as well as with resentment. The rulers of the barbarian kingdoms which arose when the empire broke up willingly preserved some parts of its structure and absorbed some of its values; while the bishop of Rome still claimed that his dilapidated city was the centre of Christendom. In the second capital, Constantinople, the imperial institution survived, and its authority still extended around the Eastern Mediterranean. The first attempt at revival of one empire under Justinian (reign 527-65) lasted but a few years. Less than a hundred years later the Eastern Mediterranean region was lost partly to the Sassanid Persians and then wholly to the Muslim power which burst out of the Arabian desert. A bare half century later the Imperial City withstood siege by an Arab navy.

The second attempt to restore the empire came from the West, and was the joint achievement of the king of the Franks and the bishop of Rome. The pope crowned Charles the Great Holy Roman Emperor on Christmas Day 800. The rivalries of his descendants reduced the empire to a fiction. When it was more effectively restored, by Otto I (reign 936-73), its real power was based not in the lands in which the Latin language had remained dominant in several 'Romance' variants—France and Italy—but in Germany. From this time onwards, the Western Empire was essentially a German institution, although the emperors long claimed a certain shadowy authority over the other rulers of Western Christendom; and for several centuries these rulers did not openly repudiate the claim, though in practice they pursued their own dynastic interests. The same is true of the attitudes of rulers to the other potentate who claimed universal authority, the pope. It was perhaps above all the bitter, and frequently renewed, conflict between emperor and pope, leading to repeated wars between Italian cities and between German feudal magnates, and to frequent invasions of Italy by German troops, which fatally undermined the authority of both, and strengthened the secular rulers, especially the kings of France and England. The kidnapping in 1303 of Pope Boniface VIII by soldiers of King Philip IV, which set off the Great Schism in the Church of Rome, is a useful symbolic landmark in this process.

Similar tendencies can be seen in the Roman empire of the East. The institution of emperor was directly descended from Constantine, though numerous individuals and dynasties succeeded each other, with or without violence. The church of Constantinople grew ever further apart from the church of Rome: there were periods of acute quarrelling and periods of conciliation, but in effect they had become separate churches by the eleventh century, becoming generally known to historians as the 'Catholic' and the 'Orthodox' churches. Within the empire, however, the secular and spiritual authorities remained much more closely united than in the West: quarrels between individual eastern emperors and patriarchs never took on the same dimensions as those between western emperors and popes.

The rulers of the barbarian kingdoms beyond the empire, converted at different periods to the eastern form of Christianity—the Bulgarians, Russians and Serbs—looked to the empire with the same combination of admiration and resentment as had the converted barbarians of the West towards the empire of Rome. King Simeon of Bulgaria (reign 893-927) wished to become associate emperor in Constantinople. The rulers of the second Bulgarian empire (1185-1393) aimed, in their wars with the Frankish rulers of Constantinople after 1204,[1] to make themselves emperors. Still later, Stephen Dushan of Serbia (reign 1331-55) had himself crowned emperor of the Serbs and Greeks in 1345. However, no Serbian or Bulgarian Charlemagne was enthroned in Constantinople. Before this could happen, the kingdom of Russia was conquered by the Mongols between 1237 and 1241, and both Bulgaria and Serbia were reduced to submission by the Ottoman Turks in the late fourteenth and fifteenth centuries. Constantinople itself held out, under a restored Greek dynasty, until 1453. The disaster of Ottoman conquest thus forestalled the process by which eastern equivalents of the sovereign kingdoms of France and England might have arisen.

The rise of the centralised sovereign state in the West was accompanied by the rise of new social groups. City burghers, secular state officials and medium landowners acquired some of the power which in previous centuries had been monopolised by great landed magnates. These new social groups often supported the monarchs, and were often welcomed as allies, or manipulated as political instruments, by them. These groups continued to have conflicting interests, yet were also increasingly linked by a common loyalty. Horizontal links between the subjects grew strong, in addition to the vertical links between ruler, feudal superior and inferior. The interests and wishes of the people began to form part of the basis of legitimacy of government.

It is important to recognise not only that the modern nation, which came into existence in this period, was something different from the medieval *natio*—a word which had various meanings in different places and periods—but also that the process of the formation of a modern nation did not take place in all the sovereign states which emerged from the fifteenth century onwards. Two outstanding sovereign states—France and England—can rightly be described as 'nation states'. In these two cases, the formation of the state and the formation of the nation advanced together: the nation was formed within the boundaries of the state, and those who lived outside those boundaries did not belong to the nation. The words 'sovereign state' and 'nation state' are not however interchangeable: it is a regrettable mistake of many distinguished historians, especially of Britain and America, to use them as if they were. Scotland, Holland, Castile and Sweden became both sovereign states and nation states. This is not, however, true of the kingdom of Spain, and still less of the numerous principalities (some of which possessed for long periods effective sovereignty and considerable power and influence) which arose in the geographical areas usually known as Germany and Italy; and it is very questionable whether the phrase 'nation state' should be used of Poland or of Hungary, though both of these were sovereign states, arguably already in the eleventh century, certainly by the fourteenth.

Despite great regional variety, the main lines of the political and social order of medieval Catholic Europe were similar. The essence of this order was the existence of mutual obligations between social groups, guaranteed by law and by institutions. In particular, the upper class had certain rights which the ruler was bound to recognise. There were bitter struggles, for centuries on end, between the central power and the social elite, with each gaining and losing battles, enjoying ascendance or suffering inferiority sometimes for long periods at a time. Nevertheless, looking backward for many centuries from modern times, one sees that there was always a balance between monarchy and nobility. This system of balances was feudalism, a word which should properly be used for this phenomenon and not simply to denote all types of pre-industrial economy in which land is mostly held by a rather small number of landowners, who obtain their wealth by the serfdom, or some other form of dependency, of the peasant majority.

In medieval Europe a third element appeared in the balance, the organised merchants and manufacturers of the cities, who also won their rights and institutions guaranteed by law. The feudal order continued to exist long after the city population had become numerous and wealthy. Capitalism coexisted with an agriculture based on serfdom or on a poor and dependent tenantry. Both belonged to the feudal order. In the course of time, in north-western Europe urban capitalism came to dominate the economy, and landowner-directed agriculture to play a secondary part; while in parts of eastern Europe urban capitalism receded after a period of growth (the so-called 'second serfdom' in Poland and Prussia). But in the whole of Catholic Europe feudalism left its mark on political and ethical thinking.

The process by which privileges were won by successive social elites, and expanded (not without bitter struggles) to lower levels of the social pyramid, was the precondition for the development of individualist thinking, and for the growth of a rather large politically conscious upper stratum, bound together by horizontal ties of solidarity and no longer linked only vertically in hierarchical subordination. Individualist thinking and horizontal solidarity were the starting-points for the growth of national consciousness. To attribute these phenomena solely to the rise of capitalism and of a bourgeoisie is an error: they must be traced back much further, to the feudal order. This was, however, much less true of the Byzantine empire (though elements of feudalism are not wholly lacking), and was unknown in Muscovite Russia (though perhaps not in Kiev Russia before the Mongols).

A second feature of medieval Europe was a hindrance to the growth both of the sovereign state and of national consciousness. This was the tendency of monarchs, who had accumulated power over a great territory, to divide it up between heirs and thereby dissolve a great centre of political power, and postpone the growth of both state and nation. This was to be seen in Anglo-Saxon and Angevin England, in the separation of Burgundy from France by King Jean in 1360, in the break-up of Poland in the thirteenth century and in the rise and fall of the Christian kingdoms of northern Spain. The same phenomenon occurred in Kiev Russia. In Muslim states, however, and in China after the reign of the First Emperor, it was not of comparable importance.

A third subject for brief comment is the Reformation. The rejection of the papal authority over the church was a result partly of increased learning and individual religious thinking (in the England of Wycliffe as well as in the Bohemia of Hus); partly of growing pride in the developing secular language; and partly of objections by monarchs, secular officials and even bishops to the claims of the pope in distant Rome to interfere in their affairs. Economic and social forces became closely interwoven with religious, and those countries in which Protestantism prevailed were those in which both the enterprise and the political influence of capitalists grew most strikingly—though not until quite a long time afterwards. Arguments as to whether capitalism bred the Reformation, or the Reformation capitalism, may be left to those who specialise in determining the priority of hens and eggs. It is here of interest to note the different influence of the Reformation in different countries, as regards the growth of sovereign states and of national consciousness.

The Reformation was a long period of latent or overt civil war in most of Europe, but the results varied from country to country. In Spain, Portugal and Italy the reformers were crushed. In England, Scotland and Scandinavia they prevailed. In Ireland a small minority of foreigners imposed their rule, but not their new faith, on a Catholic people. The Netherlands and Germany were partitioned, after decades of war which brought economic prosperity to the first and disastrous devastation to the latter. In France half a century of cruel civil war ended with strengthened national consciousness and unity, and with the strongest single state in Europe stronger than ever. In Poland the Counter-Reformation drove back the initially successful reformers without bloodshed or severe persecution. In Hungary an uneasy coexistence of Christian faiths was made possible only because the disastrous defeat by the Ottomans at Mohács in 1526 led to its partition under three rulers—the Catholic Habsburg emperors, the Muslim sultans indifferent to quarrels among Christian dogs, and the Calvinist princes of Transylvania.

A few words may be added on the three cases of England, France and Germany.

In England the initial drive came from the monarch's desire to become sovereign. Henry VIII enjoyed substantial support in his resistance to the pope, but his treatment of Catherine of Aragon made him unpopular. The confiscation of the monastery lands won support from those who expected to enrich themselves, but also antagonised large numbers of Catholics who rebelled and were crushed. In the following reigns religious conflicts became more open and more bitter. Protestantism gained ground, though the old religion still remained strong and smouldering discontent sometimes broke out in conspiracies or armed rebellion. For decades on end England was in a condition of latent civil war. The dependence of Catholics on foreign support strengthened the association of Protestantism with

English national independence; and by the end of Elizabeth's reign the process of formation of English national consciousness had been virtually completed. The civil wars of the seventeenth century did not shake it.

In France religious division developed into open war, with each side looking to foreign support—the Guises to Spain and the Huguenots less successfully to the Netherlands and England. Already in the late fifteenth century national consciousness had deeply penetrated the French people. It was at first indissolubly identified with both the monarchy and the Catholic Church. As Protestant heresy grew, the Catholics regarded it as a threat to both nation and monarchy. Finding the monarch against them, the Protestants tended to shift the emphasis of loyalty from king to nation. When the king turned against the Guises, the Catholics did the same. Thus at the accession of Henri IV both Catholics and Protestants claimed to be fighting for the nation: national unity was being treated as a greater good than religious truth. Henri IV himself seemed to confirm this view by the acceptance of the Mass which won him Paris. The Guises now became the anti-national party, servants of Spain. At the end of it all, France, thanks to its large population and great resources, was stronger than ever, and all Frenchmen professed devotion to the French nation. This by no means meant that unity of religious or political views existed, or that civil dissension was over. Thereafter, contending parties were to claim to speak for the French nation: as in England in the seventeenth century, no higher focus of loyalty was sought.

In Germany the Reformation was very largely a movement of growing national consciousness, directed against the Italian pope, extolling the German language as the equal of Latin for the expression of Biblical truth. There was no German sovereign state which could command the loyalty of Germans, for the authority of the emperor was little more than a shadow of past glory, and the strength of the Habsburgs lay not in Germany but in the Netherlands and Spain. The growth of German national consciousness, which coincided with the Reformation, was not, as in England, canalised by a centralising single monarchy, or, as in France, contained within the limits of a single powerful state. German Protestants became dependent on the protection of a number of territorial princes, and this was reinforced by the alarm felt by merchants and smaller landowners at the Peasant Revolt of 1525 and the excesses of the Anabaptists. Wars between German princes, with the Habsburgs as the champions of the Catholic Church, ended with the adoption at the Peace of Augsburg of the principle of *cujus regio, ejus religio*, which was rather favourable to the Protestants. Sixty years later the Thirty Years War was triggered off by the revolt of the Bohemian Protestant nobility in 1618, and began with a successful counter-offensive in Germany of the Habsburgs and their Bavarian allies. This, however, provoked intervention from outside, and the war became a struggle of the Spanish and Austrian Habsburgs against Sweden, France and the northern Netherlands. When it ended, the forces making for German unity and a single German national consciousness were reversed for at least a hundred years.

## The old continuous nations

This chapter is concerned with some of those peoples among whom, at least in a substantial political class, there developed many centuries ago a national consciousness which was never interrupted by external blows. The two oldest are the French and the English. The formation of the national consciousness of each of these two is indissolubly connected, not only with the growth of two sovereign states, but with the unscrambling of the links between them caused by the claims of the king of France on the homage of the king of England, and of the king of England on the territories of the king of France. The growth of both nations coincided with the growth and consolidation of two states; but the evolution of the French language and the creation of the English had a great part in the process, as did the breach of the English church with the pope and the persistence of the French church in loyalty to Rome. The English nation shared the British Isles with three other nations. One of these, the Scots, became a nation in the process of defending its own state against English invasion. A second, the Irish, was conquered by the English, but stubbornly defended its culture and forged its national consciousness in unending struggle. The third, the Welsh, never possessed its own state, but it too preserved its national identity. France was built by the conquest of regions of widely different culture. The centralising French monarchy, and its successors the centralising republics, seemed to have succeeded in imposing a single French nationality on all; yet in the late twentieth century there were signs that this process was not quite so complete as it had appeared. The complexities of the relations between the four nations of the British Isles make it necessary to devote more space to them than to the French; but this does not imply that the history of France is less complex or less rich, and no one is more convinced of the contrary than the present writer. However, I am not undertaking a comprehensive political, cultural or social history of the French or the British or any other peoples, but attempting briefly to interpret the process of the formation of nations.

An equal degree of complexity marks the development of the peoples of the Iberian peninsula, which has at times been contained within one state, in the last three centuries in two, but has been inhabited for much longer than that by several nations. Scandinavia is another naturally definable region in which three nations grew up in alternating association or discord with each other, while two more grew on the periphery, the Finns in the east and the Icelanders in the north-west.

The formation of the Dutch nation is a case of the division in two of a community which, with an economy and a culture as advanced as any in Europe, was growing into a single modern nation; but religious division, foreign military power and new economic opportunities in distant seas pulled and kept the two halves apart, making one into a nation and leaving the other in uncertain status.

The Swiss were and remained unique in their peculiar free institutions, their neutrality and their still more peculiar quality of a multi-lingual as well as multi-religious nation.

The last case considered in this chapter is Russia, a nation not less than five hundred, and perhaps over a thousand, years old: the argument on this subject is not only charged with political emotion but is itself dependent on what community should be described historically as the Russian nation.

The reader is reminded once more that the following sections are not histories—not chronological or political or social or cultural, though elements of each of these aspects are touched at times. They are summaries and interpretations of the process of formation of nations. Those moments in time which seem to the writer important are those which are mentioned, and they range from the ninth century to the twentieth; and those forces or tendencies which were most effective—state, language, religion, social class—vary from one period to another.

## The British and Irish nations[2]

The island of Britain was inhabited in the first century BC by peoples organised under various territorial rulers, who spoke languages of the Celtic group. Beginning with Julius Caesar's invasion of 55 BC, Roman armies conquered most of the island, establishing a line of forts between the Firths of Forth and Clyde but penetrating also into Fife and the Highlands, occasionally reaching the extreme north. Roman rule, and a mixed Latin-Celtic civilization, lasted about four hundred years in most of Britain; and even in the remoter parts of Wales and Scotland, which the Romans never governed, and in Ireland, which they never invaded, some influence of their culture was felt.

In the half century which followed the departure of the Romans, the southern part of the island was contested between Angles, Saxons and Celts, and in the north-west Irish invaders settled in Argyll and the Hebrides. In the ninth century, and again in the late tenth and early eleventh, raiders from Denmark and Scandinavia ravaged the coasts of Britain, and also of Ireland, and settled in large numbers in some regions.

This well-known story need not be told here, but a few words are needed on the emergence, fusion or disintegration of states.

An Anglo-Saxon state of Kent in the south-east kept fairly close contact with the continent, and in 597 its ruler accepted Christianity from the Roman emissary, Constantine: the see of Canterbury was founded. A more powerful Anglo-Saxon state emerged in Northumbria. Essentially this state extended from the Humber to the Forth, and its population spoke overwhelmingly the Angles' language. Its boundaries, however, fluctuated as a result of frequent wars, and their precise location for the last half of the first millennium AD is not known. Christianity came to Northumbria in the early seventh century from Ireland through Scotland. In 664, however, the Northumbrian king was persuaded by emissaries from Canterbury to transfer the allegiance of his church to direct subordination to Rome. Northumbria, which became one of the main centres of learning and culture in Western Europe, was under constant attack from the kingdom of Mercia, in central England, whose main rulers were the pagan Penda (630-55) and the Christian Offa (757-95). Mercia was also engaged in warfare against the Celtic peoples of Wales, who succeeded in maintaining independent principalities. Northumbria and Mercia succumbed to the attacks of the Norsemen, and a Danish state embraced a large part of eastern England. The kingdom of Wessex, in the south and west, remained as the stronghold of Saxon England. Of the several dialects spoken in England, it was that of Wessex which was first established in a considerable literature, protected by the encouragement which the great king Alfred (871-99) gave to schools and learning. His grandson Edgar (957-75) united the greater part of what has become known as England, though its boundaries in the north and west were uncertain. Forty years later King Canute of Denmark became ruler of England from 1017 to 1035. After his death nearly all the Anglo-Saxon lands became united for the first time under King Edward, the Confessor, from 1042 to 1066. This success was short-lived. Disagreement as to the succession enabled Duke William of Normandy (of Scandinavian descent but French by culture) to defeat all rivals, and to conquer England up to the Northumbrian, Cumbrian and Welsh borderlands. The consolidated English monarchy dates essentially from the Norman Conquest of 1066.

Meanwhile also in the northern part of the island several states emerged. The largest in area was that of the Picts, the character of whose language is still a subject of controversy. The Pictish kingdom embraced the Highlands and the eastern lands down to the Firth of Tay. Living south of the Pictish kingdom, in the lands from Solway to Fife, were other Celtic peoples, whose language was of the Welsh ('P-Celtic') rather than Irish ('Q-Celtic') variant.[3] The most important state to emerge in this region was called Strathclyde. This territory was also known by the name Cumbria, which applied to most of the land between Clyde and the Solway Firth, and sometimes also to the land beyond the Firth, later known as Cumberland. Christianity reached this region in the fifth century; its pioneer was St Ninian, who was active in the Solway region, but the extent of its penetration has not been determined. In Argyll the kingdom of Dalriada was formed from several chieftaincies of Irish Gaelic-speaking people,[4] known to writers in Latin as *Scoti*. Through them Christianity spread more widely, being introduced by St Columba, who was active at his base on the island of Iona from 563 to 597. Finally the south-east, or Lothian, had a predominantly Angle population.

The Northumbrian kingdom might well have remained with its boundary on the Firth of Forth had it not been hard pressed first by Mercia and then by the Danes.[5] The early history of all these people remains obscure and controversial, but the union of Picts and Scots under Kenneth McAlpin in 843 can be conveniently accepted as the date of the foundation of the kingdom of Scotland. In 1018 the kingdom extended to include Strathclyde. In the north, however, it was not possible to defeat the invading Scandinavians. When the kingdom of Norway became effectively organised,[6] it extended its rule over the Western Isles, the Orkneys and Shetlands, and the mainland of Caithness.


The island lying to the west of Britain, on the far fringe of Europe, was never conquered by the Romans, though they knew of its existence. The Irish Gaels—not the island's earliest inhabitants, but the first of whom there is written evidence—visited or raided the coasts of Britain, and, as noted above, founded the kingdom of Dalriada in the part of Scotland later known as Argyll.

Christianity reached Ireland in the first half of the fifth century. Its first missionary, St Patrick, was a Roman citizen from England. In the sixth century all Ireland was Christian. Its church was differently organised from that of Rome, for the monasteries had greater authority than the bishops. Irish monks spead the Gospel, not only in Scotland and northern England but also on the continent. In the recovery of Europe from the disasters of the Germanic invasions and Muslim assault, and in the foundation of medieval Christian civilisation, Ireland had a great part to play.

In this Irish golden age, the island was ruled by a multiplicity of minor and major territorial chiefs, whose Irish designations have traditionally been rendered in English as 'king'. In the ninth century there emerged the office of High King, who had certain limited powers to speak on behalf of all.[7] Ireland also had its intellectual elite. Side by side with church and monks, and absorbed into the new Christian culture, was a secular profession, derived from the pre-Christian past, the *fili* or traditional poets and wise men. The Irish language grew into a fine vehicle for poetry and religious thought. Irish civilisation was different from, but not inferior to, that of the Latin West.

In the mid-ninth century began the series of blows from outside which have plagued Ireland until the most recent times. The first invaders were the Vikings, who raided all her coasts but established themselves most successfully along the eastern and southern shores. At the end of the tenth century the Irish were able to stop the tide, under the High King Brian Boru (from 976 king of Munster and high king 1002-14). The Viking colonists remained where they were established, but were largely absorbed into Irish culture.

England under the Norman monarchy became a strong medieval kingdom. The monarchs and the higher nobility spoke French, introduced a French type of feudal organisation and partook of the growing northern French culture, which spread into a substantial part of the Saxon population. At the same time the Anglo-Saxon language, some Saxon institutions and ways of thinking survived.[8] The two societies coexisted, the one superimposed on the other, the two perhaps more nearly mixed within the church than within the secular machinery of government. One can hardly speak of an English or a French nation before the thirteenth century: rather there were two French-speaking monarchs, with capitals respectively in Paris and in London, and many French-speaking territorial magnates, with obligations to and claims on each other, recognising and violating each other's laws, combining with or combating each other as circumstance moved them.

The Scottish monarchy too had, after the victory of Malcolm Canmore over Macbeth in 1057, a strong Norman French element, in the court and in the noblemen to whom Malcolm gave lands and influence. The land frontier and the legal relationship between the two kings were subjects of confusion and repeated warfare. The king of Scotland held English lands of the king of England, for which he owed liege to him, but he did not accept the claim of the English Crown, that he owed liege for all his lands, which would have made Scotland a dependency of England.[9] This claim was on the whole successfully resisted and it was also much helped by the bull of Pope Celestine III *Cum universi* of 1192, which declared that the Scottish church was immediately subject to the Holy See, thus ending the rights of the Archbishopric of York over Scotland. A Scottish state, and Scottish loyalty to its king, began to take shape. The king's hold over the Highlands was dubious, and it was not until 1266 that the king of Norway (after an unsuccessful naval expedition against the Firth of Clyde in 1263) ceded the Western Isles and Caithness to Scotland. In the islands Gaelic and Norse languages and cultures coexisted, and partly fused, as is shown by the mixture of place names surviving to modern times. Orkney and Shetland remained Norwegian for two centuries more. Four languages were still spoken in Scotland: French at the Court and in the upper class; Anglo-Saxon in the south-eastern lands; Gaelic in the Highlands and Islands; and the Celtic language of Strathclyde-Cumbria in diminishing areas in the south-west.

At the close of the thirteenth century the end of the male line of Malcolm Canmore's dynasty coincided with the presence on the English throne of an exceptionally able and aggressive ruler, Edward I (1272-1307).

When the direct line of the Scottish royal house died out in 1290, the rival claimants, John Balliol and Robert Bruce, both descended from grand-daughters of David I, appealed to the English king. Edward chose Balliol in 1292, but claimed that the king of Scotland should do homage to him for his kingdom. Balliol's halfhearted attempts to escape vassalage were crushed in 1296. However, the humiliation of Balliol provoked armed Scottish resistance. There followed seventeen years of mainly guerrilla-type warfare, led first by Sir William Wallace and then by Robert Bruce, grandson of the unsuccessful claimant of 1292. Bruce was crowned king in 1306 at Scone, but he had to go into hiding for two years before resuming the struggle. His triumph came with the defeat of a large English army led by Edward II at Bannockburn in 1314, and the recognition by the English of Scottish independence by the Treaty of Northampton of 1328. Even so, the English threat to Scotland continued throughout the fourteenth and fifteenth centuries. Scotland was able to survive thanks not only to the efforts of its rulers and people (which were greatly impaired by quarrels of rebellious magnates with each other and with the crown) but also to the preoccupation of the kings of England with France—linked with Scotland by the frequently renewed 'Auld Alliance'—and to their involvement in the English civil wars of the late fifteenth century.

Nevertheless, it is safe to say that by the time of Bruce a Scottish nation was arising in this poor and polyglot country. The most important single agency in bringing this about had been the monarchy, and the institutions which it had created. In the words of an eminent recent historian, 'the homogeneity was not racial or linguistic but feudal and governmental. It was expressed most clearly in the habit of a common feudal allegiance to a strong monarchy, and in the observance of a substantial body of accepted law and custom'.[10]

The formation of the Scottish nation was marked by great suffering and barbarity, but it was still more fortunate than that of the Irish. It is a striking paradox that the Scots, a heterogeneous multi-lingual population with a rather low level of culture, emerged as a nation capable of securing its political independence, while the Irish, a homogeneous people with a higher as well as an older culture, remained a conquered nation. The reason is perhaps that the rulers of Scotland, being surrounded by a Norman aristocracy and reigning over Angle, Celtic and Scandinavian subjects, were respected by the Norman rulers of England who were in a similar predicament; and that the decisive clash between the two monarchies did not come until the Scottish state was strong enough, and had sufficient moral support from the papacy and indirect physical support from France, to withstand the shock.

The Irish did not have these advantages. There was no unified Irish state; and it was the quarrels between contenders for the high kingship which enabled the Norman invaders to set foot in Ireland in 1169. They were followed in 1171 by King Henry II himself, who assumed sovereignty over all Ireland. Henry's action was supported by the pope, who was keen to see the Irish church reorganised on what he considered a proper basis of episcopal hierarchy, and effectively subordinated to Rome. From the first the English crown regarded the Irish as mere subjects, and respected neither their institutions nor their culture. However, effective Norman or, later, English rule was confined to the east and south-east. Anglo-Norman aristocratic families acquired great domains across the south and south-west, but in these lands the intruders were in fact repeatedly absorbed into Irish culture; and in the north and north-east of Ireland there was little, if any, change.

In 1315 Edward Bruce attempted to accept the offer of the high kingship of Ireland, with help from his brother King Robert of Scotland; but this enterprise, attractive in distant retrospect to seekers after Celtic unity, failed through unwise strategy and inadequate support. In the second part of the century the English monarchy tried to tighten its grip. In 1366 the Duke of Clarence imposed the Statutes of Kilkenny, intended rigorously to separate English from Irish, to restrict contacts between the two communities and to ensure an inferior status for the Irish, who were regarded with contempt by the English monarch's English counsellors. Richard II later established the English 'Pale', approximately between Dundalk and Waterford, with the originally Viking settlement of Dublin as the centre of English power. During the fifteenth century the English aristocracy in Ireland became involved in the wars of the various pretenders to the English throne, chiefly on the Yorkist side. The ultimate victor in England, Henry Tudor, decided that he must make his authority over Ireland more effective. His governor, Sir Edward Poynings, introduced in the Irish parliament of 1495 the so-called 'Poynings' Law', which made the calling of a parliament in Ireland subject to the specific consent of the king of England, and was designed to ensure the permanent subjection of Irish to

English interests. In fact, the new policy was directed not so much against the Irish population as a whole, as against the great Anglo-Irish families, the so-called Geraldines, descended from Maurice Fitzgerald, one of the invading barons of 1169.

The Welsh had even less of a united state than the Irish. Speaking various 'P-Celtic' or Brythonic dialects, they were, like the Irish, organised in tribes with chieftains. Like the Irish, they accorded a high place in their society to poets and to music; and a Welsh literature, not inferior to Irish literature, emerged. The chieftaincies of Wales were in practice grouped into three main territories—Gwynedd in the north, Powys in the centre, and Deheubarth in the south. There was at the same time among most Welshmen a sense of membership in one community, known by the name Cymry, roughly equivalent to 'fellow-countrymen'.

The first Norman kings, preoccupied with the establishment of their feudal monarchy over the Anglo-Saxons and with their claims on the French mainland, paid little attention to Wales. In the borderlands and along the south coast Norman magnates (the 'marcher barons') established their power: in Chester, Hereford and Pembroke. It was the Earl of Pembroke, Richard 'Strongbow', who led the Norman-English invasion of Ireland in 1169.

In the early thirteenth century the strongest principality in Wales was in Gwynedd, ruled from 1200 to 1240 by Llywcllyn ab Iorwerth. During repeated wars with the marcher barons, and at times with the king of England, he held his own and became the leader of the Welsh princes. His grandson, Llywellyn II, reasserted twenty years after his death the supremacy of Gwynedd, and was recognised by Henry III of England, in the Treaty of Montgomery of 1267, as hereditary Prince of Wales. It was his mistake to refuse to Edward I, on his accession, the homage to which the king considered himself entitled.[11] In the summer of 1277 Edward invaded Wales, and Llywellyn accepted a reduced status and territory but was still treated as Prince of Wales. However, the new English regime caused discontents which burst into a rising in 1282. Llywellyn himself was killed in a minor skirmish, and Welsh resistance was crushed. A last Welsh revolt was suppressed in 1295. The heir to the English throne was given the title of Prince of Wales in 1301, and this remained the custom until present times. Wales was incorporated in the kingdom of England, though for a long time local government remained in Welsh hands and there was no systematic interference with Welsh language or culture.

In the fourteenth and fifteenth centuries there slowly emerged a factor of decisive importance for English national consciousness: the formation of the English language.

At first two languages coexisted in England. The conquerors spoke a rather provincial form of French. Anglo-Saxons of the upper classes, and those who aspired to higher office or higher social status under the conquerors, learned this Norman French. The bulk of the population spoke various Anglo-Saxon dialects: the earlier supremacy of the Wessex dialect disappeared as there was now no significant Anglo-Saxon literature. For their part, many of the Normans learned an Anglo-Saxon speech in order to converse with their subjects. The accession of Henry II in 1154 brought an influx of Frenchmen from central France or Provence who were influenced by the literary renaissances of both Paris and Languedoc. From this time the cultural links of the upper class of England with France no longer went through Normandy. During the next two centuries, though higher French culture prevailed in court circles, the nobility of England came to speak increasingly the language of the country. However, this language itself rapidly changed. It was approximately from 1250 to 1400 that the language became flooded with French words: something like 10,000 can be traced to this period. In the fourteenth century the dialect of the area north-east of London, the most densely populated and commercially prosperous region, prevailed over other dialects, and from it emerged the language of the capital. The year 1362 is a date of symbolic importance: it was then that English replaced Norman French in the law courts, and that the opening of Parliament was conducted for the first time in English.

This process is usually known as the replacement of Old English (pre-Norman Anglo-Saxon) by Middle English. It is, of course, true that there is a continuity between Anglo-Saxon and English. The basic structure and syntax remained, and the basic words most used by simple people remained the original Anglo-Saxon words, somewhat modified. One may therefore say that what had happened was that English had been enriched by the addition of French words. Yet this seems an inadequate description. The process was more than the acquisition of foreign loan-words—as Latin words passed through the church into German and Polish, or as Arabic words passed into Spanish. Rather, one should say that two languages, Anglo-Saxon and French, flowed together, and from them emerged a new language, neither Anglo-Saxon nor French but English. As English grew into a modern, rich, flexible language, evolving under the guidance of Wycliffe, Chaucer, Spenser and Shakespeare, innumerable concepts became expressible in synonyms of Anglo-Saxon or French origin. For this process, which remains essentially hidden from the historian, the best major European parallel is the emergence of the Romanian language, in which a Romance speech derived from Latin flowed together with Slav.[12] In both processes there were periods of systematic borrowing, more intense in the Romanian case (which was quicker, more conscious and more artificial) than in the English.[13]

One might therefore risk the generalisation that, though England was a land of human civilisation from the time of Julius Caesar, and even earlier, an English nation and an English language only came into existence in the fourteenth century. From this time only dates the history of England, as opposed to the history of the peoples of Britain. In Scotland, the diversity of peoples and languages remained greater until later: it is arguable that the formation of a Scottish nation was hardly completed before the sixteenth century.

English national consciousness, and the pride of educated Englishmen in their own language, were strengthened by the long wars with France and by the fluctuating discontent of churchmen with the claims made on their devotion by the foreign hierarchy of a church torn by schism.[14] In the sixteenth century various forces came together to forge a strong sense of national identity. The Reformation was both a movement of ideas and a rejection of foreign domination. The English translations of the Bible, the religious polemical literature in English, enriched the language, and coincided with a great flowering of poetry. Tudor despotism appealed both to the greed of landowners and merchants for the wealth of the monasteries and to resentment against foreigners—both the Frenchmen who had been enemies of England for two hundred years and the Spaniards whose seaborne wealth offered prizes to English raiders. In the reign of Elizabeth the upsurge of literature, the ferment of religious and political ideas, the rise of new social forces and the sense of mortal danger and crisis, all contributed to the emergence of an English nation. For hundreds of thousands, if not perhaps yet for all, subjects of the crown loyalty was now given not only to feudal superior, or church, or distant sovereign, but to the nation: the links which bound the population together were not only vertical but also horizontal.

The growing strength of the English proved to be a mixed blessing for the Welsh. In September 1400 a Welsh landowner, Owain Glyn Dwr (or Glendower), led a rebellion in the north. Its origin lay at least largely in Owain's personal grievances and land disputes, but it soon became a rising of the Welsh against the English, extending to a large part of the principality. The rebels were rather successful until 1406 when the English reconquest began to gain ground. By 1410 the revolt was almost over, and Owain had mysteriously disappeared. The accession of Henry VII, a Welshman, to the English throne aroused some hopes in Wales, but it was in fact the Tudor monarchs who effectively centralised government and insisted on the status of English as the sole official language, while Welsh continued to be spoken by the humbler classes among themselves.

In Scotland, too, a language developed from the flowing together of

Saxon and French, though with less of the latter, and with rather more from Celtic and Scandinavian sources, than in the south. This language was spoken not only in the east of Scotland but also in northern England. Scots, or 'northern English', was spoken at the Scottish court and by the social elite (who might or might not also speak Gaelic), as well as by the Lowland population as a whole. It was the language of the poets Robert Henryson and William Dunbar. It might have developed as a distinct literary language into modern times had not the union of the crowns in 1603 brought the predominance of southern English through its extension to the court, administration and upper class of Scotland.

The Reformation in Scotland brought divisions which lasted longer than in England. Henry VIII's dictatorship prevailed against the rebellion of 1536, and the accession of Elizabeth made it possible to undo the effects of the Marian reaction without major upheavals, though rebellion was long latent and briefly exploded in 1570. England was spared the civil wars which ravaged France and Germany. The Scottish Reformation took place against the familiar background of rivalry between the French and English parties. The first successes of the Reformers were defeated by French troops which, based at Leith from 1550 to 1560, upheld the regime of Mary of Guise. Mary Stuart's tumultuous reign (1560-67) ended with the victory of the Reformers, dependent on English support.

After James VI became effective ruler of Scotland, and his power had been increased when he also became James I of England, he began his efforts to reconstruct an authoritarian episcopal structure in a Protestant Scottish church, to make it amenable to his form of royal despotism. Charles I continued this effort, and provoked a mighty reaction. The Scottish national Covenant of 1638 set up a democratic structure for the church which was incompatible with royal despotism. Roman Catholicism had become a minor force in Scotland, but Scottish Protestants were bitterly divided between Covenanters and Episcopalians. This was a matter of strongly held religious convictions, but it was also a political division, which can perhaps fairly be described (though the words are an anachronism) as a struggle between dictatorship and democracy, or between social conservatism and social change. These things were of course also at issue in the English Civil War. Covenanters and Cromwell were uneasy allies from 1643 to 1648, but Cromwell's decision to execute Charles I antagonised the Scots. The result was a war which Cromwell's general won, and from 1652 to 1660 Scotland was under English rule. Though this rule was comparatively humane, and Cromwell's religious policy did not greatly differ from Scottish aims, yet English rule was resented as such. The restoration of Charles II was welcomed, but it was followed by vindictive reprisals (execution of the 8th Earl of Argyll on 24 May 1661) and by persecution of the Covenanters. Scots were still divided into religious camps when James VII and II was driven out of the British Isles by Dutch William.


In Ireland the Reformation had quite different, and disastrous, consequences. The Irish would not accept Protestant doctrines, the common people even less than the upper nobility. Little attempt was made by the English Protestants to persuade them by theological argument and intelligent propaganda; and the neglected condition of Irish education and secular culture made the Irish people more impermeable to propaganda than most. Rather, the English relied on brutal force, and this served only to strengthen Irish devotion to the old faith, and to create hatred against England. For their part the English rulers thought of the Irish as a barbarous and inferior people, ever inclined to provide help to the internal enemies of the rulers of England, or to seek help from the foreign enemies of England, and therefore to be watched with vigilant suspicion, and coerced into submission. As so often happens in such historical processes of escalation, each side behaved more and more as the other side expected it to behave. This was the essence of the relationship between Ireland and England from the late sixteenth century up to the mid-twentieth and beyond. The fact that at most times during these tragic centuries there were Irishmen, Englishmen, and Scotsmen, both Catholic and Protestant, who loved their own and each others' country deeply, who knew and understood both cultures, and who believed that Irish, English and Scottish cultures could and should coexist in peace and mutual respect, and might even fruitfully influence each other, barely affects the truth that the predominant trend on both sides was distrust and hatred. Irish national feeling and national hatred was inextricably bound up with the religious schism.

The main events in this long tale are well known. In the war which began in 1595, not only the defence of the old faith, but also the particular interests of the O'Neills and O'Donnels and their followers were involved. Spanish aid was inadequate. Defeat of the rebellion, which had not been confined to the north, was followed by the Plantation of Ulster, settling Scottish and English Protestants in what had been the most uninterruptedly Irish part of Ireland. Forty years later, Ireland was on Charles I's side in the English Civil War. A Confederacy of Kilkenny, of Irish Catholic notables, was formed, with hopes of at least ending Protestant persecution of the old church, even if it were not to be restored to the status which would enable it to persecute Protestants. In any case the defeat of Charles, and Cromwell's brutal repression of 1649-52, destroyed these hopes, caused further severe legal discrimination against Catholics, and brought further large-scale settlement of English and Scots in Ireland. The Restoration did little to improve the lot of the Irish. Charles II was too weak, and too afraid of English anti-popery, to do much; but Presbyterians in Ulster as well were victims of discrimination. Finally, in the crisis of 1688 most of Ireland took the side of the Catholic James II against Dutch William III. Once more, the Catholics were defeated, this time largely by the brave and effective opposition of the Ulster Protestants, for whom the defence of Londonderry and the Battle of the Boyne (14 June 1690) have remained proud battle-cries ever since.

Already in the sixteenth century the formation of English national consciousness had been completed, and the bitter political, social and religious conflicts and the civil war of the seventeenth did not break English national identity; no more than the firmly established French national identity was broken by religious wars or *Frondes*. The case of Scotland around 1700 is more complicated.

The majority of Scots were united behind the Presbyterian Church, and almost all Scots cherished the tradition of Scottish independence going back through Bruce and Wallace to the medieval realm and the distant Celtic past. They knew very well that they were not Englishmen. At the same time deep divisions separated Highlander from Lowlander, Gael from Saxon; and unreconciled religious minorities still survived. These various frustrations expressed themselves in the conflict latent between Jacobites and Whigs.

To the English statesmen of Queen Anne's reign and their friends in the government of Scotland, the best solution seemed to be the union of the two kingdoms in one state. The Hanoverian prince who was to be the queen's successor in London would then not have to fear that his rival might be constitutionally accepted by a neighbouring kingdom in the same island. The economic conditions of the Act of Union, as passed by the Scottish parliament on 16 January 1707, were favourable; the whole structure of Scottish law and the Scottish legal profession was preserved; and separate Acts guaranteed the supremacy of the Church of Scotland in its Presbyterian form, derived from the Covenants of 1638 and 1643. In return, the Scottish parliament ceased to exist, and the kingdoms of Scotland and England were merged in the United Kingdom of Great Britain. There was to be one state, but there remained two nations, Scots and English.

The Union was not popular, and it was at least partly brought about by corruption or pressure upon members of the Scottish parliament. It did not prevent the Jacobite rebellions of 1715 and 1745, both of which started in Scotland, and the second of which was followed by cold-blooded killings after the battle of Culloden and persecution of Highlanders for many years.

Yet in the longer term the Union worked rather well. Scots and English together went through the horrors and the triumphs of the Industrial Revolution: made, ruled and then dismantled the British empire; and fought two world wars, in which the blood tribute of Scotland was proportionately greater than that of England. All this while Scotland's kirk and law and schools remained in Scottish hands, the Scots remained a nation, and Scots and English on the whole respected, even liked, each other.

The English and Scottish nations were formed by the historical process summarised above, and both existed long before modern doctrines of nationalism were formulated. English nationalism never existed, since there was no need for either a doctrine or an independence struggle.[15] English national consciousness certainly existed for five centuries or more; but it is arguable that during the nineteenth century it disappeared, merging into a British national consciousness, which the English tended to appropriate to themselves.[16] Many Scots and Welsh also acquired this British national consciousness; but others continued to feel themselves members of Scottish and Welsh nations, while sharing loyalty to the British state and British empire, and being moved in turn by British patriotism, British imperialism and (after 1947) British inverted imperialism. However, among Scots and Welsh not only national consciousness but also nationalism existed, since varying but considerable numbers of those who constituted the Scottish and Welsh nations felt, as the English nation could not feel, the need to defend their national identities within the British state, or even to seek independence.

The Welsh were less disturbed by the Reformation than the English or Scots: they remained obedient to the old faith for longer, and passed over to the new with less commotion. It was in the eighteenth century that important religious differences appeared between Welsh and English, owing to the rapid spread of Methodism. The chapel became no less the symbol of Welsh nationality than the kirk of Scottish. The struggle to disestablish the official Church of Wales, which continued until the eve of the First World War, mobilised Welsh national feeling. Still more important was the revival of Welsh as a literary language, which dates, like Methodism, from the eighteenth century. The yearly *eisteddfod* festivals were instituted in 1789, their prime mover being Thomas Jones of Corwen. In the early nineteenth century Welsh was spoken by the great majority of the population of the still very rural principality. The threat to Welsh came from the industrial revolution, based on the rich southern coal fields. Industry brought to the Welsh, as to other peoples before and since, both wealth and misery, but it also brought floods of English immigrants into Wales as well as drawing Welshmen to jobs in England. At the beginning of the twentieth century less than half the population of the principality spoke

Welsh, and by the mid-1970s only about a fifth. Massive unemployment in the 1930s brought mass support for socialism; but by the 1960s fear for the future of the language and resentment of the impact of uniform English-controlled bureaucracy (which did not diminish when Labour came to power) was helping the nationalist party Plaid Cymru, which called in deliberately vague terms for Welsh self-government.

In Scotland difference of language was comparatively unimportant. Gaelic was still spoken by about 80,000 persons in the 1970s and there was a remarkable renaissance of Gaelic poetry. But though this gave hope that the language would be saved, it could not be seriously expected that it would become the chief language of Scotland. Attempts were also made to develop a literary non-Celtic language, Lallans, continuing the tradition of Henryson and Dunbar. This too produced some fine poems by Douglas Young and others; but the Scottish political revival in the twentieth century could not, to the same extent as the Welsh, be based on language. In Scotland industrial development had much the same effect as in Wales, a growth of both wealth and poverty and considerable immigration; but the latter consisted less of English than of Irishmen, coming usually from material conditions worse than those of the Scots. Scottish industry, like Welsh, suffered from greater unemployment than English in the 1930s and from greater loss of export markets after 1945; and as in Wales the resultant discontent was largely expressed in socialism or communism. However, the belief that the Scots as a nation should have not only their own kirk, law, and schools but also their own political institutions never died out after 1707. It was stimulated by the Irish movement for Home Rule, and grew with the combination of economic hardship and cultural revival in the 1930s and afterwards. In the 1970s the Scottish National Party made good use of the hopes aroused by oil exploitation in the North Sea, most of which was in Scottish rather than English waters. But national unease among Scots was much more widespread than the electoral support, let alone the active membership, of the SNP. There was resentment at the attitude of so many Englishmen who, while sincerely believing themselves not to be in any sense English imperialists, yet refused to recognise the distinct nationality of the Scots, talking as if the future of Scotland were simply a problem of decentralisation. There was also a growing feeling that not only had the British empire ceased to exist but that the actual and potential rulers of Britain (of whatever political persuasion) had lost all belief in themselves. These views might be mistaken, but the English politicians of the mid-1970s were doing very little to prove it.

The case of Ireland, where nationalism became a powerful force, and created bitter and apparently insoluble conflicts, needs fuller discussion.

In eighteenth century Ireland, in a climate of religious scepticism, the discriminatory laws, though still legally in force, were mildly applied. Dublin became, like Edinburgh, a centre of thought and culture in the English language which was yet distinct from that of England. Demand grew among the Anglo-Irish upper class, which thought of itself as Irish, for greater independence. The example of the American colonies showed the danger, while the good behaviour of the Irish Volunteers during the war with America strengthened the Dublin leaders' case. The result was the establishment in May 1782 of an independent Irish Parliament, that is, the abandonment of Poynings' Law.

This Parliament represented only the educated Protestant Anglo-Irish. A partial enfranchisement of Catholics in 1793 made small difference: the great mass of the Irish nation was outside political life. Radical ideas began to make themselves felt, especially after 1789. In October 1791 Wolfe Tone and some of his friends formed the Society of United Irishmen. They were radical democrats, dedicated to the liberty and progress of the Irish nation, regardless of religion. Their original strength was in Ulster, especially among Presbyterians—still subject to civil disabilities—but they also won support from Catholics. In 1795 Tone left Ireland for America, and next year went to France, to plan French aid for a rebellion in Ireland. In May 1798 the rebellion took place; French aid arrived too late, and was defeated; Wolfe Tone was captured by the English from a French ship and later killed himself, while several others, arrested before the rebellion, were executed. The rebellion convinced William Pitt that the Irish Parliament must be abolished, and Ireland represented directly in the English Parliament at Westminster. The Union was brought about by a vote of the Irish Parliament of 7 June 1801. The rebellion led by Robert Emmet in 1803, ending with his execution, was an epilogue.

Nineteenth century Irish politics were played before two distinct audiences: the British Parliament and the people of Ireland. The leading figure in the first period was Daniel O'Connell. It was he whose talents as an orator and as an organiser brought the Irish Catholic people into Irish politics. His victory in the Clare election of 1828, even on the unfavourable restricted franchise of the time, caused Parliament to pass the Catholic Emancipation Act of 1829; but the rest of O'Connell's career, devoted to the mass campaign for the Repeal of the Union, was a failure.

From 1845 to 1848 Ireland was devastated by the Famine resulting from the failure of the potato crop. It reduced more than a third of the people to destitution, cost perhaps a million dead, and set in motion the mass emigration overseas which, together with a drastically lowered birth rate, reduced the population of Ireland between 1845 and 1880 from around eight million to five million. It was not until the 1870s that the Irish political elite had sufficiently recovered from the disaster to resume the parliamentary struggle.

A great leader appeared in Charles Stewart Parnell, a Protestant landowner from Wicklow County. He was able to harness the agrarian discontent of the Irish peasants to his movement for Irish Home Rule, and to weld together the Irish members of parliament in Westminster so as to play, by negotiations or by obstruction, a decisive role in the rivalries between the Conservative and Liberal parties at Westminster. He showed equal understanding of, and equal ability to direct, the parliamentary and the agrarian struggle, neither publicly committing himself to the use of force nor abjuring it. He persuaded Gladstone to adopt Home Rule. The split in the Liberal Party in 1886, the exploitation by the Conservatives of Ulster Protestant mistrust, and the ability of the House of Lords to frustrate Commons majorities, were formidable obstacles; but what defeated the Irish cause was the scandal of Parnell's divorce case in 1890, which led to the disintegration of the Irish Nationalist parliamentary group. In the following years some good things happened in Ireland: in particular the system of landholding and the quality of Irish agriculture were improved. But these were things done for the Irish by officials responsible to an English government, not by the people of Ireland.

Throughout these years there had been Irishmen who cared not for social reforms or for some new federal relationship between Ireland and England, but quite simply wanted to get rid of the English altogether. Ireland must be herself, even if poor and weak, and all means, including physical force, should be used. They were influenced by European revolutionary nationalism (Italian, Polish and Hungarian); took a romantic interest in the Celtic past, as Balkan nationalists in Byzantine past; and idealised the devout Irish peasantry while insisting that the Irish nation comprised Protestants as well as Catholics. The first significant group, Young Ireland, was responsible for a minor attempt at an armed rising in August 1848 at Ballingarry in County Tipperary, which led to the transportation to Australia of several of its leaders. More important was the secret society founded in 1858, mainly by James Stephens and John O'Mahoney, whose Irish branch became known as the Irish Republican Brotherhood (IRB), and the American as the Fenian Brotherhood. The Catholic hierarchy repudiated the society. Several of its leaders were arrested, and spent long years in prison. In March 1867 an armed rising by small numbers of conspirators in Dublin, Cork, Tipperary and Limerick was quickly suppressed. The most efficient of the men of 1867, John Devoy, escaped to America, where he actively financed and organised Irish conspiracies for another fifty years.

At the turn of the century Irish nationalism acquired a cultural dimension. Some of Ireland's ablest minds devoted themselves to creating, or reviving, an Irish culture as different as possible from English. Around

1830 there had been some two million Irish-speakers in Ireland. Public education, which from this time onwards made rather substantial progress, was in the English language: at the time, O'Connell and other prominent Irishmen favoured this. The Famine dealt a terrible blow to the language, since both mortality and emigration were highest in the Gaelic-speaking districts. At the end of the century Irish-speakers were a small and dwindling minority. To combat this, the Gaelic League was founded in 1893, its two leading figures Douglas Hyde and Eoin MacNeill. Years of hard work succeeded in introducing the teaching of Irish into primary schools, and somewhat extending it at secondary and university levels. During the same years appeared the first works of a great poet, William Butler Yeats, and the plays of J. M. Synge, as well as much lesser literature, written in English but profoundly influenced by Irish traditions and customs, or at least by serious efforts to discover and understand these. Their efforts were inevitably marked by frustrations and polemics. There was much denunciation—in English—of 'Anglo-Irish' attitudes as a corrupting force. Yet who were the Anglo-Irish? Who were the Irish? Were only Catholics, or only peasants, or only Gaelic-speakers, entitled to use that proud name? Could literature and the arts be made a substitute for politics, to keep the Irish nation strong at a time when politics in Ireland seemed doomed to stagnation? Or should literature be subordinated to politics? These questions could find no answer, nor could the Irish escape the fate which trapped them in the language of their conquerors.

The advent of the Liberals to power in England in 1905, and their conflict with the House of Lords, gave the Irish members of the British Parliament a new chance to make themselves felt. Led by John Redmond, they pressed for Home Rule, and the British prime minister, Herbert Asquith, cautiously agreed. However, the growing opposition of Ulster, encouraged by the Conservative Party and enjoying strong sympathy in the British officer corps, blocked the way. In this situation the earlier hostility to all cooperation with any English recovered ground. Its most effective spokesman was Arthur Griffith, editor since 1899 of *The United Irishman*, who launched in 1905 the slogan *Sinn Fein* ('Ourselves'). Griffith urged complete abstention from parliamentary politics and an uncompromising priority for Irish national interests in all fields, especially in the economic. He took, rather strangely, as his model for action the policies of the Hungarian patriots of the 1860s which had led to the 1867 compromise.[17] Another important development of these years was the growth of working-class action, still on a small scale, with militant transport workers in Belfast and Dublin as the vanguard. From this movement emerged a leader of unusual talent and of an original, socialist and Marxist, turn of mind, James Connolly.

The Home Rule crisis reached its climax in the summer of 1914. Ulster

Volunteers in the north were matched by Irish Volunteers in the south, and both secretly obtained arms from Germany to use against each other. The outbreak of war in August postponed the crisis. Redmond accepted Asquith's proposal that the Home Rule Bill of 1912 should be placed on the statute book, to come into force at the end of the war when Parliament should have discussed amending legislation to meet Ulster's wishes.

War, however, inevitably made some Irishmen revert to the old policy of alliance with the enemies of England. The Germans, cast in the role of the Spaniards of 1601 and the French of 1798, responded tepidly to the overtures of the old American Irish veteran, Devoy, and of Sir Roger Casement. The IRB successfully infiltrated the Irish Volunteers, but conspiratorial confusion at the last stages made it impossible to mobilise large numbers of men for the armed rising. This took place on 24 April 1916. About 1600 men took part in Dublin, and held parts of the city for a week; there were smaller armed actions in the counties of Wexford and Galway. James Connolly and Patrick Pearse, the schoolmaster poet, expected to go to their deaths: success was of lesser moment to them than their determination to make themselves a blood sacrifice. They were among the fifteen executed after the rising was suppressed. As a military enterprise, it was a pathetic failure, but its romantic circumstances, and the capacity of Irishmen to be moved by fallen martyrs, made it almost a victory. All revolutionary movements treasure their martyrs, but the constant invocation of the glorious dead by the extremists of Irish nationalism far exceeded normal practice, and amounted almost to a mystery religion of an esoteric sect.

In the next two years it became clear that Home Rule liberalism was dead in Ireland, and that Sinn Fein had triumphed. Under this name all uncompromising nationalists came together, and the Irish nation, outside Ulster, followed them. At the 1918 election to the British Parliament, Sinn Fein won almost all the seats that did not go to Ulster Unionists. The seventy-three elected Sinn Feiners constituted themselves the provisional parliament of the Irish Republic, *Dail Eireann*, in January 1919. There followed almost three years of war against the English in the name of the Dail, led by the most eminent survivor from Easter 1916, Eamon De Valera, and the ruthless guerrilla chief, Michael Collins. It was fought not in regular military actions but in raids, explosions, murders and reprisals, in which the irregular Black and Tans, recruited as auxiliaries by the English, did their best to compete in brutality with the Republicans. The war ended in December 1921 with a compromise which gave twenty-six counties the substance of independence at the cost of the secession of six counties and the acceptance of Dominion status and a link with the British crown. This was less than De Valera could agree to, and there followed a year of civil war, more murders and counter-murders among whose victims was Michael Collins. A cease-fire agreement ended the civil war in May 1923. In 1928 De Valera decided to accept the facts and to return to political life, but the irreconcilables kept on the struggle as the Irish Republican Army (IRA). Seeking aid from the enemies of the English, they came in the 1930s under strong fascist influence.

The Irish Free State did reasonably well, and the British government tried hard to conciliate it. In 1938 Neville Chamberlain agreed to evacuate the Irish ports which the 1921 treaty had left to Britain. In 1939 he agreed to Irish neutrality in the Second World War, though this seriously weakened Britain's defences. The Irish government behaved as a genuine neutral, but 50,000 Irishmen fought in the British army against Hitler—more than counterbalancing the sporadic efforts of the IRA on Hitler's behalf. In 1948 Ireland became a republic, with British consent.

There were also negative aspects. Ireland remained very poor, its welfare services primitive. Intellectual life was largely dominated by the Catholic Church, and at times and in parts of the country (though not always or everywhere) this domination was obscurantist. The sincere and energetic efforts of the Irish government to revive the Irish language had disappointing results. The fact that Irish was taught in all schools, and that a knowledge of Irish was necessary for employment in government service, hardly seemed to help. Official statistics claimed that in 1961 there were 716,420 Irish-speakers (27.2 percent of the population), but an unofficial expert estimate in 1951 was that only 35,000 persons used Irish as their ordinary medium of speech, and only 3,000 were ignorant of English.[18] These wide discrepancies were, of course, due to different notions of what was meant by speaking Irish. The efforts of devoted scholars and patriots were thwarted by the indifference of millions who paid lip service to Irish culture but ignored it, and by the appeal to simple people of the joys of Mammon purveyed by television and tourists. Still, Irish remained a living language, and while it lived there was hope that it would survive.

The greatest frustration of all to Irish patriots was the division of the island. From 1921 the Unionists firmly controlled Ulster. The Catholic minority enjoyed the welfare services, and were represented at Westminster, but they were kept out of political life. This was how the great majority of Protestants wanted it. Hopes that the rise of the labour movement would bridge the gap between the two communities were disappointed: for most Ulster workers, the pope was a bigger menace than the boss. Captain Terence O'Neill, who became prime minister of Ulster in 1963, set himself to improve relations with the Republic. Belated gestures of reform set off massive discontents. The Civil Rights Association started demonstrations in the winter of 1968-69 which led to violence. Before long the IRA had taken over the struggle. Its political orientation had changed since the 1930s: Hitler was dead, fascism discredited, and the patrons of anti-British action were the communist states. In the late 1960s the IRA leadership was penetrated with growing success by communists, and adopted Marxist or quasi-Marxist terminology. This brought a split in the organisation: while the 'Officials' kept to the new trend, the 'Provisionals' repudiated the Soviet form of state, and preferred unlimited murder and arson while mouthing slogans increasingly influenced by Trotskyists. It was the Provisionals who made most of the running in the early 1970s.

What was now being demanded was no longer that Ulster Catholics should have full and equal rights, but that Ulster should be forcibly incorporated in the Republic: the claim was not, of course, being officially advanced by the Dublin government, but it was not repudiated with much enthusiasm south of the border. The British army was inevitably brought in to keep order. Its presence reduced, but could not eliminate, the murders, bombings and torturings of Irishmen by Irishmen. At first the Catholics echoed the IRA's denunciation of the British army as foreign invaders and oppressors, then some Protestants, too, saw British soldiers as their enemies because their own efforts at murder and torturing were opposed. The IRA hoped so to disgust the British with Ireland that it would compel the British government to withdraw the British army, opening up the prospect of a new Irish civil war, by no means confined to Ulster, since it would bring in volunteers from Scotland and from the Republic to fight for each side, and might well lead to mass reprisals against the hundreds of thousands of Irish workers employed in England and Scotland. If the British remained, they would be hated. If they cleared out, they would still be hated, and would have betrayed a community more loyally devoted to them than any other in the world outside Britain. Violence was being used, one side argued, to force two-thirds of the people of a free country to accept dictation by one-third. Not so, said their opponents, it was being used to make one-third of the population of one island accept the wishes of two-thirds. The arguments continued, while the gunmen exercised their trade. Of Yeats's terrible beauty, only the terror remained.

From the beginning, the Irish national movement was intended to bridge the religious differences; yet the fact of two religious communities remained the essence of the problem. In the south the Catholic Church wielded cultural and political power in an increasingly liberal spirit, but it could not overcome the mistrust of the Protestants in the north. They were not going to be won over by promises of new welfare legislation in the Republic: they might or might not believe these promises, but the conflict between them and the Republic was not about welfare services.

Ireland in the early 1970s was not a country of two nations. There was a nation in Ireland: it comprised the people of the Republic, including most of its few remaining Protestants, and most of the Ulster Catholics. The remaining million people were Irishmen, but did not belong to the Irish nation, or form a nation themselves. They were devoted to the union with Britain, but they were not Englishmen or Scotsmen. Their descendants might become part of the Irish nation at some future date, but this would take time, and it would require more than a few secularising or welfare laws in Dublin.

In 1976 the United Kingdom was not united, and Great Britain was no longer great, due to the actions not of its enemies but of its own citizens.

The centuries-long process of union of Saxon-Danish, Anglo-Celtic and Celtic-Norse territories into one kingdom appeared in the first half of the twentieth century to have been rather successful. It also seemed to have been accepted by the Celtic Welsh; and the wounds left by the separation and partition of Ireland seemed to be healing.

A quarter century later none of this was true. Yet loyalty to a common British homeland, devotion to the British crown and pride in the British form of civilisation were not dead, and were not confined to the middle-aged or the middle class.[19] This is not less true because these sentiments were seldom expressed by politicians or media-merchants. The truth was that the four nations were bound together, whether they liked it or not, and that it would be better to live together peacefully in some sort of agreed confederation than to hate and tear each other to bits. It was for English and Irish politicians to show not only that they were able to be generous to each other and to the Scots and Welsh, but that they cared sufficiently for Britain and for Ireland to put the lives of the people who lived in both islands above their dogmas, vanities and fears.

**The French**

The French were the first European people to be formed into a nation, and French governments were the pioneers of the European form of centralised administration and uniform national culture. This does not mean that the homogeneity of French national consciousness and culture were absolute, even in the 1970s; but that they were more substantial than any other nation's it would be difficult to deny. The process by which this result was achieved was long, and was attended by appalling sufferings, yet for the last millennium the direction has been unchanged. This is why it has been found possible to discuss the French case much more briefly than the British: it is not because French history and culture are less interesting, or less valuable to the human race, than British. Such a view could hardly be maintained by any moderately intelligent person acquainted with the bare facts: least of all by the author of these pages.[20]

The land known in modern times as France was mostly inhabited, in the first century BC, by peoples of Celtic speech, organised in several tribes or confederations. This land was conquered by the Romans, and became known as Transalpine Gaul. In it Latin-speakers and Celtic-speakers coexisted, but in the course of four hundred years of Roman rule Latin imposed itself on most of the country. Islands of Celtic speech remained, especially in Brittany in the north-west; and in the western part of the Pyrenees, stretching north into the plains and along the coast, the non-Celtic and non-Latin Basque language was spoken.

We must briefly refer to the basic facts of the formation of states in France in the second half of the first Christian millennium. The bare chronology is well known, but its cultural and social content are vigorously disputed by erudite men. At the end of the fifth century most of Gaul came under the rule of the Franks, a people of Germanic speech who had previously lived in the Rhine valley and Low Countries, between Verdun and Tournai, and who gave the country the name by which it has since been known: France. Their chief, Clovis, became a Christian in 496, and started the so-called Merovingian dynasty. Germanic Franks and Gallo-Romans coexisted in the new kingdom, with the latter providing the skilled administrators in church and state. In the course of time the local variant of Latin, the 'Romance' language, prevailed over the Frankish, taking only a few Germanic words into its vocabulary. In time also, as a result of quarrels between rival Christian princes, the Merovingian rulers lost their grip over large territories. In the mid-eighth century unity was restored when Pépin, son of a powerful general and 'mayor of the palace', was anointed king by the pope at Rheims, and founded the Carolingian dynasty whose most illustrious member was Charles the Great (Charlemagne), founder in 800 of the Holy Roman Empire which claimed authority over Christian Western Europe. The partition of this empire between rival heirs in 843 resulted in the recreation of a separate kingdom of France, which excluded a broad strip of territory, from the coast of the Low Countries down to the Rhone valley, later known as Lorraine.[21] The Carolingians suffered frequent raids on their Channel coast by Scandinavians. In 912 the Scandinavian leader Rollo was given a large territory in the north, which became the land of the Northmen, or Normandy. Here, as four hundred years previously in the case of the Franks, the Romance language soon came to prevail over that of the invaders, and the Normans were French-speakers by the end of the tenth century.

In 987, after the Carolingian dynasty came to an end, Hugh Capet was elected king of France, and founded a dynasty which lasted for three and a half centuries. His power was in practice limited to the region around Paris, known as the Ile de France. From this centre the French state expanded, despite periodical setbacks, until it reached its modern frontiers on the

Pyrenees, the Alps, the two seas and part of the Rhine. With the French monarchy and the French state there grew the French nation. It was a painful process, achieved by the expenditure of blood and iron on a scale which makes the words later attributed to Bismarck seem like tea-time patter. It was by no means inevitable. It required the subjection of territories as great as the Ile de France, with rulers no less powerful and talented, and with their own cultures no less capable of flowering than that of Paris. The story of the incorporation of these territories forms the larger portion of the story of the growth of the French nation.

Normandy was united with the kingdom of England after 1066, with the exception of the years 1079 to 1106 when it was held by a younger son of William the Conqueror. When the crown of England passed in 1154 to Henry of Anjou, who had previously acquired lands in the south-west by his marriage with Eleanor of Aquitaine, a huge Angevin empire emerged, on both sides of the Channel, surpassing in power the kingdom of France. However, the French kings obstinately resisted, by diplomacy and by economic skill as well as by force. In 1204 Philippe II Auguste conquered Normandy, and after his victory at Bouvines in 1214 was able to reduce the French possessions of the king of England in the south-west. The settlement of 1259 (Treaty of Paris) between Louis IX (Saint Louis) and Henry III of England made changes, but did not strengthen the power of the English king on French soil.

In the reign of Philippe Auguste the French state also expanded to the south. Beyond the Loire was Occitania, in which there lived essentially a different people, with a different culture and a different language (the *langue d'oc* as opposed to the *langue d'oïl*).[22] The Mediterranean culture of the south, with its troubadour literature, more sophisticated social relationships and easier manners, its *douceur de vie* and unbroken continuity with the Roman world, inspired both jealousy and contempt in the belligerent and puritanical northerners. The desire of the northern rulers to seize these lands acquired moral respectability thanks to the spread in the south of doctrines which were not so much a Christian heresy as a different religion: Manicheanism, which began in Iran a thousand years earlier, and was taken up successively by the Paulicians in Armenia, the Bogomils in the Balkans and the *cathari* in Italy. Its disciples in Languedoc were known as Albigensians, from the city of Albi in the lands of the Count of Toulouse. Exhortations from Rome could not make the counts act against their subjects on the scale required by papal orthodoxy. In 1209 Pope Innocent III declared a crusade against the Albigensians. It was led by a French-speaking nobleman, Simon de Montfort. The northern invasion led to an alliance between Raymond of Toulouse and Peter II, king of Aragon. They were, however, defeated at the Battle of Muret in September 1213.

This must be regarded as a historical landmark, comparable to Bannock-burn a century later but leading to the opposite result. The formation of a state based on Mediterranean sea-power, extending from Catalonia to the Rhone and including the Balearic Islands, is something that might have happened, in no way more impossible than the survival for four hundred years of an independent Scotland. If so, the history of both France and Castile would have been different. However, the north prevailed. The counts of Toulouse became humiliated vassals of the saintly King Louis IX, whose soldiers in 1244 captured the last Albigensian fortress of Montségur, burning men and women prisoners alive in a vast holocaust on the spot. In 1251 most of the lands of Toulouse passed to Alphonse, younger brother of the king of France, and twenty years later became part of the royal domain.

The duchy of Burgundy, which included part of the lands of the middle kingdom of Lotharingia, was united with the kingdom of France in the eleventh century, but King Henri I gave it in 1031 to his brother Robert, whose descendants ruled it as a separate principality until 1361, when it reverted to the French crown. At this time the French King John was engaged in war with the king of England: the so-called Hundred Years' War which began as a result of Edward III's claim that he, not Philip of Valois, should inherit the French throne in 1326. This war, it should be noted, began as a struggle between two French-speaking monarchs, supported by a heterogeneous collection of more or less loyal French-speaking mag-nates. The armies not only of the king of France but also of the king of England consisted very largely of French-speaking soldiers, as well as of persons whose language was Breton, Basque or Dutch. The war at first went against the French king both in the north and in the south-west. John, however, saw fit to give Burgundy in 1363 to his son Philip the Bold, and under his successors it continued to be a separate principality.

In the last decades of the fourteenth century the struggle between the Plantagenet and Valois monarchies continued; and it began to be seen as a struggle between Frenchmen and Englishmen. Both France and England were torn by the rivalries of princes and by bitter class conflicts, yet in both countries national consciousness also grew. In France, control of govern-ment in the name of the insane King Charles VI was disputed between the factions of the Duke of Orléans and the Duke of Burgundy. In 1407 Philip of Burgundy's men murdered Louis of Orléans, and in 1419 John of Burgundy was murdered by the Armagnacs (as the Orléanists became known, owing to the prominence in their cause of the ferocious Count of Armagnac). France was thus torn by civil war when Henry V of England invaded.

In this second phase of the Hundred Years' War, the English prevailed not only by their military valour, but because the new Duke of Burgundy, Philip the Good, allied himself with them. This alliance can be explained not only by the passions of the French civil war, but also by the fact that the Burgundian state, enormously strengthened by its union, through a series of ducal marriages, with the Low Countries, England's principal trading partner, had common economic interests with England against France. Under Burgundian pressure, Charles VI in 1420 promised the French crown to Henry V. When Charles VI died in 1422, his rightful heir the *dauphin*, who became King Charles VII, was in reality hardly more than a minor territorial prince (scornfully described by his enemies as 'roi de Bourges'). However, the tide turned; and this (whatever the latest and future discoveries of historical research may reveal) has been and will perhaps always be symbolised by the relief of Orléans, the last important city loyal to the dauphin, from siege by the English under the inspiration of Jeanne d'Arc, followed by the coronation of the dauphin as Charles VII in Rheims in 1429, also the work of Jeanne. Thereafter Charles VII's forces began to gain ground; Burgundy was reconciled with France by the Treaty of Arras in 1435; a French army was built which in 1450 beat the English at the battle of Formigny; and soon afterwards the whole south-west was liberated.[23]

In the second half of the fifteenth century England was in its turn too much weakened by civil war to threaten France seriously. Louis XI (1461-83), the earliest of the modern centralising kings, built up the military, financial and administrative structure of France, and by skilful diplomacy outwitted the dukes of Burgundy and Brittany, and the king of England, who together would have been more powerful than he was. In 1477, when Charles of Burgundy was killed fighting the Swiss at Nancy, most of Burgundy came to France and was never again lost.[24] Louis XI's son Charles VIII married Anne, the heiress of Brittany, and this valuable strategic territory too came under direct jurisdiction of the crown. The Bretons continued to speak their Celtic language, and retained some of their institutions and customs, but they too became Frenchmen, contributing greatly to the power of the French state, especially perhaps to its navy.

By 1500 the essential steps had been taken towards the creation of the French state and the French nation. There was further territorial expansion, east of the Rhone, up to the Alps, into Lorraine and to the upper Rhine, as well as failure to expand into the Low Countries; but, for all the blood and treasure which these successes or failures cost, they are of secondary importance when compared to the earlier incorporation of Normandy, Brittany, Aquitaine, Languedoc and Burgundy.

France was the strongest Christian state, with the most fertile land and richest economic resources. Its supremacy was, however, threatened in the sixteenth century by the emergence of Habsburg power based on Spain, the Low Countries, Germany, Italy and America; and still more, by the effects of the Reformation.

The spread of Calvinism in the mid-century alarmed the monarchs, was treated with alternating tolerance and repression, but could not be prevented. Compromises were made but were of short duration. From 1562 to 1598 France was in overt or latent civil war about religion. Inevitably, the war involved political, territorial, social and economic issues. It is arguable that the relative success of Huguenot (Protestant) doctrines in the south was promoted by continued resentment against northern Catholics by those who were still deeply permeated by the old southern cultures, including even something of the heritage of the Albigensians. The small kingdom of Navarre, the region of Béarn, under the rule of Jeanne d'Albret, was in effect a Calvinist state in which an Occitanian dialect was spoken. Jeanne's son, Henri IV of France, spoke this language more naturally than he spoke French.

In the course of the civil war new political and philosophic ideas emerged, expressed by Bodin, Montaigne and lesser men. More and more people came to feel that France was more important than specific theological doctrines, the nation more important than the sect. At first the Catholics profited from the people's reverence for the monarchy, the symbol of unity and greatness of France: it was the Huguenots who were the rebels. Later, when the rightful king was a Huguenot and the extreme Catholics, the party of the Guises, allied themselves with Spain, it was the Huguenots, or the *politiques* on the middle ground, who were the patriots. Henri IV, accepting the old faith in 1593 in recognition that 'Paris was worth a mass', united the majority of Frenchmen. In his later years France marvellously recovered from its sufferings, no doubt because its people were still the most numerous, intelligent and skilled in Europe; and Henri was remembered as one of the greatest kings of France, wiser and more generous than Philippe Auguste and perhaps the equal of Saint Louis. To Occitanian patriots of modern times, however, Henri IV is an ambivalent figure: he was a great leader and ruler, but his victory had the effect of merging Occitanian culture with French.

France suffered, though less severely than England, from internal strife in the seventeenth century. Richelieu, Mazarin, Louis XIV and Colbert pursued centralisation. This provoked opposition from regions with their own traditions, from the tolerated but insecure Huguenots and from the nobility. In the long struggle centralisation prevailed. The process continued right through the eighteenth century. In the revolutionary upheaval after 1789, there was a strong demand for decentralisation, for a federal France in which the peoples of the different regions would have their own cultures, and in which the surviving languages would have their place. This demand was rejected and suppressed first by the Jacobins and then by Napoleon. In the lesser revolutionary crises of 1851 and 1871 the demand for federalism again appeared in the Occitanian lands. In all cases centralism prevailed. It became part of revolutionary and republican orthodoxy that regionalism was 'reactionary'. Revolutionaries, no less than monarchs, gave a high priority to the military strength of France. Centralisation made France powerful, but a heavy price was paid, not only in frequent foreign wars and financial exhaustion but also in the persecution of talents.

Perhaps the main instrument of centralisation and of national greatness was the French language. We have seen already how Romance derived from Latin survived, with very few additions from Celtic, Frankish or Scandinavian sources. After the conquest of Languedoc, the northern variant became the only language of the political and cultural elite, though in several provinces of the south the people kept their own distinct speech, and this was also used in local public institutions. The central government however became more aware of the importance of language for political power. In 1539, by the Edict of Villers-Cotterets, François I made French the sole official language. This meant that, though southern speech continued to be used in private life, it lost its institutional basis. The Renaissance brought a flowering of French literature, to which southerners richly contributed. Under Henri IV the supremacy of northern French was maintained. In the seventeenth century the Académie Française, founded by Cardinal Richelieu, became a mighty instrument for moulding and controlling the language. Both academicians and great writers contributed to the process, making French the most perfect instrument of human speech and the language of all civilised men for some three hundred years. The diffusion of French language and French culture throughout the world became a highly specialised task, a form of diplomacy which maintained French power in the world long after its basic material foundations had been weakened. It was a magnificent achievement, comparable with the invention of the Chinese script: it did not operate for so long, but it affected a wider area.

The French nation, like the English, was formed by historical process, and needed neither a doctrine nor an independence movement to assert itself. The idea behind the expansion of the revolutionary armies was no French nationalism: rather it was an enthusiasm to spread the new liberating ideas to other peoples, which later turned into the desire to impose French imperial rule upon these peoples. There was, in the years after 1870, something called French nationalism, or *nationalisme intégral*, propounded by Charles Maurras and others; but this was essentially a political ideology designed for internal political struggle between Frenchmen.[25] It was rejected by the majority of Frenchmen; but national consciousness, awareness of the cultural identity of the French nation, was common to the great majority of Frenchmen, even if they also treasured their local traditions and resented the passion for uniformity of Parisian bureaucrats.

In the twentieth century other languages were spoken in France besides French: Dutch on the borders of Flanders, German dialect in Alsace, Italian in Corsica and Nice, Catalan in Roussillon, forms of *langue d'oc* from Limoges to Provence, Basque in the western Pyrenees, Breton in Brittany. In the 1970s there emerged militant groups which demanded respect for their languages and resorted to violence.[26] These groups were still more peripheral to French political life than were the Scottish and Welsh nationalist movements to British; yet their potential importance for the future could not be ignored.

## The Iberian nations

Hispania was the name given by the Romans to the whole Iberian Peninsula: from it derive the names España and Spain. In the peninsula in ancient times lived various Celtic peoples, and along the north-east Atlantic coast and on both sides of the Pyrenees the Basques, speaking a language utterly different from the Celtic, Latin or Germanic languages. On the Mediterranean coast were Phoenician and Greek colonies; and a large part of this region was brought under Carthaginian rule in the late third century BC. Roman conquest began after the Carthaginians left in 206 BC, but was not completed for centuries. Roman rule lasted nearly seven hundred years, and during this time most of the population came to speak dialects of Latin, with the notable exception of the Basques.

During the fifth century AD several Germanic peoples passed through, or settled in, the peninsula. From these emerged the kingdom of the Visigoths. The Germanic conquerors were not very numerous, and Latin speech continued to prevail. The fact that the Visigoth rulers followed the Arian heresy[27] not only placed them in conflict with Catholic rulers, but also separated Spain for some two centuries from Catholic Europe, thereby contributing to strengthen Spanish cultural identity. Conversion of King Recared to Catholicism, probably in 586, ended the schism and strengthened the Latin influences. Before long the Visigoths became absorbed in what survived of Roman culture, their language yielding to Latin.

In 711 the first Muslim armies invaded Spain, and within a few years had conquered almost all the peninsula. The Muslim rulers were at first subject to the Umayyad Caliph in Damascus, but became independent after the victory of the Abbasids over the Umayyads;[28] and in the tenth century the ruler of Cordoba declared himself caliph.

In Muslim Spain, known in Arabic as Al-Andalus, which reached its highest level of civilisation in the tenth century, a large part of the population were the descendants of the pre-Muslim inhabitants, who continued to speak Romance dialects, derived from Latin, though many of them also learnt Arabic. There were also large numbers of new settlers, brought by the conquerors. Among these, persons of Arab origin were only a minority, though they constituted the political elite and brought with them not only their Arab pride of race but also the tribal rivalries and hatreds of Arabia. Far more numerous were Berbers from North Africa, who had the status of *mawali*—persons converted to Islam, emancipated from servile status by an Arab patron, and taking Arabic names, often that of their patron. Subsequent generations abandoned their Berber language and adopted Arabic. There were also numerous converts to Islam among the Spanish population. These too adopted Arabic names and became gradually less and less distinguishable from the other elements of the Muslim population.

Those persons who remained Christians enjoyed the rights granted by Muslim rulers to 'people of the book'. Their connections with the Catholic world were inevitably sporadic, and their church was thus to a large extent independent, maintaining its own ritual, divergent from that of Rome. These Christians were known as *mozárabes*. They had many bilingual scholars, who made translations from Arabic (including some ancient Greek literature previously translated by Arabs) which became widely known in Catholic Europe. In Muslim Spain there was also a flourishing Jewish community, whose leaders had command of several languages and made great contributions to the common culture.

In the north the residual Christian territory was reduced to Asturias and Galicia, the land between the mountains and the Atlantic. In 718 the Christians defeated a Muslim army at the Battle of Covadonga, after which a more organised state was established. At the eastern end of the Pyrenees the French established a 'Spanish March' on the Catalan coast. This was formed into a County of Barcelona centred on that city, which was recovered from the Muslims in 801. By the end of the ninth century the counts, who ruled most of the Catalan lands up to Tarragona, had made themselves independent of their Frankish overlords.

In the tenth century Oviedo, the capital of Asturias, was surpassed by León, which gave its name to the whole kingdom. The kings of León considered themselves the heirs of the Visigothic kings, and claimed the title of *emperador* (emperor) as a symbol of their supremacy over other Christian rulers in the peninsula. The eastern neighbour of León was Navarre, based essentially on the region of Basque population. The two kingdoms were alternately allies and rivals, their dynasties were closely interrelated, and they exchanged rulers and territories according to a complicated system of succession. From León emerged the county, later kingdom, of Castile. During the eleventh and twelfth centuries, Castile gradually came to surpass León in real power. Dynastic successions led to repeated union and separation between the two kingdoms, until they were finally reunited in 1230, under Ferdinand II of Castile. Navarre expanded eastwards to include the county of Aragon in the eleventh century. In 1134 Aragon separated from Navarre, and in 1137 the count of Barcelona, who had married the heiress to Aragon, united the Catalan and Aragonese lands in a single kingdom. The institutions of Aragon and Catalonia remained separate. In the far west, a County of Portugal was established at the end of the eleventh century, as a lordship subject to Castile. In 1139 the first count's successor, Afonso Henriques, declared himself king of Portugal. His position was strengthened by the decision of the pope to recognise Portugal as an independent kingdom in 1179.

The kingdom of Asturias increased in stature and power after the alleged discovery of the tomb of St James the Apostle in Galicia. On the site of the tomb arose the shrine of Santiago de Compostela. This became the centre of pilgrimages from all over Catholic Europe. Along the pilgrims' route towns and commercial centres arose. The pilgrimage brought economic prosperity and artistic influences, attracting monks and builders as well as volunteers for the wars against the Muslims.

The expansion of the Christian states southwards proceeded in three directions: from Castile, from Catalonia and from Portugal. This process, known as the *Reconquista*, had something of the quality of a crusade, and lasted some two hundred years. The collapse of the caliphate of Cordoba, after the death of the great Muslim statesman Al Mansur in 1002, gave the Christian rulers the opportunity to place many small Muslim principalities in vassalage to them. The first series of Christian successes culminated in the capture of Toledo in 1085; but the tide was reversed when the Almoravids, a Berber dynasty from Morocco, brought fresh forces against the Christians in 1086. The Christian advance was resumed in the twelfth century, but was once more reversed by the still more formidable Almohads, who came with fierce religious fervour from beyond the Atlas and the borders of the Sahara. In the first half of the thirteenth century the reconquest entered its decisive stage. The Castilians of Ferdinand II (1217-52) took Cordoba in 1236 and Seville twelve years later; under Ferdinand's contemporary, Jaime II of Aragon (1212-76), the Catalans took the Balearic Islands, and captured Valencia in 1238. The Portuguese captured Lisbon in 1147 and cleared the so.. th by the mid-thirteenth century. All that remained under Muslim rule in the peninsula was the emirate of Granada, where the Nasrid dynasty maintained itself for two hundred years more.

Relations between the Christian and Muslim states had not been uniformly hostile throughout the period of the Reconquista. There were long periods of peace, and there were men on each side who understood and respected the culture of the other. This was more true of Castile than of León. The *mozárabes* and Jews played the part of interpreters not only in the literal sense as translators of books but also in the wider sense of cultural intermediaries. The reconquest brought large numbers of Muslims under Christian rule. These were known to the Spaniards as *mudéjares*. In the first hundred years and more they enjoyed protection and religious toleration. Muslim, Jewish and Christian communities coexisted in such cities as Toledo or Zamora under Christian rule no less than had previously been the case in Cordoba or Valencia under Muslim rule. The *mudéjar* contribution to crafts, architecture and sculpture was very important. All this changed abruptly in the late fifteenth century, when a new spirit of fanaticism made itself felt in the Catholic hierarchy in the whole peninsula, but chiefly in Castile.

From the beginning of the Reconquista period, the three sections of the peninsula began to develop on different lines. This was especially true of language. In the late eleventh century the spoken Romance forms began to be used increasingly in literature. From this period also dates the growing supremacy of the dialect of the central area (Castilian) over those of the north-west (Galician and Leónese) which had been more important in earlier literature as well as in public usage. *The Poem of the Cid*, written some time in the mid-twelfth century and relating to the exploits of the great soldier adventurer Rodrigo Dias de Vivar, known as the Cid Campeador, was the first great work of secular literature in Castilian. In the thirteenth century, under the influence of the *troubadours* of Langue-doc, Catalan poetry flourished, and the works of the great Christian philosopher Ramon Lull (1232-1315) were written in Catalan as well as in Latin. The Portuguese language, which developed from the dialect of Galicia, was well formed by the fourteenth century, when it was used for poetry and historical chronicles.

Geographical situation, military and economic opportunities, gave the peoples of the three regions different political and social development. Castile remained primarily a continental state, its power centred in the central plateau, though it had access to the Bay of Biscay in the north and to both the Atlantic and the Mediterranean in the south, the latter from Seville through the straits of Gibraltar. Military and religious influences were always very strong. Expansion was to the south, with the crusading mission of ending Muslim rule in the peninsula, and perhaps in north Africa too. Portugal was more oriented towards the ocean. With their long coastline the Portuguese were well fitted to be seafarers, and it was they who in the late fifteenth century became the pioneers of European oceanic exploration. The Catalans faced the Mediterranean, and from the earliest times had been interested in trade. The Catalans made themselves felt, in the thirteenth and fourteenth centuries, not only as traders but as sea-borne conquerors, from Sicily and Naples as far as the Aegean. These overseas enterprises were the work of an urban patrician class in Barcelona, as well as of the landed nobility.

The distinctions are of course approximate. The Castilians, too, took part in oceanic exploration, based on Seville, and their discoveries in America exceeded those of the Portuguese in Africa and Asia: while the Portuguese no°less than the Castilians sought, with no more long-term success, to conquer part of north Africa from the Muslims. Nevertheless, the stereotype of bourgeois trading Catalans, hierarchical military Castilians and exploring naval Portuguese is not very far from the truth.

In the fifteenth century one may say that there existed three Christian nations in the peninsula—three Spanish nations, not one—in addition to the Muslim people of the Granada state. The word Spain was rather a geographical than a national term. It was in fact used in the plural *las Españas* even as late as the eighteenth century. For Portuguese and Catalans the word *Hispania* included their own homelands, and they would certainly not agree to the exclusive appropriation of this name by the Castilians. Finally, there still remained, in the corner where the Pyrenees met the Atlantic, the Basque people, living partly in Aragon, partly in the new small kingdom of Navarre which was a dependency of France, and partly in Castile.

The fourteenth and fifteenth centuries were a period of internal strife in Castile, and to a lesser extent also in Aragon. In 1383 the Portuguese dynasty came to an end, and the king of Castile, whom the last king Fernando I had recognised as his heir, claimed the throne. He was resisted by a Portuguese pretender, John of Avis, and years of war ensued in which the Castilians had French armed support and the Portuguese English. The battle of Aljubarrota on 14 August 1385 was an important Portuguese victory, and after some more years of war the independence of Portugal under the Avis dynasty was recognised. A civil war in Castile from 1467 to 1469 ended when King Henry IV (1454-74) accepted his sister Isabella as his heir. Aragon too was devastated by a civil war between 1461 and 1472. It, too, concerned the succession to the throne, but was also a bitter struggle between social classes. In 1469 Princess Isabella married Ferdinand, heir to the throne of Aragon, and the two kingdoms became united in 1479. From the union arose the kingdom of Spain, which under the Habsburg rulers Charles I (1516-56) and Philip II (1556-98) became the greatest power in Europe. In 1580 Philip II successfully claimed the succession to the Portuguese throne, and thus a single monarch ruled the whole peninsula.

In 1492 the Muslim kingdom of Granada ceased to exist. The *reyes católicos*, Ferdinand and Isabella, promised the Muslims free exercise of their religion and respect for their property, dress and customs, as well as maintenance of their local government. Within a few years, however, these promises had been broken, and a revolt broke out in the Alpujarras region in November 1499. After its suppression an official policy of conversion of the Muslims was adopted, but it was not in fact very vigorously pursued.

The *Moriscos*, as the supposed converts were called, were nominally Christians, but in practice lived and believed as before. This stalemate came to an end in 1568 when the accumulated religious and economic resentments of the *Moriscos* found expression in an armed revolt which lasted for two years. After it was over, the population of the former kingdom of Granada was forcibly deported and distributed throughout Castile. The last chapter in this tragic story came in 1609 when the government of Philip III decided to expel all the *Moriscos* from Spain. This drastic step was taken in order to eliminate once and for all a dangerous potential ally of the Muslim enemy: even after the suppression of the 1568 rising, *Moriscos* had remained in touch with Ottoman and Moorish raiders from the Barbary coast. It is also arguable that the expulsion was in part a gesture to win public approval at a time when the Spanish government had been compelled to make a truce with the successful Netherlands heretics.[29] About 275,000 persons suffered this fate. Their removal, like that of about 150,000 Jews expelled from Spain in 1492, strengthened the national and cultural homogeneity of Castile, at the cost of losing many of its economically valuable citizens.

Though there was now one king of Spain, the earlier principalities— Portugal, Aragon and Catalonia—retained their separate institutions. Philip II was obliged to respect the rights of Aragon. In the seventeenth century, as the strains of war in distant lands, and of the mismanagement of the peninsula's economy and foreign trade, made themselves felt, it seemed increasingly desirable to centralise and simplify the administration, if only to ensure that all regions made adequate military and financial contributions to the common cause.

This was the aim of the Conde-Duque de Olivares, who from 1621 to 1643 was the most powerful minister of King Philip IV. In particular, after the outbreak of war with France in 1635, he increased his pressure on the Catalans. The result was disastrous for him. The commercial classes and the peasants objected to the financial demands, the people of country and cities objected to having Castilian troops billeted on them, the priests encouraged them to resist, and the nobility and educated classes were worried by the obvious intention of Olivares to tamper with Catalan constitutional liberties. Individual armed clashes, and an ill-advised attempt to arrest a member of the elected *Diputació* of Catalonia, led to the outbreak of armed rebellion in May 1640. In December 1640 the leaders of the revolt proclaimed Catalonia an independent republic under French protection; and when they found that this was not acceptable to the French, they declared the allegiance of Catalonia to the king of France. On 26 January 1641 a joint Catalan and French force defeated the Spanish army at Montjuich outside Barcelona. For nine years Catalonia was separated from Castile. However, the Catalans were disunited, the anarchical tendencies of the Barcelona radicals worried the upper classes, and above all French rule was soon found to be no less arbitrary than Castilian. In 1652 Barcelona surrendered to Philip IV's forces, a general pardon was given, and for the next fifty years there was no question again of suppressing Catalan rights.

The same year 1640 also brought the secession of Portugal. The Madrid government could spare few troops from its main war fronts, and the Duke of Bragança was able to make himself king. The restoration of Portuguese independence was generally preferred to union with Castile. Supported by their overseas resources, and by help from France and England, the Portuguese were able to hold out. After Spain had made peace with France in 1659, Philip IV prepared to reconquer Portugal, but his armies did not do well. Defeated at the battle of Vila Viçosa in June 1665, they were unable to reassert themselves. Spain formally recognised the independence of Portugal in February 1668. The separation proved to be lasting.

The Catalan problem reappeared in the War of the Spanish Succession. The French candidate, Philip V, was determined to modernise his kingdom through centralisation, on the model of the Bourbon monarchy. He repeatedly refused to commit himself to recognise traditional Catalan liberties. The Catalans therefore supported the Austrian Habsburg candidate, Archduke Charles. The Catalan revolt of 1705 was at first successful, with British naval support and some Austrian land forces. However, it soon became clear that the allies were only temporarily interested in the Catalans. When Charles became emperor in 1711, he had to return to Central Europe, and when the Tories came to power in England they were resolved to make peace quickly. In the diplomatic negotiations that ended with the Treaty of Utrecht, the English and Austrians went through the motions of asking for the protection of Catalan rights; but Philip V refused to yield, and the Catalans were abandoned. The city of Barcelona nevertheless decided to resist, and after a heroic siege it was stormed by Philip's forces on 11 September 1714.

Under the Bourbon monarchy, Spanish administration was centralised as it had never been before. The country was probably better governed, as a result of the reforms of Charles III (1759-88), but the intention was certainly to submerge the identity of Catalonia in the larger unit. Yet the differences remained, and when Spain had been weakened by the war against Napoleon, the loss of the American colonies, the revolution of 1820 and its suppression by the French in 1823, and finally by the miseries of the Carlist war of 1833-40, both Catalan and Basque nationalism reemerged to challenge the Spanish state. Both became more important as a result of industrial development (textiles in Barcelona from the mid-nineteenth century, and metallurgical industry in the Bilbao region at the beginning of the twentieth); but in both cases this development was also a source of weakness for nationalism, since both capital and labour were attracted from other parts of Spain, and the aims of Catalan and Basque nationalism were liable to conflict with those of Spanish capitalism as a whole and of the wider Spanish socialist movement.

The revival of the Catalan language dates from the 1830s with the poetry of Aribau, and still more of the priest Verdaguer. In the 1870s there was a large literary output in Catalan, ranging from poetry to journalism: the first regular daily newspaper in Catalan, *Diari Català*, started in 1879. The unsuccessful attempts to set up a federal republic in Spain in the five troubled years which followed the overthrow of the monarchy in 1868 had a strong support in Catalonia. Leading Catalans submitted a *Memorial* to King Alfonso XII in 1885, calling for a political system based not on centralism but on autonomies, and extolling the superior vital forces of the Catalans. In 1894 was published a *Catechism* by Prat de la Riba, which asked for a 'Catalan state in federative union with the other nations of Spain'. This view was expressed in the Bases of Manresa, which summed up the demands of moderate Catalan nationalists for home rule within Spain. A further stage was the formation of a political party, the *Lliga Regionalista*, in 1901. Ten years later the Lliga took part in a coalition government in Madrid, and obtained a concession in the form of *Mancomunidad*, an officially approved cultural authority with some powers over the four provinces of Catalan population. This, however, still fell far short of the kind of self-government that nationalists desired. In 1906 an attempt to form a single Catalan front, the *Solidariedad Catalana*, had failed; and in 1922 a new party, the *Acció Catalá*, was formed under Colonel Francisco Macia. Whereas the leaders of the Lliga, Prat de la Riba and Francisco Cambó, were socially conservative and were willing to cooperate with monarchist politicians in Madrid, Macia and his colleague Luis Compañys preferred alliance with the republicans.

Meanwhile the swelling working class of Barcelona had become an important political force. Recruited not only from children of peasants from the overpopulated Catalan countryside, but also from numerous immigrants from Andalusia, who did not speak Catalan, it came under syndicalist and anarchist leadership, organised in the powerful trade union *Confederación Nacional del Trabajo* (CNT), the rival of the socialist *Unión General de Trabajadores* (UGT). Though the CNT was not against Catalan self-government, it had to take account of its non-Catalan members, put workers' interests first, and was suspicious of big industrialists like Cambó.

Basque nationalism was inhibited by the extreme divergence of the Basque language from any other known tongue. To develop a modern literature in this tongue was a formidable task. Another difficulty was that the Basques were an overwhelmingly peasant people, with a very small middle class. From their ranks emerged men of intellectual distinction, but they tended to be absorbed in Spanish culture, to write in Castilian. Nevertheless, among the people of the Basque lands, whichever their language, there was a strong desire for self-government. The association of the Basques with the defeated Carlist cause led to the loss of their medieval local liberties, and it was from a demand for their restoration that a nationalist movement arose. Its founder was Sabino de Araña, who founded the *Partido nacional vasco* (PNV) in 1894. His aim was a united Basque homeland, Euzkadi, which was to comprise the Spanish provinces of Vizcaya, Guipuzcoa, Alava and part of Navarra, as well as the Basque-speaking lands on the French side of the Pyrenees. The party did its best not only to revive interest in Basque traditions and customs but also to promote literature in the Basque language, and to resist the penetration of Castilian at the expense of Basque through industry and the schools.

The unsuccessful disorders in Barcelona in 1917, and the dictatorship of General Primo de Rivera from 1923 to 1929, strengthened the radical forces. Macia's Catalan Left Party (*Esquerra*) joined with the Spanish Republicans, and when the Republic came into existence in 1931 they were rewarded by the creation of a Catalan regional government, the *Generalitat*, which prepared a draft for Catalan autonomy which was submitted to the Constituent Cortes in Madrid, and accepted by it with small modification. This looked like a real victory at last for Catalan nationalism, but it did not last long. The CNT would not cooperate with the *Esquerra*, and there were strikes and riots in Barcelona which helped to bring about the defeat in Madrid of the moderate Left and the victory of the Right. When a still more right-wing government was formed in October 1934, there were revolts in Barcelona, as well as in Madrid and the Asturias mining towns. The Barcelona rising was put down by the army, loyal to the Madrid government, and was not supported by the CNT workers. Catalan autonomy had lasted two years.

The Republic in 1932 offered an autonomous statute to the Basques, which was rejected by the Navarrese, still Carlist in sympathy, but accepted by the other three provinces. The Basques did not revolt in 1934, but they disliked the victorious right-wing government because it clearly stood for centralism.

The year 1936 brought a Popular Front of the parties of the Left, which included the Catalan *Esquerra*. The Basques did not join it, but they preferred it to the centralist Right. The CNT and Anarchists also did not join it, but they showed a relative benevolence which caused many of their workers to vote for it, bringing about its electoral victory on 16 February 1936. Under the Popular Front government, the Cortes began to consider a statute of autonomy for Galicia, but legislation had not yet been enacted when the military revolt of 17 July started the three years of civil war.

During the war Catalonia was a stronghold of the Republic, but its people were far from united, and their relations with the government, first in Madrid and then in Valencia, were far from happy. The *Generalitat* was revived, and for six months (November 1936 to May 1937) the CNT not only cooperated with Compañys, the founder of the *Esquerra*, having learned the lesson of the 1934 disaster, but even took part in the Madrid government coalition. This came to an end as a result of a feud between the increasingly influential and efficient Communist Party (which succeeded in taking over the *Partido socialista unificado de Cataluña* (PSUC) and a Trotskyist group known as *Partido obrero de Unificación Marxista* (POUM). Their quarrel arose not from Catalan or Spanish problems, but from the distant fanaticisms of Soviet Russian internal politics. The POUM made an ineffectual insurrection, was crushed, and its members then pursued with ruthless cruelty by the Communist and PSUC leaders, with the expert aid of Soviet security policemen sent for the purpose. These events antagonised the CNT and Anarchists, and brought odium on the Catalan nationalists. To the more conservative Republicans, they appeared to be aiding and abetting bloodthirsty anarchists, while to Spanish socialists they seemed perversely to be putting Catalan interests before the common cause. When General Franco won the war, Catalan nationalism was at first persecuted as ruthlessly as socialism.

The Basques, too, supported the Republic in the three provinces, though not in Navarre. The Republic enacted a Basque statute of autonomy in 1936. Strongly Catholic, socially conservative, but based on strong popular support democratically expressed, the Basques fought bravely, and more humanely than most of their fellow Republicans, but Franco completed the conquest of the Basque lands by 1937. After that they, like the Catalans, lost their autonomy.

In the first years of the Franco regime public use of both the Catalan and the Basque language was forbidden, and persons known to have nationalist sympathies were subjected to persecution of various kinds: their leaders either had fled the country or had been imprisoned.

Twenty years of economic recovery and industrial progress brought a certain mellowing of the regime. The Basque and Catalan lands were in the forefront of progress, and so had a higher standard of living than Castile (with the sole exception of Madrid). Prosperity did not compensate for national subjection: on the contrary, as in so many other cases that will be discussed in this work, the effect was rather to stimulate national consciousness and discontent. The large influx of Castilian labour to both Barcelona and Bilbao benefited the Catalan and Basque standard of living, but aroused the fear that Catalan and Basque cultures were facing a new danger of being submerged. At the same time the central authorities began to show more tolerance for national cultures. Folklore festivals were permitted, periodicals were allowed in both Catalan and Basque, and some hours of broadcasting time, though not of television, were allotted to them. One school in San Sebastian used Basque as its language of instruction. Voluntary part-time schools, called *Ikastolas*, were created from private funds to help the use of Basque both in speech and in writing, and priests played an active part in them. All these limited improvements (as seems to be usual in such situations) provoked not gratitude but resentment. Catalans and Basques felt that the wealth which they were producing was being consumed by the less industrious and enterprising Castilians, and that while they made the economy work, the Castilians were getting the best jobs in government and armed forces, and the best opportunities for education and careers were going to Castilian children.

The leaders of the PNV were in exile in France. That they had considerable influence among the Basques in the homeland was shown by the impressive general strike of 1947. However, this demonstration of Basque solidarity had no tangible results. It was probable that the PNV still had the passive support of the professional elite which formed the potential leadership of Basque nationalism, including a large part of the Catholic clergy. However, in the 1960s appeared a new type of nationalism, a conspiratorial group devoted to armed struggle and assassination. This was the ETA (*Euzkadi ta Azkatsuna*, or 'Basque homeland and freedom'), founded in 1959, which carried out a number of violent acts culminating in the killing of the Spanish prime minister on 20 December 1973. ETA suffered not only from police repression but from dissension and sectarianism within its ranks; yet its activities drew world-wide attention to the Basque problem and strengthened the national consciousness of the Basque people in Spain and to some extent also on the French side of the Pyrenees.

Catalan nationalism used less sensational methods, but was potentially more dangerous to the Spanish state. Indeed, the fierce reaction of the Madrid government to Basque terrorism was probably largely due to its fears of indirect effects in Catalonia. The most important event of these years in Catalonia was the Assembly of Catalonia which was held illegally outside Barcelona in November 1971, attended by representatives of the PSUC, the *Esquerra*, and several new nationalist parties. All agreed in demanding the restoration of the 1932 statute, a full political amnesty, political and civil liberties. The Anarchists also still existed in Catalonia, though it was impossible to estimate their strength. That Catalan nationalism was still alive was shown by the demonstration in Barcelona at the time of the first visits of King Juan Carlos after the death of Franco. Both Catalan and Basque nationalism faced not only the hostility of the defenders of the old regime, but the certainty that, whatever their short-term common interests, they were bound to conflict, as they had in 1936-37, with all-Spanish movements of socialism, communism and anarchism.

In the 1970s the existence of a Spanish nation was a matter of dispute, as it had been for centuries past. Doubtless a majority of the population of the Spanish state considered themselves to be Spaniards, and most of these identified 'Spanish' with 'Castilian'. Others felt themselves to be both Spaniards and Catalans, or both Spaniards and Basques, in much the same way as many considered themselves to be both British and Scots, or British and Welsh. For them, Spain was, like Great Britain for the British, the name of a state and of a culture rather than of a nation. Still others felt themselves to be only Catalans or only Basques, and would be content only with sovereign statehood.

The Habsburg rulers had called themselves kings not of Spain but of the Spains (*las Españas*), as the Romanov rulers had called themselves emperors of 'all the Russias'. In this sense Portugal had been one of the Spains, though it had finally broken away in 1640, thereby depriving the Spanish kings of the right to consider themselves rulers of all the Spains—as the Portuguese delegates to the peace conference of Utrecht in 1713 had pointed out.[30] In the late twentieth century there was no question of Portugal giving up its independence. Yet Basque and Catalans were as different from Castilians as were Portuguese. There were also the Galicians, neighbours of Portugal in the north, speaking a language very close to Portuguese, neither asking for union with Portugal nor claimed by the Portuguese, yet also without doubt different from Castilians. Some observers would argue that modern mass media exerted so strong a pressure that Castilian culture and a centralised Spanish national consciousness were bound to impose themselves. Others would reply that national languages and cultures were not so easily absorbed, and that a better answer to Spain's problems would be a federal state, perhaps even a federation of the whole Iberian Peninsula.

## The Netherlanders

Even a brief glance at the map will show that the Low Countries, with their centre in the Rhine Delta, from which they extend westward to the narrows between England and the Continent and northward to the point where the coast of Europe turns sharply and permanently towards the east, occupy a position of the greatest strategic and commercial importance.

In Roman times, the Low Countries were a remote frontier outpost. It was not until the medieval German empire had been consolidated, and comparatively stable social and political conditions had been established in France, England and Scandinavia, that their economic and cultural potential could be developed. In the eleventh century trade from the British Isles and the Baltic lands passed through the Netherlands, up the Rhine and across the Alps into Italy, while the products of the Mediterranean took the reverse road. The Low Countries, and especially Flanders, became not only a commercial but an industrial centre. Prosperous cities arose, with bourgeois and artisan classes, first among them Bruges and Ghent.

This region was divided into a number of territorial sovereignties, of which Flanders was subject to the king of France and the others to the German empire. Its cities produced not only material goods but a unique culture, including the beginnings of a secular literature in a distinct Germanic language—*Dietsch*, as it was called by the thirteenth century poet Jan Maerlant. Side by side with the traditional lords, the cities became territorial and military powers. It was the plebeian infantrymen who defeated the feudal army of the king of France at the Battle of Courtrai in 1302.

At the end of the fourteenth century Flanders and Artois came into the possession of the Duke of Burgundy (1384) Philip the Good through marriage; and his successors acquired Hainault, Holland and Zealand (1428) and Brabant (1430). Though princes of the French royal house, the dukes of Burgundy became independent sovereigns and indeed bitter rivals of the French kings. The Burgundian and Netherlands portions of their domain were never welded together by a common patriotism. The leading courtiers, soldiers and political figures were Burgundians, while the Netherlands played the main economic role. French was the language not only of Burgundy but also of Artois, Hainault and southern Flanders. However, the main division was not between the language groups but between Burgundy, with its feudal social and political order, and the increasingly bourgeois society of the Netherlands. Within the Low Countries there were also differences. The north was already specialising in seafaring and maritime trade, while the south was occupied with industry and with land-borne trade. The people of Flanders, from long experience, had a deep hostility to France, while those of Holland had no such feeling.

When Duke Charles the Bold of Burgundy was killed in battle with the Swiss in 1477, most of the Burgundian lands passed to Louis XI of France, but Charles's daughter Mary, who married the Habsburg Archduke Maximilian (later emperor), retained the Low Countries. Their son Philip married the heiress to the Spanish throne. As he died young, it was his son Charles who combined in his person the sovereignty of the Low Countries and Spain, and was also elected emperor in 1519.

It was in the time of Charles V[31] that the Reformation made itself felt in the Low Countries. The minds of these most intelligent and cultured of Europeans, whose outstanding example was the great Erasmus of Rotterdam, were well prepared for the new ideas. The influence first of Martin Luther, and then of the Baptists, spread from Germany, and somewhat later the doctrines of Calvin from Geneva and France. It was the latter which proved to be the most effective. The upper classes of the Low Countries were tolerant to the reformers, but also wished to avoid a breach with Rome and were alarmed by the tendencies to social radicalism contained in the new ideas. Emperor Charles V was a firm enemy of heresy, and issued decrees against it, but these were not fiercely applied. Charles was by upbringing a Netherlander rather than a Spaniard and did not press his people too hard.

All this changed with the accession of Philip II to the throne of Spain. He insisted on centralisation of government and church, and on the extirpation of heresy. In 1567 he sent the Duke of Alba to the Netherlands with Spanish troops to suppress opposition. The result was to drive even moderate men into revolt. This movement had three distinct aspects, closely intertwined: no neat separation or exact labelling of them is possible. There was the revolt of the nobility, in defence of its political rights, against the autocracy of Philip II; the revolt of the great majority of the people against domination by arrogant foreigners from Spain; and the revolt of Protestants (themselves divided into several subdivisions and sects) against the persecution of the Inquisition.

At first Alba was successful, and his enemies were crushed without pity. In 1572, however, Calvinist refugees from England captured the island fortress of Brill, and set up the rule of the 'Sea Beggars', controlling the mouths of the great rivers and commanding the sea approaches. Zealand and Holland were liberated by them, and Calvinist rule was imposed by force.

The second stage came when, exhausted by the horrors of war and repression, the leaders of south and north combined in opposition to the Spanish government to make the Pacification of Ghent of 8 November 1576. This was essentially a territorial division, with Calvinism to be predominant in the north and Catholicism in the south. However, the agreement did not last. Extreme reformers, who were also social radicals, seized power in Ghent and other Dietsch-speaking cities of Flanders. William the Silent, Prince of Orange, did his best to preserve the union: consistently, he fought and worked for unity of the Low Countries against Spain regardless of religious differences. He failed, however, for the nobility of the southern provinces, mainly of French speech, frightened by the social radicalism of the reformers and to some extent also animated by dislike of the Dietsch-speaking population, formed the Union of Arras, and submitted to Philip II. In January 1579 was formed the Union of Utrecht, consisting of the northern provinces only.

The third stage of the struggle began with great victories for the Spanish commander, Alessandro Farnese, Duke of Parma. In the summer of 1584 he occupied most of Flanders, and on 10 July 1584 the assassination of William of Orange deprived the Netherlanders of a great leader. However they recovered, partly because Spanish power was diverted first to the Armada against England and then to war with Henri IV of France; and partly because the Netherlands had a brilliant general in William's successor, Maurice of Nassau. During the next years Maurice recovered Friesland, Groningen and Gelderland, while Parma completed the conquest of the south. In 1609 a twelve-year truce was signed. The frontiers then established as provisional proved—with some modification—very lasting.

The result of forty years of war had thus been a territorial partition of the Netherlands. The process of the formation of a single Netherlands nation, which had begun at least in the twelfth century, was arrested. The division between the two halves of the Netherlands was now based on religion: Calvinism became one of the foundations of the new Dutch nation, while the people of the southern Netherlands remained Catholic. At the beginning of the war, the various religious groups had been scattered all over the Netherlands. However, the military strength of the Protestants had become concentrated in the north; and the frontier eventually accepted by both sides corresponded approximately to the line of the great rivers. This was to some extent a strategic boundary, although this should not be exaggerated: during the war the rivers, especially when frozen in winter, had not proved so formidable an obstacle to the armies of either side.[32] The fact remained that the Low Countries were now divided, and that the people of the north, in which Protestants predominated numerically and held all the political power, grew into a new nation, while the people of the south remained subject to foreign rule and lost the elements of national identity which they had once had.

The division was not quite so simple. Protestants from the south took refuge in the north, and contributed greatly to the subsequent economic, cultural and political achievements of the new state—which was known correctly as the United Provinces (of which there were seven), but was widely known abroad by the name of the most powerful of these provinces, Holland. There still remained many Catholics in the north, about a third of the population, who were tolerated, though subject to political disabilities. In the south no Protestants were tolerated. In the north, the language of the whole people, and of public administration, was Dutch. In the south, a large part of the population spoke French (though the proportion diminished as a result of the direct annexation to France during the seventeenth century of Artois, Cambrai and parts of Flanders and Hainault by Louis XIV), and French was the language of public business.

During the seventeenth century there was a splendid flowering of economic enterprise, overseas expansion, art and literature in the north. This was the great age of Dutch painting, and the age in which the Dutch seaborne empire was established, from Brazil to the Moluccas. It cannot be said that the south stagnated. Its economy was more efficient and prosperous than most parts of Europe, and the Counter-Reformation had its artistic achievements. Nevertheless, it lagged far behind the north.

The belief in a single Netherlands nation, the bitter regret at its partition, survived for many years, but by the end of the century it had almost faded away. This was mainly because Holland had become a world power, with interests in many distant lands, and also because its relations with other European powers had become transformed. The two states which, in the struggle for independence, had from time to time given some direct or indirect aid to the Dutch (as the people of the northern Netherlands were henceforth called in English)—France and England—had become her rivals or enemies, while her old enemy—Spain—had ceased to be dangerous. The English were competing with the Dutch in the seas of the world; and even the mutual sympathies of Cromwell and de Witt (both Protestants and republicans) did not counterweigh the conflict of state interests. The French had designs on the southern Netherlands, and proposed to the Dutch, when they were still their allies, partition schemes. These the Dutch rejected because they did not wish to be brought into direct physical contact with France: a southern Netherlands buffer state, under Spanish rule, seemed better suited to Dutch interests. In 1672 began the long period of war against Louis XIV, in which the Dutch were at times in deadly danger, but from which they emerged victorious though weakened. By the Treaty of Utrecht of 1713 the southern Netherlands were transferred from Spain to Austria, but the partition remained.

During the eighteenth century French and British interests contended with each other in Dutch politics. This rivalry to some extent coincided with the long conflict (which had also dominated the seventeenth century) between Republicans and supporters of the House of Orange. In 1787 Prussian forces, with British approval, forcibly restored the Prince of Orange against the pro-French Patriot party. In the same years, the reforms of Joseph II antagonised pious Catholics in the Austrian Netherlands, while failing to satisfy the more enthusiastic pupils of the European Enlightenment. The revolt of the southern Netherlands against Austria in 1789 was an uneasy alliance of conservatives and radicals. In December the rebels proclaimed the United States of Belgium. A year later the Austrian army reconquered the country, but in April 1792 the army of the French Revolution invaded. Dumouriez defeated the Austrians at the Battle of Jémappes on 6 November. In February 1793 the Austrian Netherlands were annexed to France, and this included the people of the French-speaking bishopric of Liège, which had joined Belgium in 1789. In Holland the division between conservatives and radicals remained deep. When the French invaded the United Provinces in January 1795, the Patriots welcomed them while the Prince of Orange went into exile. A Batavian Republic was proclaimed, with genuine support from a large part of the people. In 1806, however, Napoleon decided to make his brother Louis king of Holland, and in 1810 Holland was annexed directly to France. Thus the whole Netherlands was united after two hundred years, but under French rule.

The defeat of Napoleon brought the restoration of the House of Orange. The great powers, especially Britain and Prussia, wishing to build substantial states on the border of France, decided that the Netherlands should become a single kingdom. Though the reason for its creation was to be found in great power strategy, it might have been expected, from a twentieth century perspective, that the enterprise would have been a success, and that the Dutch-speaking peoples of the two parts of the Netherlands would be happy to be reunited with each other. This did not prove to be the case. The religious difference proved to be more important than the unity of language. Even this unity was imperfect, as the standardised literary Dutch of the north differed from the spoken tongue of the southerners, or Flemings. In the south, the upper and middle classes were overwhelmingly French-speaking, and the solidly French-speaking territory had been increased by the accession of the territory of Liège. The attempt to introduce the much more modern, but secular, system of Dutch schools into the south produced hostility. Essentially, the Catholic convictions of the great majority in the south were antagonised by Dutch attitudes and policies; the political class, being French by speech, was actively hostile; and the Dutch-speaking majority was too passive, and too little involved in political life, to give countervailing support. The result was that the united kingdom only lasted from 1815 to 1830. In the latter year, the successful July Revolution in France triggered off a revolt in the southern Netherlands; and a long diplomatic crisis ended with the establishment of a new kingdom of Belgium, while the kingdom of the Netherlands was reduced to the old seven provinces.

In Belgium, however, the existence of two languages soon led to conflict. As the economy became more complex, and schooling improved, great numbers of children of plebeian Dutch- (or Flemish-) speaking families entered the professional and business classes, and the demand grew for equal opportunities for members of the two communities, and equal status for the Flemish-Dutch language with French in public life and education. This movement was strengthened by the development of Flemish literature in the second half of the century; and Flemish demands were more pressing after the suffrage law of 1892, which brought the Flemish-speaking masses into political life. Flemish hostility to the French-speaking Belgians (or Walloons) was so bitter that, in the First World War, the German occupying forces were able to find a good deal of support. With their encouragement, a Flanders Council (*Raad van Vlanderen*) was formed and held a meeting in Brussels in February 1917. In December 1917 the Council repudiated the authority of the government of Belgium (still allied to France and commanding the Belgian army fighting against Germany), and proclaimed territorial autonomy for the Flemish districts. After the war Belgium was restored, and the wartime events did not prove too bitter to allow the two communities to live together. Nevertheless, between the wars Belgian political life was much influenced by the Flemish-Walloon conflict, which was not eliminated by the usual democratic divisions between conservatives, liberals and socialists. In the Second World War less damage was done than in the First, as the division between resisters and 'collaborators' did not coincide with the linguistic division: there was no less fascism among the Walloons than among the Flemings. After the war the conflict resumed, though in peaceful form.

The situation in 1974 was that there were 5,527,094 persons in the 'region of Netherlands speech'; 3,142,378 in the 'region of French speech'; and 1,054,970 in Brussels, which was regarded as bilingual.

An interesting feature of the Flemish nationalist problem was that the great majority of the people of Holland showed no interest in uniting with the Flemish: at the most, there was a mild sympathy for their cause. Equally, the Flemish nationalists were not much interested in uniting with Holland. The idea of a single state of twenty million Dutchmen seemed to have no appeal on either side of the border. This could not be explained simply by the religious factor, for about 40 percent of the population of Holland were Catholics, and these had for long ceased to be excluded from political life by legal restrictions. Relations between the two states after 1830 were normally good. In both countries, support for the European movement of the 1950s was strong, and both did well in the European Economic Community. The Flemish-Walloon conflict therefore seemed likely to produce continued grumbling and hard political bargaining, but nothing more dangerous. It is probably true that religion was the most important single factor in the historical process of the creation of a Dutch nation, though strategic and economic factors played a great part too, as this brief summary should have shown. It was unquestionable that in the 1970s there existed a Dutch nation. The Belgians, by contrast, did not fit into the category of 'nation', but were, without doubt, a most successful community.

## The Scandinavians

The history of the peoples of the Scandinavian peninsula begins in earnest with the irruption of the Vikings into Europe in the early ninth century. The reasons for this human explosion, which took Norwegians down the outer coasts of Scotland and Ireland and through the straits of Gibraltar, and

Danes to the east coast of England, northern France and northern Germany, remain obscure. It seems possible that there was a large increase of population in the preceding period, which in a country with limited agricultural resources and with inhabitants accustomed to the sea, would be likely to drive people to overseas expeditions. Quarrels between rival leaders, in small communities separated from each other by mountain ranges, probably also played their part. What is certain is that the Norwegians designed, and produced in sufficient numbers, a new and outstandingly successful type of ship, capable of transporting invading forces for long distances over the open ocean. Why this technological leap forward came in Norway, and not elsewhere, is also obscure.[33]

The peoples of Scandinavia, very similar to each other in language and culture, became organised into three states, in all of which Christianity became officially established despite prolonged fierce resistance, and political institutions became deeply influenced by those of the German-Latin West. These processes were essentially completed by the early twelfth century. Each of the three was pulled by geographical forces in different directions.

Denmark, the most populous of the three, the richest in agricultural resources and the nearest to Christendom, was pulled towards the North Sea and the western part of the south Baltic coast. The first Danish bishoprics were founded in the mid-tenth century, King Harald Bluetooth was converted in 960, and the archbishopric of Lund was established in 1104. The great king Canute united England, Norway and Denmark under his rule, but after he died in 1035 his kingdom broke up. Denmark itself, however, remained the nucleus of a strong state, competing with the German Hansa cities for the Baltic trade, in alliance or in conflict with the German emperor.

The Norwegian state was based essentially on the south-western 'bulge' of the Scandinavian peninsula, its main centres being Oslo, Bergen and Trondjem. The far north was very thinly inhabited. The first Christian ruler was Olaf Tryggvason, who returned from England in 995 a devout Christian. He was defeated and killed in battle at Sold in 1000, and Norway came under Danish rule for twenty years. The next Norwegian ruler, Olaf Haraldsson, later canonised as St Olaf, waged war with variable success against the Danes, while forcibly Christianising his own subjects. He was killed at the battle of Stiklestad on 29 July 1030 by an army of rebellious peasants. This event can be variously interpreted as the martyrdom of a saint and national hero, or as the victory of the embattled people against a Viking ruler bent on personal revenge, using Danish and Swedish troops to make good his claims, and backed by lesser noblemen greedy for the lands of bigger noblemen. His successor Magnus (1030-54) completed the conversion of Norway by milder methods and made efforts to reconcile ruler and people. Norway essentially faced outward to the ocean, and poured forth its manpower on distant lands. They colonised Iceland and Greenland, and the Norwegian empire survived in the Hebrides until 1263 and in Orkney and Shetland until 1450. The Scottish and Irish nations were largely descended from Norwegians, whose role in human history has thus been a good deal larger than the formal record of the Norwegian state, the weakest of the three Scandinavian states, would suggest.

The Swedish state came into being by the union of two peoples, the Svea and the Goths, under King Sverker in 1134. Its nucleus was in the region around lakes Mälar, Väner and Vätten. The south of the Scandinavian peninsula (the provinces of Scania and Halland), except for a few brief intervals, formed part of the kingdom of Denmark; while the far north had a sparse population of Finns and Lapps. Christian missions came to Sweden in the eleventh century, but the pagan religion, centred on its shrine in Uppsala, resisted well into the twelfth. Uppsala only became the archiepiscopal seat of Sweden in 1164, and the first coronation of a Swedish king by an archbishop was that of Erik Knutsson in 1210. Sweden faced eastwards, across the Baltic to the rivers whose course led up to the watershed from which much greater rivers descended through Russia to the Black Sea and the Caspian. Trade went by these river routes to Byzantium, Damascus and Baghdad: Umayyad as well as Abbasid coins were found on the island of Gotland. Swedes played a part (subsequently much contested owing to the nationalist passions of historians) in the foundation of the Russian state of Kiev. In the thirteenth century Swedish rulers also advanced, further to the north, across the Gulf of Bothnia into Finland, claiming for their conquests over the pagan Finns the character of crusades. The resistance of Russian princes was overcome, and by the Peace of Nöteborg of 1323 most of Finland became Swedish. The people became Christians but kept their own absolutely distinct language. Swedish noblemen acquired large tracts of land, and in the few cities the merchants were mostly Swedes or Germans. For Swedish medieval rulers the main enemy in the Baltic were the Russians. Relations with the German Hansa cities, which had in Visby on the island of Gotland one of their most important trading centres, were seldom cordial, but they tended to be uneasy allies against their common rival the king of Denmark.

During the fourteenth and fifteenth centuries contradictory forces operated for and against the union of the Scandinavian kingdoms. The ambitions of individuals and of cliques were tied up with fluctuating political and social discontents affecting larger numbers. Norway and Sweden came under one ruler in 1319, but the union was dissolved in 1363. Princess Margaret of Denmark married the king of Norway, and succeeded to the thrones of both Denmark and Norway after the deaths of her husband and son. In 1388 rebellious Swedish noblemen invited Margaret to become sovereign of Sweden as well. In 1397 an assembly of representatives of all three kingdoms at Kalmar agreed on a Union of Denmark, Norway and Sweden, each of which was, however, to preserve its own institutions. Margaret's successor antagonised leading Swedes by his reliance on Danish and German advisers even in the governing of Sweden; and his involvement of Sweden in Baltic wars damaged wider Swedish economic interests. In 1434 and 1436 the miners and peasants of the Dalarna region, in alliance with part of the nobility, revolted against the king, and in 1439 he was deposed. Thus in the third quarter of the fifteenth century Sweden was in fact an independent state, though the Danish king still had claims to sovereignty, and was still supported by powerful factions in Sweden. A formal restoration of the Union of Kalmar in 1483 soon became a fiction. Sweden, under the regency of three members of the aristocratic Sture family, was again independent.

These protracted struggles had three distinct but related aspects. One was the effort by part of the Swedish nobility and free peasantry to win constitutional rights, in the face of the Danish kings' attempts, backed by another part of the nobility, to set up a form of centralised royal absolutism. In this effort the social aspirations and economic grievances of peasants and townsmen also played an important part. At the same time there was, especially in the central provinces of Sweden, growing awareness of the difference between Swedes and Danes, and an unwillingness to be ruled by Danish monarchs. Thirdly, in these years the discontent with the abuses of power by the Catholic hierarchy, which was growing on the European mainland, was spreading also to Scandinavia—especially in Denmark, less in Sweden and least of all in the more distant Norway and Iceland.

All three trends came together in the crisis of 1518-23, when Christian II of Denmark, an energetic and gifted monarch with strong absolutist inclinations, invaded Sweden with a large army to reclaim his heritage, supported by the hated archbishop of Uppsala, Gustav Trolle. Christian's aim was to create a single centralised monarchy over all Scandinavia, which would have been a major European power. He was at first successful. He captured Stockholm, and had eighty leading Swedes executed on charges of heresy which, it was quite clear, were politically motivated. But Christian's triumph was brief. A leading Swedish nobleman, Gustav Vasa, raised rebellion in Dalarna, thousands joined his cause, and with the help of the Hansa city of Lübeck the Danish forces were driven out of Sweden.

This in turn led to the overthrow of Christian II by his Danish subjects. In the following decades both Denmark and Sweden were ravaged by disputed successions, aristocratic factions and popular insurrections. In both countries Protestantism prevailed, partly through religious conviction and partly through the desire of the monarchs to get their hands on the wealth of the bishops, and of the nobles to seize monastic lands. From this period of social, political and religious upheaval there emerged not only two states, but also distinct Swedish and Danish national consciousnesses, by no means confined to the upper classes but extending also to townsmen and peasants. The two states became bitter rivals for supremacy in the Baltic. For a short time at the end of the sixteenth century—when the German cities were in decline, the Dutch were struggling for their lives against Spain, and Sweden and Poland were involved in a dynastic struggle—Denmark was the leading Baltic power. However, once the Vasa dynasty was firmly established, the army reformed and a strong armament industry created (with some help from the economically more advanced Dutch), Sweden far outdistanced her rival, and became one of the great powers of Europe.

Norway remained united with Denmark. An attempt by Christian II in 1531 to use Norway as a base from which to recover his kingdom, with the help of the Norwegian hierarchy and of some Swedish Catholic exiles including Gustav Trolle, was defeated, and brought the wrath of the victor on the Norwegians. Christian III (1535-59) declared in 1536 that Norway 'hereafter shall not be or be called a kingdom apart, but a dependency of the Danish realm and Crown for all time'. This threat was only partly achieved. Norway still retained its old judicial and administrative structure, but a swarm of Danish landowners and officials descended on its people. The advance of Protestantism was slower than in Denmark or Sweden, and still slower in Iceland, but it was essentially completed by the end of the century. In 1660 Norway's position in relation to Denmark somewhat improved, when the introduction of royal absolutism in Denmark placed the two kingdoms on a footing of equality under the same ruler. This was followed by improvements in the material condition of peasants and townsmen. Norwegian national consciousness was less developed than Danish or Swedish, but it survived in dormant form.

The involvement of both Denmark and Sweden on the Protestant side in the Thirty Years War, Sweden's territorial expansion on the southern Baltic coast, and the conflict between Sweden and Russia under Charles XII and Peter the Great do not belong to the main theme of this book. One must however mention the repeated struggle between Sweden and Denmark for the southern extremity of the Scandinavian peninsula and for the islands of the western Baltic. Sweden's trading interests could not be secure as long as both sides of the Sound (the sea passage connecting the Baltic with the North Sea) were in Danish sovereignty. At the end of the sixteenth century Sweden's only direct access to the North Sea was by a narrow strip of coast between Norwegian and Danish land, on which the port of Gothenburg was built. It became a main aim of Swedish policy to annex Halland and Scania, and so attain natural frontiers along the whole coast.

By the Peace of Bromsebrö in 1645 the Swedes acquired Halland, as well as the Baltic islands of Ösel and Gotland. In 1658 by the Peace of Roskilde Charles X of Sweden acquired Scania. Charles now nourished much the same ambition as Christian II a century and a half earlier to create a single Scandinavian empire, this time under the supremacy of Sweden. However, the peasants of Scania felt allegiance rather to the Danish than to the Swedish crown, and they did not like the regime installed by the Swedes. When war broke out again, the Scanians revolted against Sweden, but by the Peace of Copenhagen of May 1660 Scania was returned to Sweden. In the next Swedish-Danish war, from 1675 to 1679, the Scanians again welcomed and helped the Danes, but once more Scania was left to Sweden by the peace treaty (signed at Fontainebleau in September 1679). In the next thirty years it would seem that Swedish national consciousness replaced Danish in Scania; for when the Danes again invaded the province in 1709 the Scanians showed themselves loyal to Sweden. Though the people of the southern provinces continued right up to present times to speak dialects in some ways closer to Danish than to Swedish, they became Swedes.

In the eighteenth century the rise of Russian power became a threat to the Swedish hold over Finland. Russo-Swedish wars were fought in Finland in 1741-43, 1788-90 and 1808-09. The last of these ended with the separation of Finland from Sweden, approved by Napoleon who was then the ally of Tsar Alexander I. The tsar recognised the legal system which had been in operation during five centuries of association with Sweden, and the Protestant religion which the Finns had acquired as a consequence of the Swedish Reformation. He established an elected Diet of Finland, based on estates as the Swedish *Riksdag* had been. It was generally believed that the Grand Duchy of Finland was a state distinct from the Russian empire but sharing a common ruler, *not* that Finland had been incorporated in Russia. The first Diet met at Borgå in 1809, and was addressed by the tsar in person, but was not summoned again for more than fifty years. The practical conduct of affairs was in the hands of Swedes, who formed almost the whole landowning class and most of the more prosperous townsmen. Swedish was the official language of the country, though about 85 percent of the population were Finnish-speaking. Higher education was conducted in Swedish, and primary education was still very sparse.

Gradually during the first half of the nineteenth century there emerged from the Finnish majority a small educated elite, which had benefited fully from Swedish culture but began to demand on behalf of its uneducated compatriots an education in Finnish, and the use of Finnish side by side with Swedish in public life. The Finnish national movement which now developed was based essentially on language, and was directed not against the Russian government but against the Swedish-speaking privileged classes. It resembled closely the national movements, based on language, which arose in Central Europe and the Balkans, and which are discussed in a later chapter; but we mention it here because the formation of the Finnish nation is most conveniently treated in connection with the other Scandinavian nations.

As in Central Europe, the leaders of the national movement were persons whose profession largely consisted of the handling of language: writers, teachers, pastors and lawyers. The study of folklore and the rediscovery and piecing together of popular epic poetry went together with the publication of grammars and dictionaries, and led to the appearance of periodicals which served to standardise a Finnish literary language, on behalf of which stronger political demands could be advanced.

A distinction must be made at this point between Finns (whose language is Finnish) and Finlanders (a term which includes both Finns and Swedish-speaking inhabitants of Finland). Finlanders showed themselves loyal subjects of their grand-duke even in the Crimean War, and the government of Sweden resisted the efforts of the British and French to bring it into the war against Russia. The grand-duke (who was also Tsar Alexander II of Russia) was well pleased with his Finlanders. In 1863 he decided to summon the Diet. It passed several reforms in finance and education, and introduced on 1 August 1863 a Language Ordinance which laid down that Finnish should be placed on an equal level with Swedish in all public business within twenty years. The implementation and extension of this measure during the next decades was a central issue in the politics of Finland: the Swedish-speaking minority, better educated and better placed in the machinery of government, tried to retard the process, while the main nationalist party, the Old Finns, pressed their case and enjoyed a good deal of sympathy among the higher civil servants in St Petersburg.

This situation changed in the 1890s. There now existed substantial Finnish professional and business classes, with friendly attitudes towards the Russians. It was the Russian government which forfeited this loyalty and friendship by denying the separate statehood of Finland and insisting that it was a province of the Russian empire. This changed attitude was part of a general policy commonly known as Russification, which is discussed later. It suffices here to say that the new policy had the effect of bringing Finns and Swedish-speaking Finlanders together in a common hostility to Russia. This remained true until Finland became an independent state in 1918. It is also true that independence was the result of a bitter civil war, but it was fought between classes, not between language groups: there were Finns and Swedish-speakers among both Reds and Whites.

The course of Finland's history in the next half century was far from smooth, but it included one remarkable achievement, which made Finland unique among the new states of the twentieth century. Though the Finns formed an overwhelming majority, they not only preserved equal status for the Swedish language in areas which had Swedish-speaking populations, but genuinely accepted their Swedish-speaking fellow-citizens as equals. For their part, Swedish-speaking Finlanders genuinely accepted Finland as their country, while retaining their Swedish national culture. Thus one equal citizenship and two nations existed peacefully side by side within one state.

During the last stages of the Napoleonic wars Frederick VI of Denmark (1808-39) remained loyal to the French emperor, while King Charles XIV of Sweden (the French-born former Napoleonic marshal Bernadotte) persuaded first the Russian tsar and then the other allies that he should be compensated for the loss of Finland to Russia by his predecessor in 1809, and rewarded for his military contribution to the defeat of Napoleon, by annexing Norway. When Frederick renounced Norway on 14 January 1814, the Norwegians themselves wished to be completely independent, and an assembly held at the Eidsvold iron works near Christiania[34] adopted on 10 April a new constitution. The Norwegian crown was offered to Prince Christian Frederick of Denmark, who accepted it. The Swedish king was obliged to invade Norway, but there was not much armed resistance. The constitution which Charles XIV accepted was a modified version of the Eidsvold document. Norway was declared to be an independent kingdom united with Sweden by a common monarch.

During the nineteenth century Norwegian national feeling grew stronger. This was closely connected with controversy about the language. There had always been several dialects in Norway. The Reformation came to Norway in Danish translations of the scriptures, and the educated class learned Danish, while the people as a whole continued to use their respective dialects. Written and printed Norwegian was essentially the same as Danish, though it included a certain number of specifically Norwegian words and expressions. In the 1840s there was a growing interest in folklore, popular stories and poetry. From this developed a movement to create a genuinely Norwegian written language. The outstanding figure was Ivar Aasen, who produced in 1848 a new Norwegian grammar, and in 1850 a Norwegian dictionary. He and his followers urged the adoption of *landsmal* (language of the country), based to a large extent on old Norse, in contrast to the existing literary language (*riksmal*). Even before Aasen's time the written language had been pronounced quite differently from the Danish which it so closely resembled on the printed page. From Aasen's time onwards, as writers and journalists felt the need to introduce more and more popular expressions into their work, written Norwegian diverged increasingly from Danish. Nevertheless the differences between written and spoken Norwegian, which from the 1930s came to be called *boksmal* ('book language') and *nynorsk* ('new Norwegian'), remained real up to the present.

At the end of the century Norwegian nationalism had become a strong force. It was partly stimulated by the international reputation won by such great figures as the writers Ibsen and Bjørnson and the explorers Nansen and Amundson. More important were growing differences between the trading interests of Norway and Sweden. In 1895 the Norwegian government demanded a separate consular service for Norway, which the Swedish crown, backed by Swedish public opinion, refused. The final crisis came in the spring of 1905. The prime minister of Norway, a Bergen shipowner named Peter Michelsen, passed a bill through the Norwegian parliament (*Storthing*) creating the separate consular service. The king vetoed it on 27 May. There was a deadlock, as no Norwegian politician would form a ministry to carry out Swedish policies. On 7 June the *Storthing* declared that, as the king was unable to find men to govern on his behalf, the royal power had ceased to function, and the union with Sweden under one monarch was dissolved. The Swedish government, unwilling to use force against Norway, accepted the facts, and by the Karlstad Conventions of 23 September 1905 Norway became an independent kingdom.

The last Scandinavian state to come into existence was Iceland, which separated from Denmark in several stages. It obtained effective home rule in 1874; was recognised as an independent state linked with Denmark only by a common monarchy in 1918; and formally proclaimed the union dissolved in 1944. The union had always been loose. Icelanders ruled themselves, and their separate national character was preserved not only by the utterly different physical conditions in which they lived but still more by their language, which had remained close to the old Norse of the Sagas during the centuries in which modern Swedish and Danish had evolved and grown simpler. The still more remote and very thinly populated Greenland remained under Danish sovereignty.

In the century and a quarter following the Napoleonic wars all Scandinavia had enjoyed almost uninterrupted peace.[35] All the Scandinavian nations grew prosperous, and adopted successful democratic institutions, in very much the same way. The notion of Scandinavian solidarity was widespread, though it stopped short of any serious attempt at political union. When Finland became independent, it was regarded as a Scandinavian state, though its people were much poorer and its political life much stormier than those of its western neighbours. As long as peace and neutrality prevailed, Scandinavian fraternal sentiments were an inexpensive luxury. But the Second World War engulfed all Scandinavia except

Sweden. The spectacle of Swedes growing richer on neutrality, while they themselves suffered occupation by Hitler's armies, revived latent ill-will among Danes and Norwegians against Swedes. On the other hand it may be argued that Sweden's armed neutrality helped to dissuade the Soviet leaders from treating Finland harshly in the hour of victory, and that Soviet reluctance to align Sweden with her enemies in the 1950s saved Finland's independence.

Scandinavian solidarity in the 1970s was not just rhetoric. There were five nations, each with its independent state: Swedes, Danes, Norwegians, Icelanders and Finns. The five were bound by an awareness that they had very similar cultures and social systems, yet they were certainly five nations, not one.

## The Swiss

Switzerland has long been an exception, from the point of view of nationality, in Europe, and indeed in the whole world. In Switzerland several languages were spoken, but it was not a multinational state: rather, in the nineteenth and twentieth centuries the Swiss were a multilingual nation. In 1960 the language of nearly 75 percent was German, of 20 percent French, of 4 percent Italian and of 1 percent Rhaeto-Romansch. The first of these figures is slightly misleading, for the normal language of these three-quarters was a speech substantially different from German; however, almost all were also capable of speaking German, and learnt it at school. The French spoken in Switzerland also differed significantly from that of France: it was closer to Provençal, and was claimed as *occitan* by Occitanian nationalists.[36] Rhaeto-Romansch was a Latin dialect which developed into a distinct language: in 1938 it was recognised as the fourth 'national' language of Switzerland, while only the other three remained 'official' languages.

The classical date for the formation of the Swiss Confederation is 1291, to which is officially linked the *Bundesbrief* (Federal Charter) which united the three original cantons of Uri, Schwyz and Unterwalden; but a more appropriate date is 1315, when the army of these cantons defeated the army of Leopold of Habsburg. Zürich joined the Confederation in 1351, Bern in 1353, and in the mid-sixteenth century there were thirteen confederates. The Confederation survived the Reformation, which divided the population not only between Catholics and Protestants but also between Protestant disciples of Calvin, Luther and Zwingli. After 1515 no new territories were admitted to full membership of the Confederation, but close alliance was maintained with the imperial city of Geneva and other French-speaking lands which succeeded in escaping the sovereignty of the king of

France. Some lands of Italian speech were also annexed, and became in effect subject territories.

A drastic reorganisation occurred when the army of the French Revolution overran the country and set up a centralised Helvetic Republic, to which eight new cantons were added, and in which all citizens were given equal rights including the use of their language. In the peace settlement of 1815 the territorial changes of the revolutionary period were recognised, and the Confederation now had twenty-two cantons. The unresolved conflicts between the conservative and radical forces (which to some extent also coincided with the cleavage between Catholics and Protestants) came to a head in the civil war of 1847, in which a *Sonderbund* of seven cantons sought to break away but was defeated. There were no further changes. The Swiss shared respectively in the modern cultures of France, Italy and Germany-Austria, but were not tempted to forego the individuality and unity of their common homeland in order to merge themselves severally in three great neighbouring national states. The dynamism of Fascist Italy and of National Socialist Germany made rather little impression on them: as conservative bourgeois, many Swiss might agree with the anti-communist rhetoric, but the claims of the *Duce* to infallibility and the delights of the *Führerprinzip* left most of them cold.

The multilingual nature of the Swiss state was no fiction, and Swiss of different speech undoubtedly felt themselves to belong to the same single nation. It would be too much to say that most Swiss were deeply impregnated with two or more cultures, or that Swiss nationality was based on a synthesis of the three main continental West European cultures. Most Swiss had at least a smattering of one other language of Switzerland besides their own, though the third language of those who knew three was as likely to be English as a third Swiss language. The equal status of the languages was due to a mutual tolerance which was probably closer to indifference than to understanding or admiration.

Nevertheless the successful coexistence and the formation of a multilingual nation seem marvellous achievements when they are set beside the long series of Franco-German wars and the disintegration of Austria-Hungary owing to the identification of language groups with distinct nations.

Perhaps the basic reason for the success was geographical. Switzerland lay across some of the most important trade routes between north and south, west and east. The trade gave rise to prosperous cities at the head of the Rhine and Rhone and beside the larger lakes; while behind the cities were mountain valleys, difficult of access to armies until modern times. Experience proved that it was to the interest of the more powerful rulers to leave the Swiss alone rather than to try to conquer them. The Swiss were excellent soldiers; they proved admirable allies to King Louis XI of France, bringing Charles the Bold of Burgundy to his ruin in 1477, and they defeated the emperor Maximilian in the Swabian War in 1499.

Left to themselves, they did not neglect the military virtues: first-class mercenary soldiers remained one of their principal exports. They also prospered in business. The stormy interlude of the French revolutionary invasion (including the brilliant retreat conducted through their land by a Russian army under Suvorov in 1799) was the only major breach of Swiss neutrality, which may be said to have dated from 1515 and to have kept Switzerland out of the Thirty Years War and the big European wars of the eighteenth century. In 1815 Swiss neutrality became part of modern international law, but was subjected to certain conditions required by the European powers. Some of these the Swiss later disregarded with impunity; and this has entitled them to claim that their neutrality is something declared and imposed by themselves, not a concession obtained by petition.[37]

Neutrality made possible the long and increasing economic prosperity of the Swiss, especially in the twentieth century when neighbouring lands were plunged in two world wars. Prosperity reinforced the preference of the Swiss for their status: perhaps increased their national self-satisfaction.

If geography made possible independence and neutrality, and neutrality prosperity, this does not mean that the Swiss are not themselves responsible for their great achievement. In particular, the Swiss confederal system based on cantons, though derived from the facts of separation of valley communities from each other by high mountain barriers, which made self-government in small units natural, could not have developed without exceptional political skill among leaders and an unusually constructive and public-spirited attitude among the majority. The Swiss record of religious tolerance is also quite exceptional, and also testifies to great qualities among the people.

The Swiss example shows that it is possible for language groups and religious groups to grow together into one nation, without destroying the individual culture of any. It is not possible for other peoples to adopt, ready-made, either the geographical situation or the historical experience of the Swiss; but other nations, both new and old, can learn from them.

**The Russians**

The first Russian state grew along the valley of the river Dnieper. Its capital was Kiev, built on the river in the border zone between the northern forests and the southern steppes. Its people spoke dialects from which are derived the modern eastern Slav languages—Russian, Ukrainian and Byelorussian. The early history of the peoples of Slav speech, and the extent of the land which they inhabited, remains obscure. The Dnieper valley formed an important part of the trade route between Sweden and Byzantium, and there were Scandinavians among the founders of Kiev Rus, as the state came to be called. However, among its subjects Slavs formed the overwhelming majority, and soon the rulers too adopted the speech and customs of the people.

Christianity reached Kiev from Bulgaria at the end of the ninth century, and a century later the Great Prince Vladimir made it the official state religion, with the blessing of the emperor and the patriarch of Constantinople. The language known as Church Slavonic, which had developed in the Bulgarian church as a result of the labours of St Cyril and St Methodius, the emissaries of the patriarch of Constantinople, became the language of the Russian church. The Slavo-Byzantine mixed culture which had been growing up in Bulgaria took on a new form in Russia. Kiev Rus became part of the Byzantine Commonwealth.[38] The new state also extended its cultural influence and its political authority to the north and north-west, far into the forest zone, coming into contact with peoples of Finno-Ugrian speech, stretching from the Estonians on the Baltic coast to the Udmurts of the middle Volga valley.

Kiev Rus did not long remain a large single state. The complicated rules of the princely succession led to subdivision of territory and to armed struggles between rival claimants. The southern lands were also open to repeated attacks, varying in scale from minor raids to major invasions, by nomadic peoples of Turkic speech. The steppes to the north of the Black Sea were sparsely inhabited; there was not much settled agriculture; and vast areas were a no man's land in which small or large bands of armed horsemen roved and raided. The resources of the grand prince of Kiev were largely employed in meeting the danger from the steppes and resisting rebellions by his relatives. Kiev itself ceased to be an effective centre of power. In the mid-twelfth century Vladimir in central Russia and Novgorod in the north-west had stronger rulers and greater wealth. During this period large numbers of Finno-Ugrians in the central forests adopted not only Orthodox Christianity but also Slav speech. The people of the centre and the north were of mixed Slav and Finno-Ugrian stock, those of the south a mixture of Slav and Turkic. They shared one church and one written ecclesiastical language, but the spoken languages had begun to diverge, giving rise to what were later called Great Russian and Little Russian.[39] The ruler of Kiev had a shadowy sovereign status, but his practical authority was negligible. In reality there was not one Russian state but several.

The results of the disastrous conquest by the Mongols between 1237 and 1240 are a matter of controversy among historians. The prevalent view of the nineteenth century Russian school was that most of the people of the south migrated northwards, leaving the south almost empty, and providing a physical continuity between the pre-Mongol and post-Mongol Russian peoples and states, between Kiev and Moscow. Against this, historians of Ukrainian nationalist outlook maintained that the people of the south remained where they were, and that the Mongol conquest further increased the national differences between Great Russians and Ukrainians. The truth probably lies between the two extremes. It is certain that the metropolitan of Kiev moved to the north at the end of the thirteenth century, and it may be assumed that some of the people followed. It is, however, also indisputable that in Galicia and Volhynia independent Russian principalities continued to exist after the Mongol invasion. Galicia was for a time without doubt the most flourishing Russian cultural centre to survive. In the mid-fourteenth century Poland acquired western Galicia, while the lands to the east of this, as far as the Dnieper, became part of the Lithuanian state, whose rulers were pagan at the time of its foundation, and spoke a language of Indo-European type which is neither Slav nor Germanic.[40] As it expanded its territory, however, a majority of its subjects consisted of Orthodox Slav-speakers. The dynastic union between Poland and Lithuania in 1386 did not bring much change.[41] Lithuania had its own institutions, and may be regarded as a West Russian state of Orthodox population, one of two heirs to Kiev Rus. This situation was changed by the Union of Lublin of 1569, which created a Polish-Lithuanian Commonwealth with a single government. Lithuania retained some institutions of its own, but its southern lands—the city of Kiev and the provinces of Podolia and Volhynia—were incorporated in the Polish portion of the commonwealth.

The second heir to Kiev Rus emerged in central Russia. Here several Russian principalities existed, their princes descended from the Kiev princely family. All were vassals of the Great Khan of the Golden Horde, the Tatar state based on the Volga valley which was the heir to the Mongols. These were the principalities of Rostov, Tver, Ryazan, Yaroslavl and Moscow. To them should be added the city states of Novgorod, Pskov and Vyatka. During the two hundred years which followed the Mongol invasion, the princes of Moscow succeeded in obtaining first place among the Russian princes. In this they usually had the support of the Tatar khans, whom they handled with skilful diplomacy. They were also supported by the Orthodox Church. The Tatars, like other Muslim rulers, recognised non-Muslim religious communities, and gave their ecclesiastical leaders authority over the lay population of their faith. The metropolitans of the church from the early fourteenth century onwards gave their support to the princes of Moscow. In 1326 the title of Metropolitan of Kiev was replaced by that of Metropolitan of Moscow and all Russia.[42]

During the reign of Ivan III the Great (1462-1505) both Novgorod and

Tver were subjected to Moscow by force, and the lesser territories in practice submitted to Moscow's leadership. While the power of Moscow had grown within the region of Russian population, the power of the Tatar state had declined. In 1480 Ivan III felt strong enough to refuse tribute to the Golden Horde. Soon after this the Horde broke up into separate khanates of Kazan, Astrakhan and the Crimea, whose rivalries could be exploited by the Muscovite rulers.

The establishment of Moscow's sovereignty over northern and central Russia was accompanied by a strengthening of the power of the grand prince over his subjects, including his nobility. In this, too, the princes enjoyed the support of the church. The growth of the Russian autocracy reached a first climax under Ivan IV the Terrible (1533-84). Three partial explanations of this process may be mentioned. First is the physical character of the Russian land, a vast plain in which forests and rivers were insufficient barriers, surrounded by enemies to the west, south and south-east. In order to resist these dangers, society had to be militarised and the central power had to be strengthened, more than in smaller countries with more effective natural barriers. Secondly, the Byzantine doctrine of autocracy was handed down by the Orthodox Church. Thirdly, the Russian rulers had before them the example of the centralised, despotic and militarised form of government which existed in the Tatar state. It is not possible neatly to disentangle the Byzantine and Tatar elements in the Russian political tradition. Both must have made their contribution. It is worth noting that in Kiev Rus there were representative institutions, unknown in the Byzantine empire: there was in fact a balance between autocracy and oligarchy which suggests rather the pattern of feudal Western Europe than that of Constantinople. After the Mongol invasion this balance disappears. This may perhaps give grounds to argue that it was rather the Tatar than the Byzantine form of centralised rule which influenced the Muscovite rulers; or that the difference between Muscovite and Kievan methods of government corresponds to differences between the Great Russian and Ukrainian national characters; but certainly neither hypothesis can be supported by conclusive evidence.

In practice of course some Muscovite rulers were weak men dependent on their favourites and their ministers. In Russia, no less than in other countries, government was at times oligarchical, and individual members of the higher nobility (called in Muscovy 'boyars') manipulated princes and took great power and wealth for themselves. But in contrast to the feudal West, privileges were not institutionalised, there was no formal division of power between the monarch and the social elite, and there were no effective corporate organisations with legally defined and legally defensible rights.

The close identification of the church with the autocracy was also connected with the fact that Muscovy was the only sovereign state whose ruler was Orthodox: the Orthodox of the Balkans were under the Turkish yoke (thought by many pious Muscovites to be a punishment from the Almighty for the treachery of the Greek prelates who in 1439 had bowed before the pope[43]), while the Christian peoples of the rest of Europe owed allegiance to the Roman schismatics from the true faith. The growth of the Muscovite state at the expense of its neighbours thus had something of the character of a crusade. This was especially true of relations with the Muslim Tatars and the Catholic Poles. The most extreme formulation of the religious mission of the Muscovite prince was the doctrine of the Third Rome, expressed in a letter of 1511 from the monk Philotheus of Pskov to Vasily III (1505-33). Moscow was the heir to Rome and Constantinople: 'Two Romes have fallen, a third stands, a fourth there shall not be'. This never became the official doctrine of Russian governments, but the mentality of which it was a reflection was rather widespread in the political class of Muscovy for a very long time.

The expansion of Muscovy, like that of Castile, was a crusade against the infidel. However, as in Spain, there was respect for the Muslims and their civilisation. Tatar princes in conflict with their kinsmen took refuge in Muscovy, were well treated and given lands. Ultimately they or their descendants became Christians and partially russified their names, but the process of assimilation took time, and these Tatars not only were influenced by but also influenced their Russian neighbours. The Muscovite view of Poland was also a mixture of hate and admiration. In the sixteenth and seventeenth centuries Polish culture held great attractions for educated Russians.

Ivan IV increased the power of the ruler, and he was the first to take the title of *tsar* (derived, like *kaiser*, from Caesar). But partly because of the weakness of his successor and his lack of an heir, and partly because of the strains and discontents caused by Ivan IV's exceptionally tyrannical rule, the state underwent a severe crisis at the beginning of the seventeenth century. Polish and Swedish armies invaded, while boyars and pretenders tried to dispute the throne. Moscow itself was twice occupied by Polish troops. Peasant revolts against landlords added to the chaos. During nearly a decade of this 'time of troubles' there emerged a strong popular patriotism, affecting not only nobles and townsmen but also peasants. Whether this patriotic feeling, mobilised into effective military resistance by the nobleman Dmitri Pozharsky and the Nizhnii Novgorod merchant Minin, can be equated with national consciousness is difficult to say. The predominant emotions were religious and traditional. Russians came to the defence of Orthodoxy, of Holy Russia and of the Russian land (*russkaya zemlya*). A national assembly, the *zemskii sobor*, elected Michael Romanov to be tsar, and once more the autocracy became the focus of loyalty. It would be doctrinaire to deny that the people of central Russia had begun to behave like a nation. Perhaps one may say that this great movement represents approximately the same stage in the development of Russian national consciousness as the movement in France against the English at the time of Jeanne d'Arc.

Under Tsar Michael (1613-45) the power of the state was built up once more, with the close cooperation of the church, whose patriarch in the first part of the region was the tsar's own father, Filaret. The process continued under Tsar Alexei (1645-76). Serfdom was for the first time firmly established in the Statute (*Ulozhenie*) of 1649. The *zemskii sobor* did not become a permanent or an important institution. The autocracy was reinforced. Alexei himself was open to Western—mainly Polish and Swedish—cultural influences. He encouraged the brilliant Nikon, patriarch of Moscow from 1652 to 1667, in his reforms of the liturgy, the sacred texts and the organisation of the church. The new ideas were brought largely by graduates of the Kiev Academy, which under Polish rule had become the most advanced cultural centre in the Orthodox world. They aroused bitter hostility in the Russian church, which was split by a profound schism. Great numbers of priests and laymen broke with the church, and sought escape in communities of the faithful in remote forests. Despite official persecution, a very large part of the Russian people remained schismatics or sectarians right up to modern times. The schism was never healed. The view held by the dissenters of the mid-seventeenth century, that the state and the tsar were instruments of Antichrist, profoundly influenced later Russian religious and political thinking.

Tsar Alexei backed Nikon against the dissenters; but when Nikon began to claim, like a medieval pope, that the church as the spiritual power was superior to the state, Alexei broke him. The partnership of the state with the church, which had brought so much advantage to the state, was to be like the partnership of the rider with the horse. This was carried still further by Tsar Peter I the Great (1682-1725), who abolished the patriarchate and subordinated the church to a department of the civil government, the Holy Synod. Peter devoted his reign to the strengthening of the state. His first priority was military and naval power, and next came measures to improve the efficiency of the civil government machine and to foster both industry and education as means of making Russia more powerful. Peter learned all that he could from more advanced countries—Sweden, Holland, England and France—not because he considered Western values superior to Russian but because he wanted to make Russia strong. He was immensely energetic, ruthless and cruel, indifferent to moral or religious values yet also to a large extent personally disinterested. He spoke of himself as a servant of the state, and this probably represented his real feelings.

Already under Alexei, Russia had gained territory in the south-west; the result of the wars between Poland and Muscovy arising out of the Cossack rebellion was that Muscovy acquired the Ukraine east of the Dnieper and the city of Kiev. Peter beat the Swedes at Poltava (1709), acquired a stretch of Baltic coastline, and built his new capital St Petersburg on the marshy banks of the Neva. The Great Northern War (1700-21) made his country one of the great powers of Europe. Its name was now no longer Muscovy but Russia, and Peter himself took the Roman title of *Imperator*.

Peter's reforms had involved not only the adoption of Western habits and techniques but also the employment of West Europeans in Russian government service. This continued in the eighteenth century. The annexation of the Baltic provinces offered career opportunities to the relatively well educated German noblemen and burghers of these lands as well as to subjects of more westerly countries. Peter's succession passed to a series of German princesses. However, the institution of autocracy proved stronger than the persons who served as autocrats. The demand for a legal division of powers between monarch and nobility was extremely small. An attempt to do this at the succession of Empress Anna in 1730 was prevented by the Guards officers in the capital. Though they themselves were to some extent an elite of the noble class, they upheld unlimited autocracy. In 1762 another German woman assumed power after her husband, Peter III, had been murdered. As Catherine II the Great (1762-96) she proved as strong and resourceful an autocrat as any pure Russian tsar.

During the eighteenth century Western cultural influences grew in Russia, and became extremely attractive to the upper classes. In the highest circles French was spoken, but still more Russian noblemen learned German. Admiration for foreign culture coincided with pride in Russia's achievements, and the two emotions were often in conflict within the same mind. For the first time Russians began to take an interest in their own language. In the first beginnings of a secular Russian literature, foreign models and styles were imitated, but serious attempts were now made to purify and to develop the Russian language. Ungainly foreign words and phrases were to be removed, but there were two schools of thought as to the best way to develop the language in the future. Some thought that it should be based as closely as possible on the old Church Slavonic, others on the spoken language. The Russian Academy, founded in 1783 and modelled on the *Académie Française*, was especially concerned with these matters. It published between 1789 and 1794 a six-volume Russian dictionary, and in 1802 its official Russian grammar. The controversy between the traditionalists and the modernists, whose chief respective spokesmen were Admiral A. S. Shishkov and the historian N. M. Karamzin, somewhat resembled the controversy which developed around this time among the Greek patriots between the supporters of the 'pure' and the 'demotic' languages.[44] In Russia it was essentially the modernists who won. They were justified by the rapid and brilliant flowering of Russian literature, whose greatest exponent, the poet Alexander Pushkin, reached the height of his powers in the 1820s.

Growing pride in the Russian language coincided with growing pride in Russian military achievements, which reached a climax in the defeat of Napoleon on Russian soil in 1812 and the subsequent victorious campaigns in Europe, ending in the entry of Russian troops into Paris. Thousands of young Russians of the upper classes, serving as army officers, saw European countries, conversed in French or German or English with Europeans, and became familiar with the culture and with the social and political ideas of contemporary Europe. Into two decades from 1805 to 1825 were packed mortal danger and heroic achievement, a marvellous flowering of language and literature and a sudden ferment of new and exciting ideas. In these years the formation of national consciousness at least in the upper layers of Russian society was completed, and there were stirrings even among the peasant masses. Unfortunately, in the short term military victory strengthened the reactionaries, who argued that the old regime, including serfdom and brutal despotism, had been justified by Russia's defeat of Napoleon. The minority who felt otherwise were too weak to make themselves felt by legal means, resorted to conspiracy (the Decembrist Rising of 1825) and were destroyed. There followed thirty years of almost stagnant bureaucratic rule under Nicholas I (reigned 1825-55).

However, things were not the same. In 1832 Count Sergei Uvarov, who shortly afterwards was made minister of education, propounded in an official report to the emperor the doctrine that Russia should be based on the three principles of Autocracy, Orthodoxy and Nationality (*natsional-nost*).[45] The first two of these were very old, but the third was new. Not only the emperor and the church, but the Russian nation, claimed the loyalty of the Russian citizen. Nearly half these citizens were still serfs, who could be bought and sold as goods and chattels. More than half spoke a language other than Russian. What then was the Russian nation, and what was its place in Europe?

The so-called Westernisers believed that it must evolve as the European nations had evolved. Hitherto its history had been barbaric. Russia belonged neither to Europe nor to Asia, for it had learned nothing from the culture of West or East. In the words of P. A. Chaadaev, in his 'Philosophical Letter' published in 1836, 'nous faisons lacune dans l'ordre intellectuel'. By contrast, the so-called Slavophils believed that pre-Petrine Russia had been a comparatively happy and healthy society, with its own culture based on Orthodoxy, and with mutual understanding and respect between autocrat, nobility and people. This essential unity and harmony had been broken by Peter, with his hasty and brutal enforcement of foreign methods and institutions, and his creation of a bureaucracy, staffed by Germans and other foreigners, which kept the ruler and the people apart. Nicholas I and his advisers disagreed with both Westernisers and Slavophils. They wished to modernise Russia in order to make her strong, and in this they considered themselves the heirs of Peter the Great. At the same time they rejected modern Western political and social ideas and most Western-type reforms, while sharing with the Slavophils a certain moralising nationalist belief in the superiority of Russia to the West. Only defeat in the Crimean War brought about (in 1861) the emancipation of the serfs, and so made it possible to include the whole population in the nation and to extend Russian national consciousness from the social elite down into the masses.

Already under Nicholas I there was pressure from the Orthodox Church for the abolition of the Uniate Church[46] and for forcible conversion of Muslims, and to a lesser extent of Catholics and Protestants. There was also pressure from the armed forces to make frontier regions safer by settling reliable Russians among the untrustworthy peoples of the Baltic coast and of the Caucasian region. But these pressures still fell far short of a systematic application of Uvarov's principle of *natsionalnost*. What was required of a subject of the empire was still essentially that he should be loyal to the tsar, not that he should be a Russian.

A new attitude emerged gradually in the 1880s. It was connected with the growth of the bureaucracy, and with a conscious attempt by Tsar Alexander III (1881-94) to reverse the reforming trends of his father's reign. It was accompanied by a great outpouring of ostentatious religious piety and of conservative rhetoric. The political, social and cultural origins of the new attitude, and of the policy which resulted from it, were rather complicated and remain in some respects obscure, but of the phenomenon itself there can be no doubt.

The essence of the new policy, which became known as 'Russification', was the claim that all subjects of the empire should consider themselves Russians, and should owe allegiance not only to the monarch but also to the Russian nation. The Russian language and culture, to which less than half of the population of the empire belonged, must be imposed in the course of time on all subjects. Provided that they put Russia first, and preferred Russian culture to their own original culture, there was no objection to their using their own languages in their homes or in personal friendships.

The first measures of Russification were directed precisely against those nations which hitherto had been impeccably loyal to the tsar—especially the Baltic Germans and the Armenians.

In 1887 Russian was made compulsory as the language of instruction in all state schools in the Baltic provinces above the lowest primary classes, and this was later extended to private schools. The ancient and famous *Domschule* in Reval was closed down. In 1893 the University of Dorpat, which had long been outstanding among Russian universities but whose language of instruction was German, was closed, and shortly afterwards a new university was established in the city with instruction in Russian. Russian was also made the language of courts of law. These measures bitterly antagonised the Germans, who formed the landowning and business classes of the three Baltic provinces; but did not in any way benefit the majority peoples, the Latvians and Estonians, to which belonged almost the whole peasantry as well as the incipient urban working class and a small intellectual elite of school teachers, Protestant pastors and a few lawyers.[47] For the Latvians and Estonians, Russian was as much a foreign language as German, but did not have, like German, the advantage of making available to those who learned it a wide European culture.

The Armenians had long been among the most devoted subjects of the tsar, above all because Russian military power was their main hope for the liberation of the majority of the Armenian people, who still lived under Ottoman rule. The Armenians were a highly educated Christian nation, with a long history and culture, centred around their monophysite church. Their schools were maintained by the church, which covered the cost from tithes paid to it by the population. The Russian bureaucrats, with their passion for uniformity in administration and their growing nationalist zeal, could not tolerate this situation. In 1896 Armenian schools were transferred to the Russian ministry of education, and their costs were to be defrayed by the appropriation of a part of the Armenian church funds. When the population objected, the Russian governor-general decided to confiscate the whole of the church's cultural funds, and this was eventually done in 1903. It was met by passive resistance in the form of a mass boycott of Russian schools, law courts and public authorities: the necessary functions were carried out by unofficial Armenian bodies which commanded the respect of the population.

Finland was a third special case. In the mid-nineteenth century the movement of the Finns to achieve equality with the Swedish-speaking minority[48] had enjoyed Russian support. However, pressures were building up in Russia to change this situation. Bureaucratic uniformity was felt necessary; there were complaints that Russian businessmen were prevented from operating in Finland while Finnish industry had access on favourable terms to the Russian market; and it was felt intolerable that Finlanders, whose security was guaranteed by Russian military strength, should not serve in the Russian army. In response to these pressures a new policy was adopted in the 1890s. Military service was introduced, Russian officials and businessmen tried to install themselves in Finland, and efforts were made to introduce Russian as a subject (but not as language of instruction) in most Finnish schools. In the last years before the First World War things got much worse. The claim was raised in St Petersburg that the laws of the

Russian empire should be binding in Finland, and the competence of the Finnish parliament was reduced to that of a provincial assembly dealing with local matters. Russian political leaders insisted that Finland was an integral part of the Russian empire, and denied the Finnish view that there was no more than a personal union through a monarch who was a tsar in one country and grand-duke in the other. The new Russian doctrines met with bitter resistance from the Finns, first at the turn of the century and then after 1908. It is arguable that Alexandar III's and Nicholas II's officials were concerned only to assert the sovereignty of the Russian state, and to subordinate Finnish to Russian interests, and that no attempt was yet made to impose the Russian language on the people of Finland at the expense of their own: Finnish and Swedish still remained the languages of schools, courts and public affairs.

The Russian Revolution of 1905 was as much a revolution of non-Russians against Russification as it was a revolution of workers, peasants and radical intellectuals against autocracy. The two revolts were of course connected: the social revolution was in fact most bitter in non-Russian regions, with Polish workers, Latvian peasants and Georgian peasants as protagonists. The tsar's concession in October 1905 of a national parliament (State Duma) elected on a fairly broad franchise, benefited non-Russians. They were strongly represented in the first two Dumas, and their various voluntary cultural organisations were allowed to operate freely, while Finland had a new constitution with a virtually sovereign parliament based on universal (including women's) suffrage. All these gains were whittled down after the dissolution of the Second Duma in 1907. Finland was reduced to provincial status; the cultural organisations of Poles, Ukrainians and others were so restricted by the authorities as to be almost useless; and representation of non-Russians in the Duma was drastically reduced by a new electoral law. The result was widespread and growing discontent among half the tsar's subjects.

It would be wrong to imagine that Russification was the wish only of a handful of reactionary ministers and bureaucrats. The truth is rather that aggressive nationalism was popular among a large part of the Russian people, of all social classes. Extreme Russian nationalism was in fact the only effective means available to the Russian politicians of the Right to mobilise popular support, and promised well for the future organisation of a conservative mass movement. However, the revolutions of February and October 1917 and the Bolshevik victory in the civil war resulted in a different course of policy. Even so, Russian nationalism and measures of Russification by no means came to an end as a result of the victories of Lenin and Stalin.

# 3  Europe: Movements for National Unity

The movements discussed in this chapter aimed at the union within one large state of communities divided among several sovereignties—in some cases scattered over great distances—which those actively engaged in the movements believed to constitute a single nation. In three of the five cases here chosen as examples of this phenomenon (Poles, Greeks and Yugoslavs) the overthrow of foreign rule was also a central aim: the struggles for independence and unity advanced together. In the other two (Germans and Italians) foreign rule was only a marginal factor, though opposition by foreign governments was more important.

Three general characteristics may be noted, which apply in varying degrees to most of these movements.

First is a sort of Messianism which transcends the normal pattern of nationalistic rhetoric and arrogance, a conviction that the great united nation for which the struggle is being waged is the bearer of universal values, beneficial for all mankind, which give this nation a divine mission, or confer on it a moral or cultural superiority over all others. The peculiar profundity of German culture, the incomparable purity of the future *Italia del popolo*, Poland the Christ among nations, the fusion of the glories of Hellas and the glories of Constantinople in modern *Ellinismos*—all are examples of a similar state of exaltation. Only the Yugoslavs operated at a more mundane and sober level—which does not mean that fanaticism was not abundant among them too, creating innumerable human tragedies.

Secondly, these nobly motivated champions of unity laid claim to territories where others lived, and had little of their nobility to spare for the treatment of their inhabitants. Examples are German attitudes to Czechs, Italian to Slovenes, Polish to Ukrainians, Greek to Anatolian Turks and Serbian to Albanians.

Thirdly, the combination of exalted claims and excessive territorial greed brought disasters on a heroic scale. The triumph and collapse of the Second and Third Reichs left the lands of German culture divided in three. Poland was shifted hundreds of miles westward and kept in bondage to one of its previous conquerors. Hellenism was driven out of Asia and Africa and grievously diminished in the easternmost of its islands. Those which had come closest to their aims, after their full share of disaster along the way, were the Italians and the Yugoslavs, though both had found in the course of their disasters that unity was something different from what they had imagined.

The German and Italian movements held the centre of the stage in international politics for more than half of the nineteenth century, and continued to threaten world peace until the mid-twentieth, or later. Italian unity was not completed when King Vittorio Emmanuele's troops entered Rome on 20 September 1870. Greater Germany remained unrealised when the Second German Reich was proclaimed in the Hall of Mirrors at Versailles in 1871; and though it was achieved in the Third Reich of Adolf Hitler, it only lasted five or seven years.[1]

The German and Italian struggles involved military action by one non-German great power—France—and by two whose population was predominantly German—Austria and Prussia; and affected the diplomacy of two more—Britain and Russia. Both movements cut across and intensified several of the main conflicts then raging throughout most of European society; between monarchy and republic, church and state, conservative landowner and liberal bourgeois, town and country, employer and worker. I shall not discuss these conflicts as such, nor argue about the virtues and vices of the political and social regimes which resulted from national unity, or from the efforts towards it. I shall mention some of these political and social issues, as well as the great international conflicts known to any person with even a smattering of historical knowledge; but my attention will be concentrated on the demands, actions, political attitudes and social recruitment of the nationalists.

The Polish movement was designed to reunite a people, among whose political class national consciousness was without doubt profoundly rooted. The struggle had to be conducted against the governments of three great powers, but it was not simply a matter of detaching the regions of Polish speech from three empires. There was a hard core of territory, inhabited by unquestionable Polish majorities, but there were also broad bands of mixed population in the west where Poles and Germans lived side by side; and still more in the east, where Poles overlapped not with Russians but with Lithuanians, Byelorussians and Ukrainians. Definition of the boundaries in west and east, and the claim of Poles to rule over large populations of the border peoples, were inseparable from the struggle for Polish independence and unity. The extreme complexity of these issues makes it necessary to devote more space to earlier periods than in the German and Italian case.

There had been a Polish state with known frontiers, but there had never been anything that could be called a Greek state. The Byzantines, it should be remembered, considered themselves Romans (*Romaioi*). Greek culture, whether in its Hellenic or its Byzantine form, had however deeply penetrated the peoples of the whole eastern Mediterranean basin. Inevitably, Greek nationalists conceived fantastic plans for the future Greater Greece. As in the Polish case, independence and unity were inseparable from expansion at the expense of neighbouring peoples.

In the Balkans a Serbian state came into existence in the first decades of the nineteenth century, and expanded its territory in the next hundred years. In the north-west of the peninsula, Slovenes and Croats and Serbs lived under Habsburg rule, and had national movements with mutually conflicting aspirations. In opposition to these contradictory nationalist aims, there was another political movement which aimed at a single state of all southern Slavs. Those who upheld this 'Yugoslav Idea' were essentially trying to create not only a new state, without historical precedent, but a new nation. In the Yugoslav case, as in the Polish, extreme complexity of the linguistic and regional divisions makes it necessary to devote more space to it than to the much more generally known German and Italian cases.

Some movements for greater unity have been given names beginning with the classical Greek word for 'everything'—*pan*. It has not seemed to me necessary to devote a separate section to 'pan-movements' as such. In the present chapter Pangermanism is discussed in connection with the German movement for unity. It has, however, seemed worth while to devote a brief section to Panslavism, whose importance has sometimes been exaggerated by historians but which must be seen in broader perspective. This section is placed immediately before the section on the more historically interesting movements for Polish and South Slav unity.

## Greater and lesser Germany

The word *Germania* is the title of a famous work by Tacitus, in which the customs and national character of 'the Germans' are discussed at length. Since then, however, the peoples described as Germans, and the country known as Germany, have greatly changed. The valleys of the Rhine and upper Danube, with their populations, were incorporated in the Roman empire. Countless thousands of persons, descended from people who spoke a language that might be called German and whose original homes were in some part of Germany, became absorbed into the populations of France, England, Spain and northern Italy. The Holy Roman Empire created by Charlemagne included the formerly Roman portions of Germany, but his wars against Bavarians and Saxons brought further territories into it. The empire reconstituted by Otto I was based on

Germany; but it maintained its claim to sovereignty over Italy, as well as to disputed lands of French and Dutch speech on its western border.

In the following centuries Germany seldom approximated to a unified single state. The emperors were frequently in conflict with the popes, and German noblemen, prelates and armies were to be found on both sides, fighting in Germany and in Italy. Powerful vassals on the periphery, defending the empire's borders against Danes, Poles and Hungarians, built up increasingly independent states of their own. Elections of emperors were occasions at best for intrigues and at worst for civil wars between rival parties.

Yet though the emperors' authority was little more than a shadow, the myth of the empire continued to have some meaning, and was associated with the growth of a German culture which owed much to the prosperous cities of the Rhine valley, Bavaria and the North Sea and Baltic coasts, centres of international trade and of magnificent buildings and plastic arts. Growing pride in this culture led to the growth of a certain German national consciousness. The expression 'Holy Roman Empire of German nation' ('*Das heilige römische Reich deutscher Nation*'), whose first use is difficult to establish but dates essentially from the mid-fifteenth century, symbolised this consciousness.

German national feeling was a powerful factor in the German Reformation. This was a time not only of new religious thought and social ferment but also of national reaction against domination by despised Italian priests. German literature, which goes back into the Middle Ages, was greatly stimulated by the Reformation: Martin Luther's Bible was a literary as well as a religious landmark.

These trends towards the formation of a German nation were retarded by the religious wars of the sixteenth century, and still more by the campaigns of Swedish, Spanish and French as well as German armies on German soil which are conventionally known as the Thirty Years' War (1618-48). These disasters impoverished the German economy, but they did not destroy German culture. German national consciousness remained, but was essentially passive: educated Germans at least were aware that they were Germans, but they felt no pressing need to form a single German state that would be unlike the still nominally existing Holy Roman Empire, a political reality. The German rulers—from the Habsburgs in Austria, the kings of Prussia and the electoral princes of Bavaria to the archbishops of Mainz and Köln and the patricians of the free cities of Lübeck, Hamburg and Bremen—managed their own sovereignties, and had no wish for unity.

The European Enlightenment produced a further flowering of German literature in the eighteenth century, culminating in the poetry of Goethe. The French revolutionary armies were at first welcomed by many Germans in the west and south-west, but Napoleon's wars and tyranny eventually produced a reaction, starting with the educated but also spreading to large numbers in the poorer classes, at first simply against the French and then for a united German 'fatherland'. This movement was used by the Austrian emperor[2] and the king of Prussia, but they and their advisers distrusted it profoundly, and would hear no more of it once their enemy Napoleon was defeated.

Germany after the defeat of Napoleon was divided into a much smaller number of states than in the eighteenth century, but still there were thirty-nine. The German Confederation which now replaced the defunct Holy Roman Empire was hardly less fictitious. It had no central parliament. There was a Diet (*Reichstag*) in Frankfurt which was in fact a place for negotiations and bargaining between the delegates of the thirty-nine state governments. There were also arrangements for the provision of military contingents for common aims.

All the states were ruled by German governments. It is true that the king of England and the king of Denmark were sovereigns in three territories of German speech (Hanover, Schleswig and Holstein), but these lands were ruled quite independently of those kingdoms. There were persons of German speech in Switzerland (recognised as sovereign and neutral by the Treaty of Vienna), in Alsace under French rule and in the Baltic provinces under Russian rule, and in several small communities in southern and eastern Hungary. However, these people did not feel themselves to be nationally oppressed, nor was their condition a source of much indignation in Germany.[3]

There was thus no question of Germans suffering from foreign rule. The problem was not independence but unity. To large and growing numbers in all parts of Germany, and mainly among the urban educated classes, national unity now seemed a pressing need. This was inextricably connected with the problem of constitutional reform, both for individual states and for Germany as a whole. The demand for the unity of the German people could not be separated from the demand that the people should have political rights. Nationalism and liberalism were interconnected, though the admixture varied according to person, class, region and circumstances.

The two giants among the German states, Austria and Prussia, were inevitably involved in these aspirations. The dynastic rivalry which had set them against each other in the previous century reappeared in the form of competition for the leadership of Germany. Metternich was strongly opposed to both nationalism and liberalism, and did his best to discourage German rulers from giving their subjects constitutions. In this he was not entirely successful: representative institutions of a sort existed in six states of central and south-western Germany, Baden being the most successful. However, student demonstrations in 1817, and the murder of a Russian writer and former official by a German student in 1818, enabled Metternich to force through the Reichstag the 'Karlsbad decrees' of August 1819 which tightened censorship and all forms of control over intellectual life. In 1837 the new king of Hanover abolished the constitution, and then dismissed seven Göttingen professors who refused to take the oath of allegiance, arousing widespread indignation throughout Germany.

An important factor working towards German unity, though its motive was essentially economic, was the formation of the customs union between Prussia and Hesse-Darmstadt in 1828. It was extended in the following years to cover all except Austria in the east and Oldenburg, Hanover and Brunswick in the north-west. The German *Zollverein*, as it was called in 1834, powerfully contributed to the economic unification of Germany, and to the influence of Prussia within it.

During the 1840s public discussion in general, and the demand for unity in particular, became more pressing, especially in the more liberal south-western states. The accession of Frederick William IV to the throne of Prussia in 1840 also aroused hopes, for he showed some sympathy for German national feeling, and his attitude towards liberal ideas was, if not friendly, at least vacillating. In northern Germany nationalism was stimulated by the fact that Danish voices were raised in favour of simply annexing Schleswig and Holstein to Denmark, and of pushing the Danish border south to the river Eider, so as to include in Denmark that portion of the population of Schleswig which was Danish in speech and national feeling.

The crisis in German affairs came in 1848. The news of the February Revolution in Paris produced results all over Germany. New governments of liberal complexion were formed in Baden, Hanover, Würtemberg, Hesse-Darmstadt and Bavaria. On 14 March there was a revolution in Vienna, Metternich was dismissed by the emperor, and a constitution was promised. On 18 March there was revolution in Berlin, and similar promises were made. During March and the first half of April there were peasant risings in south-western and central Germany, and riots by workers in the Rhineland and Saxony. A meeting in Heidelberg on 5 March set up a committee to organise an assembly to prepare for a national German parliament. Former and present members of state assemblies and some city councils were invited to attend. Several hundred persons came to Frankfurt, and the German Confederation's Reichstag was induced to give its formal approval to the electoral law for the proposed future German parliament. The franchise was obscurely worded and variously applied, but in the next weeks about 800 persons were elected, and about 500 were present when the parliament opened in the Paulskirche in Frankfurt on 18 May 1848.

The task of the Assembly was to produce a constitution for a united Germany. With the arguments about the form of government, and the consequent differences between the liberal majority and the conservative and radical minorities, we are not here concerned. The problem of German unity at once raised the question, what was Germany? The easiest answer— states with predominantly German population, or with German rulers— raised a number of difficulties. Switzerland was excluded from the first, and Alsace could not be included without a war with France. Bohemia had been for centuries a part of the Holy Roman Empire, but the majority of its population spoke Czech and were becoming increasingly convinced that they were a nation distinct from the Germans. The Czechs, led by the historian Palacký, refused to take part.[4] This was also the attitude of politically conscious persons among the Slovenes, who formed the majority in the south-eastern part of the Alpine provinces of Austria. In Prussia the Poles began to put forward claims, and for a time the Berlin government, from liberal sympathy and anti-Russian feeling, showed some sympathy for them. However, local German and Polish populations in the Poznań (Posen) province clashed, and by mid-May the Poles had been suppressed by Prussian military force. In Schleswig and Holstein the German population set up a provisional government in Kiel, and announced its intention to join united Germany. On 10 April Prussian troops invaded Holstein to support their claim. The attempt of the British foreign secretary, Lord Palmerston, to negotiate a compromise, leaving areas of Danish population to Denmark and allowing the rest to join Germany, was unsuccessful; but Russian pressure on the Prussian government brought about an armistice, signed at Malmö on 26 August, and the evacuation of Danish territory. In February 1849 the Danes denounced the armistice, war was renewed, the Prussians advanced into Denmark, but Russian pressure again brought about an armistice, on 10 July.

During 1848 opinion in the Frankfurt Assembly was polarised between the 'greater German' (*grossdeutsch*) programme, which would include all the German-speaking territories of the Habsburg Monarchy in Germany, and the 'lesser German' (*kleindeutsch*), which would leave Austria out and in effect give supremacy to Prussia. The *grossdeutsch* programme was supported both by some conservatives, who expected that Austrian participation would counterbalance radical policies, and by some radicals, whose principles caused them to insist that the whole German people must be included in free Germany. The situation in Austria was extremely confused throughout 1848.[5] Vienna was in revolt and the imperial court was forced to move to Innsbruck from May till July. In October a new revolutionary outbreak in Vienna caused the court to flee to Olomouc (Olmütz) in Moravia. Austrian armies were fighting in Italy and in Hungary. It was not until November that the German-speaking Habsburg lands were brought under control. Effective power in Austria was in the hand of Prince Felix Schwarzenberg. A traditionalist and a conservative in his determination to maintain the monarchy, unaffected himself by national preferences and contemptuous of democracy and of politicians, yet in some ways modern-minded and even socially enlightened, Schwarzenberg wished simply to include the whole monarchy, with all its different peoples, in the new Germany, and so dominate the whole of Central Europe. He was not so much *grossdeutsch* in outlook as a champion of a Greater Austria which would have swallowed up Germany.

This was an unacceptable prospect to the vast majority of the Frankfurt Assembly, and when Schwarzenberg on 4 March 1849 dissolved the Austrian parliament, and then imposed a new constitution on Austria, he became even less attractive. The *kleindeutsch* school of thought prevailed at Frankfurt, and on 28 March the assembly elected the king of Prussia as emperor of the future Germany. However, Frederick William gave a vague reply, and at the end of April the Prussian government decided that it could not accept the constitution now proposed by the assembly unless it were substantially modified. All delegates to the assembly from Austria and from Prussia were ordered by their governments to return home. The remnant of the assembly, which included some admirable liberal leaders but had no power behind it, was asked to leave Frankfurt. It moved to Stuttgart, where it was finally suppressed on 18 June by the soldiers of the Würtemberg government. There was a brief armed uprising in protest in Dresden, in which such picturesque figures as the composer Richard Wagner and the anarchist Michael Bakunin played their part, and a more serious revolt in the Palatinate and Baden led by a Polish democrat, General Ludwik Mierosławski.

There was a minor epilogue in the form of proposals by a close friend of Frederick William, General Joseph von Radowitz, for an association between a narrower German empire, dominated by Prussia, and a wider confederation, to include the whole Habsburg Monarchy. The scheme had insufficient support from the smaller German states, and was opposed by Austria. In the conflict which developed during 1850 between Prussia and Austria on a number of points, Austria had the support of Russia. At a meeting in Olomouc on 29 November 1850 between Schwarzenberg and the Prussian premier, Edwin won Manteuffel, Austria views prevailed.

The apparently complete victory of Austria, backed by the formidable Tsar Nicholas I, was short-lived. Schwarzenberg died in 1852, and was replaced by men of far less political ability. In Prussia, Otto von Bismarck became premier in 1862. The wars in the Crimea and Italy transformed the European diplomatic and military scene. In 1866 Prussia went to war with Austria and most of the other German states. The Prussians were victorious. In the peace settlement, Austria was thenceforth excluded from German affairs; Hanover and some smaller north German states were annexed to Prussia; and the rest were united in a North German Confederation under Prussian leadership. In 1870 came the Franco-Prussian War, in which the south German states also took part on Prussia's side. Prussian victory was followed by the proclamation of the German empire, which was joined by Bavaria and the other southern states. Defeated France had to cede not only German-speaking Alsace but also French-speaking Lorraine. These territories were incorporated in the new empire as a *Reichsland*, for which the imperial government was directly responsible.

The new empire preserved the identity of the smaller states, including the royal or grand-ducal titles of some rulers, and a considerable variety of institutions and laws. But Prussia contained about two-thirds of the population and more than two-thirds of the industrial resources. The political life of the empire had some striking contradictions. The imperial Reichstag was elected by universal suffrage, but the Prussian parliament by a three-class franchise weighted heavily in favour of wealth and landowner-ship. Thus two-thirds of the inhabitants of the empire, while democratical-ly electing the central parliament, enjoyed much less than democratic rights in most matters of internal politics and social policy most directly affecting their lives. There were often great contrasts between the policies of Prussia and of the other states, for example in the treatment of the growing socialist movement, or of Catholics (who formed a large minority in Prussia, and included a substantial number of Poles). Yet despite these contradictions, under the empire the sense of German national identity steadily increased. This was probably least true of the old upper classes and of the peasants in the more backward rural areas, most true of the rising business and professional middle classes. As for the rapidly growing working class, its political spokesmen were in bitter opposition to the whole regime (always in words, but perhaps less strongly in practice as the years passed), but they certainly considered themselves to belong to the German nation.

The German empire had brilliant military and economic progress to show. The *kleindeutsch* programme appeared to have triumphed. Yet the *grossdeutsch* idea had not died, least of all in Austria. It is a commonplace that after the *Ausgleich* of 1867 Austria-Hungary was based on a German-Hungarian condominium, with each of these two nations predominant in one half of the monarchy. The truth is more complex. It is true that German was the language of the dynasty, the higher bureaucracy and the armed forces, as well as of the flourishing business and cultural life of the western part of the monarchy. Austrians of German speech could play a full part, in trade and science, literature and journalism, in the wider German world, and at the same time they could be proud of their role as the most advanced people within the monarchy, contributing most to its progress. In the 1870s and 1880s, when political and cultural leadership of the German-speaking people of Austria was in the hands of Liberals, many of whom were of Jewish origin, there was not much discontent with this situation: it was possible at the same time to feel oneself a German, to pride oneself on German culture, and to be a devoted servant of the dynasty and the monarchy.

Imperceptibly, towards the end of the century, the climate of opinion changed. Already in the 1870s there were some fanatics who wished to tear the German-speaking lands away from Austria and join them to the German Reich. In order to overcome Bismarck's objections, some even launched a movement, with the slogan *Los von Rom* ('away from Rome'), to convert Catholics to Protestantism. This was a failure. Yet in the following years a strong German nationalist movement, anti-Semitic and anti-Liberal, grew up in Austria.

This was in part a reaction of a younger generation against the complacency of its elders, a fairly general phenomenon in Europe at the *fin de siècle*. It owed much to the rivalry of Germans trying to enter business and the professions with the Jews whom they found securely established in these fields, especially in Vienna. It was unusually strong in the borderlands of Bohemia and Carinthia, where Germans found their entrenched positions threatened by the Czechs or the Slovenes, who were rapidly advancing in education, in economic activity and in national feeling. The new German nationalists were bitterly critical of the Habsburg Monarchy. They did not believe that the Germans were dominant in the Austrian half of the empire. On the contrary, as they saw it, the ruling class consisted of men of German origin who had betrayed the German national ideal, and by their tolerance towards non-Germans were allowing the latter gradually to take over the whole country. And it must be admitted that there was a certain truth in this argument. The Habsburgs and their senior government servants were in no sense German nationalists. They had no desire to Germanise the Slavs or to drive the Jews out of business or cultural life. The Czech and Slovene nationalists sincerely hated the Vienna rulers for imposing German hegemony, but the German nationalists hated them no less sincerely for failing to do so. It is a strange irony that the one large mass movement among German-speaking Austrians which wished the Monarchy to survive was the socialist movement. Though in principle republicans and revolutionaries, Karl Renner and Otto Bauer, each in his different way, wished to reorganise the state in such fashion as to satisfy each nationality but to maintain the whole, giving no nation hegemony over the others.

The extreme German nationalists in Austria were essentially Pangermans. Their aim was to unite all Germans, but not to relinquish rule by Germans over the lesser peoples of the Danube Basin. Their plans were similar to those of the All-German League which existed in the Reich, and which enjoyed some support from German business and from professors and journalists of imperialist inclination. The All-German League aimed at a reversal of Felix Schwarzenberg's designs of 1849. Both he and they had planned to combine the whole of Germany with the whole of the Habsburg Monarchy; but whereas Schwarzenberg had wished the Habsburgs to dominate this vast area, the All-German League and its Austrian well-wishers regarded most of the Habsburg lands as a colonial area to be dominated by the Germans, the master people to whom 'pure' (non-Jewish) Germans from Austria should also belong.

The Pangermans were only a minority group in Austria, and the extent of the All-German League's influence in the Reich before 1914 is debatable. However, during the course of the First World War there is no doubt that both gained ground rapidly. The peace of Brest-Litovsk, imposed on Russia in March 1918, was a victory for them; and there is not much doubt that if the central powers had won the war, the peace settlement both in the west and in the south-east would have corresponded to their wishes.

Instead of this, Germany was defeated, and gave up Alsace-Lorraine to France, some small territory to Belgium and large areas of predominantly Polish speech to the restored Polish state; while the Habsburg Monarchy disintegrated, the traditional Austrian lands were forbidden to unite with Germany and made into a separate republic, and the Bohemian and Moravian Germans were incorporated against their will in the new state of Czechoslovakia. Germany itself became a republic, but the old internal state boundaries were maintained, and considerable powers still reserved to state governments. As before 1914, about two-thirds of the population and of the economic resources were in Prussia. The peace settlement was generally felt to be unjust. In particular, Prussians resented the very existence of a Polish state; many—perhaps most—Austrians continued to resent their separation from Germany; and nearly all Bohemian Germans objected to being placed under Czech rule.

These resentments remained strong even in the period of greatest stability and prosperity of the Weimar Republic, and were enormously increased by the sufferings of the great economic depression from 1929 onwards. Both economic misery and nationalist resentment were systematically and successfully exploited by the Austrian-born Adolf Hitler, who himself had grown up in Linz and Vienna in the climate of anti-Semitic, anti-Slav German nationalism of the last years of the Habsburg Monarchy. Hitler abolished the old state boundaries within Germany; proclaimed the Third Reich that was to last a thousand years; annexed Austria, the German-speaking part of Bohemia (or *Sudetenland*), and conquered the whole of Europe. In his plans he made good use of the smaller German minorities scattered through south-eastern Europe, and created a burning hatred of Germans as such in most of the continent, especially in Poland and Russia. His version of the Greater German Reich would have appalled the medieval emperors, the *grossdeutsch* spokesmen in the Paulskirche and Prince Felix Schwarzenberg, but was accepted with enthusiasm by the pupils of the All-German League in the Reich and in Austria.

When Hitler's Third Reich collapsed in 1945, a terrible fate overtook the Germans of the eastern lands. More than ten million people were expelled from the lands taken over by Poland and from the Bohemian and Moravian borderlands. How many hundreds of thousands perished in the process will never be exactly known. Not only the territory held by Poland after 1918, but all the lands east of the Oder and western Neisse rivers were lost. Part of East Prussia was annexed to the Soviet Russian empire, and Immanuel Kant's city of Königsberg was renamed Kaliningrad. Austria once more became a separate republic, and was committed by the peace treaty of 1955 never to unite with Germany. Most disastrous of all for Germans, the line of demarcation between the occupation zones of the Soviet Union on the one hand and of the British, French and Americans on the other, became a frontier between two states, while the former capital of Berlin was also divided in two, the western sector being entirely surrounded by the territory of the Soviet-controlled German Democratic Republic.

Thus in the 1970s there were in Europe four states of German speech. Of these, Switzerland had survived unchanged all the catastrophes of the twentieth century. The condition of the other three presented a striking historical irony. The two states which had dominated German history in modern times, and which had also in varying degrees represented the absolutist and military traditions of the German people, were far excelled in power and prosperity by the regions in whose history peaceful economic enterprise and cultural achievement had been more notable than triumphs in diplomacy or war. Austria was a small but comfortable state of eight million inhabitants; residual Prussia and its southern neighbours were a most uncomfortable home for eighteen millions; while Hamburg, Munich, Frankfurt and Cologne were the main centres of a successful modern polity with more than fifty million citizens living in nine federal units.

There was plenty of evidence in the 1950s of the hatred felt by the subjects of the East German state for their rulers. There was a steady drain of emigration to the West through the democratic island of West Berlin. In June 1953 there was a massive working class rising in East Berlin and other industrial centres of East Germany, but the intervention of Soviet Army tanks caused the abandonment of resistance, without many casualties. The Soviet and East German rulers found the existence of West Berlin an intolerable nuisance, but neither the blockade of 1948-49 nor the threats of 1960-61 could abolish it. In the summer of 1962 a wall was built right through the city, and East German frontier guards were given orders to shoot to kill all who tried to cross it. This put an end to the emigration westwards. In the following years more intelligent economic policies led to striking material progress in East Germany. A quarter century after the division of Germany, those who had grown up in the eastern rump state not only accepted it as a fact, but felt pride in its economic and social achievements, and a certain loyalty to the state as such, even if they had little love for its actual rulers, and still less for their Soviet Russian imperial masters. At the same time some of them felt a certain moral superiority to the people of West Germany, who seemed to them to live in a degenerate capitalist plutocracy, a land of great luxury and continued poverty, morally decadent and dependent on American patronage. In this view they felt strengthened by the violent denunciation of the West German regime which poured forth from West German spokesmen, especially from students and younger writers.

Yet though the two German states were kept apart by external force, by divergent economic policies and by the mentalities and loyalties of their citizens, the consciousness of the Germans as a single nation remained a fact, and the desire for reunification was strong. However, two points should be distinguished. It was felt as an injustice that Germans should not be members of a single state; but what was still more intolerable was that one-third of the German nation should be deprived of political and cultural liberty and be subject to exploitation and humiliation by the Soviet Russian imperialists. The existence of two German states was resented; but if there were to be two genuine German states, whose citizens could form their own institutions and policies within their own country, this would at least be tolerable. An independent Prussia, forbidden by international treaty to be reunited with the rest of Germany but with true internal sovereignty and free institutions, would be acceptable to most Germans. It was not, however, acceptable in 1970 to the communist leaders of the East German state or to their overlords in Moscow, and it did not seem likely to become so for a long time.

The case of Austria provided an example of what might be achieved if there were the will to try it. By the treaty of 1955, signed by the great powers, Austria was forbidden to join itself to Germany. Two German-speaking states, both possessing free institutions but with rather different political systems, existed very happily side by side. Austrians could take their full part in the cultural life of the German-speaking world. There was no personal or professional or business relationship that an Austrian might wish to have with a West German which he could not have. The *Anschluss-verbot* did not inhibit Austrians and Germans in those contacts with each other which mattered to both. Austrians were content to live in the Austrian republic; Austria was their homeland; they felt a normal patriotic loyalty to Austria, and did not need to ask themselves whether their deeper loyalty was to an abstract *Grossdeutschland* not yet created. If ever a similar situation could be produced between West and East Germany, with a free Prussia bound by an *Anschlussverbot*, then the ideal of which so many generations had dreamed in vain, a healthy Germany within a healthy Europe, might be within sight.

### Italian unity

The peninsula and islands known in modern times as Italy were lands of advanced civilisations (Hellenic, Carthaginian, Etruscan, Roman) long before the Christian era. When the Roman empire broke up, these lands became divided between various Germanic rulers and Byzantine emperors, and later both Muslim Arabs and Norman adventurers established themselves in Sicily and, more briefly, on the mainland. Rome itself remained the residence of the pope of Christendom. From the eleventh century new centres of power arose around the trading cities of the north and centre: one of these, the republic of Venice, became an imperial power in the eastern Mediterranean, founded on commerce but also on the annexation of territory inhabited by Italians (Verona) and by Croats (Dalmatia).

From the vigorous economic life of medieval northern Italy there developed a uniform written Italian language, used by the social and intellectual elite and expressed in a literature whose greatest figure was the poet Dante Alighieri. Though political rivalries and small-scale wars continued, a certain sense of a common Italian culture, of Italian solidarity against foreigners, became widespread. There were thus the beginnings of an Italian national consciousness—something which had never existed in Roman, barbarian or Byzantine times. One may argue that the Italian nation derives from the fifteenth century, especially from the years after the Peace of Lodi (1454), when a conscious attempt was made to preserve within Italy a balance of power based on five Italian states: the duchy of Milan, the republics of Venice and Florence, Rome of the popes, and the kingdom of Naples.

This balance was broken by the French invasion of 1494, followed by a Spanish counter-invasion. Italian culture still flourished but Italian politics were dominated by foreign states—first France and Spain, then Austria. The main exception, Venice, was not so much an Italian as a Mediterranean state.

The ideas of northern Europe made their impact, and in the eighteenth century Italy had its own splendid Enlightenment, extending even to backward Naples and producing a rich crop of philosophical, scientific, legal and humanitarian figures. Inevitably, democratic thought led Italians to think of the liberty and unity of Italy. The French Revolution aroused great hopes, but the reality of French imperial rule disappointed most.

After 1815 the European victors tried to restore the pattern of small states, with Austria directly or indirectly dominant over the whole peninsula. All these states were ruled by Italians, in the sense that the administration was carried out by persons who spoke Italian. However, two of the territories (Lombardy and Venetia) were subject to a monarch, the centre of whose power lay outside Italy (the emperor of Austria); several others, of which the most important was the Grand Duchy of Tuscany, were in fact Austrian protectorates; Austrian power was maintained by the presence of non-Italian troops (mostly German or Croatian); and Austrian political influence was everywhere used to maintain absolutism against reform. One other state also had a quite peculiar status: the pope was not only a temporary ruler but also Supreme Pontiff of the universal Catholic Church. For the next three decades after 1815 the church clearly supported absolutism. The papacy was considered by liberals to be, and in truth was, a centre of European Reaction.

Many Italians objected intensely to absolutism and resented the power of foreigners in Italy. They believed in freedom for the citizen and Italy for the Italians. This state of affairs might be brought about in one of three ways. The first was a league of the Italian states to exclude the foreigner, and to set up some sort of Italian confederation. The second was that the people of Italy should rise against all its oppressors, domestic and foreign, and create a democratic Italian republic. The third was that one Italian state should unite Italy under its leadership. The first was considered at different times by practising politicians as well as by intellectuals, but nothing came of it. Under the 1815 settlement Italy did not even have anything corresponding to the ineffective German Confederation north of the Alps. The second was the dream of revolutionaries; it was attempted from time to time, but the attempts were crushed. The third, in 1815, was perhaps the most improbable of the three, yet it was by this means that Italy was unified in the end.

Most Italians were but little concerned with such ideas. The economic and cultural level of Italy as a whole was far below that of Germany. Most Italians were peasants, devoted to the church and—especially in the kingdom of Naples—to their rulers. In the upper and middle classes strong established interests—landowners, bureaucrats, priests—upheld the existing regimes. New political ideas were found among the liberal professions in the cities, and to some extent also in the aristocracy. The spread of these ideas can in large measure be attributed to French influence in the Napoleonic period, but it would be wrong to ignore the strong native tradition of reforming thought of eighteenth century Milan, Florence and Naples. Another important factor in the Italian situation was the patriotism of individual cities, proud of their glorious past. Sometimes this took the form of antagonism to another city with which one had been incorporated in the course of the series of international changes—for example, of Genoa against Turin, or of Livorno against Florence. Political ideas had to some extent trickled down to the medium and lower strata of society in the more advanced Italian towns. Hostility to the outsider came naturally to them, and this developed easily into the idea of freeing Italy from foreigners.

The first armed actions against the 1815 settlement—the military revolutions in Naples in July 1820 and in Piedmont in March 1821—were primarily directed against absolutism and in favour of a constitution, but the idea of Italian unity was part of the objectives of the secret society of the *carbonari*, who were involved in the Naples action. Both revolutions were crushed by Austrian troops, which invaded at the request of the rulers. There were further minor insurrections in 1831 in Modena, Parma and Bologna: these too were crushed by Austrian intervention. In the same year Giuseppe Mazzini founded in Marseille the organisation *Young Italy*, grouping radical republican exiles and maintaining illegal links with Italy. In 1833 some followers of Mazzini were involved in a conspiracy in Piedmont, whose discovery by the police was followed by executions.

During the 1840s some Italian writers began to put their faith in the papacy as a rallying point for a new Italy: they became known as the 'neo-Guelph' movement. In 1843 Vicenzo Gioberti published in Brussels his *Moral and Civil Primacy of the Italians*, dedicated to Silvio Pellico, the former political prisoner and author of *Le mie prigioni*. Hopes of the papacy greatly increased with the election in June 1846 of a new pope, Pius IX, who favoured some reforms, and was widely though wrongly credited with sympathy both for liberal policies and for resistance to Austrian hegemony in Italy. He was distrusted by the Austrians; and the belief in a common cause of Italy and the pope was strengthened when in 1847 Austrian troops used an excuse to occupy the city of Ferrara on papal territory. In the same year appeared in Turin the first number of a periodical with a title which was to become immensely popular: *Il Risorgimento*. Its editors were Count Cesare Balbo and Count Camillo Cavour.

The first events of the revolutionary year 1848 in Italy took place in the south. On 9 January there were riots in Palermo, which soon grew into an insurrection. By the end of the month the whole island was lost to the Bourbon king except the citadels of Syracuse and Messina. On 29 January King Ferdinand II granted a constitution to his subjects in Naples, but this did not cause the Sicilians to return to their allegiance. On 8 February King Carlo Alberto of Piedmont and Sardinia gave a constitution; on 15 February the Grand Duke of Tuscany, Leopold II, did the same. On 14 February Pius IX appointed a commission to examine the reform of the secular institutions of the Papal States, and a month later it published its proposed Fundamental Statute.

Meanwhile there had occurred the more important revolutions in Paris and in Vienna. The news of the second of these inevitably and rapidly produced repercussions in Lombardy and Venetia. The first disorders occurred in Venice on 16 March, three days after the Viennese events; and a week later the crowds had captured the Arsenal, distributed arms, and set up a revolutionary government under Daniele Manin. On 18 March revolution broke out in Milan, and after five days of heroic and costly fighting the Austrian commander, the octagenarian Field-Marshal Count Joseph von Radetzky, was forced to retire from the city. Knowing that they could not hope alone to defy the might of Austria, the Milanese and the Venetians appealed to King Carlo Alberto of Savoy to help them. This irresolute, ambitious and enigmatic man decided to act. Moved by a combination of dynastic and national enthusiasm, he went to war with Austria. His action aroused enthusiasm far afield. There were revolutions in Parma, Piacenza and Modena, all three of which sent some troops to help Lombardy. There were also volunteers from Tuscany, the Papal States and Naples. Enthusiasm for Italian unity and independence, for the complete expulsion of the Austrians, spread throughout the peninsula.

Events did not live up to expectations. Carlo Alberto seemed more interested in organising a plebiscite for the union of Lombardy with Piedmont (held with highly gratifying results on 29 May) than with fighting the Austrians. Pius IX on 29 April made a speech in favour of peace, to the rage of his subjects who wanted to fight Austria. On 15 May King Ferdinand recovered power in Naples after suppressing some street riots, but nominally maintained the new constitution in force. Meanwhile Radetzky received reinforcements and supplies, regrouped his forces, recaptured Vicenza on 11 June, and between 25 and 27 July defeated the Piedmontese in a series of engagements known as the Battle of Custoza. Carlo Alberto retired, and on 6 August the Austrians reentered Milan. Three days later an armistice was signed, which left almost all Lombardy and Venetia in Austrian possession. Only the city of Venice, protected by its lagoons and with open access to the sea, remained unvanquished.

During the autumn and winter, while the Austrian government was occupied with troubles in its own dominions north of the Alps, as well as in Germany, politics in central Italy moved to the left. On 15 November the prime minister of the papal government was murdered, and nine days later Pius IX fled to Gaeta. At the end of the year it was announced that a National Assembly would be convoked in Rome. It met on 5 February 1849, and three days later issued a decree in four points: the temporal power of the papacy was abolished; the Roman Pontiff was to be guaranteed independence in the exercise of his spiritual power; the Roman state was to become a republic; and 'the Roman Republic would have with the rest of Italy the relations which common nationality requires'. On 21 February the Grand Duke of Tuscany fled to join Pius IX in Gaeta. On 5 March Mazzini arrived in Rome, and at the end of the month the Assembly elected a triumvirate in which Mazzini was the leading figure. This was the brief heroic period of the Italian Revolution. Rome was to be in every sense the capital of Italy, its government and the expression of the Italian idea in its purest form, and of the most perfect democracy. Rome of the Caesars and Rome of the Popes had passed away, to be succeeded by Rome of the People, the most glorious of them all.

Unfortunately reality was less kind. Hopes were revived when on 20 March 1849 Carlo Alberto renewed hostilities with the Austrians, having chivalrously given them twelve days previous notice. Three days later, at the Battle of Novara, the Piedmontese were defeated. Carlo Alberto abdicated the next day, and his successor Vittorio Emanuele II made a new armistice with Radetzky on 26 March. This was not universally obeyed. The Genoese revolted against the armistice and against the hated Piedmontese on 31 March, but were militarily occupied by Piedmontese forces on 10 April. The people of Brescia fought the Austrians for ten days, from 23 April to 2 May. This bitter affair cost about 1,000 Italian and 500 Austrian dead—higher casualties than the regular battle at Novara. During April the Austrians entered Tuscany, and had to fight hard for Livorno, where there were executions and acts of brutality after surrender. At the end of March the Bourbons began the reconquest of Sicily, where the revolutionary forces were led by the Pole Mierosławski. Palermo was occupied on 15 May. Mierosławski went off to fight again for revolution in south-west Germany.

At various times in the preceding year Italians had hoped that France might help the Italian cause, or might at least defend Piedmont against Austria. These hopes had failed. However, in April 1849 the French government at last took a hand in Italian affairs—not to help the Italians against Austria, but to anticipate the Austrians in suppressing the Roman republic. There was a first attack by the French expeditionary force, under General Oudinot, on 30 April, then a month of negotiations. In June fighting was resumed. The outstanding figure in the defence of Rome was Giuseppe Garibaldi. He and Mazzini would have resisted longer, but on 30 June the Roman government decided to capitulate. There was little brutality or persecution of republicans. Both Garibaldi and Mazzini left Rome.

The last Italian resistance came to an end when Venice surrendered on 24 August, having been free for fifteen months, the longest period of any Italian territory. Manin and his colleagues were able to leave in a French ship. On 6 August Piedmont and Austria formally made peace. As in Germany, so in Italy the revolutionary period ended with an apparently complete victory for the Austrian and the absolutist cause.

Within little more than twenty years, however, Austrian power was broken, and Italy united, by a combination of Piedmontese diplomacy and armed force, great power politics and renewed Italian revolutionary action. Count Cavour, who dominated the Piedmontese scene from 1850 to 1861, was a conservative reformer, well aware of economic and military realities, determined to strengthen Piedmont internally, set on the territorial aggrandisement of his own country yet also inspired by the notion of a united independent Italy. His foreign policy was marked by diplomatic skill and failure, good and bad luck, and he was forced to adapt himself to the wishes of stronger powers; yet in the end it was essentially successful. In April 1859 he provoked Austria into attacking him, the French came to his aid, and French military victories in June at Magenta and Solferino resulted in the annexation of most of Lombardy to Piedmont. Meanwhile new governments in Tuscany, Parma, Modena and Bologna demanded union with Piedmont. Cavour was able to obtain French consent to this by ceding Savoy and Nice to France in March 1860. In April followers of Mazzini revolted in Sicily: in this movement there was the usual combination of narrower Sicilian hostility to Naples and wider enthusiasm for an Italian republic. In May Garibaldi landed with his thousand volunteers, was welcomed in Palermo, and crossed to the mainland; and by September he had made himself master of Naples. The Piedmontese army moved south through the papal lands of Umbria and the Marches, and Garibaldi had to submit himself to Vittorio Emanuele. In all these intermediate lands plebiscites were held, in which large majorities voted for union with Piedmont, in its new guise as the kingdom of Italy. There remained Venetia, which was won in 1866 (five years after Cavour's death) as a result of the Prussian victory over Austria, and Rome itself, which the Italian army entered on 20 September 1870, after the defeat by Prussia had compelled the French to remove the armed force which had kept the Italians out ten years earlier.

Italian unity was still not complete, for the province of Trento and the city of Trieste, both with a predominantly Italian population, remained in Austria, and extreme Italian nationalists also laid claim to lands of Slovene population further inland, to the whole of Istria, and to Dalmatia, which though inhabited by Croats and Serbs had once belonged to Venice, and whose historic cities bore an unmistakably Italian appearance. Some or all of these lands were the objective of Italian patriots: they were known as 'unredeemed Italy' (*Italia irredenta*), a phrase which introduced a new term to the vocabulary of international politics.

More important was the question of the attitude to Italy of its own people. The statesman Massimo d'Azeglio, former prime minister of Piedmont, is said to have observed: 'We have made Italy: now we have to make Italians'. The pope was irreconcilably opposed to the new state, and forbade Catholics to take part in its political life: a substantial proportion obeyed. The rejection of the regime by the socialist movement was something which Italy shared with other European countries, but was the more alarming because it coincided with Catholic abstention. The rise of socialism among both industrial and agricultural workers brought bitter struggles and violence in Emilia, Romagna and Sicily. Anarchist influences were also important. The class struggle was fiercer in Italy than in Germany, though Germany had a far larger industrial proletariat and was regarded as the main stronghold of Marxism.

Finally there was a profound cleavage between north and south, so profound that it could well be said that there were two nations. In the former kingdom of Naples loyalty to the Bourbon dynasty took a long time to die out. Sicilian separatism remained a force. Brigandage in the south had both economic and political undertones. Resentment against the northerners, and especially the Piedmontese, who assumed the key posts in administration and business south of the Apennines, was very strong. Piedmontese domination of Italy was less institutionalised than Prussian domination of Germany, but it was possibly more substantial. To speak of Italy as a colony of the Piedmontese, in which the Lombards had the second best share, is an exaggeration but not a gross distortion. As Italy made progress in industry and in education in the first decades after unity, the contrast between the flourishing north and the backward south only grew.

Forty-five years after unity, the nation was once more bitterly divided in 1915 on the question of neutrality or belligerence in the European War. The war party, which had its way, was an unnatural alliance of extreme nationalists of authoritarian views with democrats and radicals devoted to the cause of liberty for which they believed France and Britain to be fighting. Against intervention was the veteran Liberal leader Giolitti, the symbol of the old regime, who by a combination of electoral corruption, manipulation of vested interests and genuinely progressive social policies and political reforms had made an outstanding contribution to Italy's progress. Also against intervention was the majority of the powerful socialist movement. Baron Sonnino, the foreign minister of the war years, was determined to sell Italy's military help at a high price: he got from the Allies a promise not only of Trento and Trieste but also of the Brenner Pass (leaving thousands of Austrian Germans inside Italy) and of all Istria and most of Dalmatia (placing about a million Croats and Slovenes under Italian rule). Sonnino's policy was in direct conflict with the former ideas of Mazzini, who had believed that Italy should be the ally, friend and protector of the South Slavs. Mazzini's ideas were unsuccessfully defended by the socialist Leonida Bissolati and the radical professor Gaetano Salvemini. When it came to the final post-war settlement, largely owing to the objections of President Wilson and his American expert advisers who were not bound by the Treaty of London of April 1915, Italy got less than had been promised. She had to give up Dalmatia, but still she got a quarter of a million Germans in the South Tyrol and more than half a million Croats and Slovenes in Istria and to the north of Trieste.

The divisions caused by the arguments about intervention in the war were carried over into the post-war years, and were added to economic troubles and class struggles. From these years of fear and hatred, amounting almost to civil war, emerged as victor Benito Mussolini and his Fascists. It is worth noting that the struggle between the Fascists and their enemies took place almost entirely north of the Apennines: the people of the south were for the most part a passive object of policy. The division between north and south remained in the Fascist era. Nor did Mussolini, for all his rhetoric, unite the people of northern Italy. His regime was ruthless, and for a time enjoyed the support of the prosperous West European powers. However, the struggle against Fascism never ceased, and it was fought by the working class and by the intellectuals, including a minority among active Catholics. To the leaders of anti-Fascism, especially to radical and socialist intellectuals, this was a new Risorgimento. They were the heirs to Mazzini and Garibaldi, and Mussolini was the successor to King Bomba of Naples or Emperor Francis of Austria. This was felt still more strongly when Mussolini made his alliance with Hitler's Third Reich. Italians were no less bitterly divided on the issue of entry into war in 1940 than they had been in 1915; but Mussolini's dictatorial powers enabled him to drag Italy on to Hitler's side. The defeats which the Italian armed forces suffered were certainly due in large part to the fact that millions of Italians had no wish to fight for Fascism. Defeat brought the overthrow of Mussolini, and this led to the occupation of Italy by German forces. Most Italians now saw Hitler's armies as the enemies of Italy. The resistance movement which was then organised, with support in all social classes, was truly a struggle for national independence as well as for political freedom and social justice.

In alliance with Hitler, Mussolini had annexed in 1941 large territories from Yugoslavia—most of Dalmatia, a large part of Slovenia and a protectorate over Montenegro. In defeat, Italy not only gave up these gains, but also had to yield Istria and the surroundings of Trieste. This meant not only that almost all the South Slavs of the borderlands became subjects of Yugoslavia, but also that the cities of western Istria, which had until this time had almost solid Italian populations, were lost. This may be regarded as a retribution for the greed of Sonnino. If, in 1919, the Italian government had accepted the 'Wilson Line', dividing Istria more or less according to nationality, Parenzo and Pirano might have remained Italian.

At the beginning of the last quarter of the twentieth century, the fabric of Italian society and political life was still fragile. The division between north and south had not been eliminated. Industrial development and better education had made some impact in the south itself. The great cities of Turin and Milan, and smaller industrial centres in the north, had attracted hundreds of thousands of southerners, whose behaviour and mentality seemed strange and barbarous to the northerners, and isolated them in ghettos of their own. Italy still contained within its frontiers the headquarters for the whole world of the Catholic Church, whose power, wealth and influence profoundly affected the Italian people. The church after 1945 fully re-entered Italian political life, but it was the turn of the working class (growing in numbers and economic power as industry progressed) to secede, under the leadership of the communist party. There was talk of an 'historic agreement',[6] of cooperation or even reconciliation between these two great forces, but little sign that it could be achieved; while perhaps a third of the people remained unwilling to subject themselves either to priests or to commissars.

Even so, it could be argued that the forces working for a single Italian national consciousness and culture were stronger than those pulling the nation apart. Massimo d'Azeglio's task of 'making Italians' had been completed. In the process, force and fraud and external misfortunes had had their part; but the myth of the special moral quality and European mission of the Italian nation, the convictions of the modern prophets from Gioberti to Salvemini, had also made their contribution.

### The Greeks and the 'Great Idea'

In the eighteenth century Ottoman empire, Orthodox Christians tended to be identified—by the Ottoman authorities, by foreign Europeans, and by themselves—with Greeks.[7] Nearly all Christians who held high rank in the church, or possessed wealth from land or from commerce, or occupied secular posts of importance under the sultan, were, and considered themselves to be, Greeks. They described themselves not by the classical name of Hellenes, but by the Byzantine name of Romans (*Romaioi*), of which the Turkish form was *Rum*.

Though successful Greeks were surrounded by the contempt and envy of Muslims, and though their lives were in consequence sometimes unpleasant and always insecure, Greeks under Ottoman rule had undoubted opportunities to make good, even brilliant, careers. From the Phanariot elite, the lay officials and rich Greek families which surrounded the patriarch of Constantinople, the sultans took, from the end of the seventeenth century onwards, many of the highest dignitaries of the central government, as well as the rulers of the two Danubian principalities inhabited by Romanians—Moldavia and Wallachia. In those two lands, the Phanariot princes built up a court and an upper bureaucracy composed of Greeks. Christians were not supposed to bear arms, but there were Greeks in the Ottoman navy in large numbers, and some even held high rank. There were areas such as Suli in southern Epirus and Mani in the southern Peloponnese which were in effect ruled by Greek tribal chieftains, who paid their tribute to the Ottoman government but were not troubled by the presence of Turkish officials. Another important element on the Greek scene were the *klephts*, rebel bands who lived in the mountains and maintained themselves by plunder. These fugitives from the law at times professed, or had attributed to them, patriotic motives. They were surrounded in the popular mind by heroic myth, and they acquired considerable skill in irregular warfare. There were also officially sponsored Christian irregulars, known as *armatoloi*, who were supposed to guard villages and transport routes against the *klephts*, but who would sometimes go over to them, individually or in groups.

The sea-borne trade of the Ottoman empire was predominantly in Greek hands: there were many Armenian, Turkish, Arab and Jewish merchants, but they kept to the land. In the late eighteenth century trade substantially increased, and Greek seafarers did well out of it. In the Aegean islands, especially Hydra and Chios, bigger and more modern ships were built, and shipbuilding and trading families made substantial fortunes.

It is important to note that the Greek population was widely and thinly distributed within the Ottoman empire, and that there were also Greek communities in foreign cities. In the peninsula and the Aegean islands the population was compactly Greek, though considerable numbers of Turks dwelt among them in some of the towns. Greeks formed large urban minorities in Constantinople, Alexandria, Bucharest, Iaşi, the ports of the lower Danube, and in the coastal cities of Asia Minor both in the Aegean and the Black Sea. There were also many Greek villages in the interior of Asia Minor. Outside the Ottoman empire, the Ionian islands had a mainly Greek population. They belonged to the republic of Venice until 1797, were then occupied in turn by French, Russians and British, and came into British possession by the Vienna peace settlement. Further afield, there were Greek merchant communities in Trieste, Venice, Vienna, Amsterdam and other West European cities.

During the eighteenth century European education and ideas made themselves felt among a considerable part of the Greek people. The Phanariot princes of Moldavia and Wallachia supported some excellent schools and collected libraries of European books. Knowledge of French was quite widespread at their courts. Constantinople also had good schools, and foreign languages were spoken and foreign literature read. Wealthy islanders founded schools from their trade and profits. Under Venetian rule the Ionian islands offered Greeks the chance of education and access to Italian culture. Small but growing numbers of Greeks from the Ottoman empire studied abroad, especially at Padua but also at Vienna, Leipzig and other German universities. Greek colonies in Western Europe helped the education of their compatriots both by inviting individuals to study in the West and by sending money to found and support schools on Ottoman territory.

Increasing contact with the West introduced the ideas of the European Enlightenment to Greeks. This process was encouraged by many of the Phanariot rulers of Moldavia and Wallachia, but was disapproved by the patriarchate, although individual priests and even bishops favoured it. Natural science and rationalism were felt as a threat to Orthodox piety. Especially important was the cult of ancient Greece in European Enlightenment literature. Classical learning and thought were praised by the *philosophes* of the West as older than, and superior to, Christianity. Greeks in the West learned through this literature about their own past, which, if not entirely ignored, had at least been very little known to the intellectual elite of Constantinople either in the last period of the Byzantine empire or under Ottoman rule. The presentation to the educated Greek public of ancient Hellas, as seen through the eyes of French encyclopaedists and sentimental Western philhellenes, was above all the work of Adamantios Korais (1748-1833). A native of Smyrna, who had spent six years in Amsterdam and six in Montpellier, and from 1788 until the end of his long life lived in Paris, Korais was an indefatigable author of translations, original works, articles and letters. He devoted himself to the propagation of the Enlightenment among the Greeks and of the Greek cause among the French, and above all to the development of a literary modern Greek language, to be formed by the infusion of classical words into the spoken tongue and by the systematisation of its formal structure. Korais took care not to attack religion or the Orthodox Church as such, but he fought bitterly against all customs, institutions and ideas which seemed to him to be superstitious survivals from an age of darkness, preventing a return to a glorious past which would also embody in itself all the wisdom of new enlightened Europe.

The Orthodox hierarchy disliked this mixture of classics and rationalism. They too were becoming impatient of Ottoman rule as they saw it declining, they too were becoming affected by a new pride in being Greeks. But if the Ottoman empire were to be destroyed (and this did not seem imminent, nor did it seem wise to take big risks on so distant a prospect), they hoped that it would be replaced by something like the old Byzantine empire, based on autocracy and Orthodoxy, probably under the protection of autocratic Orthodox Russia.

The Greek educated class was in fact divided between the followers of the Enlightenment and the followers of traditional Orthodoxy, and this division remained long after independence was achieved. In the educated class the views of Korais certainly gained ground, but they did not rout the opposing views; while for most Greeks the old values long remained unchallenged. The division is one which has its parallels in the history of other nations exposed to a sudden influx of modern ideas and practices. It recalls, for example, the contrast between Slavophils and Westernisers in

Russia, reformers and traditionalists in mid-nineteenth century Japan, and Panislamists and Turkish nationalists in the last decades of the Ottoman empire. In Greece the division was for a time concealed in the enthusiasm of the War of Independence. The Greek rebels needed both religious and secular rhetoric, appeals both to classical glory and to Orthodoxy. The word Hellene was soon accepted as the name of the Greek people, and the new word *Ellinismos*, which combined the two meanings of Greek civilisation and of the whole Greek community in the world, came into general use by politicians and intellectuals.

The first Greek who had a plan for an insurrection and for a liberated Greece was Rhigas of Velestino, a Thessalian who served in high posts in Wallachia, spent some years in Vienna, and was handed over by the Austrians to the Turks in Trieste in 1798 as a revolutionary conspirator, and hanged in Belgrade. Rhigas was the author of poems, revolutionary proclamations and a constitution, closely modelled on the French constitutions of 1793 and 1795. In this document he spoke of the sovereign people of the proposed state as including 'without distinction of religion and language—Greeks, Albanians, Vlachs, Armenians, Turks and every other race'. It is clear that Rhigas envisaged a state much larger than the territory compactly inhabited by Greeks, and that he wished to ensure equal rights to all its inhabitants. Whether he regarded the Albanians and Vlachs as separate nations, or as Greeks of different speech, is not clear.

The *Philike Hetairia* (Society of Friends), founded in Odessa in 1814 by three Greek merchants, was a better organised and more ambitious conspiracy. Much of its history still remains obscure and controversial. It is however certain that its leaders hoped to enlist the support of all the Balkan Christian peoples, and to liberate the whole peninsula from the Turks with Russian aid. It seems that in their minds the distinction between 'Greek' and 'Orthodox' was still blurred. It is not known how they intended to demarcate 'Greece' from the rest of the liberated Balkans. They attempted to enlist support from Serbs, Romanians and Bulgarians for their projected insurrection, but with little success.[8] A small force led by Prince Alexander Ypsilanti, who held the rank of general in the Russian army, crossed the border into Moldavia on 22 February 1821. At first it was welcomed as it advanced. However, Tsar Alexander I denounced the action, and when Russian aid was seen to be an illusion the enterprise was doomed. Ypsilanti's men fought bravely against the Turks, but by June they were crushed. However, another rising broke out in the Greek peninsula, led by local notables, and it was not crushed. Fighting went on from 1821 to 1827 in the Peloponnese, Roumeli and the islands. In the end the Greeks were saved by the great powers, who prevented the Egyptian fleet and army, summoned by the sultan, from conquering the Peloponnese, and still more by Russia, which went to war with Turkey in 1828 and whose army reached

Adrianople in August 1829. By the London Protocol of 3 February 1830 Greece was recognised as an independent state. Its territory was restricted to Roumeli, Attica and the Peloponnese with the western Aegean islands. The majority of the Greeks of the Ottoman empire were not included in the new state.

A Greek state now existed, but a Greek nation still had to be made. This was rendered difficult by the division, already noted, between the traditionalists and the westernisers. It was still further complicated by the problem of the language. Korais had intended to create a new language, enriched by much of the classical past. At first he was supported by the liberals and opposed by the traditionalists. However, in the new state the new artificial language soon became accepted by the educated upper stratum as a whole, progressive and conservative alike. This 'pure' language (*Kathairevousa*) was unintelligible to the people as a whole, which continued to use its 'demotic' speech. The differences between the two languages became a difference of class and it accentuated the division of the nation; or rather, by dividing the Greek population it retarded the emergence of a Greek nation. Later in the century, progressive Greeks advocated the use of demotic, and the division between *kathairevousa* and *dimotiki*, which had previously cut across the division between left and right in politics, tended to coincide with it. In imaginative literature demotic prevailed, but in the press and official business the 'pure' held sway. The controversy was still alive in the third quarter of the twentieth century, though demotic steadily gained ground.

One thing on which all Greeks could agree was that the Greek state must be expanded to include the unredeemed brethren. Progress was slow. There were unsuccessful revolts by the Greek population of Crete in 1841, 1858 and 1866. In 1864 the British government ceded to Greece the Ionian Islands, which Britain had held since 1812. In 1881 Greece received nearly all Thessaly and a corner of Epirus.

It was not until the Balkan war of 1912 and 1913 that Greek aims in the north were achieved. This was largely the work of Eleutheros Venizelos, the Cretan politician who in 1910 became prime minister in Athens and who made the alliance with Bulgaria and Serbia which defeated Turkey. In June 1913 Greece and Serbia together defeated Bulgaria. The result was that Greece acquired all southern Macedonia, southern Epirus and the islands of the eastern Aegean from Thasos to Samos; but she failed to obtain the islands of the Dodecannese, including Rhodes, which were taken by Italy after its war with Turkey in 1911.

It remained to liberate the Greeks of Asia Minor and Thrace and to possess the imperial city of Constantine, replacing the Crescent once more by the Cross in Justinian's cathedral of St Sophia. This was the Great Idea which had for long inspired some Greek patriots, and since the Balkan

Wars had become the passionate desire of millions. Greece had suffered humiliation and national frustration during the First World War, being used as a pawn by both belligerent sides; but Venizelos had stood firmly by the Western powers, and their victory promised to be his. The Allies in 1915 had promised Constantinople to Russia. The Bolshevik Revolution had put an end to that, but Venizelos agreed that the city should for the time being be placed under some international control. Greece, however, claimed all Thrace and a large slice of Asia Minor based on Smyrna. In May 1919 Greek troops landed in Asia Minor, and in the early summer they did well, occupying both Thrace and western Anatolia. The Treaty of Sèvres of 10 August 1921 granted most of Venizelos' demands. According to available statistics, in Thrace without Constantinople there were 416,000 Greeks and 524,000 Turks, and in the province of Smyrna 629,000 Greeks and 974,000 Turks. This still left about a million and a half Greeks as minority communities living among Turkish majorities, in the capital and in Anatolia.

Meanwhile the Turkish nationalists were organising themselves under Kemal Atatürk. Guerrilla actions were making themselves felt in the area occupied by the Greeks, and it was clear that there would be bitter resistance to any further Greek advance. In November 1920 a Greek general election brought a sensational swing. Venizelos was defeated, his enemy King Constantine returned, and the bitterness which had divided Greek political life in 1917 revived in more acute form. The new government tried to outdo its predecessors in patriotism, and ordered a general advance into Anatolia. The Turks defeated them on the Sakarya river in August 1921, and in the following year there were more defeats, ending in disorderly retreat and evacuation of the army, and massacre and arson in Smyrna. This was followed by a convention of 30 January 1923 which provided for compulsory exchange of populations between Greece and Turkey. In practice the Turks expelled those Greeks who had not already fled. In the process, as they escaped or were driven out of their homes scattered through Asia Minor, there were heavy losses. There had been about 2,500,000 Greeks in Turkey in 1910: the number who reached Greece was about 1,400,000, of whom later official statistics showed that 1,221,849 had been settled by 1928. Some thousands of Greeks still remained in Turkey, and were allowed to live and work there, others emigrated to distant lands; but the number who perished in the convulsions of 1922 must have amounted to hundreds of thousands.

The Asia Minor catastrophe had deep effects on Greek political life. The returning Venizelists executed several of the Royalist politicians and the commander-in-chief under whom the disaster occurred, thereby starting a blood-feud between Royalists and Republicans which made itself felt for decades afterwards. The economic effects were also drastic. The refugees brought with them skills which enriched the Greek economy; but a sudden increase of total population by about a quarter was bound to place an intolerable strain on Greek society. Greece is naturally a barren country, and the creation of new jobs lagged well behind the population pressure, both between the world wars and after the Second World War. This was a major cause of the class conflicts, ideological divisions and political hatreds which continued to plague the Greeks well into the third quarter of the twentieth century.

Greece acquired Western Thrace from Bulgaria, lost it in 1941, and recovered it in 1945. After the Second World War Italy gave up the Dodecannese.

The one remaining territory with a large compact Greek population not united with Greece was the island of Cyprus, leased by Britain from the Ottoman empire in 1878 and annexed in 1914. The British government considered ceding it to Greece in 1915 if Greece would join the Allies in the war, but difficulties on both sides put an end to the proposal. In 1945 it might have been ceded to Greece, but at that time Greece was torn by civil war, the Turkish government objected to having a Greek government close to its south-eastern coast, and the increasing strategic importance of Turkey to the British and their allies caused them to pay more attention to Turkish wishes. In the mid-1950s the Greek government started a diplomatic and propaganda campaign for the union of Cyprus with Greece (*énosis*); and Greek nationalists in Cyprus itself organised guerrilla forces whose main occupation was the assassination of other Greeks or of British soldiers. In 1959 the British, Greek and Turkish governments agreed on the establishment of an independent republic of Cyprus, in which the civil rights of both Greeks (80 percent of the population) and Turks (20 percent) should be guaranteed.

In practice this soon failed to work, as the president, the Orthodox Archbishop Makarios, ignored the rights of the Turkish Cypriots. Various districts of Turkish population formed miniature states within the state; both Greek and Turkish army officers from the mainland commanded rival militias; and an uneasy peace was kept by United Nations forces. In 1974 the military dictators who then formed the government in Athens, probably in a desperate attempt to stem their own unpopularity with the Greek people by a 'national victory', brought about, through their officers in the island, the seizure of power by a former terrorist who proclaimed *énosis*. The result was a massive invasion of Cyprus by the Turkish army, which proceeded to occupy about half the island. There were massacres on both sides and nearly half the Greek Cypriots lost their homes. It was a repetition, on a smaller scale and with less bloodshed, of the Anatolian tragedy of 1919-21.

The history of the Greek national cause since 1821 is thus dominated by a bitter paradox: the Greek state steadily expanded its territory, while *Ellinismos* steadily retreated. The Asia Minor expulsions were the single most dramatic episode in the retreat, but there were others. Thousands of Greeks were forced out of Russia—from the Black Sea ports, the Crimea and the Causasus—not in a single flood but in a trickle whose volume depended on the changing policies of the Soviet regime. Many met their deaths in collectivisation and the purges of 1936-39. The great Greek community in Egypt, with its centre in Alexandria but stretching up the Nile valley into the Sudan, was also steadily worn away by the pressures of the new Arab nationalism. The prospects of the Greek trading communities in eastern and southern Africa were less than brilliant. The Turkish invasion of Cyprus seemed likely permanently to reduce the population and the territory of Greeks on the island. Nevertheless the Greeks remained a seafaring and trading people, and especially in the Americas there were Greek communities which, though they had become American, maintained interest in Greece. It would be too much to say that the international role of the Greeks had come to an end. Yet without doubt in the lands around the Mediterranean and Black Sea, where Greek culture, in its various forms, had flourished in classical, Roman, Byzantine and even Ottoman times, the modern age brought decline. Millions of talented people were forced out of the rich lands and challenging opportunities of the Mediterranean periphery into a small, beautiful, barren peninsula and its attendant islands, cooped up together with the millions of talented people who were already there. Too much unused, or insufficiently used, human talent of exceptional quality is as explosive as dynamite, as Greek history of the twentieth century showed.

Judged by the standards of average modern nationalism, Greece did well enough: its territory expanded, and its output of chauvinist rhetoric was well up to the norm. But by the standards of the apostles of *Ellinismos*, who saw more than this in the revival of Greece, the story has been a failure. It is a tale of high idealism and cruel misfortune, of *hubris* and *nemesis*, which has yet to find its Aeschylus.

## Panslavism

The word 'Slav' belongs essentially to the field of philology. There are Slav languages, as there are Latin (or Romance), Germanic (or Teutonic), Finno-Ugrian and Turkic languages.

The early history of the peoples of Slav speech remains obscure, despite the achievements of recent historical research. Slavs appear in the writing of Byzantine and German chronicles, as Slav-speakers penetrated into the Balkans or German-speakers colonised lands around or beyond the Elbe.

The nearest thing to a 'Slav culture' known to history was found in early medieval Bulgaria. It resulted from the adoption of the invading Bulgars—a Turkic people from the Volga steppes—of the Slav speech of the people whom they conquered in the lands south of the Danube, which became known as Bulgaria; from the translation of the scriptures into this Slav language by the Orthodox missionaries St Cyril and St Methodius; and from a certain fruitful cultural interpenetration between Greek- and Slav-speakers within the wider community of the Byzantine common-wealth. This 'Slav culture' also extended from Bulgaria into Kiev Russia and into Macedonia and Serbia. Even so, the separate development of the Bulgarian, Kievan and Serbian states set limits to the unity of the culture; and the conquests by Tatars and Ottomans had the effect of splintering and provincialising it. The Muscovite culture, which emerged as the Tatar declined, inherited this Slav-Byzantine culture but turned it into something different.

Among the Western Slav-speaking peoples the only common culture was Catholicism. That there was ever a specifically 'Slav' culture common to Poles, Czechs, and Croats is a myth. It may be argued that there was something of a common culture between Czechs and Slovaks in the Great Moravian empire, or between Slovenes and Croats in the days of the Croatian kingdom, but these things are wrapped in barely penetrable early medieval mists. Common acceptance of Catholic culture, or common subjection to the predicament of medieval serfdom, of persons of Slav speech, does not constitute a specific Slav culture. There were Polish and Bohemian cultures, and Polish and Bohemian states—usually at enmity with each other.

Something can be made of evidence of a feeling of Slav solidarity against Germans at the Battle of Grünwald of 1410, at which the Teutonic Knights were defeated by a Polish army which included Czechs and Byelorussians. However, this was but a brief political episode. Grünwald was an important event in the history of the Polish state, which thereafter incorporated Byelorussian and Ukrainian subjects to whom its rulers extended no more Slav brotherly love than to the rulers of neighbouring Bohemia.

It was from the South Slav lands under Turkish rule that the first spokesman of modern Panslavism emerged. The Croatian priest Juraj Križanić in 1659 handed to Tsar Alexei of Moscow a work entitled 'Russia's policy', in which he argued that six Slav peoples (Russians, Poles, Czechs, Bulgarians, Serbs and Croats) looked to Russia for liberation from Turks and Germans. It made but small impression on the tsar, and Križanić spent more than fifteen years in exile at Tobolsk in Siberia.

More influential was the chapter on Slavs by Herder in his *Ideen zur Geschichte der Menschheit* of 1784, in which 'the Slavs' were credited with propensities to democracy, love of peace, music and folk poetry, and contrasted with the arrogant warrior Germans. This chapter which, written by a German with a guilt complex, strangely foreshadows the European guilt complex on imperialism of the mid-twentieth century, was most influential among the educated minority in the lands of Slav speech. The presence of Russian troops in Bohemia in 1805 and 1813 made ordinary Czechs aware of the similarity of their languages. Jungmann, Hanka and their friends sought contact with Russians. Through the travelling Russian nationalist professor Michael Pogodin they came into contact with Count Uvarov, the powerful minister of education of Nicholas I, and received some small financial help.

It was among the Czechs that the pioneers of scholarly Panslavism were to be found, and they were joined by two Slovaks—Jan Kollar (1793-1852) and Pavel Josef Šafarík (1795-1861). Both were Lutherans, and both had frequent contact with the other peoples of Slav speech in the Habsburg Monarchy, but very little knowledge of Russia. Kollar studied in Bratislava and in Jena. He attended the Wartburg festival of German students in commemoration of Luther in 1817, and was much influenced by the ideals and mentality of the German student movement. His love-hate relationship with the Germans is symbolised by the fact that the girl who inspired his long poem *Slavy dčera* ('daughter of Slava'), which idealised the noble past and character of the Slavs, in Herder-like spirit, and appealed to the unity of All-Slavdom (*Vseslavie*), was the daughter of a Saxon pastor who became his wife. Kollar became pastor of the Slovak Lutheran church in Budapest for more than twenty years. In 1837 he published in German, in Budapest, a work on 'literary reciprocity' between the Slavs, a strong mixture of learning and national passion.[9] The Slavs, he claimed, were one nation, the most numerous in Europe. They must only unite in order to make their strength felt. Every educated Slav should therefore learn three other Slav 'dialects' in addition to his own.

The Poles, too, had a Panslavism of their own. Mickiewicz's concept of the Polish nation as a Christ among the nations, and Czartoryski's interest in the fate of the smaller nations of Slav speech in the Ottoman empire and in the Habsburg Monarchy, of whom the Polish nation was the natural leader, were to some extent combined in the political outlook of many nineteenth century Polish patriots. Poles could be considered the largest Slav nation only on the assumption that the Russians were not Slavs at all, but Finns or Mongols or Tatars who had adopted a Slav language. This view was widely held by Polish nationalists.

In competition in Panslav demagogy, the Russians, with their larger numbers and powerful state, could always outbid the Poles. Panslavism in Russia was a doctrine justifying the imperial expansion of the Russian state, propounded by independent Russian intellectuals and profoundly distrusted, though sometimes exploited, by Russian rulers. Panslavism might be useful to arouse Slav-speaking subjects of the Habsburg Monarchy against the Vienna government; but Nicholas I, as a conservative monarch, had no wish to disrupt the Habsburg Monarchy, even when its policies conflicted with his own. Panslavism was more useful against the Ottoman Turks: the Balkan Slavs were Orthodox (and therefore more desirable subjects than the Catholic Czechs), and their 'liberation' could promote Russian strategic ambitions in the Black Sea and the Straits. In the international diplomatic crisis of 1875-78 Alexander II's foreign policy was significantly influenced by a Panslav lobby, but the disappointment of the 1878 peace settlement caused it to diminish rapidly.

There was a certain revival in the years before 1914, in the form of 'Neoslavism'. Its main spokesmen were Poles and Czechs who hoped to reconcile Austria and Russia, isolate Germany, and improve the situation of the Poles in a more democratic Russia. The movement failed owing to the refusal of Russian governments to make concessions to Poles, as well as to conflicts between Poles and Ukrainians and between Serbs and Bulgarians.

In the Second World War the hard-pressed government of Stalin resorted to Panslav propaganda (until then disapproved as characteristic of 'tsarist reaction') in order to arouse support in German-occupied Europe. In the following thirty years this was revived from time to time, though it never played a very large part in Soviet propaganda. It was clear that it was no more than a minor weapon of Soviet Russian imperialism, important chiefly as a theoretical justification for the falsification, on Soviet orders, of the history of the Slav-speaking nations of Central and Eastern Europe. Among the peoples themselves 'Slav solidarity' was no longer a living issue: the Soviet invasion of Czechoslovakia in 1968 destroyed whatever had survived of earlier illusions.

However, though Panslavism proved to be fantasy, the idea of the unity of the South Slav peoples became a real political force, as will be shown later.

### The Poles: from partition to unity

On the north-eastern border of Catholic Europe arose in the late tenth century (traditional date 966) the kingdom of Poland, which was a powerful state in the early eleventh century, and from the mid-fourteenth onwards for three hundred years. To its east lay the Orthodox Russian principality of Kiev and the pagan Baltic peoples, of which the most important were the Lithuanians.[10]

As has been shown above, about a hundred years after Tatar conquest had destroyed the first Russian state, the western and south-western

Russian lands, including Kiev itself, were conquered by the Lithuanians. After a century of vacillation by his predecessors between Christianity and paganism, the Lithuanian prince Jagiello, faced with the hostility of the German Knights of the Teutonic Order[11] and the Muslim Tatars, came to terms with his third neighbour, the kingdom of Poland. In 1386 he accepted Catholic Christianity and married the heiress to the throne of Poland, of which he became king: his Lithuanian subjects also became Catholics, but most of his Russian subjects remained Orthodox. During the next century the relations between the two parts of this Polish-Lithuanian common-wealth fluctuated. Lithuania always had its own institutions, and at times its own independent ruler; yet essentially Lithuania and Poland were allied against other states. In the sixteenth century Polish influence greatly increased. This was a period when Poland became a European great power, and when Polish arts, literature and architecture flourished as part of Renaissance Europe. At this time too Protestantism made rapid progress in Poland among the landowning and urban classes, though it had much less effect on the peasantry. All these influences also made themselves felt in Lithuania. Whereas in the previous century a majority of the people of Lithuania had been Orthodox of Slav speech, with those speaking the Lithuanian language only a minority of the population—so that Lithuania was essentially no less entitled to be described as a Russian state than the still frail but growing principality of Muscovy—in the sixteenth century Lithuania became largely polonised, and Muscovy, which had now cast off Tatar sovereignty, emerged as unquestionably the leading Orthodox and Russian state. This trend was reinforced when the ties between Lithuania and Poland were made still closer by the Union of Lublin of 1569. Though Lithuanian institutions were to some extent preserved, the two countries became one, with a single parliament (*Sejm*) and government.

During the last years of the sixteenth century Protestantism lost ground in Poland, largely through the work of the Jesuits, who were encouraged by King Sigismund III (1587-1632). Their successes among the Polish educat-ed classes (which were won not by persecution but by argument, supported, it is true, by material inducements and pressures from the secular authori-ties) encouraged them to turn their attention to the Orthodox population of Lithuania. Their aim was to restore the Union of Florence of 1439, by which, in a desperate attempt to obtain West European help for Constan-tinople against the Turks, the Orthodox oecumenical patriarch had agreed to the reunion of the Orthodox Church with the Church of Rome on terms dictated by the pope. The Lithuanian Orthodox leaders hoped for a comprehensive union which would include the churches of Muscovy and of Constantinople, and would be connected with action by Christian Europe against the Turks; whereas the aim of the Jesuits was simply the subordina-tion of the Orthodox of Lithuania to the pope. It was this latter conception which prevailed at the meeting of Orthodox and Catholic churchmen from 6 to 10 October 1596 at Brest-Litovsk. A majority of the Orthodox churchmen agreed to Union, on the basis that they should accept the supremacy of the pope, but should keep their liturgy in church Slavonic, the married priesthood, and other lesser points. They thus remained a distinct group within the world-wide Catholic community, usually known as Uniates, or Greek-Catholics.

However, the Orthodox Church continued to exist, side by side with the Uniate, in the territory of Poland-Lithuania. Those who remained loyal to the old church suffered disabilities, and their hierarchy was not recognised until 1634, by King Sigismund's successor. Orthodoxy remained especially strong among the Ukrainian Cossacks of the south-east, whose resistance created the first historical foundations for the emergence of Ukrainian national consciousness, discussed in the next chapter.

In the eighteenth century the grievances of the Orthodox population in Poland were used as an excuse by the Russian Empress Catherine II for her numerous interventions in Polish affairs. These culminated in the three partitions of 1772, 1793 and 1795, by which Poland was divided between the Russian empire, the Habsburg Monarchy and the kingdom of Prussia.[12] By the partitions, most of the lands of the former grand duchy of Lithuania came under Russian rule. In these lands Poles in the strict sense (persons of Catholic faith whose first language was Polish) were a minority, though they included most persons of education, most landowners and a considerable number of peasants. Most peasants however were Lithuanians, Byelorussians[13] or Ukrainians, while the commercial classes consisted overwhelmingly of Jews.

The Uniates within the territories annexed to Russia were viewed with bitter hostility by the hierarchy of the Russian Orthodox Church. In 1839 they were forcibly reunited with Orthodoxy, and the Uniate Church was deprived of legal existence within the Russian empire. Within the formerly Polish territories acquired by Austria the Uniate Church survived, and played an important part in the development of a national movement among the Ukrainians of Eastern Galicia. It is a historical irony that, in the only part of former Poland in which the Uniate Church struck strong roots, it played a role directly opposite to that which had been intended for it by the rulers of Poland: instead of promoting polonisation, it helped to build a nation which challenged Polish national claims.

Poles did not accept the partitions as final. Their leaders placed their hopes of restoration first in the Russian Tsar Alexander I[14] and then more seriously in the French emperor. In 1806 Napoleon, with Polish volunteers fighting in his army, entered Poland in the course of his war against Prussia and Russia, and by the Treaty of Tilsit of July 1807 a much reduced and semi-independent Polish state was resuscitated in the form of the grand duchy of Warsaw, composed of most of the Polish lands formerly taken by Prussia, and placed under the sovereignty of the king of Saxony. In 1809 its territory was increased by part of the lands taken by Austria, which was defeated in that year by Napoleon with Polish help. In 1812 Napoleon's invasion force in Russia included nearly 100,000 Polish troops. The defeat of Napoleon in Russia, the recovery of Prussia and Austria and the final victory of the Allies over France had the effect of a restoration of the Partitions, with substantial territorial changes to the advantage of Russia at the expense of both Prussia and Austria.

Though the Polish state had disappeared, the Polish nation survived. Under the old commonwealth, the nation had consisted, in law and in fact, of the nobility (*szlachta*), a class which comprised about a tenth of the population (in some districts as much as a fifth), and many of whose members were small farmers or members of urban professions. It was the nobility which in the first half of the nineteenth century formed the core of the national movement. The peasant majority were rather passive, though this should not be exaggerated: the peasants' national consciousness was weaker than that of the *szlachta*, but it existed.

It is, however, important to distinguish between those who were Catholics and whose language was Polish, and those of whom neither of these things was true. In the post-Napoleonic age, only those were Poles who felt themselves to be Poles. Polish patriots were determined to restore the Polish state in its old frontiers, yet the truth was that the Polish nation and the population of the former Polish state were not the same thing. There were persons of Catholic faith and Lithuanian speech, and of Polish speech and Jewish faith, who considered themselves to be Poles; but among persons of German, Byelorussian and Ukrainian speech and of Protestant, Uniate or Orthodox religion, loyalty to the memory of the Polish commonwealth was weak and rapidly waning.

The movement for Polish independence in the nineteenth century had, in the eyes of its own members and of a large part of liberal and democratic opinion in Europe and America, a peculiarly heroic and universal character. The Poles considered themselves, and were widely considered to be, a nation martyred in the cause of liberty, fighters for the freedom of mankind. The immediate occasion for the Second Partition, which was decisive in the destruction of Poland, had been the Constitution of May 1791, a document inspired by the French and American Revolutions, which had enabled Catherine II to smear the Poles as 'Jacobins'. Tadeusz Kosciuszko (1746-1817), leader of the revolt of 1794, was a hero to all European democrats, and his name was celebrated, among other things, by being given to the highest mountain in Australia. The Polish legions founded by Henryk Dąbrowski believed themselves to be soldiers of liberty everywhere. Their slogan was: 'for our liberty and yours' (*za naszą i waszą wolność).* Poles played a prominent part in the revolutions of 1848 in Italy, Germany and Hungary. It was not only on the European Left that the Poles were admired: they were also the darlings of the Catholic Church, above all in France. Many Polish leaders combined religious with social revolutionary zeal in a manner which was becoming rare in Europe in the mid-nineteenth century. The most striking expression of this attitude was in the writings of the poet Adam Mickiewicz, who attributed to the Poles a Christ-like role among the nations: by its sacrifices, Poland would redeem the nations as Jesus had redeemed humanity. This imagery fell into disuse later in the century, but a religious dimension remained in Polish nationalism: the nation became an *ersatz* deity to men who had lost traditional faith.

There was an obvious contradiction between this passionate and unselfish devotion to the Polish nation and the refusal to admit the right of Byelorussians, Ukrainians or Lithuanians to have national identity and national aspirations of their own. Polish insistence on the recovery of all the eastern borderlands made it difficult for Russians even of liberal outlook to support the Polish cause. In the first half of the nineteenth century the conflict between Polish and Russian aims was in fact mainly due to the argument about historical Lithuania. Russian patriots regarded the old grand duchy as mainly a 'Russian land'. They, no less than the Poles, refused to recognise the rights of Byelorussians and Ukrainians to separate national status.

The Polish movement was also divided on political and social problems. The aristocratic trend, whose outstanding exponent was Prince Adam Czartoryski (1770-1861), favoured an oligarchic liberalism, while the radicals, represented by the exiled Democratic Society, considered themselves heirs to the Jacobins. Even the radicals, however, paid rather little attention to the interests of the peasants, and to the need for land reform: this cost them some popular support in the revolts of 1830 and 1863.

Throughout the nineteenth century Polish political leaders fluctuated between the two tactics of insurrection and of compromise. Insurrection twice brought defeat, and was followed by a reaction towards compromise. But compromise too brought poor results, and a later generation once more inclined towards insurrection, which was once more crushed. This was Poland's tragedy, determined by the overwhelming force of her enemies and the indifference, or merely verbal support, of those governments which were regarded as Poland's friends. It was these bitter facts, far more than the inevitable faults of judgment of individual Polish leaders, which accounted for Polish failures. Nevertheless the failures invariably produced bitter recriminations and mutual accusations.

The tactic of compromise consisted sometimes in attempts to bring the Polish Question before the governments of the great powers through personal contacts with prominent West European statesmen. At other times it consisted in cooperation with the governments of the three partitioning powers, in the hope of improving the lot of the Polish people. At other times again, it consisted in cooperating with one of the three powers, in the hope that it would support Polish interests against the other two, and perhaps even reunite the Polish lands within its boundaries. In this hope leading Poles urged cooperation with Russia between 1815 and 1830, from 1857 to 1863, in 1905 and in both world wars; with Prussia in 1848 and briefly in the early 1890s; and with Austria in 1865 and 1914.

These major aspects of the Polish movement should be apparent from a brief survey of the fluctuations of the Polish cause from 1815 until recent times.

Emperor Alexander I of Russia was a sincere friend of the Poles, though he did not hesitate to sacrifice them when it seemed to him that the most urgent interests of Russia required it, or when the pressure of Russian national feeling against Poland was too strong to resist. His aim was to unite all the Polish lands in a single kingdom, of which he would be the sovereign; but pressure by Austria and Britain at the peace congress of Vienna forced him to accept less than he had intended. The result was the formation of a small kingdom of Poland (known to Poles as 'the Congress Kingdom'), corresponding roughly to the territory of Napoleon's grand duchy of Warsaw after the war of 1809. Alexander was king, and the government apparatus and army of his kingdom was distinct from those of the Russian empire. A constitution, with a parliament elected on a restricted franchise, was prepared by Prince Adam Czartoryski and approved by Alexander in November 1815. All this made Alexander for a time genuinely popular with the Poles. They had still, however, one major unsatisfied wish: that the lands annexed by Catherine II, corresponding essentially to the former Lithuania, should be reunited with the kingdom. Alexander gave vague private assurances that he would do this, but Russian national feeling was in practice too strong to permit it. He did however allow the university of Vilna to become a centre for the polonisation through education of a growing number of Ukrainians and Byelorussians. In 1823 a conspiracy was discovered among Vilna university students, followed by arrests and prison sentences. From this time Polish-Russian relations steadily deteriorated. Tsar Nicholas I, who succeeded his brother Alexander in December 1825, maintained the constitution in the Congress Kingdom, but he distrusted and was distrusted by the Poles. New conspiracies were formed, and in November 1830 rebellion broke out in Warsaw, followed by a war between the Polish and Russian armies. The capture of Warsaw by General Paskievich on 8 September 1831 ended

Polish resistance. The constitution of 1815 was abrogated, and in Lithuania and the Ukraine strenuous efforts were made to replace Polish by Russian education. A new university was set up in Kiev in 1833 for this express purpose.

For the next quarter century the Polish emigration in Western Europe regarded Russia as the supreme enemy, and sought ways of enlisting help from any quarter. Of the partitioning powers, the least objectionable appeared to be Prussia. King Frederick William III regarded himself to some extent as a German, but he did not think of his kingdom as a purely German state. If his subjects were loyal to him, they were entitled to respect for their nationality. He was willing to consider Prussia as a state of two nations. In a Manifesto of 15 May 1815 to the people of the grand duchy of Posen (Poznań)—the main territory of Polish population left to Prussia by the 1815 settlement—he said: 'You will be incorporated in my Monarchy without having to deny your nationality. . . . Your language will be used side by side with German in all public business, and every one of you shall have access, in accordance with his abilities, to public office in the Grand Duchy as well as to all offices, honours and dignities of my kingdom'. These generous words were belied by the practical policies of governor Flottwell of Posen from 1830 to 1840, who consciously set himself the task of absorbing the Poles into the German nation by the introduction of the German language into the schools and administration. However, with the accession of Frederick William IV in 1840 hopes revived, and Germanising pressure diminished.

In Austria there was no glimmer of hope: Metternich's regime combated the national aspirations of the Poles as relentlessly as those of the other nations of the Habsburg Monarchy, and his rejection of all democratic ideas was uncompromising. The radical wing of the Polish emigration in Paris, the Democratic Society, attempted a rising in Galicia in 1846. This evoked positive hostility from the Polish peasants, who were more bitterly opposed to the Polish landowning class on social grounds than to Vienna on national. A savage civil war broke out, in which peasants killed landlords and plundered manors while the Austrian authorities looked on, or even encouraged the peasants.

In 1848 there were Poles fighting in the revolutionary ranks in several countries, but little was achieved for Poland. Ludwik Mierosławski, one of the leaders of the Democratic Society, fought for the Sicilians in January, and led the revolt in south-western Germany against the suppression of the German Assembly in June 1849; the Piedmontese army's chief of staff in March 1849 was a Polish general, Chrzanowski; and in Hungary the Polish general Bem proved a brilliant commander. Yet nothing stirred in Russian Poland. In the first weeks after the revolution in Paris and Berlin, there was talk of war against Russia, in which the French and German peoples would help the Poles to recover their independence. Tsar Nicholas was for a short time genuinely afraid. However, the French government had no intention of risking war, and in Prussia the honeymoon period of German-Polish friendship did not last long. At the beginning of May 1848 Prussian troops forced the Poles of Posen into submission. The Poles still placed some hopes in their German friends. Their delegation in Frankfurt asked on 23 May for recognition by the Assembly of an independent Poland, while promising that all frontier districts in which the majority of the population should freely ask for inclusion in Germany, should be ceded to Germany. This request was not well received, and in any case the Frankfurt Assembly was unable to do anything. Meanwhile in Austrian Poland the authorities encouraged the Ukrainians at the expense of the Poles, and repeated their policy of playing peasants off against landowners. Minor acts of resistance by Poles in Cracow on 26 April and in Lwów on 2 November were easily suppressed.

The Polish emigration had new hopes with the outbreak of war between the Western powers and Russia in 1854. However, they got no more from French and British statesmen than a few amiable words. In particular, Louis Napoleon, who had plans for action against Austria in northern Italy, did not intend to get involved in an all-out war with Russia for the sake of Poland while Austria stayed neutral and grew relatively stronger. He fought a limited war, won his prestige victory with the capture of Sevastopol, and prepared to find in a chastened Russia a useful diplomatic partner for the future.

The beginning of major social and political reforms in Russia under Alexander II promised some improvements for Poland. The new tsar was anxious to conciliate the Poles, and found in Marquess Alexander Wielopolski a prominent Pole who was willing to implement moderate reforms. He failed to win Polish support. The conservatives agreed with his general aims, but did not dare to incur odium in the eyes of Polish patriots by saying so in public, unless Wielopolski could get from the tsar an undertaking that Lithuania would be brought under the same form of government as the Congress Kingdom: this was something that no Russian ruler could give. For their part, the radicals were opposed to any cooperation with the Russian government. In 1861 and 1862 there were demonstrations and attempted assassinations, and Wielopolski was forced into repression. When he announced that he would conscript young Poles into the Russian army, the radicals decided on armed rebellion. Fighting began in January 1863, and went on for more than a year, in the form not of open war between armies as in 1831 but of a guerrilla movement in many parts of the country.

Repression in Russian Poland was accompanied by distribution of land to the peasants on rather favourable terms. The aim was to persuade the

Polish peasants that the Russian government was their friend, the Polish
landowners their only enemies, and that Polish independence was a crazy
dream of these enemies. There now began a policy of systematic Russification, not only in Lithuania and the Ukraine but also in the Congress
Kingdom. Schools and universities were used as instruments of Russification; Russian replaced Polish as the language of instruction as well as of
public administration; and numbers of Russian officials were brought to
serve in Poland. The policy was unsuccessful, for Poles retained their
language and their national consciousness: in fact, just because they were
more prosperous the Polish peasants became more aware of the Polish
nationality. During the last decades of the century industry made great
progress in Russian Poland, and Poles became factory workers, professional and business men in growing numbers.

In Prussia, a new policy of forced Germanisation began in the 1880s. It
was connected with Bismarck's policy of *Kulturkampf* directed against the
Catholic Church, but was not confined to religious affairs: the exclusion of
the Polish language from schools and administration went ahead, and the
government gave public funds to assist the purchase of Polish landed
property by Germans. In 1899 was founded the *Deutsches Ostmarkenve-
rein*, which directed anti-Polish propaganda and organised the campaign
against Polish language and ownership of land. There was much inflated
nationalist rhetoric, including talk of a 'policy of extermination' (*Ausrot-
tungspolitik*) as an aim. In practice the methods used were fairly mild, and
they were not effective. The Poles clung to their land, their language and
their national culture. In fact, the proportion of Poles in the province of
Posen (Poznań) rose between 1867 and 1910 from 62 to 71 per cent.

From 1865 onwards the partitioning power which treated the Poles best
was Austria. A Galician Diet, elected on a limited franchise, met in Lwów,
and the Galician provincial authorities were given wide powers over local
economic affairs, public health and schools. Poles were also elected to the
central parliament (*Reichsrat*) in Vienna. The main objectionable feature
of this system, from the Polish point of view, was that the civil and political
rights which they enjoyed were also available to the Ukrainian population
in East Galicia. The demands of the Ukrainians became still more pressing
when universal suffrage was introduced into the Vienna parliament in
1907. Some Polish leaders tried to persuade Vienna to show a more marked
preference for Polish over Ukrainian claims; some sought an understanding with the Ukrainians against Russia, and to some extent against Vienna;
while some even sought cooperation with Russia against the Ukrainians.

If one considers the whole Polish nation, in the three partitioning
empires, on the eve of the First World War, one must note two main
divisions in political outlook. The first was between socialists and bourgeois democrats: the two main parties, the Polish Socialist Party (PPS) and

the National Democrats (*Endecja*) whose outstanding spokesman was Roman Dmowski, had their followers in all three territories. The second division was between those who believed that some cooperation with Russians was possible, and those who regarded Russia as the implacable enemy and the German powers as the lesser evil. This division cut across the parties, and was to be found in all three empires. Dmowski believed that the main danger came from Germany, and that Austria was too weak to provide a counterweight to it. He hoped for reforms within Russia which would give the Poles self-government in their homeland while offering them the chance of splendid careers in the vast Russian empire, where their superior abilities and culture would favour them in competition with Russians. He also favoured 'neoslavism', the purpose of which was to persuade the Austrian government that Austria should be not the second German but the second Slav great power in Europe; should in effect replace her alliance with Germany by an alliance with Russia. His more distant aim was, with Russian help, to detach Prussian Poland from Germany. In the socialist movement there was also a strong trend in favour of cooperation with Russians—not with the government but with the working class. This trend became very powerful during the revolutionary year 1905. The opposite view was that Poland's hope lay in the destruction of the Russian empire, and that this could only be brought about by the German powers. The chief champion of this view was a socialist, Josef Piłsudski. He disliked having to side with Germany, but he believed that Austria could protect Polish interests within the German camp, and that one day Germany in its turn would be defeated by the Western powers. Similar, though less far-sighted or complex, views were held by some Polish conservatives, especially in Galicia.

When the European War broke out in 1914, Piłsudski led legions of Polish volunteers to fight with the Austrians against Russia. When the Russians had been driven out of Poland, he quarrelled with the Germans, and was imprisoned in Magdeburg fortress. The final result of the war fulfilled Piłsudski's hopes, for Russia was beaten by Germany, and Germany by France and Britain. Polish independence became a fact in 1918.

At this point the difference between the Polish nation and the historical Polish state emerged in acute form. In the West, the victorious great powers gave the benefit of the doubt to the Poles at the expense of the Germans in drawing the frontiers in Pomerania and Silesia—though they gave a good deal less than Polish nationalists would have liked, and created an awkward problem through the separation of East Prussia from Branden-burg by a belt of Polish territory, the so-called 'Polish Corridor'. In the East, Piłsudski wished to revive the old Polish state, and indeed extend its territory, in a new form, by a federal union between Poland and a

Ukrainian state. These plans failed, and after the Polish-Soviet Russian war of 1920 a compromise frontier was accepted which had the effect that the old partitions of Poland were replaced by partitions of both Byelorussia and the Ukraine, with the larger share of each of these two countries going to Russia but a substantial slice to Poland.

German nationalists were not only embittered by the inclusion of nearly a million Germans in Poland, but resented the very existence of a Polish state. The Soviet rulers intended in the course of time to annex the rest of Byelorussia and Ukraine. In the 1920s both Germany and Russia were weak, but once they had recovered Poland was in grave danger. In September 1939 the fifth partition of Poland[15] took place, between Hitler's Third Reich and Stalin's Soviet Union. The Second World War cost the Poles about six million dead, more than half of this number consisting of Jews. When Hitler had been defeated, the Soviet Union kept almost all that it had taken from Poland in 1939, but compensated the Poles by giving them most of East Prussia and by advancing their western frontier to the Oder and Western Neisse rivers. About eight million Germans were expelled, and their places taken by Poles from the East or from the overpopulated provinces of Poland proper. In the following quarter of a century the high Polish birth rate had filled the gap: the Polish nation and the population of the Polish state now coincided.

This brief survey of the Polish national struggle requires a short comment. In the Polish case extremes of generosity and meanness, of high idealism and of fanatical disregard for the rights of other nations, exceed the normal pattern of nationalism. Repeatedly, the determination to impose Polish rule on Lithuanians, Byelorussians and Ukrainians deprived the Poles of an opportunity of viable independence for the Polish people with Russian consent (in the 1820s, 1862, 1920). The early prophets of the Polish cause set very high standards, and against them the judgment of reality must at times be harsh. 'For our freedom and yours' was a noble aspiration, and it was indeed often transformed into reality. Therefore, when Polish troops marched into Czechoslovakia in August 1968[16] they were defiling the essence of Polish history: it was as if they had inscribed on their standards the words 'for our enslavement and yours' (*za naszą i waszą niewolę*). It is also a bitter truth that Poland's heroic efforts had been callously exploited in the past by other powers to their advantage, and that the help of France and Britain, often sought and sometimes promised, invariably proved useless. Poland indeed suffered from false friends; yet the spectacle of Polish troops marching into Bohemia side by side with Brezhnev's Russians and Ulbricht's Prussians was shocking even in the world of 1968. With such allies Poland had no need of friends.

These things must be said, and yet it must be admitted that they are less than just. The tragedy of the Poles was that for two hundred years, save for a few brief intervals, they were at the mercy of two nations far stronger than they, whose rulers at times showed great cruelty, and seldom showed themselves capable of generosity.[17] Foreigners have blamed the Poles for reckless insurrections and for abject cooperation. Yet both have been equally fruitless and equally inevitable. Revolt is crushed, so one accepts the conqueror; the conqueror replies with another round of oppression, so one revolts. Revolt is crushed. . . . The idiot cycle repeats itself. There is no escape in sight.


**The Yugoslavs**

At the beginning of the nineteenth century almost all the land stretching from the south-eastern Alps to the Black Sea, bounded by the rivers Drava and Danube in the north and by the Adriatic and Aegean in the south, was inhabited by people speaking Slav dialects. These merged into each other as one travelled from north-west to south-east. During the first half of the century, as the result of pioneering work by native scholars, three distinct literary languages were formed—Slovene, Serbo-Croatian and Bulgarian. Intermediate dialects continued to be spoken, such as the *kajkavski* variant in central Croatia, the *shopski* dialect in the border districts between Serbia and Bulgaria, and a number of dialects in Macedonia.

These Slav-speaking people were divided between three religions. Those of the north-west, and of the Adriatic coastal strip, were mainly Catholics. Those of the lower Danube, Morava, Vardar and Maritsa valleys and of the lands between them were mainly Orthodox. In the central region of Bosnia, and on the southern slopes of the Rhodope Mountains, were many Muslims of Slav speech.

The peoples still had dim memories of past historical greatness. The triune kingdom of Croatia, Slavonia and Dalmatia had not been forgotten, nor the kingdoms of Serbia, Bosnia and Bulgaria. In 1800 not much was left of them. Part of Croatia had remained under Habsburg rule even at the height of Turkish power; more had been reconquered at the end of the seventeenth century; and the southern frontiers of the Monarchy had been settled with Serbs who had fled from Turkish rule and had received land in return for military service. These 'military frontiersmen' formed a distinct political unit in the Habsburg Monarchy. Dalmatia had been separated from Croatia in 1420 and became part of the lands of the Venetian republic: it remained Venetian until the republic was dissolved in 1797. After this it passed first to French and then to Austrian rule, but was kept separate from Croatia. In the mountains behind the south-eastern corner of the Adriatic was the principality of Montenegro, whose Orthodox Slav people had never been conquered by the Turks. The rest of the region, from Bosnia to the Black Sea and from Belgrade to the Aegean, still belonged to the Ottoman empire.

It is easy to exaggerate or to underrate the collective consciousness of these peoples in 1800. The historic names of Croat and Serb were widely used. The name Slovene was also coming into wide use among the people of the Alpine north-west corner of the region, who had never possessed a firmly organised state of their own, but were certainly aware of the difference in language and culture between themselves and their German- or Italian-speaking neighbours. In the mountainous central regions and in Serbia, life was largely based on the patriarchal extended family (*zadruga*) which has been rightly represented as the core of Serbian national culture in the centuries of Turkish rule. Another important influence were the popular epics (*narodne pesme*), preserved orally, largely concerned with the heroic days of the Ottoman conquest of the old kingdoms. In the eighteenth century southern Hungary, where the exiled Serbian Orthodox Metropolitanate was established in Sremski Karlovci, was a centre of education for Serbs. In Croatia and in the Slovene Alps opportunities for school were rather better. A few learned South Slavs made their appearance. One was Jernej Kopitar, a Slovene living in Vienna, a most erudite librarian and linguist. Another was an Orthodox priest, Dositej Obradović, who travelled widely in Europe, was deeply influenced by the Enlightenment, and published works in his language. Still more important was the Herzegovinian Serb, Vuk Karadžić, who published five volumes of popular epics from 1841 onwards, and did more than any other single person to create a modern Serbo-Croatian language, based on his own Herzegovinian dialect, but broadly accepted in the following years by both Croats and Serbs as their own.

The first major political event in the modern history of the South Slavs was the revolt of the Serbs under Kara Djordje in 1804. This was essentially a movement of discontented peasants, directed against the lawlessness of local Turkish potentates and usurpers, and not designed to overthrow Ottoman rule as such. The rebels freed a substantial region south of Belgrade, between the Drina and Morava rivers, the so-called 'land of forests' (Šumadija). Their success was facilitated by the fact that from 1806 onwards the Turks were at war with Russia in the Danubian principalities: although not much direct Russian aid reached the Serbs, the Turks were too occupied elsewhere by the main Russian army to make a major effort to reconquer Serbia. This changed in 1813, when Russia had made peace with Turkey; all Europe was convulsed by the last stages of the war against Napoleon, and the sultan had the chance to punish his rebellious subjects. It now became a direct fight against the Turks as such, and a national struggle for Serbian freedom, inevitably aggravated and embittered by the explosion of the latent hatred between Christians and Muslims. Serbia was crushed in 1813, but in 1817 a new leader, Miloš Obrenović, a more cunning politician and an abler diplomat than Kara Djordje, achieved a limited success; and as a result of the Russo-Turkish war of 1828-29 and of great power diplomacy an independent Serbian state was established, owing only nominal allegiance to Ottoman suzerainty.

Further west, five years (1809-14) of annexation of Slovene and Croatian lands to Napoleon's French empire as the province of 'Illyria' left their mark on at least an educated minority. The study of Slav dialects and grammar, the influence of Herder's ideas about language in general and about the Slavs in particular, and the appearance of romantic Panslavism, especially among the Czechs, had effects also in the South Slav lands of the Habsburg Monarchy. The outstanding figure was the Croatian writer Ljudevit Gaj, who became the leader of an 'Illyrian movement'. In his periodical *Danica* he argued that there was a single Illyrian people, of Slav speech, stretching from the Alps to Varna. Though this was only talk, and there was no question of any action to create a great Illyrian state, it was objectionable to the authorities in Hungary, with which Croatia was united under Habsburg rule. Metternich in 1843 formally forbade use of the name Illyria. The idea of South Slav nationality and unity survived however.

In 1848 both Croats and Serbs found their national aspirations rejected by the makers of the Hungarian Revolution,[18] and in consequence support-ed the Habsburg government against the Hungarians. While the fighting went on in Hungary, the rulers of Serbia, beyond the Danube and Sava rivers at Belgrade, remained prudently inactive, not daring to antagonise both Austria and Russia. However, they were interested in the liberation of their kinsmen under Turkish, and eventually also under Habsburg, rule. The chief minister of Prince Alexander Karadjordjević, Ilija Garašanin, prepared in 1843 a far-reaching project (*nachertanie*) for South Slav unity.

The Habsburgs showed no gratitude to Croats or Serbs. Under the restored absolutism, the South Slavs had the advantages of fairly good government and some material and cultural progress, but no concessions were made to their national aspirations. In 1867 the Habsburgs, having made the Compromise with Hungary, left the Croats to make the best terms they could with the Hungarians on their own. All they got was a limited regional autonomy, with a provincial Diet and the use of Croatian as the language of administration. Dalmatia remained under the rule of Vienna: thus the former triune kingdom continued to be divided. There were also Croats in Istria, a separate province, in which Italians formed nearly half the population and were both culturally and politically domi-nant. The Slovenes were divided between four provinces—Istria, Gorizia, Carinthia and Carniola (only in the last of which they formed an over-whelming majority), and in the city of Trieste.

In Dalmatia under Austrian rule the Croatian majority succeeded over the years in winning control of public life from the Italian minority which had long been favoured by Vienna. Dalmatia however was an exceedingly poor country, and very little was done from Vienna to develop its resources or protect the economic interests of its people. Croats in both provinces agitated unsuccessfully for the union of Dalmatia with Croatia. In both Dalmatia and Croatia there were also large Serbian minorities. Here as elsewhere, the normal distinction between Serb and Croat was religious. Both spoke the same language (differences of dialect were a matter of regional not of religious division), but Orthodox were Serbs and used the Cyrillic alphabet, while Catholics were Croats and used the Latin alphabet. However, in southern Dalmatia there was also a rather small number of Catholics who considered themselves to be Serbs.

The relations between Croats and Serbs became a matter of great importance in the political life of Croatia. There were two main trends among the Croats. One may be called the Greater Croatian idea. Its chief exponent was Ante Starčević. Essentially, he reinterpreted the Illyrian idea of Gaj. In his view there was one nation living between the Alps and the Black Sea, but its name was not Illyrian but Croatian. The Croatian nation should include those who, in the course of time, had become Orthodox or Muslims. The other names used by people living in this region were regional descriptions, not national names. It was possible to speak of those who lived in the region known as Serbia as 'Serbs', but it was wrong to speak of Serbs as a nation. Those who insisted on calling themselves a Serbian nation Starčević viewed as enemies. Starčević was a bitter enemy of both Austria and Hungary, though he was willing if necessary to accept a Habsburg as ruler. His aim was a great independent Croatian state, extending far into the existing lands of the Ottoman empire, possibly as far as the Black Sea. This state could at most be linked by personal dynastic union with Austria and Hungary: its institutions must be completely separate. Starčević was a fanatical defender of the constitutional rights of the medieval Croatian State (*hrvatsko državno pravo*). He gave to his party the name of Party of Pure Right.[19]

The alternative trend may be called the Yugoslav Idea. Its chief exponent was Ivan Juraj Štrosmajer (1815-1905), for many years Catholic bishop of Djakovo. He recognised that Croats and Serbs were different, but believed that they were fraternal nations, belonging to a great South Slav (Yugo-slav) community. He too wished to see a great free South Slav state, but he did not believe that it could be simply called Croatia or Serbia. The main task was to liberate South Slavs from Ottoman rule. Štrosmajer's attitude to the Habsburg Monarchy was ambiguous. He had no love for Austrian rule, and still less for Hungarian, but he did not see any prospect of the break-up of the Monarchy, nor perhaps did he even desire this. His generation and the next had as their task to make the best they could of life within the framework of the Monarchy. This did not mean that they would not have liked a completely independent South Slav state, only that this did not arise as a serious possibility. The accusation sometimes made later against Štrosmajer and his followers by extreme Serbian nationalists, that they were subservient to Austria, is irrelevant. Certainly Štrosmajer did as much as anyone to promote the notion of solidarity between the South Slav peoples, not least by his use of the rich income of his diocese for education, including the foundation of the first academy of arts and sciences in a South Slav land. Established in Zagreb in 1867, it was significantly entitled 'Yugoslav Academy'.

The government of the small free state of Serbia was chiefly interested in liberating fellow-Serbs who lived both to the south and to the west of Serbia under Ottoman rule. Prince Michael Obrenović had ambitious plans for a league of Balkan states and peoples to drive the Turks out of Europe, but he was assassinated in 1868 before this could be attempted. Whereas Prince Michael thought in terms of the extension of the Serbian state to include Serbs and perhaps Bulgarians, younger Serbs of radical outlook, above all the socialist Svetozar Marković, opposed policies of state aggrandisement, bitterly criticised the Balkan type of bureaucratic absolutism which had grown up in Serbia, and aimed at an alliance of free and equal Balkan nations.

In 1875 there was a rebellion of Serbs in Herzegovina against Turkish rule, followed some months later by a rebellion in Bosnia. Both had been encouraged by revolutionary activities based on Serbia and Montenegro, and were also supported by the Serbs of southern Hungary. Serbia itself went to war with Turkey in 1876 and was defeated, and in 1877 Russia went to war. In the complex international diplomatic crisis of 1876-78 the Russian government sacrificed Serbian interests; and Bosnia and Herzegovina, the two Serbian lands most ardently desired by patriots in Serbia, were placed under Austrian administration while still nominally subject to Ottoman suzerainty. This decision created bitter hatred against Austria in Serbia. With the Monarchy, Štrosmajer was greatly disappointed, and in Hungary those Serbs who had expressed support for the Serbian cause against Turkey were persecuted by the authorities in Budapest. Their outstanding leader, Svetozar Miletić, was imprisoned for some years. It must be admitted that the people of Bosnia gained from the change, for Austrian rule was more civilised than Ottoman, and some material progress was achieved in the next thirty years. The followers of Starčević were not entirely displeased, for it seemed to bring nearer their long-term aim of a Greater Croatia, in which they insisted that Bosnia must be included, even though Serbs were twice as numerous in that province as Croats. The Bosnian Serbs remained fundamentally hostile to Austria, and in Serbia a growing number henceforth considered Austria to be Serbia's main enemy, more deadly than the traditional but declining enemy Turkey.

An equally important result of the 1878 settlement was the creation of an independent Bulgarian state.[20] Already for some decades past, the literary language and the national identity of the Bulgarians had greatly developed. It was definitely no longer possible to consider them part of the same nation as the Croats and Serbs, as Gaj had considered them at the time of the Illyrian movement of the 1830s, though it was still possible to include them in the notion of a Yugoslav community of fraternal nations. Unfortunately the trend of the last decades of the century was not towards fraternity. The separate Serbian and Bulgarian states became centres of rival interests. The masters of the two state machines wished to expand, and inevitably clashed with each other. This trend was reinforced by the fact that, under the 1878 Congress of Berlin settlement, Serbia was designed to be a vassal of Austria and Bulgaria of Russia. This division of spheres of interest, which agreed with the conventional wisdom of which Bismarck was the outstanding exponent, did not work. Austria had antagonised the Serbs by seizing Bosnia, while the Russians made themselves disliked in liberated Bulgaria by their arrogant behaviour. Consequently each small state looked to the rival of its official protector—Serbia to Russia and Bulgaria to Austria. Thus Austro-Russian rivalry was not appeased but exacerbated by the Berlin settlement.

The main object of rivalry between Serbia and Bulgaria was Macedonia, lying to the south of Serbia and to the west of Bulgaria. This was assigned to Bulgaria by the original draft Russian peace treaty with Turkey at San Stefano in March 1878, but as a result of British and Austrian pressure had been restored to Turkey by the Berlin treaty. The people of Macedonia were of five languages and of both Orthodox and Muslim religion, but the largest single group spoke Slav dialects which were closer to Bulgarian than to Serbian. Among them were two political trends: one favoured simple annexation to Bulgaria, the other aimed at an independent Macedonian state, and argued that the Macedonian Slavs were a separate South Slav nation, distinct from both Bulgarians and Serbs. At first the Serbian government was not much interested in Macedonia, though it certainly wished to push Serbia's frontiers further to the south and south-west. However, after Bosnia had been denied to Serbia, the idea of compensation on a larger scale in the south seemed more attractive. During the last decades of the century armed bands, supported by the governments of the neighbouring states, fought each other and the Turks, making Macedonia a byword for plunder, murder and anarchy. There were Greek bands, Serbian bands and Bulgarian bands, Turkish regular and irregular troops, Albanian bands and bands of Macedonian autonomists, some of whom sometimes combined with each other but more often carried on a struggle of all against all. In 1903 there was a large-scale rising of Macedonian Slavs against the Turks, followed by reprisals and the establishment of an international gendarmerie of the European powers.

In Croatia from 1883 to 1903 Count Khuen-Héderváry maintained a political balance which satisfied the Hungarian government. He played off Serbs against Croats, fixed election results (on a very restricted franchise) by corruption and intimidation, and could always find a sufficient number of subservient persons to ensure a majority in the Diet. However, in 1903 long repressed discontent burst out in a series of street demonstrations and minor violence, and Khuen-Héderváry was removed. In the same year a number of Croatian and Serbian members of the several regional assemblies signed Resolutions in Fiume (Rijeka) and Zara (Zadar) in favour of the reunion of Dalmatia with Croatia and of cooperation between Croats and Serbs. A Croat-Serbian coalition was formed from some of the existing parties, which offered its cooperation to the Hungarian Opposition, then engaged in a bitter struggle with the Vienna government for control of Hungary's army and finances. This cooperation was a failure, for soon after the Hungarian Opposition came to power, it broke its promises to the Croats. In Croatia the normal working of legitimate institutions virtually came to an end between 1908 and 1913. Only one small faction of the successors of Starčević were willing to cooperate with Vienna against both Hungarians and Serbs, in the hope of obtaining a Greater Croatia, including Bosnia, with the consent of the Vienna government.

Cooperation with the Vienna government was still the prevalent attitude among the Slovenes. For them the essential aim was union of all the lands of Slovene population and protection of their language and culture against German and Italian. They did not share the hostility of Starčević's disciples towards the Serbs, but it was clearly essential for them to cooperate with the Croats, the only neighbouring people which did not threaten Slovene national interests. The Slovene People's Party, the largest group, led by Catholic priests and strongly influenced by the Church, still had confidence in the Monarchy, believing the dynasty to stand for a policy above nationalism, German or other. The Slovene Liberals were more sceptical about the Monarchy and more inclined to a Yugoslav ideal which would embrace the Serbs as well.

For their part the Serbs of the Monarchy were divided between the Yugoslav and the Greater Serb ideas. The latter was simply that all lands of Serbian population should be annexed to Serbia. This view was predominant among the Bosnian Serbs. The Serbs of southern Hungary and of Croatia and Dalmatia were divided. Very few positively wished the Monarchy to survive, but had to make their plans on the assumption that it would. The Yugoslav trend put fraternity and cooperation with the Croats as their first priority, whereas the Greater Serbs simply pursued whatever tactics were recommended by the Belgrade government.

The formal annexation of Bosnia to the Habsburg Monarchy in 1908 turned the attention of the Serbian government once more to the south. With encouragement from the Russian government, it sought alliances with Bulgaria and Greece. These were made in 1912, and in the autumn of that year war was declared on Turkey. In this war the Serbian army had brilliant successes, and these aroused enormous enthusiasm among all the South Slav subjects of the Habsburg Monarchy, especially among the educated younger generation, including students and schoolchildren. In this generation the idea now became widespread of a single 'nation of three names' (*troimeni narod*)—Slovenes, Croats and Serbs. Their aim was a single state to include them all. This could only be achieved by incorporating Serbia in the Monarchy or by destroying the Monarchy. The first was morally impossible in view of Serbia's heroic record and of Austria's sinister political methods and persistent hostility; therefore the second was the only possibility. This attitude was of course still a minority trend, but it was gaining ground among the most active and intelligent of the Monarchy's South Slav subjects.

The victories of the Balkan allies against the Turks were followed by inability to agree on the spoils. The Austrian government's refusal to permit Serbia access to the Adriatic, let alone to yield Bosnia, made gains in Macedonia seem still more important to the Serbian government, whose troops were in control of most of that province when the fighting with the Turks stopped. But to the Bulgarians Macedonia was their most sacred aim, and the Serb-Bulgarian treaty of 1912 had promised most of it to them. The result was the Second Balkan War of June 1913, in which the Bulgarian army attacked the Serbs and Greeks and was repulsed, and in which Bulgaria was also invaded by Romanians and Turks. The greatest part of Macedonia was thus annexed by Serbia, whose authorities simply denied not only that the Macedonian Slavs were Bulgarians, but even that they had any peculiar character of their own: they were simply declared to be 'South Serbs', and woe betide them if they denied it.

The First World War was triggered off by the murder of the heir to the Austrian throne by a Bosnian Serb, and it ended with the creation of a Yugoslav state. During the war the Croatian and Slovene, and even the Serbian, soldiers of the Austrian army fought bravely for the Monarchy, mainly because they objected to Italian designs on their homelands, but the desire to unite all three peoples, whether inside or outside the Monarchy, did not diminish. When the Austrian parliament was recalled in 1917, the South Slav leaders demanded unity of the South Slavs and independent institutions, while proclaiming their loyalty to the Habsburg dynasty—in individual cases from real conviction, but more usually from obvious prudence in wartime.

In December 1914 the Serbian parliament passed a resolution in favour of liberating all its Serbian, Croatian and Slovene brothers. This was also the aim of exiled Slovenes, Croats and Serbs from Austria-Hungary who were active in Britain, France and Italy during the war. However, acute disagreements arose between them and the Serbian government, led by Nikola Pašić, when it became known that Italy had been promised Istria and Dalmatia in return for its entry into the war on the Western side. The exiles now had reason to fear that Croatia would be divided into three parts—some given to Italy, some (southern Dalmatia) to Serbia, and the rest left as a rump still united with Hungary. Pašić did not like this prospect, but he took the conventional diplomat's view: he would get as much as he could, and wait for a more favourable time to get the rest, by diplomacy or by war. For him, Bosnia and southern Hungary were the most important territories, while Macedonia had to be kept at any cost. Dalmatia and Croatia had in his eyes a much lower priority.

Later in the war a further conflict developed between Pašić and the exiles. Pašić was immensely proud of the Serbian state, and he saw the future South Slav state as an extension of Serbia. Pašić stood in the nineteenth century radical tradition which considered centralism to be progressive, and regarded far-reaching regional autonomies as reactionary and disruptive. Therefore he wanted a large centralised state, to be formed by an extension of the Serbian administrative apparatus, but inhabited by a single 'three-named nation'. On the other hand the exiles from the Monarchy, while admiring Serbia, felt that the Serbian state should cease to exist, to be replaced by an entirely new state, Yugoslavia. They also wished the new state to respect older historical and regional distinctions, and to preserve some of the older institutions. Pašić was obsessed with the example of Piedmont. The exiles argued that Piedmont had been swallowed up in Italy. Pašić knew that, on the contrary, Piedmont had dominated Italy after unity. Serbia in the new state, was, in his scheme, to be a mixture of Piedmont and Prussia.

In November 1918 Pašić had his way. He was able to exploit the fear both of Italian aggression and of revolutionary disorder in Central Europe, to force the political leaders of the South Slavs of the disintegrated Habsburg Monarchy to accept union with Serbia with no preliminary conditions. The new Serb-Croat-Slovene state was proclaimed on 1 December 1918. Less than three years later a centralist constitution was voted by the assembly, against the opposition of federalists, including the most powerful Croatian group, the Croatian Peasant Party. There followed seven years of political intrigue, in which all the main parties kept changing their tactics, but nothing was solved. In 1928 the Croatian Peasant Party leader Stepan Radić was shot in parliament, and later died of his wounds. In January 1929 King Alexander introduced a dictatorship. He professed to be acting on behalf of a single Yugoslav nation, transcending Serbian no less than Croatian nationalism. In practice the supporters of the dictatorship were almost exclusively Serbs (though many, perhaps most, Serbs detested it), and the Croats were against it almost to a man. The result was that it operated in fact as a dictatorship of the Greater Serbs over the rest. This was even more true in Macedonia than in Croatia: government was considerably more brutal, and Macedonians were forced to call themselves 'South Serbs', while supporters either of independent Macedonia or of union with Bulgaria were pitilessly repressed.

Attempts at Serb-Croat reconciliation in the late 1930s had some success, but fundamentally a majority of the population detested the regime and was at best lukewarm about the survival of the state. In 1941 the invasion by the Germans and their allies brought the collapse of Yugoslavia within a few days. On its ruins was created a Croatian state, headed by the Croatian fascist Ante Pavelić, while the Slovene lands were partitioned between Germany and Italy, and Macedonia was given to Bulgaria. Pavelić's state seemed for a time a victory for the Greater Croatian idea, for the dreams of Starčević. Though Pavelić had to surrender most of Dalmatia to Italy, he was allowed to annex all Bosnia. However, the massacres by Pavelić's men of Serbs and Jews, the armed resistance of the survivors, and the successful national and civil war waged by the communists led by Tito, reduced the Croatian state to anarchy.

The communists won the civil and national war of 1941-45 not only by their courage and military skill, and by the military supplies which they received from the British and Americans, but also because they were able to offer the people of Yugoslavia a better prospect than endless mutual massacre. They consistently preached unity of all Yugoslavs against the fascist conquerors, the enemies of all alike. At first their propaganda fell on deaf ears; but their own example, and the demonstration by their opponents of the horror and vanity of extreme nationalism, attracted to them growing numbers of recruits from all parts of the country.

After they had won, they introduced a constitution, closely modelled on that of the Soviet Union, in which there were to be six republics: Slovenia, Croatia, Bosnia, Serbia, Montenegro and Macedonia. It now became official doctrine that there was no Yugoslav nation but four nations—Serbs, Croats, Slovenes and Macedonians—living together within one state, as well as several national minorities, of which the most important were Albanians and Hungarians. In practice the Yugoslav state was no more a federation than was the Soviet: at most there was some devolution of power, under the tight grasp of a highly centralised communist party. However, the new rulers made sincere and successful attempts to stop discrimination on grounds of nationality.

After the breach with the Soviet Union in 1948, the political system underwent a series of changes, both formal and informal. In the late 1960s not only the six republican governments but the republican communist parties began to pursue divergent policies. National tensions reappeared, partly in the form of conflicts between the economically advanced and backward republics (the former objecting to the use of the product of their labour to finance the latter, and the latter protesting that the aid which they received was too little) and partly in the form of arguments about culture and language, especially between Croats and Serbs.

The Yugoslav communists hoped to end the old rivalry between Serbs and Bulgarians for Macedonia. They maintained that the Macedonians were a distinct nation, with a language and a history of their own. All attempts to impose Serbian domination on them were definitely abandoned. Press, literature and education in the new Macedonian literary language, derived from what had previously been no more than a spoken dialect, were very successfully promoted, and Macedonian became the accepted language of public business in the republic. Though the communist government of neighbouring Bulgaria was not convinced, the people of Macedonia themselves appeared to have accepted their new national identity; and Macedonian communist leaders spoke from time to time of the need to incorporate in the Macedonian republic the people of 'Aegean Macedonia' (described by the Greek authorities as 'Slavophone Hellenes') and of 'Pirin Macedonia' (whom the Bulgarian government declared to be perfectly ordinary patriotic Bulgarians).

An interesting situation arose in Bosnia, where the Muslims increased more rapidly than the Serbs and Croats, and in the early 1970s were the most numerous of the three communities. What were they? They were certain that they were not Serbs or Croats, and official doctrine now denied (realistically) that there was a Yugoslav nation. They could hardly be called a Bosnian nation, because this would deprive the Serbs and Croats who lived in Bosnia of their Bosnian character. It therefore seemed difficult to resist the conclusion that they formed a Muslim nation. Speaking the same Serbo-Croatian language as their neighbours, but united by religion, historical and cultural tradition, they formed a compact community, as the people of Pakistan had never done. It seemed arguable that a million people in the centre of Yugoslavia were one of many nations of Muslim faith in the world, but the only 'Muslim nation'.

Another national problem of importance in Yugoslavia was the Albanians. Divided between a subordinate territory of the Serbian republic (known as the Kosovo-Metohija autonomous region) and the republic of Macedonia, they numbered about 1,200,000. This was a larger population than that of the whole Macedonian or Montenegrin republic; it was also over one-third of the total number of Albanians in the world, and was concentrated along the northern and eastern borders of the Albanian state. The claim either to form a seventh republic of Yugoslavia, or to be united with the Albanian state, was difficult to refute on grounds of principle. The rate of natural increases of these Albanians was about double that of the Serbs who lived among them.

Nationalism had not disappeared in Yugoslavia: on the contrary, its disruptive effects caused alarm, which led to a reassertion of authoritarian policies by the communist party in the early 1970s. Nevertheless, it remained true that the forces working for the strengthening of a single Yugoslav state, based on equality for its constituent nations, were stronger than they had ever been; and that the Yugoslavs were the only communists who had genuinely achieved progress towards solution of national conflicts within a multinational state, though they had begun their task in exceptionally difficult circumstances.

# 4   Europe: Multi-National Empires and New Nations

## Multi-national empires

At the beginning of the nineteenth century there were three great empires in Europe whose subjects had included for centuries many different religious communities and language groups. These were the Habsburg Monarchy, the Russian and the Ottoman empires. It was in the nineteenth century, under the influence of the penetration of the ideas of the Enlightenment of the previous century, that religious belief, pride in language, historical legends and discoveries and various social and economic discontents fused together to create, in the minds of growing educated elites, the conviction that their respective communities constituted nations, and should be recognised as such. When this belief had spread from the pioneers to a significant part of the population, genuine national movements came into existence. At this point, what had previously been multi-lingual and multi-religious states became multi-national empires; and the question arose whether they could accommodate within their borders the new claims to recognition of different nations, or whether the leaders of the movements could be contented only with sovereign territorial independence.

The first of the three empires to be seriously affected was the Ottoman, not because the new national elites were more numerous or better educated than those in Austria or Russia (the contrary was the case); but because the Ottoman state was being unmistakably weakened by unsuccessful wars against Christian powers, from whose governments they could expect help.

Since the Ottoman conquest, the Balkan subjects of the sultan had been ruled according to the *millet* system, an application of the principles traditionally applied to non-Muslim communities in lands ruled by Muslims. Recognition was given to religious communities as such (Orthodox, Armenian, Jewish) and the religious leader became the leader in all matters, spiritual and secular, of the whole community, subject to the sultan.[1] Wishing to centralise all Orthodox communities under a single head, the sultan reasserted the authority of the patriarch of Constantinople. Appointments within the religious hierarchy were within the exclusive jurisdiction of the patriarch, subject to the agreement of the synod of the church.[2] The patriarch's courts judged not only ecclesiastical cases, but also secular disputes between Orthodox; but disputes between an Orthodox and a Muslim were left to Muslim courts. The patriarch was committed to support the government's demands for taxes from the Orthodox. He had no responsibility for collecting them, but it was his duty to put pressure on those who failed to pay taxes, if necessary to excommunicate them. In his capacity as secular leader (ethnarch) the patriarch required lay officials, including persons of a high level of education and skill. Thus a certain secular bureaucracy grew up around the patriarch's headquarters in the Phanar quarter of Constantinople. This incipient Christian elite of officials and merchants, some of whom acquired considerable wealth, and all of whom were Greeks even if their origin was not necessarily Greek, became known as Phanariots.

Conversion of Balkan Christians to Islam took place on a considerable scale in three regions in the Balkans. The first was Bosnia, where a large number of people of Serbo-Croatian speech became Muslim and remained Muslim until the present time.[3] The second region was the Rhodope Mountains to the north of the Aegean. Here considerable numbers of persons of Bulgarian speech became Muslims. They became known as Pomaks. The third region was Albania. This mountainous country was not conquered until 1467: the Albanian Skanderbeg was the last Christian leader in the Balkans to resist the Turks. After the final conquest, the majority of the Albanians embraced Islam, though there remained some Catholic Albanian tribes in the north, a large number of Albanian Orthodox in Epirus, and scattered communities of Orthodox Albanians as far into peninsular Greece as Attica.

The condition of the Balkan Orthodox under Ottoman rule was precarious and humiliating, but it was not intolerable. In any case, as the sultan's government was strong, they had no choice but to submit to it. At a more sophisticated level, this was also the attitude of the Orthodox hierarchy and the Phanariots. To some extent they regarded the sultan as the successor of the emperor: the habit of deference to autocracy, inculcated by Byzantine traditions, was transferred to the Muslim lord of the imperial city. For one thing at least they were grateful to the Turks: they protected them from the aggression and the pernicious doctrines of the Western Roman schismatics.

After the Austrian victories over the Ottomans at the end of the seventeenth century, the perspective gradually changed. At least in the hierarchy and in the secular educated class the possibility of Turkish collapse began to be taken seriously, and contacts were made with

Christian governments, especially with the Russian, since Russia was an Orthodox power. In 1770 when the Russian fleet of Empress Catherine II, engaged in war with Turkey, appeared off the Mani peninsula in the Peloponnese, the local Greek population, which had been prepared beforehand by Russian emissaries, rebelled. However, Turkish reprisals were so severe that there was no rising by Christians during Catherine's second Turkish war (1788-92).

During the eighteenth century, as European ideas began to reach at least a small elite of the Balkan Christian peoples, interest developed in the specific traditions and languages of each of them, as opposed to their common predicament as members of the Orthodox *millet* and subjects of an infidel ruler. This trend prevailed in the next century, leading towards the emergence of several Balkan nations, based on language and on historical mythology, and the break-up of the unity of Orthodoxy. Already early in the century Dimitrie Cantemir, Prince of Moldavia, wrote historical and descriptive works about his country; and the writings of Transylvanian Romanian Uniate priests about the history of the Romanians became known across the Carpathians. The Serbian Orthodox Metropolitanate at Sremski Karlovci, established by the Austrian authorities, became a centre of Serbian learning. Another work of great importance was the *Slavic-Bulgarian History* written in 1762 by a Bulgarian monk of the monastery of Hilendar on Mount Athos, Father Paisii, which was read in manuscript by his more educated compatriots and became the classical text of early Bulgarian nationalism.

The revolts of the Serbs against the Turks in 1804 and of the Greeks in 1821, and their consequences, have been considered in the previous chapter; the Romanian national movement will be discussed at greater length in this chapter. It remains to say a little here of two other Balkan national movements under Ottoman rule—the Bulgarian and the Albanian.

Bulgaria remained under Ottoman control after the Crimean War. Here too, however, national consciousness was spreading. Its bearers were the small but growing number of Bulgarians educated at schools in Constantinople, in Russia, in Romania or in countries further west. A native Bulgarian merchant class also began to make itself felt, and provided some leadership. Foreign scholars took an interest in the Bulgarian language, outstanding among them the Russian Yurii Venelin. A collection of Bulgarian popular epic poetry was published in 1861 in Zagreb, with the help of the Croatian bishop Josip Štrosmajer. A decisive moment in the Bulgarian national revival was the establishment in 1870, by a *firman* of the sultan, of a separate Bulgarian Orthodox Church, with its own exarch at its head. This was the result of ten years of struggle by the Bulgarian priesthood, essentially a nationalist movement in ecclesiastical form. The priests, forming a very high percentage of the still very small educated elite of the Bulgarians, were national leaders. In the next years Bulgarian revolutionaries, based in Romania, created a conspiratorial network in Bulgaria, and in April 1876 there was an armed rebellion, quickly and savagely suppressed by the Turks. However, a year later Russia went to war with Turkey, and at the Congress of Berlin in 1878 there came into existence a Bulgarian state, which was enlarged in 1885, and took its place in Balkan politics.[4]

The last Balkan people to develop a national movement were the Albanians. For them, religion was a dividing rather than a unifying factor. The majority were Muslims, among whom the Bektashi sect were extremely important, but others were Orthodox or Catholic. It was not until late in the century that the idea took root that the common factor of the Albanian language should be considered more important than the conflict between Christians and Muslims. The Albanians were also divided between the two main groups of Ghegs and Tosks, living respectively north and south of the river Shkumbi. The Ghegs were organised in clans, while the social structure of the Tosks was based on large landowners and dependent peasants. There was also a difference between Gheg and Tosk dialects. The Albanians provided excellent soldiers for the Ottoman armies, and scattered communities were to be found in Romania, Greece and Italy.

The first joint political action by leading Albanians in opposition to the Ottoman government was the League of Prizren, formed in 1878, which asked that all lands of Albanian speech should be regrouped into a single territory (instead of four provinces), and that it should be given autonomy under the sultan. These demands led to serious fighting in 1881, after which some minor concessions were made. During the next decades the Albanian tribal leaders and landowners made efforts to develop schools for Albanians, and some were established by Austrians and Italians. Albanians also obtained education abroad, especially in Italy. The Albanian cause suffered a serious reversal as a result of the Balkan wars of 1912-13. Territories of Albanian population, amounting to more than a third of the whole Albanian people, passed to Serbia, Montenegro and Greece. The remaining two-thirds were formed into an Albanian state in 1914.

After another thirty years of domination or direct annexation (from 1939) by Italy, Albania obtained effective independence only under communist rule in 1945. The Albanian government not unjustifiably viewed all neighbouring states with suspicion, and received some support from distant China. The Albanian communists' solution to the religious diversity which had weakened Albanian nationalism was to persecute Islam, Catholicism and Orthodoxy with equal ferocity: the unity of the Albanian nation was at least outwardly impressive.

The second of the European empires to become a multi-national state, and to be threatened by national movements from within its frontiers, was the Habsburg Monarchy.

For the Habsburg rulers, *Kaisertreue* (loyalty to the emperor) was the essential requirement. When the Austrian Habsburgs first became a considerable power in Europe, they practised religious discrimination among their subjects—against Protestants in Bohemia and Hungary, to some extent against Orthodox in Transylvania but not against Orthodox Serbs settled on their southern military frontier, and against Jews. This discrimination became much milder in the eighteenth century and came to an end after Joseph II's Edict of Toleration in 1780. As for languages, all were supposed to enjoy official respect: the primacy of German or Latin in administration was a matter of common sense, not of national discrimination. The concept of nationality was, however, rejected by Metternich and his successors as a part of the body of liberal democratic doctrine. There was no Austrian nation, and no other nations either. The word *Nationalität* was introduced into official parlance to designate the admittedly existing distinct communities of culture and language among the emperor's subjects: the whole point about the promise to give each *Nationalität* its rights was that the existence of one or more nations was denied. German, Italian and Hungarian nations were denied in 1848-49. It was only the two disastrous wars of 1859 and 1866 that forced the emperor first to give up his Italian territories and then to make concessions to his Hungarian subjects: in 1867 Hungary became essentially a distinct state, and its rulers thereafter declared it to be a national state. In the rest of the Monarchy, however, though attempts were frequently made to satisfy specific claims of nationalists, or to play them off against each other, *Kaisertreue* remained the basic principle of legitimacy. It was far from ineffective. Millions of Austrian subjects served the emperor loyally in peace and war until the end. However, nationalism was not overcome: it steadily gained ground, and when Austria was defeated in war in 1918 the Monarchy broke up into national states.

The Russian tsars too asked in the first instance for loyalty to themselves and their dynasty. There was substantial discrimination in favour of the Orthodox and against Jews and Muslims: there was certainly less religious toleration than in Josephine Austria. The ranks and privileges within the empire were however based on social class, not on language; and there was no question of one nation being privileged, since the very idea of the nation was repudiated. The Poles were punished by Tsar Nicholas I in 1831 not because they were Poles but because they were rebellious subjects. There were Russians in the early nineteenth century who wished to make non-Russians into Russians, but they did not receive imperial support.

However, in the second half of the nineteenth and the first half of the twentieth century, there came into existence a doctrine which, in two multi-national states, overshadowed, or indeed replaced, the principle of dynastic loyalty as the basis of legitimacy of government. This doctrine I will call 'official nationalism'. The leaders of the most powerful nations considered it their task, and indeed their moral duty, to impose their nationality on all their subjects—of whatever religion, language or culture. As they saw it, by drawing these people upwards into their own superior culture, they were conferring benefits on them; while at the same time they were strengthening their state by creating within it a single homogeneous nation.

There are two outstanding examples of the application of this doctrine in Eastern Europe: Magyarisation in Hungary after 1867, and Russification in the Russian empire under Alexander III and Nicholas II. Of the latter something has been said in a previous chapter, and there will be further references to it later. Here the main emphasis will be on the Hungarian case, with occasional comparison between it and the Russian.

The most important factor in the determination of national movements in modern times in Central and Eastern Europe, in the three multi-national empires, was language: this does not of course mean that religious and economic factors did not also play their part, and massive social discontent always underlay them all.

In this chapter five national movements are considered. The brief sections on each are intended to note specific features of each, including certain decisive moments and a few decisive personalities; but it may be useful to begin with a brief comparison.

Four—Czechs, Slovaks, Romanians and Ukrainians—were at the end of the eighteenth century, or even later, submerged groups which had no officially recognised place in the political life of their states. The fifth—Hungarians—had legal status but were dependent, to an extent which was increasingly unacceptable, on foreign rulers. Social and cultural developments, brought about by the policies of consciously modernising rulers, created in all five cases intellectual elites which increasingly identified themselves with the uneducated and underprivileged majorities of their language groups; they came to think of the language group as a nation; and spread this language-based national consciousness down into the lower strata of the community. The process was accelerated by international forces—war and diplomacy—which were beyond their control, but which were used by their leaders to obtain independent state sovereignty based on their nation. In four cases independence was achieved, in one (the Ukrainian) it was denied. In three of these four cases (the Czech, Slovak and Romanian) the achievement of independence and unity was felt, at least at the time, to be a victory; in the fourth case (the Hungarian) there was a series of partial victories and partial defeats which defy simple classification.

Three of the five nations (Czechs, Slovaks and Hungarians) emerged from the Habsburg Monarchy; and one (the Romanian) from three: Habsburg, Russian and Ottoman. The unsuccessful Ukrainian national movement began to emerge from the Russian empire and the Habsburg Monarchy; the Ukrainian nation was divided between the Soviet Russian empire, the Polish and the Romanian states, and was finally incorporated wholly in the first of these three.

Certain unavoidable difficulties are involved in any examination of these five cases.

The development of the language community of Czech speech into the modern Czech nation is indissolubly connected with the movement for German national unity. The wider German movement has already been discussed in outline; but a narrower sector of it will have to be discussed again in the Bohemian context.

The national movement of the Hungarians was directed in its first phase mainly against the Habsburg Monarchy, and contained an element of anti-German nationalism: this struggle led to brief victory and then defeat in 1848, followed by an incomplete victory in 1867. In its second phase Hungarian nationalism was directed primarily against the non-Hungarian nations living in Hungary—though this tendency had also been present before 1848, and the anti-Habsburg tendency remained important after 1867. Thus in its first phase the aim was to liberate the Hungarian nation from foreign rule, in the second phase to impose Hungarian nationality on other nations which the Hungarian leaders did not recognise as nations. These two distinct phases, of which the second is especially significant as an example of Official Nationalism—which is found in other parts of the world at other times—makes it necessary to devote considerably more space to the Hungarian case than to the others.

It is hoped that the reader will put up with these asymmetries and inconveniences; and will respect the author's assurance that he tried hard to avoid them but could not.

## Czechs and Germans in Bohemia

The kingdom of Bohemia existed from at least the tenth century and the language of the majority of its subjects was Czech. During the Middle Ages considerable numbers of German-speaking immigrants established themselves, especially in cities and in mining districts. In the fifteenth century Bohemia had become a country of two languages. Bohemia was the first

Catholic country in which a large-scale Reformation movement appeared. Associated with the name of the great religious leader Jan Hus, it provoked the wrath of the pope, who summoned Catholic rulers to crusades against it. In the series of Hussite wars from 1419 to 1437, the Bohemians held their own against their enemies. The invading forces consisted mainly of German soldiers, but there were Czech-speakers among them, just as there were German-speakers fighting in the Hussite ranks. As a result, in the two centuries following the Hussite wars, there grew up something which may reasonably be called a Bohemian national consciousness, with an incipient Bohemian nation of two languages. Different Protestant faiths coexisted with Catholicism.

The trend was, however, reversed when the revolt of the Bohemian nobility against the newly elected King Ferdinand II in 1618 triggered off the Thirty Years' War, which cost the lives of about a third of the Bohemian population as well as ruining a once prosperous and advanced economy. The victorious Habsburgs imposed the Catholic faith by force. Politically conscious Bohemians were killed, driven into exile or reduced to silence. A new upper class was formed from the foreign families whom the Habsburg emperors brought in from other parts of Europe. The old Bohemian nation, which had extended from the aristocracy down through the smaller nobility into the middle levels of the social pyramid, had virtually ceased to exist. At the end of the seventeenth century German was spoken by the upper class as a whole, and by merchants and officials in the towns. Czech remained only as the language of peasants. There were Bohemian noblemen who knew Czech, but they would speak it to their servants rather than to their social equals. This was the age of the triumphant Counter-Reformation, pursued by the Catholic hierarchy with both persecution and persuasion, and outwardly symbolised by the splendours of baroque architecture.

From the mid-eighteenth century things began to change. Population and resources recovered. From the Czech-speaking masses there emerged an upper stratum of rich peasants and traders, who began to claim more respect and wider opportunities for their language. This may be put in general terms, as a phenomenon characteristic of similar situations which later arose in other countries: upward social mobility of persons involves a demand for upward social mobility of their language. This demand was viewed with sympathy by the reforming bureaucrats of Maria Theresa and Joseph II. The latter emperor insisted that German should be the language of the higher administration in all his empire, but he was not opposed to the use of other languages in public affairs at the local level. He was eager to educate his subjects, and wished this job to be performed by the church, which he was determined to subordinate to the state. At the same time he gave (by his Patent of Toleration of 1781) opportunities of careers to

Protestants and Jews, and abolished (by a decree of 1 November 1781) serfdom, though not ending all forms of forced labour. Chairs of Czech language were established at the Military Academy and at the universities of Vienna and Prague; school textbooks, agricultural manuals and religious works were published in Czech; and officials in regions of Czech speech were officially encouraged to learn Czech.

Thus spontaneous forces and official policy combined to favour a revival and development of the Czech language, and this in turn produced a growing identification of nation and language. The concept of a Czech nation really dates from this period.[5] The leading figure in the revival was a Catholic priest, Josef Dobrovský (1753-1829), the author of the first systematic grammar of Czech, and of a history of Czech language and early literature. Dobrovský was essentially a man of the Enlightenment, believed in the power of reason and learning, had no use for any national fanaticism, and wished from philanthropic motives to benefit his people by improving their knowledge of their own culture. For most of his life he was financially maintained by an enlightened noble family, the Counts Nostitz, who keenly favoured his researches. Dobrovský was interested in all the Slav languages, and indeed felt that there was essentially a single Slav language, divided into several major dialects (*Mundarten*). This idea was carried further in the next generation by Josef Jungmann (1773-1847), the son of a peasant, whose career was secondary school teaching. He published in 1825 a history of Czech literature, and between 1835 and 1839 appeared his pioneering five-volume Czech-German dictionary. The third great figure was the historian František Palacký (1798-1876), who became the archivist of the brothers Count Kaspar and Count Franz Sternberg, and played an active part in the foundation of the Bohemian Museum in Prague, of which the Sternbergs were the most active initiators. The museum was completed in 1822, and it published a monthly review in both languages from 1827. However, after four years the German monthly expired for lack of support, whereas the Czech periodical, under a new title *Časopis českeho muzea*, continued vigorously.[6] This contrast is of symbolic significance: the museum in fact became essentially a Czech affair, an object of pride to the Czech people, though Prague for some time yet was a half-German city. In 1829 Palacký and others founded *Matice česká*, a fund contributed by private subscribers to finance the publication of books in Czech. It too had striking success in the following decades. From 1836 onwards began to appear the successive volumes of Palacký's History of Bohemia. Written originally in German, it was a pioneering work of scholarship, but it was also the classic expression of what became the national Czech historical myth, like all myths a combination of truth and invention, setting against each other the peaceful, cultured, freedom-loving Slavs and the brutal, aggressive Germans. An important event in the construction of the mythology was the discovery, by Jungmann's pupil Vaclav Hanka, an expert on Czech popular poetry, of two ancient manuscripts which showed the existence of epic and lyric poetry in Czech in the Middle Ages. The two manuscripts, revealed in 1817 and 1818, were viewed with scepticism by Dobrovský, but were generally accepted. In the 1880s they were shown, after careful examination by Czech scholars, to have been deliberate forgeries. This episode too is of some symbolic significance in the history of the development of the modern Czech nation.

The leaders of the Czech national revival were technicians of language, and language became the criterion of national identity. The Czechs were surrounded by the far more numerous German nation. They badly needed a powerful friend, and the assurance that they were part of a great and irresistible force. This friend and this force most of their leaders thought that they had found in the notion of united Slavdom, led by the mighty Russian empire.

Czech national feeling must be distinguished clearly from Panslavism, but it is beyond doubt that it received comfort and encouragement from it. Slav solidarity was and remained an emotion of some complexity and many variations, from the expertise of the philologist to the rhetoric of the Russian imperial propagandist. Not all Czech nationalists took much interest in other Slavs. Not all Czech panslavs had much enthusiasm for the Russia of the tsars. Palacký regarded tsarism as a menace to Europe, and felt that Slav solidarity obliged him to sympathise with Poles, who were Slav victims of Russian oppression. One Czech who had lived two years in Russia, Karel Havlíček (1820-56), a radical democrat and the most brilliant journalist the Czech people has produced, had no illusions. He later wrote:

> So I returned to Prague as a simple Czech, even with some secret sour feeling against the name Slav which a sufficient knowledge of Russia and Poland has made suspect to me. Above all, I express my firm conviction that the Slavs, that means the Russians, the Poles, the Czechs, the Illyrians etc., are not one nation. The name Slav is and should for ever remain a purely geographical and scientific name.[7]

The Czech cultural revival enjoyed widespread sympathy from liberal Bohemians of German speech, both noblemen and middle class. Under the Metternich regime, the main concern of those who opposed the government was to win constitutional and civil liberties. To some extent these aims, characteristic of European liberalism as a whole, were shared in Bohemia by persons of Czech and of German speech. To some extent also liberal aims overlapped with aspirations for provincial autonomy, which set a large part of the Bohemian nobility against the centralised and increasingly uniform bureaucratic system preferred by the government in

Vienna.

In 1848 the example of the revolution in Paris produced radical stirrings in Prague slightly earlier than in Vienna. During March 1848 two successive petitions to Vienna demanded equal status for the two languages in all official business, and administrative unity for the three provinces of Bohemia, Moravia and Silesia. In April there came into existence a National Committee of over a hundred persons. German-speakers were at first included, but most of them soon resigned. A Provisional Government Council was set up on 28 May, under Count Leo Thun, of which Palacký was a member. At the beginning of June a Panslav Congress in Prague was attended by more than three hundred persons, mostly from the Monarchy but including the Russian anarchist Michael Bakunin. Meanwhile the relationship of the new authorities to Vienna was uncertain. There were anti-Jewish riots and workers' unrest. Barricades were set up, and Prince Alfred Windischgrätz, commanding the imperial troops in Bohemia, decided to suppress what he regarded as rebellious activities. After a few days of desultory fighting, on 18 June Prague was under his complete control.

The most important consequence of 1848 for the Czechs was the revelation that Bohemia had become a land of two nations. Even later than this there were still persons, in the nobility and civil service, who felt themselves to be Bohemian patriots, but there was no doubt that this was a dwindling minority. The cleavage, within the politically aspiring middle classes, had been most clearly revealed by the arguments as to whether Bohemia was or was not part of Germany. The organisers of the elected German Assembly in Frankfurt, planning a new united democratic Germany, had invited the Bohemians to send their representatives. Palacký replied in an often-quoted letter of 11 April. The Czechs, he argued, were not Germans. The links of Bohemia with the German empire had been purely dynastic. The Czech nation was distinct from the German nation. The Czechs, however, would be loyal to the Habsburg Monarchy, provided that they were able to take their place beside the other nations within it. 'If Austria did not exist it would be necessary to create her, in the interests of humanity itself.' Palacký's words reflected the predominant opinion of politically conscious Czechs of his time. Equally, from this time onwards the predominant opinion among Bohemians of German speech was that they belonged to the German nation, and that the Czechs did not.

In the second half of the nineteenth century the conflict between Czechs and Germans in Bohemia grew steadily more bitter. It was not simply an argument between federal and centralised government, or a claim by Czechs for completely equal status for their language, though both these issues were important. Beneath these specific issues lay a growing mutual intolerance, a determination by each nation to dominate the other. The Germans believed themselves to be culturally and morally superior to the

Czechs; regarded the Czech language as an outlandish form of speech; and considered it absurd that it should be placed on an equal footing with German. The extreme German nationalists hoped to compensate for their numerical inferiority within Bohemia by the backing of the German empire. As the Vienna government refused to identify itself with the German nationalist cause as such, they detested Vienna; and a lunatic fringe favoured secession from Austria and incorporation in Bismarck's Reich.[8] In this they received no encouragement from Bismarck. For their part, the extreme Czech nationalists regarded the Germans as intruders, and were determined to dominate them. At the end of the century, some Bohemian Germans proposed that Bohemia should be administratively divided in two, into a German land and a Czech land. This was bitterly opposed by the Czechs, who insisted on the historical, physical and economic unity of Bohemia. The case for the unity of Bohemia could indeed be defended by strong arguments; but it was not so much that the nationalists were convinced by the arguments as that they brandished the arguments as weapons in a war of words.

Throughout the century the Czechs made economic and cultural progress. At the end of the 1840s almost the whole population of school age in Czech-speaking districts went to school. A class of Czech small businessmen was formed, among whom brewers and millers were especially important. Textile, mining and metallurgical industry developed steadily: at first the leading capitalists were Germans, or Jews of German speech, but in time Czech industrialists too made their appearance. Industry created a large Czech industrial working class. The cities became Czech, and after a time-lag city government too passed into Czech hands. At the end of the 1860s was founded the first Czech-owned large bank, the *Živnostenska Banka*, based at first largely on small savings but developing into a major capitalist enterprise. These were also years of progress in literature, music and drama. In 1862 the National Theatre, built by massive subscription in small amounts from a large part of the nation, was opened, only to be burnt down within a few weeks. A fresh campaign of popular subscription continued for nearly twenty years, and in 1881 it was at last opened. Another very important institution was the gymnastic society *Sokol*, founded in 1862, designed not only to improve the health of its members but also to strengthen discipline and to inculcate nationalist emotion.

For twelve years after 1848 Bohemia, like the rest of the Monarchy, was ruled bureaucratically. In 1860 the emperor began to experiment with quasi-constitutional government. The Czechs were dissatisfied, and in 1867 their representatives withdrew from the Austrian parliament (*Reichsrat*), and remained away until 1879. In 1866 Palacký, embittered by his experience of the rulers of Austria, to whom he had declared his loyalty in 1848, wrote in his book *The Idea of the Austrian State* the very different statement: 'before Austria was, we were: and when Austria no longer is, we still shall be.'

Defeat of Austria by Prussia in 1866 led to an agreement with Hungary, but the hopes of the Czechs that Bohemia too would be recognised as a kingdom with its own rights, and that they would control it, were disappointed. Attempts made by the Austrian rulers between 1895 and 1898 to legislate for equality between the two languages aroused the opposition of first German and then Czech members of the *Reichsrat*; members became howling mobs throwing ink-pots at each other; and the emperor had to rule Austria by decree. The introduction of universal suffrage in Austria in 1907 increased the parliamentary strength of the socialists, who were strong in Bohemia; but the impeccably internationalist sentiments expressed by some leading socialists did not eliminate strong nationalist passions among workers of both nations.

In the First World War Czech politicians had widely different aims. Karel Kramář, leader of the Young Czech Party, hoped for Russian victory, and planned a Slav Union under Russian sovereignty, with Bohemia one of its units under a Russian prince. Most Czech radical nationalists had little faith in an independent Bohemia: they wished to stop being subjects of the Habsburgs and to become subjects of the tsar, whom they fondly imagined to be animated by benevolent Slav sentiments. Czech Social Democrats hated the regime of the tsars, and hoped that the Habsburg Monarchy would be replaced by a socialist republic, in which Czech workers and the whole Czech people would be equals of the other nations. A third point of view was that of Professor Thomas Garrigue Masaryk, one of those who had exposed Hanka's forgery, an opponent of extreme nationalism but a nationally conscious Czech and a bitter enemy of German imperialism. Masaryk put his faith in democracy of the Anglo-Saxon type, believed in the victory of the western powers and desired an independent state of the Czechs and Slovaks.

The course of the war favoured Masaryk. After the central powers had defeated Italy at Caporetto, and imposed their will on Soviet Russia by the Peace of Brest-Litovsk, the western powers had no choice but to support the dissolution of the Habsburg Monarchy. In 1918 Masaryk's outstanding diplomat Eduard Beneš extracted from the Allies recognition of a Czechoslovak provisional government. When the Monarchy began to collapse from within in the autumn of 1918, the Czech political leaders in Prague took over, and elected Masaryk, who had travelled from London to Russia and the United States, as president of the new republic.

Within the new Czechoslovak republic were three and a half million Germans, forming a quarter of the population. In 1919 these Germans wished to join either residual Austria or the German republic: they were prevented by the Allies, who accepted the usual Czech historical, economic and strategic arguments. This decision can be defended on firm grounds, but it was without doubt a denial of the principle of self-determination of nations. The Czechs also had an uneasy relationship to the Slovaks, which will be discussed later, and a Hungarian minority of three-quarters of a million was incorporated against its will. The First Czechoslovak Republic had a democratic and humane form of government, and admirable social institutions; but it was never willingly accepted by much more than half its inhabitants. The great economic depression of the 1930s and the advent of Hitler made the Bohemian Germans fanatically opposed to the republic; and the surrender of the western powers at Munich brought the amputation of the Bohemian borderlands, followed in March 1939 by the annexation of all the Czech lands to Hitler's Third Reich. Thereby the wildest dreams of the Bohemian German extremists of the 1890s were exceeded: not only was German Bohemia removed from Czech control, but all Bohemia was swallowed up, not by a medieval Holy Roman Empire, but by a totalitarian empire whose *raison d'être* was the supremacy of a master race of Germans.

Hitler is on record as planning to destroy the Czech people by the three methods of forced Germanisation, deportation and extermination. He went some way towards applying his principles to the educated elite of the nation, of whom tens of thousands were destroyed. The Czech workers and peasants, however, proved too useful for his war effort, and so were allowed to enjoy (at least by the standards of the beleaguered *Festung-Europa* of 1942-45) rather good material conditions. Meanwhile the exiled Czechoslovak government of President Beneš agreed with the Soviet leaders that the whole German population should be expelled from Bohemia and Moravia, and this was accepted by the British and American leaders. In May 1945 Bohemia was liberated, with very little fighting or destruction, by the Soviet and American armies. About a million Germans fled, and two millions more were subsequently expelled. They were robbed of their possessions, and several hundred thousands of men, women and children perished in the process. German property was cheaply acquired by the Czech peasants and workers who had previously worked for Hitler. All they had to do in return was to support the Communist Party of Czechoslovakia, which had this valuable source of patronage at its disposal.

With the seizure of power by the communists three years later, something rather similar to the plans of Kramář of 1914 was achieved. The Czech lands became a province of the Russian empire. However, in place of a Russian grand-duke the Czechs were ruled by compatriots—ideological fanatics who had at their side Russian advisers expert in the invention of conspiracies, judicial murder of opponents and falsification of the nation's history. The latter item included the need to denigrate any Czech historical figure whose actions were displeasing to the new masters: foremost among these was the late President Masaryk.

Nevertheless these methods proved no more successful than previous attempts to destroy the national consciousness or remould the national identity of the Czechs. Within twenty years they had begun to tell at least part of the truth about themselves and to reform the regime to which they were subjected. The attempt at 'communism with a human face', associated with the name of Alexander Dubček, failed in 1968; Soviet Russian imperial rule was reimposed; and refalsification of history was launched. Experience suggested that it was unlikely to work in the long term.

The long history of the Czechs shows more tragedy than happiness, more fanaticism than measured judgment. The Czechs have shown more talent for music than for politics, for rhetoric than for action. Yet they have been a complex and contradictory people. To foreign visitors the modern Czechs appeared kindly, reliable and rather prosaic; but important episodes in their past contradict this impression. One need only recall the sectarian frenzies of the Hussite wars or the crazy fantasies of the Panslavs, buttressed by Hanka's forgeries. Nature has been kind to them, but man has not. Bohemia is a land washed for longer by deeper streams of native and foreign blood than almost any other; restored again and again by patient toil; adorned by some of the noblest buildings man has raised, the birthplace of much of his greatest music; often threatened and never secure; the very heart of Europe.

## The Hungarians

The Hungarian nation, as it existed before the Turkish victory of Mohács in 1526, was confined to those who had the legal status of nobility. This class amounted to more than 5 per cent of the population, and included many poor people who lived like peasants. Hungary was a country of many languages, and not all Hungarian noblemen had Hungarian (or Magyar) for their first language.[9]

When the Turks were driven from Hungary at the end of the seventeenth century, and the whole former kingdom came under Habsburg rule, Hungarians had many reasons for discontent, even if they were glad to see the last of the Turks. The country was very sparsely populated, and cultivable land had fallen into disuse on a vast scale. To improve it, and to defend the new southern frontiers against the Turks, the Habsburgs brought in settlers who were not Hungarians. German peasants acquired land west of the Danube and in the south-east (Bácska and the Banat of Temesvár). Serbs were settled in large numbers along the southern border—the so-called Military Frontier—which was administered separately from the rest of the kingdom. In the east, Romanian settlers spread westwards from Transylvania into the Tisza plain. It was a major grievance to the Hungarians that Transylvania was not reunited with Hungary, but was preserved as a distinct principality, as it had been in Ottoman times. Further resentment was caused by the activities of the Catholic Church, whose emissaries busily set themselves to spread the Counter-Reformation in the newly liberated lands, to defeat the Calvinist and Lutheran heresies which had been allowed to flourish while the infidel held sway. All these discontents contributed to the revolt led by Francis Rákoczi in the first decade of the eighteenth century.

During the eighteenth century the population increased rapidly, the agricultural economy began to prosper, and the Hungarian character of the administration was strengthened. In return for its support of Maria Theresa against Frederick II of Prussia, the Hungarian Diet insisted that she should regard Hungary as a separate kingdom of which she was queen. In practice Hungary, though administered by Hungarians, was ruled much as Vienna wished; but when Joseph II tried to apply his reforms to Hungary, he met with fierce resistance. The nobles objected to his efforts to improve the situation of the peasants, and his decree on the use of German in administration aroused more widespread hostility. In 1790 Hungary was in a state of preparation for rebellion, and Hungarian emissaries were discussing with the king of Prussia action against Austria. Joseph II's successor, his brother Leopold II, retreated. The decree about German was withdrawn, and Latin became again the official language. Leopold repeated the assurance of his predecessors that Hungary was a separate kingdom, and had himself crowned in Buda.

The crisis of 1790 gave an added impetus to a movement which already existed for the development, and for the public use, of the Hungarian language. The situation was rather different from that in Bohemia. The Czech language by this time had ceased to be used by the Bohemian upper classes, and it was but little used in writing. It had to be rescued from its lowly condition, and made a suitable instrument for modern literature. In Hungary, Hungarian had always been used by the upper classes, not only in speech but also in writing, though not in public business. It was, however, a very crude instrument. The initiative for improving it came from persons familiar with modern European and especially German literature, and influenced by the ideas and the literary fashions of the Enlightenment. In the Hungarian revival it was writers who played the main part, rather than grammarians and philologists as in the Czech case. This is not to say that Hungarians did not both need and receive the attention of grammarians. The outstanding figure was Nicholas Révai, who was at work on Hungarian philology already in the 1780s, and produced his main work, a historical grammar, between 1803 and 1805, two years before his death. But the leading personality in the whole movement was Francis Kazinczy

(1759-1831), who became known as the father of modern Hungarian literature.[10]

Budapest, to which the university was transferred in 1784 from the small provincial town of Trnava, was the main centre of intellectual life. The first literary reviews, however, appeared in Kassa[11] in the north-east, and in them Kazinczy played a leading part. He was above all an organiser. He spent most of his time at his country home, from which he conducted an enormous correspondence, encouraging writers to further efforts and criticising them sternly, even pedantically, if he thought their work below the high standards he set them. He took his part in the controversies, customary in the early stage of development of national literature (for instance, of Russian and of modern Greek), between the champions of neologisms and those who wished to keep the old forms and vocabulary unchanged. He laid the foundation for the later flowering of poets and writers greater than he.

As the language developed, the demand for its use in public business in place of the dead language Latin grew more urgent. This demand was inevitable, but it raised difficult new problems. Hungarian was the language of only half the population of Hungary proper, of one-third in Transylvania, and of a small minority in Croatia. The citizens of Hungary of non-Hungarian speech were willing to accept Latin as the official language, but objected to being made to use Hungarian, a difficult tongue with no resemblance to any of the main languages of Europe. They were also beginning to develop their own languages, to take pride in their growing literatures, and to feel that they were something more than language-groups—that they were nations, distinct from the Hungarian nation.

As long as political life was confined to the traditional *natio*—the nobility—the problem was not acute. Virtually all members of the nobility knew Latin, and (with the exception of the Croats) nearly all had a working knowledge of Hungarian. But the demand for the use of Hungarian in public business was bound to be an inseparable part of the programme of the democrats, who aimed to extend political rights from the nobility to other classes. It was a matter of faith to them that all who belonged to the Hungarian nation must know the Hungarian language. Increasingly, the criterion of membership of the nation was not class but language. Slovaks, Serbs, Ruthenes or Romanians who did not speak Hungarian could not become members of the Hungarian nation, but peasants and others of lowly social origin who did know Hungarian could. Since Hungarian nationalists of democratic outlook were generous men, they wished to make available as soon as possible to as many as possible the chance of entering the Hungarian nation and of enjoying civil rights. The only way was to develop public education rapidly, and to make the school the instrument for enabling children of non-Hungarian speech to learn Hungarian.

The division within the ranks of Hungarian liberals and nationalists concerned the speed at which this process of education should take place, and the status which should be given to languages other than Hungarian. The radicals wished to make Hungarian the sole language of administration and of instruction. Instruction in the new schools was to be in Hungarian, and those schools which already existed, in which instruction was given in another language, should be forced to change over to Hungarian after as short as possible a period of transition. The radicals agreed that there was no objection to the use of other languages in private houses and in personal relations, but as far as possible these languages should not be used in public. The moderates asked only that Hungarian should be the official language, that public officials should know it and that it should be thoroughly taught in the schools. They did not consider it inadmissible that officials should communicate in languages other than Hungarian with persons who knew no Hungarian, or that there should be schools in which instruction was given in other languages—provided that Hungarian was also taught. They were opposed to any contemptuous treatment of other languages and cultures. Slovaks or Romanians had every right to develop and to take pride in Slovak or Romanian culture. They must not, however, think of themselves as belonging to a Slovak or Romanian nation: there could be only one nation in Hungary, the Magyar. The only exception to this rule concerned the Croats, who had always had a peculiar legal relationship to Hungary, and were perhaps entitled to consider themselves a nation too.

The political classes of non-Hungarian speech consisted mainly of moderate, rather conservative men. Their loyalty was to the dynasty, to the ruler (whom they thought of as 'emperor' more than as 'king of Hungary'), rather than to the Hungarian state or the Hungarian nation. However, they did not wish to quarrel with the Hungarians, and they recognised that it was reasonable that Hungarian should be the state language. At the same time they refused to consider their own languages as in any way inferior to Hungarian. They were proud of their own recent and accelerating cultural progress. They took a growing interest in the affairs of neighbouring peoples whom they felt to be their kin: the Serbs of the kingdom of Serbia, the Romanians of the semi-independent principalities beyond the Carpathians, and the Slovaks, the other Slav peoples in general. Indications of this interest alarmed the Hungarians. The Slovaks, they feared, were infected with Panslavism, and Romanians with Daco-Romanism. These fears, though exaggerated, were not absurd: the fantasies of some Slovak and Transylvanian Romanian journalists lent weight to them. If these dangerous infections were at work, then it seemed to the Hungarian nationalists to be a matter of urgency, of the very security of the Hungarian state, that a vigorous policy of Magyarisation (or inculcation of the Hungarian language through the schools) should be adopted. But the more the nationalists clamoured for Magyarisation, the more the Slovaks and Serbs and Romanians distrusted the Hungarians, and the fiercer became their own nationalism. This escalation of national antagonisms was already far advanced before the explosion of 1848.

The contrast between radicals and moderates in the Hungarian ranks is personified in the relations between Count Stephen Széchényi and Louis Kossuth.

Széchényi was the son of an enlightened aristocrat who had been chiefly responsible for establishing the National Museum at the beginning of the century. He himself travelled widely in Western Europe, and had read more widely still. His aims were economic and cultural progress for Hungary. His speeches, books and actions were constantly devoted to this end. He was in favour of social reform, especially in the interest of the peasants; and he did not fear to oppose the policies of the rulers in Vienna. However, he had the eighteenth century preference for reason over passion; he was not in a hurry; and he believed that enormous improvements could be made without violent political struggles and without insulting and injuring other groups.

Kossuth came from a small noble family whose more distant origin was Slovak. He shared Széchényi's aims, but he wished to go further; he was in a hurry; and he was a passionate political fighter, with a genius for oratory and agitation. With the passage of years he became more radical, and the mood of the Hungarian politically conscious class increasingly followed his lead. Essentially his aims were the sovereignty of the Hungarian state, the liberation of peasants from the remains of serfdom, the political enfranchisement of the Hungarian people and the Magyarisation of the whole population—all to be achieved as quickly as possible.

Kossuth's methods and personality became ever more distasteful to Széchényi. They clashed, especially on the language question. Széchényi favoured gradual introduction of Hungarian into public business and education, and careful consideration for those of different speech. Pressure of Hungarian public opinion was for more drastic measures. In fact a series of laws were enacted —in 1836, 1840 and 1844. The last laid down that Hungarian was to be the exclusive language of parliament, government and administration, and was to become the sole language of instruction in schools as soon as the necessary additional legislation could be completed. Exceptions were made for Croatia. Széchényi had vainly warned against such intolerant haste in an address to the Academy on 27 November 1842. The idea that the superiority of Hungarian culture could be demonstrated by violence against the culture of Hungary's inhabitants of non-Hungarian speech was especially repugnant to him. However, his influence was waning, while Kossuth grew ever more popular.

Kossuth's great moment came in 1848. The Hungarian Revolution, which was set off by the events in Paris and Vienna, may be said to have started on 15 March, when a deputation of the Hungarian parliament came to Vienna with an Address to the Crown containing far-reaching political demands, and a mass demonstration in Pest was addressed by the poet Sándor Petőffi and other Radical speakers. The demonstrators' demands were largely satisfied by the parliament's 'April Laws'. These included extension of parliamentary franchise to all males aged twenty (subject to a small property qualification and the ability to speak Hungarian); abolished exemptions of noblemen from taxation and all labour obligations of peasants to landowners; set up a National Guard; and promised equality before the law, equality of all religions, a free press and free education. The mood of revolutionary enthusiasm extended to most of the population of the cities, and gradually penetrated the peasantry too. The heroic events of the following year and a half undoubtedly extended Hungarian national consciousness to most people of Hungarian speech.

Two major problems arose however: what would the Vienna government do, and what liberties were the Hungarian democrats willing to give to their fellow-citizens of non-Hungarian speech?

The Austrian government, preoccupied by unrest in Vienna, Bohemia and northern Italy,[12] sought a compromise with the Hungarians. Meanwhile the resistance of the non-Hungarian nations to the Hungarian government, in which Kossuth was the leading figure, grew. It provided the Vienna leaders with an opportunity to play them against each other.

Kossuth's attitude, which was without doubt approved by most Hungarian political leaders, was a combination of unrealistic benevolence and national intolerance. The non-Hungarians were culturally inferior, and must be so treated: it was intolerable that they should have the status of equality with the ruling Hungarian nation. However, they need have no grounds for discontent, for as Hungarian citizens they would enjoy all liberties, and every effort would be made to transform them into Hungarians, after which all would be well with them. Kossuth and his friends genuinely believed that they were doing the non-Hungarians a kindness by giving them the chance of becoming absorbed in the superior Hungarian culture. To refuse this kindness was nationalist fanaticism: to impose it by force was to promote progress. The suggestion that Romanians, Slovaks or Serbs were nations, with a national culture of their own, was simply ridiculous nonsense. Later in life, in his long exile in Western Europe, Kossuth recognised that he had been wrong, and devised various schemes for federation in Central Europe which had no chance of being carried out. In his own country, his national intolerance remained accepted doctrine.

The final overthrow of Kossuth's government in August 1849 was followed by executions, imprisonments and absolutist government. Defeat by France in 1859, and by Prussia in 1866, forced the Austrian government to reverse its policies. In 1867 the centralised empire was transformed into a dual monarchy, to be known as Austria-Hungary. Hungary was to have its own government in Budapest, which was to enjoy a very wide measure of sovereignty. The army command, diplomacy and certain economic powers remained common to the whole Monarchy, and were handled by common ministers in Vienna appointed by the crown.

From 1867 to 1918 Hungary was a semi-sovereign state, ruled by a small political class based on a very small electorate. It still formed part of the Habsburg Monarchy, and its leaders professed loyalty to that dynasty; yet they claimed that it was a national state—the state of the Hungarian nation, of those whose language was Magyar. Hungarians formed rather more than half the inhabitants of Hungary, excluding Croatia.[13] If the population of Croatia were included in the population of Hungary, then the Magyars were in an overall minority in their own country.

The Hungarian political class was divided by the Austro-Hungarian Compromise of 1867. A large minority continued to profess the principles of 1848: to them nothing less than complete sovereign independence was acceptable. They were willing that the emperor of Austria, Franz Josef, should be king of Hungary, but his Hungarian kingdom was to be separate from all his other dominions, in complete control of its armed forces and foreign policy, and free to regulate its external trade as it wished. By contrast, the majority of the political class accepted the Compromise, on the grounds that it was the best settlement available, and that it brought Hungary solid advantages. However, even the supporters of the Compromise still viewed Vienna with suspicion. They maintained an attitude of constant and grudging vigilance.

Hungarian governments fought in fact a two-front war, against Vienna and against the non-Magyars within Hungary. The 1867-ers (or supporters of 'Dualism') tended to see Vienna as preferable to the non-Magyars, while the 1848-ers (or Independence party) tended, at least as long as they were in opposition, to express some hope that they might get support from the non-Magyars against Vienna in return for some concessions. However, both sections of the Hungarian political class fundamentally regarded both Austria and the non-Magyars as opponents—the first to be resisted, the second to be absorbed.

This requires some qualifications. The Hungarian political leaders, of both groups, were men of liberal outlook: they still regarded themselves as heirs to the ideals of 1848. They believed that all Hungarian subjects should enjoy the civil and political rights appropriate to their class (which excluded the poor and uneducated majority), whatever their origin. They also believed that Hungary should be equipped with modern industries and a modern school system, and set themselves to this task with great energy.

Their attitude to the non-Magyars was set out in the Nationality Law of 1868, the work of Baron Joseph Eötvös. This laid down that non-Magyars should be educated in their own language at primary school level, and in certain cases also at secondary level, and that they should be able to use their language—either directly or through interpreters—in dealings with the public authorities. However, it also stated that there was in Hungary only one nation (*nemzet*), the Hungarian nation: it alone was entitled to sovereignty in its own territory. Hungarian citizens of non-Magyar language were entitled to equal rights, provided that they learned the Magyar language and regarded themselves as Hungarians. They must not suffer any discrimination because they spoke their original languages at home or among their friends. But they must not be allowed any sort of collective institutions as a community, still less be given any sort of territorial autonomy. It was of course obvious that these non-Magyar language groups did in fact constitute distinct communities; but the word appropriate to designate them was not 'nation' but 'nationality', a word taken from Austrian legal terminology (in German, *Nationalität*, in Magyar *nemzet-iseg*). This did not apply to the Croats: they were a 'nation', and in their historical territories Croatian, not Magyar, was the official language in administration and in schools.

The trouble about the Eötvös policy was that it did not correspond to reality. The non-Magyars were no longer mere language groups. They had had nationally conscious social elites since the beginning of the century, and national consciousness had been spreading steadily downwards into the lower social levels ever since, largely of course as a result of the propaganda of the elites. The events of 1848 had shown that Romanian, Serbian and Slovak nations existed and that they were in process of drawing the peasant masses into their national movements. In the second half of the nineteenth century most of their leaders would certainly have been willing to remain Hungarian subjects, to recognise that the Magyars were first among the nations of Hungary, and that Magyar must be the official language of the state, provided that they too were recognised as nations, and were allowed their own autonomous institutions and control of their own schools within the territories where they formed a clear majority of the population. This the Hungarian politicians absolutely refused to consider. The legalistic doctrine with which a whole generation was deeply imbued permitted of no argument: the dogma of the single Hungarian political nation was not open to discussion. They also feared that, if they granted any territorial autonomy, this would only be a first stage towards the break-up of Hungary: the Serbs and Romanians would secede to join the neighbouring kingdoms of Serbia and Romania; and the Slovaks would demand union with either Moravia or Galicia, outside the Hungarian frontiers. In the light of subsequent history, one must admit that this fear was not unreasonable, but it was certainly exaggerated. The warnings of Panslav and Daco-Romanian[14] separatist dangers, as justifications for repression, proved to be self-fulfilling prophecies.

The Eötvös policy was therefore basically unacceptable to Romanian, Serbian and Slovak subjects of Hungary. As for the 'Ruthenes' of northeast Hungary, akin to the Ukrainians of eastern Galicia, they were economically and culturally so backward that it is hard to say what their attitude was. The one non-Magyar group which accepted the new regime enthusiastically, and made the most of the chances that it offered, were the Jews.[15]

In practice, however, Eötvös's Nationality Law was honestly applied only for a few years. In 1875 the three main political groups of 1867-ers united to form a Liberal Party, and its leader, Kálmán Tisza, became premier, and held office until 1890. He was the initiator of the policy which became known as Magyarisation, both in the schools and in the general administration. For a short time in the early 1890s pressure was somewhat relaxed, and permission was given to hold a Nationalities Congress in Budapest in April 1895. It was attended by Slovak, Romanian and Serbian representatives, who issued a statement of their political wishes. In the next years pressure increased again.

Judged by the methods of the mid-twentieth century, in Europe or beyond, the forcible Magyarisation of Kálmán Tisza and his successors was comparatively mild; yet in an age which was accustomed to humane standards in government it was resented as unjust and brutal. The 1879 Education Act made it compulsory to teach Magyar in all primary schools, and enforced this through school inspectors who behaved in a brutal and insulting manner in non-Magyar regions. In practice the non-Magyar children reacted by obstinately refusing to learn. The Hungarian government spent a large part of its education budget on largely unsuccessful efforts to force Magyar on non-Magyar children while neglecting the schools in regions of pure Magyar population, where peasants and agricultural labourers continued to be neglected by the Ministry of Education. Another weapon of Magyarisation was the use of vague clauses in the press laws, forbidding incitement of class against class, or of nationality against nationality, or 'insults to the Magyar nation', imposing of fines on newspapers appearing in non-Magyar languages, or sending editors or writers to prison for a year or so. Repeated fines drove newspapers into bankruptcy. It was possible for the surviving editorial staff to found a new paper under a new name, but it was then subjected to further petty persecution until it too was driven out of business. These cat-and-mouse tactics, and the persistent perversion of the law, created more and more enemies for Hungary, and brought the law itself into contempt. The courts were simply regarded as enemy strongholds, in which no justice could be obtained. Political redress was equally unobtainable, because the narrow suffrage excluded the great majority of non-Magyars, as well as most Magyar peasants and workers. Even with the very small electorate, elections were falsified and electors were intimidated. Sometimes villages which were polling centres would be simply surrounded by gendarmes, who would not admit the assembled electors until late at night, when they were told the poll was closed and the officials had gone home.

From 1903 to 1906 Hungary was in a state of virtual rebellion against Vienna, owing to the demand by Hungarian politicians for a separate army, which the king refused.[16] The 1848-ers were swept to power, and they even permitted the holding of free elections in constituencies of non-Magyar population, in the hope of obtaining support from the non-Magyars against Vienna. In 1906 the number of representatives of non-Magyars in parliament was doubled. However, hopes were soon disappointed. Terrified by the king's threat of universal suffrage, which would not only have strengthened the non-Magyars but would have given the Magyar small tenants and agricultural labourers a vote, the 1848-er leaders gave up their demands about the army. Their government reverted to the policies of its predecessors towards the non-Magyars. The Education Act of 1907 was even more objectionable than that of 1879. The new government even gratuitously antagonised the Croats, with whom it had previously formed an alliance, by introducing the Magyar language on the Croatian railways. In 1910 the 1867-ers came back to power. Their leader Count István Tisza paid occasional lip service to the idea of universal suffrage, and went through the motions of negotiations with the Romanians and Slovaks; but his only real aim was to split their leadership by intrigues, and no constructive results were achieved.

Not all politically articulate Magyars accepted forcible Magyarisation: it was criticised by Hungarian radical democrats and socialists, who were, however, prevented by the electoral system from exercising any political influence. Eminent among the critics was the sociologist Oszkár Jászi. He pointed out that the policy of the two Tiszas was counter-productive. If only they had given the non-Magyars equal rights and had shown respect for their languages and cultures, he argued, they would in the course of time have become loyal Hungarians and would have been absorbed in Magyar culture. He pointed to the increase in numbers of the Hungarians since the eighteenth century. The cities which had grown up in the last hundred years had absorbed great numbers of non-Magyars into an increasingly attractive and sophisticated culture. This process had been not promoted but arrested by the tricks and coercion of the Tiszas. Jászi hoped that, if only the degenerate political class could be removed from power, land be distributed to the peasants, and the vote be given to all citizens, a new Hungary could arise in which one Magyar culture could coexist with many languages.

Jászi's vision was noble but unconvincing. His model was the United States. He argued that, as a new nation and a new culture had been created in America from immigrants from many different nations, so a new Hungarian culture could be made from the confluence of several half-developed cultures based on several different languages. But his analogy was misleading. In the United States the immigrant communities were small groups, uprooted from homelands which they had left thousands of miles behind, and positively seeking absorption in a new nation which, at the time when they arrived, had taken firm shape, though it was still capable of modification as they grew into it. In Hungary the non-Magyar nations lived in compact communities in their old homelands. Even in the cities, which were indeed islands of Magyar culture in a non-Magyar sea, there were growing up counter-cultures with their own cultural elites. Thus Kolozsvár, the centre of Magyar culture in Transylvania, was at the same time Cluj, the centre of the Romanian counter-culture; and Kassa the Magyar city was also Košice the Slovak city. Urbanisation of a peasant people in a country whose urban civilisation has been created by another people does not necessarily lead to the loss of national identity by the former: it may rather intensify this identity, as the late twentieth century cases of French Canadians and of negro communities in the North of the United States suggest. Jászi's analysis of the failures of Magyarisation was right, but the opportunity which he thought Hungary had missed probably never existed.

It is instructive to compare Magyarisation with Russification. The similarities are obvious, but there were also differences. First, the Magyarisers were in a basically more difficult situation than the Russifiers, because most of the non-Magyars lived in compact settlements next to the frontiers of independent states ruled by their kinsmen, and consequently the incentive to separatism was genuinely present. It may be argued that Serbs and Romanians living under Hungary before 1914 lived better and were ruled in a more civilised manner than the subjects of the two Balkan states, though this argument must be received with some scepticism. But even if they had been much better ruled, if men such as Oszkár Jászi had been in power, the attraction would still have been very strong. In the case of the Slovaks, the spectacle of the Czechs living in Moravia and Bohemia, closely akin to them and living under far more favourable conditions within the same empire, was also disruptively attractive; thus the desire of many Slovaks to come under the same rule as the Czechs constituted, from the Magyar point of view, a sort of 'separatism'. The Russifiers hardly faced this problem. The only non-Russian peoples who lived next to a sovereign state of their kinsmen were the Romanians in Bessarabia and the Azeri Turks in Azerbaidjan: in the second case it was uncertain whether their 'kinsmen' were the Turks with whom they shared a language or the Persians with whom they shared devotion to the Shii branch of Islam; and in any case it is doubtful whether either state exercised much attraction on them. As for the Poles and Ukrainians, they knew that their kinsmen under Austrian rule were better treated than they were, but this did not make them wish to be Austrian subjects. Thus the Russian rulers were in a basically much more favourable position than the Magyar. Separatism was not a serious danger for them, and if they had set themselves to treat the non-Russians in a humane manner, they would have had a much better chance of winning their loyalty than the Magyars could have had.

The point was that they did not wish this. The dogma of autocracy, and in later years the dogma of the superiority of Orthodoxy and of the Russian nation, had to be put into effect, regardless of consequences. The Magyar statesmen were men of a liberal past, who showed their liberalism by their attitude to the Jews, but betrayed it by their policies to the non-Magyars.

Criticism by liberal Russians of Russification was very similar to criticism by liberal Hungarians of Magyarisation. The outstanding Russian liberal thinker, P. B. Struve, attacked Stolypin's treatment of the non-Russians from essentially the same point of view as Oszkár Jászi. Like him, he had as his model the United States. He thought of a new Russian 'nation in the making', into which the cultures of the non-Russian peoples could be absorbed in the course of time, modifying and enriching it in the process. Like Jászi, Struve was ignored by the rulers. From a broader historical point of view, looking back from the 1970s, Struve's views are open to precisely the same objections as Jászi's. In Russia, as in Hungary but unlike the United States, the subject nations lived in compact communities in their traditional homelands. In Russia, as in Hungary, the cities were centres not only of officially sponsored culture but of the counter-culture of the subject nations, whose new national elites were formed in them.

Defeat in war in 1918 brought the disintegration of Hungary. For a time it seemed possible that the Russian empire would disintegrate too, but it revived in a new form, with comparatively small losses of territory. A vast empire, remote from other centres of power, was less vulnerable than a rather small country situated in the centre of Europe.

The Hungarian state lost more than half its territory, and nearly one-third of the Hungarian nation was placed under foreign rule (in Romania, Czechoslovakia and Yugoslavia). Before and during the Second World War some of these lands were restored to Hungary by Hitler in his years of victory; but these were lost again in 1945.

The policy of Official Nationalism was not however abandoned in Central Europe after the defeat of Hungary. The Hungarian minorities in the three successor states experienced a treatment not unlike that which the rulers of Hungary had meted out to the non-Magyars before 1918. The government of Poland also adopted a policy of Official Nationalism towards its non-Polish subjects between the world wars. The communist governments which came to power in these countries after 1945 had quite different principles, but their practices were not so different as might have been expected.[17]

## The Slovaks

In the late ninth century there existed, on both sides of the middle Danube and in the lands lying to the north-west of it, a state of considerable power, the Moravian empire. There are but few references to it in historical documents, but good archaeological evidence has become available in recent years. It was destroyed by the Hungarian invasions at the end of the century, and its people became Hungarian subjects. Many were no doubt absorbed in the Hungarian population and adopted its language. However, those who lived in the valleys and foothills of the Carpathians, which became the northernmost region of the Hungarian state, retained their Slav speech. These were the ancestors of the modern Slovaks.

The Slovaks were united with the Hungarians for more than a thousand years. When Hungary was divided by the Turkish conquest, the Slovaks remained in that part which was effectively ruled by the Habsburgs. A small number of Slovaks had the status of noblemen, and so formed part of the Hungarian nation. The great majority were peasants. Most Slovaks were Catholics, but about a fifth of them were Lutheran Protestants. The Slovak Lutherans had acquired their faith from contact with the German minorities which lived in some of the towns in their midst; but there had also been some earlier contacts with the Bohemian Hussites.

During almost a thousand years there was nothing which could be called a Slovak nation, and it is arguable that there had never been a Slovak state (even though the Moravian empire was later claimed as such). The creation of a Slovak nation in the nineteenth century is essentially the emergence of a language group into national consciousness. There is no more striking example than the Slovak case of the role of language in nation-forming; and for this reason, though the Slovaks were and are still a very small people, their case deserves some detailed attention.

It was the reforms of Joseph II which gave new opportunities of education to at least a significant number of Slovaks. The Protestants made quicker use of these opportunities than the Catholics. As in other countries, they were more aware of the value of schools. It is also worth noting that a married priesthood is a factor favourable to the growth of an educated class, since the taste for learning can be transmitted directly from parents to children. However, Catholic priests also played their part in developing schools. The single most eminent figure of the Slovak Enlightenment was Father Anton Bernolák, author of a grammar of Slovak, published in 1787, and of a dictionary in six volumes which did not appear until after his death. In 1789 Bernolák and some friends at the General Seminary in Bratislava founded a Slovak Scientific Society (*Slovenske učene tovarišstvo*), which later had its centre in the small town of Trnava, formerly the seat of the Hungarian University. The society published works in Slovak, including improving works on agriculture and economics which were the speciality of Juraj Fándly. About three-quarters of the membership of nearly 450 were Catholic priests. During the same time the Protestants had developed their own intellectual group in Bratislava. The leading figure was Juraj Palkovič, who established in 1803 a teaching post in 'Czechoslovak literature' at the Lutheran *lycée* in Bratislava. There was also a learned society in the small mining town of Baňska Bystrica from 1810.

The Catholic and Protestant groups disagreed on the basic problem of language, and behind this disagreement lay conflicting views on the national identity of the Slovaks. Bernolák had based his grammar and dictionary on the dialect spoken in the western part of the Slovak lands, in the valley of the Vah. This dialect he and his friends hoped to make into the common literary language of all Slovaks. The Protestants preferred the language of the Czech Bible, to be adapted and enriched by words in common use in Slovakia. The Protestants were well aware of the Bohemian Hussite tradition, which they accepted as their own. They believed that there was essentially a single language of Czechs and Slovaks, and that this needed only to be efficiently worked out and then adopted by both alike. They believed that Czechs and Slovaks could and should be made into a single nation. Hence their use of the word 'Czechoslovak' for both literature and nationality. They also tended to think of the Czechoslovaks as forming a single 'tribe' (*kmeň*) within a wider Slav nation. The Catholics could have no sympathy for a Hussite tradition, but they too had some sense of kinship with the Czechs and with the other peoples of Slav speech. Their main concern was, however, with their own small Slovak nation.

During the 1830s the growing pressure for official use of Hungarian, and the growing mutual mistrust between Hungarians and educated Slovaks,

made Catholic and Protestant Slovaks conscious of the need to work together. In 1834 was founded an association of lovers of Slovak speech and
literature, of which the panslav ideologist Jan Kollar[18] was president
and Martin Hamuljak—a follower of Bernolák—was secretary. Its journal
accepted contributions in both variants of Slovak. Kollar in these years
made great efforts to secure a compromise, on the basis of Biblical Czech
but with a large addition of popular words. However, he could not
persuade the Bernolák party, and he was also repudiated by Jungmann,
Palacký and the Czech intellectual leaders. In 1842 a petition to the
emperor, protesting against an attempt by the Hungarian government to
force the Lutherans into fusion with the Calvinists in order to ensure
domination of Hungarians over all Protestant affairs, was signed only by
Lutherans, and was ignored in Vienna.

The man who settled the language dispute was Ludovit Štúr. He was a
Protestant, was educated in Germany at the University of Halle, and
returned to Bratislava to act as assistant to Palkovič at the *lycée*. He
believed that the Bernolák party were right in seeking to base the literary
language on the popular speech of Slovakia rather than on Biblical Czech,
but that the dialect of the western region which they had chosen was the
wrong one. He preferred the dialect of the central region (Turec country).
In 1844 he was dismissed from his post in Bratislava *lycée* by the Hungarian
authorities, but in the following year he obtained permission from
Vienna—in opposition to the wish of the Hungarians—to publish a
periodical, *Slovenskje Národňje Novini*. This was written in his preferred
dialect, and he also published a book in justification of the dialect, and in
1846 a new Slovak grammar. He was one of the founders in 1844 of the
Tatrín Society, to which both Catholics and Protestants belonged. In 1847
a meeting of this society at Čachtice brought about an agreement to adopt
Štúr's proposed form of the language, and to prepare a mass petition to the
government with the demands of the Slovaks.

These plans were overtaken by the revolution in Hungary in 1848. The
principles proclaimed by the Hungarian revolutionaries were attractive to
politically conscious Slovaks, but sympathy for the Hungarian cause
waned rapidly when it became clear that the Hungarians would not
consider Slovak wishes. These were most fully formulated in the demands,
prepared by Štúr and his friends, which were addressed to the emperor and
to the Hungarian government in May 1848. They asked for a parliament of
the nations of Hungary, in which all these nations and their languages
would have equal status; additional separate assemblies for each nation;
and the use in public affairs of the mother tongue of the population, not of
Hungarian exclusively. They also proposed that each nation should have
its national system of education, from the elementary up to the university
level. For Slovaks, the language of instruction must be Slovak, and

arrangements must be made for Slovak to be taught to Hungarian children and Hungarian to Slovak children. The demands also included the liberation of the various categories of peasants from their remaining labour duties to the landowners. They were rejected, and the leaders were forced to escape from Hungary and to form a Slovak National Council on Austrian territory. Inevitably, since the main enemy in the eyes of the Slovak democrats was henceforth the Hungarian government, they drifted into support of the Austrian counter-revolution. When Jelačić advanced on Hungary in the autumn, Slovak armed bands attacked the Hungarians; and when Jelačić retreated, the returning Hungarians imprisoned, and in some cases hanged, Slovaks whom they considered guilty of rebellion. When the Habsburgs had reconquered Hungary, the Slovaks hopefully asked the new emperor Franz Josef, in a petition of 19 March 1849, for equal status for the Slovaks among the nations of the Monarchy, and for the removal of the Slovak lands from Hungarian sovereignty; but the petition was disregarded. Their only reward for their loyalty to the dynasty was a small increase in the number of Slovaks employed in official positions, and a few vague words of encouragement to both Kollar and Štúr.

The revival of parliamentary life in the Monarchy in the early 1860s revived Slovak hopes. A new memorandum was drawn up in June 1861, asking for the formation of an autonomous Slovak district (*okolie*) in Upper Hungary. This was refused, but some concessions were granted. A senior secondary school (gymnasium) with Slovak language of instruction was set up in 1862 and a second in 1867, and a lower-grade secondary school two years later. In 1863 was founded the *Matice Slovenska*, in Turčiansky Sväty Martin. It became the centre of Slovak cultural life—publishing literature, holding exhibitions and meetings, advising farmers on economic affairs and generally spreading national consciousness into lower levels of Slovak society.

The establishment of a Hungarian government in Budapest, under the Compromise of 1867, brought renewed pressures against the non-Hungarians. The Hungarian nationalists asserted that Slovak cultural institutions were being used to spread Panslavism. In 1874 both the Slovak gymnasiums were closed, and in 1875 *Matice Slovenska* was suppressed.

In the next decades various political groups arose among the Slovaks, but they made no impression on the official political life of Hungary. In the First World War Slovak political activity came to an end. On the Russian front, Slovak as well as Czech soldiers deserted to the Russians in considerable numbers. Masaryk in his exile in the West spoke on behalf of Slovaks as well as of Czechs, and argued that the Slovaks must be included in the future Independent Bohemia. In May 1918 he met the leaders of Slovak immigrants to the United States at Pittsburgh. He signed an agreement with them, promising that within the future Czechoslovak state the Slovaks should have their own administrative and judicial system, that Slovak should be the official language in Slovakia, and that there should be a Slovak Diet.

As the Habsburg Monarchy began to disintegrate in the autumn of 1918, some Slovaks set up a National Council, which on 30 October met in Turčiansky Sväty Martin, and proclaimed the union of Slovakia with the Czechs. The statement included the words: 'The Slovak nation is part of the Czech-Slovak nation, united in language and in the history of its culture'. This was accepted by most politically prominent Slovaks, but not by the leader of the People's Party, the nationalist Catholic priest Andrew Hlinka, who went into opposition from the earliest days of the new Czechoslovak republic.

During the next twenty years the Slovaks were divided into three main groups. On the left were the socialists and communists, closely linked to their Czech comrades. In the centre, the former followers of Masaryk supported the Agrarians, a party of both Czechs and Slovaks. On the whole these accepted the idea of a single Czechoslovak nation. On the right, the followers of Hlinka insisted on the separate nationhood of the Slovaks and demanded far-reaching autonomy. The relative strength of the three groups varied, but for most of the history of the republic Hlinka's followers had something like half the Slovak electorate behind them.

At the time of the formation of the republic, the national consciousness of the Slovaks had not yet been completed. There was no doubt that they were nationally distinct from the Hungarians, but the nature of their relationship to the Czechs was in doubt. Even those Slovaks who were eager to call themselves Czechoslovaks expected that their people's different traditions and outlook would be respected. But many of the Czechs who now poured into Slovakia, as officials and businessmen and members of skilled professions (in all of which fields there were far too few Slovaks available to provide for the country's needs), behaved inconsiderately or even contemptuously, treating the Slovaks as country bumpkins who had to be civilised, and despising their religious beliefs as primitive superstition. These brash and energetic Czech democrats, made dizzy by the sudden victory of their nation, clearly identified Czechoslovak with Czech, and were in no doubt that it was their task quickly to transform the backward Slovaks into Czechs. All this embittered the Slovaks, and strengthened Hlinka's movement. Things got worse in the 1930s, with the high tariffs which cut Slovakia off from its natural market in the Hungarian plain, and with the steep fall in farm prices and the massive industrial unemployment, made still more painful by the fact that the birth-rate was much higher among Slovaks than among Czechs. The rise of National Socialism in Germany also had its effects. The Germans were the enemies of the Czechs, therefore the extreme wing of the Slovak autonomists regarded them as good friends of the Slovaks. Anti-semitism was also, for historical reasons, popular among Slovaks. The result was that Hlinka's party was strongly penetrated by Nazi influences, still more after the death of Hlinka in 1938. When Czechoslovakia was forced to capitulate to the Third Reich at Munich, Slovakia obtained autonomy under control of the People's Party, and in March 1939 when Hitler annexed the Czech lands, Slovakia was made an independent state under Hitler's protection.

Within Hitler's Fortress Europe from 1940 to 1944 the Slovaks did rather well. The effects of the war were less than elsewhere, and few Slovaks were expected to serve in the army. Slovak politicians emitted the requisite fascist rhetoric, but in practice they treated their opponents mildly: personal and family connections, and a kind of parish-pump solidarity, mitigated the impact of Hitlerism. The terrible exception to this statement were the Jews, who were handed over to Hitler's mass exterminators.

In the summer of 1944 the Soviet army approached Slovak territory. At this point a national rising took place, in which communists and Slovak nationalists joined. It was crushed by the Germans, and followed by merciless terror. Those Slovaks who were left in power had to act as servile agents of Germany, and as the Soviet army advanced Slovak villages and towns were laid waste.

When the new Czechoslovak republic was set up in 1945, all the political leaders formally recognised that Czechs and Slovaks were two nations, that the old concept of Czechoslovakism had to be abandoned. It was in fact abundantly clear that the Slovaks had achieved full nationhood, that the Slovak nation was now coextensive with the Slovak-speaking people; but formal recognition and practical implementation were not the same. Czech and Slovak politicians continued to distrust each other, and this was exploited by the Communist Party and its Soviet Russian patrons to impose their will on both alike. Under the communist regime introduced in 1948, the autonomous institutions granted to Slovakia after the war were emptied of all content, and prominent Slovak communist politicians were persecuted as 'bourgeois nationalists'. Suppressed Slovak national feeling made itself felt in the 1960s, and indeed provided the first impulse towards the pressure for liberty which reached its climax in 1968. During the short period of freedom in that year, it looked as if Czechs and Slovaks were at last beginning to find a balanced and durable relationship, based on the recognition both of their distinct nationality and of a special solidarity between them. Disappointment followed: the Soviet Russian yoke was clamped down on both Czechs and Slovaks, and the federal constitution introduced in 1968 was unlikely to give the Slovaks significantly more than the earlier arrangement of 1945, since it too was rapidly emptied of real content by foreign domination.

## The Romanians

The most striking thing about the Romanians is that, living in the east of Europe, between the Carpathians and the Black Sea, they have a predominantly Latin language. This language has been in modern times the main identifying mark of the Romanian nation and the basis of its national movement.

Transylvania and most of Wallachia were conquered by the Roman Emperor Trajan in 101 AD and were evacuated by the Romans under Emperor Aurelian (275-80 AD). During this period the people who inhabited the region—those indigenous Dacians who survived the war of conquest and the immigrants from other parts of the Roman empire—adopted Latin as their language. After the Roman withdrawal these lands suffered successive waves of invasion, and very little is known of the history of their population. It is not until the fourteenth century that reasonably solid documentary evidence shows the presence of people speaking what was then known as the Wallachian language. This language had acquired a very large number of Slav words, but its Latin structure and mainly Latin vocabulary remained. From this time the history of this people can be traced adequately.

Modern Romanian historians believe that during the 'missing' centuries the Latin-speaking descendants of the Dacians and of Trajan's legions remained in their homeland and preserved their language, with the inevitable modification of vocabulary caused by the invasions. Transylvania, Wallachia and Moldavia (the last of which the Romans never systematically subdued, but which came under Roman influence and later was filled by immigrants from the south and north-west) form, in their view, the three historic homelands of the Romanians, in which they have been continuously present.

Hungarian historians claim, on the contrary, that the Latin-speaking population left with Aurelian or was destroyed by the invasions, and that Transylvania was inhabited for centuries by Slavs, who in their turn were partly destroyed and partly absorbed by the Hungarians who conquered the country at the end of the ninth century; while the Latin-speaking people south of the Carpathians were similarly displaced or absorbed by the Bulgarians. The surviving Latin-speakers lived for the next centuries in the Balkan peninsula, played a leading part in the second Bulgarian empire in the thirteenth century, and penetrated north of the Danube and up into Transylvania in the period which followed the devastations of the Mongol invasion.

These rival theories are of course inspired by nationalist motives, and neither can be proved by adequate evidence. It seems more probable that considerable numbers of Latin-speaking people remained throughout the centuries in these lands than that they all disappeared and a completely new lot took their place a thousand years later. This does not of course exclude the probability that there was large-scale immigration also at the later date. In any case, certainty will never be attained. What concerns us in this work is that already before 1400 people speaking this language formed a majority of the population in Moldavia, Wallachia and Transylvania, and that from them emerged the Romanian nation.

The people of Moldavia and Wallachia were Orthodox Christians, and their rulers resisted the Ottoman invasions during the fifteenth century, after which they became vassals of the sultans, enjoying substantial sovereignty within their lands. In Transylvania their kinsmen too were Orthodox, but were subjects of Hungary until 1526 and then of a Hungarian prince, who was also a vassal of the sultan, but was in practice less effectively controlled by the Turks than the other two princes. For one year (1600-01) Michael the Brave became ruler of Wallachia, Moldavia and Transylvania at once. This was a result of international diplomacy and war, not of any national programme to unite the Orthodox people of Latin speech in one kingdom. However, there were some signs of something that could be called, in later terminology, Romanian patriotism; and the exploits of Michael the Brave inevitably furnished arguments to Romanian historians two centuries later. At the end of the seventeenth century the Ottoman government, alarmed by the tendency of the princes of Moldavia and Wallachia to combine with their enemies, and particularly with Russia, replaced them by right Greeks from Constantinople (Phanariots).[19] These new rulers, obliged to buy the princely appointment with huge sums, compensated themselves by merciless extortion of taxes from their subjects: Phanariot rule therefore worsened the lot of the peasants. Some of the Phanariot rulers however were men of great culture, who surrounded themselves with learned men and developed education. The culture which grew around the two courts was mainly Greek, and the princes also encouraged Western, especially French, science and ideas. From this at least the upper class Romanians benefited, and some progress was also made in education in the Romanian language. In Transylvania, the Uniate Church introduced in 1691 by Emperor Leopold I made it possible for a minority of Romanians to obtain a good education and to take part in public life.[20] Thus the eighteenth century was the time when modern Romanian national consciousness began to grow, on both sides of the Carpathians.

In Transylvania the Uniate bishop Inocentiu Micu defended the Romanian cause in the Diet. In a speech in 1737 he referred to the 'the Wallachian nation' but was met with shouts of: 'The Wallachians are only a *plebs*'. He appealed without success to Vienna and to the pope in his struggle for political rights for his people. He was forced to resign his see in 1751 and ended his days in Rome. In the second half of the century there appeared a number of scholarly studies in the Romanian language, the work of the so-called Transylvanian School, designed to show that the Romanians were not only the original inhabitants of Transylvania, but true Romans, descended from Trajan's legions. These works were the earliest clear statement of what became the Romanian national historical mythology, the foundation of modern Romanian nationalism. Transylvanian Romanian scholars also worked on the adoption of the Latin alphabet for the Romanian language in place of the Cyrillic, which had long been in use in the Orthodox Church. The development of schools under Joseph II also benefited the Romanians, especially those living in the region of Arad and Temesvár, outside Transylvania proper. The number of Romanians under Habsburg rule was increased in 1775, when Austria annexed the north-western corner of Moldavia (known as Bukovina).

The discontent of the Romanian population of Transylvania was not confined to the aspirations for political equality of the educated minority. In 1784 took place a large-scale revolt against the landowners, led by a peasant, Horia, with undertones of national resentment of Romanians against Hungarians. In 1791 a petition to the emperor set forth the grievances of the Transylvanian Romanians, and was signed by the two Romanian bishops, Orthodox and Uniate. Entitled *Supplex Libellus Valachorum*, it insisted that the Romanians were the autochthonous people, that they formed the majority of the population, that they had been unjustly robbed of their rights and that they should be recognised as a fourth *natio* in addition to Hungarians, Székély and Saxons. It called for a national assembly to prepare measures for the achievement of full equality for the Romanians. Emperor Leopold II merely passed the petition to the Transylvanian Diet, whose Hungarian and Saxon members rejected it.

During the eighteenth century Moldavia and Wallachia became theatres of war between Russian and Turkish armies. As a result of the war of 1806-12 Russia annexed the eastern half of Moldavia, between the rivers Prut and Dniester, which became known as Bessarabia. It seemed inevitable that all Moldavia and Wallachia would be annexed to the Russian empire.

In the next years the Greek nationalist secret society *Philike Etairia*[21] energetically recruited support in Moldavia and Wallachia, including some Romanians. One of these was Tudor Vladimirescu, a small landowner from western Wallachia (Oltenia) who had served as an officer in the Russian army. He raised a rebellion in Oltenia in February 1821, shortly before the Greek forces of Ypsilanti entered Moldavia. Vladimirescu's movement was as much social as national: he was followed by peasants who wished to be freed from the oppression of the landlord and the tax-collector. Vladimirescu believed that the Russian army would shortly march, and that the defeat of the Turks by Russia would bring liberty. When it became clear that there was to be no Russian support, Vladimirescu was unwilling to fight the battles of Greeks, for whom neither he nor his followers had sympathy, against the overwhelming Ottoman power. He tried to negotiate his own terms with the Turks, but was captured by the Greeks and killed.

Vladimirescu's rising was not however without result. It became clear to the Turks that the Romanians disliked the Greeks, and that only the latter were dangerous to Ottoman interests. In the next years Greek influences were eliminated, Greek schools abolished, Greek traders discouraged and Greek officials dismissed. Romanians took their place. In the next years new schools were founded, teaching methods were improved, and a standardised literary Romanian language was formed. The Romanian language reformers brought thousands of neologisms of Latin, French or Italian derivation into use, and succeeded in replacing the Cyrillic by the Latin alphabet. In the growing published literature, where—as was frequently the case—Latin and Slav synonyms existed, it was the Latin form which was preferred. Similar trends were at work in Transylvania, where Romanian cultural life was centred round the leaders of the two churches, who cooperated with each other to support and develop the existing Romanian schools and to found periodicals using the Romanian language. A younger generation of professional people—lawyers, teachers, small businessmen—began to appear.

The revolutions of 1848 had important effects both in Transylvania and in the two Danubian principalities (as Moldavia and Wallachia were called in European diplomatic language).

At a meeting at Blaj, the centre of the Uniate Church in Transylvania, the view was expressed that Transylvania should only be united with Hungary if the Romanians were given fully equal status within the common kingdom. On 15 May 40,000 Romanian peasants assembled on a meadow outside Blaj, which became known as the 'field of liberty', in the presence of the bishops of both churches. The meeting asked for an election to the Transylvanian Diet, in which Romanians should be represented in proportion to their share of the population, and that the Diet should then decide whether Transylvania should be united with Hungary. The meeting also asked for a system of Romanian schools in Transylvania, to culminate in a Romanian university. The Diet ignored the demands, asserted that political and social liberties had already been promised by the April Laws of the Hungarian parliament, and advised the Romanians to go to Budapest to discuss their claims with the Hungarian government. The Orthodox bishop, Andrei Şaguna, took a delegation to Budapest from July to September to plead the Romanian case, but without result. In the Hungarian parliament, Baron Nicholas Wesselényi, the outstanding liberal nationalist of the preceding decades, spoke in favour of concessions to the Romanians, but he was overruled by Kossuth.

In Moldavia and Wallachia during the 1830s and 1840s there emerged groups of young men of upper class families, educated in Western Europe or familiar with Western ideas, who opposed the political regime (established, by Russo-Turkish agreement, in 1832) which left power in the hands of the richer landowners and denied freedom of speech and political organisation. Several of them went into exile in Paris, where they were in touch with French radicals and with the followers of Mazzini and the Polish revolutionaries. In May 1848 they returned to Bucarest, and at the end of June they and their friends seized power in Wallachia. The revolutionary government remained in power for about three months and tried to negotiate with the Turks. However, Russian pressure forced the Ottoman government to refuse a compromise, and at the end of September Turkish troops occupied Bucarest.

The Wallachian revolutionaries, whose most brilliant leader was Nicolae Bălcescu, and their Polish friends, regarded the Russian tsar as their main enemy, and therefore passionately desired cooperation with Hungary. Unfortunately this was now quite impossible. As the complete breach between Vienna and Budapest approached in the autumn, the Transylvanian Romanians took the side of Vienna. A Romanian National Committee was set up, and in large parts of Transylvania Romanian officials took over the administration. In the autumn of 1848 Romanian armed forces, led by Avram Iancu, began to fight the Hungarians, declaring their loyalty to the dynasty. In February 1849 Bishop Şaguna, together with Romanian leaders from Transylvania, from the province (Banat) of Temesvár and from Bukovina, presented a petition to the new Emperor Franz Josef in Olomouc. They asked for a single Romanian duchy, under the Habsburg crown, with representation in the imperial parliament and the central government, with its own annually elected representative assembly, and with Romanian as the language of administration in its territory. It had no success. The constitution of 4 March 1849 did no more than abstractly proclaim the principle of equality of all the nationalities and languages. Meanwhile in Transylvania Iancu's forces held out against the Hungarians. In May Bălcescu met Kossuth, and in July he saw Iancu, in a vain hope of reconciling Hungarians and Romanians. At this stage all the Hungarians could offer was empty verbal assurances: the Russian army marched, and Hungary was soon crushed.

By a Russo-Ottoman Convention of May 1849, both Russian and Turkish troops were stationed in the two principalities. In 1851 the Russians withdrew, but in 1853 they were back again, and their return was the immediate cause of a Russo-Turkish war which escalated into the

Crimean War. In June 1854 Austrian pressure caused the Russians to retreat from the principalities, and Austrian troops took their place, with Ottoman consent. For a time it looked as if the Romanian lands, having escaped Russian domination, would fall under Austrian. To some Romanians this was not altogether an unwelcome prospect, since it would mean that all the lands of Romanian population would be united under one ruler. However, the mutual mistrust and concern for balance of power of the European great powers prevented this. By the Treaty of Paris of 1856 the Russians ceded to the Ottoman empire the southern half of eastern Moldavia (Bessarabia) and the powers set to work to prepare a suitable political system for the principalities.

In February 1859 the two principalities were united under one ruler, Alexander Cuza, and in February 1866 he was replaced by a prince of the German family of Hehenzollern-Siegmaringen. Thus the modern Romanian state came into existence. It was undoubtedly the result of the efforts of the minority of politically conscious Romanians, but it was also largely due to a favourable international situation. At both moments of crisis, in 1859 and in 1866, the two powers most capable of frustrating Romanian aims were otherwise preoccupied: Austria in 1859 faced war with France in Italy, and in 1866 with Prussia, while Russia sought good relations with France or Prussia. The European government which most consistently supported the Romanian cause was the French; the British government, which was at first opposed, was persuaded by Napoleon III to change its policy. The last formal stage towards Romanian sovereignty was achieved in 1877, when Romanian troops took part in the Russo-Turkish war on the Russian side. Romania had to pay a price, by ceding southern Bessarabia once more to Russia, but the prince was rewarded in 1881 by being recognised by the powers as King Charles of Romania.

In Transylvania the Romanians were not rewarded for their loyalty to the Habsburgs: the mere fact that the Hungarians were repressed did not improve the Romanians' lot. When Franz Josef made the Compromise with the Hungarians in 1867, he had to approve the union of Hungary with Transylvania. In the following decades the Romanians were subjected to Magyarisation. The Romanian National Party, founded in 1881, demanded the restoration of Transylvanian autonomy, universal suffrage and the use of Romanian language and Romanian personnel in the administration. In June 1892, just over a hundred years since the *Supplex Libellus Valachorum*, a Memorandum was submitted to Emperor Franz Josef, listing Romanian grievances against Hungarian policy and appealing for reform. Franz Josef simply passed it on to the Hungarian prime minister, who returned it unopened to its authors. In May 1894 the leaders of the Romanian National Party were put on trial for 'incitement against the Hungarian nation', the evidence being the Memorandum itself. Fifteen persons received prison sentences, and the party was officially dissolved. This repression did not prevent Romanians from contesting seats at elections despite the unfavourable electoral law. In the 1906 elections they, like the Slovaks, won more seats than usual in the Hungarian parliament, but in the next years the old Hungarian methods of corruption and intimidation reduced their numbers again.

On the eve of the First World War the Romanians of Transylvania were in a difficult situation. Their traditional loyalty to the Habsburgs had brought them no protection against Hungarian misrule. Some of their ablest leaders hoped that the heir to the throne, Archduke Franz Ferdinand, would soon succeed his aged uncle and would help them. They were encouraged in this belief by many politicians in the kingdom of Romania, who above all feared Russian expansion and therefore did not wish the Habsburg Monarchy to break up. Others preferred cooperation with the Hungarian Left, above all with the socialists. They hoped that, if once universal suffrage were carried in Hungary (as it had been in Austria in 1907), a new democratic system would emerge which would give Romanians their rights within the Monarchy. Others had lost all hope of fair treatment from either Vienna or Budapest, and aimed only at the disruption of the Monarchy and the union of Transylvania with the kingdom of Romania. This was also the view of the more radical political groups in the kingdom. The outstanding spokesmen for this 'Daco-Romanist' separatism were the poet Octavian Goga in Transylvania and the historian Nicolae Iorga in the kingdom. Inevitably, the Romanian national movement in Transylvania was rent by these competing factions, and its official leaders had difficulty in keeping all options open and retaining everyone within the fold.

In the first years of the war, Romanian soldiers in the Austro-Hungarian army fought loyally on the Russian and even on the Italian front. The Romanian government dragged on negotiations with the Western Allies, determined to get the maximum territory at minimum risk. When Romania came into the war in August 1916 it met with military disaster, though its armies rallied in defence of Moldavia in 1917. The collapse of Russian military resistance to the central powers caused Romania to make separate peace with Germany in 1918, but also made it possible for Romanian troops to occupy Bessarabia, whose population was in majority Romanian.

The collapse of the Habsburg Monarchy in the autumn brought the secession of Hungary. The new Hungarian government's expert on relations with the non-Hungarians, the sociologist Oszkár Jászi, was unable to persuade the Romanians to remain within Hungary on any terms. In Transylvania the Romanians took over the administration of their homelands. In conscious imitation of the Blaj meeting of 1848, the leaders summoned the peasants to Alba Iulia. Here an assembly of many thousands acclaimed a resolution in favour of the union of all Romanians in one state. After protracted arguments at the peace conference, most of the Romanian claims were obtained: not only Transylvania and Bukovina, but most of the Banat of Temesvár and a broad strip of plainland between the Transylvanian mountains and the river Tisza. Now the Romanians were the masters, and a million and a half Hungarians were subject to their rule.

The political regime in Romania between the wars was unpleasant for most Romanian citizens. Though progress was made, especially in education and in industrial development, and though some leading politicians were convinced democrats and some of these held power for some years, yet on the whole the administration remained both corrupt and brutal. The economic depression of the 1930s and the rapid increase of population combined to increase the poverty of the peasants. These things affected both Romanian and Hungarian citizens of Romania, but inevitably the Hungarians tended to regard themselves as victims not only of social injustice and political repression, but of specifically anti-Hungarian policies pursued by Romanian governments. It is probably true that Hungarians suffered more than Romanians. For example, when the sweeping land reform of the 1920s took land from the big landowners in Transylvania (who were Hungarians), the land was redistributed among Romanian peasants, and very little was given to the landless or very poor Hungarian peasants who lived in the region. When new employment was created by new industries, jobs tended to be given to Romanians rather than to Hungarians. In any case the government of Hungary did its best to exploit discontent, and conducted an energetic campaign, by propaganda and by diplomacy, for revision of the frontiers.

Hungary was not Romania's only enemy. The government of Soviet Russia was also determined to recover eastern Moldavia (or Bessarabia), in which more than half the population consisted of Romanians and the other half was a mixture of Ukrainians, Russians, Bulgarians, Turks and smaller groups. The collapse of France in June 1940 enabled the Soviet government, with the approval of Hitler, to seize Bessarabia. Stalin also surprised his German ally by taking the northern part of Bukovina, on the grounds that its population was Ukrainian. It was now the turn of the Hungarians to ask for their share. In August 1940 the German and Italian governments dictated a partition of Transylvania which gave nearly 1,000,000 Hungarians and nearly 1,500,000 Romanians to Hungary, while leaving rather less than 500,000 Hungarians and 2,000,000 Romanians to Romania. This of course satisfied neither side, but enabled Hitler to extract more soldiers and more resources for his war in Russia from each government in turn by threatening to modify the 1940 decisions to the disadvantage of one or the other.

In 1945 the old frontier with Hungary was restored, but the Soviet government kept Bessarabia and northern Bukovina. At first the new Romanian government made great efforts to satisfy its Hungarian subjects (within the framework of communist party dictatorship). In particular, instruction in Hungarian in schools was much increased, and a separate Hungarian university was set up, beside the Romanian university, in the Transylvanian capital of Cluj (in Hungarian, Kolozsvár). In the late 1950s, however, a more nationalist attitude appeared in official policy, the Hungarian university was suppressed, and the Hungarians complained of discrimination on national lines in the administration, education and the economy.

The unique feature of Transylvania is that it has been for centuries a country of two nations, each with its own history and culture. Neither Romanians nor Hungarians can rightly be called 'minorities': Transylvania is historically both a Romanian land and a Hungarian land. There has also been a 'minority'—the Saxons—who have also made a great contribution to the history of Transylvania. The happiest solution for Transylvania, in the age of nationalism, would have been that it should be an independent state with equal rights for all three nations, or that it should have been incorporated, together with all the Romanian lands, in a larger unit. One such unit might have been a federation of Hungary, Transylvania and trans-Carpathian Romania. Another combination, actually suggested by some Romanians in 1848, might have been the union of Moldavia and Wallachia with the Habsburg Monarchy. Yet no such scheme was ever acceptable to those who had the power of decision. The Austrian government had no wish to antagonise Russia for the sake of the Romanians. When the Hungarians had a political majority in the Diet, they forced through union with Hungary; and when in 1867 Hungarian politicians had Franz Josef at their mercy they obtained union from him. The Romanians then pleaded for Transylvanian autonomy, and were ignored. Later, when the Romanians were in a position to use their majority of the population, they imposed their solution. It was now the turn of the Hungarians to plead for autonomy, and they in turn were ignored.

There was a strange love-hate relationship between the two nations. Hungarian politicians in Budapest displayed a frivolous arrogance, based on a very thorough ignorance, towards the Romanians whom they saw as sub-human barbarians, natural serfs, stinking Wallachs whom Magyars were entitled to order about and to insult. Romanian politicians in Bucarest replied with an impenetrable resentment, and obstinate defensive hostility, based on equal ignorance, seeing in the Hungarians savage Asiatic oppressors whose pride it was the duty and the pleasure of Romanians to humiliate. Yet among Romanians and Hungarians in Transylvania who knew each other, who spoke each other's language and knew each other's literature, art and folklore, this attitude did not always prevail. There were those on both sides who felt more in common with fellow-Transylvanians of the other language than with men of their own speech from the centres of power beyond Transylvania.

In the 1970s Hungarians in Romania could use their language in public affairs, and books and periodicals were published in Hungarian in large numbers. The trouble was that this was not enough for them. The government in Bucarest was eager to treat them generously (within the limits set by the communist party dictatorship), provided that they regarded themselves as Hungarian-speaking Romanians. This they were not willing to do. They accepted the Romanian state as a fact, and recognised their duties as citizens, but they considered themselves as part of the Hungarian nation. The only long-term solution seemed to be to diminish the importance of the frontier by improving relations between the two states, so that ultimately a situation could arise similar to that which prevailed between Austria and Germany: one in which Hungarians from Romania could move freely to and from Hungary, and maintain any personal or professional relationship they might desire with any one in Hungary, while remaining citizens of the Romanian state. This state of affairs in 1970 seemed far away, as a result of international circumstances beyond the control of either government.

As we have seen, the Latin mythology (in which, as in all mythologies, truth and imagination were blended) played a dominant part in the Romanian national movement. In 1945 Romania came under Soviet Russian domination, and it looked as if the situation had returned to 1853: as if the process of absorption of Romania in the Russian empire, predictable in the first half of the nineteenth century and reversed by the Crimean War, was being resumed. Particularly striking was the attempt to attack Romanian Latinity: to sever cultural relations with France and Italy, to tinker with the Romanian language by stressing the Slav words in the vocabulary at the expense of the Latin, and to falsify Romanian history in order to show that not the Latin peoples but the Slav peoples (and especially the Russians) had been the best friends of the Romanians since the distant past. This policy was reinforced by the policy adopted by the Soviet government to the people of conquered Bessarabia. Massive deportations of indigenous Romanians to distant parts of Russia, massive immigration of Russians or Ukrainians, reimposition of the Cyrillic alphabet and a conscious attempt to manufacture a Moldavian language and a 'Moldavian nation' distinct from the Romanian appeared to have achieved some success. In Romania, however, Russifying policies produced resentment and passive resistance, and failed in their object. Romanian schoolchildren simply failed to learn Russian, while very large numbers learned French from their parents. When in 1962 the Romanian government decided, mainly for economic reasons, to defy Soviet wishes, there was a nation-wide outburst of resentment against the Russian culture which had been thrust down Romanian throats in the preceding years. The defence of the Romanian language and of Romanian Latinity, and the resumption of cultural cooperation with France and Italy and other Western countries, were officially encouraged. It was abundantly clear that there was to be no reversion to 1853, and that Romanians of all levels of society were intensely conscious of their national identity.

## The Ukrainians

The differences between the people of southern and central Russia, which, as has been shown, can to some extent at least be traced back to the twelfth century, increased in the years following the Union of Lublin (1569), by which the lower Dnieper region was incorporated in Poland. These years were marked by a rapid increase in the demand for grain on European markets. Polish landowners, who acquired new lands in the south-east, sought to increase output by importing labour, by tying peasants effectively to the soil and by extracting greater efforts from them. Not only did their material conditions get worse, but they were subject to pressure to abandon the Orthodox for the Uniate church.[22] Many thousands escaped social and religious persecution by migrating into the south-eastern steppes, where they became Cossacks or continued to farm land, in easier conditions, under the protection of the Cossacks.

The word Cossack (*Kazak*) is of Tatar origin. It was first used to denote armed forces of Tatars who served the Christian rulers of Muscovy and Lithuania in defence of the borderlands of the steppes.[23] In the sixteenth century the word is increasingly used to describe Christians from the borderlands, who tended more and more to operate on their own, cooperating with the official Muscovite or Lithuanian forces but not permanently controlled by them. As Cossack numbers grew, being increased especially by peasants escaping from serfdom in both the Russian states, they developed into a kind of military democracy, combining warfare with agriculture and electing their leaders. The most important centre was the Zaporozhian *Sich*, situated above the rapids of the Dnieper some two hundred miles south-east of Kiev. This grew into a substantial military power, capable of negotiating with or fighting against the Poles, Muscovites, Crimean Tatars and Turks. There were also other Cossack centres: in the Kharkov region (*Slobodskaya Ukraina*), on the Don, in the steppes north of the Caucasus and in Siberia. The first of these consisted mainly of persons of Little Russian speech, originating from Lithuania; the last two were composed mainly of Great Russians from Muscovy, and in fact were to a large extent controlled by the government in Moscow.

The Dnieper Cossacks reached the height of their power under the *hetman* (or elected leader) Bohdan Khmelnitsky, who held this office from 1648 to 1657. He defeated Polish armies, and for a time ruled a large independent state, strategically placed across the Dnieper and extending to Galicia and to the north-western corner of the Black Sea. For a time the Crimean Tatars were his allies, but when they abandoned him he was compelled, in 1654, to make an agreement with Tsar Alexei of Muscovy. This Treaty of Pereyaslavl was differently interpreted by the two sides. Khmelnitsky intended to make the tsar his overlord and protector but to maintain the system of self-government that had grown up in the Ukraine.[24] The tsar and his advisers considered that the Ukraine had been simply incorporated in his domains, and should be administered by his officials in the same way as his other domains, with only minor concessions to local traditions and sentiments. During the next fifty years Muscovite authority was not effectively enforced. The hetman who succeeded Khmelnitsky collaborated in turn with Muscovy, Poland or the Ottoman empire. As a result of a series of wars between Poland and Muscovy, the border between the Polish-Lithuanian commonwealth and the Russian empire became established along the Dnieper,[25] and the Ukraine was thus divided in two parts for more than a century.

The situation changed when Hetman Ivan Mazeppa sided with Charles XII of Sweden against Peter the Great. After his victory at Poltava (1709), Peter imposed a harsh regime on the Cossack lands east of the Dnieper, even insisting on the replacement of Little Russian by Great Russian as the language of administration. By the partitions of Poland the rest of the Ukraine was carved up: in 1772 Austria acquired eastern Galicia, and in 1793 Russia took Volhynia and Podolia. Thus the great majority of the people of the Ukraine were placed under Russian rule and a substantial minority under the Habsburgs.

In the eighteenth century the Russian type of administration and the Russian type of serfdom were imposed on the people of the Ukraine. They were resented, and there was much hostility to the *moskaly* (Muscovites) among the peasants and townsmen. The upper classes—the Cossack officers and landowners—were well treated, and most of them became more or less assimilated into the Russian nobility. Russian was the official language, and Ukrainian was at most tolerated as the 'Little Russian dialect' spoken by the country yokels. However, the language did not disappear. As in the case of small peoples in Central Europe, there appeared in the Ukraine persons of education who wished to use the language of the people as a vehicle for literature. The first important work was a satirical poem about life in the Ukraine entitled *The Aeneid*, by Ivan Kotlarevsky, which appeared in 1798. After the foundation of the University of Kharkov (1804), that city became a centre of Ukrainian literary activity, which included the publication in 1819 of the first Ukrainian grammar. The most productive period was between 1830 and 1840. In these years were published works by Taras Shevchenko, the greatest poet of the Ukrainian language. The formation of an accepted Ukrainian literary language owes more to him than to any other individual. The use of this language was the decisive stage in the formation of an Ukrainian national consciousness. It was this which transformed mere knowledge of differences, pride in local traditions and resentment of domination by outsiders, into a conviction that the Ukrainians were a nation. Those who had this conviction were not yet numerous, for they were confined to a small intellectual elite. However, they were too numerous, too talented and too strongly convinced to be destroyed. In the second half of the nineteenth century the people of the Ukraine suffered from the same economic hardships as the Russians, somewhat aggravated by the fact that it was in the Ukraine that the metallurgical industry made the most rapid progress from the 1890s onwards. Increasingly, the resulting popular discontents were canalised into nationalist channels, and the intellectual elite of Ukrainian nationalists began to win mass support.

It was a long and painful process. The first Ukrainian nationalist organisation, the Society of St Cyril and St Methodius, founded in Kiev in 1846 by the historian N. I. Kostomarov, wished to see a federation of Slav peoples, one unit in which would be the Ukraine. It was discovered by the police, and those arrested included Shevchenko. The great poet was sent to Orenburg in the Urals as a private soldier, and Tsar Nicholas personally ordered that he should be prevented from writing or drawing (he was a talented painter as well as a poet). He was allowed to return to St Petersburg only in 1858, and died three years later, a broken man. In the following decades there were periods of relative freedom, when literary and historical works in Ukrainian could be published, and of relative severity when they could not. In 1876 the south-western section of the Geographical Society, located in Kiev, which had been the main centre of Ukrainian cultural activity, was closed down, and a government decree forbade the use of the 'Little Russian dialect' for the publication of anything except historical documents, and the importation from abroad of publications in that 'dialect'. In the last decade of the century Ukrainians were among the main victims of the new policies of Russification. During these years, however, illegal political parties of a radical or a socialist type were being created in various parts of the Russian empire. In 1901 was founded the Revolutionary Ukrainian Party, which soon split up into a radical liberal, a social democratic and a more conservative nationalist group.

Meanwhile in Galicia, under Austrian rule, Ukrainian nationalism developed freely and successfully. Already in 1848 a Ukrainian nationalist movement appeared, and was tolerated by the Austrians as a counter-weight to the Poles. Under the much freer political system from the mid-1860s onwards, Ukrainian political parties were able to organise, to publish and to hold meetings. As a result of their action, virtually the whole population was affected. The Galician Ukrainians, still poor and little educated, undoubtedly formed a conscious nation. Only a small minority considered themselves Russians and hoped to be incorporated in the Russian empire. Similar trends were to be found among the Ukrainian population in Austrian Bukovina, south of Galicia.[26] In north-eastern Hungary (or Ruthenia) lived an exceptionally backward population whose national identity was uncertain: a few thought themselves Ukrainians, a few Russians, the rest accepted the Hungarians' designation of them as 'Ruthenes'.

Galicia provided an asylum for the leaders of Ukrainian nationalism persecuted within the Russian empire. Outstanding were the historians Michael Drahomanov and Michael Hrushevsky: the first was active as a socialist in the 1880s, the latter held a Chair at the University of Lwów (Lemberg) and was the leading figure in the Shevchenko Society which was the embryonic Academy of Sciences of the Galician Ukrainians. In 1905 Hrushevsky and others returned to Russia. In the first two Dumas, there were about forty Ukrainian nationalist members of various political shades. For a few years Ukrainian literary and social organisations and activities were permitted. The St Petersburg Academy of Sciences officially declared that Ukrainian was a distinct language, not (as had been the official view) a mere 'dialect'. From 1908 onwards however the authorities reverted to Russification and repression.

The Russian Revolution of March 1917 brought a great outburst of Ukrainian national feeling. In Kiev was set up a National Council (*Rada*) of well known Ukrainian political and cultural figures. It negotiated inconclusively with the successive provisional governments. After the Bolshevik Revolution of November it declared the independence of the Ukraine. Having very few military forces of their own, the Ukrainian leaders saw their country invaded by Bolshevik forces from the north and by the German army from the west. They came to terms with the Germans, who compelled the Bolsheviks, under the Treaty of Brest-Litovsk of March 1918, to recognise an independent Ukrainian state. When the *Rada* government failed to provide the occupying Germans with as much grain as they demanded for their armies, the German general deposed the government and installed General Pavel Skoropadski as hetman.

The defeat of Germany at the end of 1918 led to the fall of Skoropadski, which was followed by two years of three-cornered civil war in the Ukraine, between Bolsheviks, Russian monarchists (Whites) and Ukrainian nationalists. The latter included not only the political groups from the Russian

Ukraine (of whom the strongest were the Ukrainian Socialist Revolutionaries led by Simon Petlura) but also the Ukrainian nationalists from
Galicia, who in 1919 were driven out of Lwów by the Polish forces of Josef
Piłsudski, who claimed all Galicia for Poland. Petlura in 1920 made an
agreement with Piłsudski to form a joint Polish-Ukrainian federation, to
include all the Ukrainian lands. The Polish army, invading the Russian
Ukraine with this aim, had some initial successes, but was then driven back
into Poland by the Red Army of the Bolsheviks. The Polish-Soviet war
ended in 1921 with a partition of the Ukraine between Poland and the
Soviet Union.

It is impossible to show with certainty what were the feelings of the
Ukrainians themselves during these confusing and immensely tragic
events, which brought death to hundreds of thousands and misery to
millions. At different moments, the *Rada*, the Ukrainian Socialist Revolutionaries, the Bolsheviks and the Russian monarchists had substantial
support in the Ukraine, but it was perhaps the anarchist bands led by the
Ukrainian peasant Nestor Makhno which most genuinely reflected Ukrainian peasant feelings.[27] It was the Bolsheviks who won, because they had
the strongest military force.

Events had clearly shown that Ukrainian national feeling was a force to
be reckoned with. The victorious Bolsheviks recognised this by setting up a
Ukrainian Soviet Republic as a member of the Union of Soviet Socialist
Republics. Its rulers were persons who had not been chosen by the people
of the Ukraine, but had been imposed by the government of Moscow. The
political dictatorship and social policies of the communist party were
carried out in much the same way as in the rest of the Union. In the cultural
field, however, the Ukrainians gained some advantages. Ukrainian was
made the language of administration, nominally superior but in practice
about equal in status to Russian. Literature in Ukrainian, provided that it
avoided political issues, was genuinely encouraged.

Mykola Skrypnik, who was Soviet Ukrainian commissar for education
from 1927 to 1933, was a genuine communist and a genuine Ukrainian
patriot, and this combination was expressed in his policies. He was a victim
of the great economic crisis of agricultural collectivisation and forced
industrialisation which began in 1929. The Ukraine, Russia's richest grain
land, suffered still more than central or northern Russia. Millions died of
starvation, millions more were deported to labour in conditions which
rapidly shortened their lives. The consequent popular discontent inevitably
took nationalist form: the rulers who imposed these cruel policies were
hated not only as tyrants but as *moskaly*—Muscovite foreigners. Skrypnik
and his friends were accused by the Moscow authorities of 'bourgeois
nationalism' and disappeared from public life.

Four years later another disaster hit the Ukraine with special severity—

the Great Purge. Once this police action had escalated to the point at which people were being arrested in hundreds of thousands, nationalist hatred of Russians by Ukrainians, and Russian suspicion of Ukrainians as a hostile nation, potentially friendly to Russia's foreign enemies, reached fantastic proportions. The whole of the *Politburo* of the Ukrainian communist party, all the members of the Ukrainian republican government and four-fifths of the members of the central committee of the party in the Ukraine were removed from their posts, and nearly all of these perished either by execution or in labour camps. The purge reached down to the lower levels of the party and to the masses outside the party.

The fate of the Ukrainians who became citizens of Poland after 1921 was somewhat better. Nevertheless they were badly treated by the Polish authorities, and did not in fact enjoy the rights which were guaranteed to them under the Minorities Treaty prescribed by the League of Nations. In 1930 Piłsudski, who since 1926 had assumed dictatorial powers, sent punitive expeditions to 'pacify' the Ukrainian districts of the south-east.

It was not surprising that Hitler's destruction of Poland pleased Ukrainian nationalists. When in 1941 Hitler attacked Russia, his forces were welcomed by the Ukrainians both in eastern Galicia (which had been transferred from Poland to the Soviet Union in 1939 by favour of Hitler), and also further east. However, Hitler himself insisted on treating the Ukrainians and Russians alike as 'subhuman' slave peoples. Ukrainian resistance forces appeared, some under the leadership of the Soviet High Command, others in opposition to both German and Soviet forces. The latter continued the fight for at least two years after the Soviet Army had driven out the Germans: they enjoyed considerable support from the population in Galicia.

As a result of the Soviet victory in the Second World War all the Ukrainian lands were united in a single state. Not only eastern Galicia, but also northern Bukovina (Romanian between 1918 and 1940) and Ruthenia (Hungarian until 1918, included in Czechoslovakia from 1918 to 1939 and Hungarian again until 1945) were annexed by the Soviet Union. The northern and southern extremities of Bessarabia (or eastern Moldavia), which contained substantial Ukrainian populations, were also incorporated in the Ukrainian SSR. Unity in itself was a source of satisfaction to Ukrainians, but their pleasure was modified by the fact that they were subjected to a form of government determined not by them but by the government in Moscow, and that decisions in economic and cultural policy were taken from the point of view of the interests of the central regime rather than of the Ukraine. In the last years of Stalin's life political pressure and economic hardships were very severe. In the years of Khrushchev's ascendancy things improved. The new boss, who had served for twelve years as first secretary of the Ukrainian communist party, brought a number of his colleagues from those times to positions of power in the centre. The tercentenary of the Pereyaslavl Treaty in 1954 was celebrated with much pomp, and flattering speeches were made about the Ukrainians. However, the Soviet press continued from time to time to denounce 'bourgeois nationalism' in the Ukraine, and in the 1960s and 1970s leading Ukrainian writers were arrested for 'anti-Soviet' activities.

The extent of Ukrainian national feeling, and the extent of opposition to the Russians, or even of the desire for an independent Ukrainian state, remained difficult to judge. On the one hand there was evidence that many Ukrainians were being absorbed into Russian culture. Foreign travellers reported that in the cities of Kiev and Kharkov only Russian was spoken in the streets and shops. Against this was the evidence that the influx of peasants from the countryside was Ukrainianising the industrial labour force, and that Ukrainian was spoken in the home circle. There is little doubt that both these things were happening, that contradictory trends were operating side by side. Intellectual opposition was clearly strong, and was not eliminated by periodic public denunciations or arrests. Education in Ukrainian history and Ukrainian literature, which continued in the Soviet schools in the Ukraine, kept Ukrainian national consciousness alive, and spread it more deeply in the population as the general economic and cultural level improved. The most nationally militant intellectual elites had, of course, less opportunity to put themselves at the head of a popular movement, or to canalise mass social discontents into nationalist channels, than had those of the 1890s. But it remained clear that a Ukrainian nation existed, and that no way had yet been found to enable Russians and Ukrainians to live together in mutual trust and respect.

# 5  European Nations Overseas

### The expansion of Europe

The great voyages of exploration at the end of the fifteenth century, round
the coast of Africa and out into the Atlantic, were made possible by new
methods of shipbuilding and of navigation, pioneered by the Portuguese.
The Atlantic, no longer the Mediterranean, became the main route for the
movement of men, commerce and political power. The explorers, and the
rulers who sponsored their voyages, had various motives: to win individual
fame, to grab wealth, to glorify a particular monarch, to search for distant
eastern allies against the Ottoman threat, and to convert the heathen to the
true faith. This tremendous outburst of navigating skill, commercial greed
and military aggression also coincided with the outbreak of the Reformation. The expansion of European Christian power over the world went
together with the warring of Christians against each other, in the name of
their faith. One of the consequences of the religious conflict was the
emigration of defeated religious communities to the new world of North
America, to build there a new society.

The expansion flowed in two directions, with very different results. The
Portuguese, followed by the Dutch, the French and the English, discovered
the great civilisations of the Far East, of which they had heard dim rumours
for centuries past: and in time they imposed their rule on large tracts of
Asia. There were never, however, many Europeans settled in these lands;
and the civilisations of India, China, Japan and the Archipelago, though
modified by contact with Europeans, remained essentially unchanged.

Those who ventured across the Atlantic, above all the Spaniards,
discovered continents of which nothing had ever been known, and communities ranging from the primitive to the highly sophisticated, all far more
different from their own than were those of Asia. Having subdued these
communities, the European invaders set themselves to create New Spain,
New France and New England.

A number of separate cultures existed, some of which produced magnificent sculpture and architecture, and possessed advanced knowledge of

mathematics and astronomy. The finest artistic achievements were those of the Mayas, who flourished approximately between the fifth and tenth century AD in Yucatan and Guatemala. The most powerful states of which there is documentary evidence, in the form of accounts by Spanish eye-witnesses, were those of the Aztecs in the valley of Mexico and of the Incas in Peru. In Mexico irrigation works were of great importance. In Peru a highly regimented and efficient social and political system existed, with complex public works. Unfortunately the deliberate destruction of indigenous documents by the Spanish conquerors, and the ruined condition of surviving buildings, have severely limited the ability of historians to reconstruct the nature of these societies.

The first landing of Europeans in North America, by Norsemen led by Lief Ericsson around 1000 AD, in the region later named the Gulf of St Lawrence, left no traces and brought back no information. The Genoese sailor Christopher Columbus, in the service of the Catholic sovereigns of Spain, discovered in 1492 the two largest Caribbean islands, of which one became known as Cuba and the other as Little Spain, and on later voyages explored the Atlantic coast of Central America and the mouth of the Orinoco. In 1519 Hernán Cortés invaded the mainland with 400 men, 15 horses and 6 cannon, and within two years by diplomacy, deceit and fierce fighting conquered the Aztec kingdom. In 1532 Francisco Pizarro had led a small expedition to Peru, and by cruder methods of fraud and violence, and no less bravery and endurance, destroyed the great kingdom of the Incas. By the mid-sixteenth century the coasts of America, from Florida to the Orinoco and from the Pacific shore of Mexico round Cape Horn to the Rio Plata, had been explored, and the sovereignty of the king of Spain asserted. Mexico became the capital of New Spain.[1]

The north-eastern part of South America was explored by the Portuguese. A fleet under Pedro Álvares Cabral reached the coast of Brazil in 1500, and Portuguese settlements were made in the following years, with their chief centre at Bahia.

The first expedition from Europe to North America since Lief Ericsson was led by a Genoese, John Cabot, who sailed from Bristol in 1497 in the service of the king of England, and discovered Newfoundland and Cape Breton Island, but his English patron took little interest in these achievements. Between 1534 and 1541 Jacques Cartier, of St Malo, in the service of François I, made three journeys to the St Lawrence, noted the two natural strongholds which later became the cities of Quebec and Montreal, and heard from the Indians the name Canada. In 1608 Quebec became the capital of New France.

In the seventeenth century English settlements, some by religious exiles and some by officially sponsored merchant companies, were made along the eastern coast from Massachusetts to Carolina. The northern part was known as New England.

The Dutch, whose main seafaring achievements were in the Far East, also founded a colony of New Netherlands around the mouth of the Hudson River, with New Amsterdam as its centre. In the same year they established themselves in Pernambuco in Brazil. Neither enterprise proved lasting. In 1654 the Portuguese colonists drove the Dutch out, and in 1664 the Dutch government ceded New Amsterdam to the English, who renamed it New York.

During the eighteenth century North America was a theatre of war between the English and French, each of which obtained allies against each other among the Indian tribes. The French were the pioneers in exploration. They travelled up the St Lawrence to the Great Lakes, and down the Ohio and the Mississippi, while English settlements were confined between the Appalachians and the ocean. The French colony of Louisiana seemed likely to extend up the Mississippi valley and then far away to the west over the Great Plains until it might conflict with the shadowy authority of the kings of Spain, whose dominions nominally extended up the coast of California. However, in the struggle between France and England it was the English who won. Wolfe captured Quebec in 1759, and the Peace of Paris in 1763 put an end to French America.

The last European state whose citizens established themselves on the mainland of North America was Russia. In the 1730s Captain Vitus Behring, a Danish sailor in Russian service, explored the Straits between Asia and America to which his name was later given. Russian settlements on the mainland of Alaska were administered by a Russo-American Company under a statute granted by Emperor Paul in 1797.[2]

Two comparatively empty regions in the southern hemisphere, outside the American continent, were also settled by Europeans—at the southern tip of Africa and in the South Pacific.

The Cape of Good Hope was first discovered in modern times by Bartholomew Diaz in 1487. (It is possible that Greek or Phoenician sailors sailed round it in ancient times, or that it was known to traders from southern India, but conclusive documentary or archaeological evidence is not available.) The Cape was used as a staging post for obtaining fresh water and food on voyages to India by Portuguese, Dutch and English, who traded with the few indigenous inhabitants. It was only in 1652 that the Dutch decided to make a more solid settlement. Jan van Reebeck was the first governor of Cape Colony. In the Napoleonic wars the British occupied it, then returned it to the Dutch, but finally acquired it in the peace settlement of 1814.

In the South Pacific too the Dutch were the pioneers. They first sighted Australia and named it New Hollandia. The island lying south of the south-east corner of Australia was first called after Van Diemen and then after Tasman. New Zealand too was named after a Dutch island. It was, however, the great English navigator, Captain James Cook, who explored the eastern coast of Australia and circumnavigated the two islands of New Zealand. The first substantial colonisation began in New South Wales in 1788, in the form of a penal settlement. Free settlers began to outnumber the original convicts after the Napoleonic wars. Tasmania, South Australia and Victoria also emerged as settled colonies by the middle of the century. It was not until 1839 that the British government decided to assume sovereignty over New Zealand, and British immigration developed in the next decades.

### From settlement to independence

In the lands of European settlement there grew up large communities whose origins were European but whose conditions of life and work were not. These communities were bound to separate themselves from the metropolis in Europe. The fundamental cause was simply geographical: climate, flora and fauna and human neighbours were different from those in Europe, and it was impossible in the long term that men living thousands of miles across the oceans, preoccupied with other and more pressing issues, could take decisions on the colonists' behalf. Geographical distance was in fact responsible for the many conflicts of economic interest which arose between colony and metropolis, and for the political controversies which broke out when doctrines first formulated in Europe were transplanted overseas. The movement from colony to independence was made in practice by war in British and Spanish America and in South Africa, but by consent in Portuguese America, Australia and New Zealand.

The population of British North America consisted of various elements present in Britain itself but combined in quite different proportions.

A large part consisted of religious dissenters. The most obvious examples are the Puritans of Massachusetts and the Quakers of Pennsylvania. These were followed in the eighteenth century by 'Scotch-Irish' from Ulster (Presbyterians squeezed in their homeland between an Anglican ruling group and a Catholic majority), German sectarians and French Huguenots. It was largely these latter immigrations which enabled the population of the colonies to rise between 1713 and 1763 from 360,000 to 1,400,000. In the 1730s and 1740s a mass movement of religious revival (the Great Awakening) took place, similar to Methodism in contemporary England, led by Jonathan Edwards and George Whitefield. Religious dissent and Methodism cannot of course be equated with political radicalism: indeed, they may be regarded as obstacles to radicalism in so far as they direct attention to the after-life. Nevertheless, a society in which religious dissenters play an outstanding part tends to be a society less disposed to respect the political hierarchy than one in which an established church is dominant.

Colonial society was also much influenced by the fact of the open land frontier. To say this is not to accept the claims for the role of the frontier in American history and national character made by Frederick Jackson Turner, whose ideas have been much modified by modern American historians. But it remains true that the struggle along the frontier—against flood and forest as well as against Indians—was a major fact of early American history. When a region had been settled, and its inhabitants had become accustomed to a more stable life, others came after them and advanced the frontier. The hard frontier life remained a fact for a minority, and the memories or the mythology of the frontier were still important to the sedentary descendants of earlier frontiersmen. Self-reliance, egalitarianism, help between neighbours and a healthy contempt for chair-bound authorities in the rear became part of a way of thinking very widespread among Americans.

The Indians of the north-east had no great monuments of civilisation like Mayas, Aztecs or Incas in the south. To the Europeans they appeared at best as likeable children, at worst as savages. The skills which they possessed, in agriculture and hunting, were quickly acquired, without any feeling of respect for the autochthonous Indian culture which had given rise to them. Indians were respected as fighters—sometimes as allies, more often as enemies—but were not regarded as equals. Intermarriage was on a small scale. It was the metropolitan government, rather than the colonists, which made some—though ineffectual—efforts to protect Indian interests.

The other non-European element present in the colonies were the black slaves, brought from Africa in the inhuman slave trade after they had been sold by their compatriots to European traders. They were regarded with contempt by the colonists, and were too defenceless to be able to make their needs recognised.

The upper classes in the colonies consisted of businessmen, landowners and professional people. In New England and the central states in the eighteenth century shipbuilding and sea-borne trade prospered, and manufacturing industry was growing. In the South, large estates and plantations worked by negro slaves brought great wealth to their owners. Of the professions, the church had lost some of its earlier predominance, while the law was growing, in response to the needs of a more complex economy and as a result of the increased activity of schools and colleges. It would however be wrong to suggest a breach between the religious and the secular elites: the Great Awakening stimulated the foundation of more and better schools, and their graduates strengthened the secular professions. Educated Americans were familiar with the ideas of the European Enlightenment, and especially with radical and democratic ideas in England. The case of John Wilkes was widely known. It was not only the intellectual elite which was concerned with political ideas: arguments about English liberties, their alleged suppression in corrupt contemporary England, and the need for Americans to defend their rights as Englishmen, extended to quite a wide public, and there was a considerable pamphlet literature on these themes.[3]

The colonial economy was subject to the Navigation Acts, and to the 'enumeration' of products that could be exported only to England. These measures, introduced in the seventeenth century, were the English form of mercantilism, the economic doctrine then prevalent in Europe. They were more objectionable in retrospect, when Americans were understandably inclined to blame all policies of the metropolitan government, than they were at the time: large sectors of the economy thrived on them, and they did not provoke much opposition.

Economic and political grievances became serious after the conclusion of the victorious peace with France in 1763. The British government needed revenue to pay for the expenses of the future defence of the colonies, whether against the Indians or the Spaniards in the West, or conceivably against France which still held firm bases in the West Indies. This was what caused it to impose a number of unpopular taxes, culminating in the Stamp Act of 1765. It had also infuriated the people of the southern states by its Proclamation of 1763 which, designed to protect the Indians beyond the Appalachians, prohibited further westward expansion by the colonists. This was followed by the Quebec Act of 1774, which placed the lands north of the Ohio under the government of Quebec and so cut off the states of Pennsylvania and New York from expansion. These actions brought out the latent distrust of the metropolitan government, and revealed how far apart was political thinking in the colonies and in England. American opposition to the Stamp Act, the vocal demand for 'no taxation without representation', led to its repeal; but other objectionable laws remained in force, and British officials were instructed to enforce their execution. In the 1770s the radicals agitated for a breach with England: their outstanding figure was Samuel Adams, who through his network of Correspondence Committees in New England and the central states sought to arouse his compatriots to defend what he claimed were their rights. More moderate men hoped to reach agreement with London, but as they met with no understanding they drifted towards the radicals.

The series of violent incidents and reprisals from 1770 to 1773 did its work. In September 1774 the first Continental Congress met in Philadelphia, with delegates extra-legally elected from twelve colonies. It protested against the British government's coercive acts, ordered boycotting measures against British goods and passed a Declaration of Rights and

Grievances. During the winter of 1774-75 various proposals were published, by Thomas Jefferson and others, which amounted to something like what was enacted in the twentieth century British empire under the name 'dominion status'. London would not however consider them. In April 1775 the first clashes took place between British and American troops, at Lexington and Concord. The second Continental Congress, meeting in May 1775, appointed George Washington as commander-in-chief of the continental forces. In August 1775 the British government declared the American colonies to be in a state of rebellion. The irrevocable formal step was taken on 4 July 1776, when the Congress accepted Thomas Jefferson's Declaration of Independence.

The War of Independence was as much a civil war as a war between the people of two territories. In England there was widespread sympathy for the American cause, and in America a large minority of Loyalists supported the British. During the war British forces held New York, Philadelphia and southern Atlantic ports. But the war was decided against the British in the summer of 1781 when a French fleet, based on the West Indies, obtained command of the sea around Chesapeake Bay, and combined French and American land and sea forces were concentrated against the British General Cornwallis at Yorktown, Virginia. His surrender brought the war to an end, and the existence of the United States of America was assured.

The Spanish empire in America was composed of territories varying enormously in climate, comprising mountains and deserts, great rivers, open uplands and thick jungles; for the most part sparsely populated but containing peoples of widely differing beliefs, social habits and languages; poorly served by land communications and linked by sea and river.

Europeans of families established in America were known as creoles. They were distinguished from Spaniards recently arrived from Europe (*peninsulares*). In the course of time the latter merged into the former, but there was always a fresh supply of new arrivals.

Of the Indian population of Central America, which may have numbered between twelve and fifteen million before the Spaniards arrived, it seems that at the middle of the seventeenth century only about one-seventh survived. The Inca empire, whose population had been about six million, lost half its inhabitants in the first thirty years of Spanish rule, partly through mass butchery by the conquerors, but still more by epidemics of European diseases hitherto unknown across the ocean. From the early stage of Spanish rule there was a clear conflict between the attitudes of the conquerors, who regarded the Indians as a semi-human labour supply from which to enrich themselves; of the church, which regarded them as possessors of souls capable of redemption, and therefore not only conducted cruel religious persecution but also at times came forward as their active champion; and of the crown of Spain which endeavoured by legislation to regulate the relations between all its subjects. In practice, it was more often the exploiters on the spot than the philanthropists in the hierarchy or in distant Spain who triumphed. Oppression was, however, mitigated by intermarriage. In the course of time throughout a large part of Spanish America *mestizos*, persons of mixed origin, came to outnumber both pure Europeans and pure Indians. The church became a genuinely popular institution, accepted by all as their own; and the Spanish language was widely diffused. It was in the viceroyalty of Peru that the largest compact mass of Indians remained, speaking the Quechua language and living in communal villages. It was here that memories of the past were most alive. In 1780 a large-scale rebellion, caused by accumulated social discontents, was led by a descendant of the Incas who took the name Tupac Amaru. Suppressed with merciless cruelty, it terrified the European upper class.

Spanish statistics from the late eighteenth century showed Indian majorities in the populations of the vice royalties of New Spain (60 per cent) and Peru (57 per cent). *Mestizos* in these two territories were 22 and 29 per cent. In Chile about half the population were *mestizos* and about a third were white.

The other main component in the Spanish American population were black slaves, imported during three centuries of imperial rule into the Caribbean islands and the coastal regions of Venezuela. Smaller but considerable numbers were brought to the Rio de la Plata and to some of the Atlantic provinces of Central America. With negroes too there was large-scale intermarriage.[4]

Spanish rule was based on a hierarchy of officials, rising from the local Indian boss (*cacique*) or creole mayor (*alcalde*), through the governors of provinces of varying importance, to the viceroy.[5] The viceroys and governors (sometimes called captains-general) had advisory councils (*audiencias*), of senior bureaucrats, which were primarily judicial bodies but had some powers of supervision over the administration, and were sometimes in conflict with the governors. This machinery of government, reproduced in each of the main regions, gave them distinct frameworks, and to their creole inhabitants the sense of forming distinct communities. Greater distances, greater geographical obstacles and more rigid state apparatus thus caused the main Spanish regions to differ more significantly from each other than the colonies of British North America.

A special case was Paraguay, where in the seventeenth century the Jesuits established a paternalist dictatorship over the Guaraní Indians. This was on balance a benevolent regime, and these Indians fared better than any others under Spanish rule. However, the general odium attaching itself to the Jesuits in the Europe of the Enlightenment made itself felt in Spain too. In 1767 they were expelled from Spanish America, and Paraguay was transferred to the viceroyalty of Rio de la Plata.

The economic policy of Spain was strictly mercantilist. This was of benefit to some regions and some interests, harmful to others. Mexico, New Granada and Peru had a privileged position in relation to the other regions. Local industries in the Andean states benefited from protection. Opposition to Spanish policy came especially from landowners in Venezuela and in the maritime provinces of Rio de la Plata, who wished to sell the produce of their estates or plantations directly to Europe. There was considerable ill feeling between creole merchants and merchants from Spain, who enjoyed special privileges.

Discontents were increased by the vigorous policy of reform adopted by the Bourbon King Charles III of Spain (1759-88), who set himself to modernise Spain and her empire. New senior officials (intendants) were introduced in 1786, and most of them were sent from Spain. Their task was to control the execution of policy more efficiently, to improve collection of taxes, and to some extent to protect the Indians from their exploiters. An aggressive policy of promoting the importation of European goods via Spain damaged existing American industries. This trade was kept firmly in the hands of Spanish merchants. The key position of Spaniards in high executive posts was also reinforced. All these things increased resentment among creoles against Spain.

Growing numbers of creoles thus began to think in terms of self-government. During the late eighteenth century the ideas of the Enlightenment became known to educated creoles: indeed, the Bourbon regime to some extent encouraged them. The American Revolution inevitably made its impression. The French Revolution appealed only to a smaller number, especially as one of its consequences was the revolution in the French Caribbean island of Santa Domingo in 1791. This negro insurrection, led by the great Toussaint l'Ouverture, which created the first independent American state south of the United States—the republic of Haiti—filled Venezuelan landowners, however liberal-minded in theory, with terror. The most important figure in the Spanish American Enlightenment, Francisco Miranda, a native of Caracas, looked rather to the ideology of Jefferson and the military support of Britain for his attempts (which were unsuccessful) to liberate Venezuela.

The last occasion on which South Americans rallied behind Spain in war was in August 1806, when a British force which had occupied Buenos Aires was defeated by a creole army. However, the discontents were accumulating beneath the surface, and a drastic change in the situation of Spain rapidly made this clear.

In 1808 Napoleon invaded Spain and dethroned the Bourbons. The

Spanish authorities had to choose between Ferdinand VIJ and Joseph Bonaparte, and their dilemma gave the politically-minded creoles an opportunity to make themselves felt, combining patriotic rejection of the French with the assertion of their own aims. The first outbreaks were in Chuquisaca in May 1809 and in Quito in August 1809. More important movements followed in 1810: in April in Caracas, in May in Buenos Aires and in Bogotá, and in September in Santiago. Also in September 1810 began a rising in Mexico, which unlike the others had a marked social revolutionary character.

The emancipation of Spanish America was fought over an immensely wider area than the war of the North American colonies against the British. It was also immensely more painful, with heavy casualties to civilians as well as soldiers, and mass acts of reprisal cruelly performed on both sides. It was spread over nearly twenty years instead of five.

A general pattern may be noted. At first the new leaders proclaimed their loyalty to the king of Spain, but soon this 'mask of Ferdinand' wore thin, and independence was declared as the aim. In Mexico there was a revolutionary war, in which the creole leaders were forced into alliance with the Spanish authorities, which they won. In Peru the Spanish authorities were not at first seriously threatened. Elsewhere the independence movements were fairly successful until Napoleon had been defeated in Europe. Ferdinand VII then made renewed efforts to suppress the rebels, but his armies were decisively defeated by 1824.

The declaration of independence of 5 July 1811 in Caracas and of 11 November in Cartagena were followed by eight years of fighting in which the Spaniards several times defeated the rebels. In 1817 and 1818 the revolutionary leader Simón Bolívar built up an army in the remote southern regions of Venezuela, led it across the Andes in the summer of 1819 and liberated most of New Granada. In 1821 his forces finally defeated the Spaniards, and a single Republic of Gran Colombia came into existence, covering all the lands of the former viceroyalty of New Granada and Venezuela.

In the south the Spanish viceroy of Rio de la Plata was overthrown in May 1810, but this was followed by several years of conflict between centralists and federalists, conservatives and radicals, the city of Buenos Aires and the outlying provinces. Spanish rule however was not restored, and a military base was established for the liberation of the Pacific territories by José de San Martín, who in·1815 and 1816 created an army in the western province of Mendoza and in January 1817 crossed the Andes into Chile. With the help of the forces of the Chilean revolutionary leader Bernardo O'Higgins he defeated the Spaniards and liberated Chile.

In Peru Spanish power remained effectively unchallenged, not least because the creoles, remembering the Tupac Amaru rebellion of 1780, feared Indian revenge if Spanish rule should collapse. Risings by creoles and by Indians were suppressed in turn. In the end Peru was liberated not by its own people but by the forces of San Martín and of Bolívar.[6]

In Mexico the first rising was led by a priest, Miguel Hidalgo y Costilla, in September 1810. This was as much directed against the landowning class, in the interest of the peasants and in the name of true religion, as against Spanish rule. It was crushed after four months, but another rising broke out in November 1813 under the leadership of one of his followers, another priest, of *mestizo* origin, named José María Morelos y Pavóu. It too was suppressed.

For the next five years Spanish rule in Mexico not only survived, but was supported by the creole upper and middle classes, whom the peasant rising had greatly alarmed. The next movement of opposition came not so much from radicals as from conservatives. The Mexican church objected to the anti-clerical legislation of the 1820 revolutionaries in Spain, and the army officers to attacks on their privileges. In February 1821 Colonel Agustín de Iturbide led a revolt, supported by the church. After an interval of two years, during which Iturbide declared himself Agustín, emperor of Mexico, there was another revolt, of some of his subordinate officers. In October 1824 the first republican constitution of Mexico was adopted.

Events in Mexico had repercussions in the southern part of Central America. Some favoured independence for Guatemala, others union of Guatemala with Mexico. In July 1823 a constituent assembly met and proclaimed the republic of the United Provinces of Central America— Costa Rica, Guatemala, Honduras, Nicaragua and El Salvador. These five did not however remain together. The process of separation into five republics was completed in 1838. By this time Bolívar's Gran Colombia had already broken up: Venezuela's formal separation took place in April 1830, and Ecuador seceded in August of the same year. Of the Spanish empire in America all that now remained was the islands of Cuba, Santo Domingo and Puerto Rico. In the place of the empire were fifteen sovereign republics.[7]

During the sixteenth century a number of Portuguese settlements were set up along the long northern and eastern coast of South America, between the mouths of the Amazon and the estuary of the Rio Plata. It was only towards the end of the century that sugar and cotton plantations, worked by African slave labour brought by the shortest Atlantic route, began to be profitable. In the seventeenth century the Dutch established themselves in Pernambuco province, and the French at Rio de Janeiro, but these rivals were driven out by the Portuguese Americans themselves without help from the homeland.

Portuguese economic policy was based on the same mercantilist principles as that of other colonial states. At the end of the seventeenth century
discoveries of gold and diamonds brought substantial European immigration, which from that time began to counterbalance the overwhelmingly
negro population of the north. The capital was moved from Bahia to Rio de
Janeiro and the centre of political power was increasingly in the south.

When Napoleon's armies occupied Portugal in 1807, the regency and the
court were transferred under British naval protection to Brazil. Free trade
with the rest of the world was permitted: this, together with the presence of
the court and the Portuguese upper class, brought both economic and
cultural development and a growth of Brazilian national consciousness.
Once Portugal was liberated from Napoleon there was a pressing demand
from the metropolitan country for the return of King John VI. He did not
leave until 1820, and his son and heir Dom Pedro remained as regent.
When he too was pressed to return, he refused, and on 7 September 1822
declared Brazil independent. The only resistance came from a Portuguese
garrison in Bahia, which was overcome by Brazilian troops and foreign
volunteers. Pedro became the constitutional emperor of Brazil. The new
situation was recognised by the Portuguese government, and no war of
independence was needed.

After the United States had won their independence, the British crown
continued to hold vast territorial possessions in North America. The
former French colony of Quebec, conquered by the British in 1759, was left
in their possession by the Treaty of Paris of 1783. Further west, in the
region of Lake Ontario, were British settlements, whose population was
greatly increased by United Empire Loyalists from the thirteen former
colonies who preferred exile under the British crown to citizenship of the
new republic. Further vast lands with sparse population stretched to the
north and west.[8]

The Canadian Constitutional Act of 1791 established the two provinces
of Lower and Upper Canada, each with a lieutenant-governor, an appointed legislative council and an assembly elected on a narrow franchise. In
Lower Canada (or Quebec) the great majority of the people were French,
but there was a growing minority of British, especially in the city of
Montreal. Many of the leading French commercial families, who had
developed the fur trade in the period of French rule, left Canada after 1759.
Whether for this reason or for others, the commercial life of Montreal
largely passed into British hands. The remaining French *seigneurs* and the
French church hierarchy accepted British rule. As social conservatives and
devoted Catholics, they disliked the American republic, and after 1789 they
detested the French republic: the British crown was preferable to either. At

the same time there was no cordiality between French and English. The French sullenly acquiesced, determined to preserve their traditional way of life and thought unchanged. The British rulers declared that they had—and indeed had—no intention of infringing these values; but there were English-speaking Canadians in both provinces who did not trouble to conceal their hostility to all things French. Dislike of Catholicism, propagated especially by the Orange Order in Upper Canada (or Ontario), played its part. At the same time Upper Canada had growing political difficulties. Immigration from Britain, especially from Scotland and Ireland, grew rapidly after the Napoleonic wars. The immigrants outnumbered the United Empire Loyalists by the 1830s, but positions of authority in the province were concentrated in the hands of a small number of families, most but not all of which were Loyalists. This local oligarchy, which became known as the Family Compact, provoked bitter opposition from the more recently arrived colonists.

The two currents of discontent developed independently towards a crisis in the year 1837. A democratic programme put forward by the French Canadian leader, Louis-Joseph Papineau, in February 1834 was rejected. British counter-proposals of 1837 led to protest meetings in French districts, a boycott of British goods, and in November and December 1837 a series of encounters between armed French Canadians and British troops. Also in December 1837 William Lyon Mackenzie, the leader of the Upper Canada radicals, made an unsuccessful armed attack on Toronto.

The British government set up an enquiry into Canadian affairs under Lord Durham. His main constitutional proposal, the establishment of a single parliament with an equal number of seats allotted to each province, was carried out by the Union Act of July 1840. Equality of seats was objectionable first to the French Canadians, who outnumbered the English-speaking Canadians by about three to two, and then to the English, who obtained an overall majority of the population in the 1850s owing to immigration. However, the system worked tolerably well in practice, and the rival political parties could only obtain a majority if they recruited both supporters and leaders among people of both languages. The objectionable part of the Durham Report was the contempt shown for the French-speaking people. Writing with the zeal of a mid-nineteenth century centralising radical, Durham dismissed the French Canadians as an inert and backward people. Philanthropic concern for their interests could only point to speedy assimilation to their English-speaking neighbours, either in Canada or in the United States. Fortunately for Canada, British governments were too cautious and conservative to act on these lines.

The main problem, for thoughtful Canadians after the mid-century, was the protection of the scattered North American territories of the British crown against the United States, which was viewed with a mixture of admiration and dislike. The view emerged that a strong union of all the provinces, from Pacific to Atlantic, should be brought about. Canadians should look not south—whether in hope or in fear—but west, up the St Lawrence, across the Great Lakes and prairies and Rocky Mountains to the other ocean. The formula of Sir John Macdonald and George-Etienne Cartier was a Confederation of British North America, not a loose association which might bring about the disintegration which threatened the United States from 1861 to 1865, but a strong centralised system. After much negotiation and hesitation, this aim was brought about by the British North American Act of July 1867.[9] The name of Canada was extended to the whole great country. Its unity, along the west-east axis, was enormously strengthened by the completion of the Canadian Pacific Railway in 1885.

From the beginning there was a lack of sympathy between the British administration of the Cape Colony, installed in 1815, and the Dutch population. The British government was anxious to avoid expenditure, and so to avoid conflict with the African tribes on the colony's eastern border; and the British missionaries, who became an important pressure group, demanded more humane treatment for the Africans, and more serious efforts to spread Christianity among them, than the Dutch settlers and their Dutch Reformed Church were willing to make. The conditions for the emancipation of slaves, passed by the British parliament in May 1833 and coming into force at the end of 1834, gave very unfavourable conditions of compensation to slave-owners in the Cape.

The discontent of the Dutch (or *Boers*, as they became generally known, from the Dutch word for 'farmer') was expressed in the mass emigration known as the Great Trek, which began in 1835. These pioneers, or *Voortrekkers*, moved with their families, servants and mobile possessions in ox-waggons. They crossed the Orange River, and then some moved on to the Vaal and across it, while others crossed the Drakensberg into the coastal region. Here they came into contact with the Zulu kingdom in which there was already a small European community of traders and whalers at Port Natal (later renamed Durban). The Zulu king Dingaan on 6 February 1838 invited the Voortrekkers' leader Piet Retief and seventy companions to drink with him, then had them captured and horribly done to death on his execution hill outside his town. About 500 other Voortrekkers and servants were killed ten days later. The massacre was avenged in a battle on 16 November at the Blood River, when the Voortrekker army led by Andries Pretorius defeated the Zulus with heavy casualties. In the first months of 1839 Pretorius finished the job of destroying Zulu power. Dingaan's successor was made a vassal of the Natal republic established by the Voortrekkers. Meanwhile in the interior the Voortrekkers defeated the kingdom of the Ndebele in November 1837, and established two republics, one between the Orange and the Vaal with its capital at Winburg and the other beyond the Vaal with its capital at Potchefstrom.

The British government of the Cape had not prevented the Voortrekkers from leaving, but once they had established themselves it began to take an interest in them, urged on both by the missionaries and by the English community in Durban. In August 1843 Natal was formally annexed by Britain. Some of the Boers remained, but those who were determined to get away from the British, and run their community in their own way, moved across the Drakensberg. British policy towards the Boer republics of the interior vacillated for some years, but in 1852 the British government recognised the Transvaal republic, and in 1854 the Orange Free State. In the following twenty years the two Boer republics set up their own institutions, democratic for the white inhabitants only. The black Africans were to have no political rights at all. Attempts to unite the republics between 1860 and 1864, when Martin Pretorius was president of both, did not succeed.

In the early 1870s the Dutch-speaking Europeans of South Africa were divided into three distinct communities. Transvaal had about 30,000 white inhabitants; Orange Free State about half as many; and Cape Colony over 230,000 of whom a large majority were Dutch-speaking. The great majority of Dutch-speaking people were pious Calvinists. This was especially true of the two inland republics, in whose people a passionate conviction was implanted that they had been called by God to a special mission, to spread Christian civilisation in Africa, overcoming the hostility of both savage black pagans and godless liberal materialist Englishmen. The Trek and Blood River were commemorated as great acts of God through His faithful servants. In the Cape this conviction was also widespread, but sinful liberal materialism also made inroads into the Cape Boer community. This was shown in the different attitude of the Cape parliament (which was granted responsible government by London in 1872) towards representation of non-whites. The Cape electoral franchise was based on property qualification, but it specifically did not exclude Africans or Coloureds (descendants of mixed marriages between Europeans and Malays or other Asians or Hottentots) if they possessed this qualification. In Natal, the fourth South African colony, were very few Dutch-speakers. Here considerable immigration from Britain took place from 1847 onwards. In the 1870s Natal had about 18,000 white inhabitants, overwhelmingly English-speaking.

A new stage began in 1877 when the British colonial secretary, the Earl of Carnarvon, impressed by the results of confederation in Canada, strongly favoured the same solution in South Africa: the four territories, if united, would be stronger and more prosperous, he believed, as well as strengthening the British empire in a strategically important part of the world. In April 1877 the British declared Transvaal annexed. The Transvaalers acquiesced. In January 1875 the British went to war with the Zulus, whose military power had revived under a new king, Cetshwayo. At the outset the British army was defeated, though Zululand was conquered a few months later. Encouraged by this evidence of British military incompetence, and hoping that the new Gladstone ministry at Westminster would retreat from its predecessors' imperial policy, the leader of the Transvaal intransigents, Paul Kruger, urged the repudiation of British authority. The result was a war in which the Boers defeated the British at Majuba Hill in February 1881. The British government decided to yield, and Transvaal was again recognised as an independent state.

In 1867 diamonds were discovered in Griqualand on the north-east borders of Cape Colony, and from 1886 onwards gold mining developed on a massive scale in the Witwatersrand in southern Transvaal. Both discoveries brought rapid economic progress and a flood of immigrants. Johannesburg started on its headlong growth into a vast modern city. Virtually none of the immigrants were Dutch-speakers, and so the people of the Transvaal saw ahead the danger of being outnumbered by foreigners in their own land. Paul Kruger, president of Transvaal from 1883 to 1900, bitterly resented the foreign immigrants or *uitlanders* and refused to satisfy their grievances, not all of which were unreasonable. More important, the forward policy of British imperial expansion, associated with Joseph Chamberlain, could not tolerate the separate existence of the Boer republics. Cecil Rhodes, premier of the Cape from 1890, who had his own vision of an Africa dominated by Britain from the Cape to Cairo, became a militant exponent of imperialism.[10] The Jameson Raid, a clumsy attempt to invade Transvaal in conjunction with a revolution by the *uitlanders* which never took place, discredited Rhodes, put an end to Afrikaner-English cooperation in the Cape, and embittered relations between the Cape and Transvaal. The appointment of Sir Alfred Milner as high commissioner in the Cape in 1898 did not improve the situation. Milner and Kruger, two honourable and intelligent fanatics, could never come to terms. In October 1899 Britain and the two Boer republics were at war.

The war began with a series of British defeats, followed by a recovery under the leadership of Field-Marshal Lord Roberts, who at the end of 1900 had occupied the main centres and proclaimed the annexation of the two republics. This was followed by more than a year of guerrilla warfare, in which Boer commandos received support from the Afrikaner population of the Cape as well as from the people north of the Orange, and the British retaliated by interning thousands of Afrikaner women and children in concentration camps—where some 25,000 died in a year and a half—and by burning farm buildings and destroying livestock. Peace was eventually made in Vereeniging and signed in Pretoria on 31 May 1902.

For the next three years Milner ruled all South Africa. Like Lord Durham in Canada sixty years earlier, he wished to create efficient and progressive government and to further economic development. Like Durham, he believed that English language and culture were bound to prevail: the survival of a second culture, with a second European language, seemed as absurd to him as had the survival of French culture in Quebec to Durham. Both were wrong.

The advent to power in Britain of the Liberal Party under Sir Henry Campbell-Bannerman brought a radical change of policy. Responsible government was granted to the two former republics. From October 1908 to February 1909 a National Convention of elected delegates met to decide a constitution for a Union of South Africa: the reluctance of the people of Natal, many of whom still thought of themselves as English rather than as South Africans, to join a Union, was overcome by the prospect of economic advantage. The new constitution was unitary rather than federal, but it preserved important differences between the franchise laws in the four provinces. The Cape franchise, which permitted Coloureds and Africans with property and educational qualifications to vote (but not to be elected) was preserved, and could only be repealed by a two-thirds majority in both houses of parliament of the Union. In practice this meant that 77 per cent of the population of the Cape were entitled to 15 per cent of the seats—not much, but better than nothing. The rights of non-Europeans in Natal were in practice so minimal as to be negligible: in Transvaal and Orange Free State no such rights existed. The Convention also agreed, at the insistence of General J. B. M. Hertzog from the Orange Free State, that both European languages should enjoy complete equality in public business, and this provision was also entrenched in the constitution by making it reversible only by a two-thirds majority in both Houses. Representatives of the Coloureds and Africans, led by the former Cape prime minister, W. P. Schreiner, visited London in 1909 to try to obtain better terms for non-Europeans; but the British government was not willing to exert pressure, and parliament passed the South Africa Bill in May 1910. This was widely acclaimed as an act of generosity by the British towards a brave defeated enemy: it was only many years later that it appeared an act of betrayal of the weaker majority peoples, abandoned to the mercies of the stronger minority.

Thus, after nearly a century of conflict, including two wars for independence, the European community had obtained sovereignty in a large state, which had before it the prospect of moving towards independence in the same way as the other states of the evolving British empire—Canada, Australia and New Zealand.

However, the division between English-speaking and Afrikaans-speaking people, no less profound than between English-speakers and French-speakers in Canada, made the formation of a single European South African nation extremely difficult, while its situation in the midst of indigenous black African populations, outnumbering it six to one, added a further tragic dimension.

Sydney, the first European city in Australia, was founded by Captain Arthur Philip as the residence of his shipload of 750 convicts. After completing their sentences, the convicts could become free settlers, and their children grew up free. Gradually also the number of free immigrants increased, and sheep farming developed. During the 1830s and 1840s pioneers explored the interior, following the rivers westwards into the Murray, then into the Darling and south-west to the ocean. Others travelled northwards as far as the Gulf of Carpentaria. During these years the two cities of Melbourne and Brisbane were founded. Two enterprises of systematic colonisation, planned in England, were also carried out, inspired by the great exponent of white overseas colonisation, Gibbon Wakefield. One was on the Swan River in the far south-west, from which developed the colony of West Australia. In 1840 transportation of prisoners stopped, except for West Australia, whose settlers continued to demand convict labour until 1868.

As the population increased, the demand for representative institutions grew. In 1842 New South Wales was given a council with an elected majority on a restricted franchise, and in 1850 similar institutions were extended to Tasmania and South Australia. In 1851 Victoria became a separate colony, its capital being Melbourne, and in 1859 Queensland became another, comprising the lands from Brisbane to the Gulf of Carpentaria. In 1855 all the colonies obtained constitutions with responsible parliamentary government and democratic franchises.

This result was not achieved without violence. In 1851 discovery of gold at Ballarat led to massive immigration, which in five years increased the population of Victoria from 70,000 to 333,000. The immigrants objected to the duty raised by the government of Victoria on their mining licence, and demanded the right to be represented in the legislature. In 1854 there was fighting between miners and troops.

The Australian colonies developed on separate but parallel lines for the rest of the century. The population was mainly English and Protestant, but there was a Catholic Irish element especially in Victoria. The indigenous people, known in Australia as *aborigines*, were sparse in numbers, poorly organised, and suffered from the contemptuous arrogance, the diseases and at times the murderous zeal of the Europeans. The white population was divided into four main sectors: the coastal cities, the mining centres, the farming districts and the great areas used for sheep or cattle grazing. Conflicts on land ownership between farmers and graziers were one of the main themes of Australian politics. The public climate tended to greater equalitarianism than in Britain, and labour and school legislation were well advanced.

Federation of the five colonies was discussed as early as the 1880s, but no such pressing need was felt as had been the case in Canada in the 1860s. There was also an important economic conflict between New South Wales, which favoured free trade, and the other colonies, which inclined to protectionism. It was the growth of rivalry between the European great powers in the Pacific that made Australian politicians think more urgently about unity. Protracted negotiations between the leaders of the five colonies culminated in the establishment, from 1 January 1901, of the Commonwealth of Australia. The powers reserved to the states were more numerous than in the Canadian confederation, but residual powers were left—as in Canada but not in the United States—to the central government. Australia was now sovereign.

New Zealand was the scene of the most successful of Gibbon Wakefield's colonising enterprises. From the 1830s onwards the South Island developed as a white man's farming country, its trade in meat with England flourishing after the introduction of new cold storage methods by the New Zealand Shipping Company in 1882. The two islands received representative government in 1853 and responsible government in 1856.

The most serious problem was the series of disputes with the indigenous Maori inhabitants of the North Island. The Maoris saw their lands threatened by the immigrants, and there were frequent minor wars during the 1860s. When peace was brought about in 1870, the Maoris retained about half the land on the North Island, but remained materially worse off than the white inhabitants. Nevertheless, though it may well be argued that white immigration was in itself an act of injustice towards the Maoris, it is also true that great efforts were made and sustained to obtain an acceptable compromise, and that relations between white and Maori New Zealanders in the twentieth century were better than between white and non-white in any other overseas state founded by European colonisation.

## The United States

The thirteen colonies had rid themselves of their British overlords by 1782: the creation of a single state, and still more the creation of a single nation, were arduous tasks that still lay ahead.

The Articles of Confederation, agreed by the Continental Congress during the War of Independence, were little more than an alliance between sovereign states. In the subsequent years, as individual states pulled in different directions and conflicted with each other, it became clear that there was a serious danger of disintegration, and loss of the new-won liberty either to the British or some other European power, unless a more solid basis of unity were created. This was the task of the statesmen who eventually produced, with validity from March 1789, the Constitution of the United States. This great work was essentially a compromise between those who wished for maximum diversity and maximum sovereignty for each state, and fundamentally disliked the very idea of a central government; and those who believed it necessary to concentrate important powers at the top, to endow the United States with the necessary executive apparatus of a modern state, and to put firm restraints on centrifugal forces. The second school of thought, which became known as the Federalists, and whose leading spokesman was Alexander Hamilton, on the whole prevailed; but substantial safeguards were given to their opponents, whose most eloquent exponent was Thomas Jefferson. Though the concept of 'party' was distasteful to the founders of the republic, not least to Washington himself, there did soon develop a party system, in which for several decades the followers of Jefferson, and later of Andrew Jackson, first known as Republicans and then as Democrats, were the strongest force. The prevalence in political life of this democratic element, whose main strength lay in Virginia and New York, modified but did not reverse the tendency towards the strengthening of the federal government. An institution which unexpectedly operated in the same direction was the Supreme Court, which in the period when John Marshall was chief justice (1801-36) gave several decisive verdicts in favour of the federal power.

Not only the form of government but the territorial extent of the republic needed definition, and this took many years. Napoleon compelled Spain to cede to him Louisiana, the vast and largely unmapped tract lying between the Mississippi and the Rockies which was ceded by France to Spain in 1783. However, his preoccupations in Europe prevented him from taking possession, and the inability of his troops to recover Santo Domingo from the insurgent slaves[11] further discouraged him. He therefore offered the territory for sale to the United States in 1803; Jefferson accepted immediately, and justified himself to Congress later. In 1819 the United States bought Florida from Spain. The frontier with Canada in Maine was settled by the Ashburton-Webster treaty of 1842, and the 49th parallel was made the boundary with the Hudson's Bay Company territory in Manitoba. The Columbia river valley, which was explored by travellers both from Britain and from the United States, was an object of dispute until 1846, when both governments agreed on the extension of the 49th parallel as far as Puget Sound—leaving Vancouver Island to Britain and the Olympic Peninsula to the United States. Further north, Russia retained Alaska and its outlying islands until 1867, when they were sold to the United States for seven million dollars. In the South, American squatters in the Mexican province of Texas declared themselves a separate republic in 1836. The United States annexed Texas in 1845, and in the following year went to war with Mexico. American troops entered Mexico City, and by the peace settlement of 1848 the vast region between the Rockies and the Pacific, then known by the single name of California, became part of the United States. It remained to drive most of the Indians from their homes, to destroy their traditional way of life and to fill up half a continent.

Territorial expansion gave new content to the disputes between the states and the central government, which the Constitution and the Supreme Court had by no means solved. Already in 1807, the New England states had jointly protested against Jefferson's embargo on foreign trade. A Connecticut legislature resolution spoke of the duty of state legislatures 'to interpose' their protecting shield between the right and liberty of the people and the assumed power of the General Government'. The plans for a convention of the New England states in 1809 to 'nullify' the policy were abandoned when the federal government itself repealed the embargo. In 1828 John Calhoun, the eminent spokesman of South Carolina, advanced the doctrine of 'nullification' to defend the interests of the southern states which were seriously damaged by the protectionist trade policy introduced to the advantage of the New England states. A compromise policy was proposed in the summer of 1832, but in South Carolina a special state convention was summoned, which first formally declared the federal trade bill null and void, and then solemnly reassembled in March 1833 to repeal its nullification.

The serious conflicts in economic interests between the three geographical 'sections'—northern seaboard, southern seaboard and expanding west—were made much more bitter by the problem of slavery. A procedure was devised by which the population of a newly settled territory on the expanding western border could apply for admission to the Union as a new state, with its own state constitution. The number of states thus extended by 1820 from the original thirteen to twenty-four. Some of the new states, created by expansion from the South, were based on slavery: in those colonised from the North, slavery was prohibited. In 1820, when the North had a population of 5,152,000 and 105 federal congressmen, and the South 4,485,000 and 81, an agreement known as the Missouri Compromise was made. The new state of Missouri was admitted to the Union as a slave-owning state and Maine as a 'free-soil' state, but there was to be no slavery north of latitude 36° 30'. A new situation arose in 1846, when a proposal was put to Congress that slavery be forever prohibited in any territory to be acquired from war with Mexico. This raised the prospect that, as the continent filled up by natural increase and immigration, and as new states were in consequence created, slave-holding states would be greatly out-numbered, and the federal Congress would be in a position to impose abolition on the South by majority vote. This fear caused Calhoun, in protesting against the 1846 proposal, to talk again of 'nullification'. California, whose population was rapidly increased from all over the world by the Gold Rush of 1849, declared itself for the prohibition of slavery. In South Carolina and Mississippi there was talk of secession from the Union. The death in 1850 of Calhoun and of the anti-southern President Zachary Taylor made possible a new compromise which preserved the Union.

This time however the antagonisms grew very deep. In the North the 'abolitionist' campaign, to end slavery because it was evil, became a mass movement. Northern opinion refused to accept the fugitive slave law which had been part of the 1850 compromise: the 'underground railway' was organised by white radicals and free blacks to help slaves escape across the Ohio. In 1851 began the serialisation of *Uncle Tom's Cabin*, which depicted southern society as utterly depraved. William Lloyd Garrison's rhetoric in condemnation of the southern upper classes[12] was matched by southern rhetoric denouncing pitiless exploitation of labour in northern factories and asserting that slavery was not only not degrading or cruel but positively humane, benevolent and morally uplifting. The people of the South increasingly felt themselves an object of aggression. Southern culture, its local traditions and customs and liberties, had to be defended against merciless and hypocritical enemies. There developed something which could seriously be called southern national consciousness. In anticipation of secession, efforts were made rapidly to develop southern industries, railways and shipping, and to remodel school instruction so as to inculcate loyalty specifically to the South rather than to the Union as a whole.

The slavery issue split the dominant Democratic Party, and a new party appeared in the North, which took its rivals' earlier name of Republican. In the 1856 presidential election the Democrats still had a majority, but in 1860, as a result of further splits in the vote, the Republican candidate, Abraham Lincoln, had a relative majority. Rather than accept his leader-ship, six southern states, beginning with South Carolina, seceded in the winter of 1860-61. A convention at Montgomery (Alabama) in February 1861 founded the Confederate States of America, with its own president, Jefferson Davis, and its own constitution. Lincoln refused to recognise the secession, but bided his time. In July 1861 the Confederate artillery 'fired on the flag' at Fort Sumter, guarding the harbour of Charleston (South Carolina), and the Civil War began.

This terrible struggle, mobilising millions and arming them with the most destructive weapons yet devised by human ingenuity, ended with the victory of the industrialised, capitalist North and the reassertion of the Union. The existence in North America of two republics, with peoples for the most part of similar origin and of the same language but of different social structure and national consciousness, similar to the state of affairs in Central and South America, was averted. As the spiritual wounds healed, the sense of belonging to a single American nation revived and was strengthened; but the conflicts between whites and blacks (now formally emancipated from slavery), and between white views as to the place of the blacks in America, were not removed.

The subsequent growth and consolidation of the American nation (as the people of the United States have become known, to the mild but ineffective annoyance of the other peoples of the Western Hemisphere) was profoundly influenced by the entry of millions of immigrants from Europe. Already before 1775 considerable numbers of Germans had settled. These, together with English, Scots and 'Scots Irish', continued to flood into America after Independence. Then came Scandinavians, and after the Great Famine, a flood of Irish. The coming of the steamship in the 1850s provided quicker, healthier and less uncomfortable transport, and the number of immigrants continued to grow. After the Civil War the influx increased still further. In the 1880s immigration from northern Europe continued, but was accompanied by a growing flood from southern and eastern Europe, which continued to grow when the earlier stream began to dry up. In the first decade of the twentieth century more than two million came from Austria-Hungary, as many from Italy, and from Russia over a million and a half, in the last case consisting largely of Jews. There was also immigration from Asia to the West Coast. About 300,000 Chinese settled in California between 1850 and 1880. Japanese sought employment in Hawaii, and when this was annexed by the United States in 1898 these Japanese were able to move to the American continent.

Much has been written of the sufferings of the uprooted. Driven out of their homelands by poverty, by loss of a livelihood through the dislocation of agriculture and of the older industries, and in some cases by religious or political persecution, often travelling in horrible conditions and exploited by middlemen, they found themselves in new poverty among strange people in a strange land. Yet it is also true that the hopes of a new free life with which they had set out were not in the long term disappointed. The policy of the United States government was to welcome them, to give them work to do, and make them part of a great new nation in the making.

This policy on the whole prevailed for more than a hundred years, though not without bitter opposition. Not only among the original Americans, but also among each successive wave of immigrants which established itself, there was a tendency to resent and fear newcomers. This tendency, known as 'nativism', burst out fiercely from time to time. Agitation in California in the late 1870s led to the passing of a Chinese Exclusion Act in 1882, which put an end to Chinese immigration. At the beginning of the twentieth century there was similar agitation against Japanese. An agreement of 1907 between the United States and Japanese governments stopped further migration of labourers directly from Japan to America. Agitation against European newcomers was led by the Immigration Restriction League, founded in 1894, but it had small effect before the First World War.

The mood created by the war itself, massive patriotic propaganda and hostility to Germans and Austrians, created a climate of opinion much more favourable to nativism. In the early 1920s a Red Scare, a reaction partly to labour troubles at home and partly to the victory of the Bolsheviks in Russia, increased public distrust of East Europeans, and combined with rather widespread anti-semitic feeling and the anti-Catholicism of the Ku Klux Klan to strengthen nativism. Economic conditions had also changed since the heyday of mass immigration. America now had the largest and most skilled industrial labour force in the world, and labour leaders were more than ever determined to prevent the high American wage level from being undercut by cheap foreign labour.

All these forces contributed to the passing of the Johnson-Reed Act of 1924, which placed an upper limit of 150,000 on immigration in any one year, and gave quotas to groups from each foreign country, based on the proportion which persons born in each state formed of the total population of the United States in 1924.[13] This law thus discriminated strongly against the peoples of eastern and central Europe, and in favour of the people of countries from which immigrants had been coming for longer periods, especially Great Britain.

The effect of the Johnson-Reed Act, and also of economic and political conditions in post-war Europe, was that European immigration enormously diminished in the 1920s. There continued however to be fairly substantial immigration from within the Western Hemisphere. About a million Canadians entered the United States in the 1920s. Most of these were English-speaking, but there was also a considerable influx of French-speakers into the mill towns of New England. There was also a growing stream from the West Indies: between the wars mostly from British islands but also some from French islands and from Haiti, and after 1945 above all from Puerto Rico, which must have sent at least a million by the late 1960s. Finally there were immigrants from Mexico, largely seasonal labourers but also including large numbers who settled permanently. This mass influx dated from 1942, when the United States began to encourage employment of Mexicans in conditions of wartime labour shortage. In 1945 there were more than 2,500,000 Mexican-born persons in the United States.

From these many sources, in the hundred years which followed the Civil War, was formed the American nation. Plentiful manpower and plentiful resources combined to create the People of Plenty. Great achievements in applied science and industry, and great victories in war, created the immense attractive force, felt all over the world, of the United States of America. The immigrants were swept up into this great process; they too felt pride in their great new country, pride in the contribution which they had made to its greatness. The greatest exception (which is not by any means a complete exception) were the negroes, descendants of black African slaves brought against their will to America, including those whose ancestors had been brought to the Caribbean islands, and had moved in later generations to the mainland. Black Americans will be briefly considered later. Other partial exceptions[14] are those who remained from the indigenous American peoples, including those descended from intermarriage with Spaniards who entered the United States from Mexico.

The immigrants from Europe became Americans, but they did not entirely lose their loyalties to their old homelands. In general it is true that each generation became more American, but it is not quite so simple as that. Many of the East European peasants who arrived in the United States had very little national consciousness—as opposed to strong simple feelings for the place of their birth and childhood and for relatives and friends. Their children, who learned in American schools, and read American newspapers and books, discovered more about their homeland and their nationality than their parents had known. Thus, second generation Lithuanian-Americans and Slovak-Americans became more interested in the fate of the Lithuanian and Slovak nations back in Europe than their parents had been, and contributed valuable funds and advice to the national movements in the homelands. In the case of immigrants who had already arrived with strong national feelings, such as Irish or Poles, the national feeling often remained strong for generation after generation.

The great Americanising forces were the school and the factory. The forces which kept the old loyalties alive were the church and the foreign language newspaper. National feeling was also more strongly maintained among those who were concentrated in great cities in compact communities, protected and also directed by politicians and priests, than among those who scattered themselves across the country, bought and developed their own land and lived at some distance from each other on Midwestern farms, a very different kind of geographical and social pattern from Mediterranean or Danubian villages. To the second group belonged the Scandinavians, many of the Germans and some of the Czechs and Serbs. In the first group were the Irish, who had had the bitterest experience of farming life and preferred to be in large communities close to their own countrymen and priests; and the Italians, Poles and smaller East European groups, who had arrived later and poorer, at a time when to start a farm required more capital and knowledge than in earlier generations—more in any case than they possessed.

Immigrant communities were to a large extent grouped round their churches. The churches in their turn became Americanised as English began to prevail as their language. The American Catholic community started as English-speaking owing to the predominance of the Irish. Italian and Polish immigrants had some success in bringing their languages into church affairs, but as generations succeeded each other English began again to prevail, not as the language of Irishmen but as the language of the United States and one of the main Catholic languages of the world. The case was somewhat different with the Orthodox immigrants. There were no English-speaking Orthodox communities anywhere in the world outside America. However, by the mid-twentieth century the use of English in American Orthodox churches had become quite common.

The long-term effects of urbanisation, education and secularisation are unmistakable. The various immigrant communities were progressively integrated into the American nation, while at the same time they were modifying American culture and national identity itself. The complete control of American political leadership and social elites by White Anglo-Saxon Protestants (WASPs) began to be challenged. Not only did the more recent immigrant groups become important voting blocks, of which politicians had to take account, but individuals of more varied origins began to reach top positions. First came Irishmen in the political parties and Jews in business life. Then gradually Italian, Polish, Czech, Lebanese or other names appeared in prominent positions in industrial leadership, science, the press, the government hierarchy, municipal politics and Congress.[15]

This does not however mean that the non-WASPs—or 'white ethnics' as they were named, to differentiate them from blacks, Amerindians or Mexicans (chicanos)—were contented with this progress. On the contrary, it is arguable that, as has so often been the case in human history, visible improvements increased discontent, because they aroused much greater expectations which could not be satisfied quickly. In 1970 there were about seventy million Americans of Irish or southern or eastern European origin, and of these about fifty million were Catholics. The older generations had had to face the collective contempt, or at best the cold condescension, of the WASPs. The younger generation found themselves faced with a different kind of insult. The 'liberal establishment' of the 1970s—the intellectual elite of the north-east, which was mainly WASP and partly Jewish, and which largely dominated the mass media and the universities—in its enthusiasm for the rights of the blacks, was only too inclined to treat the 'white ethnics' as 'reactionaries' or 'fascists'. To 'white ethnic' factory workers the alliance between black militants, Jewish intellectuals, north-east coast patricians and their rich student children with their fashionable revolutionary slogans, looked like a new version of the conspiracy of the WASPs to keep them down. Resentments among non-WASP white Americans were undoubtedly an important, and possibly an increasing, element on the American political scene. The party politics of the United States are not the subject of this book, but the extent to which the 'ethnics' have or have not been absorbed into one nation is a very relevant matter. The conventional wisdom is that the melting-pot has been effective, with the single admitted exception of the Blacks. This wisdom was not however accepted by all Americans. Some insisted that what had happened was not that the immigrants had grown into a new American nation, making their own contribution to it, but that the attempt had been made to impose on millions of Catholics, Orthodox and Jews an alian WASP ethos, and that this had failed. The original languages had on the whole been replaced by American English, but the Protestant ethos had made few converts. Many 'ethnics' had lost their old values without gaining anything new except the materialist hedonism of the mass media. Others had retained their old loyalties, and stubbornly defended them against the hostility of the 'establishment'. In the words of a recent writer, 'There is no such thing as *homo Americanus*. There is no single culture here. We do not, in fact, have a culture at all. . . .'[16]

Faced with these bitter controversies, in which all concerned have powerful cases to make, I can only state my own opinion that the myth of opportunity for all to rise within a new society and a new nation contained, like most myths, a large element of truth. The American nation was the first, and remained the most powerful, of the new nations. It was a different kind of nation from the nations of Europe, yet it was justifiable to use the same word 'nation' to describe it as to describe those communities in Europe which are called nations.

## The Spanish American nations

No United States of Spanish America came into being. Even Bolívar's Great Colombia, and the Central American union, could not be preserved. Distances by sea were much longer, and communications by land were far fewer and more difficult, than on the eastern seaboard of North America. The mountains and jungles, which the pioneers encountered as they penetrated the interior, were more inhospitable. The institutions, set up by the officials of the Spanish monarchy, were more solid and rigid than those of the North (with the possible exception of New France on the St Lawrence). Within their framework, separate hierarchies of interest and ambition arose, which survived the severance of links with the sovereign overseas. Against this, it might have been expected that the great unity of Spanish culture, cemented by the one rigidly enforced faith, would have gripped more firmly together the Spanish colonists than the people of what became the United States, with their warring Protestant sects and their diversity of political ideas and even of national origins. This may have been counteracted partly by the facts that in Spanish America, too, there were differences deriving from the homeland—between Basques, Galicians, Estremadurans and Castilians; that in the Spanish colonies the gentleman-adventurer of extreme individualism was a more predominant figure than among the English-speaking; and that in the northern colonies social discipline, mutual aid and community spirit were more developed.

Whatever the reason, fifteen states arose and maintained their separate statehood; and to those were added Santo Domingo in 1865, Cuba in 1898 and Panama in 1903, the last two being due more to international pressures than to internal forces. Whether the people of these states developed into nations, as fully conscious of their difference from other nations as the nations of Europe—for example, of Germans from Italians, or even of Serbs from Bulgarians—is hard to say. A certain feeling of solidarity between Hispanic nations persisted, but did not much mitigate the operation of contradictory interests. On the other hand, wars between Spanish American states were comparatively few. The war between Argentina and Brazil about Uruguay involved a non-Spanish-speaking state ruled by a monarchy. There were territorial conflicts in the 1830s and 1840s between Ecuador and New Granada (which did not adopt the name Colombia until 1886); and an attempt by a Bolivian dictator to incorporate Peru in a confederation under his rule was defeated with Chilean armed help in 1839. More serious was the war of the Pacific of 1879-83, in which Peru and Bolivia fought against Chile for the possession of coastal provinces with rich mineral resources, and which ended with the cession to Chile of all Bolivia's coastal strip and of some Peruvian territory as well. The most terrible South American war was that provoked by the Paraguayan dictator Francisco Lopez in which for four years (1865-70) Paraguay resisted the combined forces of Argentina, Brazil and Uruguay, and in which about half the population of Paraguay perished. Paraguay also fought Bolivia from 1932 to 1935 for the possession of the Chaco province, a jungle territory which was thought to possess great unexploited mineral resources. The result of the war was more favourable to Paraguay than to Bolivia.

A few observations on the South American nations can best be based on a division into four regions. The first comprises the three southern republics of Argentina, Uruguay and Chile, whose population, as a result of massive immigration, became overwhelmingly of European stock; the second, the Andean states of Ecuador, Peru and Bolivia and the republic of Paraguay, in all of which *mestizo* and pure Indian are predominant; the third, the Caribbean islands, Venezuela, and some of the Central American states, with a large element of African origin; and the fourth Mexico, which is a unique case. There are some states which do not fit into this regional division: Colombia has elements of the second and third categories, while Costa Rica, though located in Central America, in many ways resembles the southern republics. There is also one other quite unique state, Haiti, with a black population whose language is French.

The three southern republics were favoured with good natural conditions for agriculture, especially for stock-raising, for whose products there was a growing demand in Europe. In all three there emerged a prosperous oligarchy of landowners and of exporting merchants. Foreign capital became very powerful, first in the form of big trading firms and then of investments in industrial resources, outstanding among which were the British owners of Argentine railways and later the North American owners of Chilean mines. In the second half of the century immigration from Europe grew rapidly, and was encouraged by the governments. Argentina received the largest number: about 3,500,000 up to the Second World War and over 1,500,000 in the first two post-war decades. Of these immigrants, about half were Italians and a third Spaniards; the rest included Germans, Yugoslavs and Lebanese. In Chile and Uruguay numbers were relatively smaller but still very large. The population of all three countries thus became overwhelmingly European: the negro element in the Argentine, which had been substantial at the time of independence, was reduced to a very small minority, and the same was true of the Indians, confined to a few areas of Chile and of north Argentina.

The combination of temperate climate, natural wealth and a large European labour force ready to work hard should, it is sometimes suggested, have produced three 'modernised', 'democratic' nations, rather like the nation of the United States; and surprise is expressed that this result did not ensue. This is a rather naive comment. The truth is not only that the immigrants were seldom persons coming from modern democratic societies, but also that the societies into which they were precipitated had even less of this quality, and indeed lacked many of the elements of the rule of law, as understood in nineteenth century Europe and North America. From this point of view, Chile was the more 'progressive' country: for a large part of its modern history, it was ruled by men who at least genuinely set themselves to construct an efficient and honest government machine, and to keep soldiers in their barracks. Argentina was torn by conflicts between the enormous city of Buenos Aires, in which a *bourgeoisie* of more or less liberal outlook prevailed, and the countryside, the home of the anarchically individualist cattle-hands (*gauchos*) who readily followed strong men versed in the arts of anti-city demagogy. As a city proletariat of immigrant workers grew, it adapted much of the *gaucho* outlook to its urban milieu, together with doses of more doctrinaire European anarchism imported from Italy. In both Chile and Argentina, a rich oligarchy maintained at least political influence, even if it did not usually exercise direct political power. In Uruguay, whose political history in the nineteenth century was still more stormy, there came to power in 1903 a leader, José Batlle y Ordóñez, who used his great authority to strengthen civil liberties and create liberal social institutions. For fifty years Uruguay was something like a European democracy, though this began to break down in the 1960s. To sum up, one may say that, for all the internal weaknesses and contradictory forces pulling society apart, three nations had arisen, and national consciousness extended downwards to the great majority of the population.

In the Andean states and Paraguay, power tended to be seized by soldiers, and wealth was concentrated in the hands of the richest of the landowners and capitalists, of whom some were foreigners. Most landowners and capitalists were not very rich, and it would be wrong to identify those who were rich with the military dictators; but it is at least fairly true that the oligarchy and the generals tolerated, and usually helped, each other at the expense of the population at large. The fundamental problem in all four countries were the Indians. The imprecise word 'Indian', which cannot be statistically defined, comprised both those who still spoke an Indian language and those who, though they had adopted Spanish as their language, lived 'the Indian way', whether in villages or in the cities, among which the sprawling metropolis of Lima was outstanding. Of the first category, the most numerous were those of Quechua speech, numbering probably more than six million and divided between three states—Peru, Ecuador and Bolivia—followed by the Guaraní-speakers who formed a majority of Paraguay's 2,500,000 inhabitants in the 1970s. The Indian problem, inextricably mixed with the problems of land distribution and economic growth, will be discussed later. The great variety of cultures, of standards of living and of levels of education, make it difficult to decide what meaning should be given to the notions of Peruvian, Ecuadorian, Bolivian and Paraguayan nations.

This obscurity is even greater in the Caribbean region. The most prosperous of the states of the region was Venezuela, with some 11,000,000 inhabitants and a thriving oil industry. Considerable immigration from Europe reduced the negro preponderance in its population. Its western neighbour Colombia had twice as many inhabitants, *mestizos* of both Indian and African origin. Colombian politics for most of the nineteenth century were fought between two factions of the oligarchy, while the population suffered not only from poverty but from periodical explosions of *guerrilla*. These reached a climax in the mass-scale *violencia* of 1948-64, in which probably a quarter of a million people lost their lives without any very compelling justification. The small Central American republics were a happy hunting-ground for foreign business interests and for both indigenous and foreign military adventurers. Cuba was transformed in the 1960s from semi-colonial dependence on the United States to semi-colonial dependence on the Soviet Union. The consequence, a fusion of the Soviet-type monolithic party with streamlined old-style *caudillismo*, probably involved the formation in Cuba of a national consciousness stronger than had ever previously existed in the Caribbean region.

Mexico, with 50,000,000 inhabitants in the 1970s, had a uniquely dramatic historical development in modern times: twenty-five years (1829-55) of the military dictator Santa Anna, who lost California to the United States; a period of anti-clerical reforms, civil war and French military invasion (1857-67) in which the reforming president, Benito Juárez, prevailed against the would-be emperor, the Habsburg arch-duke Maximilian; the long dictatorship (1876-1910) of Juárez's lieutenant Porfirio Díaz, who opened the country to foreign investors; a period of revolution and civil war (1910-20) in which perhaps a million Mexicans lost their lives; and the emergence of a political system moulded by the victorious generals of the revolution and handed on by them to later generations in the form of rule by a body which chose to call itself the Institutional Revolutionary Party.

The revolution was a great event, because it changed not only the ruling elite but also the nature of the national mythology, and so of the nation itself. Until the revolution power belonged to those approved by the landowners and the church, which shared the wealth with foreign business interests. In the Juárez era the church took some hard blows but recovered; and it may be argued that the main effect of Juárez's efforts was that under his pupil Díaz the foreign element in the oligarchy gained ground at the expense of the indigenous element. Throughout this period Spanish culture prevailed and was glorified. The Indians who, as in the Andes, consisted of the two categories of speakers of Indian languages and of Spanish-speakers who lived the 'the Indian way', were a despised mass. Persons of true Spanish blood were very few, even at the apex of the social pyramid; but the *mestizos* who occupied the upper levels were proud to belong to Spanish culture. Juárez, by birth a Zapotec Indian, had profound sympathy for his fellow-Indians, but did not doubt that Spanish culture must prevail. The revolution changed this situation. It took wealth and power from many great landowners; and this process was continued under the presidency of General Cárdenas (1934-40). The revolution also took the remaining wealth of the church, and forced the priesthood itself into a status of semi-legality. Few members of the elite of Porfirio Díaz's time retained power or wealth: in their place arose a new elite of bureaucrats, army officers, lawyers and business managers, recruited from the victors of the revolution.

As time passed, as the economy grew, and as the links with North American capital were strengthened from the 1950s onwards, the new elite became a new bourgeoisie, more *étatiste* and less committed to free enterprise doctrine than the old, but not less concerned to preserve and increase its wealth and power. However, this elite legitimised itself by the rhetoric of revolution. The revolution had become 'institutionalised' in the persons of the new rulers and the new privileged. They spoke not only in the name of the revolution but in the name of the Indians. In the new official mythology, Indian traditions and Indian cultures were glorified, and Spanish culture was denigrated. Cortés was no longer a national hero but a villain. The Spanish language was the national language of Mexico, but Mexicans were heirs to the Toltecs, Zapotecs or Mayas, not to the Castilians. Meanwhile the Indians occupied, as previously, the lower levels of the social pyramid. Something, it is true, had been done for the Indians in land reform and in social welfare—far more than in any Andean state. Admirable work had also been done—sometimes by Mexicans—in the study of the numerous, diverse and truly magnificent civilisations of the pre-Columbian peoples of Mexico. Perhaps most important, social mobility was probably greater than in any other Spanish-American country: talented Indians could make good careers, and the education without which careers could hardly be started was made increasingly available even to the poor. Yet the fact that politicians and rich and distinguished citizens loudly proclaimed their pride in their Indian ancestry and their devotion to Indian culture did not necessarily prove that 'the Indian problem' had been 'solved', or a new Mexican nation had been created.

Though the new nations of Spanish America successfully rejected the sovereignty of their former European rulers, their economic progress remained dependent on foreign trade, and their natural resources were developed first by European and then by North American capital. Cattle-ranches, meat-packing plants and railways in the Argentine were largely British-owned. British and other foreign capital played a leading part in Mexican oil, Bolivian tin and Chilean copper. Between the world wars North American investments increased more rapidly than European.

In so far as they opened up natural resources, these investments were obviously beneficial to the peoples of Latin America, and were welcomed by their rulers. However, inevitably also they created jealousy and resentment. Not only foreigners, but also their local associates and employees created islands of wealth amidst local poverty. The view became widespread that the wealth of the indigenous nations was being drained abroad, in the form of dividends to absentee foreigners and high salaries to foreign specialists employed on the spot. In Mexico, President Cárdenas nationalised foreign oil companies, but later presidents again welcomed foreign investments. In the smaller Caribbean republics North American business interests remained invulnerable: outstanding among them was the United Fruit Company. As a direct result of the economic strains of the Second World War, British and other European interests were greatly reduced. The British-owned railways and many other enterprises passed to the Argentine government on terms unfavourable for the owners. United States investments however forged ahead. In 1968 they formed about 70 per cent of all private foreign investments, 40 per cent being in petrol and mining.

The dominant position of the United States in Latin America was not based solely on economic power. In 1903 the political intervention of President Theodore Roosevelt in favour of a separatist movement against the government of Colombia led to the creation of the republic of Panama, which then granted extra-territorial rights to the United States over the zone through which the Panama Canal was later built. For sixty years after the Spanish-American war of 1898 the United States exercised something like a protectorate over Cuba; and during the 1920s American troops intervened in Haiti, Nicaragua and Santo Domingo. After the Second World War, United States intervention was mainly motivated by the desire to suppress communist threats to government, and so to overall American strategic interests. Two examples were Guatemala in 1954 and Santo Domingo in 1965. The relative role played in these events by different agencies of the United States government, and by American business interests, is a matter of controversy: that they increased anti–United States feeling throughout the subcontinent is beyond doubt.

The advent to power of Fidel Castro, which reduced United States influence in Cuba to the naval base of Guantanamo, was followed by an increase of anti–United States nationalism in most republics, especially strong in the intelligentsia and from time to time affecting the governments. The countries least affected were Mexico and Venezuela, whose governments were able to extract increasingly favourable terms from those North American business interests which developed their mineral resources or (as was increasingly preferred) took part in the establishment of secondary industries.

### The Brazilians

While Spanish America broke up into many states, Portuguese America remained united. This may be partly explained by the fact that it consisted, until the late nineteenth century, of a number of settlements close to the coast, and that its sea communications were protected because Portugal, and then independent Brazil, were allies of Britain, the greatest sea power during the critical centuries. Another reason is that, because independent Brazil remained a monarchy under its own emperor, who was the son of a king of Portugal, there was a continuity of personnel and of loyalty in the civil administration and armed forces.

Brazil remained a single state, but it retained a basic division, between its north and south. The north was based on a plantation economy and a black labour force, while in the south first mining and then livestock farming were developed by a growing stream of immigrants from Europe. The problem of slavery (which survived until 1888) did not lead, as in North America, to civil war: here too the cause must largely be sought in the existence of a centralised monarchical administration. Nevertheless, the division between north and south, which resembled perhaps more the situation in Italy than in the United States (with Brazil's *mezzogiorno* in the north), continued to be a grave source of weakness to Brazil.

Immigration into Brazil began in the 1820s, grew fast in the 1870s, reached its peak in the 1890s, and continued on a smaller scale between the world wars and after the Second World War. There were at first large numbers of Portuguese; in the 1870s Germans predominated; and after the mid-1880s the most numerous were Italians. Japanese came in substantial numbers after 1908; and there were also immigrants from Poland and other East European countries. Thus in the Brazilian population, expected in the mid-1970s to surpass 100,000,000, persons of European origin balanced those of African or mulatto provenance. There was no official race discrimination, and not much public expression of racial prejudice, but the relations between white and black and mixed were more complex than appeared on the surface. This will be briefly discussed in chapter 9.

Brazilian politics were not more 'democratic' than those of Brazil's western neighbours, but rather less disorderly. The habit of the rule of law was more firmly founded. From the 1930s Brazilian politics bore some resemblance to those of the Argentine. A type of mass movement, led by nationalist demagogues who offered social reforms, emerged. These movements—under Vargas in Brazil from 1930 to 1945 and from 1951 to 1954, Perón in Argentina from 1945 to 1955, Goulart in Brazil from 1961 to 1964—could not easily be fitted into conventional European political frameworks, but they were closer to fascist than to socialist models. In 1964 military rule was established in Brazil, and internal order and economic progress were pursued with some success, at the price of perpetuating social injustices and leaving the urban and rural oligarchies untouched. There was, however, little doubt of the formation of a Brazilian nation. Immigrants had been absorbed into a national culture based on the Portuguese language and thus easily distinguishable from that of Spanish- or English-speaking neighbours.

## The Canadians

The founders of confederation were both English- and French-speaking. From 1867 onwards French Canadians had two sets of leaders: in the central government and in the province of Quebec. The former were inevitably concerned with the affairs of a vast new country, of small but growing population but of enormous promise: the latter no less inevitably were preoccupied with the preservation of French culture in its peculiar North American form. This difference of priorities was bound to lead to differences of political outlook; and as the party system of Canada, like those of all democratic polities in the late nineteenth and twentieth centuries, became more organised, the voters of Quebec tended to give their allegiance to different parties at the central and the provincial levels.

The population of Quebec province was predominantly French-speaking, but the large business community of Montreal was mainly English-speaking. Thoughtful *Québécois* resented the fact that though political power in the province was in their hands it was the Anglophones who held the economic power. The resentment did not make itself felt as early as one might expect, largely because of the attitude of the Catholic church. The hierarchy and the clergy basically disliked English-speaking rule, but urged loyalty to the British crown. In the 1830s a secular, liberal-minded leadership had emerged from the professional classes which, in defiance of the church, had called for resistance. The fiasco of the Papineu rebellion had reinforced the church's political supremacy. In the 1870s there was bitter conflict between the rather liberal Archbishop Taschereau of Quebec and the ultra-montane Bishop Bourget of Montreal, which led to the foundation of the University of Montreal, in opposition to Laval University in Quebec city (founded 1852) which was accused of liberal deviation from true doctrine. Partly because of these intra-clerical controversies, and partly because of the situation of conflict arising from the presence of its large rich English-speaking minority, Montreal rather than Quebec city became the centre of militant *québécois* nationalism.

From time to time Francophone hostility to Anglophone control of Canada flared up passionately. One occasion was the execution in 1885 of Louis Riel, who had led a revolt in Saskatchewan in which people were killed. He was widely regarded as a martyr, a victim of English oppression of the French. Another occasion was the decision of the government of Ontario in 1913 to stop compulsory teaching of French in the schools of that province. Bitterness on this issue had not died when war broke out in Europe in 1914. Opposition to conscription, for a war in which Britain and France were fighting as allies, greatly increased Francophone nationalism. During the 1920s it remained clear that within Canada, whatever the views of the English-speaking majority, there existed a distinct French-speaking nation.

In 1935 two nationalist groups in Quebec came together to form a new party, *Union Nationale*, led by Maurice Duplessis, who was prime minister of the province from 1936 to 1939 and from 1944 to 1959. Under the Duplessis government the prevalent political attitudes were social conservatism and French nationalism. Despite his anti-Anglophone rhetoric, Duplessis had no objection to capitalist enterprise. American capital flooded the province and some of the new wealth overflowed into the eager hands of Duplessis's ruling team. Subservience to plutocracy, even to the point of large-scale corruption, went with repressive attitudes to labour. This was not uniformly successful. Within the Quebec Catholic church an oppositional trend appeared, in favour of working class interests. Meanwhile the social structure of the *québécois* people was rapidly changing: they were being industrialised, urbanised, educated and subjected to modern secular ideas.

The death of Duplessis in 1959 caused the *Union Nationale* to break up. A new provincial government pursued social reforms and cultural and educational development. These new policies, known as 'the quiet revolution', were not so quiet as the name implied, for a great deal of radical nationalist rhetoric was put forth in these years. Separatism now became an important political force. The central government and the central leadership of the Liberal Party, uneasily aware that for many years the French-speaking population had suffered both from neglect and from encroachments on their cultural rights, began to take seriously a policy of equal status for both languages, as recommended in 1965 in the report of the Royal Commission on Bilingualism and Biculturalism. To the *québécois* extremists, this seemed a waste of time. French culture, they argued, was already doomed outside Quebec: the surviving islands would be engulfed before long by the rising Anglophone flood. The only remedy was to create a separate sovereign state of Quebec. In this state could be incorporated as many as possible of the French-speaking communities that lived close to the existing provincial border, which should be correspondingly extended. The more distant groups would have to choose between Anglicisation and emigration to Quebec. As for the Anglophones in Quebec, they could accept a unilingual French culture, or they could go on living in Montreal as citizens of a foreign state, or they could get out. Quebec itself would then become a sovereign independent state, the second state of wholly French culture in the world.

In the mid-1960s militant Francophone nationalism grew. The separatist cause was given a certain international *cachet* when President de Gaulle of France, invited by the prime minister of Quebec to see the 1967 International Exhibition in Montreal, saw fit to address a crowd with the slogan words, *Vive le Québec libre!* The fact that France had abandoned Quebec in 1763 and 1783, and that official France had never since shown much interest in the fate of the North American French, did not prevent the separatists from making the most of this episode. A separatist party, the *Parti québécois*, was founded in 1968, and obtained 24 per cent of the votes in the provincial election of 29 April 1970. Discontent and prosperity existed side by side. Quebec with 6,000,000 inhabitants, approximately one-third of the population of Canada, had a disproportionately high rate of unemployed; the standard of living in Quebec province was lower than in Ontario; the birth-rate in the province, once higher than in the rest of Canada, was in 1970 5 per cent below the all-Canadian level. All these and other misfortunes the separatists attributed to Anglophones. Particularly resented was the refusal by the central government to permit local education authorities to force all new immigrants to Quebec province to go to schools with French language of instruction: that new Canadians from Italy, Hungary, Germany or Poland should be allowed to live in Montreal and yet choose English rather than French as the future language of their children was felt to be an affront to French civilisation.

In October 1970 a secret separatist organisation, *Front de libération du Québec* (FLQ), which professed a mixture of nationalist, anti-Catholic, anti-capitalist and revolutionary doctrines, kidnapped a British diplomat, and then a minister in the Quebec government, Pierre Laporte. The two men were to be held as hostages until a series of political demands had been met. The Quebec premier, Robert Bourassa, hesitated;[17] but the Canadian premier, Pierre Elliott Trudeau, a man of French birth but two cultures, who held rather radical social views but also believed that governments should rule, not surrender, invoked wartime powers and sent troops into the province.

Trudeau earned the hatred of the separatists, who regarded him as a traitor to the French Canadian people. Many French-speakers continued to vote for him at federal elections, as shown in 1972. Nevertheless René Lévesque's separatist *Parti québécois* steadily gained ground. At the Quebec provincial election in November 1976 it won 41 per cent of the poll, a relative majority, and received 69 out of 110 seats in the assembly. Though commentators eagerly attributed Lévesque's success to his exploitation of economic difficulties rather than to a specific desire of the *Québécois* for sovereign independence (which was belied by some opinion polls), the fact remained that he had won, and that he was committed to a plebiscite on independence within two years.

In the 1970s the single state, stretched along the St Lawrence river and then linked, across the prairies and the Rockies, with the Pacific, still existed, and indeed appeared at first sight to be doing rather well. Its population had surpassed twenty million, and had one of the highest standards of living in the world. Its material resources were enormous, and its industries flourishing. Unfortunately this outwardly prosperous and successful polity suffered from two grave maladies. The first was that the state was the home not of one nation but of a nation-and-a-half. The second was that the flourishing economy was largely owned by citizens of the neighbouring state, with a population ten times the size of its own, from whom it was separated not, like Australia, by an ocean, but by a long land frontier, beyond which everything was very much the same but just a bit bigger and perhaps just a bit better. Canada looked like a second-rate provincial version of the United States. This seemed at least to be true enough to put many of those Canadians who stopped to think about their country in a condition of uneasy irritation.

Canada was not a state of two nations. If it had been so, if English-speaking Canadians had considered themselves one nation and French-speaking Canadians another, it might have been easier to organise a fruitful symbiosis and cooperation between them. But English-speaking Canadians insisted that there was one Canadian nation, to which the French-speakers belonged but in which they must accept a perceptibly lower status. In fact, they simply identified the alleged Canadian nation with themselves. This the French-speaking Canadians refused to accept. They themselves had first been part of the French nation, and then, after the breach with the past which the metropolitan French had made from 1789 onwards, they had grown, under the guidance of their ultra-montane, politically passive but culturally vigorous church, into a new nation. This nation in the twentieth century lost ground in all Canada except Quebec, and increasingly rejected both the cultural leadership and the political passivity of the church. Increasingly, its spokesmen urged that it should concentrate on Quebec, and create an independent state.

If this should happen, there would be bitter territorial problems. There would be dangerous frontier disputes with Ontario and New Brunswick, and painful resettlement problems, affecting hundreds of thousands and causing irreparable economic damage. In the event that this programme could be carried out, with or without large-scale bloodshed, with greater or lesser bitterness and hatred on both sides, where would it leave the English-speaking Canadians? Would a residual Canada continue to exist, a nominally sovereign dependency of the United States? Would the United States wish to incorporate it in the form of another half-dozen or more states? And what sort of sovereignty would independent Quebec possess, under whose protection?

The three-cornered relationship between English-speaking Canadians, French-speaking Canadians and the United States had long been very complex. In the nineteenth century there had been a fourth partner in the game, the British empire, but from 1918 onwards it had dwindled away at an ever accelerating speed. English-speaking and French-speaking Canadians had needed each other to balance United States pressure, though each had from time to time used the United States presence to press the other. Britain too had been used in the balancing act. The *Québécois* considered the British empire the lesser of two evils, at first because the liberal heresies of the British were less pernicious and less dangerous to the true faith than those of the Americans, and later because British capitalism was less frighteningly powerful than American capitalism (though Duplessis was hardly a foe of American capitalism). Nevertheless the *mariage de convenance* of the *Québécois* with the British empire seldom stood much strain. The latent hatred for the English welled up in the Riel affair, and in the bitter refusal to fight England's wars, not only against the Boers but also against the Germans of William II or of Adolf Hitler. It might have been thought that the alliance of Britain and France in two world wars might have consolidated Canada; that the counterweight to the United States might have been not Britain alone, but Britain and France; that the St Lawrence basin might have been oriented towards Western Europe as a whole. Yet this did not happen; nor did the advent of the European Economic Community, with Britain and France in it, seem likely to have this effect.

In its new phase, in the 1960s, *québécois* Anglophobia was directed against both English-speaking Canadians and Americans. It was hard to say which was regarded as the main enemy. Rational process might appear to suggest that America represented the greater danger, and that it was good sense to come to terms with Anglophone Canadians. Irrational nationalist passion, however, would reject any cooperation with any Anglophones even against Satan himself. Some separatists believed that they could make their own terms with the United States: their aim was a sort of partition of Canada between Washington and Montreal. Others believed in a complete independence from all Anglo-Saxons. How much help France would be willing or able to give to a state which made a point of its hostility to the whole Anglo-Saxon world was not easy to predict. Another favourite answer was that Quebec should become a second Cuba. At first sight this is just silly slogan-mongering: the Gulf of St Lawrence and the Caribbean are worlds apart. In another sense however it might make more sense. Cuba in the 1960s exchanged one great power for another as its protector. This same great power was also the only non-Anglophone state in the world for whom the Arctic had vital strategic importance. This orientation towards Russia and Siberia might also become more practical should the communist party obtain power in France and in Iceland.

These open questions must arise from any consideration of Quebec's future, but they belong to a field that transcends the subject of nationalism which is our concern here. Yet mere brief mention of them suggests that the preservation of Canada, the maintenance of the West-East transcontinental axis, the search to make bilingualism a practical reality, and the working out of a relationship with the United States which conformed more genuinely to equal friendship than to satellite status, were objectives worth pursuing and capable of attainment. Possibly Grant's lament for a nation[18] was premature. Possibly the belief in a better, healthier and stronger Canada from ocean to ocean, whose supporters of both languages still far outnumbered the die-hards of Toronto or the *enragés* of Montreal, might still prevail. Perhaps even one day a Canadian nation might become a reality.

**White South Africans**

After two hundred years of Dutch settlement, the language of the majority of white South Africans[19] had begun to diverge significantly from that of the Netherlands. It was in the 1870s that a movement began to gain support which claimed that a new language and a new nation had come into being, which should be called Afrikaans and Afrikaner. The widespread adoption of these names implied not only distinction from Holland but also implicit denial that the English-speakers were 'Africans'. The English-speakers made things easier for the Afrikaner nationalist by clinging fanatically to their Englishness, standing, as it were, on the beach at Durban gazing through telescopes backwards round the Cape of Good Hope towards 'home' and the venerable figure of Queen Victoria. The English-speakers also made it easier by concentrating their efforts on business and ignoring politics, in which Afrikaners became predominant, hardly less in the Cape than in the republics.

The Afrikaner literary revival was pioneered by S. J. du Toit, a *predikant* of the Dutch Reformed Church, of distant French Huguenot descent, and the centre of the movement was the small town of Paarl in Cape Colony. The efforts of du Toit and his friends to make Afrikaans a distinct literary language were successful; but it took some time before the concept of a single Afrikaner nation developed.[20] At first it was in the Orange Free State that national consciousness was strongest, while the prevalent attitude in Transvaal was more narrowly parochial. The victory of Majuba increased the Transvaalers' own consciousness, and the prestige of their republic. However, in the Cape in the 1880s the prevalent trend among the Afrikaans-speakers was liberal rather than nationalist; and the leading Afrikaner politician, Jan Hofmeyr, was able for a time to cooperate with Cecil Rhodes. The Jameson Raid and the Boer War ended this, and cemented the union of the three branches in a single Afrikaner nation. The Milner years did not change the essential situation. The English-speaking or continental *uitlanders* in Johannesburg received their civil rights, and the population of Transvaal became less predominantly Afrikaner; yet the political apathy of these non-Afrikaners, as of the English-speakers in the Cape and Natal, left politics in the new Union of South Africa in Afrikaner hands. Among these politicians three attitudes may be distinguished.

First were those who welcomed membership of the British empire and involvement in world politics, while insisting on the sovereign independence of their country. These men believed in a white South African nation which should include two cultural communities of equal status, each with its own language. This was essentially the view of General Louis Botha, and still more of his successor General Jan Smuts, known as a world statesman. It was the predominant view of the South African Party, formed by a fusion of Afrikaner and English-speaking groups, and led by Smuts. It was able to bring South Africa into both world wars, though the first decision was followed by an armed rebellion of irreconcilable Boers, and the second decision fatally split the party.

The second group wished to make South Africa completely independent of Britain, and wished for no role in world politics. At the same time it, too, believed in a white South African nation of 'two streams', of which neither should seek to impose its domination on the other. This was the view of General J. B. M. Hertzog, who broke with Botha in January 1914 and founded the National Party. Hertzog came to power for a time in 1924, in association with the English-speaking Labour Party. During the 1930s he became much more friendly towards the Smuts group, in 1933 entered a coalition government with them, and in 1934 fused his party with theirs under the name United South African Party. Hertzog was willing to include English-speakers within his concept of an Afrikaner nation. For him the decisive criterion was not language but loyalty. He considered himself a South African patriot and an anti-imperialist. He required of Afrikaners that they should put South Africa first, and not be diverted by any sentimental feeling towards the British empire. This attitude set strict limits to the possibility of cooperation between him and Smuts. In 1939 Smuts never doubted that South Africa must enter the war beside Britain and the other dominions, but Hertzog was for neutrality. He and his followers therefore left the United Party. For a short time he was reunited with the extreme Nationalists, but separated from them again in 1940.

The third group simply identified the South African nation with the Afrikaner nation, and both with Afrikaans-speakers. Persons of English speech might have a place in South Africa for the time being, provided that they accepted Afrikaner political leadership and Afrikaner values; but in the long term they would have to assimilate to Afrikaans culture, or go.

This view was held on the extreme wing of the National Party, which rejected the fusion of 1934, and which far outnumbered the followers of Hertzog from 1939 onwards. The reorganised National Party, led by Dr Daniel Malan, was largely inspired by the elite organisation *Afrikaner Broederbond*, founded in 1919, and making its membership secret from 1922, which set itself not only to develop Afrikaans culture but also to place reliable persons in positions of political and social power. In 1938, following tumultuous celebrations of the centenary of the Great Trek, was founded another secret organisation, *Ossewabrandwag* ('Sentinel of the Ox-waggon', an allusion to the Trek). It appealed to the traditions of the Voortrekkers, but upheld the ideals of Hitler's Germany. Dr Malan disapproved of some of its ideas, but shared its hatred of Britain. When the war had been won by Britain and its Allies, the Nationalists continued to gain support. In the 1948 election they, together with a small remnant of Hertzogites, had an overall majority in parliament. From then onwards the Nationalists were politically supreme.

From the 1950s onwards the centre of the political stage in South Africa was occupied by the conflict between white and black South Africans. However, the conflict between English- and Afrikaans-speakers was latent and unresolved. It can perhaps be better seen in perspective if a brief comparison is made with the situation in Canada.

In both countries an English-speaking community coincided with another community of European origin whose language was not English. In Canada the English-speakers formed a majority; in South Africa they did not. Thus, when the metropolitan British government withdrew, it left the English-speakers dominant over the French-speakers in Canada and the Afrikaans-speakers dominant over the English-speakers in South Africa.

In both countries the English-speakers dominated business life. The two largest centres of English-speaking business, Johannesburg and Montreal, were situated deep inside the region of predominantly non-English speech, though two other large centres, Toronto and Durban, were in the English-speaking region.

Neither *Québécois* nor Afrikaners had received much support from their original homelands. The spoken languages diverged in pronunciation and vocabulary from the metropolitan languages; but whereas the claims of Afrikaans to separate status from Dutch were vigorously pressed, the *mystique* of a single French culture kept a strong hold over the *Québécois*. By contrast, the English of the Canadian English-speakers was strongly influenced by that of the United States.

In both cases the non-English-speaking communities showed a relatively greater talent for politics than the English-speaking. This should not be exaggerated in the Canadian case: Macdonald and Mackenzie King were formidable figures. In the South African case it cannot be exaggerated: even the case for common membership of a single white South African nation was put not by English-speakers but by Afrikaners: Botha, Smuts and the two Hofmeyrs, uncle and nephew.

Both Canada and South Africa were threatened by an external danger, which might have been expected to unite the two communities, to accelerate the process of forging them into a single nation. Both dangers were at first distant and nebulous, but took on more precise shape as time passed.

The danger to Canada was absorption into the United States. In the early nineteenth century the Americans were a hostile neighbour, but were too weak to prevail against the British empire. In the twentieth they were no longer enemies, but had become extremely rich, extremely benevolent and extremely powerful friends. The danger was not of invasion, but of suffocation in an over-affectionate embrace. Canadian business in the 1970s was largely owned by U.S. firms; the cultural fashions and behavior patterns of the United States were forcing themselves on Canadians; and the remaining institutions and habits of mind which still distinguished the Canadian way of life seemed threatened with extinction. The danger was not smaller for the *Québécois*; for if they felt it difficult to preserve their culture in a predominantly Anglophone Canada, how much more difficult would it be to survive within a single continental community.

For South Africa the main perceived danger was from the north, the danger of being engulfed in a flood of black nationalism. As long as the colonial empires stood firm, the danger was minimal; though this did not prevent the obsession of white South Africans with the threat to their racial purity and racial dominance. With the emergence of African national states, the danger was still more verbal than real; but the floods of black nationalist rhetoric were perhaps a portent of real threats to come.

The reactions to the dangers were different in the two countries. In South Africa, African denunciations and international isolation tended to draw English- and Afrikaans-speakers closer together; so that the single white South African nation was paradoxically nearer to achievement under Vorster than in the time of Smuts. In Canada, the growing laments in both languages about the take-over of Canada by United States capitalism coincided with strident demands for a separate republic of Quebec.

## The Australians

It was only in the twentieth century that a distinct Australian nation clearly emerged. In Australia the indigenous inhabitants were reduced to an even smaller and more insignificant proportion of the population than in North America. The overwhelming majority of Australians were English-speaking, but the larger proportion than in Britain of Scottish Presbyterian and Irish Catholic helped to produce a different, and also a more varied, cultural climate. Australians felt no strong need to separate themselves from Britain, and were content to follow Britain's lead in foreign policy in return for Britain's military protection. Surrounded by the ocean, they were not subject, like the Canadians, to the pressures or attractions of a neighbour on land. This made it easier for them than for the English-speaking Canadians to develop along their own lines, in a unique, though varied, natural environment. The Australian who emerged from this slow process was a more distinctive human type than the Canadian, and possessed a more definite national identity.

For most of its history Australian society closely reproduced British society, with the difference that the top levels of the British social pyramid were missing. It is true that some big sheep farmers (graziers) imitated the style of British big landowners; and that successful businessmen closely resembled their British equivalents. Australian universities, and a few private secondary schools, were modelled on British universities and 'public' schools. Until the mid-twentieth century a large number of the most able capitalists and members of the intellectual professions emigrated to England and made careers there. This steady 'brain drain', which was of great benefit to England but a serious loss to Australia, was drastically reduced, though not completely eliminated, after the Second World War. The middle and lower levels of the social pyramid were very similar to their British equivalents, and were steadily reinforced by immigration from Britain. This is not the less true because spoken Australian English differed in vocabulary and pronunciation from British (though rather similar to Cockney speech), and because many Australians delighted in jeering at 'Pommys'. It would be pompous to speak of a love-hate relationship between British and Australians: rather, it was a fairly friendly mutual tolerance, marked by mutual mockery but seldom turning into bitter resentment.

It was the Second World War and the dissolution of the colonial empires which accelerated the growth of Australian national consciousness. Britain was unable to defend Australia against Japan from 1941 to 1945. America took its place, and American political and cultural influences grew thereafter. In the 1950s immigration of continental Europeans, whose language was not English, greatly increased, while American predominance in its turn produced a reaction. More Australians began to understand that they must work out their own relationship with their Asian neighbours, even if this meant allowing at least token immigration from Asia—which hitherto had been completely refused. Japan became Australia's main trading partner, and after the fall of Sukarno it became possible to develop friendly relations with Indonesia, Australia's immediate neighbour with a population of more than 100 million. Australia's business and cultural elite stayed at home, and devoted themselves to making careers in a country of enormous promise. If Australians could realise that they no longer needed to prove, either to themselves or to others, that they were different from, and just as good as, Americans or British; and if they could understand that it is not enough to inherit a 'lucky country' but that it is necessary to make provision, and spend money, for its defence, then a marvellous future awaited them—far happier than seemed likely to be the fate, in the late twentieth century, of the land from which their forefathers had come.

# 6  West Asia and North Africa: Muslim Empires and Modern Nations

## The rise and fall of Muslim empires

The most important ancient civilisations, with developed social and political organisation, known to us in some detail for their buildings, artefacts, inscriptions and documents, arose around the valleys of a few great rivers. Three of these rivers—the Nile, the Euphrates and the Tigris—lay within the region which in the mid-twentieth century became known as the 'Middle East'.[1] The connection between river-based civilisations, artificial irrigation works and the emergence of despotic government systems has been brilliantly explored, if inevitably in a somewhat impressionistic manner, in the theory of 'hydraulic societies' developed by Karl August Wittfogel in his great work *Oriental Despotism*. Two patterns of growth of empire can be distinguished. One was that the state expanded its authority over the territory beyond the central river valley, and came into conflict with another state based on another irrigation system. The second was that the whole territory was conquered, and its administration taken over, by people from beyond its borders, 'barbarians', who then consolidated and expanded still further.

The Mediterranean-Persian Gulf region was for millennia on end the theatre of a struggle for supremacy between Egypt and Mesopotamia. In the mid-sixth century BC Cyrus, king of the Persians, a people of the Iranian plateau, took over Mesopotamia, and his successor Cambyses conquered Egypt. The Persian Archaemenid empire then extended to Turkestan and the borders of India, and included Asia Minor up to the Caucasus. This was the greatest empire yet seen in the Eastern Mediterranean, Persian Gulf and Caspian area. There arose however a new rival centre of power, not based on a river valley or an hydraulic society, in peninsular Greece and the Aegean islands. The Hellenes resisted Persian invasion at the beginning of the fifth century BC; and a century and a half later the Hellenised Macedonian ruler Alexander used the resources and manpower of Greece to conquer Persia and even to reach the boundaries of India. The states into which his empire broke up were later incorporated in the Roman empire, which may be regarded as in some sense the heir to the Persian and pre-Persian hydraulic empires as well as to the city-states of Greece and Italy. The Roman empire's territory was even more extensive than that of its Persian predecessors: it stretched westwards to Morocco and Portugal, north to the Firth of Tay and north-east to the central Danube valley. However, in the east the Romans never subdued Iran. A strong state emerged under the Parthians; and from 226 AD to 642 the Sassanid empire in Iran proved a formidable neighbour, pressing on Rome from the south-east while the Germanic tribes increased their pressure from the north and north-east. In the early seventh century the Sassanid king Khusru Parviz conquered part of Rome's East Mediterranean lands; but this Persian success was very soon reversed by the irruption of the Muslim Arabs from the desert. This led to the formation of an empire which, though it did not last so long as the Roman, covered a territory of similar dimensions.

The peoples of the river valleys worshipped numerous gods, associated with different aspects of life in settled society; the peoples of mountainous lands imagined various gods sitting above the mist on the high peaks; the peoples of forests found them behind trees or in springs or lakes. The vision of a single God came from pastoral peoples, who spent much of their lives looking up to a clear sky.[2] All three great monotheistic religions of mankind came out of the edge of the desert between the Nile and the Euphrates: first Judaism, then Christianity more than a thousand years later, and six hundred years later still Islam.

Unlike its two predecessors, Islam was a religion that encouraged holy war and territorial expansion. Whether because they had military leaders of exceptional brilliance, or new methods of the use of cavalry and camels in war, or because the ruling elites of the eastern Roman empire were exhausted (less than a hundred years since the tremendous campaigns of Justinian and less than two decades after the efforts of Heraclius on two fronts, against Slavs and Persians); or because in the three centuries since Constantine made it the official religion, Christianity had lost its hold over the peoples of the eastern Mediterranean; or for all these reasons and others too, the Muslims advanced victoriously in all directions: across North Africa into Spain, into Asia Minor, and through Iran to the valleys of Central Asia.[3]

This great Muslim empire was torn by dissension from its first years. Rivalry between the followers of the Umayyad family, to which belonged the fourth caliph, Uthman, the Prophet's father-in-law, and the followers of the Prophet's son-in-law, Ali, the fifth caliph, led to a split into the two great branches of *Sunna* and *Shia*.[4] In 750 a revolt, based on Mesopotamia and Iran, overthrew the Umayyad dynasty of caliphs based on Damascus. The victorious dynasty of the Abbasids, descendants of the Prophet's paternal uncle, came to power largely through the support of the Shi'is or followers of the descendants of Ali, but once in power they gave their support to the Sunnis, who remained the orthodox majority in the Muslim world from then onwards. The *Shia* split in turn into a number of sects, which at different times won support in different parts of Persia, Mesopotamia and North Africa. These sects expressed varying combinations of religious, social and regional discontent, and even established themselves for considerable periods of time as strong territorial powers.

Nevertheless, for about three hundred years there was a more or less united Muslim empire and a caliph recognised as the successor of the Prophet and supreme ruler of Muslims, with a great new civilisation; and at first sight a plausible case can be made for describing both the empire and the civilisation as Arab. The original Muslim conquerors were Arabs, nomads from the desert and merchants from a remote part of the peninsula. They established their rule over settled populations which were heirs to thousands of years of civilisation, layer upon layer of rich and diverse cultures. The Arab conquerors became the lords of these civilised peoples, and gave to them their faith and their language.

It was not their fixed intention to convert their subjects. Christians and Jews were allowed to practise their own religion, in return for the payment of taxes from which Muslims were exempt. As the Muslim rulers needed revenue, they even had an interest in preserving large non-Muslim communities among their subjects. However the new faith spread rapidly, whether because Muslim preachers could not restrain their enthusiasm or because Christians were disillusioned with their spiritual leaders and longed for a new truth, or for other reasons. The institutions, laws and habits of thought which emerged were certainly derived in part from earlier times, but the contribution of Muslim doctrines and social patterns was also profound and lasting.

The Arabic language was well developed for poetry and rhetoric before Muhammad. With the advent of the Prophet it became a sacred language, in which the Koran and other sacred texts were expressed. All over the Muslim world, religious learning was thereafter acquired through the Arabic language. More than this, spoken Arabic gradually became the language of the people in the central and western lands. Syriac and Aramsic disappeared, Coptic was reduced to being the liturgical language of the surviving Christian minority in Egypt, and the Berber dialects of northwestern Africa were banished from the coastal plains into the mountains. Only Persian in the east, and Turkish in the north survived as major languages of Islam, but both received a massive injection of Arabic words, not only of religious concepts and political-administrative terms but also of abstract notions in general. Arabic literature extended from poetry and religious teaching to numerous highly sophisticated works of law, history, philosophy, mathematics and natural science. Thus the new civilisation was inextricably interwoven with the Arabic language; and yet it is a historical distortion to speak of an Arab empire created by an Arab nation. Families descended from pure Arabs, who could trace their descent back to Arabia, enjoyed for the first period a superior status and prestige; but in the course of time they became merged in the much larger Arabic-speaking population, whose ancestors had been Copts or Phoenicians or Berbers or Greeks or Latin Spaniards or Visigoths. The essence of the civilisation was not Arab but Muslim; and Islam transcended the boundary between the religious and the secular which is part of European Christian thinking.

The Baghdad caliphate began to lose most of its authority in the tenth century. This process was connected with the reassertion of Persian culture, which led to the loss of control from Baghdad over the Iranian lands; with the increasing importance of Turkish mercenaries; and with the movement westwards of whole tribes of Turks, converted to Islam. New centres of power, and new states, emerged within the Muslim world, but they cannot be compared to the stable sovereign states which emerged in Catholic Christendom. Each of their rulers claimed to be the sole true ruler of Islam rather than the ruler of a specific territory; and none of these states survived for very long in a stable form.

Already in the eighth century Muslim Spain seceded, and its ruler, who came of the Umayyad family, claimed to be the true successor to the caliphate of Damascus, usurped by the Abbasids. The Spanish caliphate of Cordoba later broke up into a series of smaller principalities. In Iran and Asia Minor the Seljuk Turks established a strong state in the eleventh century, but they claimed to be acting in the name of the caliph, who still resided in Baghdad without any power. In North Africa another powerful state arose at the end of the tenth century under the Fatimids, who were Shi'is, claimed to be descended from the Prophet's son-in-law Ali, and sought authority over the whole Muslim world. The Fatimids conquered Egypt, and set up a powerful state based on their new capital of Cairo. After Fatimid and Seljuk power had declined, and the invasions of the European crusaders and of the Mongols had been repulsed, a new state emerged in Egypt, under the dynasty of Mamluks, soldiers of slave birth, originating in Central Asia or the Caucasus or southern Russia. This was the strongest state in the Muslim world in the late thirteenth and fourteenth centuries, and its authority was legitimised by the presence in Cairo of a descendant of the caliph of Baghdad, which had fallen in 1258 to the Mongols. Another Muslim state also emerged in the Volga valley, where the Tatar successors to the Mongol conquers adopted Islam, and flourished in the fourteenth century.

Meanwhile a small Turkish tribe, the Osmanlis, settled in western Asia Minor on the Byzantine border, grew steadily stronger, acquired land on the European mainland, conquered a large part of the Balkans and in 1453 captured Constantinople. Its sultan Selim in 1517 conquered Syria and Egypt, and in the sixteenth century the Ottoman empire emerged as a new universal empire of Islam, as extensive as the early Umayyad and Abbasid caliphates. Its supremacy remained until the nineteenth century. It did not however rule all Muslim lands. In the mid-sixteenth century the Russian tsar of Muscovy conquered the Tatar states of the Volga valley. At the end of the fifteenth century a new Shia empire emerged in Iran, under Shah Ismail. In the far west, a Moroccan kingdom remained independent of Ottoman authority. Finally, the Moghul empire was established over the greater part of India by the middle of the sixteenth century, and also had two hundred years of power, until it succumbed to British conquest.

The history of the Muslim lands, in terms of state power, may be viewed as the disintegration of the universal empire of Baghdad; the rise and fall of several dynasties, most of which claimed to be the only true successor of the universal empire; and the restoration of a second universal empire—the Ottoman—even more powerful than the first. None of the states of the period 1000-1500 resembled the consolidated secular sovereign states of early modern Europe; not even Egypt, of which it may be argued that a certain continuity of government was preserved from the Ptolemies to the Mamluks.

## The revival of Iran

In this brief survey, the emphasis has inevitably been on the lands of Arabic speech—Syria, Egypt and North Africa. However, despite the conquest by the Muslims, the culture of Iran maintained a continuity with the past, and developed on different lines, which must now be considered.

The Iranian state is 2,500 years old, second in antiquity only to the Chinese, yet its existence has been interrupted for long periods. One can hardly argue that an Iranian nation continuously grew, together with the process of formation of the state, as was the case with the French, Scots and English, or with the Russians and the Japanese. Perhaps a better parallel would be with the Greeks, whose history is about as old and also had periods of breach in the tradition. Yet the history of Hellas is that of a civilisation, not of a state. Classical Greece was not encompassed by one state; the empire of Macedon lasted but a few decades; and the Byzantine state considered itself to be the Roman empire—its people spoke Greek, but they were *Romaioi*, not Hellenes. In Iranian history, too, there was a great civilisation (even if the Hellenes called it 'barbarian'), but it is the state that is the dominant feature. Though the state's existence was interrupted, first by Alexander and then by Islam, the idea of the state—the Persian historical mythology—survived, and played its part in the emergence of the modern nation. In this the Iranians perhaps resembled the Serbs, whose medieval state was destroyed but left a memory in poetry: the *narodne pesme* are the equivalent of the *Shahname*. Both the Parthian and the Sassanid rulers claimed descent from the Acheamenids; and both consciously strove to maintain the religion and the culture of their distant predecessors, though the content of the culture and in particular its language had changed considerably.

The Muslim invasion and conquest of Iran, which was completed approximately between 637 and 651 AD, was followed by the settlement of considerable numbers of Arabs, especially in the province of Khurasan, to the south-east of the Caspian Sea. Those who remained loyal to the Zoroastrian religion were treated on the whole more harshly than the Christians or Jews, and many of them emigrated to Gujarat, in Western India. During the following century or more, the great majority of Iranians became Muslims. The movement which led to the overthrow of the Umayyads by the Abbasids in 750 started in Khurasan, and both Arabs and Iranians played active parts in it. Though the Abbasid victory was not a victory of Iranians over Arabs, there is no doubt that an element of Persian culture was injected into Muslim civilisation in the Abbasid period: this change was symbolised by the movement of the caliph's capital from Damascus to Baghdad on the Tigris, near to the old Sassanid Iranian capital of Ctesiphon. It is also arguable that the strength, from this time onwards, of Shi'ism in Iran, together with the adjacent Arabic-speaking part of Mesopotamia (Iraq), had something to do with the difference between Iranians and Arabs, though it is an anachronism and an oversimplification to regard Shi'ism, either then or later, as a 'national religion' of Iran.

At the time of the Arab invasion, several variants of Iranian speech were in use in Iran, of which the most important were Pahlavi, the official language of the priesthood and of government, and *dari*, the spoken language of the region around Ctesiphon, the capital. With the triumph of Islam, Pahlavi fell into disuse, but the spoken language extended eastwards, increasingly displacing the other Iranian languages as far as Khurasan and Central Asia, and at the same time changing its nature by the absorption of a very large number of Arabic words. In the ninth and early tenth centuries Arabic was the language of culture in Iran, and the educated class (whether indigenous or Arabian in origin) became bilingual, writing or reading Arabic and speaking Persian. Gradually however a new literary Persian language arose, based on Persian vernacular and Arabic, rather as English arose from Anglo-Saxon and French. First oral and then written poetry emerged in this language. Lyric poetry had a very high proportion of Arabic words and closely followed Arabic literary models; but in epic narrative poetry, which was an indigenous Persian *genre*, there was a marked preference for Persian words, even for abstract notions, to some extent consciously derived from the ancient language. Persian epic poetry reached its climax at the hands of the great poet Firdausi, who was born probably between 932 and 942 and died between 1020 and 1026. His *Shahname* ('Book of Kings') not only was a literary masterpiece, but also formed the foundation of Iranian historical mythology, for it put together all that was then known or believed about the history of the past Persian empires. Its importance in the formation of an Iranian national consciousness cannot be overestimated.

The revival of Persian literature and of pride in Persian culture was promoted by the weakening of the Abbasid caliphate. In Iran independent principalities emerged. During this period the people of Iran came into close contact with the Turkish people of Central Asia. Whole Turkish tribes moved south and west. Some were pagan, others had already nominally accepted Islam. They gradually became absorbed in Muslim civilisation, and were intermingled with the Persians in Iran and the Arabs in Syria and eastern Asia Minor. The most successful were the Seljuks, who in the eleventh century created an empire extending over Iran, Iraq and most of Asia Minor, with its two great cultural centres at Isfahan in central Iran and Konya in Anatolia. The Seljuk sultans were Sunni, and recognised the Abbasid caliph in Baghdad. They and their soldiers were Turks by origin and by speech, but they admired and encouraged Persian culture, and many of their administrators and advisers were Persians. Persian became the cultured language of the northern half of the Muslim world, the vehicle of literature and science. There developed a symbiosis of Persians and Turks which recalls that between Greeks and Latins in the Roman empire. It continued after the fall of Seljuk power, and remained after the great thirteenth century Mongol invasion, in the states created in Iran by the Ilkhans, successors to the Mongols, and by the successors of the last great Central Asian conqueror Timur in the fifteenth century.

All this time there were states in Iran, but no great Persian state, yet the national identity of the Persians was latent, and was nourished by a continuously vigorous literature which produced several truly great poets, and by a living historical mythology. In the sixteenth century there came into being a great Persian empire. It was founded by an Azeri Turk named Ismail, leader of a religious sect which dated from the early fourteenth century, had long been confined to the Ardabil district of the north-west, and merged with Shi'ism in the mid-fifteenth. Ismail in 1501 conquered all Azerbaidjan and proclaimed himself in Tabriz as shah of Iran. In the next ten years he brought most of the Iranian lands under his rule, from southern Mesopotamia to the Oxus. This was not only a military and political triumph, but also a religious enterprise. Social discontents and Iranian national feeling played their part in the movement. Ismail's *kizilbash* ('red head') missionaries penetrated Asia Minor, arousing the wrath of the Ottoman Sultan Selim I, who defeated Ismail at the battle of Chaldiran in 1515. However, the new empire preserved its Iranian conquests, and Ismail's successors, known as the Safavid dynasty, became less zealous in religion and more interested in the strengthening of secular power.

The Safavid empire was multi-national and multi-religious. There were two main languages, Persian and Turkish: there were Persian-speaking cities and Turkish-speaking cities, Persian-speaking pastoral tribes and Turkish-speaking pastoral tribes. The subjects of the Safavids also included two distinct Christian communities, each with its own languages: the orthodox Georgians and the monophysite Armenians. In the southwest there were Arabs. Shi'i Islam was predominant, but there were also Sunni, and these included persons of Persian, Turkish and Arabic speech. These varied peoples were united by a powerful dynasty, and their educated elites shared a pride in Persian culture and in the Persian past. The Safavid empire reached its climax in the reign of Shah Abbas I (1588-1629), whose efficient government and justice, and magnificent buildings at Isfahan, won the admiration of travellers from most parts of the civilised world.

## European domination

The crusader states created in Syria by European invaders in the twelfth century were an ephemeral episode, and the Muslims placed under Christian rule by the *Reconquista* in Spain were either absorbed or expelled. From the sixteenth century onwards, however, substantial Muslim populations began to be conquered by Christian states, and to go on living under Christian rule while remaining Muslims.

The first example is central Russia. After Ivan the Terrible of Muscovy had captured Kazan (1552) and Astrakhan (1555), large numbers of Tatars became his subjects. They were subjected from time to time to incentives or persecution to make them Christian. Some, especially in the upper classes, were converted, but the great majority were not; and from the time of Empress Catherine II (1762-96) pressure was greatly reduced if not completely eliminated. In the nineteenth century the Russians conquered much larger territories, in Transcaucasia and in Central Asia, with compact Muslim populations.

The major conquerors of Muslims were the Dutch in Indonesia and the British in northern India: it is true that the latter was not a region of predominantly Muslim population, but most of it was subject to Muslim rulers and many millions of Muslim people lived there. French conquest of Muslims began with Napoleon's ephemeral seizure of Egypt in 1798, but was followed by the conquest of Algeria from 1830 onwards and by the French protectorate over Tunisia in 1881 and Morocco in 1912. The British set up their protectorate in Egypt in 1882. In the colonies carved out of

Africa by the European powers were also many Muslims.

At the same time the two most important Muslim empires, the Ottoman and the Persian, though not placed under direct Christian rule, were objects of frequent intervention by European powers, as a result of which they lost not only some territories but also a large part of their internal sovereignty. Their condition has been well described as 'semi-colonial'. Something must be briefly said of the way in which this came about.

In the nineteenth century, as not only Western goods but Western ideas penetrated Muslim lands, resentment of European domination spread. It took somewhat different forms in those lands ruled by Europeans and in the still sovereign Muslim empires.

As the number of European merchants in oriental markets increased, from the sixteenth century onwards, their presence raised difficult legal problems. The Ottoman sultans and Iranian shahs at first welcomed them, since the trade which they brought was lucrative. They were therefore willing to offer them favourable working conditions. In 1535 Suleiman the Magnificent, the most powerful of all the Ottoman monarchs, made a treaty with François I, king of France, under which civil and criminal cases affecting French subjects were to be judged, according to French law, by French consuls. This was the first of the 'capitulations' granted to Europeans. In 1583 British subjects received similar rights. In 1600 Shah Abbas I, the most powerful of the monarchs of the Safavid dynasty, granted similar rights to British subjects in an agreement made with Sir Anthony Sherley. During the eighteenth century all the main European powers obtained capitulation agreements in Turkey.

These were originally agreements made between equals. However, as the balance of military and economic power changed to the overwhelming advantage of the West, they became in effect guarantees of foreign domination, increasingly resented by the Turks and Iranians. European citizens often, though not always, treated the people of the host nation arrogantly. Ottoman and Iranian rulers were keen to introduce those European innovations which they expected to strengthen their economies and their armed forces; and as these were expensive, they borrowed money from Western banks. Western capital thus began to obtain a stranglehold over some of their resources. The Iranian government became indebted to British and Russian banks, and foreigners were placed in charge of the Customs, or appointed as advisers to the Iranian Ministry of Finance. The Western economic stranglehold became especially tight in Egypt, where Khedive Ismail, who was no more than a nominal vassal of the Ottoman sultan, pursued reckless financial policies, combining useful works of modernisation with extravagant expenditures on personal luxuries, and being ruthlessly squeezed by his creditors in both types of enterprise.[5] In 1876 the *Caisse de la Dette* was set up, enabling the representatives of European creditors to control a large part of Egyptian revenues; while in the field of justice, the old consular courts were replaced by the mixed tribunals, under which European judges were able to interfere widely in the whole system of Egyptian courts of law. The obvious dependence of Egypt on foreigners provoked the nationalist rebellion of Arabi Pasha, which led to the military occupation of Egypt by the British.

## Islamic modernism and Panislamism

Muslims disliked being directly ruled by infidels, but accepted the facts. The great majority had always been accustomed to despotic government. The new European rulers were in some ways better than the old. The interests of the peasants were directly damaged only when, as in the Bashkir lands in the eighteenth century, in Algeria from the end of the nineteenth and in Turkestan in the first years of the twentieth, Russian or French settlers began to take their lands. As for the ruling classes, a good deal of wealth and power was left to them, and their religion was not attacked. The conquerors wished on the whole to preserve things as they were, but in the course of time the penetration of European industrial goods and of European ideas made this impossible.

The old intellectual elite, the Muslim *ulema*, tended at first simply to reject the new ideas as impious. But there grew up alongside it a new intellectual elite, of persons who had received a European-type education, at first just a few sons of the upper classes but gradually also a substantial number from humbler origins. Some of these simply repudiated the Muslim world, and adopted the most advanced European ideas of their time. Most, however, tried in some degree to combine new ideas and old beliefs to modernise Islamic society and doctrine. Their attitude to the West was ambivalent. To some extent, they admired the ideas and institutions of the West, and wished to westernise their own societies and to develop friendship with Western peoples. To some extent they wished to acquire Western skills in order to make their peoples strong, so that they could fight against the European Christians and drive them out of their countries.

An early Islamic westerniser was Sayyid Ahmad Khan (1817-98), an Indian Muslim who already as a young man founded modern schools. After the Indian Mutiny of 1857,[6] which was among other things a confrontation between the traditional Islamic elite and the British, Sayyid Ahmad actively promoted European-type education through the medium of the Urdu language. He founded in 1875 the Anglo-Oriental College at Aligarh, which was modelled on a Cambridge college. Sayyid Ahmad considered himself a good Muslim, but in the eyes of the orthodox his doctrines were full of heresy. He was concerned with the fate of all Muslim peoples but in the first place with those of India. He was an Indian patriot, but was also concerned to defend Indian Muslims against eventual Hindu domination.

The second place in which Islamic modernism became a force was the Russian empire. The most active were the Tatars of the Volga valley. Here there existed a substantial merchant class, who largely managed the land-borne trade between European Russia and Central Asia, and some of whom built quite large fortunes. These rich Tatars spent some of their money on founding schools based on 'new principles': the Arabic word *jadid* ('new') gave the modern schools movement the name by which it became known in Russia. There was a genuine demand among the Tatars for knowledge such as could not be obtained from the traditional Muslim schools (*medrese*) which taught Koranic law. There arose in the last decades of the nineteenth century a new intellectual elite of school teachers who spread European learning, and also European democratic ideas, including the most un-Muslim idea of the emancipation of women. The Tatars continued however to be faithful Muslims: they engaged in a fierce, and rather successful, competition with the Russian Orthodox church for the conversion of the smaller pagan peoples who inhabited part of the Volga and Urals area. The movement in the Russian empire for the modernising of Islam, and the interest among Muslims in modern political and social ideas, were not confined to the Volga Tatars. Similar trends were to be found in the Crimea and Azerbaidjan, and in the first years of the twentieth century the *jadid* schools began to spread even to the Kazakh steppes and Turkestan, though in both these regions they only affected a very small number. All this activity alarmed the Russian authorities, who were much afraid of Panislamism. However, the emphasis in the movement was now beginning to change, from the idea of solidarity of Muslims in the world to the narrower concept of solidarity of peoples of Turkish speech.

Panislamism became a more serious force towards the end of the nineteenth century in the Ottoman empire, after Sultan Abdulhamid had repressed the constitutional movement and was looking for some way of winning support for his internal and foreign policies from a wider Muslim public. In his efforts to spread a kind of Panislamism which would strengthen his regime, he received some help from a mysterious personage, who has been the subject of a large literature, and whose true character still remains obscure. This was Jamal al-Din al-Afghani (1839-97), either an Afghan or a Persian by birth, who spent his life travelling round the Muslim world and Europe, fluent in many languages, possessing personal magnetism, appearing to some a pious Muslim to others an atheist, professing at times devotion to autocracy, at others the most radical democratic views, taking money from the sultan and the shah of Persia, the governments of the French Republic and the Russian tsar, asking but not getting funds from the British Embassy in Constantinople; an inexplicable mixture of mystic, adventurer, political agitator and prophet. Perhaps all that can be said of him with certainty is that most of the leaders of resistance to European domination in the Muslim world in the first third of the twentieth century felt themselves to be direct or indirect disciples of Jamal al-Din.

This is especially true of Egypt, where Muhammad Abduh (1849-1905) came under his influence while he was still studying at Al-Azhar University in Cairo in 1869. Abduh was involved in the resistance to the British in 1882 by Arabi Pasha, and was thereafter exiled for six years. He was allowed to return to Egypt in 1888, paradoxically as a result of British pressure on his behalf. He made a good career in Muslim law, and became chief *mufti* of Egypt from 1899 until his death. He was prominent as an adapter of Islam to modern needs, though there are grounds for thinking that he was himself, like Jamal al-Din, an atheist. The main idea which he left to his disciples was not so much Panislamism as Egyptian nationalism. The first prominent nationalist politician in Egypt was Mustafa Kamil (1874-1908), who founded a National Party in 1907. From this beginning developed, after the First World War, the *Wafd*, the great mass nationalist Egyptian movement, led by Saad Zaghlul Pasha. Abduh also had influence in Algeria, where there emerged in the 1920s a puritanical nationalist movement of so-called reforming *ulema*, in opposition to the trend which was already making itself felt for educated Algerians of Muslim birth to forsake Islam for the attractions of French civilisation.

By the 1920s there was not much left of the Panislamic dream which had at times so much alarmed the Russian, British (Indian) and French governments. In its place, however, other forces had appeared. One was nationalism based on a clearly identifiable territory: such were Egyptian, Algerian and Tunisian. The second was the attempt to identify nationality with language, though this must mean that existing territorial boundaries would be transcended. The three languages were Turkish, Persian and Arabic. The concept of a Turkish nation revolutionised the whole conception of the Ottoman empire, and it also potentially affected peoples of related Turkic speech within the Russian empire, Iran, Afghanistan and even China. The identification of the Iranian nation with persons of Persian speech conflicted to some extent with the notion of the unity of all Shi'i Muslims, and also raised the question of the loyalty of Turkic-speakers within Iran and of Persian-speakers outside Iran. The concept of an Arab nation was the most difficult of all, affecting the largest number of people, who shared one Arabic language but were spread out over a vast area from the Atlantic to the Persian Gulf.

As far as the active nationalists, and the politically conscious population as a whole, were concerned, it was these three national concepts which prevailed in the next fifty years, and they will now be briefly considered in turn. However, it still remained true that in the mind of the vast majority in all these lands the main difference between them and their foreign rulers or dominators was that they were Muslims. Even after independence had been achieved, religion remained, side by side with language, as the identifying mark.

## The Iranians

The Safavid empire broke down in the eighteenth century, and Iran was at the mercy of Afghan invaders. In 1796 Aga Muhammad, like Ismail a man of Turkish speech, established his rule over most of Iran, and founded the Qajar dynasty. It was his misfortune that his rise to power coincided with the emergence in the vicinity of Iran of two great European powers: Russia, which in 1801 annexed Georgia and embarked on a career of conquest in the Caucasus and Central Asia, and Britain, which in the same years consolidated its Indian empire and came to dominate the Persian Gulf. In the nineteenth century Persia escaped conquest or physical partition only because British and Russian power and mutual distrust balanced each other. Their rivalry enabled Iranian rulers to some extent to play them off against each other, but this policy had narrow limits: Britain was not prepared to fight Russia in order to restore Transcaucasia to Persia, nor Russia to fight Britain in order to give Herat to the shah. The Anglo-Russian balance of power served chiefly to preserve Iran in a condition of social and cultural stagnation.

However, towards the end of the nineteenth century modern ideas began to penetrate, through the influence of Iranians of the upper classes who had travelled abroad, through the Christian-influenced new religious sect of the Babis, and through the activities of the versatile Jamal al-Din al-Afghani. Oppositional periodicals were published in Persian in London, Calcutta and Istanbul. At the end of the century also Western capitalist enterprise began to penetrate Iran on a more serious scale, and this provoked hostility from both conservative and modernist opinion: from the first as a threat by infidels to Islamic ways, from the second as attempts to enslave the people of Iran to foreign business. The first effective protest was the agitation from 1890 to 1892 against Nasiruddin Shah's granting of a tobacco curing and sale monopoly to a British company. Under pressure, the shah withdrew the concession.

This success for incipient nationalism did not long hold up Western economic penetration. Government debts to foreigners caused the Iranian customs revenue to be placed under foreign control, and growing imports of Western goods damaged Iranian merchants. At the turn of the century there was a growth of more or less secret associations (*anjuman*). These had long existed, but had been little more than local groupings of friends or professional associates to discuss things of common interest: now they took on a more political character, and persons influenced by modern political ideas played a more active part in them. Tabriz, the first capital of the Safavids, situated in Turkish-speaking Azerbaidjan on old trade routes towards Asia Minor and the Caucasus, was a still more important centre than Tehran, the Qajar capital. Tabriz lay near the Russian border, and at least its upper social stratum were both aware of the Russian threat to Iranian independence and influenced by the radical political ideas which were then stirring in Russian Transcaucasia.

The Constitutional Movement (*mashrutiyat*) first burst into public life on 13 December 1904, when two thousand prominent persons, mainly learned Muslim doctors (*ulema*) and bazaar merchants, retired to a mosque in a Tehran suburb to 'take refuge' (*bast*), refusing to come out until some promises of equal justice were made and some unpopular ministers dismissed. This threat, a strange procedure to non-Iranian minds, was at first effective. However, the shah's promises of reform were not kept, and in July 1906 a second *bast* took place. It was on a larger scale, and affected two distinct though allied groups: merchants and intellectual secular reformers, who took refuge in the British Embassy compound in Tehran (with the consent of the *chargé d'affaires*) and religious leaders, who went in solemn procession to the holy city of Qum nearly a hundred miles south of the capital. This time the protesters demanded a Constitution and an elected Assembly (*majlis*). The shah again yielded, and the Assembly met in October 1906.

Cooperation between shah and *majlis* did not last long. On 3 June 1908 the shah's elite armed force, a Cossack battalion trained and commanded by a Russian officer, bombarded the *majlis* building. By this time the original unity between the religious and secular opposition, between the traditional elite and the modernist elite, had broken down. One of the Muslim notables, Shaikh Fazlullah Nuri, supported the shah's counter-revolution. In Tabriz however the radicals, organised in a committee of political *anjumans* and led by Sayyid Hassan Taqizadeh, held out. Events and opinions in Tabriz were much influenced by the events then in course in Russia, and there was some contact between Tabriz revolutionaries and the socialist movements in Russian Azerbaidjan and the city of Baku. Russian government troops, at the shah's request, besieged Tabriz in April 1909 and captured it, but there developed in southern Iran a strange alliance between the democrats and the chiefs of the Bahtiyari tribe of the Zagros mountains. In July 1909 the Bahtiyaris captured Tehran, enabling the democrats to hang Shaikh Fazlullah Nuri.

After this the politics of Iran entered a confused and stagnant period. With help from the Russian government and from Russian-trained Persian troops, the shah to some extent reasserted his authority. He was dependent on the good will of the tribes and on the balance between Russian and British influence. The British had some sympathy for the reformers, the Russians for the reactionaries; but as each needed the other's alliance in the imminent struggle against Germany in Europe, neither was prepared to go too far in antagonising the other's *protégés*. When war came in Europe, Iran was a happy hunting ground for emissaries of all the belligerents, not least of the Germans, who had the advantage of being enemies of both Britain and Russia which Iranian patriots had come to dislike profoundly. Revolution in Russia and defeat of Germany left Britain for a short time in the strongest position; but despite the bold plans of Lord Curzon the British public was in no mood for further imperial ventures, and so Iran escaped from further subjection. Meanwhile the conflict between the old and the new elite, between xenophobe Muslim theocracy and modernising secular democratic nationalism, remained unresolved.

In the end neither the old nor the new elite won: both were defeated by an enterprising soldier, the Russian Cossack-trained Reza Khan, who seized power in February 1921 and made himself shah in December 1925, proclaiming a new Pahlavi dynasty. Reza modelled himself to some extent on Kemal Atatürk. He made great efforts to modernise the economy and culture of Iran. He did not replace the Arabic by the Latin alphabet, but he did encourage the replacement of many Arabic words by neologisms adapted from Persian roots. He saw himself as a protector of the people against the upper classes, but the dictatorial rule which he imposed bore more heavily on the poor than the rich. He fought the religious establishment (though less bitterly than did Atatürk). Above all, he set himself to develop a militant secular Iranian national consciousness. Like Atatürk, he stressed the pre-Islamic past. He did not attack Muslim beliefs as such, but he insisted that Iranian culture was much older than Islam, and that this great culture, and memory of the glorious Persian empires, must be the foundation of Iranian national consciousness. In this he had substantial success: he had the advantage that the glorious Persian past was real, whereas Atatürk's much vaunted Turkish past (with the exception of the pre-Turkish Hittites and the only partly-Turkish Seljuk and Ottoman cultures) was largely an invention. His version of Iranian national consciousness was spread by a growing, though still rather sparse, network of schools. It was in part a measure of his success that a fairly large modern-minded Iranian intellectual elite came into existence, of whom the great majority loathed him and his ways because he denied the political freedoms which western-type education had taught them to desire.

Reza Shah had the misfortune to fall foul simultaneously of Churchill's Britain and Stalin's Russia: he made the mistake of believing that Iran's two traditional enemies would be defeated by Hitler's Germany. In 1941 British and Soviet forces occupied Iran, and Reza was deported. The first years of the reign of his son, Muhammad Reza Shah, were uncomfortable. First the Soviet forces encouraged the formation of separatist states among the Azeri Turks and the Kurds of the north-west; and soon after Soviet troops had been withdrawn (by a combination of American atomic diplomacy and diplomatic sharp practice conducted by his prime minister, Qavam es-Sultaneh), Muhammad Reza was involved in a conflict with the British government about the nationalist mass movement which placed the shah in the position of being denounced as an agent of foreign powers, and in August 1953 led to his flight abroad for some days. However, when the crisis was over, he returned, and in the next twenty years showed himself to be an outstandingly able ruler. In this he was helped first by the military support and economic assistance of the United States, and second by the abundant oil resources of Iranian soil, but his success was also due to his own skill and courage.

Essentially he continued the work of his father. He set himself to destroy all rival sources of authority. The Muslim religion was firmly supported, but the *ulema* were allowed no share in secular power. This antagonised not only the learned Muslim dignitaries but also many pious bazaar merchants, but they were forced to yield. The tribes were brought under central control, at the cost of injustice to their leaders and hardship to the Qashgai or Turcoman nomads who were forced into a sedentary existence. More important still, the great landowners were forced to give up their lands. This had two important consequences. It improved the material conditions of a large part, though by no means all, of the Iranian peasants, and won their gratitude. It also replaced the power of the landowners, until then a series of local despots ruling as they saw fit, by a centralised bureaucracy. More important even than the industrial progress achieved under Muhammad Reza Shah was his creation in Iran of a modern apparatus of state. This was buttressed by an efficient system of coercion, a very well-equipped and numerous army owing allegiance to him directly, and most efficient security police (*Savak*). Through the state apparatus, through the means of publicity and through the school system, he set himself to mobilise the rural masses into the nation, and to develop an Iranian national consciousness, intended not to deny but to comprehend Islam, placing Islam in the wider context of Iranian culture.

Several millions of Iranian citizens were Turkish, not Persian, by speech. It did not however follow from this that they did not consider themselves Iranians. Azeri Turks were Shi'is, as were Persians, while the Turks of Asia Minor were Sunni. During the Soviet-sponsored regime in Azerbaidjan there seemed to be more interest in social reform, promised by the (communist) Democratic Party, than in Azeri nationalism or separation from Iran. The Kurds continued to cherish the hope of independence and unity, but they were better treated over the years by the Iranian than by the Iraqi or

Turkish governments. The most potentially disloyal non-Persian community were probably the Arabs in Khuzistan, living near the Iraqi border in oil-producing lands and an object of dispute between the two states.

Another element of potential weakness was, by the same paradox as obtained in the reign of Reza Shah, the modern-educated intellectual elite. Created by the modernising policies of the two shahs, they were as disaffected and alienated from the regime as the intelligentsia of Russia under the last three tsars, and for similar reasons. It is perhaps worth noting that many Iranian intellectuals of the left were children of landowning families which had suffered from the shah's land reform. In the early 1970s many intellectuals in Iranian cities, and many Iranian students abroad, were bitter enemies of the shah, who appeared not only to have Iran in his firm grip but also to be holding out to his subjects a concept of a modern Iranian nation which many found acceptable.

## The Turks

The words 'Turk' and 'Turkey' in European usage contain a certain ineradicable ambiguity. Europeans long understood, by these names, the great Muslim empire of the eastern Mediterranean and the Middle East, and its Muslim inhabitants, in particular its ruling element. 'Turks' however has also, for a long time past, meant persons whose language was Turkish, and who were descended from peoples whose original homeland had been Central Asia. However, it was not even right to speak of a single Turkish language; rather, there had been for centuries a group of Turkic languages, spoken by peoples living between the Volga and the borders of China, between Siberia and the Aegean, differing from each other in about the same degree as languages differ within the Latin, Slav or Germanic groups. The variant of Turkish which developed in Asia Minor formed the foundation of the language of the greater part of the educated elite of the Ottoman empire, though it is also true that the higher culture of this political class was trilingual—in Turkish, Persian and Arabic. In the Turkish language there existed an ancient word—*türk* (in modern Turkish spelling)—to denote persons of Turkish speech. The members of the Ottoman educated elite, however, did not use this word to describe themselves, for it had until the twentieth century a plebeian and socially disparaging flavour: rather, they spoke of themselves as *Osmanlı* (Ottomans). For them the legitimacy of government was religious and dynastic. They were subjects of the sultan, who was also the Commander of the Faithful. There was no suggestion that persons of Turkish speech were a politically significant category, still less that government should be carried on in their name. This does not of course mean that there was not a passive feeling of identity between users of the same language, and a certain contempt for those who used other languages—for example, Kurds, Iraqis or Persians.

The first impact of European political ideas in the Ottoman empire—which resulted from the series of military defeats during the eighteenth century and from the attempts of the rulers, especially Mahmud II (1808-39), to strengthen the empire by economic and military reforms—took the form of liberalism and constitutionalism.

The reforms of Mahmud II did much to modernise the armed forces, education and the legal system. It was his misfortune that the need to resist Greek and Egyptian rebels, supported in various degrees by the European great powers, absorbed most of the resources of his declining empire. A further period of reforms, known in Turkish history as *Tanzimat*, and extending, with some interruptions, from November 1839 until the end of the 1860s, also brought some solid achievements. However, the serious efforts of the reformers were frustrated both by the opposition of the beneficiaries of the old order and by the lack of qualified and honest subordinates. New laws created confusion, and ill-paid officials could seldom resist the temptation to eke out their earnings by bribes. It is even arguable that the reforms actually increased the incidence of corruption, while creating among the small but growing modern intellectual elite expectations that could not be satisfied.[7] In exile in France, a group of Turkish writers planned for a democratic state, to be based on French or English practices. This group became known as the Young Ottomans, and their most eminent member was the poet Namik Kemal (1840-88). For a short time it looked as if their plans might be fulfilled. On 30 May 1876 Sultan Abdulaziz was deposed, and three months later his successor Murad V had the same fate. Sultan Abdulhamid proclaimed an Ottoman constitution on 23 December 1876.

The victory of the reformers was very brief. In February 1877 Abdulhamid dismissed its main author, Midhat Pasha (1822-83), while allowing the first Ottoman parliament, elected on a narrow franchise and under pressure from the administration, to meet. Even this cowed assembly proved too lively for the sultan's taste, and he dissolved it in February 1878.

Meanwhile another reform movement had been developing among the people of Turkic speech in the Russian empire, especially among the Tatars of Kazan and the Volga valley. The Tatar leaders were at first concerned with social and educational reforms, and with equality between Muslim and Christian subjects of the Russian empire; but they became increasingly aware of the specific unity of language which bound together the peoples of Turkic speech. Panislamism began to give way to Panturkism. The chief exponent of this new tendency was not a Volga Tatar, but a Crimean, Ismail bey Gaspirali (1851-1914), who published from 1883 onwards at Bahçesaray in Crimea a bilingual journal, *Tercümen* ('The Interpreter', the Russian edition *Perevodchik*). Gaspirali sought to create a uniform Turkish language, to be derived from Osmanli, Crimean and Volga Tatar. In this he was not successful, but his campaign for solidarity of the Turkic peoples, with its slogan of 'Unity in language, in thought and in work' (*dilde, fikirde, işte birlik*), made a considerable impact.

The Ottoman rulers of the late nineteenth century were not interested in such things, but some younger Ottoman intellectuals began to take notice. In 1897 the poet Mehmed Emin used the despised word *türk* in a patriotic poem which declared: 'I am a Turk, my faith and my race are mighty'. A few years later a periodical entitled *Türk* was published in Cairo by some exiles from the Ottoman empire, and in 1904 it published an article by a Russian Tatar named Yusuf Akchura entitled 'Three kinds of policy', in which Turkish nationalism, based on language, was put forward as an alternative to the respectable doctrines of Ottoman patriotism and of Panislamism. After the disappointment of the hopes raised in 1906 of a parliamentary form of government in Russia, Akchura went into exile in Ottoman territory. Here in intellectual circles an interest in Turkic languages and peoples was beginning to appear, stimulated partly by the publications of West European scholars on the history and culture of Central Asia, and partly by the influence of Polish and Hungarian exiles, who began to make known to their Ottoman friends the connection between nationality and language, as shown by Central European experience.

The years which followed the overthrow of Sultan Abdulhamid by the Young Turks' revolution of 1908-09 brought a sharp conflict between the three policies outlined in Akchura's 1904 essay. Panislamism was in disfavour owing to its association with Abdulhamid. All-Ottoman patriotism, on a new basis of equal democratic rights for all Ottoman citizens whatever their faith or language, proved to be a mirage: the neighbouring Balkan states were not dissuaded by the creation of an Ottoman parliament from their plans to take the Ottoman lands inhabited by their kinsmen, nor did these kinsmen give up their hopes of such a result. After the lost war of 1912-13 many thousands of Turks arrived as penniless exiles on the new Ottoman frontiers. Only Turkish nationalism still seemed a sound foundation of policy. Several Tatar exiles from Russia, including Akchura, joined with Ottoman intellectuals of similar views in organising from 1911 the periodical *Türk Yurdu* (the Turkish homeland). Among the Ottoman members of this group was the poet and sociologist Zia Gökalp (1876-1924). The government did not commit itself to a Panturkic policy, but it was quite glad to see the expression of such ideas. Inevitably, Russia was regarded by nationalists as the main enemy, since it was within the Russian empire that the largest number of Turkic-speaking people were to be found. The outbreak of war with Russia in 1914 strengthened the trend. Gökalp used, in a famous poem of 1914, the name *Turan*, originally popularised by Hungarian and other experts on Central Asia, to denote the greater Turkish fatherland which, enthusiasts claimed, stretched from the borders of China to the Bosphorus, or even to Hungary.

In the First World War the Turkish armies fought bravely, in the Caucasus against the Russians, and at the Dardanelles under the command of the brilliant general Mustafa Kemal Pasha against the Australians and New Zealanders; but it was not until the collapse of Russia at the end of 1917 that Panturanian ideas seemed capable of becoming reality. In 1918 the Turks entered Azerbaidjan and took Baku, but the victory of the Western Allies over Germany caused them to withdraw very soon. The last faint hope was the attempt of Enver Pasha, who had been the leading figure in the wartime government, to organise a Turkic state in Russian Central Asia in the first years of the Soviet regime. Enver perished, and Russian rule was restored in communist form.

Meanwhile the Ottoman empire had been reduced to Asia Minor, and a new state had come into being, based on a Turkish nationalism which owed something to the ideas of Akchura and Gökalp, but more to the fortunes of war and the bravery of Mustafa Kemal and his armies. Revolting against the residual government of the helpless sultan in Istanbul, who had accepted the will of the victors, Kemal organised in 1919 in Anatolia a new political authority, based on the centrally placed city of Ankara, and new armies. These first held the invading Greeks, and then in 1921 drove them out of Asia Minor. There was also a war in the east against the Armenians, conducted with terrible savagery on both sides and ending with the massacre or expulsion of the Armenian population of that region.[8]

The war of 1919-21 had a threefold character. It was a national war against the Greeks. It was also, in the minds of the peasant soldiers if not of Kemal, a holy war of Islam against infidels. It was also, in the mind of Kemal if not in those of his soldiers, a revolutionary and civil war against the old political and religious leadership. The sultan-caliph, the *şeyh-ul-Islam* and the *ulema* had surrendered to the foreigners. The new state should repudiate all international connections with Islam, give up all pretentions to the loyalty of Muslims who were not Turks, and become a secular state, though Turks as individuals could continue to be Muslims. A series of decrees in 1924 and 1925 put secularisation into effect. The religious law of Islam (*Şeriat*) ceased to have authority, religious schools (*medrese*) were abolished and replaced with state schools under the ministry of education, religious properties were taken over by the state, and the various dervish orders and brotherhoods (*tarikat*) were suppressed, and their property confiscated. These measures provoked widespread opposition and some attempts at rebellion, which were repressed with executions and imprisonment.

A further breach with the past was the abolition of Arabic script and its replacement with Latin, decreed in November 1924. Kemal was influenced by the plans for the introduction of the Latin script in Soviet Azerbaidjan in 1925. His aims were not dissimilar to those of the Soviet leaders: like them, he wished to cut off the new generation from the literature and culture of the past, which were contained in the Arabic script. His brutal action met with a need which had long been felt by specialists in language. Turkish speech, with its great variety of vowel sounds, is not well suited to the Arabic script. From the beginning also the Turkish nationalist movement had stood for the reform of the language. The cumbersome official vocabulary and style, full not only of words but of whole phrases from Arabic and Persian, had to be replaced by a language close to common speech. Already for several decades the press of Istanbul had contributed to a process of simplification and modernisation. Under Kemal the process was accelerated. The Turkish Linguistic Society, set up in 1932, had the task of rapidly eliminating Arabic and Persian words, and manufacturing new words from Turkish roots to take their place. This hasty and artificial action produced many ridiculous results, and after a few years the pace was greatly reduced, and many widely used words of non-Turkic origin were allowed to stay. However, in the course of time public practice achieved more than deliberate policy. The changes which took place in spoken and written Turkish between the 1940s and the 1970s were as great as those which had been achieved during the 1930s, and neologisms multiplied and came into popular use.

Kemal Atatürk's conception of the Turkish nation comprised the people of Turkish speech living within the state whose frontiers were settled by the peace treaty of Lausanne of 1923. He renounced any claims either to the peoples of other formerly Ottoman territories or to peoples of Turkic speech living in the Soviet Union, Iran or Afghanistan: Panturanian and Panislamic aims were equally repudiated. The state was officially described by the word *Türkiye*, which had only come into use in the last years before the war and had had no official status until the Law of Fundamental Organisations of 20 January 1921. From this time the word used by Turks and by foreigners was the same. Kemal encouraged the creation of historical myths designed to link the Turks with the past inhabitants of Asia Minor and to glorify the pre-Islamic history of the Turks. Thus it was claimed that the Hittites had been Turks: symbolically, one of the new state banks was named Hittite Bank (*Eti Banka*). However, the Turks had not always lived in Asia Minor. The original Turks had lived in Central Asia, the cradle of the human race. Thence, the nationalist ideologues now claimed, some Turks had proceeded to the Nile valley, where they had created Pharaonic civilisation, others to Mesopotamia, where they founded Sumerian civilisation (Atatürk also set up a Sumerian Bank). In the course of time the peoples of these and more distant lands, who owed their culture to distant Turkish forebears, had lost their Turkish speech. Only in Asia Minor and in some of the lands to the east had it survived.

Atatürk died in 1938. For a time during the Second World War Panturanian plans were revived by individuals, but they were never approved by the rulers. After the war genuine competition between political parties was introduced into Turkish public life. Turkish democracy proved fragile: it was interrupted by military intervention and embittered by acts of vengeance, above all the execution of the former prime minister Adnan Menderes in 1961, which threatened to replace the earlier monolithic cohesiveness of the Turkish nation by the mutual hostility of two camps which the executions of 1923 had produced in the Greek body politic.

Kemal left a legacy of progressivist, anti-religious, blandly authoritarian orthodoxy, designed to lead the common people forward into the glorious heritage of the secularist westernised twentieth century, which it could hardly be expected to find for itself. Yet the desired modernisation was only partly achieved. Old-style bureaucracy flourished, while among the common people the old religion remained strong. When at last an indigenous Turkish business class began to appear, it contributed to a revival of Islam: the connection between the merchant class and the Muslim piety, so striking a feature of the history of the Muslim peoples from Morocco to Indonesia, manifested itself in post-Atatürk Turkey. Another trend of the 1960s was that from the intellectual-bureaucratic dominant class a minority detached itself to challenge, from a more or less Marxist point of view, the prevalent Western-democratic ideal, which was simultaneously under attack from the Muslim traditionalists. Interest in the Arabic-speaking Muslim world and in the Turkic peoples under Soviet rule was latent but not negligible; and the uncertain prospects of both might cause it to revive. The quality of Turkish nationality remained elusive half a century after Kemal's victory. The views which Turks might take of their nation's place in the world were confused. Yet that a Turkish nation existed, of which a hundred years earlier there had hardly been a sign, was beyond doubt.

### The Arab nation

Under Ottoman rule the centre of gravity, cultural as well as political, moved to Istanbul and the lands surrounding it. Though a Muslim state, it is arguable that the Ottoman empire was the successor rather to the Byzantine empire than to the caliphate of Baghdad. The Arabic-speaking lands sank to a provincial status, even though they were comparatively rich and populous, and provided the Ottoman army with soldiers and the Ottoman political elite with able men. The Arabic-speaking subjects of the sultan accepted this state of affairs with resignation as long as the Ottoman empire remained a powerful and respected state.

The modern movement to make the Arabic language the basis of nationality, and to create an Arab nation whose will should form the foundation of the legitimacy of government in the lands of Arabic-speaking population, resulted from the growing domination by European powers over the Ottoman empire and neighbouring territories during the nineteenth and early twentieth centuries. However, an important distinction should be noted from the start.

In Algeria, Tunisia, Egypt, Morocco and Libya, which were annexed or made into protectorates by France, Britain, Spain and Italy between 1830 and 1911, political opposition to European rule developed, but it was at first based essentially on the identity of the peoples as Muslims, and its aims were some form or other of constitutionalism. As political parties emerged, and secular nationalism challenged specifically religious claims, this nationalism was at first territorial rather than linguistic. Claims were made for the independence of Egypt, Tunisia or Morocco rather than for the creation of a single free Arab homeland.

In those territories which remained under Ottoman rule until the end of the First World War—Syria, Mesopotamia and Arabia—demands were also made for constitutional liberties or territorial autonomy. Nevertheless, increasingly the aim of the small oppositional elite was an independent Arab homeland. The claim was advanced on behalf not of a religion or of a territory but of those who spoke a single Arabic language.

Arab nationalism was not anti-Muslim, but inevitably it diminished the importance of Islam while laying greater stress on language. It is not surprising that its pioneers should have included a high proportion of Christians and of unbelievers. Arab Christians, especially the Catholic Maronites in the Lebanon and the Copts in Egypt, were more easily and quickly accessible to European ideas than were Muslims. There were two Christian universities in Beirut, the American college founded in 1866 and the Jesuit University of St Joseph established in 1875. American Protestantism made few converts, but American secular democratic ideas made an increasing appeal. For an Arabic-speaking Christian the idea of nationality based on language was understandably most attractive, for it made it possible for him to claim inclusion, as a patriot, in the community from which his religion had hitherto excluded him. The trend towards Arab nationalism, directed against the Turks, now regarded not as fellow-Muslims but as foreign rulers, was accelerated by the Young Turkish Revolution, whose All-Ottoman democratic principles in practice looked more and more like Turkish centralism with a Turkish nationalist flavour. Several Arab nationalist secret societies came into existence. At the same time, in Arabia proper, there was a growing desire among local notables, quite unaffected by liberal or nationalist ideas, to make themselves independent of the Ottoman empire and to set up territorial rule of their own. Outstanding among them were the Hashimite family, descendants of the Prophet and rulers of the Hejaz and the holy cities; and the Wahhabi religious community, led by Abd al-Aziz ibn Saud, who ruled over Najd. Both rulers, while on bad terms with each other, kept in contact with the British in Egypt.

During the First World War the British made promises to the Hashimites which were not compatible with the promises made in 1917 by Balfour to the Zionists of a Jewish national home,[9] or with the Sykes-Picot agreement of 1916 dividing the Arabic-speaking Ottoman territories between Britain and France. The revolt of 1916-18 against the Turks by the Arabs of the Hashimite Sharif Hussein of Hejaz made some contribution to British victory, but the consequent settlement bitterly disappointed the Arabs, for it did not create a single Arab state over the whole Fertile Crescent of Syria and Mesopotamia. Instead five states were set up, as 'mandated territories', of which three were to be held by the British and two by the French. The two 'mandatory powers' were to report regularly to the League of Nations, and were to prepare the territories for ultimate sovereign independence.

Feisal, son of Hussein, was driven out of Damascus in July 1920 by the French. The British installed him as king of Iraq, a new state with extremely artificial frontiers, carved out of the Mesopotamian provinces of the Ottoman empire. Shi'i Arabs were twice as numerous as Sunni; and the north, inhabited by Kurds, who spoke a language related to Persian and had no wish to be ruled by Arabic-speakers, was incorporated because of its petroleum resources, which the British wished to control through their new vassals. Feisal continued to cherish his Panarab schemes. His Sunni subjects, only a quarter of the population but providing most of the elite, had a strong vested interest in Panarabism, for much the same reasons as the Christian Arabs of Egypt and Lebanon discussed above. Only if Iraq were merged in a single Arab state, with a large Sunni majority, would they cease to be a minority in their own country. The new Iraqi ministry of education set itself to spread Panarab ideas through the schools, and had considerable success in the following years, at least in the towns. Shi'i Iraqis had no enthusiasm for Feisal.

Still less did the settlement please the Kurds, who inhabited the highlands around the upper Euphrates and Tigris, stretching across to the south-east of Lake Urmia in Iran. Numbering several millions (but never precisely counted by any reliable census), the Kurds were divided by the peace settlement between four states—Turkey, Iran, Iraq and Syria—all of whose rulers refused to recognise them as a distinct nation.

The French government created two states, Syria and Lebanon. It might have been more natural if Lebanon had been confined to the region of predominantly Christian population, in which there had been a strong French influence for centuries. The French however decided in favour of a *grand Liban*, about half of whose population consisted of Muslims.

In the south the British set up a kingdom of Transjordan under Feisal's brother Abdullah, while Palestine, in which the contradictory claims of Jews and Arabs were somehow to be reconciled, was placed directly under British administration. Sharif Hussein fared less well than this two sons. In 1925 he was driven out of Hejaz by the Wahhabi leader, who founded the kingdom of Saudi Arabia, covering the greater part of the Arabian peninsula. In the south-western corner of the peninsula the Yemen, with a comparatively dense population, remained independent.

Nationalist movements in the lands of Arabic speech between the world wars were based on each individual territory. Self-government for the individual peoples and strategic guarantees for the European sovereign, protectorate or mandatory powers could in principle have been compatible. In reality the willingness of the various British and French authorities to make concessions, and the willingness of the political leaders of the various Arab peoples to accept either direct foreign rule or indirect dependence on a foreign protector, varied greatly. As a new generation of better educated persons of humbler social origin entered the Arab elites, political demands became more radical, and hostile suspicion of British and French policies more profound.

In Egypt a strong nationalist party, the *Wafd*, emerged under the leadership of Sa'ad Zaghlul.[10] After widespread anti-British riots in 1919, Egypt settled down to a parliamentary form of government, based on a limited suffrage. Treaties of 1922 and 1936 arranged for the maintenance of large British forces in the country, in order to ensure British control of the Suez Canal, but in internal politics Egypt was sovereign.

In Iraq, the British also had major strategic interests: the security of the Persian Gulf and the western approaches to India (protected by an airforce base at Habbaniya), and the rapidly growing exploitation of oil in the Mosul area. These interests were guaranteed by treaty when Iraq became an independent state in 1930.

In Syria the French had to put down in 1926 a revolt of the Druse religious sect and large-scale riots in Damascus. In Lebanon their situation was easier, since the population was divided almost equally between Muslims and Christians, and the Catholic (or Maronite) majority of the Christian half was well disposed to French rule. In 1936 the Popular Front government of Léon Blum signed treaties with both countries, granting independence on condition that French military bases remained; but the treaties were not ratified by the French parliament.

The political problems of the French territories in North Africa differed substantially. Tunisia and Morocco were protectorates, but Algeria was legally an integral part of the French republic. In Algeria and Tunisia there were large communities of European settlers, of Italian and Spanish as well as of French origin, but increasingly absorbed into French culture; in Morocco, settlement was on a smaller scale, though substantial French business interests had grown up. The people of Tunisia, and of the coastal regions and cities of the other two lands, were Arabic in speech and culture; but in the mountains of Algeria, and still more in Morocco, a large part of the population were Berbers, who shared little with the people of the plains but their Muslim religion. Population pressure in Algeria had caused emigration of Muslim workers to France, where they were employed in low-grade jobs in industry.

The first active political movement in Tunisia, the *Néo-Destour* founded in 1934 by Habib Bourguiba,[11] demanded sovereign independence for Tunisia, and in 1937 and 1938 was responsible for riots which were met with martial law and arrests. In Morocco the French aroused bitter opposition by the so-called *dahir berbère* of 1934, which separated the administration of the Berbers from that of the Arabic-speaking people, placing them under French criminal law. This measure was inspired partly by genuine paternalist concern for the more primitive Berber peoples, partly perhaps by a desire to play off Berbers against Arabs. Its opponents accused the French not only of trying to de-arabise the Berbers but of planning forcibly to convert them from Islam to Christianity. Opposition to the *dahir* strengthened nationalism, and led to the formation of the first nationalist party. In Algeria two trends emerged among the Arabic-speaking people. The first, whose spokesman was the French-educated Ferhat Abbas, was towards closer integration of Algeria with France, provided only that Muslims were placed on a level of legal and social equality with Christians, and that there was no attempt to replace Arabic culture by French through crude methods of assimilation. The obstacle to this policy was the hostility of the French settlers, largely people of plebeian origin with little interest in any culture of any sort. These *pieds noirs* simply regarded the Muslims as an inferior race, destined to be their servants, and strongly objected to any plan to give them equal status. The second trend was towards Muslim nationalism, with a strong socialist and proletarian content. It derived an important part of its support from Algerian workers in France.

These various movements viewed each other's efforts with sympathy, and their leaders had some contact with each other. The notion of a wider Arab national struggle, for a single Arab state, was at first confined to a few intellectuals, but gained more support, from Iraq to Morocco, as a result of the conflict between Arabs and Jews in Palestine.[12] The arguments used by Jews to persuade Arabs that their conditions would be improved by the presence of skilled and enterprising Jewish immigrants did not convince them. This was partly due to the influence of Arab large landowners who feared for their possessions, and of fanatical Muslims; but suspicions of Jewish immigration were also deeply rooted in the Arab population as a whole. When the number of immigrants increased as a result of the anti-semitic policies of Hitler in Germany and the fear that these policies would be imitated in other Central European states, Arab opposition escalated into an armed rising against the British in 1936.

There is no doubt that among the younger generation of educated people, from Iraq to Morocco, the concept of a single Arab nation had been steadily gaining. It had its strongest support in Syria. In the 1930s it was popularised, for those whose first European language was French, by the periodical *La nation arabe*, directed in Geneva by the Lebanese exile Chekib Arslan. The Palestine revolt caused the idea to spread to those whose first European language was English. It was propagated in Iraqi schools, and also began to make an impact on Egypt, where both Western languages were known to educated people. The events in Palestine were understood as a threat to the whole Arab nation. Here, it was felt, was a matter not just of rule by a more or less benevolent European power, but of Arab lands being seized from Arab cultivators and given to foreign invaders. Panarab feeling was exploited by the Italian and German governments (although in Libya the Italians had shown themselves ruthless oppressors of Arabs). Young Arab nationalists increasingly looked to the two fascist powers as future liberators.

These fascist sympathies in fact produced small results during the Second World War. The British were able to defend their position in Egypt. In this they had the sullen acquiescence of King Farouk and the more genuine support of the *Wafd*, whose leaders took seriously the notion that Britain was fighting for democracy against Hitlerian tyranny. A pro-German government in Iraq, led by Rashid Ali, attempted to capture the RAF base at Habbaniya, but was defeated in April 1941. In June 1941 British and Free French forces invaded Syria. In North Africa, after their invasion of November 1942 the Americans showed a certain benevolence towards Moroccan nationalism. In 1943 Ferhat Abbas published an Algerian Manifesto with demands for autonomy and democratic reforms, which the French rejected. As the tide of war moved into Europe, French authority was restored under General de Gaulle's government. Algerian discontent and nationalist hopes were not appeased, and on 8 March 1945 violent riots broke out at Sétif, Frenchmen were murdered, and many more Muslims were killed in reprisals. Meanwhile the British supported Syrian and Lebanese claims against the French, and were largely responsible for the removal of French power and for the admission of both countries as sovereign states to the United Nations in 1945.

In the first post-war years Panarab nationalism became stronger, and extended at least to a large part of the educated class in Egypt and across North Africa. In the eastern lands, which now enjoyed sovereign independence, the rulers adopted Panarab rhetoric even if their devotion to the cause was half-hearted. They were uncomfortably placed between the pressures of radical political movements, which demanded the liquidation of British military bases, and the British government, which argued unsuccessfully that the bases were needed to defend the common cause of democracy against the threat of Soviet expansion. British and American determination to keep the bases was also motivated by the immense increase in the output of oil in Arab states. The greatest oil resources of all were in Saudi Arabia, which was thereby brought out of its medieval backwardness into active Arab politics. This was also true of minor Arab principalities along the Persian Gulf in which oil was found. Even the isolated and primitive Yemen, which had no oil, was influenced by Arab politics. Most important of all was the rapid increase of the modern intellectual elite, which now turned away from fascism (which had been discredited by Hitler's defeat) and learned at least some Marxist catchwords (now fashionable because Soviet Russia had won the war). A few even went so far as seriously to study Marxism. The new intellectual elites were now passionately opposed to the privileged classes in the Arab lands, which both obstructed their social advancement and offended their new ideological principles. The struggle for social revolution became closely interwoven with the struggle against the British military presence in the eastern lands and French rule in the Maghreb.[13]

British attempts to gain acceptance of their military interests by treaties which made further concessions were rejected in both Egypt and Iraq. A three-cornered struggle developed in Egypt between *Wafd*, King Farouk and the British, involving guerrilla attacks on British forces in the Canal Zone and riots in Cairo.[14] The situation changed radically when in July 1952 a group of Egyptian military conspirators led by Colonel Gamal Abdel Nasser overthrew King Farouk. Nasser was the first ruler of Egypt to declare himself a supporter of the Panarab cause, but he did not simply identify Egyptian interests with it. As he saw it, Egypt was involved in three loyalties: was an Arab state, a Muslim state and an African state. In practice, events showed that his aims were Egyptian hegemony among Arab states (of which Egypt was undoubtedly the most populous and most powerful, though not the richest, since it lacked oil); Egyptian imperialism in Africa and on both sides of the Red Sea; and, if possible, a strong Egyptian influence on non-Arab Muslim states.

In North Africa in the early 1950s French policy reverted to repression. In 1951 negotiations with the Tunisian *Néo-Destour* were abandoned, and Bourguiba was arrested. In 1953 the sultan of Morocco, who had shown public sympathy for the nationalists, was deposed. These policies were reversed by the government of Pierre Mendès-France, who released Bourguiba in 1954. His successors gave Tunisia first autonomy and then, in March 1956, independence. The sultan of Morocco was also allowed to return in November 1955, and in May 1956 Morocco too became independent.

In Algeria no such progress could be achieved. The bitter resistance of a million European settlers, and the insistence in Paris on the legal status of Algeria as part of France, made agreement impossible even with the moderate Ferhat Abbas. A group of extreme nationalists set up a secret military organisation. Its leader, Ahmed Ben Bella, escaped to Cairo, where Nasser helped him to enlist and train Algerian volunteers. Ben Bella succeeded in organising on Algerian soil a *Front de libération nationale* (FLN), which in November 1954 began an armed insurrection. As the savage guerrilla conflict dragged on, the majority of Algerian Muslims, of Arabic or Berber speech alike, became either by conviction or by fear supporters of the FLN. Ferhat Abbas himself went to Cairo and put himself at its disposal.

Support of the FLN made Nasser the enemy of France. His relations with Britain were at first rather good, and he made a treaty with them by which the Suez Canal military base was transferred to him, while he recognised the independence of Sudan.[15] Later in the year, however, relations deteriorated when Britain persuaded the government of Iraq to join an alliance (the Baghdad Pact) under British and American auspices, intended as a defence of the 'northern tier' of the Middle East against Soviet expansion. This Nasser regarded as a manoeuvre to split the unity of the Arab states. He sought arms from Czechoslovakia and the Soviet Union, and when the United States government refused to finance his planned Assuan High Dam, he annexed the Suez Canal Company. This led to the joint invasion of Egypt by Israelis, British and French in November 1956. The Israeli army had rapid successes, but the outcry at the United Nations and the hostility of the United States as well as of the Soviet Union caused the Western powers to abandon the enterprise. Nasser was triumphant.

This led to a rapid growth of Panarabism and to onslaughts on the remaining pro-Western Arab rulers. In Jordan King Hussein narrowly escaped being overthrown in April 1957.[16] In February 1958 the Syrian government declared its union with Egypt in the United Arab Republic. In July 1958 a military revolution in Iraq overthrew the regime which had existed for the last decade under the effective leadership of Nuri-es-Said, a veteran Arab nationalist who had, however, believed in cooperation with the British. Nuri, a social conservative and symbol of the old regime, was done to death by the revolutionary mob, together with the regent and the young king. In 1962 the Algerian war came to an end when de Gaulle's government conceded complete independence to an Algerian republic ruled by the FLN. Nasser also succeeded for a time in making himself master of Yemen, to which he sent large numbers of Egyptian troops to take part in a civil war between 1962 and 1967. In 1967 the British abandoned their Red Sea base at Aden, and its Arabian hinterland, after futile attempts to organise a federation of the rulers of the South Arabian protectorates. The new state called itself the Republic of South Yemen. On Nasser's western border the kingdom of Libya, established in 1951 in place of the former Italian colony, became a republic after a military *coup d'état* led by Colonel Muammar Ghadaffi in September 1969. This was followed by the closure of British and American bases and the seizure of the rapidly developing Western-owned oil industry.

The lands of Arabic speech were now freed of all West European domination, but unity was still far off. The hostility between Arab governments and political factions was as fierce as the hatred of Arab nationalists for their former European masters. The conflicts appeared to be ideological, though territorial rivalries had by no means disappeared. Monarchies remained in Morocco, Jordan and Saudi Arabia, as well as in the small oil-rich sheikdoms of the Persian Gulf. They were socially conservative, and still hesitated to abandon friendly relations with Western powers. While indulging from time to time in Panarab rhetoric, they were in no hurry to unite with the other Arab states. Elsewhere various forms of dictatorship existed, with various forms of 'socialist' programme. The *Ba'ath* party, which emerged in Syria and Iraq after the Second World War, sought to combine a genuinely radical socialism, more or less Marxist, with the pursuit of complete Arab unity. President Nasser of Egypt appealed to the *Ba'ath* as a hero of the Arab cause, but they distrusted his military methods of government and doubted whether he was a genuine social radical. These ideological misgivings were not overcome by the creation of the United Arab Republic in 1958, and resulted in its dissolution three years later. In February 1963 the Iraqi branch of *Ba'ath* seized power, and a month later the Syrian *Ba'ath* returned to power in Damascus. Iraqi and Syrian *Ba'ath* leaders conferred with Nasser in Cairo with a view to resuscitating plans for union of all these states, but again without success. The Iraqi and Syrian *Ba'ath* then quarrelled with each other, being divided on whether first priority should be given to Panarabism or to socialism, and there followed in both countries a bewildering succession of *coups d'état*, repressions, persecutions, and acts of revenge, from which it is difficult to extract any deeper significance.

The main cementing force on the diverse and fluctuating Arab scene was hostility to Israel, which in June 1967 and October 1973 led to war. Ever since 1948 the Arab states had refused to recognise the existence of Israel, and about 600,000 Palestinian Arabs, who had fled or had been expelled at that time, and whose numbers had risen to about 1,500,000 through natural increase by the 1970s, remained a strong pressure group which Arab governments could not ignore. Whereas the governments of Germany and Finland had made tremendous efforts to absorb hundreds of thousands of expellees in their economies, the governments of Arabic-speaking countries, with the partial exception of Jordan, had done nothing. On the contrary, they had left the Palestinian refugees in miserable conditions, deliberately inciting them to hatred and revenge against Israel. For their part the

Arabs could reply that, whereas Germans and Finns had been expelled as a consequence of German or Finnish aggression against their neighbours, the Palestinian Arabs had been peaceful residents in their own country, whom foreign Israeli invaders had driven from their homes. The Israelis could reply to this that as many Jews had been expelled, after being robbed of their possessions, from Iraq, Morocco and other lands of Arabic speech, as Arabs had been expelled from Palestine. Right and wrong were in fact to be found on both sides, but to say so solved nothing.

For the first decade after the expulsion the Palestinians were essentially instruments of the Egyptian, Syrian and Jordanian governments, from whose territories from time to time raids were made into Israel, resulting in reprisal raids by Israelis across the border. In time however the Palestinians began to create their own organisations. In 1964 was founded the Palestinian Liberation Organisation (PLO), led by Yassir Arafat, which claimed to include fourteen different groups. After the 1967 war between Israel and its neighbours,[17] while the defeated Arab states recovered slowly from disaster, the Palestinians developed new skills in taking hostages from nations not involved in their quarrel. Their targets were not only Israelis but any victims whom they could use to compel other governments into anti-Israeli action. At the same time they declared that their aim was a democratic Palestine, in which Jews too could be citizens provided that they abjured Zionism. Their aims were not nationalism and hatred but socialism and love.

Possibly more effective than Palestinian gunmen and incendiaries were the highly conservative rulers of oil-rich Persian Gulf states, led by the king of Saudi Arabia, who began in November 1973 to use the manipulation of oil prices and the withholding of oil supplies to European and American states as a means of forcing them to put pressure on Israel. These Arab statesmen were convinced that, rather than sacrifice the comforts expected by their voters, Western statesmen would hand over Israel to their tender mercies. It should also be noted however that the foundations of Saudi or Gulf Coast sheikhly power were far from firm. Not only were sheikhs vulnerable to assassins' bullets, but the Saudi policy of creating modern industries, dependent on imported engineers, teachers and labour force, was leading to mass manufacture of hostile intelligentsia, from whom the teachers of assassins and the assassins themselves could best be recruited.

The oil sheikhs also endeavoured to use their money power to influence Arab governments towards more moderate internal policies. Economic development, financed by Saudi capital, was potentially more attractive to Syrian and Iraqi rulers than support for Palestinian terrorists. The markedly more moderate stance of both governments in 1976 may have been due no less to the inducements of Arabian plutocrats than to the magic of Dr Kissinger's diplomacy.

The history of the peoples of Arabic speech, their states and their political and social movements in the twentieth century, is more complicated than that of any other group of people from whom a movement for national unity has been formed. In the mid-1970s the future of the Panarab idea appeared quite unpredictable. Originally it had been confined to the eastern Arabic-speaking lands. It then had the support of a small but growing number of young educated people, including army officers. It was also supported, for their own reasons, by the rulers of Arab states: first the Hashimites tried to bring the Fertile Crescent under their rule; then King Farouk patronised Panarabism in rivalry with the Hashimites; then Nasser played the same game, while Saudi Arabia manoeuvred between them. Gradually, however, Panarabism was extended first to Egypt and then to all North Africa. In the early 1970s it was clear that this wider Panarabism had a hold on two generations of urban educated people, those who had grown to manhood in the 1940s and their children. Its impact on the millions of workers and peasants was more difficult to judge. Panarabism is based essentially on language, yet the unity of the language is not a simple matter. Classical Arabic was the same for all who knew it well; and the modern written Arabic of the newspapers and of secular literature was the same from the Maghreb to the Persian Gulf. But the written language affected mainly the secular and religious elite. The spoken language, used by educated and uneducated alike, differed very widely from Morocco to Egypt, Iraq and Yemen.

The sovereignties of more than a dozen states of Arabic speech were still a powerful obstacle to unity. The states were spread out over a far greater distance than had been the sovereign German states of the nineteenth century, and some of them had a history as states of more than three thousand years.[18] The variety of political and social institutions and habits was also far greater than it ever was in Germany or Italy. Nevertheless, there existed a genuine solidarity among Arabic-speaking peoples, affecting the masses as well as the elites and uniting them against external threats. This solidarity operated against Israel, against Western governments and against foreign business firms in their midst. It might operate one day against Soviet interference; but the experience of Muslim peoples under Soviet rule did not suggest that the type of tactics used by Arabic-speaking nationalists against French and British rulers would have much scope if Soviet rule were extended to those lands.

It is especially hard to disentangle, in this solidarity, the elements of Arabism and of Islam. Admittedly the solidarity was stronger between Arab Muslims than between all Muslims: a Moroccan would feel himself closer to an Iraqi than to a Turk or an Indonesian. Yet it might be argued that this was not so much because Arab nationalist intellectuals had convinced the Arab masses that the Arabic language was a more important link than the

Muslim faith, as because they had convinced themselves that Islam was an Arab invention, and that all true Muslims ought to be Arabs. This conviction could not of course be imposed in Anatolia, Bengal or Java because in those lands Arabs had no coercive power; but attempts could be and were made to impose it on Kurds, Berbers and Sudanese. Some Arab intellectuals of Christian origin were only too willing to denigrate the Christianity in which their parents had believed, in order to be accepted in an *umma* which was now supposed to comprise not true believers but members of a nation. Some Arab intellectuals of Muslim origin were also willing to argue that the true merit of Islam lay not in its religious content but in the fact that it had been created by Arabs. In their opinion all true Arabs ought to be Muslims. They were however at best lukewarm believers: essentially, what they were doing was to demote Islam from a great universal religion to a theatrical prop for Panarab rhetoric.

The land in which the latent hostility between Muslims and Christians of Arabic speech placed the greatest strain on Arab unity was Lebanon, where Christians of Arabic speech lived in a compact mass in the central part of the highlands and part of the coastal area. When Lebanon became independent, a complex system was devised to ensure equal distribution of political power between Muslims and Christians. This system was always fragile, and in 1975 it broke down altogether.

The overall impression in the mid-1970s was that a large part of the driving force behind Panarabism came from traditional Muslim fanaticism; that a modern Arab national consciousness had penetrated the intellectual elite in all Arab lands, but had not reached down very deep into the social structure of the various and scattered Arabic-speaking peoples; and that the fulfilment of the vision of a single Arab state still lay far beyond the horizon.

# 7 East Asia: Empires, Colonies and Nations

## Empires and cultures

Two great areas of culture existed from ancient times in the lands south and east of the Himalayas: the Indian and the Chinese. From these two centres, influences radiated outwards and contributed to the formation of other cultures: especially Japan, Vietnam, Cambodia and Java. Much later, Muslims entered many of these regions, followed shortly afterwards by explorers, traders and conquerors from Christian Europe. From their activities emerged European colonial empires in some lands and indirect domination, mainly economic but partly political, in others. European imports included European concepts of nationalism. These combined with indigenous political traditions to produce national movements and the emergence of new states. These processes are the subject of this chapter.

The earliest available evidence from the Indian region is archaeological but not documentary, and insuperable uncertainty remains about the beginnings of Indian civilisation. It seems possible that the peoples of the Mohenjo-Daro and Harappa communities, in the Indus valley, were akin to the Dravidian peoples who inhabited southern India in historic times. Whether there were societies and states of a comparable degree of civilisation in the valleys of the Ganges and its great tributaries, may perhaps be shown by future archaeological discoveries. More may also perhaps be learned of the Aryan conquerors who entered India from the north. The most important evidence concerning them comes from their ancient literature and the language in which it is written. Sanskrit is the basic Indo-European language, and the fact that it is the language of the early Hindu scriptures suggests that the authors of these scriptures came from peoples related to the people of Iran, though they must have moved into India long before the foundation of the Persian empire by Cyrus. The epic poems and philosophic-religious doctrines contained in the literature doubtless derive from the Aryan conquerors; but to disentangle the Aryan and Dravidian components of the theogony and of the social and cultural fabric which emerged in the subcontinent over a period of many centuries, and which became generally known as Hinduism, seems to be a difficult task even for the specialists. It suffices here to say that from the fourth century BC onwards there is documentary evidence on the rise and fall within the subcontinent of several powerful kingdoms with a Hindu culture, especially the Mauryan empire (c. 320-180 BC) and the Gupta empire of the fourth and fifth centuries AD; but that there was no single Hindu empire, comparable with the Persian, Roman or Muslim empires. From the eighth, and particularly from the eleventh century AD, Muslim states arose on Indian soil, and by the victory of Panipat of 1526 a great Muslim empire was founded by Babar, a descendant of the Central Asian conqueror Timur. Known as the Moghul empire, it extended over most of India. Before and after this, Muslim and Hindu communities, and Muslim and Hindu states, coexisted within the subcontinent; and even at the height of Moghul power there were still Hindu states in the south.[1]

Of the other region there is more abundant and older documentary evidence. The first powerful Chinese state of Shang, which lasted approximately from 1766 to 1122 BC, was based on the Yellow River basin. In China—the classical case of the hydraulic society, which provided Wittfogel with the main example for his theory—publicly organised irrigation works were of primary importance. Between the eighth and sixth centuries BC a number of states arose in China, some of which were centred in the Yangtse basin. What is not clear is whether the Yangtse basin had been the theatre of an earlier civilisation, significantly different from that of the Yellow River basin. If so, then this civilisation became fused with that of the north, as Dravidian civilisation in India became fused with Aryan. There is not, however, in the case of the Yangtse and Yellow rivers, any more than in the case of the Ganges and the Indus, evidence of a continuous rivalry between strong civilisations and states, comparable with that which existed between ancient Mesopotamia and the Nile basin.

It is necessary at this point to make some reference, however superficial, to certain features of the Chinese civilisation, unique in its survival for almost four thousand years in the same land, which set it aside from any other in human history.[2]

First is the ideographic script, which was in use already in Shang times, but was elaborated and perfected in the course of the following millennium. Depicting concepts, not sounds, it enabled persons who knew it to communicate with each other even though their spoken languages were different. It was of course useful only to those who had undergone a difficult process of education, a small minority of the population—though how small is a matter of controversy between historians of China.

The second main feature is the body of ethical and political doctrine, derived from the teaching of Confucius (551-479 BC), which, alternately adopted and denounced by rulers, modified and reinterpreted by later thinkers, still determined for more than two thousand years the attitudes of Chinese to their families and to civil authority. It is worth noting that Confucius lived in the age of the warring states, before the creation of the unified empire.

The third feature is the centralised bureaucracy, based on the system of examinations at provincial and central level, which produced China's political and cultural elite, conventionally described by European historians as the *literati*. Those few who passed at the highest level had access to the highest posts of the imperial government. Those who passed only at lower levels, and many who studied for examinations but never passed, filled the lower ranks of the bureaucracy, and formed the landed class or 'gentry': they did not own great landed estates, but they were the most influential people in their local communities. Clearly, children of rich and learned families had great initial advantages in the competition. It was even sometimes possible for children of the very rich and powerful to get to the top without taking the examinations. Nevertheless education remained the main criterion for advancement, and there was greater social mobility on grounds of merit than in contemporary societies in other lands.

The Chinese states were first brought together in a single great empire by the ruthlessly centralising and autocratic First Emperor (221-205 BC). The great subsequent periods of Chinese unity and power, the Han dynasty (206 BC–220 AD), the T'ang (618-907), and the Sung (960-1125), were separated from each other by periods of disunity and weakness, with several states in rivalry with each other, or with barbarian tribes from the north and west conquering Chinese territory. The greatest of the invaders were the Mongols of Kublai Khan (1260-94), who established a new dynasty, the Yuan, which ruled all China until 1368. Its overthrow by a peasant-born leader, Chu Yuan-chang, who made himself emperor and founded the Ming dynasty (1368-1644), was the result of a great movement both of social revolt and of national reaction against Mongol domination. The Ming government in its turn broke up, and power fell to other northern barbarians, the Manchus, who founded the last of China's dynasties, the Ch'ing (1644-1912).

The frequent barbarian invasions, and periods of partial or complete conquest of the country, led to a coexistence of Chinese and other authorities (Turks, Mongols, Tungus, Manchus) on Chinese soil. The ruling groups of conquering peoples, including many thousands of soldiers, preserved their distinct way of life, including their languages. At the same time the Chinese structure of government and society continued to function, with little modification. The barbarian rulers were obliged to administer the vast country through its own traditional political and cultural system, but they kept their own in being alongside it, and reserved many positions of power to their compatriots, many of whom however in the course of time became absorbed into Chinese culture. This dual system existed in the north Chinese states of Liao (947-1125) and Chin (1115-1234) as well as in the all-China empires of the Yuan (1275-1368) and the Ch'ing.

China resembled the Roman empire in its vast extent, the variety of its lands and peoples, and its tolerance of many religions, but it was more closely united by a common culture; it lasted for very much longer; and it showed a certain growing ossification, a confirmed habit of contempt for all outsiders as barbarians, which made it exceptionally difficult for the Chinese to adapt themselves to the new disruptive forces brought by the Europeans.

North-east and south-west of China were two lands in which states emerged which alternated between direct subjection to China and a semi-independent tributary status. These were Korea and Vietnam. Both adopted the Chinese script, were profoundly influenced by Confucianism and adopted a government system similar to the Chinese. Buddhism acquired a strong influence in Korea, but not in Vietnam.

Beyond Korea lay the Japanese islands. Here a state grew up around the Inland Sea and extended its power east and north on the central island of Honshu at the expense of the aboriginal people of the Ainu. Its ruler was an emperor, who was supposed to be descended from the sun goddess. Under the regent for an infant emperor, Prince Shotoka (572-622 AD), the influence of T'ang China became very strong. The Japanese adopted the Chinese script, and Buddhism also spread rapidly. The impact of Confucian doctrines and of Chinese forms of government were, however, less profound. In Japan during centuries of internal struggles a certain balance was established between the central power of the *shogun* (who ruled while the emperor was little more than a symbol) and the regional power of the nobility. Already by the tenth century a uniform Japanese language had developed, and Japanese literature flourished. Successful resistance to sea-borne invasions from Korea by the armies of Kublai Khan, in 1274 and 1281, strengthened the national cohesion of the Japanese, though civil wars continued for another three hundred years, reaching a climax at the end of the sixteenth century. The final victor, Tokugawa Ieyasu, made the shogunate hereditary in his family. His successors deliberately isolated Japan from the rest of the world for two centuries. On their islands the Japanese were a homogeneous and fiercely patriotic people, with a refined culture of their own, a large population and prosperous economy, and a comparatively large warrior class which was to some extent involved in political life. Japan was thus more similar to a European sovereign state than was China, and the Japanese had what can reasonably be called a national consciousness.[3]

It is worth noticing the difference in attitudes of the Chinese and Japanese rulers to foreign religions. Buddhism spread to China, and thence to Korea and Japan. The Chinese emperors took rather the same attitude to religions as had the Roman emperors. Provided that the leaders of the religious community accepted the secular rulers and made the appropriate obeisances, and provided that they were not associated with a menacing foreign power, they were allowed to operate in China. Buddhist monks were not dangerous emissaries of an aggressive Indian empire: there was no association between the new religion and military threats, as was the case between Christian Europe and Islam in the Middle Ages. Consequently, Buddhism seldom suffered persecution in China, but was allowed to flourish, and to influence and be influenced by the established learning of the Confucians and the doctrines of the Taoists. All three made a lasting contribution to Chinese civilisation. The Chinese emperors adopted a similarly tolerant attitude to Christianity, seeing no reason to fear Christian military power. This tolerance enabled the Jesuits to acquire considerable influence at the court of Peking, until the pope forbade them to observe Chinese rituals. This, like the refusal by the early Christians of emperor worship in the Roman empire, caused the emperor to forbid their activities—though there were not mass-scale persecutions of the Roman type. Islam, too, had little impact on China. The peoples of eastern Turkestan, who came from time to time under Chinese sovereignty, accepted Islam, but they made few converts among the Chinese themselves.

The Japanese attitude to Christianity was different. In the late sixteenth centuries Portuguese and Spanish missionaries, following in the steps of St Francis Xavier, spread the Gospel in Japan with great success, until the shoguns, fearing the combination of religious propaganda with Spanish military power, already installed in the neighbouring Philippines, persecuted Christianity to the point of extermination.

## European domination

The concept of 'European' invasions of 'Asia' is misleading. What happened was rather that persons from European Christian lands invaded lands of Muslim, Hindu or Buddhist culture, sometimes as merchants demanding advantageous trading conditions and sometimes in armies impelled by religion and by greed to conquer whole kingdoms. The first effort of this sort left few traces—the conquest by the crusaders of Palestine and Syria in the twelfth and thirteenth centuries. More lasting were the effects of the wave of conquest which began in the sixteenth century, starting from Russia by land and from Portugal by sea. This effort affected three distinct regions, which may be described as northern Asia, India and south-east Asia. Of these three only the second was more than a geographical expression. Though there was no single Indian state, there was an

Indian culture, of which its members were well aware, located within the easily definable subcontinent. By 'northern Asia' we mean the vast expanse between the Caucasus and the Pacific which became the Russian empire. By 'south-east Asia' we mean not only the south-west corner of the Asian mainland but the great semicircle of islands extending from Sumatra to Luzon. In this region four great cultures met—the Hindu, Chinese, Buddhist and Muslim; it was the last two which became most firmly established, with the distinction between them corresponding approximately to that between Malay islanders and Thai or Mongol mainlanders.

The Russian expansion into Muslim lands began in the valley of the Volga, whose people in the sixteenth century were Tatars and other smaller peoples, speaking languages of the Turkic or Finnish type. In 1555 Tsar Ivan IV captured Astrakhan at the mouth of the Volga. By the end of the century Russians had penetrated far into Siberia and had also expanded southwards to the mountain barrier of the Caucasus. The conquest of Siberia was similar to that of North America. Small and rather primitive peoples sparsely inhabited a vast land of forests and great rivers. Russian fur traders and gold prospectors explored the lands, armed actions subdued the people, and in due course the tsar's officials caught up with the colonists: the autocratic government of Russia, whose writ ran continuously (even though with long delays) overland, was able to keep its distant subjects under control in a way that the constitutional government of England could not do with its constitutionally-minded American subjects separated by the ocean.

In the Caucasus the Russians faced a great variety of peoples, speaking languages widely differing from each other. Some were Christian, and welcomed the Russians as protectors against the Turks or Persians; others were fanatical Muslims, and fought the Russians bravely and successfully. The kingdom of Georgia, whose people were of Orthodox Christian faith, freely united with Russia in 1801. Other regions of Georgian or related speech, as well as the northern half of the homeland of the Azeri Turks along the Caspian Sea, were annexed in 1813. Persian Armenia was ceded to Russia in 1828. The Armenians became loyal subjects of the tsars, because they hoped that they would liberate the much larger population and more extensive lands of those Armenians who were subjects of the Ottoman empire; but this never came to pass. In the main Caucasus mountain range itself the Muslim Circassians in the west and Chechens in the east were not finally subdued until 1864 and 1859 respectively.

Further east, in the steppes south-east of the Urals, the Turkic-speaking Bashkirs and Kazakhs became loosely subject to the tsars in the mid-eighteenth century, but Russian authority was not made effective until the 1840s. To their south lived the Turkic and Iranian peoples of the Central Asian mountain valleys, a region of extremely ancient civilisation; these people were not nomads like the Kazakhs but skilled agricultural peoples, with such famous urban centres of culture as Samarkand and Bokhara. These lands, generally known as Turkestan, were conquered by Russian armies in the 1860s. The process of Russian expansion in Central Asia was completed with the annexation of the lands of the Transcaspian Turcomans between 1882 and 1885. Twenty years before this, Russia had forced China into ceding to her, by the Treaty of Peking of 1860, the Pacific coastline between the Amur and Ussuri rivers, at the southern tip of which a Russian port was founded with the arrogant name of Ruler of the East (Vladivostok).

In India the first European settlement was the Portuguese trading centre of Goa, founded in 1510. In the seventeenth century the English established themselves in three widely separated trading settlements: Bombay (a gift from their Portuguese allies), Calcutta (granted by the Bengal vassal of the Moghul emperor) and Madras (in the remnant of the former kingdom of Vijayanagar). In the eighteenth century the French too appeared in India. The British[4] and French, bitter rivals in Europe, in America and in India, sought to enlist the support of Indian rulers against each other. It was this warfare between the two European powers which caused the British East India Company to extend its power inland. By the end of the century the three British presidencies included a large part of the subcontinent. In the first half of the nineteenth century, the strongest remaining states, the Maratha Confederacy and the Sikh state in the Punjab, were subdued. In 1858 the East India Company was dissolved, and its possessions were taken over by the British crown. Thus the whole of India was dominated by Britain: the most important regions were directly ruled, while a host of larger and smaller Indian principalities accepted a British protectorate.

In south-east Asia Europeans first appeared on the islands, and on the coasts facing them. The pioneering Portuguese captured the powerful Malay trading principality of Malacca in 1511, and then established bases in the Moluccas. Their sea-borne empire extended from points on the East African coast across to Ceylon and east to Macao on the coast of China, and to the island of Formosa. The island group lying south of Formosa, first discovered by Magellan in 1521, and named in 1542 Philippines after the king of Spain, had been mainly conquered by the end of the sixteenth century;[5] its inhabitants were converted to Christianity in the following decades.

The next European intruders, the Dutch, organised in the Netherlands East India Company (founded in 1602), successfully resisted English attempts to install themselves in the islands, and forced the Portuguese out of Malacca in 1641 and most of Ceylon by 1658. The centre of Dutch power was the settlement of Batavia in western Java, captured by the great conqueror and administrator Jan Pieterszoon Coen in 1619. From the mid-seventeenth century the Dutch dominated the whole archipelago, but it was not until the second half of the eighteenth century that direct Dutch rule was imposed over the interior of the islands.

At the end of the Napoleonic wars the Dutch recovered their possessions in the archipelago, but the British kept Ceylon and established themselves on the Malay peninsula, with their main base the city of Singapore, built on an island ceded in 1819 by the sultan of Johore.[6]

In the Philippines, Manila became a centre both of commerce and of Spanish culture, with its university founded in the seventeenth century. In 1898 during the Spanish-American War, the island peoples, or Filipinos, revolted under the leadership of Emilio Aguinaldo, but the war ended with the annexation of the Philippines by the United States.

On the mainland to the north of Malaya the main historical line of division was between the Vietnamese in the east, long subject to Chinese influence, including Confucianism and the Chinese script (though they had not been directly ruled by the Chinese since 939); and the peoples west of the Mekong who were Buddhists of the Hinayana school. These were the Khmers, whose ancestors had made their land Cambodia the centre of a splendid civilisation, mainly Hindu but partly Mahayana Buddhist, from the ninth to the thirteenth centuries; the Thais, who had been organised in a series of states in the land known to Europeans as Siam, since the late thirteenth century; and the Burmese, who had also been organised in a number of states between Arakan and the delta of the Irawaddy since the mid-eleventh century. Siam and the Vietnamese states had comparatively homogeneous populations, but in Burma there were several substantial smaller religious and language groups in addition to the Burmese.

European contact with these countries began in the sixteenth century. French Catholic missionaries were active in southern Vietnam or Cochin-China. The British rulers of Bengal became neighbours of Burma. In the nineteenth century both countries fell victims to imperial expansion. British conquest of Burma was completed in three wars between 1826 and 1886. French expansion on the mainland lasted from 1862 to the late 1880s, and resulted in the establishment of the French colony of Indo-China. Siam—or Thailand— remained an independent state between the British and French zones.

## China: decline and revival

China was never conquered by a European power, though portions of its territory were annexed, and indirect domination made itself felt in the economic field.

In the eighteenth century European merchants were permitted to trade with China through Canton, subject to numerous restrictions and exactions by Chinese officials, to which they adapted themselves with some success. Thanks to these limitations of contact the Chinese empire was effectively insulated from the overseas enterprises of the Europeans. There was no meeting of minds. To the Chinese, the Europeans were impudent barbarian intruders. The Europeans felt entitled to security in the performance of their peaceful tasks, and believed that they were not just making money but bringing civilisation to the Chinese. Each side remained ignorant of the other. In particular the Chinese government was unaware of the growing disparity between its own military and economic resources and those of the Europeans.

In the 1830s the British government became involved in a series of quarrels about traders' rights. The most important concerned the trade in opium, highly profitable to British merchants, which the Chinese government decided, not less from concern for its own economic advantage than from moral revulsion, to suppress. The result was an Anglo-Chinese war from 1839 to 1842. The Chinese were unable to defend their coasts against British warships, and had to make peace between 1842 and 1844, transferring the island of Hongkong to British sovereignty and opening five Chinese ports to British merchants. Other European governments, as well as the United States and Japan, obtained similar rights. The great international settlements in Shanghai became small modern states inside the Chinese empire, administered by foreigners but employing thousands of Chinese. Trade in Chinese coastal waters and up Chinese rivers passed largely to foreigners. The Chinese government became indebted to foreign banks, and foreigners staffed the Imperial Maritime Customs Service.[7]

During the first half of the century European Christian missionaries, both Protestant and Catholic, began to operate in China, and after the Opium War they found their task much easier. Among those influenced by a Chinese translation of the Bible was a frustrated scholar who had failed in the examinations in Hongkong. His name was Hung Hsiu-ch'uan, and he came from the Hakka language group. He became the leader of the so-called T'aiping Rebellion, which convulsed all China in the 1850s.

One cause of the rebellion was the misery brought about by the shifting of the course of the Yellow River, which caused massive loss of life through floods and famine, and made millions more homeless, sending off an influx of refugees into southern China. The rebellion started by Hung in Kwangsi province in July 1850 was in the tradition of the great popular revolts which had brought earlier Chinese dynasties to an end. It also had a national character, being directed against the Manchu rulers of China, much as the revolt of 1368 which established the Ming dynasty had been directed against the Mongol rulers. It also had a religious character, as Hung took the title of Heavenly King, proclaiming the Great Peace (*T'ai-ping*). His doctrines owed a good deal to Christianity, and he proclaimed himself the Heavenly Younger Brother of Christ. His policy of social revolution owed some of its ideas to those of the radical reformers of Han and Sung times, Wang Mang (9-23 AD) and Wang An-shih (1069-74). The rebellion was at first very successful. In large parts of the empire the apparatus of government crumpled up. The T'aipings for more than a decade held a vast area on both sides of the middle and lower Yangtse, and had their capital in Nanking.

In the end however the Ch'ing dynasty survived. This was largely due to the efforts of two high officials who organised efficient armies over a period of years: Tseng Kuo-fan (1811-72) in Hunan province and Li Hung-chang (1823-1901) in Anhwei. It was also due to the help of a force of European mercenaries, led first by the American Frederick Townsend Ward and then by the Scotsman Charles Gordon from 1862 to 1864. In July 1864 the capture of Nanking by Chinese government troops brought the rebellion to an end. It had cost many millions of Chinese dead.

While the T'aipings were still at the height of their power, further quarrels between the Chinese and European governments had led to a further war, of Britain and France jointly against China, with intermittent military operations from 1856 to 1860. In October 1860 the allied forces entered Peking. In the next years eleven more treaty ports were opened to European traders. The Russian governments made use of China's weakness to obtain large territories between the confluence of the Ussuri and Amur rivers and the Pacific.

During the next thirty years an attempt was made, at first under the leadership of Tseng Kuo-fan, to repair the damage of the T'aiping rebellion and to make the government of China more efficient and more modern without abandoning the main principles of Confucian doctrine or bureaucratic structure, and without adopting pernicious European ideas. It looked as if progress had been made; but the fighting which broke out in Korea in 1894 against the Japanese brought a bitter reawakening. This disastrous war introduced the period when China found itself at the mercy of the European powers and their Japanese pupil; when railways were built and policed for the advantage of Russian empire-builders and their French bankers;[8] when China's alliance with Russia brought not protection but exploitation; when Russian and Japanese armies fought each other on Chinese soil without regard for the government of China; when foreign business communities in Shanghai lorded it over Chinese; and when the only reason why China was not entirely occupied by foreign powers was that the operation would have cost them too much.

There were attempts at reform. The most important was that of K'ang Yu-wei, a Cantonese who tried to interpret Confucius so as to justify the introduction of western political institutions, in order to strengthen China in the face of its aggressors. Though he convinced the young emperor, his period of reform lasted only 'a hundred days' in 1898, and he was overthrown by the Empress Dowager Tzu-hsi. She encouraged the activities of a secret society which became widely known as the 'Boxers'. Originally both anti-Manchu and anti-foreign, it concentrated its hatred only against the Europeans, and was able to win wide popular support among the people of north China, which in these years suffered heavily from both drought and floods. In 1900 the Boxers beseiged the European and Japanese embassies and communities in Peking and Tientsin, which led to a joint punitive expedition by armed forces of the European powers and further economic concessions by China. The defeat of Russia by Japan in the war of 1904-5 on Chinese soil merely substituted Japanese for Russian predominance in north China.

From the 1870s onwards young Chinese began to go abroad to study, in America and Europe and increasingly in Japan. In 1906 there were over 13,000 Chinese students in Japan, of whom only some hundreds completed serious studies, but all of whom were subjected to new cultural and political influences. In China in 1905 the old examinations system was abolished, as being incompatible with a modern system of schools, the need for which was now officially admitted. In practice the creation of a modern education system, despite some initial successes, was bound to be a long process, and in the short run the effect of abolishing the old system was not so much to improve as to dislocate the means of social mobility. Those who had studied abroad were the main source of new ideas, a varying mixture of western-style liberalism, nationalism and material progress. The man who emerged as the leader of a new democratic trend was Sun Yat-sen (1866-1925), the son of a peasant from the Macao area, who spent many years in the United States and Japan, and visited Europe. Sun became a professional revolutionary, and organised a number of unsuccessful risings in the south, backed by financial help from overseas Chinese, mainly in Hongkong and Singapore. Of the successive names given by him to the political groups which he founded, that which became permanently known in China and outside was Kuomintang (National People's Party). The famous 'three principles of the people', which Sun enunciated as the essence of his policy, have been conventionally translated as Nationalism, Democracy and People's Livelihood. Essentially all Chinese radicals had a double aim: to free China from European domination and to reorganise Chinese public life. Social reform and national independence were inseparable in their minds: the phrase 'Chinese nationalism' does not satisfactorily describe them, but no better name has been found.

Anti-Manchu feeling grew, and was by no means confined to the southern provinces. An army mutiny in Wuchang on 10 October 1911 set off revolts in the southern, central and north-western provinces, and a provisional republican government was set up in Nanking. Sun Yat-sen returned to China in January 1912 to be elected president; but the real power was in the hands of the most eminent Chinese general, Yuan Shih-kai. Yuan failed to make himself emperor, and died in 1916. During the next decade the main force in China were a number of rival generals ('warlords'), each of whom had his own army and territorial base. They alternately threatened each other or joined together in temporary combinations to direct the nominal government in Peking.

Meanwhile reforming and revolutionary ideas were spreading in the educated class. The main intellectual centre was Peking National University, whose chancellor from 1917 was Ts'ai Yuan-pei, a classical scholar of liberal inclination who had been minister of education in 1912. Under his protection two outstanding scholars made themselves felt. One was Hu Shih, a former pupil of John Dewey at Columbia University in New York, who was the chief spokesman for the modernisation of the language. He wished to replace the classical style, with its artificially rigid use of the script, very difficult to understand, by a freer style, more closely related to the spoken language, known as *pai-hua*. The model was the popular novels of the late Ming and early Ch'ing eras, which the Confucian scholars had affected to despise as being in vulgar taste. The campaign was successful, and a flourishing new literature began to appear in periodicals using the *pai-hua*. This sustained action by Hu Shih bore lasting fruit, and was felt long after the moderately liberal ideas of its champion had been forgotten in China. The second outstanding figure was the dean of letters of the Peking University, Ch'en Tu-hsiu, who was mainly interested in political philosophy, and responded with enthusiasm to the ideas inspiring the Bolshevik Revolution in Russia as soon as they filtered through to China.

On 4 May 1919 there were big student demonstrations in Peking to protest against the decision of the Paris Peace Conference to approve of the occupation by the Japanese of part of Shantung province, which had formerly belonged to Germany. This May Fourth Incident triggered off nationalist demonstrations, press campaigns and anti-Japanese trade boycotts in other cities, and started a stronger nationalist movement, with deeper popular support, than had yet been seen. Sun Yat-sen was able to establish a government in Canton. Soviet Russian military and political advisers helped to make the Kuomintang a more efficient political instrument. Sun Yat-sen collaborated, until his death in 1925, with the newly formed Chinese Communist Party, led by Ch'en Tu-hsiu. A new army, led by General Chiang Kai-shek, moved north, and at first Kuomintang and communists, though they had previously clashed several times and basically distrusted each other, marched together. This cooperation came to an end in 1927 when Chiang Kai-shek suppressed the communists in Shanghai. What was left of communist armed forces retired to mountainous parts of Kiangsi province.

For the next ten years the greater part of China was at least nominally under the rule of the Kuomintang. Chiang's aim, like that of Kemal in Turkey and Reza in Iran, was to modernise and strengthen China, to develop industries and schools, to improve the conditions in which the people lived and to bring them into the process of government. On balance he failed. Firstly, the Kuomintang never really took over China: considerable regions were left under the control of regional warlords with whom Chiang had to compromise. Secondly, his attention was largely concentrated on improvements at the top of the government machine, for which he recruited both Western advisers and Chinese trained in the most modern Western skills. Many of these men had excellent aims, but they had too little contact with the middle levels of the bureaucracy, and even less with the people at large, least of all with the peasants. Thirdly, Chiang's preference was for military hierarchy and military methods: he would give orders, and expect them to be carried out, but never mastered the skills of persuasion, and of involvement of large numbers as willing executants of policy, essential to civil government. Chiang was a conservative at heart. He believed that China should be ruled by the elite of *literati* and gentry, but he did wish to make the elite understand and use modern methods of government. In practice, most of them learned little if anything, and little changed. Something like a modern Chinese business class began to appear in the cities, but it too was not averse to using traditional methods to enrich itself. Finally, Chiang had the misfortune to have his country attacked by the Japanese, in Manchuria in 1931, in North China a few years later, and an all-out invasion in 1937, which led to the loss of all the richest parts of the country and the retreat of the government to Chungking, in the remote province of Szechwan. Inevitably, a much higher proportion of much reduced resources had to be devoted to military purposes, and isolation from the rest of the world, except by inadequate air contact through Burma, still further hampered economic or social progress.

Meanwhile the Chinese communists emerged as a strong rival. Regrouped under Mao Tse-tung, after the 'Long March' from 1934 to 1936 which led them from Kiangsi west and then north over a six-thousand-mile journey to Yenan in Shensi province, they there set up a state of their own. By a combination of coercion and persuasion, by lowering land rents and developing schools and propaganda, and by fighting the Japanese in guerrilla actions, the communists won growing support from the peasants, and drew more and more people into political life on their terms. Their action spread far outside the Shensi region. 'Liberated areas' were established between the main lines of communication, which remained in Japanese hands. By 1945 the communists claimed to have nineteen bases with a civil population between 70,000,000 and 90,000,000, and to have around a million persons under arms. The communists fought more actively and continuously against the Japanese than did the Chungking government in the 1940s. This active resistance won widespread support among the peasants and among intellectuals, especially perhaps among the students of Peking University, which was operating under the rule of a Japanese-sponsored Chinese government, set up in rivalry to the Chungking government. Essentially, the communists were mobilising to their purposes the Chinese national feeling which Japanese conquest had provoked, were claiming a monopoly of patriotism, and were completing the process of transformation of the Chinese from a civilisation into a nation. The process in many ways resembled that which was going on, parallel and without significant mutual influences, in occupied Yugoslavia.

When Japan was defeated in 1945 the rivalry between Kuomintang and communists grew into a large-scale civil war, which the communists won. Thereafter China became a major military power (as was shown in the Korean War in 1951) and an industrial power. In a world united by communications as it had never previously been in Chinese history, China was again a great power. China was also very vulnerable, having on its vast western and northern frontiers the Soviet empire, ruled by ruthless despots of immense arrogance and self-righteousness, and to its east an economically resurgent Japan, and beyond it the unpredictable but extremely powerful United States.

Looking back at Chinese history, the temptation to pay more attention to the continuity than to the breaches in it is almost irresistible. The Chinese is the only one of the great empires which imposed a single culture on the vast majority of its subjects and maintained, with only a few short intervals of confusion, its sovereignty over the same territory for three thousand years up to the present time.

At the beginning of the twentieth century it looked as if this great and durable civilisation had come to an end; that China would, like the Ottoman empire, be a dependency of the modern powers; that huge chunks of its territory would be lopped off. First came the European scramble for concessions, then Japan's Greater East Asia Co-Prosperity Sphere, then the rhetoric in the 1950s about the American Century, then the monolithic Socialist Camp led by Stalin, the Teacher of Genius of all Progressive Humanity. In each of these stages, great benefits were promised to the Chinese people by its arrogant self-constituted protectors. It may be argued that the brief period of American ascendancy differed from the others in so far as Franklin Roosevelt truly believed that a renascent China would become one of the Big Four (or more than four) albeit made over in an American image.

None of these blueprints was put into practice. Looking back from the 1970s one may see the hundred years from the Opium War to the triumph of Mao Tse-tung as another of those troubled interludes which have brought suffering and humiliation to the Chinese people, yet cannot destroy Chinese civilisation. Mao made China again one of the main centres of power in the world. He founded not a new hereditary dynasty but a new empire, based on a political elite, differing less radically than its members and contemporary observers thought from that of past dynasties. The future of the elite and of the empire, however, were full of uncertainties.

The continuity should not blind the observer to the change. European ideologies—both nationalism and communism—had left their mark. Everything was now done in the name of the people, which under earlier dynasties had been a passive factor. The Kuomintang half-heartedly, and the communists effectively, set themselves to mobilise hundreds of millions of peasants and workers, to draw them into political life. Thus it may be argued that the European Enlightenment made itself indirectly felt, and the Chinese became a nation. The social structure and the culture of this nation was also transformed by the revolutions which the communists introduced, and repeated in various forms. The whole Confucian heritage was repudiated, many historical documents and works of art were destroyed, and the printed and broadcast word and the schools were used to indoctrinate everyone with Mao's interpretation of Marxism-Leninism. Only the ideographic script, though modified, remained, as a special barrier between China and the rest of the world except Japan and Korea.


## The Japanese

Under the Tokugawa shogunate, from the beginning of the seventeenth century until the mid-nineteenth, Japan was almost completely isolated from the rest of the world. However, on these islands there existed an efficient system of government, a rather prosperous economy and a flourishing and homogeneous national culture. Political power was based on balance between the shogun, with his capital at Edo (modern Tokyo) and the 'outer' *daimyo*, the big aristocratic families who controlled the western, southern and northern regions. The *daimyo* had their castle towns and their peasant subjects. They were served by the lesser nobility or warrior class (*samurai*), who numbered perhaps as much as 6 per cent of the whole population. The *samurai* did not often have to do any fighting, but they were brought up on a code of military virtues, the way of the warrior (*bushido*). They were not landowners: they resided in the castle town, and received regular incomes, measured in a quantity of rice contributed by the peasants. The *daimyo* were obliged to send members of their families to Edo, as hostages to their good behaviour, and to come there themselves for part of the year. This system of 'alternate attendance' (*sankin kotai*) involved them in large expenditures, which provided a demand for the services of merchants. Nominally the merchants were the lowest in social esteem of the four officially recognised classes of Japanese society, ranking below peasants and artisans. In reality many of them were able to acquire great wealth and considerable political influence. Edo, and to a lesser extent the smaller castle towns, were centres of crafts, painting and literature. Tokugawa Japan also had an unusually developed system of schools. It seems possible that by the early nineteenth century something like 40 per cent of male children in Japan were literate, which was a higher proportion not only than in China but also than in most European countries at the time.

From the beginning of the nineteenth century the rulers of Japan became aware of growing external pressure to break down their isolation. The Dutch, who had been the strongest European power in the Far East in the seventeenth century, and who had been allowed by the shoguns to keep a trading station in Nagasaki harbour—the only authorised presence of foreigners in Japan—were now much less important. The growing pressures came from Russia in the north and from Britain and America in the east and south. The first European attempts to open regular relations were rejected. The decisive effort was made by the government of the United States, which sent a fleet under Commodore Matthew Perry to Edo Bay in July 1853. On his return in February 1854 negotiations were resumed, and during the next five years treaties were made with Russia, Britain, France and the Netherlands regulating future commercial and diplomatic relations.

By accepting the foreigners' demands the shogun and his government (the *Bakufu*) had incurred odium from the most patriotic elements, as traitors to the national cause. There was already considerable internal discontent with the *Bakufu*, from the *daimyo* who wanted to free themselves from the shackles of the *sankin kotai* system, and from both *samurai* and merchants who were socially frustrated in various ways. These different forms of discontent became increasingly fused in the 1850s. The *Bakufu* was the object of hatred, and resistance to the foreigners was the aim. At the same time, there was a growing feeling of national unity in the face of external danger, and of a need for a rallying point for national resistance, which the *Bakufu* could no longer provide. The answer was found in the exaltation of the emperor, whom it became the object of the extreme patriots to restore to his rightful position, usurped by the Tokugawa. The emperor, descended directly from the sun-goddess, was the very essence of the special Japanese 'national polity', or *kokutai*. This became the key-word of the nationalist ideology, compounded of Confucianism and Shinto religious beliefs, which in changing forms dominated the

Japanese scene for more than eighty years.

The patriots' plan of action was summed up in the slogan 'Honour the Emperor, expel the barbarians'. The second part of the plan proved harder to put into effect than the first. The centre of resistance to the foreigners was in the two main 'outer' *daimyo* domains of Choshu (in western Honshu) and Satsuma (in southern Kyushu). In June 1863 Choshu forts fired on an American ship, and some days later French and Dutch ships were attacked. In Satsuma territory a British subject was killed in 1862, the authorities failed to take action against his murderers, and in August 1863 there was fighting between British ships and Satsuma ships and land batteries, ending with the destruction of part of the city of Kagoshima by the British. These incidents showed the Japanese that they could not resist the foreign powers. Instead, the two *daimyo* governments built up military forces of their own, some of which were commanded by young Japanese who had been sent to study in the West. In January 1868 Satsuma and Choshu forces seized Kyoto, the ancient capital, and proclaimed the Restoration of the Emperor (whose reign was given the name of Meiji) and the deposition of the shogun. There followed a civil war, in which the last Tokugawa forces surrendered in May 1869.

The Meiji Restoration introduced a radically new era in Japanese history. The replacement of shogun by emperor was of no more than symbolic significance. What was essential was that a modern state, based on European models, was set up, and that all the old legal privileges were abolished. The *daimyo* domains and the Tokugawa lands were split up into prefectures; *samurai* stipends were abolished in return for a lump sum in compensation; a modern army was based on conscription; the main source of revenue was a new uniform land tax; and a system of schools and universities of a Western type was rapidly erected. These great changes were enacted in the early 1870s. They provoked some discontent, which was expressed in 1877 in an armed rising led by Saigo Takamori (1828-77), one of the leaders of the Restoration; but by the end of the decade they were working, and by the end of the century Japan had become both a military and an industrial great power.

The contrast between Japan's quick adaptation to the world of modern capitalism and the modern sovereign state and China's failure to do this has often been discussed. Several reasons have been suggested by modern specialists. One is the obvious physical difference. The Japanese islands formed a small and compact territory, all parts of which were accessible to foreign sea-power, and in which it was impossible for one region to be affected without the rest of the country being aware of it: China was half a continent, in which the centres of power, wealth and population were not mainly on the coast. A second is that Japanese culture had arisen from a combination of several influences, of which the political class were aware, so that the addition of new elements did not seem in principle unacceptable; whereas to the Chinese elite their culture seemed homogeneous and unchangeable (although new influences had from time to time been brought in during their history), and was indeed regarded as the only true culture, immensely superior to that of any barbarians who were merely clever or strong. The fact that warriors and merchants were the two most vigorous elements in Japanese society was also important, because it was precisely in military and in economic skills that the Western barbarians had shown themselves most efficient, and therefore perhaps worth imitating.

Be this as it may, the rapid adaptation took place, and it strengthened the coherence of Japanese society. By the end of the century there could be no doubt that the Japanese were a nation, and that Japan was not only a sovereign state but a national state.

### Hindus, Muslims, and British in India

British rule in India, and the growth of nationalist movements against it, were complicated by the existence of two great religious communities in the subcontinent. Some consideration must first be given to the history of the relationship between them.

As a result of the repeated invasions, and the rise and fall of principalities, a large part of the population of India became Muslim. The largest proportion of conversions were in three regions—the north-west, the lands north of Delhi, and Bengal. One of the attractions of Islam was liberation from the fetters of caste, though it is doubtful whether historians will ever be able to estimate with any precision the relative importance, in the success of Islam in certain regions, of force and persecution, of genuine conversion to a new faith and a new order, of the settlement of immigrants of Turki or Iranian stock, and of chance. In the greater part of northern and central India, the bulk of the population remained Hindu, and Muslims lived among them. The first intolerant zeal of the Muslim invaders ebbed away. The two communities influenced each other. Muslims adopted elements of the caste system in their social organisation. Both the doctrines of Muslim Sufis and of Hindu Sikhs contributed to the mystic *bhakti* movements of the fifteenth century, of which the most important was that led by Nanak (1469-1533), the founder of the Sikh religion.

Under the Moghul emperor Akbar (reigned 1556-1605), the coexistence of Hindus and Muslims was officially encouraged. Akbar took Hindus into his service both as military commanders and as civil officials. Rajput nobles were equal in his confidence to the Turkish or Afghan soldiers of his own people. The language of the Moghul court was Persian, though the mother tongue of the elite was Turkish.[9] The Hindu elite which Akbar patronised also began to learn Persian, which in the seventeenth century became the language of culture in most of India.

At the time of the Muslim invasions of India, the Hindus' language of culture had been Sanskrit, which was standardised as a written language by the fourth century BC, in the grammar of the great scholar Panini. From Sanskrit were derived a series of simpler spoken languages, varying substantially from Sind across to Bengal. These spoken tongues were promoted by the *bhakti* movements of the fifteenth century, and they began to take their place as literary languages as well. The situation in the south of India was different. Here the prevalent languages belonged to the Dravidian group, of completely different origin from the Aryan or Indo-European languages derived from Sanskrit. Tamil literature went back to about the time of Christ. Two other Dravidian languages, Kannada and Telugu, were widely spoken at the end of the first Christian millennium, and a fourth, Malayalam, spoken on the Malabar coast, became a written language in the fifteenth century.

The Hindu language spoken in the Delhi region at the time when the Delhi Muslim sultanate was established was that which has become known as Hindi. During the eighteenth century there emerged a new language, formed from both Sanskrit and Persian origins. The basic structure was Indian, but a large part of the vocabulary was Persian (that is, largely Arabic, since so many Persian words denoting intellectual concepts were loan-words from Arabic, the sacred language of Islam). This new language was known as Urdu (derived from the Turkish word for 'army'). In the eighteenth century it was not only convenient as a *lingua franca* for spoken communication between different parts of northern India, but produced its own imaginative literature. Under British rule in the nineteenth century, it became known as Hindustani. The Indian intellectual elite which emerged under British rule was attracted by the idea of a single language for all India, and later still Mahatma Gandhi accepted the name Hindustani, and regarded it as the future language of free India. It could be written in both the Arabic script (which was used for Urdu under the Moghuls) and the Devanagari Hindu script. A suggestive parallel is the use of the Serbo-Croatian language in both the Latin and the Cyrillic alphabet.

The Indians whom the British fought, in order to establish their empire, were both Muslims and Hindus in the Madras region; Muslims in Bengal; Hindus in the Maratha lands behind Bombay; and Sikhs in the Punjab. Among those rulers and their descendants who most resented British predominance, as well as among those who gladly became allies of the British or accepted their protection, there were both Muslims and Hindus. Towards the vast peasant majority of the population of India the British government adopted the traditional function of earlier rulers: it demanded taxes and soldiers, performed certain communal services and provided courts of justice. In 1857 some of the traditional rulers, both Muslim and Hindu, revolted against the British (the so-called Indian Mutiny), with heroic support from some of their subjects, and were defeated. It was only after this great tragedy that new elites, influenced both positively and negatively by European forms of education, appeared as claimants to speak for the people of India. The elites emerged among both Hindus and Muslims, and both were entitled to consider themselves Indian.

In Bengal and Bombay Hindus proved more capable than Muslims of adapting themselves to the modern economic and social trends which prevailed with European rule, more willing to pursue British-type professions and to seek employment in the British administrative apparatus. It is however a mistake to generalise this superior Hindu ability to the whole of India: it was definitely not true of the central part of northern India.[10]

Those Hindus who did successfully adapt themselves found that their efforts met with little encouragement from the British authorities, and that they were viewed with mistrust and contempt by the non-official British communities. One of these men was Surendranath Banerjea, who was rejected as a candidate for the Indian civil service. In 1876 he founded the Indian Association, which pressed for greater opportunities for Indians to enter the government service of their country. During these years there was also some growth of political discontent among orthodox Hindus, who resented British rule and wished to maintain traditional values, while realising that they also had to face the challenges of the modern world. In 1875 Arya Samaj was founded by Swami Dayananda, a Gujarati Brahmin. It made some headway in the Punjab, where it alarmed the Muslim community. In 1883 the hopes of modern-minded Hindus aroused by judicial reforms proposed by a new viceroy, Lord Ripon, were bitterly disappointed when fierce opposition by the British community in Bengal caused them to be abandoned. With the help of some liberal-minded British friends, they founded in 1885 the Indian National Congress. This became the main Indian political organisation, appealing at first only to a small social elite but including among its supporters both orthodox Hindus and westernised Indians. The Congress gained further support in 1905, when Lord Curzon divided Bengal into two provinces. The effect of the division was to give a Muslim majority in the eastern province, and to place Bengalis in a slight minority among Biharis and Oriyas in the western province: both results were objectionable to the educated Hindu Bengali elite. In the next years, however, the outstanding leaders of Congress were two men of Mahratta origin from Bombay presidency. Gopal Krishna Gokhale (1866-1915) was essentially a liberal westerniser, willing to take part in British-made institutions in order thus to extract political advantages for Indians. Bal Gahandhar Tilak (1856-1920) looked back to the glorious Mahratta past and upheld Hindu values against western. The two men stood for conflicting trends within the Congress, which led to a breach at its 1907 meeting in Surat which was not healed until 1916. Meanwhile the nationalist movement was based not only on the political aspirations of the intellectual elite, whether westernised or orthodox, but also on the growing influence of Indian business groups whose interests had been harmed in various ways by British economic policies.

The Muslims too were divided between modernisers and orthodox. They were increasingly aware that they were a vulnerable minority in India, threatened not only by their new masters the infidel British but also by the revival of their old victims the no less infidel Hindus. Muslim political leaders were compelled tactically to side with the Hindus against the British or with the British against the Hindus. At first the modernisers, who were politically the more effective group, chose the second alternative. They welcomed the division of Bengal. In 1906 it was a disciple of Sayyid Ahmad,[11] named Muhsin al-Mulk, who founded in 1906 the Muslim League. When the British introduced in 1909 the India Councils Act (usually known as the Morley-Minto reform), providing for the election of Indians to provincial assemblies and governments, they placed Hindus and Muslims in separate electoral colleges. This accorded with Muslim wishes, but was understandably regarded by Congress as a piece of imperialist 'divide-and-rule' tactics. In 1911 however the British government decided to restore a unified Bengal, which annoyed the Muslims.

The First World War brought regulations and economic hardships which affected the civil population, both Hindu and Muslim, both peasants and businessmen. The war was, however, especially objectionable to the Muslims because one of the enemies of Britain, against whom Indian soldiers were obliged to fight, was the largest Muslim state in the world, the Ottoman empire. When the war was over, and it appeared that Turkey was to be partitioned by her conquerors, a movement for the defence of the caliphate was started.

Before this, an agreement had been made at Lucknow in 1916 between Congress and the Muslim League for common action. The most important point was that both sides agreed that any future measures that would affect the position of either religious community as a whole should become law only if it had the support of three-quarters of the members of that community. Between 1919 and 1922 cooperation between Muslims and Hindus against the British was effective. It was in these years that Gandhi rose to the front rank on the Hindu side, and began to mobilise the Hindu masses in the political struggle. The civil disobedience campaigns of 1920 to 1922 involved both Hindus and Muslims.

Gandhi was a man of genius who defies all brief explanation; and even the massive detailed research which has been devoted to his career has left much that is controversial or even obscure. Even so, any study of nations and nationalist movements must record the fact of his personal impact. Gandhi was both a religious prophet and a brilliant political operator. He could wear with equal ease the respectable suit of a London barrister or the *dhoti* of a Hindu sage. He could beat politicians and bureaucrats at their own game (though he suffered tactical political defeats from time to time), and he could make industrial magnates and party machines work for his ends. He was a convinced reformer, determined to break down the injustices of caste which no previous Hindu politician had dared to attack; and he was also able to enlist the manipulators of regional caste groups as officers of his political army. His campaigns of mass civil disobedience were planned to avoid violence, yet they let loose forces which were bound to provoke bloodshed. The mass shootings at Amritsar in April 1919 were a direct result of Gandhi's incitement, yet there is no reason to doubt his horror and repentance at the result; and after the Calcutta blood-bath of 1946, Gandhi's personal visit to Calcutta, and the brave public posture which he and the Bengal Muslim leader Suhrawardy then assumed, certainly prevented further massacres in the following tense months.

Gandhi was the first Indian nationalist leader to appeal for mass support. To what extent his 'charismatic' personality in fact 'mobilised' the masses is arguable. He undoubtedly extended the political struggle beyond the urban centres of the three presidencies to provinces whose population had hitherto been politically passive, such as Bihar, United Provinces and Punjab. Throughout the country he succeeded in enlisting new local elites, of lower social status than the previous leadership of Congress. These persons ('sub-contractors', to quote the useful expression of a recent historian[12]) were well qualified to involve much larger numbers, at least in periods of crisis or deep public emotion.

Gandhi exercised immense authority over his compatriots until his death. His well-dramatised protest marches, civil disobedience campaigns, prison sentences and hunger strikes captured the imagination of millions, not only in India. The effective leadership of Congress was however shared by others, who revered Gandhi as their leader but did not share all his ideas. The principle of *swadeshi*, or consumption of home-produced articles, was attractive to Indian big businessmen, though Gandhi's own main aim was to encourage small-scale crafts, symbolised by his praise for the peasant's spinning wheel. Jawaharlal Nehru, the son of the prominent nationalist Motilal, a Kashmiri Brahmin who was also a socialist and secular philosopher, took but little interest in Gandhi's religious beliefs. Gandhi's insistence on non-violence (*ahimsa*), and his doctrine of passive resistance by *satyagraha* ('truth-force'), undoubtedly won devoted supporters and influenced the behaviour of Indian crowds; but it is also true that there was plenty of violence by Indian against Indian during his life-time, and that he himself fell victim to a religious fanatic assassin. The limitations on the application of Gandhi's methods (which Gandhi himself recognised) did not prevent his successors from attributing their triumphs to these methods, or other nationalists in Asia and Africa from assuming the mantle of Gandhi when it suited them.

The caliphate campaign died out when Kemal himself abolished the caliphate in Turkey. In 1928, a committee of Congress led by Motilal Nehru produced a draft for a future constitution. In reply, the Muslim lawyer Muhammad Ali Jinnah (1876-1948), who from this time became the outstanding leader of the Muslims, outlined Muslim requirements in Fourteen Points, which included a federal system, far-reaching powers for its component units, reservation of residuary powers to them, and various safeguards for all Muslim citizens of the future Indian state. When these were rejected by Congress, its relations with the League deteriorated. Theoretical attempts were now made to identify a distinct Muslim nation within India. The most distinguished spokesman for a 'two-nation theory' was the poet and philosopher Muhammad Iqbal (1875-1938). A student both of Hinduism and of contemporary European philosophy, influenced by both and much addicted to unorthodox religious speculation, Iqbal maintained, in his presidential address to the Muslim League in 1930, that Indian Muslims were one nation, separate from the other people of the subcontinent. A lesser but important figure, Choudhary Rahmat Ali, published in 1935 a book entitled *Pakistan, the fatherland of the Pak nation*. This word, which means 'land of the pure', and was composed of the first or last letters of the names of various lands of Muslim population, gradually won popularity among the Indian Muslim intellectual elite.[13]

In 1937 an election was held under a new British-made constitution, which permitted the formation of ministries in the provinces by Indian political parties. Congress and the Muslim League were electoral allies. The result was a big success for Congress but a disappointingly small vote for the League. Jinnah expected that the new ministries, in provinces with large Muslim population, would include representatives of the League. However, Congress took the view that its victory entitled it to form the ministries alone. It would accept Muslim ministers only if they resigned from the League. They argued that the League was a 'communal' organisation representing one religious community, whereas Congress was a secular and nation-wide organisation, to which Muslims could belong on equal terms with Hindus.

This decision of 1937 was a landmark in Hindu-Muslim relations. From this time Jinnah began systematically to mobilise Muslim mass opinion behind the League in opposition to Congress. On 23 March 1940 the Lahore meeting of the Muslim League passed a resolution demanding that those regions which had a Muslim majority should form 'independent states'. A last attempt at agreement was made by a British Cabinet Mission which visited India from March to May 1946. Its proposals would have allowed the predominantly Muslim provinces to form Muslim states within the projected independent Indian Union. For a short time it seemed that an interim government would be formed, on this understanding, from representatives of both Congress and the League. This was, however, not achieved, and Jinnah called for a campaign of 'direct action' to create Pakistan. One of the first results was a massacre in Calcutta in which 4,000 people lost their lives.

The stalemate was resolved by the British government's declaration of 20 February 1947 that independence would be given not later than June 1948. In June 1947 the last viceroy, Earl Mountbatten, produced his plan for the partition of India. Pakistan was to be formed of the north-western lands, part of Punjab and part of Bengal. Commissions of experts were set up to define the boundaries, but meanwhile there were massive movements of refugees in both directions, accompanied by massacre, starvation and disease. More than 500,000 persons lost their lives, and more than 12,000,000 lost their homes. This was the end of the British empire in India—peaceful in the sense that there was no fighting between British and Indians; magnanimous in the sense that the leading figures showed courtesy and gratitude to each other; generous in the sense that Mr Attlee and other British socialists and liberals had long had sincerely benevolent intentions towards the Indians; yet none of these things for those who were robbed, killed or saw their children slaughtered.

Controversy will long rage as to who was to blame, in the short and long term; whose obstinacy in the last years or whose fanaticism or Machiavellian designs in preceding decades did most to bring about the tragedy. Yet the truth is probably that it was not the wickedness of mean men but the devotion of noble men that proved disastrous. Nobility is a quality that cannot be denied to Gandhi or Jinnah or Jawaharlal Nehru, to Wavell or Attlee or Mountbatten. Neither British paternalism nor British liberalism, neither the plan for a secular Indian state nor the determination to preserve Indian Muslim identity, were contemptible. The truth is rather that the aims could not be reconciled, and that the passions which nationalist leaders aroused to promote their aims were bound to claim millions of victims from those for whose welfare they were designed.

## India: Multi-lingual nation or multi-national state?

The government of independent India in 1947, even after the amputation of the north-west and of most of Bengal, found itself responsible for most of a subcontinent. India was a historical and a religious concept, but there was no Indian nation. What held the people of India together was a culture, founded on religion; but the rulers of the new state insisted, with passionate sincerity, that it was to be secular, with absolutely no preference for one religion over another. In place of the unifying force of Hinduism, they offered the vision of a great modernised industrialised democratic India, and the reality of the unifying force of the Congress Party, with its central and regional bureaucracy. What pulled India apart was variety of language, but paradoxically this was counteracted not only by political power but also by the unifying force of the language of the expelled foreign rulers, which remained the vehicle of public administration at the higher levels.

The new government was heir not only to the provinces which had formed British India, but also the princely states which had been subject to various types of British protectorate. It proceeded to deal with them without worrying too much about democratic principles. In Hyderabad the people were Hindu and the ruler Muslim: democracy therefore meant incorporation in India, which duly occurred. In Kashmir the ruler was Hindu but the people were Muslim; yet the new government of India insisted on taking all Kashmir, and succeeded in annexing most of it after some fighting against the new army of Pakistan.

When it came to deciding what should be the main territorial units of federal India, neither the old British provinces nor the old princely states necessarily had a strong claim to be preserved. Instead, against the opposition of many eminent Congress leaders, the principle of linguistic units was accepted in successive stages. Andhra, with Telugu spoken by 86 per cent of its people, was formed as the first linguistic state in October 1953, out of parts of Madras province and Hyderabad. Under a new settlement of provinces, in November 1956, each of the other three Dravidian languages predominated in one state. In Madras, which took the name Tamilnad in 1968, Tamil was the language of 84 per cent of the people; in Mysore, renamed Karnataka in 1973, 65 per cent spoke Kannada; and in Kerala 95 per cent spoke Malayalam. In 1960, after some years of nationalist disorders, the large state of Bombay was divided into Gujarat, where 90 per cent spoke Gujarati, and Maharashtra, in which 76 per cent spoke Marathi. In West Bengal 84 per cent were Bengali-speaking; and in Assam the majority spoke Assamese, with a large minority speaking Bengali. In 1966 the Indian portion of Punjab was further divided, between Hindi-speaking Haryana province and Punjabi-speaking Punjab. In the rest of India it could be argued that Hindi was predominant: the extent of this predominance depended on whether Rajasthani, Bihari and Oriya were considered to be distinct languages or dialects of Hindi.

The Indian constitution of 1950 provided that Hindi in the Devanagari script should be the official language of India. It was estimated that 30 per cent of the population could speak this language, and a very much larger proportion could learn to understand it with but little effort since it was closely related to the languages which they habitually spoke. It was however clearly not possible to introduce Hindi into government at once. There must be an interval, during which English would remain the language of central government and of the higher administration throughout the country. This had two advantages: many modern technical, scientific or political terms had no Hindi equivalent, so that many important operations simply could not be conducted in Hindi; and the people of southern Indian could in fact only communicate with northerners through the *lingua franca* of English. The year 1965 was set as the time for adaptation to Hindi.

It was obviously undesirable that independent India should continue to be ruled in the language of the former imperial power, not only for obvious moral and political reasons but also because only some 2 per cent of the population knew English. However, the proposal to replace it by Hindi produced much the same reaction among the non-Hindi-speaking peoples, and especially in the southern states, as the proposal to replace the dead language Latin by the modern living language Magyar had produced among the non-Magyar-speaking people of Hungary in the first half of the nineteenth century.

The proportion of the population which could be considered to be Hindi-speaking varied between 30 and 43 per cent, depending on the definition of Hindi.[14] During the course of the 1950s and 1960s four states and two smaller territories of the Indian Union adopted Hindi as their official language.[15] In addition, knowledge of Hindi was widespread, and it was in fact the effective second language, in the two large western states of Maharashtra and Gujerat.

During more than twenty years of independence, Hindi underwent considerable change. Systematic efforts were made to enrich and enlarge its vocabulary, and to replace Persian/Arabic words by neologisms based on Sanskrit roots. During the same years films, radio and press in Hindi increased their audience, and translation from other Indian languages into Hindi became financially remunerative for writers. All these things increased the attractions of Hindi for a large part of the educated elite, and also for large numbers of people of all social classes who were drawn, often from a great distance, into the rapidly growing cities.

Nevertheless there were two regions in which Hindi did not make much appeal.

One was West Bengal. A rather large Bengali intellectual elite had grown up in the two centuries of British rule, and in the later period there had developed a notable literature in the Bengali language. Bengalis had also become quite prominent in the professions in other parts of India, especially in Indian universities and as writers and journalists. The Bengali elite knew English, and were prepared to recognise its merits as a language of government, however strongly they might desire the independence of India from British rule. Hindi they tended to regard as a backward, upstart and artificial tongue. After the partition of 1947, Hindu Bengalis of the social elite (generally known as *badhralok*, or 'respectable people') were forced into West Bengal or into more distant parts of India. The overpopulated West Bengal countryside was one of the poorest regions of India, and the urban agglomeration of Calcutta, steadily increased by the influx from the villages, became a hotbed of all sorts of discontents. Opposition to the central government grew steadily in West Bengal during the 1950s and 1960s. Its roots were in the desperate poverty of the urban masses, but those who expressed it were mostly members of the *badhralok*, educated men and women who inherited a certain tradition of political radicalism, and who found themselves in something like the predicament of the Russian intelligentsia of the nineteenth century, driven to ever more revolutionary views.

It was thus not surprising that West Bengal was one of the two strongholds of the communists. When the communists split in 1964, it was the left faction, the Communist Party of India (Marxist), or CPI(M), which had its greatest success in West Bengal. In the 1971 election to the state legislative assembly, it alone won 111 seats against the 105 seats of the official Congress. This situation changed after the war between India and Pakistan in 1971: in the March 1972 election to the West Bengal State Assembly, Indira Gandhi's party swept the board, winning 216 seats out of 280, while the CPI(M) retained only 14. This placed the CPI(M) far behind the official CPI, which in effect supported Congress, essentially because of Indira Gandhi's pro-Soviet posture: it won 35 seats. Nevertheless, it remained doubtful how long this Congress triumph would last, since the misery which produced revolutionary feeling in Bengal remained unchanged. One may argue that twenty years of strong opposition from West Bengal to Delhi governments was above all due to economic and social causes; but it was also true that feelings of Bengali cultural superiority, resentment at the division of Bengal, and a feeling that India was being run by politicians from the wrong regions, gave latent nationalist quality even to Bengali social revolutionary protest.

The region of India in which opposition to Hindi was most clearly related to national feeling was the south.

In those parts of Mysore which had belonged to Bombay under the British Raj, and in those parts of Andhra which had belonged to Madras, some knowledge of Hindi had been fostered in the school system before independence. Though the official languages chosen by these two states were Kannada and Telugu, there was no fierce feeling against learning Hindi as a second language. In Kerala, where the official language was Malayalam, the state government actively encouraged the study of Hindi.

For this there were several reasons. One was that Kerala, with a large Christian minority, had a higher rate of literacy than any part of India, and it was thus possible to teach more children quicker and more easily. A second was that, as it was also a region of exceptionally dense population, a very large proportion of its inhabitants sought employment in cities to the north, where a knowledge of Hindi helped them to get jobs. A third was that the communist party, which was very strong in Kerala, favoured the spread of Hindi. However, though all three state governments were willing to have Hindi taught, the introduction of Hindi as the official language of government aroused little enthusiasm from them or their peoples.

Opposition was strongest in Madras. The Tamil language had its long tradition of literature, and Tamil culture had always been somewhat different from that of the north, even though Tamils and northerners shared a Hindu heritage. Under British rule, a successful Madras intellectual elite had grown up, not less proud of its status, and with not less reason, than that of Bengal. The Madras elite differed from the Bengali in that it had been especially prominent in government service. This continued after independence, with a higher proportion of Madrasis entering the Indian administrative service than of entrants from other states. The examinations had always been conducted in English. Should this be changed to Hindi, Madrasis would find themselves at a grave disadvantage. Madras therefore spearheaded the attack against making Hindi the official language by 1965, which had been the proclaimed intention of the makers of the constitution of 1950.

As early as 1921 there had been an active political group which upheld the distinct interests of the Tamils. This was the Justice Party, which not only stood for regional rights but was especially directed against the supremacy of the Madras Brahmins. In succession to it there emerged in 1949 a party with a broad programme of social and political reform, which took the name *Dravida Munettra Kazagham* (Dravidian Progressive Movement). In the 1950s it won more and more followers, and in 1967 it held a clear majority in the state legislature as well as most Madras seats in the Indian parliament. The DMK declared its intention to work for a new constitution for India, with most of the powers transferred to the states, and a 'compositive government' at the centre with the bare minimum of authority. In September 1970 the DMK premier of Madras, since 1968 renamed Tamilnadu, held an All-India States Autonomy Convention, which was attended by some members of the Punjabi Sikh party, *Akali Dal*, and of a Bengal breakaway from Congress, the Bangla Congress. There was however little practical prospect of such a change of constitution, and the DMK was not prepared to press for separation from the Indian Union. Controlling Tamilnadu through their majority, they were willing to cooperate at the All-India level with Indira Gandhi.

The proposed replacement of English by Hindi was in fact indefinitely postponed, after years of argument about the best verbal formula, by the Official Languages Amendment Act of 1968. English remained the language of parliamentary debates, and had equal status with Hindi in official communications between the central and state governments, as well as in the conduct of government business. It was official policy to encourage the teaching of three languages in secondary schools. The government's intention was that in Hindi-speaking states the languages would be Hindi, English (or another modern European language) and a second Indian language; and that in the non-Hindi-speaking states they would be the regional language, Hindi and English (or another European language). This was refused by Tamilnadu, which preferred only two languages, Tamil and English, thus deliberately excluding Hindi. Moreover, even in Hindi-speaking northern India these good intentions were not carried out, since children were encouraged to take, as their second Indian language, not a southern language but either Sanskrit or Urdu, both of which were of course very close to Hindi.

Linguistic nationalism in India was also connected with religion. The founders of independent India were determined that it should be secular, and insisted that political parties should not be based on religion. One result was that the two main religious groups organised themselves nominally on the basis of language.

The Muslims of Uttar Pradesh rallied behind the defence of Urdu. The truth was that for the northern peasants Urdu and Hindi were virtually the same language, but that the two elites, insisting respectively on the Devanagari or Arabic script, on more Sanskrit words or more Arabic/Persian words, were in fact struggling for two competing cultures derived from religion. The rulers of Uttar Pradesh claimed to speak for secular democracy while using administrative power to minimise the teaching of Urdu, and denounced those who protested as Muslim fanatics; but the Muslims were convinced that their opponents in reality stood not for secular democracy but for Hindu domination.

Muslims, though numbering many millions, were scattered throughout India, and could not hope to form a state of their own within the Indian Union. This was however a possible aim for the second religious group, the Sikhs. They rallied behind the Punjabi language, written in the Gurumukhi script. In reality, at the level of peasant speech, the difference between Hindi and Punjabi was small: what was being defended was the Sikh religion. Punjabi language and Gurumukhi script in Punjab were the weapons of Sikhism: a rather different situation from that in Bosnia, where Cyrillic script and Orthodoxy were the weapons of Serbian nationalism. In Bosnia, intermingling of population made territorial separation impossible, but nationalism was a reality. In Punjab, concentration of Sikh population was sufficient (as a result of the mass expulsions at the time of Partition in 1947) to make separation possible, but Punjabi nationalism was not so much a real force as a disguise for the organisation of Sikh religious believers.[16] The Sikhs were successful in their struggle, and in 1965 Indian Punjab was divided into two states, Punjab and Haryana.

Further smaller regional nationalisms undoubtedly existed, such as the Maratha revivalist *Shiv Sena* (army of Shivaji) in the city of Bombay; and serious disturbances threatened to break up Andhra in 1973, when there was a movement to separate the territory formerly under Madras from the Telengana region, formerly part of the princely state of Hyderabad, whose citizens had been given privileged opportunities in the state service when the state of Andhra had been set up.

Hitherto, emphasis has been laid on the forces operating against Indian unity, and certain parallels have been suggested with Central Europe. However, there were also powerful forces operating in favour of unity. First of all must be placed the religious and cultural legacy of Hinduism, affecting in different ways and with differing intensity the vast majority of the people of India. This basic unity is certainly affected by changes in the place of caste in Indian affairs, by the complex interconnections between castes, by the rise and fall, consolidation or transformation, of individual castes. At a more easily visible level, a second unifying factor has been the Congress. An alliance of disparate organisations based in the different states, linked by flexible yet firm bonds, it survived the factional struggles and splits of the 1950s and 1960s and continued to defy any attempt to fit it into doctrinaire European political categories.

The conflict about the use of Hindi or of English had lost some of its intensity by the 1970s, but the future development of Hindi seemed certain to be an important matter. The growth of a single standardised language, in press and other media, intelligible to rapidly increasing millions who passed through India's growing school system, was likely to strengthen the national consciousness of those who adopted it as their language. In this respect it might be compared with the growth of a single written modern Arabic language, the same from Morocco to Iraq, whose use by the educated coexisted with the continued use by the peoples of distinct forms of speech barely intelligible from one major region to another. A comparison with the role of Russian in the Soviet Union also had some relevance, though it was less apt. Russian was already a standardised language early in the nineteenth century, and differences of dialect (as opposed to the two distinct languages Ukrainian and Byelorussian) ceased to be important. Russian was the vehicle for a great literature, and was spoken as mother tongue by all Russians. Hindi in the 1970s was far from occupying an analogous position in India. Neither the will nor the means existed in the early 1970s for a policy of Hindification comparable to the Russification of late tsarist or Soviet times, and India possessed no instrument at all similar to the bureaucracy of the tsars or to the communist party of the Soviet Union. Indira Gandhi's choice of dictatorship in 1975, though approved by her Soviet friends and by the CPI, was repudiated by the Indian electorate in March 1977.

Nevertheless there was perhaps another trend in Indian political life which had its Russian analogy. There seemed to be a movement of the centre of political gravity, from the great coastal cities to the land-locked northern plain. Not only was Delhi the capital both of the Moghul empire and of independent India, but it was in the north and centre that the vast Hindi-speaking reserve of manpower lived. Russia had had one St Petersburg, which after two brilliant centuries yielded place once more to Moscow. India had had three windows to the outside world—Calcutta, Bombay and Madras. It was the British rulers who brought the capital back to Delhi, in 1909: it may be that this will prove as symbolically important in Indian history as was Lenin's reversion to the old capital in 1918. It is in any case interesting that the case for the supremacy of Hindi in India was viewed with sympathy from the 1950s onwards by Soviet spokesmen, and also by the Moscow-oriented communist party of India.

Whether India would survive as a single great state, or whether bits would splinter off to leave one great central heir to the Moghul empire and several peripheral smaller states, it was quite impossible to predict. Much would depend on the unforeseeable effects of the fluctuating relationships between the great foreign powers of the Far East: America, Russia, China and Japan. Tendencies similar to the formation of national consciousness in other parts of the world were at work in different parts of India, but they would not necessarily prevail. The more or less official doctrine, that India was a nation state, that there was a single Indian nation, of composite culture, speaking many languages but united by a secular democracy, or socialism, or some other term yet to be devised, might in time obtain not just passive popular acquiescence but positive assent, and might be translated into practice, so that India would become a gigantic Switzerland. Or it might become clear that India was a multi-national state; in which case the several nations might be held in common bondage as in a still more populous version of the Soviet empire; or the multi-national state might, like the Habsburg Monarchy, burst asunder. European experience could probably be enlightening at times for Indian statesmen, but there was little point in trying to force India into intellectual categories derived from European history. Great states existed for centuries in India without any need for national consciousness, and new or old types of legitimacy and allegiance might well prove more effective.

### Pakistan

Pakistan faced the same two basic problems as India, an uncertain national identity and a variety of languages; but both were made more difficult by the fact that the country was divided into two parts, separated from each other by a distance of a thousand miles.

The foundation on which Indian identity had to be built was religious and cultural, and the same was true of Pakistan. However, whereas India included virtually all Hindus in the world (the Indonesian island of Bali and the small Indian diaspora across the oceans form but a slight exception), the people of Pakistan were only a peripheral section of a much wider Muslim world community. Hinduism was specific to India, but Islam was not specific to Pakistan. Before independence, political rhetoric had stressed the Muslim character of the nation which was being brought into being, though its leaders were rather secular-minded politicians. The new state would need a constitution, and this should be emphatically Islamic. But when the practical work of constitution-making began, it was found that the *ulema* had few practical proposals to make, and modernising bureaucrats and lawyers played the main part. The constitution was adopted in 1956, but two years later Field Marshal Ayub Khan became military dictator. A new constitution was devised in 1962, but it was not of much importance. Meanwhile civil servants ruled, while landowners gradually yielded place to businessmen as the most influential social class.

More than half the population of Pakistan had Bengali for their language and lived in the eastern section, where there was no other significant language group. In West Pakistan the language of nearly two-thirds (29 per cent for the whole state) was Punjabi. The two next most important languages were Sindhi (12.6 per cent in the West and 5.5 per cent in the whole) and Pushtu (8.5 per cent and 3.7 per cent). None of these was made the official language. Instead was chosen Urdu, which was the mother tongue of less than 4 per cent but had a glorious past as the language of the army of the Moghul empire, and was understood as a second language by the educated elite in the western part. As a result of pressure from the east, in 1954 Bengali was given official status equal to Urdu. English was also retained as a language of government.

But by far the greatest problem of Pakistan was its physical division. East Pakistan, with a solid Bengali population, had more than half the population of the whole state. In 1961 its population was about 51,000,000 and that of the West about 43,000,000. East Bengal suffered especially from the economic consequences of the partition of 1947. A very large part of the former Bengali elite remained in, or moved to, West Bengal, which also had the main industrial centres: the population of East Bengal thus consisted, to a quite exceptional extent even by south Asian standards, of impoverished peasants, cut off even from the slender means of material improvement which they had previously possessed, and at the same time lacking experienced political leadership.

In Pakistan it was the western half which provided the political and economic elite. West Pakistan had a considerable business class, which grew and prospered, though there were of course large regions of West Pakistan which were extremely backward; East Pakistan however largely lost its earlier business class, which had been Hindu, and what remained made slower progress. New industrialisation was much more successful in the West than in the East. The gap between the *per capita* income of the West and the East widened strikingly in the period from 1959-60 to 1968-69 to the disadvantage of the East. This was the more bitterly resented in the East because the exports of East Bengal provided the greater part of the foreign currency which was essential to the West's industrial expansion. The highest posts in the administration were also overwhelmingly held by westerners. In the Civil Service of Pakistan (CSP), the successor to the Indian Civil Service of British rule, the proportion of easterners in the yearly intake increased notably during the ten years' rule of Ayub Khan, as a result of conscious government policy, but it still remained well below the proportion of easterners in the total population.[17]

The new political system of Ayub, founded on locally elected 'basic democracies' and designed to exclude political parties of the earlier type, did not satisfy easterners. The Awami League, founded in 1949 as the main oppositional party in East Bengal, and crippled by Ayub's Elective Bodies Disqualification Ordinance of 1958, continued to command massive support. In 1966 its leader, Mujib ur-Rahman, put forward his Six-Point Programme. This demanded that the central government should confine itself to defence and foreign affairs; that the two parts of the country (or 'wings') should have almost complete independence to make economic policy; and that East Pakistan should be allowed to form a militia of its own. The government replied by arresting the Awami League leaders. However, popular discontent remained, and in 1968 opposition grew in both 'wings', being directed in the West essentially against Ayub's rule but in the East essentially for Bengali independence. Ayub resigned in March 1969, after having released Mujib ur-Rahman from prison. Mujib publicly reiterated his earlier demands, and added further measures of a socialist type, which had been part of an Eleven-Point Programme adopted by the radical East Bengal students at the end of 1968. Ayub's successor, General Aga Muhammad Yahya Khan, restored political liberties, and allowed an election to a National Assembly, which took place in December 1970. This gave the Awami League all but two of the seats in the East, and an overall majority in the whole of Pakistan (160 seats out of 300).

From this moment the disintegration of Pakistan went rapidly ahead.

The meeting of the National Assembly was postponed; Mujib made still more radical demands; and Yahya Khan ordered troops in to suppress what he regarded as sedition. There was brief armed resistance, followed by massacres of civilians, especially of university students and teachers, and by a sustained guerrilla campaign. In December 1971 the Indian government sent its army into Bengal, and also waged full-scale war against Pakistan in the West. The result was that a new sovereign state came into existence, Bangladesh, under the leadership of Mujib ur-Rahman.

Two decades of effort to create a Pakistan nation had clearly failed, and it was clear that the Pakistan state would not be reconstituted. The problem remained whether or not new nations seemed likely to appear in its place.

In the mid-1970s there were over a hundred million Bengalis in the world, about three-quarters of them in Bangladesh and one-quarter in West Bengal in India. They were united by a common language and culture, divided by religion. In 1947 the religious division had proved stronger than the cultural unity: was it possible that after a quarter of a century these factors would be reversed? Bengal could theoretically be united either as an independent state or within the Indian Union. Neither alternative looked very promising. A single hundred-million Bengali state would start its life as the greatest centre of poverty in the world, the most permanently threatened by starvation, and with the most hideously squalid urban agglomeration of the whole human race, Greater Calcutta. If India incorporated East Bengal, it would be incorporating mass misery; and though East Bengalis in 1972 regarded Mrs Indira Gandhi and her army as liberators, only a few years later sentiments had soured on both sides. There seemed little doubt that growing misery would create growing political discontent, especially among the younger generation of the educated elite. Left-wing forms of communism had been strong in West Bengal since the 1950s, and could very quickly spread among the easterners, whose less intellectually sophisticated political climate had been an obstacle in earlier years. Much would also depend on encouragement or direct help from China. The argument that, if Mao's type of political and social organisation had revitalised six hundred million Chinese, the same could be done for one hundred million Bengalis, had a certain persuasiveness. The Bengalis were desperately poor and their economy was in a primitive condition, but the same had been true of China before Mao. The Chinese had an ancient and splendid culture that formed an indestructible national cement; but the Bengalis had their ancient culture too.

The rulers and the army of West Pakistan were able to lead their people against the easterners until Indian superior force defeated them; but this did not mean that a single Pakistani nation had been created in the West. This was unfortunately far from true. The Baluchis in the south-west were restive, and many Pathans in the north-west were attracted by the idea of a common homeland of Pakhtoonistan, to be linked in some way with Afghanistan. In the latter country both Indian and Soviet Russian influence was strong, and these two countries, allied since 1971, had a common interest in using Afghanistan against Pakistan. Even in the more central core of the country, Punjabis and Sindhis were seldom on very good terms.

It would seem that there was in fact nothing that could be called a Pakistani nation, though it was also quite possible that the state of West Pakistan might survive, under a government whose real basis of legitimacy would not in fact be national identity (though its spokesmen might continue to talk as if it were), but more ancient traditions.

There existed in fact a vast territory, extending from Mesopotamia to the Pamirs and from the Caspian to Kashmir, which shared a common tradition of Muslim religion and Persian culture. This region was divided in the 1970s between Iran, Pakistan, Afghanistan and the Central Asian republics of the Soviet Union. States had risen and fallen in this region for centuries, and would doubtless rise and fall in the future. The only state of the four which could be said to be based, in the 1970s, on a strong sense of national identity, shared by a large part but certainly not by all of its people, was Iran. The fate of the region was, however, likely to depend not only on the national consciousness (or lack of such) of its people, but also on the imperial ambitions or defensive needs of the rulers of three much greater powers: Russia, India and China.

**South-east Asia**

Of nationalist movements in the heterogeneous region known as 'south-east Asia' a brief outline must suffice.

In Burma political parties appeared in the 1920s, and a new constitution permitted the beginnings of parliamentary politics in 1937. In these years a political group of younger men made itself felt, the so-called *Thakin* party,[18] many of whose leaders had studied in Japan. When the Japanese occupied Burma in the Second World War, the *Thakins* appeared as their allies, organising a Burmese National Army to fight the British. Their aim was not so much the greater glory of Japan as the independence of Burma under their own rule. They formed themselves into a secret Anti-Fascist People's Freedom League, and in 1945, when the Allies were clearly winning, brought the Burmese National Army over to the Allied side. After some hesitation by the British authorities in Rangoon and by the British government in London, Burma was granted independence in 1948. Shortly afterwards the AFPFL leader Aung San and some of his closest helpers were assassinated by political enemies. The new state was faced with opposition from the non-Burmese peoples within its frontiers and from several brands of communist guerrillas, but it survived.

In the Dutch East Indies the first nationalist organisation, which in 1911 took the name *Sarekat Islam*, was intended to protect both the Muslim faith and the interests of Javanese merchants against the Chinese minority.[19] It also acquired before long an anti-Dutch character. In the years after the First World War, on the initiative of a Dutch left socialist group emanating from Holland, a communist party was created which made an unsuccessful armed rebellion in 1926. Several small nationalist groups appeared, led by various Dutch-educated Javanese, who had learned European ideas, especially forms of socialism, during their studies in the homeland or in Europe. Outstanding among them was Ahmed Sukarno, who studied also in Berlin, where he came under the influence of the communist-led Anti-Imperialist League. Imprisoned by the Dutch, he reappeared in public life under Japanese protection in the Second World War. Like Aung San, Sukarno was concerned more for his own people and his own career than for his Japanese protectors. Unlike Aung San, he never fought against the Japanese.

The efforts of the Dutch to restore their rule were vigorously resisted. In Java, Sukarno, supported by various nationalist parties, was not content with effective control over Java, but insisted that the new state must comprise all the Dutch islands; it was given the name, already in use before the war with Japan, of Indonesia. The Dutch tried at first to limit their recognition of nationalist power to Java, to unite all the islands in a loose federation, and to keep them in some sort of association with the Netherlands. They failed in all these objectives. Sukarno declared a unitary state in Indonesia, broke the last constitutional links with Holland in 1954, and acquired western New Guinea (Western Irian) in 1957. The last of these successes, which extended his rule over people of utterly different culture from that of the main islands, could be variously interpreted as a triumph for Indonesian unity or for Javanese imperialism.

The complex situation in British Malaya and Singapore, and in the British-ruled portions of Borneo, resulting from the immigration for many decades of Chinese and Indians, will be briefly discussed in a later chapter.

American annexation of the Philippines in 1898 was bitterly resisted by Aguinaldo's nationalists until March 1901. In the subdued islands the Americans set up representative institutions, and enlarged their powers by successive acts. In 1934 the United States government undertook to make the Philippines an independent republic by 1946. This was due partly to the generosity of the American public, expressed in Congress, and partly to the desire of the American sugar industry to put Philippine sugar outside the American tariff barrier. During fifty years of American rule a modern school system was created, and English replaced Spanish as the main language of culture, while the population continued to speak its own languages, of which the most widespread was Tagalog. Japanese occupation from 1942 to 1944 interrupted the progress towards independence, but the Philippine Republic was in fact proclaimed on the promised date, 4 July 1946.

The south-eastern territories ruled by the French were collectively known as Indochina. They included Cambodia, Laos (annexed from Siam in 1893) and Vietnam (which was in turn divided into Cochin-China, Annam and Tonkin). Nationalist activities developed among Vietnamese intellectuals between the world wars. Some had studied in France, some in Japan. French influences, ranging from some sort of liberalism to communism, were the strongest, but the Kuomintang in China also had its admirers. When the Japanese occupied Indochina in 1940, with the consent of the French government in Vichy, resistance movements began. In the resistance there was a Chinese Kuomintang trend and a communist trend. The second, represented by the brilliant Ho Chi Minh (who had lived in France and other European countries as well as in communist-controlled territory in China), was the more effective. When the Japanese surrendered, the Vietminh, a political movement led by communists, were in a strong position, especially in the north. French troops returned in 1945, but the French government sought a negotiated settlement. Like the Dutch in Indonesia, they aimed at a federation, to be united with France. They hoped to limit the authority of the republic of Vietnam, controlled by Vietminh, to the former provinces of Tonkin and Annam. The southern province of Cochin-China, and the states of Laos and Cambodia, should be combined with Vietnam in an Indochinese federation. Agreement was almost reached, but was rejected at the last moment by the French. In December 1946 the Vietminh launched an attack on the French forces.

An international conference in Geneva in the spring of 1954, after seven years of war, established Cambodia and Laos as independent states, while Vietnam was divided on the 26th parallel of latitude. In the north was a communist-ruled republic, and in the south a rival Vietnamese government supported by American economic aid. Lip service was paid on both sides to the ultimate reunification of Vietnam. However, to Ho Chi Minh and his protectors in Moscow these words meant forcible imposition of communist rule in the south, while the southern rulers in practice opposed reunification. In 1958 the Vietcong guerrilla movement started war in the south: it was led by communists, and aided with weapons and skilled commanders from the north. The southern army, though lavishly equipped from the United States and supported from 1964 onwards by American armed forces which grew to several hundreds of thousands, was unable to crush its enemy. Soviet Russia did not send troops, but delivered enormous quantities of military suppies to the northern government, which also received some aid from China. The protracted war brought terrible sufferings and massive loss of life to the people of Vietnam. War-weariness and pro-Vietcong agitation in the United States thoroughly discredited the war in a large part of American public opinion as well as creating odium all over the world against America, to whose leaders—and not to the implacable communist leaders of North Vietnam—sole responsibility for the protracted misery was attributed. In 1973 President Nixon withdrew American forces. By the spring of 1975 the northern communists, with their southern supporters, had conquered the whole country. The successes of the communists, achieved by years of heroic effort and mass suffering, were successes in civil war; but the victorious Vietnamese communists understandably identified their cause with that of the Vietnamese nation.

### From the empire of the tsars to the Soviet empire

In contrast to the British, French and Dutch empires, the Russian empire did not break up, but changed the nature of its imperial rule. No new states appeared in its place, but this was not for any lack of national movements.

The first modern nationalist movements against Russian imperial rule in Asia appeared in Transcaucasia, at the end of the nineteenth century. Among both Armenians and Georgians political activity was dominated from the beginning by some form of socialism. The Armenian revolutionary movement, directed above all against Turkish rule but largely based on Russian territory, was both socialist and nationalist. In Georgia, where agrarian discontent was very strong, and where there was not much ground for anti-Russian feeling, the strongest political movement to emerge was the Menshevik branch of Social Democracy, whose aim was to replace tsardom by a socialist republic, in which the Georgian workers and peasants should have their place.

The modernist and democratic movement among the Volga Tatars, and the rise of Panturkism, have been mentioned in an earlier chapter. Similar modernising ideas spread among the Tatars of the Crimean peninsula, and among the Azeri Turks of the west Caspian coast and interior. Modernising and Panturkic ideas also had a faint echo among the Kazakhs of the south Siberian steppes and in some cities of Turkestan, though in the latter region traditional religious and social hierarchies on the whole prevailed, and were respected by the Russians. There was however one violent outbreak, in Turkestan in 1916, whose immediate cause was mobilisation of the Muslims for labour service in the war, but which was also due to latent resentment at the growing settlement of Muslim lands by Russian and Ukrainian peasants.

The revolutionary years 1917-21 brought a rapid growth of nationalist demands, but they were not satisfied. Georgians and Armenians wished to remain within Russia, but when the government of Lenin, by the peace treaty with Germany and its allies at Brest-Litovsk in March 1918, signed away large parts of their homelands to Turkey without consulting them, they decided to secede from Russia. For a month a Transcaucasian republic was formed, but it then broke up into three—Georgia, Azerbaidjan and Armenia. While civil war raged in Russia, these were able to exist as precarious sovereign states. In 1920 the Russian Bolsheviks, who had strong support from the workers of the big industrial city of Baku, invaded Azerbaidjan. This placed Armenia in an impossible position. Rather than be subjected to the Turks, who under Kemal had suppressed the attempts of the Armenians of eastern Turkey to join their kinsmen in a large Armenian state, they preferred inclusion in Soviet Russia. Meanwhile the Tatars fared no better. Their lands were invaded and devastated in turn by Russian Whites and Reds, and huge numbers perished in the 1921 famine in the Volga valley. Their plans for a Volga-Ural (*Idel-Ural*) autonomous state collapsed: they were given nominally autonomous status, but in fact came under a new form of Russian domination. Georgia remained independent until 1921, when Soviet Russian forces simply marched in and took over the government.

In Central Asia nationalist movements appeared, led in some cases by traditional elites and in others by modernising democrats. All were suppressed. The city of Tashkent, administrative capital of Turkestan, had a substantial Russian population, including army officers, civilian bureaucrats, tradesmen and railway workers. All declared themselves loyal supporters of the Bolshevik government, though few had much understanding of what the Bolsheviks stood for. The point was that it was a *Russian* government, and in its name they sallied forth to suppress the Turkic Muslims, who tried to organise their own state based on the city of Kokand. The hatred shown by Russian railway workers to Muslim peasants was essentially the same as that of South African 'poor whites' to 'Kaffirs', or of British workers in the Rhodesian copper belt towards the Zambian 'natives'. Resistance by the Turkestanis to Russian rule continued into the 1920s, led by the guerrilla forces known as *Basmachi*, in whose ranks Enver Pasha, the former ruler of Turkey, met his death.

The Bolsheviks actually extended the borders of the Russian empire, by annexing Bokhara and Khiva, which before 1917 had been protectorates outside the imperial borders. In the Far East they significantly tightened Russian control over Outer Mongolia. This, a formerly Chinese province, whose people genuinely disliked Chinese rule, had come under Russian protection in 1914, by agreement with the Japanese government.

The new Russian state bore, from 1923, the name Union of Soviet Socialist Republics. The number of constituent Soviet socialist republics increased over the years, reaching sixteen in 1940, after the annexation of three Baltic republics, part of Romania and part of Finland, and falling to fifteen when the last of these was incorporated in the Russian republic (RSFSR). Some SSRs contained subordinate territorial units with a lesser degree of devolution—'autonomous republics' (ASSR), or 'autonomous' 'regions', 'provinces' or 'districts'.

The various Soviet constitutions, including that of 1936, have been described as 'federal', but the Soviet Union was not a federal but a unitary state. The essential feature of federal government—that the territories should be sovereign in certain fields, that they should be not subordinate to the central authority but 'coordinate' with it—did not apply. Apart from this, the apparatus of state was in reality dominated by the communist party, whose organisation was strictly centralist.

The Soviet Union has often been declared to be a voluntary association of brotherly peoples. In reality, the constituent nations were never given an opportunity to decide whether they wished to remain within the same state as the Russians; when substantial groups in these nations showed that they wished to secede, they were kept in it by force; and most of the territory whose people succeeded in seceding between 1917 and 1921 was reconquered by force in 1939 or 1944. There was a provision in the 1936 constitution which permitted a republic to secede; but persons who advocated secession would be punishable for 'anti-Soviet' or 'counterrevolutionary' crimes under the criminal code.

The practice of Soviet imperial rule was essentially the same throughout its territories, and must be considered as a whole. Thus, though this chapter is concerned with Asia, it is best, in order to avoid needless repetition, to consider also some European territories.[20] This section will also end with some discussion of indirect Soviet rule over the nations of Eastern Europe whose earlier development has been discussed in preceding chapters.

Lenin laid down that communists must fight with equal energy against two 'deviations'—'Great Russian chauvinism' and 'local bourgeois nationalism'. Russians must fiercely oppose any tendency towards domination by Russians, while non-Russians must resist all anti-Russian nationalism among their compatriots. In practice in the 1920s the first of the two deviations was regarded as the more harmful, and within the limits of communist party dictatorship the benefit of the doubt was given to the non-Russians. For some years these nations made real gains, in terms of public use of their languages, employment of their compatriots and development of their national culture. This was especially true of the Ukrainians and Tatars.

All this changed at the end of the 1920s, with the advent of forced collectivisation of agriculture and breakneck-speed industrialisation. The worst famine conditions were created in the Ukraine and in the Kazakh steppes: the former had the best grain lands and the latter the largest pastoral and nomad populations. Bad crops, confiscation of stocks and slaughter of livestock caused millions of deaths by starvation. Inevitably these sufferings, which resulted from policies whose motivation was not nationalist, but economic, created bitter national hatred. Whereas Russian peasants, when subjected to confiscations or to deportation to labour in inhuman conditions in mines or on construction sites, attributed their woes to the government, non-Russians in a similar predicament felt that their nations were being oppressed as such by Russians; and Russian communist agents of these brutal policies eagerly attributed popular hostility to anti-Russian 'bourgeois nationalism'. From 1934 to 1937 conditions improved, but the Great Purge of 1937-39, which brought hundreds of thousands of executions and millions of deportations to forced labour, frequently leading to premature deaths through undernourishment and exhaustion, hit the non-Russian nations even harder than the Russians. The leadership of the communist parties of the Ukraine, the Caucasus and Central Asia was almost completely destroyed, and there were very severe losses among the most educated and most skilled.

The end of the Purge was followed by two better years, but then came the German invasion. This not only brought appalling military casualties and destruction, but also led to excesses of Russian nationalism. Nations suspected of sympathy with the Germans suffered special repression. Some small nations—the Crimean Tatars, the Kalmyks, the Chechens and several other Caucasian peoples, and the German minority from the Volga valley—were deported from their homes to distant parts of Siberia or Central Asia on the grounds that some of their number had collaborated with the enemy and that the majority had not prevented them from doing so.[21] When the western part of the Soviet Union was recovered from the invaders, large numbers of Ukrainians and others were arrested as collaborators; and among Soviet prisoners of war repatriated from Germany non-Russians were especially liable to be sent to forced labour for having helped the enemy.

After the death of Stalin things again improved. The contenders for the succession sought to win the support of the non-Russians. Khrushchev, who for many years had been the communist party boss of the Ukraine, showed some sympathy for Ukrainian national feelings, though this did not get much beyond polite phrases. As material conditions improved for all Soviet citizens, so did those of the non-Russians, but Russian supremacy remained a fact of the Soviet empire. In 1934, at the Seventeenth Congress of the Communist Party, Stalin had declared that 'bourgeois nationalism' was the more harmful of the two deviations, and this doctrine was never reversed. In the 1960s and 1970s there were repeated propaganda campaigns against 'bourgeois nationalism' in the republics, but denunciation of 'Great Russian chauvinism' was seldom heard.

The economy was not only state-owned, but also highly centralised. Decisions were taken at the centre, in the supposed interests of the whole economy. This would seem to be, and no doubt often was, in accordance with economic rationality; but it did not always agree with the preferences of the non-Russians. It was to the interest of the economy as a whole that Central Asia should specialise in production of cotton, at the expense of food grains, which could be supplied from other regions. The argument was the same as that used by the British in Egypt. Central Asians, however, like Egyptians, wished to cultivate their own food crops rather than place themselves at the mercy of the imperial government. This argument about cotton or wheat, and in later years more complex arguments about specialisation or diversification of production, lay at the heart of Central Asian nationalist opposition to Moscow's policies. Soviet policies in fact brought great economic progress to Central Asia, including great new industries; but it was not the sort of economic progress which the Central Asians themselves would have chosen. Possibly, Moscow did know best; but Central Asians were inclined to assume that Moscow's interests were being put before their own and that they were being exploited.

Russian was bound to be the first official language of the Soviet Union, and therefore all non-Russians hoping to make a successful career in administration, industry or cultural life would have to learn Russian. Lenin, however, strongly rejected cultural Russification: other languages and cultures must be treated with equal respect. Yet over the years this is not what happened. Inevitably, Russians held most of the leading posts in the administration. Inevitably, the methods of government and the attitudes of bureaucrats to the population resembled those of the old Russian regime, including the contempt (at times merely condescending, at times harshly arrogant) habitually felt towards non-Russians. The use of Russian as the language of instruction in higher education could be justified on the grounds that the other languages lacked the specialised vocabulary, and even the necessary flexibility, for advanced modern thought. Yet little attempt was made to adapt these languages (Russian itself had needed such adaptation at the beginning of the nineteenth century, and thanks to such men as Pushkin and Karamzin it had achieved it).[22] On the contrary, Turkic languages were forced to use the Russian Cyrillic alphabet, and were systematically stuffed with Russian loan-words, while the use of Russian in public business in non-Russian republics increased.

National literatures and history were censored in order to eliminate anti-Russian opinions. Even medieval epic poems, widely known and loved, were mutilated or suppressed if they were thought likely to encourage 'bourgeois nationalism'. The history of the non-Russian nations was rewritten, not only in Marxist terms (which might indeed be expected in a state ruled in the name of revolutionary communism), but also in order to satisfy Russian national pride. Thus, Ukrainians were taught that only the Poles had been their enemies, while the Russian people had always been their friend. The heroic resistance of the north Caucasian Chechens, under Imam Shamil, from 1836 to 1859, to the invading Russian armies of Tsar Nicholas I, was represented in the 1950s as a reactionary effort supported by British and Ottoman imperialism. The conquest by Russian tsars of vast tracts of Asia was an 'objectively progressive phenomenon', because it saved the people of these lands from the much worse fate of falling under British rule, and because it brought them into contact with the superior culture of the Russian people. In the course of time, they too benefited, when the last tsar was overthrown by the progressive vanguard of the Russian working class led by the great Lenin. These arguments have a close family resemblance to those used by Victorian English champions of imperial expansion, who justified conquests in terms of the spreading of higher civilisation and morality.

Political centralisation, 'monolithic' communist party rule, subordination of local to central economic interests, and a new form of cultural Russification, were general characteristics of Soviet rule in non-Russian lands from the 1930s onwards. This can best be shown by looking at some individual cases.


The two republics in which the indigenous nation enjoyed the largest measure of practical autonomy; in which posts of command in state and party administration, the economy and cultural life were almost entirely in indigenous hands; and in which it was most easy publicly to take pride in national history and traditions, were Georgia and Armenia. Both nations had a very large proportion of highly educated and skilled people. The talents shown by Armenians before 1917 as capitalists and traders were to a large extent employed in the Soviet era in the management of state industry. Georgians had some (though less) talent in the same direction. They also revealed an unusual capacity as security policemen during the period when their compatriot L. P. Beria was in charge of state security (1938-53). Both Georgians and Armenians regarded themselves as culturally superior to Russians, and from the 1960s onwards made little effort to conceal this belief.

Less fortunate were the Estonians, Latvians and Lithuanians, whose three small republics were annexed, with Hitler's consent, in 1940; lost to the German invaders in 1941; and recovered after Hitler's defeat in 1945. Educated persons from these three nations were deported in hundreds of thousands, and Russians were settled in their place. After Stalin's death conditions improved. The future of the two Protestant nations, Estonians and Latvians, appeared bleak in the 1970s, as their populations were static or declining, but they clung with passion to their national cultures and resisted Russification. The Lithuanians retained a high rate of natural increase, probably attributable to the strength of their Catholic religion and the higher proportion of rural to urban population.

As has been shown, the culturally and politically most advanced of the Muslim peoples of Russia were the Tatars. The first attempts to create an All-Russian Muslim political party, in 1905 and in 1917, were chiefly their work. The Tatar people suffered very heavily both from the destruction of the civil war, which raged to and fro across their homeland in 1918 and 1919, and from a massive famine in the Volga valley in 1921. They did however at first make some gains as a nation under the Soviet regime. A Tatar ASSR was set up with Kazan as its capital; and because the Tatars had a more developed modern intellectual elite than any other Muslim people in the Russian empire, it was natural that they should have provided a high proportion of those communists charged with propagating the faith among the Muslims. Outstanding among them was Mir Sajit Sultan-Galiev, for some years a close collaborator with Stalin. However, in 1923 it was discovered that Sultan-Galiev had been in contact with anti-Russian Muslim leaders in Central Asia, and he was dismissed from his office: he was probably executed in 1929. Sultan-Galiev has been described, not inappropriately, as a 'Muslim Titoist'.[23]

The Tatars numbered nearly six million people in 1970, but only about a quarter of these lived in the Tatar ASSR, in which they formed less than half the population. Three-quarters of the Tatars were scattered across a number of central Russian provinces, the Bashkir ASSR, the Kazakh republic and the Central Asian republics. The Tatars were much more urbanised than other Muslim peoples of the Soviet Union, but they had, in proportion to their numbers, a comparatively low proportion of students in higher education.[24] These figures give the impression that the Soviet leaders, regarding the Tatars (in view of their past record) as a potentially dangerous elite among Soviet Muslims, were deliberately discriminating against them; but this is admittedly only indirect evidence.

In Central Asia during the civil war there emerged for a time a national movement, led by a small intellectual elite trained in the 'new' schools of the Volga Tatar modernists,[25] which aimed to create a Turkestani nation, based on the Chagatay branch of the Turkic languages. This was resisted by both 'white' and 'red' Russians, not least, as already noted, by the Russian railway workers of Tashkent.

In the view of the Soviet leaders, the main dangers in Central Asia were Panislamism, Panturkism and the idea of a single Turkestani nation. The best way of removing these dangers (apart from forcible repression) seemed to be the encouragement of distinct and rival national consciousnesses.

Soviet doctrine on Central Asia was clearly influenced by nineteenth-century Austrian thinking.[26] The word 'nation' (*natsia*) was, as far as possible, avoided; the ambiguous word 'people' (*narod*) was used for the whole Soviet people—which, it was hoped, would one day grow into a single Soviet socialist nation; while the groups to be encouraged in Central Asia were to be called 'nationalities' (*natsionalnosti*). These groups were to be based on language: their spoken dialects, which differed substantially from each other, were to be made into literary languages, as divergent from each other as possible; and those who spoke each dialect were to be provided with communist political and educational matter in the new languages, were to be organised in separate administrative units, and were to be encouraged to consider themselves distinct 'nationalities'. Thus, the local dialect of Persian known as Tadjik was to be elevated into a Tadjik language, spoken by a Tadjik 'nationality', quite distinct from the Persian language and the Iranian nation;[27] while the Turkic population were split into Uzbeks, Kazakhs, Kirgiz, Türkmen, Kara-Kalpak and some smaller 'nationalities'. The new languages were at first written in Latin alphabet, in order to diminish the cultural unity previously symbolised by the Arabic alphabet used for Chagatay Turki; and the Latin was replaced by the Cyrillic in the 1930s in order to promote Russian influence.

Despite initial resistance, this policy proved rather successful; but its result was not what the Soviet specialists in language manipulation had expected. The policy boomeranged. New Uzbek, Kazakh, Kirgiz and Türkmen nations indeed emerged, but their nationalist feelings were directed not so much against each other as against Russians.

In the 1970s the main posts in state and party hierarchies in Central Asia appeared to be in Asian hands; but on closer examination things looked different. Usually first secretaries of provincial party committees were Asians; but second secretaries were Russians, and there were well-placed Russians among heads of departments in the committees' permanent secretariats. Ministers in republican governments were usually Asians; but among deputy-ministers, heads of departments within ministries, and especially in the police apparatus, Russians (sometimes also Armenians, Georgians or Ukrainians) were strongly entrenched. Probably the same was true of major economic enterprises, but evidence was not abundant. In places of work, Asians and Russians met, and did their jobs fairly smoothly together; but when working hours were over, they went home to different parts of town and spent their leisure in different ways. Islam, not so much a body of dogma or a set of ritual observances as a way of living and thinking, a morality and a culture, remained deeply rooted in spite of sustained hostile campaigns by the Soviet mass media. Intermarriage of Muslim men with Russian girls was rare, but intermarriage of Muslim girls with Russian men was virtually unknown, if they were to live in Central Asia. Those

Central Asians who went to live, thousands of miles away, in Moscow or another great Russian city, might indeed intermarry, and their descendants lose all link with Asia but their name; but there were few of these. A very important obstacle to the absorption of the Central Asians in a new Soviet culture was the difference between the rates of increase of the populations. Asian birth rates were much higher than Russian; and between 1959 and 1970 the proportion of Russians in the population of all four Central Asian republics and of Kazakhstan diminished.[28] This trend was bound to continue, as the age composition of the Muslim republics was very much younger than that of the European.[29]

The Soviet theorists of 'the national problem' liked to distinguish between 'bourgeois nations' and 'socialist nations'. They hoped to produce the second type of nation in the Soviet Union, and hoped that in the course of time the several socialist nations would become fused into a single Soviet nation. They were of course right to point out that the social structure of the 'nationalities' of the Soviet Union was different from that of European 'bourgeois' nations or of the pre-capitalist peoples of other continents. However, the 'socialist nations' that developed during fifty years of Soviet rule proved to be less different from the earlier nations than had been expected.

Two main sets of causes account for the growth of national consciousness among the non-Russians. One was the emergence of new elites, the result of industrialisation, urbanisation and education. These elites were not bourgeoisies of the traditional type, since they did not own the means of production, and since the industries or institutions in which they worked were founded not by private profit-seeking enterprise but by state action. Yet these elites were very similar in function and in mentality (not least in a certain philistine, self-glorifying taste in the arts, literature and architecture) to the elites of industrialised Victorian England, Wilhelminian Germany or the United States of Theodore Roosevelt. The dominant Russian elite (one is tempted to call it a 'state bourgeoisie' as opposed to a 'private bourgeoisie') revealed these traits from the 1930s to the 1950s. In the 1960s substantial elites of a similar type had emerged in the non-Russian nations. They were very proud of their achievements, proud of their 'socialism' and resentful of the fact that they could not dispose of its results the way they wished because they had Russians sitting on their necks.

The second set of causes was the creation, through the same processes of industrialisation, urbanisation and education, of modern-minded workers and peasants equally aware of their national identity and equally proud of their achievements. The Uzbek peasants of the old Russian empire were passive subjects, dominated by their traditional elites of tribal chiefs or landowners, with the great white tsar far away above them. The Uzbeks of the 1970s were citizens of a modern state, their national consciousness strengthened by industrialisation, urbanisation and education.

It was undoubtedly true, as Soviet propagandists unceasingly argued, that the Asian nations of the Soviet Union had made immense economic and cultural progress since 1917. It does not follow from this that these nations were grateful to the Soviet leaders or the Russian nation. The history of all other empires shows that elites created by progressive colonial policies turned against those empires; and that more prosperous and more skilled subject nations (the Czechs in 1910 or the *Québécois* in 1970) were more militant than exploited and ignorant subject nations. It was the good things which imperial rulers did, rather than their cruelties and injustices, that turned the subject peoples against them. It is true that no demands for independence were heard in the 1970s from the Soviet Central Asian republics. The reason is clear enough: such demands would lead to immediate arrest. It would, however, be premature to regard this as proof that the Soviet Union, alone among empires, was exempt from the operation of what may perhaps be called the Law of Colonial Ingratitude. It is difficult to believe that it never occurred to Uzbeks, learning that Rwanda or Mozambique were receiving independence, that their country, too, one of the earliest centres of human civilisation, might also be independent. 'Socialism without Russians' was an aim which had its attractions in Ashkhabad and caused fear in Moscow. Meanwhile the Soviet Union remained in the mid-1970s the only one of the great European colonial empires of the nineteenth century that was still territorially almost intact.

It would be wrong to assume that Soviet-style neo-russification benefited the Russian nation. On the contrary, a strong case may be made for the view that the Russians suffered, as a nation, no less than the other nations of the Soviet empire. The Soviet rulers consistently showed contempt for Russian traditions, falsified Russian history and mutilated Russian culture, especially its religious elements. The elements in the tradition which they preserved, praised and sought to develop still further—uncritical submission to autocracy, military prowess, love of military glory, suspicion and hatred of foreigners—were only a part of the whole, and obsessive official emphasis on them distorted Russian national identity. Among the dissidents of the 1970s several varieties of Russian nationalism could be detected, ranging from a xenophobia with anti-semitic undertones, not very different from official policy, to a belief in the solidarity of the Russian nation with the other nations as victims of a non-national Moloch state whose leaders denied all spiritual values and all historical traditions. This does not necessarily mean that, if the Soviet autocracy were replaced by a regime of political freedom, Russians and non-Russians would prove capable of solidarity in practice.

The Soviet Russian imperial rulers not only directly ruled about 120 million non-Russians, constituting almost half the population of the Soviet Union, but also exercised indirect but most effective domination over another 100 million Europeans in lands lying west of the Soviet frontier. This may be regarded as the modern Russian imperialist version of 'neo-colonialism'.[30]

It was made clear between 1945 and 1948 that there was only one state in this region to which the Soviet rulers were willing to concede full internal sovereignty in return for a guarantee that its foreign policy would be coordinated with that of the Soviet Union: that is, to treat it in the traditional manner of regional great powers towards regional dependencies. This state was Finland. Elsewhere they insisted on imposing political institutions and social policies closely copied from those of the Soviet Union. In one case, in Yugoslavia, the communist leaders were men who had won power by their own efforts, and they proceeded to carry out communist policies in their own way, through persons chosen by them. For this reason Stalin viewed them with growing suspicion, and in 1948 excommunicated them as heretics. They survived this anathema, retained their hold on power, and built a political and social system substantially different from the Soviet model. In a second case, Albania, the communist leaders also won their own war, with some Yugoslav help, but were hostile to Yugoslavia, above all because more than a third of the Albanian nation remained within Yugoslavia rather than being incorporated in the Albanian state.[31] Therefore, when Stalin quarrelled with Tito, they were able to retain independence of either Yugoslavia or the Soviet empire. In six other countries (Eastern Germany, Poland, Czechoslovakia, Hungary, Romania and Bulgaria) power was held by persons chosen and installed by the Soviet leaders, and these states became vassals of the Soviet empire. When Yugoslavia was excommunicated, the communist parties were subjected to mass purges of varying intensity, designed still further to increase their subordination.

Soviet neo-colonialism was directed not only against the effective sovereignty of the states, but also against the culture and identity of the nations. In particular, historians were compelled to falsify the history of their own nations in a sense favourable not only to the cause of communism since 1917 but also to the national and imperial pride of Russians, going back into the distant past. The nation which suffered most from this process was the Romanian. Not only national history, but the national language, was attacked. Efforts were made to give greater emphasis to the substantial Slav element in Romanian vocabulary at the expense of the Latin element. Cultural relations with France and Italy were severed. It was suggested that the Romanians were not a 'Latin nation' but a 'Slav nation'. The myth of the benevolence throughout history of 'the great Russian nation' (despite admitted occasional aberrations by some tsars), which had long been forced on Ukrainians, Georgians, Tatars, Estonians and other non-Russian nations of the Soviet empire, was forced on Romanians, Poles, Hungarians, Czechs and others.

This intense political, economic and cultural pressure was relaxed after the death of Stalin. The milder regime which followed encouraged greater expectations, which led to a series of insurrections: workers' risings in Plzeň (Czechoslovakia) and in Berlin and other cities of East Germany in 1953 and in Poznań (Poland) in July 1956, followed by much larger movements in Poland and Hungary in October 1956. In all these cases the initial demands were for social justice and political liberty: it was only after the Soviet leaders had proclaimed their hostility that the movements took on a nationalist, anti-Soviet character. In Poland the Soviet leaders agreed to a last minute compromise; but in Hungary the obstinate refusal of the communist leader Ernő Gerő and his Soviet advisers to make concessions to the people led to hostilities between Hungarian police and Hungarian workers, then to a revolution which ended the communist party's monopoly of power, and finally to a short war between the Hungarian and Soviet armies.

Forcible suppression of the Hungarian Revolution restored Soviet supremacy for six years. It was next challenged by the Romanian communist leaders, who objected to Soviet demands for a degree of economic coordination between communist states which would have reversed their own industrial plans. They followed up their economic resistance by permitting a strong revival of Romanian cultural nationalism with strong anti-Russian overtones. The attempts at 'Slavisation' were completely abandoned, and the old Latin historical mythology was restored in its entirety. The Soviet leaders accepted their defeat.

In 1968 a new crisis developed in Czechoslovakia. Here, too, the movement was originally concerned with economic and social reforms and with political liberties. Nationalism was present only in the form of conflict between Slovaks and Czechs. However, the reforms accepted by the party leaders headed by Alexander Dubček, summarised in his slogan of 'communism with a human face', were rejected by the Soviet leaders, who found it necessary to invade Czechoslovakia with several hundred thousand troops, including contingents from Poland, East Germany, Hungary and Bulgaria. At this point there developed a strong anti-Soviet and anti-Russian nationalism, especially strong among the Czechs who, for reasons mentioned in an earlier chapter,[32] had always liked to consider the Russians as a benevolent brotherly nation. An important consequence of the Soviet invasion was a systematic policy of refalsification of the history of the Czechs and Slovaks (which in the 1950s had been falsified according to the pattern already mentioned, but in the late 1960s had been allowed to move back towards the truth).

The invasion of Czechoslovakia resulted in the elaboration of an official formula for Soviet neo-colonialism: the so-called 'Brezhnev doctrine of limited sovereignty'. It was declared to be the duty of the leaders of the 'Socialist states' to give joint help wherever 'socialism' was endangered in one of them. It was not for the leaders of the 'endangered' state to decide whether there was a danger or not; nor should 'help' be delayed until it was requested. The collective wisdom of all the socialist states, which meant the collective wisdom of the Central Committee of the Communist Party of the Soviet Union, which meant the wisdom of whoever spoke for the CC of the CPSU, would decide whether there was a danger or not, and would order intervention if necessary.

The essence of Soviet policy after 1945 in Eastern Europe was not only national domination, but national humiliation: the nations of the vassal states must not only obey orders from the foreign overlords, but must be deprived of their national identities. This demand was in practice abandoned in the case of Romania after 1963, but was upheld in the other countries with varying intensity—most severely in Czechoslovakia.

Yet the attempt to destroy national identities was singularly unsuccessful. The truth is rather that the processes of industrialisation, urbanisation and mass education, which in the last two centuries in one country after another had the effect of extending the national consciousness of the elite downwards into the mass of the population, or (which is the same thing) of drawing the masses upwards into the politically conscious nation, were completed in Eastern Europe under communist party governments. The public ethos, diffused through the schools and the mass media, was an amalgam of residual Marxism and nationalism; but of the two ingredients the second was by far the more important, and the actions of the Soviet leaders themselves kept national resentment vigorous. Where, despite official indifference or hostility, religion remained strong (Catholicism in Poland and Orthodoxy in Romania), it became fused with nationalism, giving it greater strength; where religious beliefs declined, nationalism increasingly filled the vacant place in men's minds, becoming an *ersatz* religion. The truth was that, as long as more than a hundred million Europeans were kept in unwilling vassalage to the Soviet empire, national resentment would remain a dangerous explosive material. It was in the power of the Soviet leaders alone to remove this danger.

# 8    Africa: Colonial Empires, New States and New Nations

## Early African states

In Africa south of Egypt one civilised state maintained itself, with changing fortunes and frontiers, for two thousand years: Ethiopia. The founders of the Ethiopian monarchy were probably immigrants from Arabia, crossing the narrow entrance to the Red Sea.[1] In the fifth century AD the rulers of Ethiopia accepted Christianity. The language of the Ethiopian scriptures, Ge'ez, belonged to the Semitic group. From Ge'ez were descended the modern languages Amharic (spoken in central Ethiopia) and Tigrinya (spoken in the northern province Tigre and along the coast). The Ethiopian church followed the Egyptian in accepting the monophysite doctrine, and remained linked to Egypt's Coptic church[2] after the conquest of Egypt by the Muslims. The boundaries of Ethiopia fluctuated during the centuries. As Muslim influence became established along the coast, the centre of gravity of Ethiopia was displaced southwards. In the fifteenth century a major Muslim invasion nearly destroyed the Ethiopian state: it was saved with the help of Portuguese forces. In the nineteenth century the Emperor Menelik II extended Ethiopian rule to the south, at the expense of peoples of Galla or Somali speech.

Other African states lasted for briefer periods and had a less splendid cultural achievement. The most important were in West Africa: Ghana, the home of the Soninke people, lying between the upper Senegal and Niger rivers, from the ninth to eleventh centuries; Mali, inhabited by the Mandinka people, lying between the Atlantic coast and the Niger river, from the thirteenth to fifteenth centuries; and Benin, the land of the Edo people, to the west of the Niger delta, in the fifteenth century. In both Ghana and Mali, Muslims were influential though not completely dominant. Another region of developed civilisation was the east coast, from the straits of the Red Sea down to the Mozambique Channel. Here several trading principalities flourished from the thirteenth to the fifteenth centuries, their peoples Muslim by religion and Swahili[3] by language, dependent on the sea routes to Arabia and India. The arrival of the Portuguese in the sixteenth century brought about their decline, interrupted by brief periods of partial revival. In the African interior, kingdoms rose and fell as pastoral peoples conquered agricultural peoples, established their rule over wider areas, and were conquered in their turn. The most important was the kingdom of Kongo, whose ruler accepted Christianity in 1506 and entered into alliance with the king of Portugal. It broke up after 1665, when a Portuguese army defeated the Kongo forces. Yet another was Mwanamutapa, which flourished in the late fifteenth and sixteenth centuries between the Zambezi and Sabi rivers and the Indian Ocean coast.

### European colonisation

It was the sea-borne exploration in search of Asia which brought Europeans in significant numbers to Africa. Its pioneers were the Portuguese, who established themselves on both the west and the east coasts of the southern third of the continent, and in the seventeenth century asserted their authority over African states in the interior. As trade with the East around the Cape of Good Hope developed, small European settlements were founded on the west coast of Africa between Cape Verde and the Congo: the English, French, Dutch, Danes and even Prussians had their trading posts.

The most lucrative European activity in these parts for three hundred years was the slave trade. In 1807 the British government declared it illegal, and took it upon itself forcibly to prevent others—Arabs and black Africans as well as Europeans—from engaging in it. In the first half of the nineteenth century the slave trade, in fact, was reduced to a trickle, and European merchants bought and sold other goods, especially palm oil along the west coast and in the Niger delta. During the century also European explorers, inspired in varying degrees by scientific curiosity, religious enthusiasm and love of adventure, penetrated the interior. Following the explorers came the missionaries, to convert pagans and to compete for converts with the Muslims and with each other.

Thus, by the end of the third quarter of the century, the commercial, religious and strategic interests of several European states were involved in Africa. European governments did not, however, give a very high priority to African affairs. There were various pressure groups among their subjects concerned with Africa, but they were not very influential. Governments were prepared to some extent to give protection to their traders and missionaries, and to take reprisals against African rulers who maltreated them; but tried to restrict their commitments geographically to a minimum. The French were installed since 1783 in Senegal, the British since 1787 in Sierra Leone, where former negro slaves from America, who had supported the Empire Loyalists in the War of American Independence, had been settled. In the next hundred years further small British and French settlements were made on the west coast, while the Portuguese kept their positions on the southern part of the east coast.

It was the British government, with its Indian empire and its world-wide sea power, which was potentially most concerned with Africa. Victorian statesmen were seldom keen to acquire new territory. They themselves disliked, and they knew that both parliament and its electors disliked, any increase of public expenditure requiring further taxes. They were, however, determined to maintain their rule over India, which gave Britain its world power status and was a great source of wealth and, if necessary, of military manpower. The routes to India must be defended. Threats to India by sea could be met by British naval power provided that the Cape of Good Hope was securely held and there were no dangerous rival bases on either the west or the east coasts of Africa. There were only two places where British communications might be threatened by either of the two powers which were Britain's potential rivals, France and Russia. These were the Straits of Constantinople and Egypt.

The rulers of Egypt had made themselves effectively independent of the Ottoman sultan since the 1830s. Instead, they had fallen into a new slavery, to the numerous Western bankers and merchants, chiefly French or British or associates of one or the other, who flocked to despoil this potentially rich country. In 1869 the Suez Canel was opened, and with it a new shorter route to India. Khedive Ismail, who had encouraged this and many other enterprises, became finally bankrupt. This gave Disraeli the chance to buy Ismail's allotment of Canal shares and so establish a strong British position in Egypt. Continued Anglo-French pressure produced fierce resistance from the religious and political classes, expressed by the army under Arabi Pasha, who seized power in September 1881. Attempts at joint Anglo-French action were unsuccessful. Gladstone's government took military action and the British found themselves in sole occupation of Egypt. Gladstone had intended to get out again as soon as possible, but it proved impossible either to establish a satisfactory regime in Egypt or to come to terms with France. Things became still more difficult when a revolt, led by a religious leader who claimed to be the *Mahdi*, the new Messiah and successor to Muhammad, swept the Egyptians out of the Sudan. General Gordon was sent to Khartoum, but the city was captured, after a long siege, in January 1885.

The disaster in the Sudan made the British aware that their position in Egypt could be threatened from the south. It was this which set off the scramble for Africa, in which Britain and France were the leading actors, but Germany also took its part, followed by Italy and Belgium, while the extent of Portuguese possessions also had to be fixed.

During the 1880s and 1890s Eastern Africa, between the Red Sea Straits and the northern boundary of Portuguese Mozambique, was divided between Britain, Italy and Germany. In the northern sector (which came to be known as Somaliland) Britain took the part facing north to Arabia, while Italy took the long curve of coastline from Cape Guardafui south-westwards. Italy also annexed a coastal strip, conquered from Ethiopia, which became known as Eritrea. The French acquired a small Red Sea coastal territory at Djibouti. The coastline between Italian Somaliland and the Portuguese territories was divided in two, the southern half (which came to be known as Tanganyika) going to Germany and the northern half (which came to be known as Kenya) to Britain. Zanzibar first went to Germany, but transferred to Britain in 1890. Uganda, a strategically important territory lying between the Great Lakes and the Sudan, was occupied by the British with German consent. Both the British and the Germans pushed inland to the Great Lakes, and the frontiers of the two territories were mutually agreed. To their west lay a vast region which became known as the Congo Free State, and was managed as a private commercial enterprise by King Leopold II of the Belgians, exploiting forced African labour on a scale and by methods which by European standards of the time were exceptionally ruthless. In 1908 the territory was taken over by the Belgian state as a colony. To the north of the lower Congo another great territory was explored by Pierre de Brazza, and was placed under French sovereignty.

In all these activities the main motivations of the governments were strategic. The British were concerned to protect their position in Egypt and the sea routes to India. As the Ottoman empire steadily lost territory in Europe and became materially weakened, and as British influence in Constantinople diminished, Egypt replaced the Straits as the main object of British strategic concern. Egypt's vulnerability through the Upper Nile valley became an important issue in great power politics. The successors of the victorious Mahdi still held the Sudan, but there was a growing possibility that France might advance from her possessions on the lower Congo and in the north-eastern corner of West Africa, to threaten the Nile from the west. For their part the Italians, established not only in Somali-land but in Eritrea, tried to expand into the heartland of Ethiopia. The army of Emperor Menelik put an end to the Italian advance at the battle of Adua on 1 March 1896. Menelik's victory was made possible partly by supplies of French weapons. A combined Franco-Ethiopian threat to the Sudan, supported also by France's ally Russia, greatly alarmed the British government. It was decided to undertake an Anglo-Egyptian expedition to reconquer the Sudan for Egypt. This culminated in General Kitchener's victory at Omdurman on 2 September 1898. Meanwhile a French expedition, under Captain J. B. Marchant, had set out from the west and reached the Nile 300 miles south of Khartoum. Kitchener and Marchant met at Fashoda for a day on 19 September. A major Anglo-French crisis developed in Europe, but it ended with a French retreat. The Sudan was re-united with Egypt, and placed under nominal Anglo-Egyptian condominium and effective British control.

West Africa was of little interest to British governments until the end of the century. Pressures from commercial interests and missionaries, to take over large parts of the interior to the advantage of peaceful trade and religious enlightenment, met with little sympathy. Reluctantly, Whitehall extended its West African territories inland. These new boundaries were accepted by the French, who were, however, determined to bypass them in the north as well as on the coast, and to establish a large empire from the Atlantic to the Congo, linked across the Sahara with Algeria and Morocco. The British government was willing to recognise French claims in the hope, consistently disappointed, that the French would recognise British supremacy in Egypt and the Upper Nile.

The exception to this statement was the territory which became known as Nigeria, and extended from Lagos and the delta of the Niger northwards to the principalities of the Fulani emirs of Sokoto and Kano. The pioneering activity of Sir George Goldie and his chartered Royal Niger Company, from the 1880s onwards, had its effect. Trading interests in this region—more populous and economically promising than the lands lying to the west under French rule—made themselves felt in Whitehall. A combination of commercial enterprise, military ambition, paternalism and missionary zeal was effective. The British government upheld British supremacy in Nigeria in the face of French pressure; Frederick Lugard conquered Sokoto and Kano in 1903; and in 1914 a single Colony and Protectorate of Nigeria came into being.

The other main British concern on the continent was South Africa. Gladstone accepted the independence of Transvaal in 1881, hoping that the republic would become dependent on Britain and confident that as long as it had no contact with potentially hostile powers it could not damage British interests. Meanwhile republican territory was bypassed on the west by the extension of British sovereignty over Bechuanaland in 1884 and by expansion into Matabeleland in the 1890s. This last was the work of the British South Africa Company, chartered in October 1889 and organised by Cecil Rhodes. From its conquests emerged the two colonies of Northern and Southern Rhodesia. All this expansion was accepted by British governments as a means of strengthening British security at the Cape; which does not of course mean that it was not also expected by many of its promoters to be economically profitable to them. The South African situation was drastically changed with the discovery of gold resources on the Rand. This made the Transvaal the object of covetous feelings by

British businessmen both in the Cape Province and further afield. It also made it possible for the Transvaal to aspire to full political independence; to seek the protection of foreign powers—especially Germany; to attract the Afrikaans-speaking people of the Cape to it instead of, as hitherto, being attracted towards them; and thus to threaten the future security of the British route to India by the Cape. Thus the economic ambitions of capitalists and the strategic anxieties of British statesmen combined to produce the Boer War of 1899.

In this brief survey I have stressed the strategic factor because I believe that it was the most important in bringing about British, French and German actions. Only in the case of King Leopold's Congo enterprise was crude economic profit the decisive aim. The well-known Hobson-Hilferding-Lenin theory of economic imperialism does not fit more than a part of the historical facts. At the same time one should not forget that economic, and also religious missionary, pressure groups, as well as personal overweening ambitions, played their part. It is still more evident that, once European imperial rule had been established over all Africa except Ethiopia, economic exploitation of African resources and African manpower grew rapidly.

Changes in European rule in the last period of colonialism in Africa must be briefly mentioned. In 1918 the German colonies were taken away by the victors and distributed among them under the system of mandates responsible to the League of Nations: Tanganyika to Britain, South-West Africa to the Union of South Africa, Togoland to France, Kamerun divided between Britain and France, and Ruanda and Urundi to Belgium. The next important change was the conquest of Ethiopia by the Italians in 1936. Italian rule ended in 1941, when British forces conquered the Italian possessions Eritrea and Somaliland, and then restored Ethiopian independence.

## Imperial policies and attitudes

In African as in Asian lands occupied by European rulers, the traditional political and religious elites complied with the policies of their new masters, while basically resenting them. As in Asia also, the new masters' policies soon created incentives and mechanisms for the formation, from among their subjects, of new cultural elites, through the development of European types of training and education. Inevitably these new elites became familiar with European ideas, and began to judge European rule by European standards and found it wanting. Thus in Africa as in Asia two types of opposition to European rule appeared. The old and new elites combined in varying degrees in the anti-colonial nationalism of the twentieth century.

Common opposition to European rule, greatly varying in intensity, coexisted with mutual distrust between the old and new elites, which also varied greatly between regions and between periods. In general it should be noted that African nationalism appeared later, met with less resistance from European rulers, and achieved its immediate aim of independence more rapidly, than Asian.

All European colonial policies had some points in common. All sought to spend as little as possible on either the military defence or the economic development of their colonies. All gave some degree of support to European enterprises seeking to gain profits from the colonies' natural resources. All introduced some element of Europeanisation, affecting the social structures and cultural life of their colonial subjects, while seeking to minimise the consequent political discontents. All used methods of political repression more severe than they would have used in their European homelands. Nevertheless there were great variations between them.

The French consciously set themselves to spread French culture, hoping in the long term to make black Frenchmen of their Africans. In practice their efforts were concentrated on a substantial but comparatively small section, who were subjected to education of high quality, with relatively greater emphasis on the highest level. Black graduates of French secondary schools and universities were welcomed as Frenchmen, at least when they were in France. There were, however, numerous Frenchmen living in the colonies who did not regard black Frenchmen as their equals, least of all when they saw that they were their cultural superiors.

The Portuguese rulers proclaimed a rather similar cultural attitude. In practice the opportunities for Africans in Portuguese colonies to obtain a good Portuguese education were much smaller, and the quality of Portuguese education at all levels was markedly inferior to that of French. Portuguese living in the colonies also tended to treat educated Africans with contempt, though possibly in practice this was less widespread than among the French.

The British did not have so generous an attitude in principle as the French. It may be argued that, in the social pattern of England (though perhaps not of Scotland), culture and learning have always enjoyed less prestige than in France. Be that as it may, it is fair to say that British colonial rulers did not set themselves the aim of making black Englishmen out of their Africans. Nevertheless the British rulers did not neglect education. In the British colonies in West Africa both primary and secondary education were extended to a larger section of the population than in the French. Access to British universities, and development of university-level colleges in British colonies, lagged behind similar institutions in French, but they were considerable, and increased rapidly in the 1940s. African subjects of British colonies also had access—admittedly on a rather small scale—to university education in the United States. Plenty of arrogance was also displayed by British subjects in the colonies towards the blacks. The belief became widespread that, whereas the French considered it a compliment when an African thoroughly absorbed French culture and French social habits, the British regarded corresponding behaviour by British-ruled Africans as impudence and deserving rebuke. The proportion of enlightened Frenchmen and of narrow-minded Englishmen was perhaps not so high in reality as the cliché would have us believe.

The fourth main colonial regime, the Belgian, inclined rather to the British than to the French model. The Belgians developed practical education at a lower level, seeking with some success to train a skilled African labour force, but until the very eve of independence they discouraged higher education. In practice it was probably harder for a Belgian African to obtain a full modern education even than for a Portuguese African.

The proclaimed political aims of the four colonial regimes also differed widely. The French aim, of making black Frenchmen, implied the spread among Africans of French democratic ideas and the formation of political parties of the French type, but at the same time strong objection to any political movement whose aim was national independence—which was bound to imply rejection of French culture and of the French political heritage. The British did not object to the goal of independence: if they preferred their Africans to be Africans rather than black Englishmen, they could hardly refuse the right to independence. However, they considered it their duty to ensure that when independence came, there should be government institutions, and a political elite of Africans, capable of ruling in what British officials and intellectuals could recognise as an orderly and democratic way. They disliked the formation of political parties of radical outlook. The Portuguese rulers were not prepared to consider independence, as it would imply rejection of Portuguese culture; and meanwhile they did not intend to make much effort to enable Africans to acquire these cultural blessings. As for democracy, being opposed to introducing it in Portugal itself, the rulers could hardly be interested in offering it to Africans. Finally, the Belgians were not prepared to consider either democracy or independence until a very late stage, and then they simply abandoned colonial rule.

It is necessary to point out several influences which made themselves felt in the policies of Britain and France towards their African colonies.

First was paternalism in the civil service. The colonial officials for the most part sincerely regarded themselves as protectors of their black subjects. Their lives were devoted to their welfare, even though they might often act as stern parents towards wayward children: the idea that children grow up, and no longer accept their parents' guidance, was abhorrent to them.

Second was the conflict between European missionaries and business-men in the colonies. Missionaries too felt themselves to be the protectors of their flock, and tended (often quite rightly) to see the businessmen as wolves threatening their sheep. Missionaries were also pioneers in the creation of schools and hospitals. Their aim was to save souls and lives. It was not their intention, by lowering the death rate, to increase population pressure on existing maladjusted resources, and so strengthen the demand for social reforms or the volume of popular misery and discontent; nor to create political opposition by the propagation of contemporary political ideas through their schools. Both these results ensued. Missionaries did not necessarily favour independence: on the whole Catholic missionaries in French, Belgian and Portuguese colonies favoured the spread of their metropolitan culture, while Protestant missionaries in British colonies thought more in terms of British ideas of self-government leading very slowly to independence. However, it is clear that the total effect of missionary activity was to promote political consciousness and activity among Africans. This did not mean that the new emergent group of African politicians necessarily felt gratitude to the missionaries: on the contrary, they often resented what they considered to be attitudes of cultural and moral superiority, arising out of the missionaries' determination to inter-pret Christianity in narrowly European terms.

A third influence was the conflict in metropolitan politics. In general, the conservative parties took a paternalist attitude, compounded of the officials' ethos of service to the colonial peoples and of the businessmen's desire to maintain valuable economic privileges. The parties of the left pressed for more rapid development of democratic institutions in the colonies, or for more rapid movement towards independence. In parlia-mentary politics, the paternalist trend was stronger for a longer period in Britain, the radical tendency in France. In reality the political balance was more even. In France, that portion of the educated elite which was excluded from overt political life after the years of the Dreyfus controversy, entrenched itself in the army and the civil administration in the colonies; whereas in Britain, where personal and social contact between right and left in the political elite was closer than in France, liberal and even radical influences deeply penetrated the colonial administration. In both cases also the passive effect of the indifferent majority should not be underrated. Paternalists and radicals (Lord Milner and Clement Attlee, Marshal Lyautey and Léon Blum) had this in common; they genuinely cared about the peoples of the colonies. This was not true of the large numbers in both countries who oscillated between chauvinism and indifference, between 'keep the map red' and 'let the damned natives go to hell their own way'.

### African nationalism

In the beginning of African anti-colonial nationalism, influences from America were important. The Panafricanism of the West Indian Marcus Garvey[4] found disciples among modern-educated Africans. Nnamdi Azikiwe from Nigeria, Hastings Banda from Nyasaland and Kwame Nkrumah from the Gold Coast all studied at colleges in the United States and came under Panafrican influence. At the sixth Panafrican Congress, held in Manchester (England) in October 1945, besides the black American pioneer W. E. B. Du Bois and the West Indian George Padmore, many nationalists from Africa were present who later became prominent in anglophone African states: they included not only Kwame Nkrumah, but also Jomo Kenyatta from Kenya. Among francophone Africans there was an equivalent influence from the French West Indies. A poet from Martinique, Aimé Césaire, was one of the creators of the concept of *négritude*, around which developed an impressive literature in French: among its leading writers was Léopold Sédar Senghor from Senegal, who apart from writing poems in French also taught classical Greek to French schoolchildren in France. The movement for *négritude* enjoyed some sympathy from French intellectuals.

The first effective African nationalist movement was in the Gold Coast. Here there was a comparatively large educated class; and a considerable number of Africans had served in the British army in the Second World War, seen something of the world and become politically conscious. There was also widespread economic hardship owing to the spread of the 'swollen shoot' disease of the cocoa tree. In February 1948 there were food riots in Accra. In the following year the main political party, United Gold Coast Convention, split: the young radical leader Kwame Nkrumah broke away to form the Convention People's Party, which he proceeded to organise on an efficient mass basis, especially in the towns. In 1950 Nkrumah proclaimed a programme of civil disobedience and 'positive action', modelled to some extent on Gandhi's methods in India. This led to his imprisonment; but when an election was held in 1951, under the reforms proposed by the constitutional commission which the government had appointed in 1949, the CPP won an overwhelming victory. Nkrumah was released to become prime minister. His centralising policy was resisted by the traditional African elite, but he won the struggle, and was supported by the British government in London. In March 1957 the colony of Gold Coast was replaced by the sovereign state of Ghana, and Nkrumah established a vigorous one-party dictatorship.

In Nigeria the first active political group was the National Council of Nigeria and Cameroons founded in 1944 by Dr Nnamdi Azikiwe, generally known as Zik. Its main support came from the growing educated class among the Ibos, whose homeland was in the east of the colony, but who were also to be found as skilled employees or in the professions in the west and north. The NCNC was not concerned only with Ibo interests, but aimed at an independent Nigeria, to be the common homeland of the many different peoples who inhabited it. In 1951 a second party, the Action Group, led by Chief Obafemi Awolowo, was founded in the Yoruba lands in the west; and in the same year the leaders of the Fulani oligarchy, who had ruled the north under British 'indirect rule', organised a Northern People's Congress, to be based on wider popular support. These three parties distrusted each other; but since all three had hopes of dominating the whole of Nigeria, they had to take part in the manoeuvres for preparing a new constitution. After six years of negotiations a compromise was agreed by all, and Nigeria became an independent federal state in October 1960.

French West Africa (AOF) was divided into eight territories. After the Second World War the French government conferred French citizenship on all its subjects; set up elected assemblies in all eight territories and an indirectly elected assembly for all AOF; and arranged for the direct election by the people of AOF of deputies to the National Assembly in Paris. During the late 1940s the influence of metropolitan political parties was felt in AOF. The socialists were most successful in Senegal, but the strongest party in the region was the *Rassemblement démocratique africain* (RDA), founded at a conference at Bamako in 1946. It cooperated in Paris with the French Communist Party until 1950, when the party split. In the 1957 elections to the territorial assemblies, RDA won majorities in Ivory Coast, Sudan, Guinea and Upper Volta, and a powerful minority in Niger. However, differences between personalities and policies were too great to allow the RDA to remain a single party unifying the whole of AOF. In 1958 General de Gaulle's new French constitution offered the territories of AOF the choice between immediate complete independence or membership in a new French Community. At first only Guinea rejected membership, but by the end of 1960 six more territories chose independence. The eighth territory, Mauritania, had French consent for its independence, but the claim by the Moroccan government that it was part of Morocco caused several years' delay in its formal admission to the United Nations. The formerly French mandated territory of Togo became independent in 1960. The island of Madagascar, and the four territories of French Equatorial Africa (AEF) became first members of the Community and then independent states.

The Belgian rulers of the Congo in fifty years made good progress in industrial development, in the training of skilled manpower and in primary education, but they neither considered political independence likely nor did much to prepare an African elite. The number of Congolese with a modern education at the end of the 1950s was extremely small. New universities at Léopoldville and Elisabethville had had little time to produce results. In January 1959 there were violent riots in Léopoldville, organised by a party based on the Bakongo people who inhabited the extreme western part of the country, around the mouth of the Congo river, and spread also into neighbouring French and Portuguese territory. The riots caused the Belgian government to hold a series of elections, from town and rural councils upwards, and to prepare the country rapidly for independence. During this process there emerged a number of politicians and parties, some of whom had plans for Congolese nationalism designed to transcend local or tribal loyalties. In the summer of 1960 Congo became independent, but within a few weeks had disintegrated, as different regional governments, backed by rival great powers and rival groups of African states, fought each other, and United Nations officials did their best to sort out the mess.

In British East Africa the struggle for independence was complicated by the presence of large numbers of British landowners and large British urban populations. This was especially difficult in the White Highlands of Kenya, on the Copper Belt of Northern Rhodesia and in a large part of Southern Rhodesia.

The most numerous of the peoples of Kenya, the Kikuyu, suffered from over-population and soil exhaustion, and believed that the well-farmed White Highlands of the European settlers should be theirs. There was also a small politically conscious elite of educated Kikuyu who founded a small political party as early as 1922. Outstanding among them was the sociologist Jomo Kenyatta, who had studied in London and published a book entitled *Facing Mount Kenya*, which combined social analysis and nationalist aspirations. In 1952 a guerrilla war began in the Kikuyu lands which became known as Mau Mau. In this movement peasant discontent, religious fanaticism and nationalism combined; its leaders included primitive magicians and sophisticated products of modern schools. The Mau Mau militants regarded Kenyatta as their leader. Whether he was or was not responsible for starting the armed struggle, he was found guilty and sent to prison, but his followers held down British troops for four years. Meanwhile successive stages of constitutional reform were hurried through. Kenyatta was released in 1959, and became president of independent Kenya in 1962. A single party regime emerged, which mobilised support not only from the Kikuyu fifth of the population but also from the many smaller peoples who make up the remaining four-fifths. The two other East African states obtained their independence at about the same time. Uganda, which had no European settler problem, was faced with serious conflicts between its peoples. In Tanganyika there were European settlers, but fewer; and none of the large number of different peoples stood out as clearly stronger than the others, or possessed any formidable traditional or institutional framework. It was thus possible for a talented school-teacher, Julius Nyerere, to build up a country-wide party with massive support—the Tanganyika African National Union—to which power was handed over.

Further south, the three territories of Northern Rhodesia, Southern Rhodesia and Nyasaland were combined in 1953 in the Central African Federation. This was the plan of Sir Godfrey Huggins, prime minister of Southern Rhodesia, which had had a form of parliamentary government based on a European electorate since 1923, and which in the mid-1950s had a population of about 2,200,000 Africans, 170,000 Europeans and 13,000 Asians. Huggins believed that a federation would be economically more successful than three territories, and he hoped to work out a form of 'partnership' between Africans and Europeans which would avoid the extremes both of white South African *apartheid* and of unlimited rule by Africans. He and his successor, Sir Roy Welensky, were opposed by all politically conscious Africans and by a growing proportion of the European settlers. In Nyasaland, with an almost completely African population, the nationalist movement led by Dr Hastings Banda soon won massive support. In Northern Rhodesia the European population, consisting mainly of highly paid workers in the mining industry, bitterly opposed African claims, but the African nationalists were too strong for them. In both cases the British government in London yielded to the Africans. Nyasaland and Northern Rhodesia became sovereign republics, changing their names respectively to Malawi and Zambia.

White supremacy was now confined to Rhodesia (from whose name the word 'southern' was dropped), the Portuguese colonies of Angola and Mozambique, South-West Africa,[5] and the Union of South Africa.[6] As Portugal itself was ruled by a dictatorship which forbade political parties, there could be no legally authorised nationalist movements. In Rhodesia such movements were permitted in principle, but the narrow limits placed on voting rights for blacks condemned the nationalists to increasing frustration, and to ineffectual extremism. In 1962 the leader of the Zimbabwe African People's Union (ZAPU), Joshua Nkomo, was interned; and in 1964 the Zimbabwe African National Union (ZANU), which had broken away from ZAPU, was banned.

The inevitable consequence was to drive nationalists into exile, conspiracy and violence. Guerrilla organisations made their appearance. These needed a safe base in a neighbouring state, and training facilities and arms. The first was provided for Angola by Congo (Zaïre) and Zambia, for Mozambique by Tanzania, and for Rhodesia by Zambia; the second by the Soviet, Chinese and East European governments. Recruits were attracted for training from inside the territories, and in due course guerrilla operations began on their soil.

The inevitable result of this was that the guerrilla movements claimed, and were considered by a growing number of foreign governments, to represent the peoples of these lands, and to have the sole right to speak in their name. The Rhodesian and Portuguese governments replied that the guerrillas represented only a tiny minority; yet even if this were true, these governments prevented themselves from proving it by their refusal to introduce institutions which would enable their black subjects to express their opinions. Those non-elected black tribal chiefs whom they put forward as alternatives were dismissed by the nationalists and their foreign protectors and sympathisers as 'stooges'.

However, it still remained true that all these territories were inhabited by several peoples, which differed from and distrusted each other. Tribal loyalties played their part in the frequent splits which occurred in the illegal nationalist movements and guerrilla forces. The exiled nationalist leaders, inevitably influenced increasingly by Marxist thinking as they found practical support to their movements coming from countries ruled by communist parties, aimed to create, within their liberated states, single new nations, commanding a loyalty which would transcend all tribal divisions. This was an understandable and laudable aim for a member of a European-educated intelligentsia; but the fact that the leaders held these views could not cancel out the fact that tribal and linguistic divisions remained strong among their peoples.

The majority of white Rhodesians remained determined not only to keep power, but to see to it that neither the school system nor the political institutions should enable Africans ever to achieve that status of 'civilised men' which Cecil Rhodes had once laid down as the qualification for citizenship. As the British government insisted on a series of conditions which (though far from acceptable to the African nationalist leaders) would have made rapid advance for Africans possible, the Rhodesian prime minister, Ian Smith, made a 'unilateral declaration of independence' in November 1965. It was felt by some at this time that if a token force of British troops had been sent to back the governor who remained loyal to London, Smith and his colleagues would have capitulated. The British government, however, believed that such action would have led to civil war, and was not willing to cause bloodshed. It therefore limited its resistance to support of economic sanctions, which were declared by the United Nations, and which were largely ignored by member states. Rhodesia survived for eleven years, but when black nationalists obtained power in Angola and Mozambique in 1975-76, the opportunities of Rhodesian black guerrillas rapidly increased. Pressed by the United States and South African governments, Smith agreed, in September 1976, to embark on a drastic constitutional revision designed to give Rhodesia a black majority government within two years.

Unmoved by the British, French and Belgium examples, the Portuguese leaders maintained for two decades more their official doctrine that all the colonies were an integral part of Portugal, and that all educated persons, black no less than white, were full citizens. The most impressive exiled nationalist movement was the *Frente de Libertação de Moçambique (Frelimo)*, based on Tanzania, which began guerrilla action in northern Mozambique in 1964. Its efforts kept considerable numbers of Portuguese troops engaged, and the assassination of its leader, the highly cultured Eduardo Mondlane, in February 1969, did not destroy it. Guerrilla fighting also grew in Portuguese Guinea. The situation was transformed by the Portuguese revolution of April 1974, which was a direct result of discontent in the Portuguese army with the protracted unsuccessful wars in Africa. The new Portuguese rulers gave full independence to Guinea, and accepted the claim of *Frelimo* to represent the African population of Mozambique, which became officially independent on 25 June 1975.

In Angola several resistance movements arose in the 1960s, divided by ideology and by tribal composition. In 1975 there were three, each recruiting its main support from different sources. The People's Movement for Liberation of Angola (MPLA) appeared the most popular among the intelligentsia, of which part was in the capital Luanda, and part in exile. It also drew mass support from the second most numerous people of the country—the Mbundu, who numbered 700,000 out of a total population of some 6,000,000. Its proclaimed ideology was Marxist, its aim the creation of a single Angolan nation, and it was supported by the Soviet Union. The National Front for Liberation of Angola (FNLA) was based chiefly on the Bakongo people who lived on both sides of the border with Zaïre: it was strongly supported by its ruler, General Mobutu. The third movement, the National Union for the Total Independence of Angola (UNITA), appeared to have support among the most numerous people of Angola, the Ovimbundu (numbering about 1,700,000).

Independence was declared by Portugal in November 1975 while civil war was raging, with FNLA and UNITA together against MPLA, which was in possession of Luanda. UNITA's forces were strengthened by some South African fighting units, but Soviet support to MPLA rapidly increased, including an airlift in Soviet aircraft across the once British- or American-dominated Atlantic Ocean, of some 12,000 troops from Cuba, possessing sophisticated modern weapons. The Cuban invasion was decisive and MPLA won the civil war. The Angolan nation was still to be created.

Hostility to the Western industrial states was not confined to those countries in which indigenous white hostility to black advancement had promoted revolutionary doctrines and guerrilla action. The rulers of those

African states which still maintained good relations with the West were under constant attack from the radicals in their own countries and abroad. The essence of the accusation was that these rulers were 'stooges' of foreign capitalism, and that they had not achieved independence, but had merely passed from colonial status to 'neo-colonialism'.

It was indeed true that in most of these countries large sectors of the economy continued, after sovereign independence had been declared, to be dominated by European or North American capital. Cities like Lagos or Abidjan had large resident European business communities. In some African states (especially in some of the former French colonies) Europeans remained also as civil servants, or as military or administrative advisers. In Kenya and Tanzania some British landowners accepted the new citizenship, and continued to farm their estates. In many African states there were European doctors in hospitals, European lecturers in universities, European engineers in charge of construction sites. Apart from this, both the former imperial governments and governments of other advanced industrial countries made gifts or loans on a considerable scale, and some economic aid was channelled through international organisations.

These various forms of continued European or North American influence could be seen in two diametrically opposed ways. From one point of view, all this added up to 'aid to developing countries', useful as far as it went but much too little in the recipients' opinion. White-skinned advisers were welcomed as experts; and indeed many of them gave their first loyalty to their African employers and served them well. From the opposite point of view, it was 'neo-colonialism', a form of exploitation just as ruthless, and in the long term at least as dangerous, as the old exploitation through direct colonial rule. The white-skinned advisers were spies for Western governments, symbols of white race supremacy; and indeed some of these advisers did treat their African employers and colleagues in an arrogant manner.

The first view was upheld by some governments whose independence did indeed appear to be little more than fiction, but also by others which had achieved considerable progress under the leadership of considerable statesmen, who had won respect and prestige on an international scale: such were Ivory Coast under President Félix Houphouet-Boigny, and Senegal under President Léopold Sédar Senghor. The first prominent exponent of the second view was President Kwame Nkrumah of Ghana, who did his best to evolve a whole theory of neo-colonialism. It was taken up by Soviet spokesmen, who stoutly maintained that political independence was insecure unless accompanied by economic independence; and that economic independence could not be achieved until not only all foreign private capital was expropriated, but 'aid' from and trade with 'capitalist' countries was replaced by 'aid' from and trade with the 'socialist' countries—which was by definition wholly disinterested and comradely.

The truth varied from country to country; but it is certain that the presence of Europeans in their midst, and the knowledge of their economic and cultural dependence on the advanced industrial nations, caused much resentment among the new intellectual and political elites in the new African states. Here there is some similarity with the situation in the independent states of the Balkans earlier in the century. In Romania in the 1920s both Jews (a recognisably distinct group) and foreigners owned a large part of the infant industries. This undoubted fact was resented by nationalists; and the resentment was eagerly manipulated by governments, which made these 'alien' groups scapegoats, to divert public discontent away from their own misdeeds.

## African states and nations

The frontiers drawn by European colonial governments in the nineteenth century, both between their territories and those of another colonial power, and within their vast domains, were often quite artificial—mere lines on the map, sometimes taking account of river valleys, sometimes not even that They cut across regions which might have formed natural units, and they divided peoples and language groups. This was more true of pastoral peoples, accustomed to drive their herds over enormous distances, than of sedentary peoples occupied with agriculture. As examples of divided peoples, we may mention the Yoruba, Ewe, Bakongo and Luo.

The early African nationalists knew who was their enemy: the colonial government of European foreigners. What was not clear was the unit for which they were demanding loyalty. Those who had been influenced by American Panafricanism replied: 'Africa'. The outstanding exponent of this doctrine was Kwame Nkrumah. He and his disciples believed in the essential unity of Africa and its peoples. The doctrine inevitably led to contradictions. In their legitimate desire to explore the pre-colonial history of Africa (which had indeed been neglected by European historians), some African nationalists made extravagant claims for Africans' historic contributions to human civilisation. Others argued that the relative lack of authentic history meant that Africans were free from a sort of original sin possessed by Europeans (and arguably by Asians too), from their long heritage of crimes, follies and misfortunes. Starting with a sort of virginal purity, the Africans could point the true way forward. Something of the same thing was to be found in the concept of *négritude*, formulated by francophone West Indians and taken up by francophone West Africans.

When Nkrumah became prime minister of the first ex-colonial African territory to become independent, he renamed the Gold Coast as Ghana, after the medieval kingdom whose territories had in fact lain north and west of his; but he also pursued the concept of a united Africa, and devoted a large part of his efforts, during fifteen years of power, to enlisting the support of the rulers of the other new African states which came into being. However, as in South America in the nineteenth century, geographical distances and diverse group interests proved too strong an obstacle. It is true that in the late twentieth century mere distance was a less serious impediment than in the time of Bolívar: it is also true that the diversity of cultures between the different parts of Africa was far greater than was the case between the different Spanish-speaking communities in Spanish America, though perhaps not between Amerindian communities.

In most of independent Africa the language of the former colonial power became the official language of the new independent state. The exceptions were Sudan (with Arabic), Somalia (with Somali from 1972), and of course Ethiopia, which was far from being a new state, and which had Amharic as its official language. Partial exceptions were Kenya and Tanganyika, in which the status of Swahili was nominally superior to that of English. It could be argued that an element of English or of French culture provided a minimum cultural uniformity on which an African unity could be built. However, these were the languages of the expelled and execrated foreigner, and the degree of penetration of English or French culture into African society could hardly be compared with the degree of penetration of Spanish or Portuguese into Central or South American.

Nkrumah's dream of African unity remained far from reality at the time of his death. Even his more limited enterprise of a union between Ghana and Guinea remained a fiction, and was abandoned after his overthrow in 1966. The federal republic of Mali, composed of Senegal and Sudan, was proclaimed in April 1959, but broke up again in August 1960, with Sudan retaining the name Mali. The attempt at an economic union of the three East African states of Kenya, Tanganyika and Uganda also ran into insuperable difficulties. Tanganyika united with Zanzibar to form Tanzania in 1964, but the two parts in effect remained separate.

Panafricanism remained an inspiration to young educated radicals in all African lands. The Organization for African Unity (OAU) maintained a certain solidarity of African states in foreign policy, publicly expressed at its periodical conferences and in its hostile posture at the United Nations towards Portugal, Rhodesia and South Africa, and to a lesser extent towards the former colonial powers. When conflicts arose between African states, and action rather than rhetoric was required, OAU proved less effective. Certain principles were generally adopted among its members. Existing frontiers, though created by the colonial rulers of the past, were recognised, since it was felt by all that attempts to improve them were likely to raise more difficulties than they solved. It was also generally agreed that secession was to be discouraged. This doctrine was applied in the case of the Congo, but was abandoned by some member governments during the Nigerian civil war. It was also agreed that 'tribalism' was to be discouraged, though no satisfactory definition of this phenomenon could be found.

Rulers of independent states did their best to unite their subjects in loyalty to a single nation which they set out to create; and to pursue political centralisation, economic modernisation and mass education. In practice there were formidable obstacles. Centralisation and modernisation often, though not always, involved hostility to traditional hierarchies. Whereas in Hungary under Dualism the champions of centralisation and modernisation had been members of the traditional nobility, in most African new states they came from the modern Europe-influenced intellectual elite, which included children of traditional chiefs, but tended, like European liberals and republicans of the nineteenth century, to regard autonomies and local loyalties as reactionary obstacles to progress. A possible partial exception was the Ivory Coast, where President Houphouet-Boigny owed his supremacy not only to his earlier espousal of progressive ideas but to the loyalty which the traditional social hierarchy enabled him to command.

In Ghana, Nkrumah enlisted support from all parts of the country, but especially from the cities of the coastal region. He was opposed by the older elite of the Akan-speaking regions, especially of the former kingdom of Ashanti. Their opposition, which was also based on the discontent of cocoa-farmers who believed themselves to be exploited by the central government, was expressed by the National Liberation Front, founded in 1954. Nkrumah however defeated the NLF and its northern Muslim allies in the election of 1956. The regional assemblies, which he had accepted as a condition for obtaining British consent to complete independence, were soon destroyed. When Nkrumah's dictatorship was overthrown, his successors in varying degrees maintained the supremacy of central government over any centrifugal forces. The Ewe people, who would have preferred to join their compatriots in the neighbouring Togo state, were denied this right by Nkrumah, and even the democratic government of Kofio Busia, who held power from 1969 to 1972, did not act otherwise.

The formation of the independent state of Uganda was long delayed by the wish of the separate kingdoms, of which the most important was Buganda, to preserve their autonomy. When independence came in 1962, Dr Milton Obote, leader of the Uganda People's Congress and a champion of centralisation and radical policies, made an alliance, against other centrifugal groups, with the king (*Kabaka*) and parliament (*Lukiko*) of Buganda. After four years, however, Obote quarrelled with the Kabaka, and in May 1966 was able forcibly to suppress an attempt at secession by the Baganda. In September 1967 he introduced a new constitution, which simply divided Buganda up into four provinces. The Kabaka escaped abroad, the army was purged and arms were received from the Soviet Union. However, Obote began to quarrel with his new army command,

and in January 1971 General Idi Amin seized power during Obote's absence abroad. Under the subsequent dictatorship the hopes of the various former kingdoms for autonomy were not satisfied.

The Congo state in 1960 seemed likely to disintegrate. For some time there were three governments: the official government at Léopoldville; a second, which professed itself socialist, in the north at Stanleyville; and a third, avowedly secessionist, under Moïse Tshombe in the Katanga province, supported by the Belgian mining interests of that rich region. After some years of warfare, involving multi-national United Nations forces and multi-national forces of European mercenaries serving various pretenders, a central government began to establish its authority. In November 1965 General Joseph Mobutu made himself dictator. With American financial support and political advice he gradually imposed his authority. Tribal diversity remained, but the military regime was obeyed. Mobutu took pains to Africanise names of people and places: the state was named Zaïre, its capital Kinshasa. The aim was to inculcate a Zaïrean patriotism, and in the course of time a new national consciousness. The regime antagonised the young intellectual elite, and the army suppressed student riots with heavy casualties. However, the first stage of Mobutu's aims, the creation of a single political authority, had for the time being been achieved.

The formerly German territories of Ruanda and Urundi, held by Belgium as 'mandates' after the First World War, became separate independent states under the names of Rwanda and Burundi. Both were inhabited by two peoples: the Hutu who formed the majority and the Tutsi who were a minority and held power and wealth. In Rwanda in 1959 the Hutu successfully overthrew Tutsi rule, killing large numbers of their enemies, before independence was granted by the Belgians. In Burundi the Tutsi remained in control until 1972, when the Hutu revolted. The revolt was crushed, and both sides committed massacres: the Tutsi, as victors, massacred more. The number of victims was variously estimated between 80,000 and 300,000, and half a million people were made homeless.

A pattern more similar to European experience is found in the Horn of Africa, the region which extends from the upper Nile to the shores facing Arabia, and includes the great curve of coastline that sweeps 1,000 miles to the south-west. The most important state in this region was Ethiopia.

The Ethiopian Christian state was dominated for centuries by persons of Amharic or Tigrinyan speech. The expansion of its frontiers by Menelik brought great numbers of Muslims, of various languages, under Ethiopian rule. The Amhara were reduced to less than half the population.[7] In the twentieth century, Ethiopian policy consciously pursued Amharic domination. Not only were the Ethiopian leaders unwilling to surrender the provinces of Haud and Ogaden to a Somali state: Ethiopian nationalists aimed to create a single empire in the Horn, with the Amhara the official nation in the same sense in which the Magyars were the official nation in Hungary under Dualism.

This was resisted not only by the Somalis but by the Muslim portion of the Tigrinya-speaking population of Eritrea. Of a total (in the 1950s)[8] of some 1,500,000 persons speaking languages of the Tigrinyan type, about 524,000 lived in Eritrea and the rest in Ethiopia. Of the latter, 329,000 were Muslims and the rest Christians. The Christian Tigrinyans tended to favour union with Ethiopia,[9] the Muslims to oppose it. When union took place in 1952, it was stated to be on a federal basis. However, the Ethiopian government paid little attention to the federal constitution, and in 1962 the Eritreans were persuaded or coerced into accepting the status of a single province in a unitary Ethiopian state. Opposition grew, supported by propaganda, money and weapons from Sudan, Syria and Iraq, with more indirect encouragement from the Soviet Union. In the early 1960s an Eritrean Liberation Front, supported mainly but not exclusively by Muslims, began guerrilla action against Ethiopia.

Among the Galla too there were stirrings of opposition. The Galla peasants were less willing than in the past to accept the domination of the landowners, who were for the most part Amhara or Amharised Galla. The ability of the Ethiopian regime to command the loyalty of the Galla elite was also in doubt. University students of Galla origin began to speak of Galla rights. In 1967 a political group appeared, putting forward demands on behalf of the Galla people and led by a Galla from the central province of Shoa named Tadäsä Biru, who had risen to the rank of general in the Ethiopian army. It was suppressed, and arrests were made.

The Ethiopian regime came under increasing attack from modernisers and radicals. An abortive revolution in 1960 was followed by army mutinies in 1974. In September the emperor was deposed, and in November the military revolutionary leaders executed more than fifty former politicians and high officials. Meanwhile the Eritrean Liberation Front continued to fight for separation, but the Ethiopian revolutionaries were uncompromising in their insistence on unity. The further danger that Galla and Somali separatism might lead to large loss of territory could also not be ignored.

The name Somali is found in Ethiopian texts of the early fifteenth century and in an Arabic chronicle of the 1540s. The peoples which bore this name, who may be physically descended from the ancient inhabitants of South Arabia, spread southwards from the Red Sea coast, mainly between the sixteenth and nineteenth centuries. They were mainly nomadic and pastoral, organised in various tribes whose dialects differed from each other but were basically related. In the third quarter of the nineteenth century, after attempts by rulers of both Egypt and Ethiopia to take over all the Somali lands had failed, those portions which had not already been annexed by Ethiopia were placed under the protectorate of three European powers—the north-western part under Britain from 1887, the region of Djibuti under France from 1885, and the largest portion, consisting of the Indian Ocean sector, under Italy from 1889. The southernmost portion of the Somali lands was included in British East Africa (later Kenya).

European occupation met with resistance, especially the revolts under the religious leader Mullah Mohammed ibn Abdullah in the British protectorate in 1898-1904, 1913 and 1920. Somali resistance was dominated by the traditional elite, and took the form of hostility to foreigners and infidels rather than any European-style democratic nationalism: the European-educated elite of the Somalis was extremely small.

The Italians attempted to exploit Somali hostility to Ethiopians when they invaded Ethiopia in 1936. During the Second World War the Italians occupied the whole of the Horn of Africa (except French Djibuti) in 1940, but in 1941 the whole was reconquered by the British. At the end of the war the Somali territories were an object of dispute between the great powers, which ended in the declaration of the former Italian territory (Somalia) as a United Nations Trust Territory under Italian administration. In 1954 the British, who had kept control of the formerly Ethiopian, but Somali-inhabited, province of Haud, restored this to Ethiopia. At the end of June 1960 the British Somali protectorate came to an end; on 1 July the Trust Territory of Somalia became an independent state; and on the same day the unity of the two territories in a republic of Somalia was proclaimed. In French Djibuti however a referendum, held in September 1958, had shown a majority for membership of the French Community. There was no doubt that the substantial element in the population who were not Somalis favoured this solution, but it was doubtful whether this was the wish of the Somalis.

During the 1950s political parties had come into existence in the Somali territories which became increasingly concerned, not only with independence from European rule, but with the unity of all Somalis in a single state. In the early 1960s it was estimated that in addition to some 2,000,000 in the new united republic there were also about 850,000 Somalis in Ethiopia (in the two former provinces of Haud and Ogaden), and nearly 100,000 in Kenya. The main object of Somali hostility was therefore Ethiopia, in which no Somali political activity was permitted, and the movements of Somali pastoral tribes across frontiers were impeded. Independent Kenya, in which political opposition was suppressed shortly after independence, was a natural ally of Ethiopia.

To the north of Ethiopia, the vast territory known as the Republic of Sudan had long been a region of contact and of conflict between Islam and other religions, and between northern fair-skinned peoples and black Africans. In the modern tragedy of the south Sudan, linguistic, religious and racial factors have played their parts.

The lands around the upper Nile are the home of a considerable number of rather small peoples, differing greatly in language and in customs. They maintained their pagan beliefs, and effectively resisted Islam, which was brought both by merchants and by armed invaders. The southern peoples had good reasons to hate Muslims and Arabic-speakers, whom they had known throughout their history as organisers of slave-seizing operations. Ethiopian Christianity, however, had barely touched them.

After the British conquest of the Sudan under Kitchener (undertaken nominally on behalf of the government of Egypt), the south was administered from 1902 to 1946 as a separate unit. This consisted of the three provinces of Bahr al-Gazal, Equatoria and Upper Nile. In the early 1950s about 40 per cent of the population of the so-called Anglo-Egyptian Sudan consisted of Arabic-speaking Muslims, living in the northern part of the country. In the west and south-west regions lived various black peoples, mostly Muslim, among whom were some Arabic-speakers. The three provinces of the south contained about 30 per cent of the whole population. They belonged to various Nilotic peoples, of whom the most important, the Dinka, numbered more than a million.

Under British rule considerable numbers of southerners became Christians. The British administrators saw themselves as protectors of these defenceless tribes against Muslim fanaticism and Arab commercial greed. For their part the Arabic-speakers claimed that British paternalism was nothing but imperialist hypocrisy. The British alone, they claimed, were responsible for any hatred of Arabs which might exist in the south. The British simply wished to keep the upper Nile for themselves in order to be able to put pressure on the northern Sudan and Egypt, whose livelihood depended on the river. Once Sudan became independent, Muslim and Christian, black and brown, Arab and Nilotic would be brothers. Any suggestion that the north Sudanese, or the Egyptians through them, had imperialistic designs on the Nilotic peoples, was dismissed as absurd: imperialism is something of which only white Christians from overseas can be guilty.

In 1946 the British government's policy changed, and it was decided to prepare Sudan for independence (largely, it may be argued, in order to deprive independent Egypt of the Sudan); and with this end in view the

British rulers began efforts to bring northerners and southerners together. A conference was held at Juba in June 1947 at which fair promises were made by Sudanese from both north and south. However, the evidence does not show that the southerners at the conference agreed to accept a unitary state of Sudan; nor that these southerners were entitled to speak for the peoples of the south, who had not elected them.

As the preparations for independence reached their final stage, it became clear that the new state would be dominated by northerners. Of eight hundred important posts in the administration, to be transferred from British officials under a 'Sudanisation' programme, only four were to go to southerners. Those Arab officials who genuinely tried to be fair to their Nilotic subjects were under heavy pressure from powerful northern traders' interests, which showed themselves contemptuous and hostile to the southerners. In July 1955 the Khartoum government of Al-Azhari arrested four southern members of parliament, and dismissed three hundred southern workers from a cotton factory. This action provoked demonstrations, and these in turn triggered off a mutiny. The rebels made themselves masters of the three provinces, except the city of Juba, but ended their resistance when British troops intervened and new promises were made to consider southern demands. The few southerners elected to the national parliamentary committee which prepared the Sudanese constitution asked for a federal state, but they were overridden. In the first elected Constituent Assembly there were 46 southern seats, and 40 of these were held by the Federal Party. The government, representing the dominant political group in the north, and the Assembly, in which northerners had a large majority, decided simply to ignore southern aspirations. In May 1958 the southern members walked out of the Assembly. The conflict between northern and southern politicians was one of the main reasons for the seizure of power in Khartoum by General Abboud on 17 November. The new regime treated the south as a conquered country. There was some lip service in Khartoum to solidarity of all Sudanese, and a handful of southerners were given jobs which brought no real power; but in the south the Arab army officer and merchant regarded the southerners as an inferior race of natural slaves, and set about grabbing their land, their shops and their women, while more and more southerners took to the jungle and organised a guerrilla, in which they treated northerners with no less cruelty than was meted out to them. Many thousands fled to neighbouring countries, and military supplies were sent to the guerrilla fighters, mainly from Ethiopia and Israel.

In 1963 refugees in Uganda formed a Sudanese African National Union to speak for southern interests, and in the same year large supplies of weapons, sent through the Sudan to rebels against the government of Congo, fell into south Sudanese hands. Thus strengthened, the southern resisters were able to form a substantial force, which they called Anya-Nya (a Nilotic name for the poison of the Gabon viper). With perhaps 12,000 men under his command, and widespread support from the people of the region, Anya-Nya's leader Joseph Lagu was able to organise a guerrilla in the south.

The fall of the Abboud government in Khartoum in October 1964 made little difference. Its successor adopted a strongly 'anti-imperialist' stance, spoke of restoring liberties after military dictatorship, gave some government posts to some southerners, and tried to put pressure on the southerners' African friends by sending arms to Congolese and Eritrean rebels. The promises soon proved unreal. In December 1964 there were armed clashes in Khartoum between supporters of northern and southern factions. In March 1965 there was a Round Table Conference in Khartoum, at which the southerners asked for a plebiscite in the south but the government would go no further than offer some more posts to southerners and some more schools. In July 1965 northern troops, infuriated by the murder of two of their comrades by southern guerrilla fighters in Juba, went on a rampage of murder and burning for two days. Resistance, repression and atrocities continued.

In May 1969 General Gaafer Muhammad Nimeiry seized power in Khartoum, and ruled in collaboration with the communists, who had a policy for the south based on Soviet 'nationality' doctrine. This made some appeal to some younger southern educated persons, but the war did not come to an end. In July 1976 the communists tried to overthrow Nimeiry, but were beaten, and their leaders, including the southerner Joseph Garang, were executed. Nimeiry now at last made a serious attempt to come to terms with the south. His envoys met representatives of Anya-Nya in Addis Ababa in February 1971, and an agreement, amounting to an armistice and promises of fair treatment for southerners, was made. In the following year it appeared that conditions in the south had genuinely improved, fighting had stopped, and officials were treating southerners as equal citizens. Nevertheless the pressures of Arabisation, conversion to Islam and economic exploitation by the north remained.

The southerners suffered from the basic weakness of linguistic and tribal diversity. Christianity and the English language were the only unifying factors; but most were not Christians, and only a small intellectual elite could speak English. In a separate state the Nilotic peoples might have created a national unity, though the examples of Uganda, Rwanda and Burundi were not encouraging. The northerners were determined that Arabic should be the basis of Sudanese culture and nationality; but to educated southerners, the acceptance of Arabic meant acquiescence in Islamisation.

Above all, racial contempt by Arabs for blacks whom they saw as their inferiors was as deeply rooted as anything to be found in the American

South or in South Africa. It was going to be a long and difficult task for even the most enlightened Khartoum politicians to remove this mentality.

Nigeria was an artificial creation of British colonial rule. This large country contained many people, languages and religions. In the north Islam predominated, while in the south Christian missionaries had made many converts from the late nineteenth century onwards, but many people still retained a variety of pagan faiths. There were three main languages. In the north Hausa was widely spoken (by 18 per cent of the population of all Nigeria). It was a *lingua franca*, spoken also in the French territories to the north and north-west. The second important language was Yoruba, spoken (by 17 per cent of the total population) in the south-west, and also a large part of the neighbouring French state of Dahomey. The third was Ibo, perhaps more a group of dialects than a uniform language, spoken (by about 18 per cent of the total population) to the east of the lower course of the river Niger.

British administrators normally described the peoples of their African colonies as 'tribes'. They spoke of 'tribal conflicts', 'tribal differences', and 'tribalism'. However, it is arguable that three peoples in Nigeria were more than tribes, that they were nations in the making. In the north there were the Fulani, ruled by emirs who were successors of the nineteenth century Muslim religious reformer Othman dan Fodio. In the south-west were Yorubas, with their long succession of rulers and their enterprising merchant class. In the east were the Ibos, whose situation was rather different. There had never been a single large Ibo state, and there was nothing that could well be described as a traditional Ibo upper class. The Ibos, however, proved apt pupils of the missionary schools, did well in British offices as clerks, and began to make their way in the professions in the growing cities—as lawyers, doctors or journalists as well as in business. They were a rather egalitarian people, with more respect for personal achievement than for status. Large numbers made careers in Lagos and in the northern cities. It was among the Ibos that Zik's NCNC[10] had its main support, but this party from the beginning considered its field of action to be all Nigeria, not just the Ibo lands. The Ibos, just because they were so successful outside their own homeland, were the most 'Pan-Nigerian' of the Nigerian peoples.

Independent Nigeria began with a federal constitution, with a northern, a western and an eastern state. Each had its own government, and was also represented in the central parliament. It might have been expected that the West and East would line up against the North. Both had a much higher level of education and modern skills than the North, and both were largely Christian while the North was mostly Muslim. However, Yorubas and Ibos soon quarrelled about the boundaries of a fourth (mid-western) state, which it was proposed to add to the original three states of the federation. This state was to be based on Benin, a city of ancient culture, and was also to include people of several languages, including some Ibos. The northern leaders had at first opposed this move, but they soon made use of the opportunity which its creation gave them of playing off West against East. The northern emirs had the advantage over the southerners that they had a docile population: the combination of religious and political authority was overwhelming, and the attempt to create a democratic opposition to the emirs had little success. The Sardauna of Sokoto proved to be a skilful manipulator of political power, and another northerner, Sir Abubakar Tafewa Balewa, was prime minister of the federation. Despite mutual distrust the eastern and northern politicians combined at the expense of the West. The most eminent Yoruba leader, Chief Obafemi Awolowo, was overthrown after his Action Group had been split, thanks to the support given by the northerners to his rival Chief Samuel Akintola in an extremely violent election in the western state in October 1965. After five years of independence, Nigerian politics seemed to be full of fraud, coercion and corruption. There was growing bitterness and hostility to all the established politicians, especially among the younger generation.

This period came to a bloody end on 15 January 1966, when a group of young officers seized power. They murdered Sir Abubakar and his finance minister in Lagos, the Sardauna in the northern capital Kaduna, and Chief Akintola in the western capital Ibadan. In Enugu, the eastern capital, there were no murders. After some hours of confusion the senior officer of the Nigerian army, Major-General Aguiyi Ironsi, accepted power from the rebels and was recognised as ruler of all Nigeria. All the rebel officers were Ibos, and there were no Ibo victims. This naturally inclined non-Ibos to think the action had been an Ibo plot to take over the country. Ironsi was himself an Ibo, and so was Colonel Emeka Ojukwu, governor of the East, who emerged unscathed from the action. Yet the truth seems to have been rather different. The action was one of middle-rank officers who were determined to put an end to the corruption and the separatist trends in Nigerian politics, and to rebuild a united Nigeria on different lines. They were a group of military radicals, arrogating to themselves a monopoly of patriotism, and believing that political problems can be solved simply by shooting the politicians. This is a fairly common phenomenon of twentieth century history, in the Balkans, Middle East and Latin America as well as in Africa. A very high proportion of officers of the rank of major and captain in the new Nigerian army were Ibos, not through conspiratorial action by sinister cliques but because more Ibòs than others possessed the educational qualifications needed in an officer, and because the army was the most promising career in Nigeria for ambitious young men.

Ironsi's policy was to unify Nigeria, using the army as the most reliable and genuinely all-Nigerian instrument to this end. The climax of his policy was a decree of May 1966, which abolished the federation and the three regional governments, and dissolved all political parties and regional associations. This was viewed in the North as an attempt by Ibos to take over the whole country. A certain parallel may be suggested with Yugoslavia—with centralised Nigeria as a Greater Iboland, as centralised Yugoslavia had been a Greater Serbia. There was also another reason why Ibos were unpopular in the North, rather similar to the reason why Jews were unpopular in Eastern Europe or Chinese in south-eastern Asia: all three appeared as an alien community, commercially or professionally gifted and concentrated in compact communities in the midst of other peoples. Anti-Ibo pogroms broke out in several northern cities, which cost some six hundred lives.

On 29 July 1966 northern soldiers mutinied in Abeokuta and Ibadan, captured Ironsi and tortured him to death. The chief of staff, Lieutenant-Colonel Jack Gowon, was taken prisoner, but then agreed to assume power. It does not seem that Gowon was in fact an accomplice of the northern military murderers (he was himself a Christian northerner) any more than Ironsi had been an accomplice of the Ibo military murderers in May; but his actions understandably infuriated and alarmed the Ibos, whose chief spokesman was now the eastern military governor, Ojukwu. Their fears were soon justified. At the end of September there were mass-scale pogroms against Ibos in the North, in which there may have been as many as 10,000 dead, and hundreds of thousands of Ibos began to pour into the East from all parts of the country. There followed some months of communication by letter or telephone between Gowon and Ojukwu, culminating in a personal meeting of Gowon and the four military governors at Aburi, in the territory of Ghana, on 4 and 5 January 1967. This meeting (detailed minutes of which have been published) ended in apparent agreement on a form of loose confederation: the colonels, as honest soldiers and old personal friends, believed that they could agree where mere self-seeking politicians had failed. When they got back to their office desks, they found things were less simple: their bureaucrats and specialist advisers told them the scheme would not work, and accusations of bad faith were exchanged all round. The conflict could no longer be bridged. On 30 May 1967 Ojukwu proclaimed an independent sovereign Republic of Biafra; Gowon refused to recognise the secession; and on 6 July the first shots were exchanged in a civil war which lasted two and a half years and in which armed combat, massacre, starvation and disease took more than a million lives.

The war was not caused by a northern or a Biafran plot to seize all power. The essence was that the Ibos did not believe that they could any longer live within one state with those who had massacred, or tolerated the massacre of, their compatriots; while Gowon and his supporters refused to accept the dissolution of the Nigerian state, which with its 60,000,000 inhabitants was the largest in Africa and could, they hoped, look forward to a glorious future. Ojukwu and his colleagues did not consider themselves to be fighting exclusively for an Ibo cause: they took the whole eastern state as their homeland, and gave it a new name, Biafra. The eastern state was an artificial region, owing its origin to a past colonial power: but so also was Nigeria. Biafra contained many who were not Ibos: the north contained even more non-Fulani, and the mid-western state was a patchwork of peoples, languages and faiths.

The governments of Africa and of the world as a whole favoured the federal side. The conventional wisdom of *bien pensant* liberalism con-demned secessionists, from Jefferson Davis and Edward Carson to Tshombe. Most enthusiastic in this sense were the British politicians and civil servants, who could not bear to think that the proudest creation of the British empire in Africa, a great united Nigeria, was to break up. They were rivalled, as patrons of Gowon, by the Soviet leaders, who saw an unrivalled opportunity to establish a strong base in Africa. On the other hand, the French government, not indifferent to the prospects of their oil companies in the oil-bearing lands which were in Biafra, supported Biafra. In the later part of the war the world press was more favourable to Biafra, as stories of mass starvation spread, and humanitarian groups organised relief, often performing deeds of heroism by flying in supplies. Four African countries also decided to recognise Biafra while maintaining relations with Nigeria—Ivory Coast, Gabon, Tanzania and Zambia. All this favourable publicity and aid served only to foster illusions in Ojukwu, to prolong the war and to increase the death toll.

Biafra, with a population of about 13,000,000, was clearly weaker than a combination of North (30,000,000), West (11,000,000) and Mid-west (2,500,000). Its aim was to put up so strong a resistance that its opponents would conclude that the effort of forcing it into submission was not worth while. The best hope was that there might be sympathy in the West, a revival of Yoruba-Ibo solidarity against the North. This hope was disap-pointed. The former Yoruba leader Awolowo, released from prison by Gowon, after some months of vacillation came down on the federal side. A brief Biafran invasion of the Mid-west turned Yorubas against Biafra. Fairly soon in the war Biafra lost its coastline and its northern districts; and the fiercest fighting, lasting over a year, was for the central Ibo heartland. In the periphery, Gowon's men successfully incited the non-Ibos against the Ibos. Gowon announced the division of Nigeria into twelve states (the North into five and the East into three). This was designed both to centralise the government of the whole country and to give more self-government to those who did not belong to the Hausa-Fulani, Yoruba or Ibo peoples. Gowon was certainly no northern imperialist. He had no wish to see an Islamic *jihad* against the Ibos. He insisted in his general orders that Biafrans should be regarded not as enemies but as compatriots, temporarily misled by rebel leaders, but with whom in peace they would all have to live together. He saw himself in fact as an African Lincoln, and was so portrayed by sympathetic American and European writers. How far these statesmanlike injunctions were carried out is another matter. Terrible massacres of Ibos occurred in many places; but it is of course arguable that these would have been more numerous and more savage without Gowon's orders.

The federal government won the war, and the Ibo lands were reincorporated in Nigeria. There was no systematic persecution of Ibos, though elementary prudence dictated that they should not hurry to resume their former careers in cities outside their homeland. Optimists hoped that the war would have forged a new Nigerian nation. Analogies with the American civil war were irrelevant: the differences between Ibos and others in 1967 were of a different order than differences between Americans of the two camps in 1861. The question was not whether Gowon was a noble figure, but whether the Ibos were a nation. This question could not be answered by ritual incantations about the evils of 'tribalism'. The Ibos survived, and they went on living in the Nigerian state of the early 1970s. This was no proof that they felt themselves to be Nigerians first; that they had put their 'tribal' culture behind them; that they would remain within Nigeria a minute longer than they had to. Nor was it proof that the Yorubas, or the Fulani, felt this way, or would feel this way much longer. Bloody defeats did not cause Poles to put loyalty to the Russian or German empires or to the Habsburg Monarchy before their Polish national identity. In Nigeria a war was won, but no nation's fate was decided.

The African scene in the 1970s thus certainly had many features which recalled the European nationalist struggles of the nineteenth and early twentieth centuries. The contemptuous references by African politicians to 'Balkanisation' seemed rather misplaced: one felt tempted to say that if the African leaders did as well in the coming decades as the Balkan leaders of the past, they would have grounds to congratulate themselves. The similarity of Amharisation in Ethiopia to Magyarisation in Old Hungary, and of Somali irridentism to pre-1914 Yugoslav or Polish movements for unity, cast a shadow ahead. The assumption that the federal victory in Nigeria would have much the same happy consequences as the Union victory in America in 1865 seemed rather facile: were the consequences of Union victory so happy as all that, and was there any parallel in Nigeria to the basic unity between Americans which existed even while the Civil War was raging? Far from having overcome or bypassed the errors and horrors of old Europe, the Africans had barely yet encountered them. They had not emerged from the dark tunnel: they had not yet entered it.

Yet dark forebodings might be as misplaced as self-righteous optimism. It might be that the future of Africa would lie neither in empires based on official nationalism such as old Hungary nor in small homogeneous national states of the Balkan type, but in multi-lingual empires ruled by centralising despots, perhaps nearer to the ancient Iranian or Indian models than to any modern European example. One obvious difficulty was to see an institution which could ensure continuity. If national conscious-ness, based on religion, language and deeply rooted historical mythologies, were not available, then the agent of continuity could only be the central power. In past empires this meant dynastic rule, with at least some long periods of peaceful succession. In the twentieth century the founding of new hereditary dynasties in Africa seemed improbable, and the one ancient dynasty—the Ethiopian—was at last overthrown. One possible answer was the monolithic all-wise political party. The fall of Nkrumah brought the collapse of this institution in Ghana: whether other dominant single parties would survive the death of Kaunda, Kenyatta, Nyerere, Sékou Touré, Houphouet or others also remained doubtful.

These questions, then, which add up to the single question, whether nationhood of the European-Mediterranean-American type has any rele-vance to the future of Africa, must be asked without any former European sense of 'superiority', but also without any optimistic self-deception.

# 9 Race and Nation: White Racialism and Anti-White Nationalism

## Racialism

As European traders and conquerors spread around and across other continents, they were brought into regular social contact with settled communities of people whose outward physical appearances greatly differed from their own. Black African slaves were known already in the Roman and Persian empires, and in medieval Christian and Muslim states. Europeans met Chinese traders in other lands long before regular direct contact was established with China. Chinese and Indians were in contact from at least the fifth century, both through sea-borne trade and through the journeys of Buddhist pilgrims. Some of the Indonesian islands were well known to the Chinese, and in the fifteenth century Chinese fleets visited the east coast of Africa. Communications across the Indian Ocean, between southern India and East Africa, were much older than this. The people of Madagascar were partly of Malaysian origin. It was not until the sixteenth century that considerable numbers of Europeans got to know sub-Saharan African and Far Eastern countries; and it was in the same period that other Europeans found and conquered the civilisations of the Americas. There grew up in the following centuries the idea that human beings were divided into 'white', 'black', 'yellow', 'brown' and 'red' races.

The arrogant belief that some human subspecies were biologically and culturally inferior was no modern invention. The ancient Aryan conquerors of India considered the Dravidian peoples of the south as their inferiors, especially because of the darkness of their skins; colour discrimination was an important element in the growth of the complex hierarchy of castes. As for cultural superiority, the belief of the Chinese that theirs was the central kingdom of the world, surrounded by 'barbarians' whose duty was to pay tribute to the Han emperor and Han civilisation, is not unlike the attitude of the Hellenes or Romans to 'barbarians'. In all these cases, contempt for the physical characteristics of the barbarians had an important part. In the nineteenth century, doctrines about the hereditary characteristics of races, based on interpretations of the scientific knowledge of that time, became popular, especially in northern Europe and North America. The content of these theories need not detain us here: it suffices to note that they insisted that the white race was morally and culturally 'superior' to the others; that the black race was the lowest on the scale; and that this hierarchy was ineluctably determined for all time by the laws of biology. At the end of the century these principles were also applied by some racial theorists, especially in Germany and Austria, to the case of the Jews, who in physical appearance did not differ very strikingly from other 'whites'.

It became customary in the nineteenth century to use the words 'race' and 'racial' to describe these physical or biological divisions among human beings. It is admittedly unsatisfactory, because the word 'race' had earlier meanings whose continued use has created confusion. Nevertheless, a special type of group identity and of group conflict, to which the name 'racial' has become attached, were an important feature of twentieth century politics; and these identities and conflicts were often related to those of and between nations.

This book is not intended to include a comprehensive survey of 'race relations'. It is concerned with the effect of racial conflicts on the formation of nations; with the possibility of the transformation of racial groups into nations, either as fragments of a larger existing nation or as new nations; and with the emergence, from situations of race conflict, of communities which are not nations, but which remain associated, however uneasily, within common states.

The most important racial conflicts of modern times have resulted from the transplantation of large numbers of people from far distant homelands into lands inhabited by other peoples who differ fundamentally from them in religion, culture, physical appearance and social habits. In some cases the new arrivals have been conquerors, in others they have been captives. Thus, European conquerors irrupted into North and South America and Southern Africa; while Africans were forcibly removed to North and South America, and Chinese and Indians were brought, in conditions of semi-slavery, to live among Malays, Burmese and Fijians. Slower expansion by land also sometimes produced this result, when the newcomers strikingly differed both physically and culturally from the indigenous people. The confrontation between Arabs and Nilotic peoples in Sudan is such an example; the interpenetration between Russians, Tatars and Central Asians was more gradual, but hardly less painful.

Thus all the most prominent examples of racial conflict have an element of historical artificiality, of which those involved are at least dimly conscious. One party to the conflict, and sometimes both parties, are felt not to 'belong': the place of conflict is not 'their' homeland. Racialists usually also insist more vehemently than do nationalists on the depth of the gulf between them and their opponents. The same is true of many alleged opponents of racialism (who in many cases are themselves racialists of a different brand). By such persons 'racialism' is felt to be an exceptionally odious doctrine, and use of the word an exceptionally vile form of abuse. As a matter of historical record, nationalists and socialists are no less capable of fanaticism, cruelty and massacres than are racialists.

Often racial conflicts combine a sense of profound cultural differences ('civilisation' against 'barbarism') with religious ('faithful' against 'infidel') and physical (sexual repulsion or attraction, or perhaps both at once). It is seldom that mere national conflicts simultaneously involve all three of these dimensions.

It is possible to distinguish situations in which persons of one racial type are settled in huge numbers—by choice or by coercion—in large compact territories inhabited by peoples of another racial type; and situations in which alien communities are scattered in small numbers over many different lands. I shall consider in this chapter the main examples of the first type: the coexistence or conflict between blacks and whites in the Americas and South Africa and between Amerindians and whites in North America, Mexico and the Andean republics. Examples of the second type, which I shall call 'diaspora communities', will be discussed in the next chapter.

This distinction is of course open to obvious objections. Both black and white Americans descend from communities transplanted from their own homelands. Both the original Dutch settlers at the Cape and the Bantu peoples of eastern Cape province were intruders into the homeland of the Hottentots. On the other hand, the Chinese in Malaya—discussed in the next chapter as a diaspora community—were immigrants into the ancestral homeland of another race. However, logical consistency sometimes must be sacrificed. This book is concerned with the formation of national consciousness and national movements, and therefore with the extent to which these are affected by race conflicts. If one examines racial problems from this point of view, then the difference between the predicament of small scattered communities and the confrontation between great blocks of population of different race does make sense. These are different realities.

## Black and white in the Americas

The ancestors of the black people of America were slaves transported in European ships from Africa two to four hundred years ago. The slave trade was an enormous crime perpetrated by Europeans against Africans, from which many Europeans settled in America profited. Some have argued that the flowering of capitalism and the industrial revolution, which gave the

Europeans and North Americans their lead in the world economy, was principally derived from these profits. It is also true that African chiefs eagerly made profits from selling their subjects or their captives to European traders, even if the latter usually fixed the terms of trade to their advantage. It is also true that an older, and no less inhuman, slave trade existed in eastern Africa between African chiefs and Arab traders, though the numbers of slaves were smaller than in the trade with Europeans.

As a result of this great mass crime against African peoples by the European Atlantic nations, there were in the 1970s in the Americas perhaps 80,000,000 people of partly or wholly African descent, including the varieties of persons of mixed descent for which numerous specific terms existed in the four European languages. This approximated roughly to a quarter of the total population of black Africa south of the Sahara. In the course of successive generations, the black people lost their original languages and learned to speak the languages of their masters, though with many variations of accent and vocabulary. Of their original social and religious customs and beliefs rather more survived, especially in Haiti (where independence was won by a revolution and long war) and in parts of Brazil which, despite the abolition of the slave trade, continued to receive new slaves until well into the nineteenth century. Thus the black people belonged and yet did not belong to the European-founded American nations among whom they lived.

The political revolt of the blacks in the United States in the 1960s led to massive reconsideration of the history of slaves in America, to which black historians richly contributed. Some of the 'black studies' initiated in American universities were no more than political indoctrination courses, but the almost universally admitted need to look at the period anew certainly led to the improvement of historical understanding. White liberal, black nationalist and both black and white Marxist schools of thought contended with each other. Old arguments from the ante-bellum period were reopened in the light of new evidence and new prejudices. White liberals had insisted on the cruelty of slavery, while southern propagandists had argued that working conditions were worse in northern factories employing slave labour. Together with the charge of cruelty came that of inefficiency, and of demoralisation of the slaves into lazy and incompetent workers. Massive evidence collected by the 'cliometric' historians Fogel and Engelman in their *Time on the Cross: The Economics of American Negro Slavery* suggested that slavery was economically efficient, and that conditions of work were indeed not worse for the most part than in the North. Their conclusion was vigorously rebutted by other historians. The demoralisation of the slave has also been rejected by some modern historians. Laziness was, it is argued, largely a matter of passive resistance to exploitation. There were also numerous slave insurrections, some serious. What is much more important, modern historians have insisted on the enormous achievement, both before and after emancipation, of black workers in America. The American economy was partly built by blacks, and blacks have been among the most productive, as well as longest established, Americans. American history is partly black history.

Comparisons have also been made between the situation of slaves in the English-speaking and the Spanish- or Portuguese-speaking lands. It has been argued that the Catholic Church had a more universal human perspective than the Protestant churches, was more insistent on the fact that blacks had human souls and that souls were equal in the sight of God. It was also claimed, above all in the works of the Brazilian writer Gilberto Freyre, that the Portuguese, long accustomed to racial intermixture with Moors before they reached America, lacked the sexual antipathy to blacks shown by the English colonists. Freyre depicted the great Brazilian plantations as patriarchal institutions within which white and black belonged to a single great family. This distinction was at first accepted by North American historians, firmly addicted to the sense of superior guilt so characteristic of the twentieth century Anglo-Saxons. Closer examination modified the picture. Perhaps the Catholic Church was in principle more humane, but it is questionable whether Catholic slave-owners as a group were better than Protestant slave-owners. The distinction between the patriarchal type of plantation and the capitalist, ruthlessly exploitative type had much validity, but both types were to be found in both countries: the patriarchal in the American South in the earlier states and in the Brazilian north-east, the exploitative in the cotton kingdom in Mississippi and in the coffee plantations of the Paraiba valley.

The Reconstruction period which followed the American Civil War, from 1865 to 1877, has been largely reinterpreted. The personalities and policies of the Freedmen's Bureaus and of the post-war administrations in the defeated states, had a much better record than the historians' consensus of the earlier twentieth century allowed. Yet it remains true that they were unable to put through such reforms as would have given the emancipated blacks a solid economic foundation, and the opportunity of quick social and educational progress. After President Hayes in 1877 had in fact given power in the South back to the white elite, the pattern of discrimination emerged which was to be the fate of the American negro for the next eighty years or more.

In the South, negroes were deprived of a vote, either in public elections or in the more important processes of election at Democratic Party primaries which, granted the permanent supremacy of the Democrats in the South, decided all other elections. This violation of the fifteenth amendment to the constitution of the United States was masked by the manipulation of literacy tests and a poll tax, and other forms of intimidation and chicanery by electoral officials. The school system was divided, ostensibly on the basis of the US Supreme Court decision of 1896 in the case of *Plessy v. Ferguson*, to the effect that school facilities must be 'separate but equal'. In practice they were separate and unequal: wretchedly small sums were spent on schools for negroes, and with some notable exceptions the quality was wretchedly low. Segregation was enforced in public—in restaurants, hotels, lavatories, trams, buses, railway carriages, swimming pools and the like. Negroes were expected to observe a ritual of deference towards all white persons with whom they had any communication. This was particularly painful for those negroes who succeeded in overcoming the huge obstacles and acquiring a high level of education and professional skill. By achieving success according to the white man's criteria, the negro acquired no merit in most white southerners' eyes: rather, he was guilty of impudence in trying to rise above his station. The predominant white southern view of the negro was of a crude and rather comic creature, at his best useful and loyal, at his worst lazy and sullen, perhaps dangerous. Underlying this contempt was fear; a hysterical fear that negroes were a sexual menace to white women—not only by violent rape but also by physical attraction—and that black masses would swamp white civilisation. Not all southern whites of course felt like this, but the more liberal minority was to be found in the social elite, while the majority of the white 'popular masses', far from being comrades of the black masses in the class struggle, were confirmed 'nigger-haters'.

From the late nineteenth century onwards, negroes began to move to the northern and western states, where the climate of opinion and the chances of jobs were more favourable to them. Nevertheless, white northerners too had a strong dose of race prejudice, which was reinforced by the numerous white southerners who also moved to industrial jobs in such northern cities as Chicago and Detroit. In the North, negro workers were the last to be hired and the first to be fired. Northern trade unions were less concerned to help negro workers than to protect white workers against having their wage rates undermined by cheap negro labour. Segregation of schools and residential districts was about the same as in the South. Negroes, being the poorest, drifted most easily into crime, and this in turn gave northern negroes a bad public reputation. Occasional horrible race riots took place in northern cities.

In the first decade of the twentieth century two trends appeared among politically conscious educated negroes. One was associated with Booker T. Washington, principal of Tuskegee College, Alabama, who urged negroes to accept social separation as a fact, and to work to improve themselves within the capitalist economy, earning and saving and educating their children, and thereby achieving in due course respect and better treatment from the whites. He himself earned the respect and cooperation of some leading white businessmen, and of President Theodore Roosevelt. His moderation, however, antagonised more radical spirits who wished not only for material improvements but the removal of discrimination. Their chief spokesman was the negro Harvard graduate W.E.B. Du Bois, the chief founder in 1909 of the National Association for the Advancement of Coloured People (NAACP). The NAACP had white as well as black members, especially Jews. It specialised in legal actions to defend individual negro victims of injustice and to enlarge the legal and constitutional rights of negroes as a whole.

Negro soldiers played their part in the First World War, and this both increased self-confidence and impatience among younger negroes and revived race hatred among white southerners. In the first years of peace there were race riots in the North, the worst being in July and August 1919 in Chicago with 38 dead. There were also numerous lynchings in the South—appalling rituals of barbarism where a negro accused of a crime, sexual or other, would be forcibly removed from the local gaol and hanged or burnt alive in the presence of a frenzied white mob. In this bitter time there appeared a new negro leader, the West Indian Marcus Garvey, who propounded a flamboyant form of black nationalism, appealing to the past glories of Ethiopia and preaching the unity of negroes with Africa in a glorious future. His Universal Negro Improvement Association, founded in Jamaica in 1914, claimed 4,000,000 members in the United States in 1920 and certainly had hundreds of thousands. Garvey's ideas survived him, influencing the later Panafrican movement on both sides of the Atlantic. During the 1930s northern negroes suffered especially from the economic depression, but there were also gains for them. President Franklin Roosevelt, and his wife Eleanor, consulted negro advisers and did a good deal to secure jobs for negroes in government service. Partly as a result of the Roosevelts' influence the trade unions paid more attention to the needs of black workers.

In the 1950s negroes formed about one-tenth of the population of the United States, and were found in three main regions. In a broad strip of territory stretching along both sides of the Mississippi through the states of Mississippi, Louisiana and Arkansas and from central Alabama east to South Carolina (the so-called 'black belts'), they formed a majority of the population, in some counties as much as 80 per cent. To the south of the black belts negroes were a minority, though substantial. Finally, in the North and increasingly in the West large concentrations of negroes had grown up in great cities, especially in New York, Chicago, Washington and Detroit, but also spreading to other newer cities such as Los Angeles and Oakland in California. In 1930 there were 8.4 million negroes in the eleven southern states and 3.4 million in the rest of the country. In 1971 the corresponding figures had changed to 10.3 million and 12.2 million. The southern negroes in the 1930s included a large element of small farmers or farm labourers, but this changed drastically in the 1940s and 1950s: the number of non-white farming households in the South decreased between 1940 and 1954 from 680,000 to 463,000 and this process accelerated later. Southern cities like Atlanta and Birmingham grew rapidly with an influx of both black and white workers.

Urban negroes could exercise more political pressure than rural, and the post–Second World War climate of opinion among the American people as a whole favoured reform. The US Supreme Court on 17 May 1954 gave a unanimous verdict, reversing the decision of 1896 and declaring that 'separate educational facilities are inherently unequal'. However, resistance in the South to the 'desegregation' not only of schools but of other public services was strenuous and bitter, and provoked mass action by negroes and their white sympathisers, both southern and northern. A landmark was the successful negro boycott of the Montgomery (Alabama) bus service in 1956, a protest against the colour bar in seating in public transport. From this action emerged the Southern Christian Leadership Conference, which had in Rev. Martin Luther King a leader who became known the whole world over. In 1960 came a second symbolic mass action, the sit-in by negro students at the lunch-counter of a store in Greensboro (North Carolina) which refused to serve negroes. The next stage were the mass marches, demanding civil rights, in which negroes were joined by whites, including many college students. These provoked violent opposition from white citizens councils and conservative white southerners. They did not stop at murder, and the world press duly reported the acquittals of known murderers in southern courts.

The recurrent scandals and crises from 1954 onwards forced the US federal government into action. President Eisenhower got through Congress in 1957 a Civil Rights Act, which empowered the federal authorities to bring civil law actions in states where persons had been deprived of their right to vote, and created some machinery to enforce it. It was followed by a stronger act in 1960. White opposition deprived them of their effect, and the resounding promises of J. F. Kennedy in his 1960 electoral campaign remained but words. It was left to President Lyndon B. Johnson to take effective measures. In January 1964 a constitutional amendment forbade poll taxes as a condition for the vote; in June 1964 a Civil Rights Act with real sanctions passed the US Senate; and in 1965 a law on the right to vote put an end to literacy tests, and provided that if local registrars failed in their duties, the federal attorney-general would have the power to register voters. These acts ended the political disfranchisement of the American negro.

However, the mass movements had acquired their own momentum. Just as the NAACP had discounted Booker T. Washington as a moderate, so the NAACP was discounted by the followers of Martin Luther King; and before long King was surpassed by more radical groups, though his murder in Memphis in April 1968 ensured his memory as a martyr to his people's cause. Two main radical trends now appeared.

One was the Black Muslims, founded by a mysterious character who called himself W. D. Fard and operated in Detroit from 1930. He was succeeded in 1934 by Elijah Muhammad (born Elijah Poole in Georgia), who exhibited great talents as an organiser, a propagandist and a business-man. In the 1950s he won a brilliant helper in the person of Malcolm X (born Malcolm Little in Omaha, Nebraska), the son of a Baptist minister, intellectually gifted and a victim of white arrogance, who led the Muslims in a politically more radical direction. This brought a breach with Elijah Muhammad in 1964, and Malcolm was murdered on 21 February 1965. The Muslims recruited their mass support from negro workers in northern cities. They had some support from black businessmen, but were on the whole disliked by black intellectuals. One of their merits was their insistence on both self-discipline and collective discipline, on a return to personal puritan morality and a rejection of the white man's luxury as a source of corruption and undermining of the negro race. They denounced Christianity as a religion of corruption, and proclaimed their devotion to Islam, though their Islamic theology hardly satisfied orthodox Muslims outside America. They also hated Jews, as another corrupting white force. Black anti-semitism, which grew especially in New York's Haarlem district, can be partly attributed to the Black Muslims, though it was also more generally due to hatred by the poor and the unemployed of local capitalists, who were largely Jews.[1] The Black Muslims aimed to withdraw from all contacts with white men, and to build up a separate economic structure of farms, business and professions. They denounced the NAACP for its cooperation with white Christians and Jews, and the more radical groups because they professed internationalist views. Their final aim was a sovereign territory of their own, to consist of 'two or three', or of 'four or five', states of the Union.

The second trend, which included a large number of smaller groups, often fiercely fighting each other, looked to a socialist revolution for the redemption not only of black but of white Americans. Stokely Carmichael, who had been chairman of the Student Non-violent Coordinating Com-mittee (SNCC) which followed King's Ghandi-type resistance tactics, abjured these methods in favour of unlimited struggle, and launched in 1966 the slogan of Black Power. In the same year the group known as Black Panthers was founded in California.

In the next years there poured forth a flood of rhetoric from black spokesmen, inciting to hatred of the whites, glorifying almost any kind of violent action, including simple criminal acts, repudiating all bourgeois morality and clamouring for the destruction of the whole 'system'. This rhetoric produced widespread fear and indignation from whites. In judging the phenomenon, several points should be borne in mind. Firstly, rhetoric greatly exceeded action. Criminal assaults by negroes, particularly by the young, grew to terrifying proportions in great cities; but these have their explanation in features of America's social structure, school system, mass media values and both public and private morality which cannot be discussed here. Mass violence by negroes was usually directed at other negroes, especially in the ghastly riots in Watts district of Los Angeles in 1965. Secondly, the total volume of hatred, contempt and brutality directed by blacks against whites was still immensely smaller than the total volume that had been directed by whites against blacks. The negro problem by the 1970s had been largely transferred from the South to the North, since the majority of American blacks now lived in the North. Less was heard of southern maltreatment of negroes, and the civil rights reforms had indeed brought great changes. Nonetheless, the negro in the South remained the underdog, while in the North he still suffered more than the white man from poverty, badly paid jobs, unemployment, bad housing and bad schools. It was still up to the white man to reach into his pocket, and to force himself into imaginative and generous thinking, to put things right.

The misery of negro ghetto schools was undoubtedly partly due to negro family ways and to the negro tendency to live only in the present and to give no thought to the future—an attitude which was of course not unknown, but for historical reasons was less widespread, among whites. But the misery of negro schools was still more due to lack of funds, to the extreme unwillingness of urban authorities and of white urban tax-payers to pay the bill for a proper education system. Tinkering about with the bad system in existence, by bussing white and black schoolchildren to and fro across metropolitan areas in order to make all schools conform with a race-statistical norm, though defended by planning bureaucrats and various champions of 'liberal' intellectual orthodoxy, could be no solution. Children are not statistical objects; neither white children forced to form a despised minority in black majority schools nor black children doomed to humiliation in white majority schools seemed likely to get a good education. Above all, the bussing plan was mainly a device to save tax-payers the necessity of paying the bill for good schools and well-trained teachers for the hitherto deprived black communities. It was this that the black spokesmen wanted, not an abstract desegregation they never asked for.

The radicals of Black Power had an ambiguous attitude, the result of the contradictions in which they were placed through no fault of their own. They rejected the moral and political values of the Black Muslims, though influenced by their nationalist pride as well as by the achievements of new African states and by the doctrine of *négritude*. 'Black is beautiful', they proclaimed. They discarded the word 'negro', originally adopted as a respectable name in place of the insulting 'nigger'. In its place they accepted the name 'black', previously regarded as contemptuous. They were Black Americans, or Afro-Americans. They did not reject America altogether; they rejected only 'the system' (social, cultural, moral), which they attributed to capitalism, and wished to replace by socialism, to be brought about by a bloody and purifying revolution. Socialist America would have to be built also by white Americans; yet the black radicals found it difficult to cooperate with any but a lunatic fringe of whites, romantically ena- moured of heroic violent exploits. Other whites seemed to be enemies, not only conservative businessmen or old-style white supremacy men but also many whites who considered themselves socialists, even revolutionaries, but whom they would describe as 'liberals', a word which had become a term of abuse. Reason would point to a political alliance with all radical reformers in the American nation, but passion counselled acts—or at least gestures—of contempt and hatred against almost all whites who came their way.

The creation of a black Israel on the territory of the United States, as desired by the Black Muslims, seemed unlikely. No elected president could agree to such action, and the chance that the United States would be at the mercy of a conquering power who would impose it still seemed small in the mid-1970s. Much the same could be said of a great social revolution, either won from within or imposed from outside, to destroy capitalism, capitalists and all their hangers-on in a flood of ritually cleansing blood.

Meanwhile there remained the NAACP and lesser organisations, much less publicised by American mass media than extremists, yet still doing their work of persuasion, education, propaganda and reform through Congress and the law courts. Such work achieved great results in the 1950s and 1960s, and had the confidence and support of many millions of blacks, who considered themselves Americans and wished to remain Americans. It was easy to denounce these men and women as a 'black bourgeoisie'; yet persons of this outlook amounted to many millions, almost certainly to an absolute majority of all blacks; and of the minority only small active factions supported either the nationalists or the revolutionaries. Yet it could also be plausibly argued against the NAACP that it tacitly assumed that blacks would be content to have a social pyramid of their own, placed at a lower level than the white pyramid, provided that its shape broadened out and that its bottom level steadily rose (though more slowly than the bot- tom of the white pyramid). In the age of rising expectations, televised pa- rading of the 'good' life of luxury, and consuming guilt complex on the part of highly articulate white intellectuals, this prospect seemed unrealistic.

We come in conclusion to the question: Were the blacks part of the American nation, or were they a nation on its own, united by a distinct physical appearance of which they were perforce aware, by a past of oppression and a present of relative deprivation? Many answers have been offered, but none could be proved. Possibly a compromise might in time emerge: blacks would come to be accepted, and to regard themselves, as Americans, and at the same time would belong to a system of cultural institutions of their own, fully provided with funds both from the central authorities and from their own membership and extending all their benefits to all blacks wherever they might live, whether in black agglomerations or among whites. In this connection black leaders might be well advised to study the ideas once proposed by Bauer and Renner for the Habsburg Monarchy. An alternative apocalyptic prospect also existed. The black problem might prove insoluble in an American society obsessed with both luxury and guilt. It might continue to poison the body politic and social, while white 'liberal' self-haters gleefully diffused the poison. The historic revenge for the slave trade and slavery would be the collapse of an undermined America in the face of an external enemy. If so, then a great evil would have brought about a still greater evil.


The problem of a black nation or nations also existed in the Caribbean islands, with a population of about 25,000,000 people, of whom the great majority were wholly or partly descended from African slaves. Here four European languages were spoken: English, French, Spanish and Dutch. Haiti was an independent republic from 1804, Santo Domingo from 1865, and Cuba from 1898, and the people of each undoubtedly acquired national peculiarities of their own. The French colonies of Guadeloupe and Martinique voted to remain *départements* of France; the Dutch islands were more loosely linked with the Netherlands; and Puerto Rico (annexed from Spain in 1898) became a Free Associated State but not a member state of the United States. The British government in 1958 brought into being a federation of the West Indies comprising the British Caribbean islands, but this fell apart in 1962. Thereafter Jamaica and Trinidad became independent states, followed by Barbados (1962), Bahamas (1973) and Grenada (1974). The remaining islands agreed to a form of associated statehood with Britain, under which their internal affairs were managed by their governments but foreign affairs and defence by the British government.

Both the English- and the French-speaking islands have produced intellectuals who have made, as we have seen, important contributions to Panafricanism and to the concepts of *négritude* and Black Power. These ideas also had their followers in the islands, and in the former British, French and Dutch colonies on the mainland of South America (Guyana,

Guyane and Surinam). However, the problem is not one of foreign sovereignty since the people of the islands rule themselves. Rather, it is a problem of national identity and of its diffusion to all levels of the social pyramid.

In the islands a phenomenon could be observed which was also found among North American blacks and in Brazil, but which is even more developed in the West Indies. This was social stratification based on relative 'lightness' or 'darkness' of skin, with the palest persons (those presumably with the smallest element of African ancestry) aiming to 'pass' into the white category. The islands were governed by democratically elected rulers, but the light-skinned had the social prestige, and many means of influencing the direct political rulers, while property and economic power was largely left in the hands of whites, to whom the pale-skinned were drawn by social snobbery. The dark-skinned masses lived in poverty, which increased as a result of population pressure. Overpopulation led to massive emigration. The emigrants swelled the black ghettos in the United States, or intensified the new 'race relations' problem in Britain, whose people, it must be noted, developed, with less objective cause, a racial intolerance scarcely inferior to that of white Americans. In the islands conditions were only partly improved by the growth of the tourist industry, which brought floods of rich, noisy and arrogant North Americans or British into contact with poverty-stricken blacks. It was not surprising that Black Power slogans had some success, or that black radicals sought to unite black masses against the white-pale privileged in what was a peculiar mixture of class hatred, nationalism and plain xenophobia. In the case of Trinidad and of the continental former colony of Guyana a large community of former immigrants from India formed a further complication.[2]

The modern Brazilian nation had been formed from four sources—the original Portuguese colonists and subsequent immigrants from Portugal; the descendants of African slaves; immigrants from foreign countries (Italians, Germans, Poles, Japanese and many others); and the descendants of the indigenous Amerindian peoples. The first group interbred with the other three, but the largest category of interbreeding, continued for the longest time, was between Portuguese and Africans. At the time of the separation of Brazil from Portugal, a large majority of the population had at least some African blood. At the time of the abolition of slavery, in 1888, this was still so, but the influx of European immigrants had already become substantial. In the mid-twentieth century the African element was relatively reduced by two causes: the flooding of southern Brazil by European immigrants, and the dilution of the African element by more and more interbreeding. This means that more and more blacks had pale children, and that more and more children of pale parents became so pale as to disappear in the 'white' population. In 1890 those of African or mixed origin were stated to be 56 per cent of the population, in 1950 only 37 per cent.

The Brazilians were perhaps even more addicted than the West Indians or American southerners to subtle distinctions between degrees of light or dark skin colour, crinkliness of hair, thickness of lips and the like: nowhere was the snobbery of colour more developed. The darker the skin the lower the social prestige. However, colour snobbery was more easily counteracted by economic snobbery in Brazil than in the United States: the Brazilians loved to claim that 'money whitens'. It was also always possible to 'whiten' oneself by intermarriage, which was of course not the case in the southern United States.

The largest proportion of Afro-Brazilians lived in the north-eastern states, the land of the great plantations and also the land in which poverty remained most serious up to present times. Brazil's northern problem was not unlike the southern problem of other countries (the United States and Italy). Poverty in these provinces was to be found not only among agricultural workers and small farmers, heirs to the agrarian slaves, but also in the shanty slums of the great cities which grew up in the north-east in the second half of the twentieth century (Recife with 1,700,000 inhabitants in 1970 and Salvador with over a million). In 1970 the total population of the north-east was about 29,000,000 or nearly a third of the population of Brazil. The impoverished agricultural population were very largely black or mulatto. Though the oligarchic system of politics in southern Brazil was modified by the 'populist', quasi-fascist dictator Getulio Vargas, who came to power in 1930 and created his *estado novo* in 1937, it was little affected in the north-east: here the landowners and plantation elite continued to manage, and deliver to the government, the rural vote. This situation began to change after 1945, and particularly in the late 1950s. Meanwhile population growth, shooting ahead of economic improvement, increased the poverty of the people. There was a severe drought in the north-east in 1958. In 1959 radical peasant movements appeared. The Peasant Leagues, founded by Francisco Julião, attracted world-wide attention. The Catholic church also gave support to peasant action, especially to the National Confederation of Agricultural Workers, in which communists too had some influence. In the early 1960s there were numerous armed clashes when peasants forcibly occupied estate lands, or refused to be dislodged from their own land by speculators who had bought it up from the landowners. These were not racial but social movements. They were not felt to be clashes between white and coloured, though the average skin-colour of rebels was certainly darker than their opponents'. After the military seizure of power in April 1964, incidents of this sort came to an end.

In the industrial south-east and south (nearly 57,000,000 inhabitants in 1970) Afro-Americans were proportionately much fewer, though their numbers were increased by the stream of rural immigrants, largely from the north-east. Racial prejudice was stronger among the whites of the city of São Paulo than in the north-east. Abundant sociological evidence showed that white attitudes to blacks and mulattos, regarding both personal and public relationships, differed little from those in North American cities. There was very little intermarriage. In São Paulo as in Detroit, the blacks had the least skilled and worst paid jobs, forming a kind of 'lower working class' on whose backs the white working class could rise to a better standard of living. This served to confirm the racial stereotype in white minds that blacks are only capable of the worst jobs, and so to confirm the reluctance of white employers to give them better jobs. The black predicament then was much the same as in the United States, with the very important difference that the reality was concealed by polite evasion rather than proclaimed with open contempt. Endless repetition of the fiction that Brazil was a harmonious multiracial society helped to smooth indignation on one side and quieten conscience on the other.

From 1931 to 1937 there existed a *Frente negra brasileira*, pursuing much the same aims as the NAACP in the United States. It turned itself into a political party; was dissolved with other parties under Vargas; and did not reappear in the post-war years. There was no sign of response in Brazil to the concept of Black Power, though perhaps if there had been no military dictatorship there might have been. There seemed little doubt that both blacks and whites felt themselves to belong to one Brazilian nation, but it also seemed likely that the self-satisfied claim of Brazilians to have 'solved' racial problems was premature.

## Black and white in South Africa

Once the Afrikaner Nationalists had defeated their white opponents in the electoral victory of 1948, they began to put into effect their plans for dealing with the non-whites: the black majority, divided into a number of diverse tribes; the coloured minority, descended from mixed marriages of Dutch with Malays or Hottentots; and the Asian minority, consisting of immigrants from India.

The great majority of the whites had long considered the blacks as an inferior race, incapable of reaching the white level of civilisation. The blacks must be denied any share in political life, and must be prevented from intermarriage with whites. They were useful as a source of cheap labour, to perform menial tasks at low pay; but white workers must be protected from the danger of black competition in the labour market.

These attitudes were common to the majority of whites of both languages, though there were in both groups some individuals of more liberal outlook, and some white legislation had been designed to defend black interests. Nevertheless, there were important differences between majority English-speaking and majority Afrikaner points of view.

The leaders of the English-speaking community tended to be mainly interested in business. They cared neither for political theory nor for general principles of social organisation: they tended to treat the blacks simply as their own interests suggested at any given moment (which usually meant badly). The Afrikaner leaders were professional politicians and Calvinist *predikants*, who regarded social organisation largely from a theological point of view, and believed that political and social order must be based on God's Word, as they understood it. They believed that the Bible had clearly laid down a position of permanent inferiority and helotry for the children of Ham. This also suited the interests of Boer farmers who employed a black labour force, treated their servants with rough justice and even a certain benevolence, but had no doubt that the black man should keep his place, which had been determined for all time. The right relationship of white to black was domination (*baasskap*).

From the combination of Boer will to rule and the search for theological truth emerged the doctrine of *apartheid*, which was accepted as the programme of the National Party government of Dr Daniel Malan in 1948. This word is rendered in English as 'separate development'. White and black civilisations, it was argued, are different, and each must develop side by side. The black people should have their own homelands, consisting of the territory reserved to them by previous governments, with substantial further additions. Blacks from these homelands should be permitted to work in the rest of South Africa, which was to be white man's land; but here they would be only temporary sojourners, without political status and without the prospect of permanent homes. As for the coloureds and Asians, they would have no homelands, but would be allowed to live and work in white South Africa subject to precise definition of their status and limitation of their rights.

Separate development was hardly a new idea in history. The essence of the caste system in India was the coexistence of mutually exclusive communities. The *millet* system of the Ottoman empire had separated religious communities and defined their status in relation to other communities. The concept of 'communal' organisation was also to be found under British rule in southern Asia. Most of these communities, though perhaps discontented with the particular status allotted to them, did not object to the principle of separateness.

There were, however, some aspects of *apartheid* in South Africa, both in theory and in practice, which were especially objectionable.

The first was the arrogant dogmatism with which the policy was expounded. The racial categories were to be permanently separated by insuperable barriers, and the inferior categories, of which the blacks were the lowest, were to be inferior for all time. Thus the black people were condemned to eternal helotry in their own country. It is true that the theorists of *apartheid* included some humane and sensitive men who did not think of blacks in this way, but theirs was not the main influence. The policy was of course consciously directed against the small African educated elite which had been brought up according to European liberal values. *Apartheid* was bitterly resented by these men as well as by white South Africans of liberal outlook. It was also bitterly resented by all politically conscious Africans outside South Africa, as an insult to their whole race, and by both the moderate and the extreme Left throughout the world. Rejection of the dogmatic proclamation of race superiority largely accounts for the special odium in which South Africa came to be held in subsequent years by the politicians and press of Europe and America.

The second objectionable feature was the manifestly unjust division of land and resources between the proposed white areas and African areas. The Africans, who formed three-quarters of the population, would be entitled to only 13 per cent of the land even after the land, promised earlier to them but not yet handed over, was in their possession. The great industries of South Africa and its great mining wealth were to remain in the white areas. There would continue to be an African labour force in these areas, but these workers were to be regarded as temporarily earning their living outside their homeland. Yet it was obvious that the homelands, some of which were overpopulated and some of which had extremely poor land, could support less than half the African people, and that South African industry could not operate without African workers. Meanwhile the situation of African wage-earners in the white areas was made miserable by pass laws which subjected them to time-wasting and degrading formalities and were administered in a gratuitously brutal manner, as well as by separation of families and constant interference in private lives.

During the 1950s a programme of disfranchisement, separation and repression was enacted by the South African parliament. Africans had never had a vote in Transvaal, Orange Free State or Natal; but in Cape Province those who passed a property and educational qualification were entitled to vote, on the common electoral roll, until 1936. In that year they were removed from the common roll, but were allowed to elect two Europeans to represent them in the Cape legislature and three Europeans to represent them in the South African parliament. They were deprived of this residual right in 1959. The coloureds were removed from the common roll in 1956, after a five-year struggle between the South African government and the Supreme Court. They were then allowed to elect Europeans specially to represent them (as the Africans had previously been allowed), but were deprived of this right in 1968.

Segregation of residence was carried out under the Group Areas Act of 1950. It affected coloureds and Indians relatively more than Africans, who had in practice already been confined to separate districts, though Africans too were the objects of mass resettlement in the following years. The new quarters to which the non-whites were transferred were in most cases fairly comfortable—sometimes much better than those abandoned—but this did not make the process of shunting human beings around like cattle any less repulsive. The Bantu Education Act of 1953 also led to a series of administrative actions, designed to give the Africans the sort of education which their masters thought would be good for them, rather than the sort which they themselves desired. Government policy was resisted by part of white South African public opinion, including some of the press and some universities, but it was forced remorselessly through. Segregation of the races was extended in all spheres of public and social life: there is no room here to enumerate the details. Finally the whole process was facilitated by an all-purpose repressive charter entitled the Suppression of Communism Act, passed in 1950. The hostility of the National Party to communism is not in doubt, but the object and the effect of this law were far less to crush the insignificant communist groups in the country than to enable the authorities to stop any political activity that they disliked by arbitrarily asserting that it was 'communist'. The system of repression was used both ruthlessly and economically, to isolate persons regarded as dangerous through the system of partial house arrest known as 'banning', as well as by imprisonment for the numerous offences created by the new laws, and by the occasional use of armed force.

African political resistance was at first led by the African National Congress. Founded in 1912 by four African lawyers (one of whom was a graduate of Columbia University), this was at first a cautious and conservative body, supported by some traditional chiefs and disliked by more radical educated Africans. It was the abolition of the African common roll franchise in 1936 which convinced the intelligentsia that mass political organisation of Africans was essential, and that the ANC was the only instrument available. In 1952 the ANC, in alliance with the South African Indian Congress, then led by a communist, Dr Dadoo, asked the prime minister, Dr Malan, to repeal a number of discriminatory laws. His refusal was met with a campaign of civil disobedience. This led to some clashes between crowds and police, but could not be long sustained. A second big effort was made in 1955. The ANC, together with the Indian and coloured organisations, an African trade union group and the white communist-influenced Congress of Democrats, adopted a Freedom Charter. Its aim was a multiracial democratic South Africa, rejecting the domination of any race over others. Its programme also included nationalisation of mineral wealth and banks. The government responded by arresting more than a hundred persons on charges of treason.

During these years communists had gained considerable influence within the ANC and the Indian and coloured movements. The communists were indeed largely responsible for the emphasis on multiracialism. In their view, all conflicts between the races were a harmful distraction from the struggle against South African capitalism and against the Western Imperialists who stood behind it. Their ideas understandably attracted many intellectuals in all the racial groups, for they alone offered the hope of a future of fraternity rather than race war. Their ideas also understandably did not appeal to those Africans who were now convinced that the white man was an incorrigible oppressor, and that the only way forward was by uniting all the blacks against white supremacy. These people were proud of their black race as such, and were encouraged by the successes of African nationalists in West Africa. A group of them in 1958 seceded from the ANC because they rejected its multiracialism, and in 1959 founded the Pan-Africanist Congress.

The PAC was responsible for a new campaign of civil disobedience in 1960. It reached a climax in the police shooting of demonstrators at Sharpeville on 21 March and in the impressively disciplined march of 30,000 Africans to the centre of Capetown on 30 March. This effort too was suppressed by the police, and Pan-Africanist leaders were arrested. Meanwhile there were also disorders in rural regions, caused largely by economic grievances but marked also by political discontents. The most serious was a rising in Pondoland, which caused the government to bring in considerable armed forces. For a short time also a group called Spear of the Nation, connected with the ANC and led by Nelson Mandela, organised acts of sabotage. However, the government declared both ANC and PAC to be unlawful organisations, and the security forces succeeded in crushing resistance. With the most able leaders—including Mandela—in prison, and many of their sympathisers isolated by banning orders, African opposition to official policies was quite ineffective, and the government proceeded with its policies.

In 1970 there were in South Africa 3,726,540 whites; 2,021,430 coloureds; 618,140 Asians; and 15,036,360 Bantus (or blacks, or Africans). The last group consisted of a number of tribes and languages. The most numerous were the Zulu and the Xhosa, each amounting to around 4,000,000 people. They were followed by the Tswana, Pedi and Shoeshoe (or southern Sotho), each numbering between a million and a half and two million. Of the fifteen million blacks, about seven million lived in the homelands and about eight million in the white areas. There were over a million Zulus in urban white areas and nearly a million in rural white areas.

The number of Xhosa in urban white areas was also over a million, but in white rural areas there were less than 700,000.

During the 1960s the government proceeded with its plans for making, out of the reserved lands of the Africans, nine homelands (or 'Bantustans'). The process of consolidating their territory by transfer of population, so as to eliminate white or black islands in the middle of larger units, and also by adding some more land for African use, was not complete by the early 1970s. The most compact homeland was Transkei, with a population of over 1,700,000 almost entirely Xhosa, occupying about 150 miles of Indian Ocean coast and stretching up to 100 miles inland. Kwazulu, with 2,106,040 inhabitants almost wholly Zulu, lay further north but was less compact. Ciskei, with half a million Xhosa, was separated from Transkei by the white-settled corridor of East London. Other homelands were Gazankulu (mainly Shangaan), Lebowa (Pedi), Bophuthatswana (Tswana), Basotho Qwaqwa (Shoeshoe) and Venda and Swazi (inhabited by peoples of those two names).

The first homeland to receive an approved constitution, with its legislative assembly elected partly by chiefs and partly by adult suffrage, was Transkei in 1963. It was followed by Kwazulu, Ciskei, Bophuthatswana and Lebowa in 1972. Government spokesmen in the 1960s more and more abandoned their previous contemptuous tone when speaking of Africans. They began to hold out a future prospect of some sort of commonwealth of largely independent African states associated with each other and with white South Africa in a friendly union. It was clear however that they intended to keep the political, military and economic power in their own hands.

Meanwhile in the white areas too the situation of the Africans was changing. Even within the framework of the Bantu education system the educated elite was growing. African businessmen and professional men were more numerous. The growth of the South African industrial economy increased its dependence on the African labour force. Though a whole armoury of rules existed to guarantee the supremacy of white workers and to keep Africans out of skilled and well-paid jobs, these were in fact increasingly evaded. Only trade unions of white, coloured and Indian workers could be officially registered. For black workers, a system of partly elected liaison committees was enacted. It was not illegal for blacks to form trade unions but their ability to act on behalf of their members was limited, since they could not be registered, and strikes by black workers were forbidden. However, in practice in the early 1970s African workers began to organise themselves, and even carried out some rather successful strikes in the Durban area in 1974. Following these, if only in order to adapt law to reality, the absolute ban on strikes by Africans was relaxed, by certain specified exemptions.

In the prevailing official view, South Africa was to be a country of many nations placed in a hierarchical relationship to each other. The Afrikaners were to be the top nation, but there was some room for argument among Nationalists as to the extent to which the English-speakers could be included within the white South African nation. The Africans consisted of a large number of tribes, some of which might perhaps even be considered to be nations. Two concepts, however, the Afrikaner leaders rejected: either a multiracial South African nation or a single black South African nation as a partner of the white nation. Coloureds and Indians could hardly be considered as nations, but it was recognised that they formed distinct communities; and there was a growing tendency among Afrikaner spokesmen to stress common interests which bound them to the whites—in the case of the coloureds, cultural links, and in the case at least of middle-class Indians, economic.

Afrikaner hostility to a multiracial nation was based partly on religious conviction, and partly on the deeply rooted aversion (shared also by English-speakers) to interbreeding between races, or 'miscegenation'. Once all Africans were given the vote, this could no longer be avoided, so they believed; and this was sufficient reason to deny political democracy outside the white community. There was a further reason why the Afrikaners opposed a multiracial democracy. Even if the imagined horrors of miscegenation could be avoided, even if one were optimistic about some agreed political and social compromise, it was clear that the specific Afrikaner culture would be submerged. A multiracial South Africa would have closer links with the African states, and probably also with the Americas. English would be the predominant language, and some sort of Afro-Anglo-Saxon culture would emerge, in which the old Afrikaner values would be swamped. As the Afrikaners saw it, they were a small nation, forged out of a long heroic struggle against heavy odds, not imperialists but victims of imperialism. They had no other country to go to. Holland had long ceased to be in any sense 'home' for them. They were not 'white settlers' but the people of the country. Defence of *apartheid* seemed to them to be defence of their national identity. Tremendous understanding, ingenuity and persuasiveness would be required of the other communities in order to reconcile them to a new order in South Africa.

Multiracialism was also unattractive to many thinking Africans. African hostility to Indians in Natal (whose situation had something of the character of a 'Jewish problem')[3] led to bloody riots in 1949; and the sincere protestations of democratic or left-inclined leaders of the ANC and the Indian National Congress in the 1950s certainly did not eliminate the underlying economic and national mutual antipathy and fear. Africans also regarded coloureds with some suspicion. It was true that the coloureds were victims of discrimination under *apartheid*; that their growing educated elite was exceptionally frustrated and alienated; and that in consequence from their ranks a rather large proportion of left-oriented persons appeared. Yet it is also true that coloureds were attracted towards European ways, whether of English or of Afrikaans expression, and that this made them unreliable in African eyes.

The Africans themselves remained divided into numerous tribal and language groups. The fact that this was stressed by apologists of *apartheid* did not make it untrue. It was fairly clear that educated Africans in the 1970s tended to think in terms of African solidarity, and to aim at a single African national consciousness transcending the divisions; but it is doubtful whether such a consciousness existed in the early 1970s at grass roots level. On the other hand, if it was true that as soon as Africans became highly educated they began to think in all-African terms, then this would suggest that African nationalism would prevail in the longer term over Zulu, Xhosa or other national consciousness; for all communities tend to follow their own educated elites rather than their politically unconscious majorities, or the elites of foreign dominant groups. This trend might be retarded by the insistence on giving all African children (whether living in Bantustans or in white areas) school teaching in their tribal language as well as in the European languages; but it was not likely to be prevented over a period of several decades. Meanwhile both the recognised leaders in the Bantustans and the black bourgeoisie in the white areas were placed in a painful predicament; they had to find a balance between the contradictory roles of carrying out or expounding government policy to their less educated compatriots, and of defending their people's interests against government policies. The emotional strains which this double role placed on them were not likely to increase their loyalty to the regime under which they lived, or make them love its leaders.

The government's desire to woo the homeland leaders was dramatically expressed by Prime Minister John Vorster's first personal meeting with them on 8 November 1973. However, even if such intention existed on both sides, it would not be possible for negotiations between government and homeland leaders to be limited to the affairs of the homelands themselves. If the eight million blacks working in white areas were considered officially to be citizens of the homelands, temporarily absent, then the homeland authorities were bound to take an interest in their living conditions and legal status, to press for material improvements and more humane treatment. The government did in fact in 1974 urge an easing of 'petty apartheid' measures: how far this directive was carried out by subordinate authorities was uncertain. In 1975 blacks were permitted to acquire leases of thirty years for their dwellings in white areas. But all historical experience suggests that it is precisely when a long down-trodden community begins to live better, and when considerable numbers of such a community obtain wider horizons through education, that their discontent increases most rapidly. Leaders of the homelands, and the persons elected to administrative positions of limited power in Soweto[4] and other black urban areas, would inevitably be pushed by this growing radicalism into demanding more from the government. Already in the first months of 1976 these pressures were revealed in different ways in the reluctance of Chief Matanzima of Transkei to accept responsibility for Xhosa living in white areas, and in the speech in Soweto by Chief Buthelezi of Kwazulu in favour of a common political struggle by all black peoples.

Much more serious were the riots in Soweto in August 1976. Sparked off by protests by schoolchildren who objected to increased teaching of Afrikaans in their schools, they soon involved thousands of persons. In the following weeks there were large-scale disorders in many other black urban areas in Transvaal, Natal and Cape Province, as well as demonstrations by coloureds in Capetown. Very various elements took part in these disorders. There were gangs of black criminals (*totsi*) whose aim was simply to smash property or to rob. There were battles between Zulu and Xhosa, some of which may have been deliberately instigated by police. But there was no doubt that the riots as a whole were an explosion of black political rage, the biggest yet seen in South African history. Observers noted especially the implacable hatred of many young blacks against whites, and their contempt for their parents' generation which still sought reconciliation. These young blacks had no doubt that the age of Black Power was at hand, and that this would mean the complete destruction of their enemy. As an estimate of the relative power of the government and of their own group, this was no doubt wildly unrealistic; but that such a mentality should be widespread was a grim comment on thirty years of South African policy.

It might well be that the indigenous Zulu, Tswana or other traditional cultures had a stronger hold on their peoples, and were more capable of healthy development within the modern world, than either black or white intellectuals thought. Yet any outsider who expressed such an opinion was bound to be considered by educated Africans a patronising reactionary. Western culture, with all its material and intellectual pleasures paraded by the mass media, was clearly attractive both to the ambitions and to the idealism of the African intelligentsia. Yet they, too, were guilty of a patronising attitude to their own peoples when they insisted that traditional culture should be scrapped, and that its maintenance was only a Machiavellian scheme devised by their enemies.

The situation of the blacks of South Africa was thus quite different from that of the blacks of the Americas, though many of the humiliations and deprivations from which they suffered were the same. It partly resembled that of the African blacks in colonial times, for they were living in their own country, ruled by foreigners. Their predicament also resembled that of the blacks of the independent African states, in that they were divided (like, for example, the blacks of Ghana and Kenya) into many peoples and languages, and could only be mobilised as a single political force by use of a European language.

The similarities and differences were clear, but the nature of the South African situation remained unique. It was not clear what kind of national consciousness was emerging, and would prevail, among South African blacks; or whether sufficient strong men of good will could be found to build an interracial compromise before the fanatics took over, and South Africa became a pawn in the struggle of distant empires for mastery of the South Atlantic and Indian oceans.


## The American Indians

The invasions from Europe had a more devastating effect on the indigenous people of America than on those of Africa. The horrors of Africa's tribute in slaves were surpassed by the suffering of the Amerindians. Their lands were taken from them, their way of life was destroyed across the greater part of both subcontinents, and their numbers were reduced, by massacre, by deprivation of their livelihood and by new diseases, to a fraction of what they had been. Nevertheless, some survived with language and culture recognisably the same, and larger numbers contributed an ingredient of varying strength to the *mestizo* nations of Spanish and Portuguese America.

In the United States it is estimated that the Indian population was less than a million when the Europeans arrived. By the middle of the nineteenth century it had fallen below 300,000 but in the mid-1970s it was approaching the original figure.[5] In colonial times, and in the first decades of the republic, some protection was given by the government to the Indian tribes; but the advent of the apostle of mass democracy, Andrew Jackson, and the growing scramble of white immigrants for resources, put an end to this. The next hundred years are a melancholy story of broken promises, robbery, exploitation and aggression, which were met on the Indian side with savage but unsuccessful resistance.[6] A new policy was introduced by President Franklin D. Roosevelt's Indian Reorganization Act of 1934, which gave firm legal status to Indian forms of self-government and land tenure. Those who were best able to profit from these opportunities were some of the tribes of the south-west (especially the Navajos, whose numbers were in fact far greater by the mid-twentieth century than they had been at the time of the conquest), and to a lesser extent those of the north-western states of Washington and Oregon.

However, this improvement did not solve the Indians' problems. As population once more increased, the reservations could not provide a living for all their people, and Indians had to find employment in the American economy. In the 1950s a policy of 'termination' of federal tutelage was announced. Its motives were mixed. On the one hand was a genuine belief, by liberal-minded officials, that Indians should no longer be treated as backward children but must be prepared for full participation in American life as equal citizens. On the other hand was the desire of businessmen to get their hands on valuable natural resources in the Indian reservations.

The various political movements among black Americans from the 1960s onwards had their effect also on the Indians. Pride in the Indian past, rejection of white claims of superior civilisation, and a general desire for Indian liberation made themselves felt. There were acts of defiance of authority, and there was sympathy among liberal whites. However, the prospect of any unity among the numerous Indian tribes, speaking languages vastly different from each other, seemed remote; while the chances of any Indian sovereign state were even smaller than of a black American republic.

Spanish rule in Mexico, and Mexican independence, as related earlier, had created an overwhelmingly Spanish-speaking *mestizo* people, the great majority of whom were small peasants or agricultural labourers, who in their way of life were closer to the true Indians of pre-colonial times than to the landowners or townsmen of Spanish origin who ruled the country. This changed after the Mexican Revolution, and still more after the land reforms of Cárdenas. Not only did millions of *mestizos* of predominantly Indian origin get the use of the land they cultivated, but the whole apparatus of propaganda put forward an ideology of Indianism. Cortés and the Castilian heritage were disowned, and the ancient Indian civilisations were extolled as ever more treasures of pre-Columbian art and architecture were discovered by archaeologists. Praise of all that was Indian went together with a substantial (even if officially exaggerated) increase of social mobility. There remained about three million persons, in a population of nearly fifty million, who still spoke Indian languages, and only a third of these knew no Spanish.[7] Mexico in the 1970s was not the revolutionary paradise which rhetoric suggested, but it was a country which Indians (whether they were Indian-speaking or only Indian in manner of life) could feel was their own. In Guatemala, where Indian languages were proportionately much more important, opportunities were less good, as the country was more backward and dictatorships and guerrilla actions impeded progress.

In South America there were primitive Indian tribes, threatened by white economic activities and population pressure, in Venezuela, Brazil, Argentina and Chile.

In Paraguay the Indian element was predominant. The Guaraní were protected by the Jesuit regime of the seventeenth and early eighteenth centuries, and held their own in spite of the rather limited European immigration in the nineteenth century, and in spite of the appalling casualties of the war of the 1860s. Paraguay in the twentieth century was in effect a country of two languages, Spanish and Guaraní. Paraguayans were proud of their Indian ancestry, and there did not seem to be serious racial tension. It was, however, possible that the calm was due to the forced stability maintained since 1954 by the dictator General Alfredo Stroessner, and that it would be broken when he ceased to rule.

The main problems concerning American Indians arose in the central Andean region of South America. Three Andean states had in the 1960s a high proportion of Indians—Ecuador about 40 per cent of its population, Peru about 45 and Bolivia about 50 per cent. The most recent figures of reasonable accuracy, the 1961 census of Peru, showed that 2,647,674 persons spoke Quechua; of whom 886,082 were also literate in Spanish, a further 407,240 also spoke Spanish but were illiterate, and 1,354,352 knew no Spanish at all. In Ecuador in 1950 about 340,000 were Quechua-speakers, of whom about half also knew Spanish. In Bolivia in the 1960s more than a million spoke Quechua and rather less than a million spoke Aymará.

The inability or reluctance of South American states to provide regular and accurate information on Indian populations makes it extremely difficult to judge either the dimensions or the nature of the problem. It would seem likely that in the 1970s there were something between five and six million Quechua in these three states; but there was no indication of the formation of a Quechua national consciousness transcending state frontiers. Hundreds of thousands of Indians had been moving, for decades past, to seek employment in the conurbation of Greater Lima, or in the smaller though considerable cities of Guayaquil, La Paz and Quito, or in the mining centres of Bolivia. Here they lived in great squalor, picked up at least some knowledge of Spanish, and became superficially assimilated in a Spanish-speaking society. The Indians who stayed behind, the least enterprising and most backward, or the most stubbornly devoted to their ancient traditions (depending on the point of view of the observer), remained excluded from public affairs, and found no politically effective leaders of their own. They lived in poverty, as agricultural labourers or members of traditional rural *comunidades*, forced to fight an unending and losing battle against the encroachments of larger landowners. The possessing classes and conservative parties regarded them with a mixture of contempt and vaguely benevolent condescension, and made no appreciable effort either to understand or to satisfy them. The politicians of the extreme left contented themselves with the belief that social revolution would solve all their problems, and assumed that the revolution would be conducted in Spanish.

There were a few exceptions. The founder of *Acción Popular Revolucionaria Americana* (APRA), the Peruvian Victor Raul Haya de la Torre, had a conception of an Indo-America, capable of developing politically, socially and culturally in its own way, quite distinct from either Europe or North America. The idea of *Indo*-America (joint creation of Indian and Spanish peoples), as opposed to *Latin* America, was attractive; but it remained little more than a slogan. APRA never became an effective continent-wide movement, though its ideas had intellectual sympathisers in several countries. In Peru, where APRA was strongest, it was repeatedly repressed by dictatorial governments, and proved incapable, in those years when it obtained the semblance of power, of putting its promises into effect. Another Peruvian who showed sympathetic insight into the predicament of the Indians was José Carlos Mariátegui. He saw the solution in social revolution, especially in land reform. He was a founder of the Peruvian communist party, and died young in 1930. Both the communists and APRA claimed to be his political heirs, but his ideas remained no more than an aspiration. However, the military regime installed in 1968 by General Velasco Alvarado not only introduced some real land reforms, but adopted an Indianist ideology, extolling the Indian past at the expense of the Castilian, much as had been done for decades in Mexico.

The real feelings of the Indians themselves remained uncertain. Plenty of 'progressive' Spanish-speaking intellectuals were ready to speak on their behalf, and to try to organise guerrilla bands in the Andes: Fidel Castro's friend, the romantic hero Che Guevara, met his death in an unsuccessful guerrilla enterprise in Bolivia. Several talented imaginative writers, of a 'populist' school which in some ways recalled the Russian *narodnik* writers of the nineteenth century, did much to bring the sufferings and aspirations of the Indians before a wider public. Ciro Alegría's novel *El mundo es ancho y ajeno* depicted the miseries of the Indians in the 1940s in terms of wicked oppression and hopeless resistance, which might seem crude to foreign readers, yet was not unlike real events as they were reported in the press at the time. More penetrating were the novels of José Maria Arguedas, *Los ríos profundos* and *Todas las sangres*. Their author was himself bilingual in Spanish and Quechua, and gave a more subtle and convincing picture of Indian society and Indian thinking. In the absence of systematic statistical information and thorough social studies, this imaginative literature had to be regarded as evidence, pointing to the persistence of an Indian culture greatly different from, and deeply suspicious of, the Spanish-*mestizo* official culture.

It seemed, however, fairly clear that there was in the mid-1970s no Quechua nationalism, though this does not mean that none might ever develop.

# 10  Diaspora Nations

## Types of diaspora

The subject of this chapter is a type of community whose essential feature is that it is scattered over a wide part of the earth's surface: hence the use of the Greek word *diaspora*. In one outstanding case a whole community, already united by ancient religious culture and a profound solidarity for which the modern phrase 'national consciousness' is perhaps appropriate, was twice forcibly uprooted and transported abroad. This community are the Jews, who were removed first by the Babylonians and then by the Romans. The Jews are the only people beside the Chinese who possess a cultural identity unbroken for more than three thousand years. Whereas the Chinese suffered many foreign invasions which their culture absorbed, the Jews had for over 1,800 years no homeland;[1] but at the end of that period their diaspora was itself split when a large minority of the Jews in the world returned to Palestine and created the state of Israel, and in it a new Israeli nation.

A second pattern is that considerable numbers of a vast continental population, attracted by business prospects or recruited as unskilled labourers, were transported to distant lands, where the new communities which they formed represented a large proportion of the population of the lands in which they settled, though only a tiny fraction of that of their original homes. To this category belong the overseas Indians and Chinese, among whom in the one case Tamils, and in the other case Cantonese and Fukienese, tended to predominate.

A third pattern is that the resources of the homeland were not sufficient to support all its people, and that a large proportion of its inhabitants sought a living by trade abroad, and settled in substantial distant communities, whose aggregate population was rather numerous in relation to the population remaining at home. In these cases the diaspora and the homelanders were fairly evenly balanced, and interacted upon each other. Examples are the Greeks, Armenians, Lebanese and Volga Tatars. Each of these cases is somewhat different. The Greeks living in the Ottoman empire outside peninsular Greece and its islands were isolated communities in a Muslim world; yet they were inhabiting lands in which their ancestors had lived for centuries before the Muslims arrived. Other Greeks established communities in more distant places—in southern Russia and the Caucasus. The Armenians' situation was rather similar, but there were also large Armenian communities living within the Russian, Ottoman or Iranian empires, far beyond the lands which had once formed the Armenian homeland. Christian Lebanese were to be found in communities in Ottoman provinces far beyond the Lebanon; but there were also Lebanese and Syrian communities, both Christian and Muslim, far from Ottoman territory, in West Africa, to which they came when it was brought under European Christian imperial rule. Volga Tatars also lived in communities in Central Asia, far from the Volga.

A common characteristic of most of these communities is that their social structure was distorted, and that they became concentrated in certain types of activity—above all in commerce, later in the modern intellectual professions—as well as bringing with them to their new lands a significant number of persons expounding the religion which was essential to their culture—priests, rabbis or *ulema*. In the case of the overseas Indians and Chinese there were also large numbers of labourers employed in particular kinds of enterprise, chiefly large-scale European-owned plantations or mines. The concentration in certain types of activity, which to the indigenous peoples inevitably tended to look like a sinister monopoly of such occupations, was a source of latent hostility between them; and this grew as the indigenous peoples acquired modern education and political consciousness.

Some of these diaspora commercial elites operated by sea and some by land: outstanding among the former were the Greeks and Chinese,[2] while the latter comprised the Jews and Armenians.

A fourth pattern of diaspora are the merchants from European countries who made a living in Asia or Africa. Some European communities of this type existed for as long as two hundred years. However, though the communities continued, the individuals for the most part did not. They were free citizens of independent states, who could and did move freely between their homelands and their overseas communities. Few of them struck deep roots overseas.[3] The Greeks, Armenians and Lebanese, on the other hand, were citizens—of second-class rank—of states ruled essentially by foreigners—Ottomans, Russians or Iranians—and were glad to make new homes with new loyalties, while never altogether losing the links with their old homes.

There is another category which might be considered to fall under the heading of a diaspora: the numerous Muslim trading communities which were to be found around the east coast of Africa and the southern coasts of Asia. They include the Arabs from Arabia, and the Persians or 'Shirazis' from the Persian Gulf, who settled in such places as Zanzibar and Mombasa; and the Muslim Gujarati merchants from western India who established themselves in the Malayan peninsula and the Malaysian archipelago. These people played an important part in spreading Islam: one might indeed argue that the Victorian imperialist slogan that 'trade follows the flag', used to justify European annexations in Asia and Africa, has less truth in it than there would be in a slogan 'the faith follows the trade' applied to Muslim penetration in the east. However, these Muslim traders did not in most cases keep themselves apart in distinct communities: rather, in the course of time they became Africans or Malaysians, contributing greatly to the emergent African or Malaysian cultures and national consciousness.

Other marginal examples also occur to one. One such are the Baltic Germans. These were essentially the descendants of conquerors or colonists planted, from the thirteenth century onwards, among the Latvian and Estonian population of the south-east Baltic lands. Up to the twentieth century they included noble landowners (some of distant Swedish or even Scottish origin, but united essentially by a German culture), but also city merchants, teachers, ministers of religion, craftsmen, shopkeepers and workers. Another example are the Scots who settled in England, from early modern times onwards. These have perhaps been especially prominent in business, government service and the intellectual professions, but also include all classes. A rather large proportion, but by no means all, became assimilated to the English culture in which they lived. In the 1970s there may well have been more persons of Scottish origin living in England than in Scotland.

A recent original essay on these problems[4] distinguished between 'mobilised' diasporas, which 'enjoy many material and cultural advantages compared to other groups in the multi-ethnic polity', and 'proletarian' diasporas, which consist essentially of workers seeking employment abroad in large numbers. Jews, Armenians, Greeks, Baltic Germans and Volga Tatars would clearly fit John Armstrong's first category. His second category does not however fit my own classification in this book—which does not of course mean that it is not valid in the context of his analysis. It would include overseas Indians and Chinese, but it would also cover immigrant workers in the New World (whom I prefer to discuss in connection with the formation of new overseas nations of European origin), and the south European *Gastarbeiter* in contemporary industrial Europe (Yugoslavs, Turks and Spaniards in Germany; Italians in Switzerland; Portuguese, Algerians and Italians in France), of whom the great majority do not remain for more than a few years. The *Gastarbeiter* constitute a major European social problem, whose future is uncertain; but they do not seem to me to belong to the theme of my book.

Something has already been said of the Greeks of the diaspora and of the

Volga Tatars. I shall confine myself in this chapter to a discussion at some length of the case of the Jews which, quite apart from its own intrinsic importance, is also, as has been noted in earlier chapters, intertwined with the growth of national movements in Central and Eastern Europe; and, more briefly, to the overseas Chinese and Indians, whose story raises problems both of national consciousness and of racial conflict.

First, however, a few words may be devoted to the Armenians, whose case has some parallels with that of the Jews.

The recorded history of the Armenian state, based on the eastern part of Asia Minor, goes back at least to the second century BC. Its ruler Tigranes (95-66), who extended his power into Syria and Mesopotamia, became a client of Rome. The Armenians became Christians at the turn of the third and fourth centuries AD, and were later separated from the main body of Christendom by their adoption of the Monophysite heresy. In the following centuries Armenia was a buffer state between Rome and Persia, and later between Byzantium and the Arabs. There were periods of relative independence, and the Armenian religion and culture were preserved. In the sixteenth century all the Armenian lands came under Ottoman rule, but in the early seventeenth the eastern region of Erivan was annexed to Safavid Iran. During this period Armenians played an important part outside their homeland as traders, establishing communities in Constantinople, Isfahan, Aleppo and Cairo, and even in Christian commercial centres such as Kronstadt (Brasov) in Transylvania and Lwów (Lemberg) in Polish Galicia. All this time however the Armenians retained something which the Jews had lost—their own homeland of compact population.

In 1828 Erivan region was annexed to the Russian empire. The Armenians proved very loyal subjects to the tsars, because they hoped that they would liberate their kinsmen in Ottoman Armenia. A nationalist movement, with a partly socialist ideology and a tendency towards terrorism, grew up in the late nineteenth century, directed primarily against the Ottoman government, but at times also against the tsars. The hopes of liberation by Russian arms from Turkish rule were not fulfilled, though some small districts were ceded to Russia and some thousands of Armenians fled to Russian territory. In April 1915 the Ottoman government gave order for the deportation of the Armenians from the six *vilayets* (provinces) in the east in which they had a compact population. This order in fact led to a massacre of hundreds of thousands, and by the end of 1916, 300,000 had fled to Russia.

The Armenians of Russian Armenia had their share of suffering in the Russian Revolution and Civil War, but their existence as a nation was not in danger. They maintained their culture and religion under the Soviet regime, and by the 1970s they, together with their neighbours the Georgians, possessed a greater degree of autonomy than any other non-Russian nation of the Soviet empire.

Already under imperial Russian rule large Armenian communities—professional, business and skilled workers—had grown up outside the Armenian homeland, in the Transcaucasian cities of Baku and Tiflis and in southern Russia. This diaspora continued to grow. In 1970 there were 2,208,000 Armenians in the Armenian SSR and 1,235,000 in other parts of the Soviet Union. There were also substantial Armenian communities in Iran, Syria, other Arab states and both North and South America, amounting in all to over 1,700,000.

## The Jews

The Jews were twice forcibly uprooted. Deported to Babylon in the seventh century BC, they were allowed by Cyrus the Persian to return in the sixth. Deported again by the Romans after rebellions in the first and second centuries AD, they returned in the twentieth to impose their rule on the peoples who had lived there in the interval.

In the centuries of diaspora some Jews came to Rome, and moved to the European provinces of the empire, especially Spain and the Rhine valley. Others spread over North Africa, Arabia and Mesopotamia. A nomadic people inhabiting the Black Sea steppes, the Khazars, adopted Judaism and became a territorial power in the eighth century AD. In Christian lands Jews received reluctant tolerance, interrupted by outbursts of persecution. In Muslim lands in the early Middle Ages, especially in Spain, they fared better. Crusading armies marching through Germany massacred Jews and destroyed houses and property. Jews were persecuted in England in the thirteenth century, and expelled in 1290.

The country most hospitable to Jews in the late Middle Ages was Poland. The charter of King Boleslaw the Pious of Great Poland of 1264 gave them better conditions than elsewhere in Europe; and this was confirmed by Casimir the Great (1333-70), king of all Poland, who welcomed thousands and assured them a means of livelihood. At the other end of Europe the great contributions of Jews to Spanish and Portuguese culture ended with the new religious intolerance of the late fifteenth century. Those Jews who remained loyal to their faith were expelled from Spain in 1492, the year of the conquest of Muslim Granada. Jewish converts to Christianity (*marranos*) were allowed to remain, but even these converts were objects of distrust and discrimination. Portuguese policy was somewhat less brutal than Spanish, but not less ruthless in its aims.

Now their kindest hosts were the Moroccans and the Ottoman Turks, under whose rule Jewish colonies were established from Tunisia to Bosnia. These Jews, who continued to speak a form of Spanish, were known as

*Sephardim*. They were outnumbered by the Jews of Poland, known as *Ashkenazy*. With the partitions of Poland in the late eighteenth century, most of the latter became subjects of Russia, but substantial numbers came under Austrian and Prussian rule. There were also older but smaller colonies in Holland, West Germany (especially in Frankfurt-on-Main) and Bohemia (especially in Prague).

The Jewish communities lived in cities. They consisted overwhelmingly of merchants, small traders, craftsmen and persons involved in the maintenance of the Judaic faith, doctrine and law. In comparison with the peoples among whom they lived, they were exceptionally gifted for commercial enterprise. It is worth noting that, like the Armenians but unlike the Greeks and the Italians, they concerned themselves almost entirely with land-borne trade: they acquired no aptitude for seafaring. Their skills as merchants, and especially as bankers, made them useful to reigning sovereigns and to large territorial magnates. They were also exceptionally gifted for intellectual activities. In this field they had to reckon with the bitter hostility of the Catholic Church, which in the Middle Ages virtually monopolised intellectual life, and regarded the Jews as purveyors of pernicious doctrines. Their commercial activities won them the resentment of peasants, who saw their few hard-earned pence disappear into the Jew's pockets, and of aspirant shopkeepers and small businessmen from the indigenous population, who saw in them hated rivals. Thus the position of the Jews was always precarious, and remained dependent on the favour of the upper classes, on the very problematic courage of princes to defend them against popular wrath. It was somewhat, but not much, better in Protestant countries, especially in Holland.

Conditions improved generally in the Enlightenment of the eighteenth century. As the prestige of learning, and the opportunities of critical thinking and writing, increased, Jews could take advantage of them. Within the Jewish communities themselves, an Enlightenment of their own appeared, the *Haskalah*. The quality of Jewish religious scholarship and of the study of Hebrew—the sacred language which had survived centuries of dispersal but had inevitably become corrupted—improved. Controversies about religious reform convulsed the Jewish communities. At the same time Christians of liberal outlook began to urge that legal discriminations against Jews should be removed; and Jews became more willing to adapt themselves to the surrounding cultural world. Liberalism went together with growing capitalism and the consequent industrial revolution. Christian and Jewish bourgeoisies grew numerous and powerful, and regarded each other as allies in the struggle against the old monarchical and aristocratic order. Instead of being dependent on the capricious protection of rulers, Jews began to be fighters for political freedom and for legal and social equality. Many Jews played an honourable part in the revolutionary struggles of 1848. Emancipation of Jews became a major claim of European democrats.

German nineteenth-century culture proved very attractive to Jews, and they made an important contribution to it. The old Jewish colonies in the Rhineland flourished, and the Jews from the east, incorporated in Prussia and Austria by the partitions of Poland, made their way to the cultural and economic centres of both countries. Berlin, which during the century evolved from a second-rate administrative capital into one of the few really great cities of the world (in the fullest sense of this expression), had a Jewish population of more than 50,000 at mid-century and of 144,000 in 1910. Not only in business but in most intellectual and artistic activities Jews became extremely prominent. This was still more the case in Vienna, which on the eve of the First World War had around 200,000 Jews. In both countries there were voluntary conversions, to the Lutheran or Catholic faiths, but these were not very numerous. More important was a falling away from Jewish religious orthodoxy and social habits, corresponding to the secularising trends visible in Christian society. In the 1850s and 1860s Jews acquired full civil rights in the German lands. Increasingly, they felt themselves to be Germans: heirs to the Jewish past, believers or at least respecters of the Judaic faith, but German or Austrian patriots and members of the German cultural community.

A similar process took place in Hungary. There were old but small Jewish communities in some Hungarian cities, especially in the eighteenth century capital, Pressburg (Pozsony, Bratislava). The main influx of Jews into Hungary however followed the partitions of Poland. Opportunities were better in the Hungarian lands than in Galicia, and Jews poured over the Carpathians. Most settled in the northern and eastern provinces, where the majority of the population were not Hungarians (Magyars) but Slovaks, Ruthenes or Romanians. A large number, however, moved to the new capital, Budapest. The growth of this city, in the last half-century before the First World War, into a great cultural and economic centre, was accompanied by a rapid growth of its Jewish population. Early in the twentieth century, of its 1,000,000 inhabitants more than a fifth were Jews. As in Germany and Austria, so in Hungary Jews were especially successful in banking, in various branches of industry and in the free professions. In both Vienna and Budapest the most important newspapers were staffed by Jews. In Hungary nearly half the doctors and two-fifths of the lawyers were Jews. All this was made possible by a liberal policy on the part of the Hungarian governments, which enacted full emanicipation in 1867, and thereafter encouraged Jews to engage in business, a form of activity for which Magyars, whether noblemen or peasants, had hitherto shown little inclination or aptitude. The Hungarian rulers also encouraged Jews to regard themselves as Magyars. This most Jews were willing to do. They gladly accepted, and played a great part in developing, the Magyar language, literature and culture. They also played their part in propagating Magyar nationalism among the non-Magyar Slovaks and Romanians in whose midst they lived, incurring thereby the resentment of these peoples.

Romania, which for three hundred years was a vassal state of the Ottoman empire and which became independent after the Crimean War, received a large influx of Jewish immigrants as an indirect result of the partitions of Poland and more directly as a consequence of the Treaty of Adrianople of 1829, which opened the country to international trade. Romania was at this time a much more backward country than Hungary. Such commerce and industry as existed was largely in the hands of Greeks. In the capitals of Moldavia (Iaşi) and of Wallachia (Bucharest) an educated elite, strongly influenced by French culture, already existed, but the intellectual professions had only just begun to develop. The upper strata of Romanian society consisted of landowners and bureaucrats. In this society the Jewish immigrants soon supplied the business class required by modern capitalism. Most became shopkeepers or dealers in wine and spirits in small towns. The more successful became bankers; or leased land from big landowners to sublet it to peasants, thereby making substantial profits. As the intellectual professions grew, Jews entered them. They were especially numerous in medicine and in the press. Romanian governments, even when led by persons of proclaimed liberal outlook, were extremely reluctant to give Jews full civil rights and opportunities of employment. Pressure to this effect by the governments of the European great powers resulted in definite undertakings by the Romanian government at the Congress of Berlin (1878), but these were by no means fully or quickly carried out.

The Jews of the Russian empire were concentrated in the formerly Polish provinces, of which the 'congress kingdom' of Poland should be distinguished from the great borderland region extending from Lithuania to the Black Sea coastal area.[5] For a short time under Empress Catherine II the Jews received rather liberal treatment, though their movements were restricted by a decree of 23 December 1791, which confined them (with the exception of a small wealthy and educated minority) to fourteen provinces.[6] Under Tsar Nicholas I (1825-55) they were harshly treated, and subjected to pressure with the aim of converting them to Christianity— with little success. A new period of promise opened with the reign of Alexander II (1855-81). During this period much greater opportunities of education and of employment became available. In the business progress which followed the emancipation of the Russian serfs (1861) Jews played their part, and some acquired fortunes. On the Jewish side there was a new willingness to accept the culture of the host nation. In the borderlands, whose main city and cultural centre was Vilna, this meant a tendency to accept Russian culture. In the 'congress kingdom' assimilation was rather towards Polish culture, and Jews tended to identify themselves with Polish national aspirations. Assimilation was however strongly opposed by the most orthodox leaders of the Jews, who in this respect spoke for the majority. Conditions of life and work for most Jews in Russia and Poland were even worse than in Romania. The majority consisted of poorly paid craftsmen, manual workers and small shopkeepers. As their numbers grew, poverty grew also, and the outlook remained dark.

## Anti-semitism and Zionism

Though the nineteenth century was on the whole a period of progress and hope for Jews, the basic hostility of the host populations to them was not removed: rather, it was aggravated by economic and ideological factors which became clearly visible by the end of the century.

The Christian priesthood and hierarchy viewed the Jews at best with distrust and at worst with passionate hostility, considering them a dangerous element likely to corrupt the faith and morals of their flock. This is especially true of the Orthodox Church, not because there is any special element of hostility to Jews in Orthodox dogma that is not present in Catholic, but because the Orthodox Church had not been subject to the influences of the Enlightenment, as had the Catholic (at least north of the Pyrenees and the Po) and the Protestant. The Orthodox attitude to Jews resembled the Catholic attitude of 1400 rather than of 1900.

In the agricultural countries, the peasants had economic grounds for hating Jews, since these represented capitalism and the power of money. Polish or Romanian peasants were often wrong to regard Jewish inn-keepers or tradesmen as richer than themselves, and almost always wrong to see in them malevolent exploiters of Christians. But it was a fact that a large part of the small cash incomes, left to the peasants from the sale of their products and after the payment of their taxes, found its way into the hands of Jews. The same applies to the growing and floating population employed in some manner in the growing cities. When politicians appeared who attributed their suffering to the Jews, these peasants and workers were easily convinced. For them, anti-semitism was, to use a phrase attributed to the German Social Democratic leader August Bebel, 'the socialism of the imbecile'.

In the industrial countries, these trends existed but were less important than another economic cause of hostility to Jews. This was the appearance among the host peoples, as a result of economic development and of modern education, of large numbers of persons seeking employment in business and in the professions. Children of peasants or of small officials aimed at a career in industrial management, banking, medicine or journalism, and found the best jobs held by Jews. For the most part, these Jews had got their jobs because they were the best persons available at the time—though it cannot be denied that there was a tendency for Jews in key positions in enterprise to give jobs to other Jews. For the unsuccessful aspirants from the provinces it was easy to believe in a monstrous 'Jewish plot'. This belief gained ground in Germany, especially in Berlin. It was much more widespread in Austria, where talk of the 'stronghold' of the Jews in Vienna found ready listeners.

Anti-semitism as a doctrine emerged in the last decades of the century all over Western and Central Europe. It derived its popularity from the religious and economic factors summarised above. It was formulated by intellectuals of nostalgic conservative outlook, of whom the most outstanding was the Frenchman Charles Maurras. To men of this outlook 'the Jew' symbolised all that was most hateful about the Europe which had emerged since the French Revolution: the ascendancy of reason over faith, of city over countryside, of money over physical labour, of competition over hierarchy, of abstract radicalism over simple truths, of internationalism over state loyalty. There were Jews in all European countries, and they maintained contact with each other: therefore they were a sinister international conspiracy, a poison undermining societies, destined—unless checked—to destroy all national culture and identities.

The attitudes of governments to instinctive and to articulate anti-semitism varied. In Germany the upper classes seldom associated with Jews (though Bismarck himself was an exception); but they did not encourage anti-semitic demagogy, still less identified themselves with it. In Austria too social exclusiveness existed, but the government was in no sense anti-semitic. The fiercest anti-semites, the German nationalists, were also bitter enemies of the whole Habsburg system. They wished Austria to be a 'German state', whereas Emperor Franz Josef and his ministers, though German was their mother tongue, considered themselves above nationalism. They required only that their subjects should be *kaisertreu*, loyal to their dynasty: on this basis they wished to accept equally the loyalty of all, whatever their speech or faith or homeland. In Austria the predominant language and culture were German, but to the rage of the German nationalists the main exponents of this culture were Jewish journalists and writers. These Jews considered themselves to belong to the German cultural community, but the German nationalists, fanatically anti-semitic, denied them this quality. The German nationalists were always a comparatively small minority. However, in the much larger Christian Social movement anti-semitic rhetoric was part of the everyday currency of politics. Its leader, Mayor Karl Lueger of Vienna, was especially addicted to it, and was for this and other reasons cordially disliked by the emperor. The truth was that the Austrian Jews, together with the Hungarian Jews, were one of the main cementing factors in the Habsburg Monarchy.

In Romania, the political class was basically hostile to the Jews, but in the course of time came to terms with them. Jews were excluded from the military and civil government service, but in business life and the professions a certain unwilling partnership developed.

Pressure by the European powers continued to limit the ability of Romanian governments to court mass popularity by discriminating against Jews. In Russia, both governments and people were hostile. This fact is somewhat concealed, in the historical literature of the period written by Russians and by foreigners, by the fact that the small but vocal intellectual elite, being predominantly radical or socialist in outlook, was not anti-semitic. However, the much more numerous adherents of the Orthodox church, and the rural and urban poor, had the motives for hostility to Jews which have been summarised earlier. Russian capitalists, or aspirant capitalists, were few, and did not for the most part feel themselves blocked in their careers by Jews. The rulers of Russia, however, especially after the assassination of Alexander II in 1881, were mostly hostile. This is true of the last two tsars and of most of their advisers—the outstanding exception being the finance minister Count Sergius Witte (1894-1903). Most leading Russian officials were conservative paternalists, distrustful of capitalism and of modern civilisation, nostalgically idealising a happy Russian past which never was. They genuinely believed that the Jews, with their sinister international connections, were undermining and poisoning Russian society, and that the Russian people must be protected from them. This was the motive behind the series of geographical, professional and educational restrictions placed upon the Jews after 1881 and maintained, in spite of pressure from liberal opinion within and outside Russia, until the end of the imperial regime.

The Russian rulers' fear of the Jews as a revolutionary force was by no means unjustified. Living in growing squalor and poverty, suffering all the miseries and injustices which were the common lot of all the subjects of the tsars, but with the addition of specific restrictions and discrimination applicable only to them, it was natural that there should be even more discontented persons among the Jews than among other Russian citizens. Moreover, the whole emphasis, in traditional Judaic culture, on the value of learning and the importance of moral ideas, made young Jews substantially more likely to take an interest in modern political and social ideas than young Russians; that is to say, made them more accessible to revolutionary ideas than other communities in Russia. The truth is that, though the great majority of Russian Jews were not revolutionaries, a disproportionate share of those Russian subjects who were revolutionaries were Jews. The process thus escalated: because the Russian government feared Jews as revolutionaries, it persecuted them, and because Jews were persecuted they sympathised with revolutionaries or become revolutionaries. It is also true that certain high officials and police chiefs deliberately encouraged pogroms (riots in which Jews were beaten or killed, and Jewish property was destroyed) as a means of diverting mass discontent against a convenient scapegoat: it was hoped that the socialism of the imbecile might replace the more dangerous variety. Even so, it is a mistake to exaggerate official complicity or leadership: many pogroms were rather popular enterprises, supported by the urban poor of Ukrainian or Lithuanian cities, led by quite unofficial local demagogues.[7]

The attitude of Hungarian governments after 1867 differed sharply from that of the Russian. The Hungarian rulers, though themselves noblemen and social conservatives, were men of liberal origin (many had taken part in the revolution of 1848-49). They welcomed capitalism, which they expected would make Hungary stronger, and they appreciated the ability of the Jews to promote it. They also favoured the growth of the professions and of Magyar literature and culture, in which also they were glad to see the Jewish achievement. They had no reason to fear revolutionary activity by the Jews. It is true that some Jews were leading social democrats, leaders of the Budapest working class; but this class they did not consider dangerous. There were two potentially revolutionary dangers in Hungary: the landless or dwarf-holding peasants and the non-Magyar nations. With the first of these the Jews had no contact, with the second no sympathy. Hungarian Jews in the northern and eastern provinces were fervent Magyar patriots, hateful to Slovaks and Romanians but most acceptable to the Hungarian government. There was anti-semitic feeling in Hungary, due to the causes mentioned earlier, but Hungarian governments gave it no encouragement.

Thus on the eve of the First World War it was in Russia, and to a much lesser extent in Romania, that prospects were dark for Jews, and that the road to assimilation and advancement seemed closed. In Germany, Austria and Hungary it would have required unusual prophetic gifts to foresee that within a few decades all Jews would be in mortal peril.

The idea that Jerusalem is the home of the Jews, and that they should one day return there, was deeply implanted in the whole Judaic religious and cultural tradition, which had been maintained for centuries in the diaspora. The idea that Jews should have their own state had been suggested in recent times by individuals, both Gentile and Jewish; among the latter, by Rabbi Hirsh Kalisher (1795-1874) and by Moses Hess (1812-75), whose book *Rome and Jerusalem* appeared in 1862.

Greater urgency was given to the idea by the anti-Jewish policies of the Russian government following the assassination of Alexander II. During 1881 and 1882 was formed an association of Lovers of Zion (*Hovevei*

*Zion*), with branches in various Jewish communities in Lithuania, Poland, Ukraine and Romania. Its leading figure was Rabbi Samuel Mohilever (1824-98) of Radom. Some of its members were able to establish agricultural settlements in Palestine, the first of which was named Rishon-le-Zion ('First to Zion') and located south of Jaffa. In 1882 also was published in Berlin a pamphlet entitled *Auto-Emanzipation*, by Leo Pinsker, a Jewish doctor in Odessa. Pinsker considered that anti-Jewish feelings were ineradicable among the host nations; that Jews could never win their esteem or friendship by acts or arguments; and that the only solution was for Jews to make themselves masters of their own destiny instead of depending on the goodwill of others. The Jews must find a homeland of their own—not necessarily Palestine—and organise their own life there.

Neither the arguments of Pinsker nor the example of *Hovevei Zion* made much impact on the Jews, even in Russia. Between 1882 and 1903 about 25,000 Jews went to Palestine: this first wave of emigration became known to later Jewish historians as the first 'ascent' (*aliah*) to Zion. They met with great difficulties, but managed to maintain themselves, largely owing to financial assistance from the French Jewish baron, Edmond de Rothschild. For most Jews in Russia two other outlets seemed preferable to Zionism. One was socialism, which in its various forms attracted many intellectuals, workers and poor middle-class Jews in Poland, Lithuania and Ukraine. The other was emigration to the New World: between 1881 and 1914 about two millions Jews entered the United States, where they made their way in that melting-pot of peoples, doing rather better for themselves than most other immigrant groups, thanks to their inherent abilities and mutual help.

The man who launched Zionism as an international political force was Theodor Herzl (1860-1904). His famous book *Der Judenstaat*, which appeared in 1896, said little that had not been said earlier by Hess or Pinsker. More important was the personality of the man. Born in Budapest, he made a career in Vienna as a journalist and writer. He wrote for the *Neue Freie Presse*, the outstanding Viennese newspaper, and the organ of successful, assimilationist, cultured *Kaisertreu* Jewish opinion. He spent several years in Paris in the early 1890s and witnessed the anti-semitism of Maurras and his school, reflected in the Dreyfus Affair. It was this which convinced Herzl of the ineradicable and dangerous character of anti-semitism. If even in France, the most civilised country in the world, hate campaigns against Jews on a mass scale were possible, then Jews could not be secure in any country in which they were only guests. There must be a Jewish state. Herzl not only proclaimed this idea, but worked tirelessly to put it into practice. He had a magnetic personality and immense energy. He travelled through Europe, interviewing princes and ministers, the German emperor and the Ottoman grand vizier. He created the World Zionist Organisation, which held its first congress in Basel in 1897, and met thereafter every year up to the First World War. He inspired loyalty and enthusiasm, and when he died others continued his work.

The results were not at first very impressive. The best offer received from a government was from the British: a portion of Uganda for Jewish settlement. This was discussed by the 8th Zionist Congress in 1904 and turned down. Immigration into Palestine increased, but was still small: it now included convinced socialists, who decided that membership of a European socialist party (German or Austrian social-democracy, Russian Menshevism or Bolshevism), or activity in a specifically Jewish socialist movement in a European country (the *Bund* in Russia and Poland), did not meet their needs; and who therefore preferred to set up Jewish socialist communities on Palestinian soil. Thus were formed the first *kvutzot*, from which later emerged the specific form of the *kibbutz*.

Very important also for the future was the development of Hebrew as a modern spoken language. For centuries past the effective language of the Jews of Eastern Europe had been Yiddish, basically German with a large admixture of Slav and Hebrew words. A considerable literature and drama existed in Yiddish. The pioneers in Palestine became convinced that the national language of the Jews must be not Yiddish but Hebrew. In the long work of developing and popularising Hebrew, over many years, the chief figure was Eliezer Perlman, known as Ben Yehuda. He, more than any other single man, is responsible for the vigorous growth of Hebrew and its adoption by successive generations of Jews in Palestine.

At the time, all this made little impression on Jewish opinion. In particular, the World Zionist Organisation received little financial help from rich Jews in Europe or America. Occasional outrages, like the pogroms in Russia between 1903 and 1906, or the Beilis Trial of 1913,[8] aroused the sympathy of Jews all over the world; but for the most part, Jews were too busy with their daily lives in the countries of which they were citizens to make much effort to support a long-term political effort on behalf of Zionism. The international Jewish conspiracy devoted to dark Zionist purposes, dear to anti-semitic polemists, did not exist. More than this, the bulk of Jews in Germany, Austria, Hungary, France and Britain were content to be assimilated to the culture of the host nation. They maintained their communal and religious loyalties (though of many, even this was not true), but they felt as Germans, Magyars, Frenchmen or Englishmen. They had no wish to create a new Jewish nation or a Jewish state: those who had this wish appeared to them a mere nuisance.

The outbreak of the European war in 1914 set the Jews of Europe against each other, while the sympathies of American Jews were also divided. Most Jews were hostile to imperial Russia, especially after the anti-semitic brutalities of Russian armies in occupied Galicia in 1914-15. Most Jews also welcomed the Russian Revolution. There were, however, influential

Jews on the Anglo-French side. The orientation of Zionism was in fact decided by one man, of a personality no less remarkable than Herzl's: Chaim Weizmann. Born in Lithuania in 1874, Weizmann lived for ten years in England, and became an admirer of British institutions and people. In 1914 he decided to stay in England and set himself to win British political leaders to the Zionist cause. His work as a chemist for the ministry of munitions increased his prestige. The desire of different political groups to ensure a strong British position in the Middle East after the war gave him his opportunity. It is indeed arguable that the Balfour Declaration of November 1917 was designed to further the aims both of Jewish nationalism and of British imperialism, which at that moment coincided with each other. However, this is not to say very much. There were other British imperialists who believed that their aims could be better secured by supporting Arab nationalists, and indeed at this same time negotiations were proceeding with them, and vague but essentially incompatible promises were given to both sides. This complex story, which has often been told with varying degrees of partiality, has many aspects; but an essential part of it is the personal relationship of Chaim Weizmann and Arthur Balfour. Weizmann's belief in Britain, and Balfour's conversion to the Zionist cause, were not simply based on material interests. In the words of a recent historian of Zionism, 'Balfour . . . had the feeling that he was instrumental in righting a wrong of world-historical dimensions, quite irrespective of the changing world situation'.[9]

The Mandate[10] over Palestine, confirmed to Britain by the League of Nations in 1922, was expected to promote both British interests and Jewish aspirations. But both were confronted with a major problem to which little attention had been given.

Palestine was already inhabited by about a million Arabs, whose ancestors had lived there for longer than the whole period of Old Testament Jewish history. A few Jewish colonists were acceptable to them, but the prospect of large-scale Jewish settlement was not. The Arabs feared that they would be deprived of this land, and that the end of the Ottoman regime would thus bring them not freedom but another form of foreign rule.[11] The Jewish leaders dismissed these fears. They argued that there would be room for all in Palestine, and Jewish enterprise and labour would so enrich a neglected but naturally rich land that the standard of living of the Arabs too could improve. However, such improvements, if they took place, would involve a transformation of the economy and of social relationships which would threaten not only the interests of the Arab upper class but the whole way of life of the Arab people. This Arab mistrust was never allayed, but grew with every year which passed.

The British government was chiefly concerned with the security of the Eastern Mediterranean and the Suez Canal area. It did not wish its Arab subjects to be in a state of smouldering discontent. It had long been the view of powerful British imperial interests, and especially of the government of India, that the Muslim world must not be antagonised. A more recent, and increasingly important, argument was that the exploitation of oil—so vital not only to military, naval and air power but also to the civilian economy—required good relations with the peoples in whose countries the oil lay, especially with Iraq, which had also been placed by the League of Nations under British Mandate. British officials tended to find Arab notables more congenial companions than Jewish intellectuals of East European origin. These Arabs combined a certain deference to British attitudes of mind with a Muslim traditionalism which was attractive to romantically minded Englishmen; while the Jews had been brought up in a German or Russian cultural climate quite unlike the British, and showed a distressing addiction to abstract political and social ideas. All these things inclined British officials on the spot to favour the Arabs and to minimise Jewish immigration. The Jewish cause had the support of the first high commissioner, Sir Herbert Samuel, and of influential groups in England; but the views of the Englishmen on the spot proved more important than those held in London.

In the first post-war years some 35,000 Jews came to Palestine, devoted Zionists determined to build a new society. In 1920 *Histadrut*, the trade union organisation, was set up, and in the following years it created banking, insurance and industrial enterprises, becoming a major economic force. Under the Mandate, both Arabs and Jews had their own institutions, which dealt with the British authorities on behalf of their communities. On the Jewish side the most important were the *Knesset*, or elected assembly, and the Jewish Agency, which controlled what were in effect government departments for the Jewish population. In 1929 was formed the first *kibbutz*, at Degania. This was a new form of large-scale voluntary collective farm. The *kibbutzim* achieved great successes in agriculture in the coastal plain and the Galilee area.

The Balfour Declaration had promised a 'national home' for the Jews in Palestine, not a Jewish state. This limited and undefinable aim was accepted by the Jewish leaders. Some attempts were made to reach agreement between Jewish and Arab leaders, but on neither side did the most influential persons take much trouble to understand the feelings of the other. Cooperation and civilised discussion between Jews and Arabs were confined to a small number of intellectuals with little following. Haj Amin al-Hussaini, who became grand mufti of Jerusalem in 1921, was an implacable enemy of the Jews. There were anti-Jewish riots in 1922. More serious was a wave of attacks by Arabs on Jewish settlements in August 1929, in which more than 100 Jews were killed.

Meanwhile in Eastern Europe the situation of Jews was worse than it had been before 1914. In Poland (where there were more than three million Jews) governments were not actively anti-semitic, but they did nothing effective to protect Jews from popular hostility, including acts of violence. Piłsudski, who became dictator in 1926, was comparatively friendly to the Polish Jews, but this was not true of the officials who carried out his policies. In Hungary the situation of Jews was transformed by the revolution of 1918 and the communist regime of 1919. The Hungarian conservative politicians, who returned to power in the counter-revolution led by Admiral Horthy, were now terrified of socialism and communism, which, as explained above, had not alarmed them before 1914. Many of the communist and socialist leaders had been Jews. The identification of 'the Jews' with 'godless revolution' and 'atheistic socialism', characteristic of the Russian political class from 1881 to 1917, was now also largely accepted by the corresponding class in Hungary. Under the regime of Count Stephen Bethlen, a conservative of the old school, from 1921 to 1931 Hungarian Jews once more enjoyed the old opportunities in economic and cultural life, but their position was now precarious. In Romania the situation was not unlike that of Poland. The ruling Romanian politicians accepted an uneasy partnership with Jewish business, and tolerated Jewish influence in the professions, but below the surface anti-semitism was strong.

The world depression of the early 1930s was a turning-point. In all three of these countries mass poverty, peasant misery and unemployment in the professions provided opportunities for anti-semitic movements. The most important of these was the Romanian Iron Guard, which acquired something of the character of a mass revolutionary movement, firmly based on the 'socialism of the imbecile'. In both Hungary and Poland, anti-semitism was to be found both within the government camp and in the radical right opposition. Most disastrous of all, however, was the advent to power in Germany of Adolf Hitler, with his proclaimed policy of 'ridding Germany of the Jewish poison'.

Between 1922 and 1926, some 60,000 Jews came to Palestine, mostly from Poland. After Hitler took over in Germany, the demand for Jewish immigration rapidly increased. The number between 1934 and 1939 reached about 225,000. Both these waves consisted far less of devoted Zionist pioneers than of refugees trying to escape persecution. Arguments for increased Jewish settlement in Palestine were now mainly humanitarian. The Arabs, however, quite justly pointed out that they were not to blame for the cruelties of European governments, and that they should not bear the cost. Jewish opinion grew more radical and impatient. Already in the 1920s the brilliant Zionist leader Vladimir Jabotinsky had been insisting that there must be a Jewish sovereign state in Palestine, and that there must be a Jewish army. The *Hagana*, the defence force supported by the *Histadrut*, was felt to be too passive. In 1925 Jabotinsky set up his own International Union of Revisionist Zionists, and in 1931 his followers created a separate national military organisation (*Irgun Zvai Leumi*).

The British authorities continued, inevitably, to vacillate between the Jewish and Arab camps. They permitted a substantial increase in immigration, and the Arabs replied by a large-scale armed insurrection in 1936. This was followed by the appointment of a royal commission under Lord Peel, which reported in July 1937. It recognised that there was an irrepressible conflict between the two communities, and proposed a partition of Palestine into a Jewish and an Arab state. The proposals did not please the Jews, for their state was to be very small, and they were rejected outright by the Arabs. The British government eventually rejected the Peel Report. Its White Paper of 1939 prohibited sales of land to Jews in most of the country; set a maximum figure for future Jewish immigration of 75,000 in the next five years, after which it was to end altogether; and proposed that at that time a single Palestine state should be established with a population three-quarters Arab and one-quarter Jewish. To the Jews this was a bitter blow. Their feelings were well expressed by the slogan that they should 'fight the British as if the Nazis did not exist, and fight the Nazis as if the White Paper did not exist'.

During the Second World War the British were able to maintain control over the Middle Eastern lands of Arabic speech, including Palestine. They accepted Jewish military contributions to the war effort, but resisted Jewish political demands in order not to antagonise Arab opinion from Iraq to Egypt. The Jewish position was truly tragic. They had to support Britain against their mortal enemy Hitler, yet the British government too showed itself by its policies to be their enemy. Even the small numbers of Jews who succeeded in escaping from Hitler's Europe in the 1940s were refused entry into Palestine.

Meanwhile Hitler passed from the stage of cruel persecution and denial of a livelihood to Jews to the stage of 'final solution'—physical extermination. Jews from the territories directly controlled by Hitler were concentrated in camps in occupied Poland; and the governments allied to Hitler were pressed to deport their Jews to the same destination. There they were destroyed in gas chambers with gases specially designed to do the job economically and efficiently. About six million persons were exterminated between 1942 and 1944. An eye-witness described in a written report how, in one of these centres, men, women and children were packed naked into the chambers, of a volume of 45 cubic metres and each containing 750 persons; how they were kept waiting in this state for 2 hours and 49 minutes until the gas could be turned on; and how 32 minutes later the last victim was dead.[12] The Romanian government of Marshal Ion Antonescu refused to deport its Jews to the death camps. So did the Hungarian regent Admiral

Horthy until March 1944, after which the Hungarian government led by General Döme Sztojay complied with Hitler's wishes. The exception were the Jews of the city of Budapest. Horthy personally protected them, and thousands of individual Hungarian families helped to give Jews refuge.[13]

Some of these things became known in Palestine, and the mood of the Jewish leaders grew more frantic. As the danger to the Middle East receded, the need to defend British interests diminished. In the international Zionist movement, Weizmann, who remained devoted to Britain, had lost much of his influence. David Ben Gurion, who now became the outstanding leader, demanded, at an extraordinary Zionist conference held in the Biltmore Hotel in New York from 9 to 11 May 1942, that unrestricted Jewish immigration into Palestine should be allowed, and that a Jewish state be established after the war. As the British refused these demands, the Jewish community in Palestine was in effect in a state of hostilities with the British. The *Irgun Zvai Leumi* resorted to armed terror against British soldiers and civilians. Lord Moyne, the British minister resident in the Middle East, was assassinated in Cairo on 6 November 1944. There followed four years of guerrilla warfare in Palestine, of international diplomacy and of argument in the United Nations. Both the United States and the Soviet Union supported the creation of the state of Israel. The British government stated that, when the Mandate ended in May 1948, British forces would be withdrawn.

The operation of British rule in the last years in effect favoured the Arabs: the Jews, who were a numerical minority, could only arm and organise themselves in spite of British repression. They faced not only resistance from the Palestinian Arabs but invasion by the armies of the neighbouring states. On 14 May 1948 the provisional parliament, the Zionist National Council, proclaimed the state of Israel in Tel Aviv. The widespread expectation that Israel would be crushed was belied by events. The *kibbutzim* and other local communities defended themselves, a regular army was formed, and on 24 February 1949 an armistice was signed with Egypt, followed in the next five months by armistices with Transjordan, Lebanon and Syria. At the cost of 14,000 casualties in a Jewish population of 650,000, a Jewish state was established in more than half of Palestine.

### Israel

The new state was small and underpopulated, since the greater part of the Arab population had fled or been expelled. The Israeli leaders were determined to attract as many Jewish immigrants as possible. Any person of Jewish origin was given by Israeli law the right to become an Israeli citizen. The first flood of immigrants came mainly from Europe, consisting of persons who had good reason to believe that there was no future for Jews in the countries of their birth. In the 1950s the European influx diminished, but immigrants from Asian and African countries increased, as renewed crises in the relations between Israel and countries of Arabic speech led to the destruction of Jewish communities in those lands (in particular, in Iraq, Morocco and Egypt). By 1970 more than 1,300,000 immigrants had come to Israel, of whom 604,451 were from Europe and America and 711,582 from Asia and Africa. The immigrants in the course of time produced children and grandchildren. Of a total Jewish population in Israel of 2,561,000 in 1970, 1,182,000 (46 per cent) had been born there (of whom 234,000 were children of parents born in Israel); 704,100 had been born in Europe or America; and 674,400 had been born in Asia or Africa.[14]

The non-Jewish population remaining in Israel in 1950-51 numbered 173,400; by 1968 it had grown to 406,000.[15] The majority had fled; some of the consequences of the flight and expulsions have been discussed above.[16]

The total Jewish population of Israel was of course only a minority of the number of Jews in the world. In 1948 it was nearly 6 per cent, and in 1972 it was about 20 per cent. The largest Jewish community in the world was in the United States (5,800,000). In the Soviet Union in 1970 the number of Jews was estimated as 2,151,000.[17] Thus the Jews have been since 1948, like the Armenians and the Greeks but unlike the Jews before the creation of Israel, a people with both a homeland and a diaspora. The diaspora is however more numerous than the population of the homeland.

Israel had to face from the beginning the implacable hostility of all the states of Arabic speech, and especially of Egypt, Jordan and Syria. This hostility proved to be the single most important factor in welding the Jewish people of Israel, of such diverse origins, into a single nation. The Arab states refused to admit the existence of Israel, and refused to establish regular diplomatic or commercial relations with it. In practice, contacts across the frontiers were sporadic and on a very small scale. Three times after 1949 Israel fought a war against its neighbours: in November 1956, at the time of the international 'Suez' crisis; in June 1967, after the Egyptian attempt to blockade the Gulf of Aqaba; and in October 1973, when Egyptians and Syrians attacked Israeli-held territory which had formerly been theirs. On the first two occasions the Israeli army won at once overwhelming victories; and on the third, after some reverses due to surprise, they drove their assailants back. Arab hostility however remained unchanged.

The second factor which welded the Israelis together was the use of Hebrew as the language of private and public intercourse. The pioneering work of Ben Yehuda has already been mentioned. A modern imaginative literature in Hebrew appeared, and the Hebrew press and broadcasting flourished. At first there were difficulties about the forms of Hebrew

(Ashkenazy, Sephardic and Yemenite), and still more about the pronunciation. The older generation of Jews from Eastern Europe continued to express themselves more easily in the language of their land of birth (German, Polish, Russian, Romanian, Hungarian and most of all Yiddish), but they learned to speak Hebrew as a new language. Their children grew up speaking Hebrew. The pronunciation favoured in public life (and especially promoted by broadcasting) was closer to the Asian, Yemeni form; indeed closer to Arabic than to European languages. The complete acceptance by young Israelis of Hebrew, and their development of it as a vigorous semitic language, was of the greatest psychological importance. It helped all Israelis to think of themselves as the people of the country, a people of the Middle East, not as an appendix to Europe.

The third factor, of great but barely measurable importance, in the creation of Israeli national consciousness was the Judaic religion. Israel was intended to be a secular state, and many of the political leaders after 1948 were not believers. The party system, however, made it necessary for governments to enlist the support of the religious parties and, in return for this, concessions had to be made—in particular, the refusal of civil marriage and restrictions to ensure respect for the Sabbath. However, the influence of Judaism on the life of Israelis, and on the formation of Israeli national consciousness, can certainly not be explained in terms of party manoeuvres, or limited to professed believers. The moral and cultural heritage of Judaism is much wider, and is certainly not less than the influence of the Christian heritage on the secularised societies of Europe and America. The important difference is of course that Judaism is limited to Jews, and the religious heritage thus directly reinforces national consciousness.

Thus all three main factors, identified in the first chapter as important to the formation of national consciousness—state, language and religion—operated in the case of Israel. An Israeli nation emerged. It is also very important that the artificial social structure, characteristic of Jewish communities in the diaspora, ceased to exist. Jewish talents in business and in the intellectual professions were of course richly available in Israel, but all the other social groups required in an advanced urbanised and industrial society—workers in industry, transport and agriculture, clerical employees and civil and military government servants—were also provided by Jews.

The international danger inevitably strengthened national unity; but this does not mean that the Israeli nation was not, like other nations, divided by conflicts of interests and ideas. There was a wide range of political parties, from left-wing socialists through the dominant *Mapai* to conservative religious groups. Another basic division, perhaps more important, was between Jews of European and of Oriental origin. The commanding posts were overwhelmingly in the hands of Europeans, who had been committed for longer to the Zionist cause, and who were better educated, than their fellow-immigrants from Asia and Africa. Discontent grew among the Oriental Jews in the early 1970s: a minority of the latter half-seriously described themselves as 'Black Power'. Connected with this was the division between generations. Younger Israelis were growing impatient with the political orthodoxy and patriotic puritanism of the *kibbutz* elite and founding fathers of the state. They would have liked less emphasis on defence, wider horizons of ideas and reconciliation with the Arabs. Yet to like something is not to obtain it, and Arab hostility remained implacable.

The Israeli nation remained only a part of the world Jewish community, yet was inextricably connected with it. Jews in America, of whom some were Zionists and some were not, provided economic aid; and the West German government, sincerely moved by a desire, shared probably by most Germans, to make some amends for German cruelty to Jews, provided a sum of reparations to the Israeli government and another sum twice as large in the form of payments to individual victims of Nazism. American and German economic resources proved essential to maintain the Israeli economy.

Independence had been supported by the Soviet Union in 1948. However, the Soviet leaders had inherited the Russian left-wing socialists' dislike of Zionism, and ruthlessly discouraged any interest shown by their Jewish subjects in Israel. The official Soviet view was that the old 'Jewish question' of the times of the tsars had been 'solved' as a result of the Bolshevik Revolution. It is true that in the first years of the regime the relative situation of Jews in Russia greatly improved, and that there were many Jews in leading positions in the communist party, in government service and in nationalised industry. The victory of Stalin over Trotsky and Zinoviev was to some extent a victory of Russian over Jewish communists (though Stalin himself was not a Russian). In the Great Purge of 1936-39 Jewish victims were very numerous. Jews became increasingly suspect to Stalin by reason of the fact that Jewry as such was an international community, and that thousands of Russian Jews had relatives abroad. In the last months of Stalin's life an unmistakable anti-semitic trend appeared in the Soviet press and public life. This diminished in the late 1950s, but reappeared as Soviet foreign policy became increasingly committed to supporting the Arab states. At the end of the 1960s, anti-semitism, which Soviet spokesmen insisted was only 'anti-Zionism', led in practice to much discrimination against Soviet subjects who were Jews. In the face of worldwide criticism, the Soviet government began to allow Soviet Jews to emigrate to Israel. To do so, these Jews had to experience economic and physical persecution, yet many thousands made this choice.

Considerable Jewish communities remained in Romania and Hungary, while in Poland a small number returned from exile in the Soviet Union. In all three countries, Jews were prominent in the leadership of the communist parties in the early 1950s. The Romanian government allowed Romanian Jews to leave for Israel, and most in fact did so. Romania established good relations with Israel, and maintained them despite Soviet disapproval. Most of those Hungarian Jews who had escaped the deportations of 1944 remained in Hungary. It seemed that anti-semitism was greatly reduced. In the Hungarian Revolution of 1956 there were Jews among the leaders both of the old regime and of the revolutionaries. The evidence does not support the view that the revolutionary movement, which for a time swept the whole country, was anti-semitic. It was in Poland, with its tiny remnant, that anti-semitism was most evident. It was encouraged by the government of Wladyslaw Gomulka for the same reason as by some of the ministers of the tsars—that it provided a scapegoat for popular discontent. Polish Jews were subjected to persecution, and then in effect expelled to Israel in a humiliating manner.

The Israelis of 1970 had much of which to be proud. They had made the desert to flower, they had built excellent modern industries, schools and universities, and they had one of the best armies in the world. Above all, they had become a nation, with an honourable place among the nations of the world.

The Zionists had been proved right. The hopes of civilised and humane Jews like Oszkár Jászi, that within a socially reformed Hungary, granting national and cultural equality to all its citizens, the Hungarian Jews could find their fulfilment, and the 'Jewish question' would cease to exist, had been disappointed—not only in Hungary but in all the European countries which had large Jewish communities. The arguments of the assimilationists, derived from nineteenth century liberal and socialist ideas, had been refuted by the realities of the barbarous twentieth century. Six million Jews were exterminated, and the Zionist survivors had to fight desperately. Some of them had not disdained in their turn to murder British officials and soldiers, to massacre the population of an Arab village and to drive hundreds of thousands of Arabs from their homes.

The Zionist triumph was won by inflicting brutal injustice on hundreds of thousands who were guilty only of wishing to keep their homeland. The Jews, who had suffered the greatest oppression in human history, themselves became invaders and conquerors. They had no choice. They had to build their own state, assure a refuge to their people, and remove them from dependence on the goodwill of host nations, none of whom could ever be trusted again. The Arabs were in their way, and they suffered. They replied with ineffective but fanatical hatred.

Israel was stronger in the early 1970s than were the Arab states, and the help given by Israel's friends was more effective, and was inspired by more genuine sympathy, than was the help received by the Arab states from those who professed to be their friends. Israel was no mere transient crusader state, a creation of feudal lords dependent on lukewarm kinsmen far away, awaiting a Saladin to destroy it. The compact Israeli nation was more formidable than that. Yet human reason could not accept that there could be no end to the merciless hatred, to the legacy of unnumbered cruelties and counter-cruelties, wrought by Christians and Jews and Muslims against each other. The end could certainly be brought no nearer by the brash contempt of shallow minds for the three great religions which arose on the borders of the desert beyond the eastern shore of the Mediterranean, or by any attempt to replace them by the ritual incantations of secular ideologies. The guilt for the cruelties was not confined to the Middle East; it was shared in varying degrees by the peoples of all Europe and most of America. There was little sign in the early 1970s of the effort of imagination, compassion and labour required for reconciliation.

Meanwhile the Israelis saw no salvation but to man the walls of the citadel; and the Palestinian Arabs saw no way but to rail against all who could not or would not give them back their homes and to kill any, Jew or Gentile, whose death might be of use to them.

### Overseas Indians

The abolition of slavery in British territories in 1833 deprived British owners of sugar plantations of cheap labour. The gap was filled by recruiting workers on contract (indenture) from British India.[18] The conditions in which these men were transported, housed and employed were little better than those formerly endured by African slaves. Protests in Britain, supported by government officials in India, caused the traffic to be stopped in 1837; but it was renewed, with some attempt to make rules for better protection of the workers, in 1843. The main recipient was at first the Indian Ocean island of Mauritius, followed by Trinidad, Jamaica and Guyana in the Caribbean, and the British colony of Natal in South Africa.

The first indentured emigrants came from the hill tribes on the borders of Bengal and Bihar, then from the heavily populated Ganges valley. In the 1870s this outflow from the north-east was far surpassed by that from the south, consisting of Tamils or Telugus. The main objective was Ceylon, followed by Burma. In the 1890s indentured Indian labourers built the railway from the east coast of Africa into Uganda. In the first years of the twentieth century the rubber plantations in Fiji became important. There was also a genuinely voluntary emigration, on quite a large scale, of persons seeking a living in commerce. These were especially to be found on the east coast of Africa, and inland to Uganda.

Some of the indentured labourers made their way back to their homes in

India, but most stayed in the lands to which they had been brought. Some improved their lot, becoming independent farmers or businessmen, or rising through the imperial education system into the modern professions. The great majority remained agricultural labourers, dwarf holders or workers in industry or mines. The Indians remained alien both to their imperial rulers and to the indigenous populations whose lands they shared. Poor Indians tended to be seen by the indigenous poor as rivals undercutting their means of livelihood and as followers of religions unknown to them; while prosperous Indians appeared as economic exploiters. The imperial rulers found them convenient, not only as cheap labourers but also as traders, clerks or professionals; but though individual British officials might show sympathy or understanding for their predicament and for their culture, most resident white men viewed them with a contempt born of ignorance. In all these respects the position of the overseas Indians resembled that of the Jews in pre-modern Western and in modern Eastern Europe.

In the 1970s there were three main types of situation in which overseas Indians found themselves.

In Ceylon and Burma they lived among peoples who had been in contact for centuries with Indian culture, who had received Buddhism from India, and who had cultures of their own in no way inferior to that of India. In Ceylon in the early 1970s there were more than three million Indians. In Burma there were over a million before the Second World War, most of whom were compelled to leave when Burma became independent. In Malaya in 1972 there were 1,230,000 Indians, a smaller community than the other two coexisting cultures, the Muslim (Malay) and the Chinese.

The second type of situation was in Africa, where the Indians lived among peoples of a lower level of culture. The parallel with the Jewish predicament in Europe was striking.

The Indians of Natal had a substantial and talented professional elite, whose members were all the more disliked by their white English-speaking South African neighbours because they had shown themselves capable of operating by European political and professional standards. It was the action of the London-trained lawyer Gandhi in defence of Indians in South Africa which led to the decision of the government of India finally to abolish indentured labour throughout the empire in 1917. The Indians of Natal were anti-colonial radicals, and as such had theoretical sympathy for the rights of the Africans, but relations between them were not good except at the top level of the two political elites. Indians no less than Africans suffered from *apartheid* policies in South Africa after 1948, but mutual antipathy, based on racial, economic and religious grounds, remained strong. It was violently expressed in the anti-Indian riots in Durban in 1949. In the 1970s a certain trend was however observable on both the white and the Indian side to recognise a common interest in the face of rising African nationalism.

In the British colonies in East Africa, Indian politicians, and still more the governments of independent India, had supported African anti-colonial movements, and expressed pleasure at the independence of Kenya, Tanganyika (later Tanzania) and Uganda. The new governments, however, were eager (like the governments of East European states fifty to a hundred years earlier) to develop commercial and professional classes from their own peoples, and adopted policies of Africanisation, designed to replace Indians by Africans (as earlier in Eastern Europe to replace Jews or Greeks by Romanians, Hungarians or Turks). Measures were directed in the first instance against those who had not opted for African citizenship.[19] Pressure in Kenya and Tanzania was comparatively mild, but in Uganda General Idi Amin in August 1972 ordered a mass expulsion of Indian holders of British passports. A large number of these unfortunate people were allowed to enter Britain, but there were innumerable legal quibbles which helped to swell political passions and racial prejudices. The outlook for Indians in East Africa, even for those who had accepted local citizenship, remained bleak. Their situation seemed much closer to that of the defenceless Jewish communities in Europe in the late 1930s than of the Chinese in south-east Asia in the 1970s. The Chinese were protected both by their own efforts and by the great prestige possessed by China in world affairs. The Indian government possessed no such prestige, and showed remarkably little interest in the fate of Indians abroad, except as one more excuse to indulge in selective anti-imperialist rhetoric.

The third type of situation was in the former plantation colonies in the Caribbean, and in the Indian and Pacific oceans. Here the Indian immigrants shared the country, in something like equal numbers, with immigrant Africans descended from slaves or (in the case of Fiji) with an indigenous people of comparatively primitive culture.[20] Here the Indians were not, as in the first two situations described above, minorities but were, as much as any other community, the people of the country. These territories, which had attained sovereign independence by the 1970s, had the task of creating new nations from disparate elements, among which the Indian was the most gifted.

Of these four territories, Mauritius seemed to have the best prospects. The Indians were sufficiently predominant to be able to divide into political groups rather than cling to a monolithic unity. Optimists could hope that from the variety of French, English, Hindu and Muslim cultures a plural society might develop acceptable to all.

In Fiji, before independence came into effect in 1972, the Fijians secured various forms of protection, in education, in government employment and in the electoral system, against the dangers of Indian political or economic dominance: the situation was not unlike that of Malays in Malaya in regard to Chinese. Fiji started its independence no less divided than had Malaya.

In Trinidad the Indians were mainly agricultural labourers. Indians worked in the sugar plantations, blacks in cocoa plantations and in the more recently developed petroleum industry. A much higher proportion of blacks than of Indians were urban. The electoral victory in 1956 of the People's National Movement led by Dr Eric Williams was a victory for black nationalism. Once in power, however, Dr Williams found himself forced to carry out policies which conflicted with his earlier social radicalism. On his left appeared Black Power groups, against which he was compelled to use military force in 1970. The Indians were unhappy with the Williams regime, but Black Power threatened them still more.

The most difficult situation was in Guyana. Here, as in Trinidad, the urban population were blacks, and the rural were Indians (except in the sparsely inhabited south, where Amerindian peoples still survived). The willingness of Indians to work hard for low wages undercut the blacks' standard of living. In the last years of British rule the Indians were under-represented in teaching and in clerical jobs in the administration, but rather successful in the professions, and to a lesser extent in business. In 1951 an Indian dentist named Cheddi Jagan founded the People's Progressive Party, pledged to unite blacks and Indians on a socialist programme. The party's communist orientation was an advantage in providing a certain clarity of vision and cement of discipline, but a disadvantage in that it alarmed the British authorities, and still more the United States government. In 1953, when PPP won a majority of the elected seats in the colonial legislature, the governor suspended the constitution. In 1955 the party split on racial lines: most of its black supporters followed Forbes Burnham into a rival People's National Congress. After ten years of rivalry between PPP and PNC, and a change of electoral law beneficial to the latter, PPP was at last reduced to a minority, and in 1966 Guayana became independent. As Jagan's followers saw it, a radical attempt at a multiracial socialist policy had been frustrated first by British repression and then by American intrigues, and antagonism between Indian and black had been encouraged in order to preserve capitalism.

In none of these cases was there much sign of an emergent national consciousness. In the two Caribbean cases, the Indian communities, living half a world away from India, were threatened both by internal Black Power forces and by the possibility of territorial expansion from either Venezuela or Brazil.[21]

**Chinese and Malaysians**

The links between China and southern Asia go back to ancient times. The Chinese word *Nanyang* means the 'southern ocean', and the Nanyang territories are those which Chinese have reached by sea, and in which Chinese communities have grown up. Strictly speaking, the expression covers only the islands, from the Philippines to Sumatra, and the Malay Peninsula.

Thailand only partly belongs, since the earliest Chinese communities there resulted from contact overland. However, in the nineteenth century Chinese immigrants also came by sea, when Bangkok became a centre of European trading interests. There is another important difference between Thailand's relation to China and that of the islands and peninsula. The Thais became and remained Buddhists, and this was a powerful link between the two cultures. Thais and Chinese intermarried on a large scale, and as the two physical types are not very different it was quite impossible to judge, in the twentieth century, what proportion of the population of Thailand was of partly Chinese descent.

The peoples of the islands were for a long period under Hindu or Buddhist influence, but as we have noted earlier, Islam steadily gained ground, and prevailed in most of the islands and the peninsula before the arrival of the Europeans, who in their turn made Christian converts, especially in the Philippines. The gulf separating Chinese from Muslim or Christian culture was of a different order from the differences between Thai and Chinese Buddhism; and the physical differences between the Chinese and the peoples who may be loosely comprehended under the name Malaysian were also far greater and far more consciously perceived, than between Chinese and Thais or Khmers. Intermarriage was much less frequent.

As early as the fifth century Chinese Buddhist pilgrims made sea voyages to the south, and trade began to develop. Under the Sung dynasty there were already Chinese trading communities in the Philippines and Java. The encouragement given by the Sung rulers to Chinese enterprise in the Nanyang was continued by the Yuan. In 1293 a large Chinese fleet was sent to conquer Java but failed. The early Ming rulers discouraged private trade, but sought to promote trade through official missions only. Between 1405 and 1433 the Chinese admiral Cheng Ho repeatedly visited the islands and the peninsula, and even crossed the Indian Ocean to the east coast of Africa. Links between China and the now substantial overseas Chinese communities increased in the second half of the seventeenth century. During this period the Manchu rulers had established their authority in most of China, but supporters of the defeated Ming were holding out in the southern provinces, backed by the wealth and naval power of overseas

Chinese. After the final Manchu victory, thousands of southern Chinese emigrated to the Nanyang.

When the Malaysian world came under European commercial domination, and then direct rule, between the end of the sixteenth and the end of the eighteenth centuries, the Chinese, though distrusted by both Europeans and Malaysians, became useful to both owing to their economic skills. When China too experienced indirect European domination, Chinese subjects could no longer be prevented from seeking jobs in the south. From the 1830s Chinese workers mined tin in Malaya, and the development of rubber on a big scale in Malaya from the beginning of the twentieth century brought thousands more. There was also a considerable influx of refugees from the Taiping rebellion in the 1860s. Many Chinese returned home after some years, but many also remained. Modern European capitalism offered trading and banking opportunities to Chinese merchants (including self-made men who had started as labourers), and careers to Chinese entrants into the modern intellectual professions which capitalism brought with it. The island of Singapore, acquired by Britain in 1819, developed into the main economic centre of the whole Asian south-east, and its population became overwhelmingly Chinese, about 1,500,000 out of 2,000,000 at the end of the 1960s. In Malaya excluding Singapore the Chinese in the early 1960s formed about 36 per cent of the total population, being chiefly concentrated in the western coastal regions. It was estimated that there were something like two and a half million Chinese each in Thailand and Indonesia and three-quarters of a million in the Philippines, but these are not precise figures. There was a clear difference between the last three countries, where the Chinese were minorities within much larger populations, and Malaya (with or without Singapore), where they were one of the constituent communities.

The predicament of the Chinese in these lands recalls the predicament of the Jews in medieval and modern Europe. The Chinese communities were easily distinguishable from the peoples among whom they lived. Their superior commercial and intellectual talents, and their propensity to rational rather than emotional behaviour, gave them the same capacity for successful careers, for the same sorts of reasons, and provoked the same type of jealousy and of bureaucratic restrictions. The rulers, like medieval European kings or great landowners, found them useful, protected them as long as that was convenient, and made scapegoats of them when it was not: the pogroms of Chinese in the Philippines under Spanish rule in 1602 and 1639 and under Dutch rule in Java in 1740 have their European precedents. The difference is that the rulers, unlike the indigenous kings and aristocrats in Europe, were as foreign to their Philippine or Javanese subjects as were the Chinese. At the same time the Chinese incurred the hostility of the Filipinos and Indonesians not only because they were richer than they, and exploited them economically, but because they appeared to them (though for the most part wrongly) to be instruments of the foreign rulers. This is also true of the attitude of the Malayan population to the Chinese; but the British rulers of Malaya did not use the Chinese as scapegoats, not because they were more noble than the Spaniards or Dutch but because they knew that the Chinese were absolutely indispensable to the economic welfare of their colony.

The overseas Chinese had one characteristic which the Jews had never had: they belonged to a civilisation whose centre was a vast and potentially strong empire. The overseas Chinese gave generously to the Chinese patriotic and reforming exiles of the late nineteenth century, especially to Sun Yat-sen. When the Kuomintang came to power in China, it expected the Nanyang Chinese to bring up their children as nationally conscious Chinese. Cultural consciousness had always been strong among the overseas Chinese: now a priority of political loyalty was being demanded which was bound to create difficulties both for them and for the rulers of the lands in which they lived, first for the colonial powers and then for the independent governments of the 1940s and 1950s. Things became still more complex when the Kuomintang was challenged by the communists in China, and when the Malayan Chinese followers of the communists organised first a successful resistance movement, coordinated with the British military headquarters in Colombo, against the Japanese occupation, and then from 1948 onwards an efficient but ultimately unsuccessful guerrilla against the restored British authority in Malaya.

Thailand, which had treated Chinese more liberally than the colonial powers, perhaps because the Thai kings exercised more absolute power and were therefore able to protect a community which was useful to them, tightened the pressure after the *coup d'état* by a nationalist general in 1932, and still more so in the years of satellite relationship to Japan from 1940 to 1945. As in Indonesia and the Philippines, the main problems were citizenship and schools. Some Chinese were willing to be assimilated, to regard themselves as citizens of the country in which they lived, and to be educated in its schools, or in European schools authorised by its government. Others insisted that they were citizens of China, required their children to be taught in a Chinese language in schools designed to promote Chinese culture, and at the same time expected to enjoy the same opportunities and protection as citizens of the country. There were of course variations between these two extremes. Citizenship laws varied in theory and in practice, but the trend in the 1950s was to squeeze out the Chinese schools. Chinese communities fared better in Thailand than in the Philippines or Indonesia.

Attitudes of governments also depended on the governments' attitude to the communist rulers of China. The Thai leaders were hostile, and so feared communist subversion from the Chinese community, and this tended also to be the case in the Philippines. In Indonesia under Sukarno, public attitudes to Mao Tse-tung's China were friendly, and a mutually satisfactory Dual Nationality Agreement was signed in 1955. In practice this was not always generously applied, and it was always possible to justify hostile actions towards Chinese on the grounds that the persons affected were capitalistic, pro-Kuomintang Chinese. When Sukarno was overthrown in 1965, the ensuing massacres of Indonesian communists were combined with pogroms against Chinese in which thousands perished, and still more thousands lost their possessions and were expelled from the country or driven from rural districts into a few overcrowded cities.

In Malaya great efforts were made not only by the British rulers but also by the leaders of both communities to prevent the communist insurrection from bringing about a racial conflict between all Chinese and all Malays. Two political parties emerged. The United Malay National Organisation (UMNO) was led by nationalist intellectuals from the Malay community, and steadily increased its popular support. The Malayan Chinese Association (MCA) represented the non-communist Chinese. The two parties formed an alliance in 1953, and gradually the negative conviction that they must combine or perish began to develop into something like mutual trust. In 1957 Malaya became an independent state, with the Alliance in power. It had been intended to include Singapore, and such was the wish of the leading Singapore politicians; but the prospect of increasing the proportion of Chinese in the population to little short of half, and to more than that of Malays, was unacceptable to the Malay leaders. After six years of diplomacy by the British and other governments concerned, a solution was found. A new and larger state was created, with the name of Malaysia. The increase in the number of Chinese by the inclusion of Singapore was to be balanced by an increase in the number of Malay-related people through the inclusion of two British territories in Borneo. This solution however created a new problem. The Indonesian government of Sukarno, whose territorial claims had hitherto been limited to lands which had once been Dutch, declared that British Borneo should be part of a single island of Kalimantan within Indonesia. The hostilities which then developed on the island came to an end when Sukarno was overthrown in 1965.

However, before this Singapore had seceded. The expectation of the Malay leader Tungku Abd-ul-Rahman that the Chinese would be content to run economic life while leaving control of the government machinery to Malays, was not fulfilled. The vigorous party of Lee Kuan Yew, the Singapore premier, began to compete for Chinese mainland votes, and the UMNO leaders pressed the Tungku to expel Singapore from the federation. This in fact happened. Thereafter Singapore survived as an independent republic, and the situation of the Chinese on the mainland became more insecure.

The understanding on which government by the Alliance, on the

Malayan mainland, had been based—that Malay should be the official language, that Malays should be privileged in the allocation of posts in the political administration, and that the employment of Chinese in business and in the professions (in reality, Chinese domination of those sectors) should be accepted by the Malays—began to break down in 1969. The election campaign of that year showed that there was large-scale defection from the Alliance by both Malays and Chinese—by Malays in the direction of Panmalaysian or militant Muslim policies, by Chinese in the direction of militant assertion of Chinese equal opportunities in government. This trend reached a climax in violent riots between Malays and Chinese in Kuala Lumpur on 13 May 1969, two days after the election.

In the mid-1970s the Chinese in Malaya were less vulnerable than the Chinese in Indonesia, but it was far from sure that in the long term this would continue. Their situation, and that of Singapore, would soon deteriorate if the new tendency towards cooperation between Malaysia and Indonesia (in itself admirable as a step towards peace) should lead to coordinated policies designed to crush the Nanyang Chinese. It is true that Indonesia was not a very attractive model for Malays in the mid-1970s. Its material prosperity and educational opportunities were far inferior to those of Malaya. Moreover, it was a country of over 100 million people, with many languages and a variety of rather impressive traditional cultures: if submerged in it, Malay identity might disappear altogether. However, it would be unwise to assume that this relative unattractiveness would be permanent. The idea of solidarity between the island and peninsular peoples of Malaysian culture, formerly expressed by Sukarno in the slogan *Maphilindo*,[22] was far from realisation in the mid-1970s, but should not be lightly dismissed as an aspiration. The notion of some hundred and fifty million Malaysians as a world force had potential attraction for the rising generation all over the Malaysian world.

The policies of the government of Malaysia rejected such a dream. They aimed instead to create a single Malaysian nation—not in the broad cultural sense of the word, but in the narrower political and legal sense of those inhabiting the sovereign state of Malaysia. Within this state persons of Malay and Chinese origin were to enjoy complete equality as citizens. The Malaysian government was certainly determined to prevent any repetition of the events of 1969, and did not hesitate to pursue more authoritarian policies to this end. Yet it was not inaccessible to pressure from the Malay population, and the population was certainly less enlightened in its attitude to the Chinese than was the government. It remained government policy that Malays were to be politically 'more equal' than the Chinese, and it was therefore reasonable to wonder for how long into the future the Malays who held political power were going to go on allowing the Chinese to be economically 'more equal' than the Malays. This question was made more acute by the growing unemployment among Malays, and the growing inability of the state machine to employ the growing output by the secondary schools of young Malays who had been encouraged to expect clerical or executive jobs. The need for young Malays to seek jobs in business, a Chinese preserve, was bound to grow.

Thus it seemed likely that the authorities hoped that, with the development of Malay as the official language, and with the rise of a new generation which had been taught in Malay-language schools, the Chinese would be gradually not only 'Malaysianised', in the sense of putting their loyalty to a bilingual Malaysian nation before their loyalty to Chinese culture, but also 'Malayanised', in the sense of being absorbed in a Malay culture based on the Malay language. The similarities to the concept of equal political rights cherished by the Magyarisers in pre-1918 Hungary were rather striking. However, the Chinese were being asked to renounce membership of one of the greatest world civilisations—a good deal more than the Magyarisers had asked of the Slovaks.

In Singapore, the Chinese were in an overwhelming majority, but their identity was in doubt. Hongkong was a Chinese land, ruled by a foreign government but destined within a few decades to be reunited with China; and Taiwan was a part of China which for the time being had a Chinese government different from that which ruled the mainland. Singapore was neither of these things. It was an island of people of Chinese origin, impregnated in varying degrees with Chinese culture, but open to all the economic and intellectual influences of the world, one of the great marketplaces of humanity. There were disagreements between those Singapore Chinese who stressed the world-wide role, and tended to favour use of the world-wide language English on equal terms with Chinese, and those who insisted on the priority of Chinese culture: the controversy was visible in school policies and in economic life. Some believed that a Singaporean nation could be formed, bearing the mark of its Chinese cultural origin yet differing from the Chinese nation as the Australian nation differed from the English. Yet even if no definite Singaporean national consciousness developed, there might yet be a place in that part of the world for something more like the trading republics of the past in the Mediterranean and Baltic and on the coasts of East Africa and Arabia; and perhaps this form of polity might even appear in other parts of the archipelago, in which attempts to introduce the European type of centralised sovereign state and uniform national consciousness had not been conspicuously successful.

# 11 Class and Nation

To define class is as difficult as to define nation; yet both have long existed and been known to exist. I have argued that none of the many attempts to define nation have been fully successful, and I have been unable to provide a definition which both covers all nations and excludes all communities that are not nations. Instead I have tried only to narrow the limits within which discussion of the nature of the nation makes sense. I should like to try to do the same for the class. Division of societies into classes clearly has something to do with wealth, with economic function, with professional outlook and with social prestige. The classical Marxist linking of classes with a specific function in the process of production has much to commend it. If we use the word 'class' solely in this sense, then we can at least minimise confusion of thought. It means however that classes are in effect reduced to four: landowners, peasants, capitalists and wage-earning workers.

These Marxian categories seem to me inadequate in regard to the middle strata of the social pyramid. Here there are several important social groups which do not have a specific relation to the process of production: for example, army officers, civil bureaucrats, priests and members of intellectual professions. Soviet Marxists, while recognising that these groups sometimes play an important role in social and political struggles, tend to regard them as satellites of the dominant class, which consists of landowners (in the 'feudal' era), of businessmen (in the 'capitalist' era) or of workers (in the 'socialist' era). Thus, Soviet writers will refer from time to time to 'feudal intelligentsia', 'bourgeois intelligentsia' or 'toiling intelligentsia'. In my opinion, though these distinctions are not without value they are not adequate. Moreover, the words 'feudal' and 'bourgeois' are too ambiguous to help analysis. These points will be discussed later. It must suffice now to say that the social categories, whose relations with national movements I shall discuss, will be more numerous than the four principal Marxist categories. Whether all the categories which I shall discuss are 'classes' or not, seems to me a rather obscure semantic question. Essentially, I am concerned with all social groups which exercise, as groups, a significant influence on political power.

The discussion in this chapter is concerned with the role of different social groups in the formation of nations and in both the leadership and the membership of national movements. It will be most convenient to consider this relationship between class and nationality in the following historical situations, which will be familiar to those who have read the preceding chapters: old nations of Europe with a continuous history as nations; old continuous nations outside Europe; new nations of America; new nations of lands recently emancipated from colonial rule in Asia and Africa; and nations of the Soviet empire. After this survey some brief concluding remarks will discuss the extent to which class antagonisms have promoted or inhibited national movements, have reinforced each other or pulled against each other; that is, how far (depending on one's point of view) class struggles have damaged national unity, or national struggles have been an obstacle to class solidarity.

### 'Feudalism' and 'bourgeoisie'

I have argued in an earlier chapter that the formation of the old nations of Europe resulted from the rise of the centralised monarchical state. Clearly, this process was not achieved solely by the wish of individual monarchs, however talented and strong-willed, but was promoted also by persons and groups among the monarch's subjects. The group which was most obviously important for this process was the feudal nobility. However, the often-used simple generalisations on this subject must be treated with great care.

'Feudal' and 'feudalism' should be used in the specialised sense in which medieval historians use them. Feudalism was a complex system of social and political relationships between noblemen and monarchs, and between different levels of vassals, from powerful landowners down to serfs. 'Nobility' is also a word which comprehended persons of varying wealth and social function, who had in common a legal status: as persons who had inherited nobility from their ancestors, or on whom nobility had been conferred by their social superiors, they had certain legal rights, privileges and obligations. Yet noblemen might be immensely wealthy landed magnates, or gentry of moderate means, or poor peasants, or city dwellers with few or no landed possessions. The word 'aristocracy' is also often used vaguely. It is best to confine this word to a small number of the richest, most powerful and prestigious families.

Some Marxist historians, especially Soviet Russian, and also a large number of writers who are neither Marxist nor Soviet but have been influenced by their terminology, use the word 'feudalism' simply to describe any society which is pre-industrial and agrarian and in which a large part of the land is controlled by a small number of large landowners. This use of the word can only confuse thought, for it ignores important differences in types of ownership and tenure of land, as well as in political status and influence. I propose to use the word 'feudalism' only in relation to the medieval political and social system in Western and Central Europe; and when I am concerned with landowners as a social or economic category, I shall call them 'landowners', preceded by the appropriate adjective.

Reverting to the formation of the centralised monarchy in Western Europe, one cannot say that '*the* nobility' or '*the* landowners' either promoted or opposed this process. Some noblemen, some of whom were great aristocrats, were on the kings' side, and others were against. Many of the kings' ablest advisers and generals were eminent noblemen: so were many of the leaders of rebellions—of the Pilgrimage of Grace in England, the *Comuneros* in Castile and the *Fronde* in France. Another large and powerful body of men of which something must be said is the Catholic Church. Many outstanding kings of England and France, and many German-Roman emperors, were locked in bitter conflict with the church, whether with their own prelates or directly with Rome; but in these conflicts they also had the active support of many churchmen among their subjects. The church provided medieval Europe not only with orthodox spiritual guidance, but also with its intellectual elite and with the beginnings of a civil government. Some of the kings' first ministers were cardinals of aristocratic origin, others were persons who had started their career as humble priests. Indeed, the institution which offered the highest degree of social mobility in medieval Europe, the nearest approach to 'the career open to talents', was precisely the church. The kings, however sincerely they felt themselves to be pious Christians, were usually jealous of the church's independence and wealth; and confiscation of monastery and church lands in the sixteenth century enabled them at the same time to increase their revenues, to reward their supporters, and to parade as patriots.

It is a well-worn cliché that the centralising monarchs made use of '*the* middle class' or '*the* bourgeoisie'. There is of course much truth in this, but these words, like 'nobility' and 'feudalism', need further examination.

In almost any society at any period of time and in any part of the world, there have been middle groups, placed in terms of power and wealth between the rulers and the mass of their subjects. There are three essential functions which have had to be performed, even in rudimentary form, by these middle groups: the buying and selling of goods, the transmission and execution of the ruler's orders, and the propagation of the orthodox ideas. We may say that even a primitive society contains embryonic capitalists, bureaucrats and intellectuals. In medieval Europe the last two functions were performed by the church, the first by the urban merchants. The cities sometimes gave valuable aid to kings in their struggle against refractory noblemen; sometimes they showed themselves stubborn and successful opponents of royal power. Taking the whole process of the growth of the centralised monarchy, one may perhaps say that kings and burghers were more often allies than enemies.

The growth of trade and of learning in the late Middle Ages led to the emergence of something which can usefully be described as the West European *bourgeoisie*, or 'middle class' in the singular (*Mittelstand* in German). To an increasing extent, a new ethos came to be accepted by the middle group, an ethos whose essence was the supremacy of individual judgment and a preference for civil over military values. The spread of this ethos was connected with the movement for reform of the church. To argue whether the bourgeoisie created the Reformation, or the Reformation the bourgeoisie, is to argue whether the hen or the egg came first. The great value of the work of Max Weber and Richard Tawney in this field is that they showed the connection: they themselves did not claim to have established a scientifically certain causal sequence, and attempts of later writers to do so cannot achieve what is clearly a pointless aim. Undoubtedly the successes of individualism in economic enterprise stimulated individualism in religious belief, and both contributed to the growth of individualism in political thought. In the course of the Reformation the old intellectual elite of orthodox Catholics were replaced by new intellectual elites which, though mostly still Christian believers, recognised a much wider sphere for secular thought than had the medieval church. This secularisation of intellectual life was not confined to the lands in which the Reformation triumphed; the culture of seventeenth and eighteenth century France was arguably more secular than that of England, however much Louis XIV, by repealing the Edict of Nantes in 1685, sought to uphold Catholic authority and to penalise dissenters. It was in France that the gulf between the secular intellectual elite and the political power became deepest: neither could destroy the other, and indeed there was, since they shared pride in French power and French culture, an element of love as well as of hatred in their mutual relations.

The individualist bourgeois ethos made some impression also on civil government: it had its disciples in the bureaucracy of Louis XV and Louis XVI, even if it was not predominant. In the Protestant countries this was much more the case, especially in Holland and England, but to a large extent also in Scotland, in Sweden and even in Prussia. In these countries it is a justifiable oversimplification, which explains more than it distorts, to speak, in the singular, of *the* middle class. In France before 1789 this is more doubtful. A large part of the French intellectual elite was completely alienated from the regime; and this was true also of a part of the business class. Thus there was not a single homogeneous middle class: rather, the values of two of the middle groups (government officials and intellectual professions) were mutually opposed, while the third middle group (business class) was divided between them. The alienation of the intellectual elite certainly contributed to the outbreak, and influenced the course, of the Revolution; but it is arguable that it was only under the regime of Napoleon that a common ethos prevailed in all three middle groups, and that a single homogeneous bourgeoisie came into being.

In the mid-nineteenth century in all Europe north of the Pyrenees and Apennines, and west of the Austrian and Russian borders, there was a fairly homogeneous social and cultural category, which embraced all three middle groups. When I use the word 'bourgeois' in the following pages, I shall be referring to this category; when I want to refer to capitalists or businessmen, I shall call them 'capitalists' or 'businessmen', not 'bourgeois'. Unfortunately the word bourgeoisie is far too often used ambiguously, even by perceptive and learned historians. The wider category is not the same as the narrower, even if, as Marxist writers would argue (in my opinion, convincingly in certain precise cases, and unconvincingly in others), the capitalists are the most significant component in the wider category. Certainly, it is necessary to note the use by Soviet writers of such expressions as 'bourgeois bureaucrats' or 'bourgeois intellectuals', corresponding to the 'feudal officials' and 'feudal intellectuals' of the medieval, or simply of the pre-industrial, era. This use is perfectly intelligible, but in my mind misleading. Just as the economic dominance of large landowners in a pre-industrial society does not constitute 'feudalism', equally economic dominance of profit-seeking private capitalists does not constitute a 'bourgeois order'.

The essential point about a bourgeois order is the existence of a common ethos uniting the three middle groups in a single social and cultural category. It would of course be wrong to exaggerate the homogeneity, or to fail to see that the relative status of the three components varied between different West European societies: that in England it was the capitalists who were the most prestigious element in the bourgeoisie, in France the intellectuals, and in Prussia the bureaucrats. Nevertheless the increasing homogeneity, from the Reformation onwards and especially in the nineteenth century, is undeniable.

The growth of this homogeneous bourgeoisie was specific to the history of the part of Europe mentioned above (with certain islands of bourgeois culture beyond its borders, of which the most important were in Catalonia, Bohemia and German-speaking Austria), and to those parts of America which were colonised from that part of Europe. Elsewhere in the world the three middle groups remained sharply distinct from, though not of course uninfluenced by, each other.

If monarchs, noblemen, churchmen and bourgeois played a leading part in the process of formation of the centralised monarchical state, within which the old nations were formed, this does not mean that persons of

humbler social status played no part. The diffusion of national consciousness downwards was a long process, accelerated in periods of religious
strife or of external danger to the nation. In such periods, craftsmen and
labourers and peasant small-holders consciously identified themselves with
the nation. Examples of such periods are the Elizabethan era and the Civil
War in England, the wars of the Covenanters in Scotland, the French
Revolution and the struggle of the Spaniards against Napoleon.

## Bureaucracies and intelligentsias

In the case of those old continuous nations in whose history neither a feudal
social and political order nor a homogeneous bourgeoisie (as described
above) existed, the pattern is substantially different.

To this category belong the Russians, although they became Christian in
the tenth century, and although from the eighteenth century onwards
Russia became a European great power. Both China and Iran belong to the
same category. The case of Japan is more questionable, since undoubted
similarities to the feudal order of Western Europe may be noted; and at
least since the eighteenth century capitalists played an important part in
national culture, though it can hardly be said that there was much sign of a
European-type bourgeois ethos.

In Russia, from the time of the rise of Muscovy and the overthrow of the
Tatar yoke, that is, from the sixteenth century, the dominance of the
centralised monarchical power was overwhelming. This, as explained
earlier,[1] was due largely to the support of the church, the heir to Byzantine
traditions; and largely to the exposure to invasion of a land without
powerful natural defensive barriers, which made necessary a permanent
militarisation of the whole society. The successive monarchs who built up
the centralised Muscovite state made use of a landowning class, but
subordinated it strictly to their own needs. This was a 'service nobility',
with no rights against the monarch. Obligations did not, as in feudal
Western Europe, work both ways: the noblemen received land only in
order to enable them to provide the military forces which the monarch
needed from them. The merchants too were subordinated to the monarch:
the butcher Minin of Nizhnii Novgorod was a symbol of the patriotic
merchant class, rallying round the tsar in times of danger to the throne and
the true faith. It was only from the late eighteenth century that the nobility,
with encouragement from Empress Catherine II, hesitantly began to play a
slightly more autonomous part. In the early nineteenth century it must also
be noted that language reformers and poets, by making uniform literary
Russian into a great and beautiful language, did much to strengthen
Russian national consciousness and to extend it to lower levels of society.

However, looking back over the history of Russia, one has the impression that the emergence of a nation was no less overwhelmingly due to the growth and maintenance of the monarchical power than was the case in China.

In China the united monarchy was brought about by the victory of the First Emperor over the several small states of the previous period. In the Chinese civilisation which continued to exist for the following two thousand years, the monarchy and its comparatively centralised bureaucratic structure played a major role, though there were periods when the empire broke up into several units, and though the dynasties ruling the united empire were several times replaced by rivals after prolonged civil war. The monarchy was based on its bureaucracy, staffed by persons recruited through the examination system, designed to reward those who had mastered the traditional Chinese literary and philosophical culture based on the ideographic script. The members of this political and cultural elite are customarily described by Western writers as the *literati*. Education, hierarchical subordination and capacity to govern, rather than noble social origin, were their first priorities. The *literati* were however largely recruited from families which possessed considerable land and wealth, which gave their children the leisure necessary to acquire culture; and *literati* who rose from poor origins obtained in their careers opportunities to acquire land, and to give their own children such leisure. Thus there was a connection between landed wealth and bureaucratic eminence. The assertion that '*the* landowners' 'controlled' the government does not appear justified; nor is 'feudalism' a suitable label for the Chinese political and social system either before or after the First Emperor, for nothing similar to the complexities of feudalism in medieval Europe existed.

The development of nationalism in China in modern times was in opposition to the whole traditional structure. A new elite of European-influenced reforming or revolutionary intellectuals appeared, who challenged, and sought to replace, the traditional elite of Ch'ing China. The first reformers hoped to combine Confucian values with Western democratic ideas, and to graft representative institutions on to the Chinese system of government. Their successors were revolutionaries, who believed that the whole system must be swept away and replaced with something new. The Kuomintang movement, initiated by the revolutionary Sun Yat-sen, enlisted the support of more conservative forces. In the years of Kuomintang government the business class, which in traditional China was viewed with contempt according to Confucian doctrine (though at certain periods it included not only rich but influential men), became one of the pillars of the regime. Kuomintang nationalism in its great days had the support of bureaucrats, capitalists, landowners, intellectuals and a large part of the peasantry. One may even perhaps argue that there was a tendency towards the formation of a bourgeoisie, as defined earlier; that is to say, towards the fusion with each other of the middle groups of society. Defeat and occupation by the Japanese arrested this process, and in the following years a large part of the intellectual elite was alienated from the Kuomintang, and came to prefer its rivals, the new revolutionaries—that is, the communists. Communist victory was achieved by a new military and political elite, enjoying massive peasant and workers' support. With the communists in power, a new bureaucratic structure took shape, which was then deliberately combated by the leaders through the Cultural Revolution. This was designed precisely to prevent a crystallisation of social forces and also to repudiate the whole tradition associated with Confucianism. The results of this remarkable struggle, continuing in the 1970s, could not be predicted.

In Japan the growth of state and of nation were marked by a prolonged struggle between rulers (at first emperors, then shoguns acting in the name of emperors) and nobility. This struggle appears remarkably similar to the struggle in medieval Europe, especially perhaps in England. The application to Japanese history of the word 'feudalism' seems to have considerable justification, though it is a matter of controversy among historians. The system which became stabilised under the Tokugawa shoguns in the early seventeenth century represented a balance between the monarchical power and the nobility. During the preceding centuries, marked by frequent civil wars, the social group which had given its essential character to Japanese national identity was the warrior class, or *samurai*. They formed the cadres of the system of government, while at the highest level the balance of power between *daimyo*, or great lord, and *shogun*, or ruler, was determined by a complex system of obligations and autonomies which worked rather well. In Japan as in China, and no doubt largely as a result of Confucian influence, merchants and capitalists had an extremely low social status; yet in practice they flourished, and some of them became so essential to the political elite that they were able to exercise a good deal of influence in the later Tokugawa period. In the overthrow of the Tokugawa in 1868, and in the establishment of the new regime in the 1870s, the leading figures were samurai. This is not to say that '*the* samurai' made the Meiji Restoration, or built the new order; indeed many samurai fought for the Tokugawa, and many more followed Takamori Saigo in his revolt against the new regime in 1879. The new order was also strongly supported by businessmen, and the new rulers strongly encouraged the development of capitalism. The intellectual elite was divided. There were some who bitterly resented the Westernising tendencies of the new regime, and resolved to reassert traditional Japanese values, using to this end the new material strength which Westernisation had brought. Others felt that the new rulers had not gone nearly far enough: they wished to repudiate the past and to accept

Westernisation without reserve—whether in the form of liberalisation or, some decades later, of Marxism. Most accepted the mixture of tradition and Westernisation offered by the Meiji era rulers, and served them with the devotion and national pride which their ancestors had given to earlier rulers.

In Iran, from the Muslim conquest until the emergence of the Safavid dynasty, the continuity of rulers and of state boundaries was lost: all that survived was the idea of Iran, its language (greatly modified) and its historical mythology. The Safavid state was created by military power and religious zeal, and ruled by a balance between regional magnates, tribal chiefs, large landowners and the officials of the shah. This was true of the successors of the Safavids up to the twentieth century. In the modern nationalist movement in Iran, at the beginning of the twentieth century, the traditional intellectual elite of devout Muslims and the new intellectual elite of European-influenced democrats fought for a time side by side. The traditionalists objected to the shah's subservience to foreigners; and the bazaar merchants who were (as in other Muslim lands) devout supporters of Muslim orthodoxy, objected to the competition of Western capitalists who were favoured by the shah. The new intellectual elite objected to the shah's despotism and to his choice of ministers. They won varying degrees of support among craftsmen and workers in northern cities, and had their friends among tribal chiefs or landowners. Millions of Iranians were passive spectators of the struggle. Neither the traditional nor the new intellectual elite won; and their defeat by the shah led to bitter disagreement between them. Some of the aims of both were adopted by the new dynasty of Reza Shah and his son. In their pursuit of modern material progress and their struggle to make Iran a strong state, they fought an intermittent but increasingly successful struggle against *ulema*, bazaar merchants and landowners, while at the same time persecuting revolutionary intellectuals. Essentially, they replaced the power of local magnates by the power of a centralised bureaucracy and a modern army. The social group on whose support their power rested was this new bureaucracy, recruited from most social strata but very largely from the peasantry, which Shah Mohammed Reza undoubtedly benefited by his land reforms. The regime also had supporters in the business class and in the peasantry at large; but it alienated a large part of the European-educated elite, while the growing industrial working class was probably for the most part indifferent or hostile.

**The Polish and Hungarian cases**

Two old European nations, whose national consciousness had a continuous history for centuries but whose existence in a sovereign state was interrupted for a long period, are the Poles and the Hungarians. In both cases, the original nation, both in the legal sense of the word *natio* and in the empirical sense of the part of the people in which national consciousness was well developed, was confined to the nobility, a substantially larger stratum of the whole population than in West European medieval states but still a small minority. It was in this social group that national consciousness was preserved during the centuries of partition.

The Polish and Hungarian national movements of the nineteenth century developed in an age when the doctrine of nationalism, derived from the Enlightenment and the French Revolution, had spread throughout Europe, and when the development of capitalism was transforming social structures. Inevitably, new social groups were drawn into both the Polish and the Hungarian national movement. The leading figures in the Hungarian parliament before 1848 were noblemen, in the legal sense, and many of them were landowners. In the revolutionary regime of 1848-49—in its armed forces, deliberative and administrative bodies—landowning noblemen were prominent. The same is true of the Polish Sejm of 1815-30, of the military and political leaders of the revolutionary regime of 1830-31, and of the leadership of the 1863 rising. However, things were not so simple. Nobility is a legal category, landownership an economic. Many noblemen had very little to do with landed estates, and some did not even possess any land. In both Polish and Hungarian political life a very important figure was the noble-born member of an intellectual profession, especially the lawyer, the journalist and the university student or teacher. The outstanding example is Louis Kossuth. Others are the leaders of the conspiratorial societies in Vilna and Warsaw in the late 1820s, and the Polish revolutionary exiles between 1831 and 1863, and after 1863. In a later period, Jozef Piłsudski belongs to this category. One may say that in both countries between 1815 and 1867 the centre of gravity of nationalist leadership was steadily passing from landowning noblemen to noble-born intellectuals, and that the politically conscious sections of the intellectual professions were being steadily reinforced from non-noble strata.

In both countries there developed during the nineteenth century a substantial business class, and in both countries the businessmen consisted mainly of Jews. Both nationalist movements received some sympathy and material help from Jews. Hungarian Jews in 1848-49 supported the Revolution; the rulers of semi-independent Hungary after 1867 emancipated the Jews; and Jewish business was encouraged throughout the Dualist period. There were also Jews among the supporters of the Polish risings of 1830 and 1863.

It may perhaps be said that, at the time when the Hungarian nationalists obtained most of the substance of independence, and became able to put forward the claim that Hungary was a national state, the landowning nobility were still politically predominant, though other social groups had played an important part in achieving that relative independence. Dualist Hungary was ruled by landowning noblemen in its government, parliament and bureaucracy, and the regime counted on the active support of the intellectual professions and the business class, both of which were largely composed of Jews. Thus the ruling stratum was a combination of landowners and bureaucrats, while the remaining two of what we have called the 'middle groups' (intellectuals and capitalists) formed the middle position. There was in Dualist Hungary an undoubted development of a bourgeois ethos and a bourgeois culture, but it was confined to the intellectual and business professions, and did not, as in Western Europe, comprise the bureaucracy.

In Poland the national struggle continued for another forty years: the relative autonomy granted to Galicia under Habsburg rule from 1865 can hardly be compared with Dualism in Hungary, for it affected only about a quarter of the Polish nation. During these forty years the social composition of the Polish national movement changed. The economic position of the whole landed nobility in Russian Poland (the largest portion of the old Polish commonwealth) had been greatly weakened by the land reforms of 1864, in which the Russian government had given Polish peasants land, on extremely favourable terms, at the expense of the former landowners, in order to win them over to Russian rule and to crush the nobility which they rightly regarded as the mainstay of rebellion. Still more than in the first half of the century, the leadership of nationalism had passed to members of the intellectual professions, from whom, as in Russia itself, there emerged a new social category—the professional revolutionaries, whose political attitudes increasingly transcended the limits of the class into which they had been born. During the same period also there appeared, especially in the Prussian portion of Poland, a Polish business class. These rising Polish capitalists competed both with German and with Jewish (German-speaking) capitalists, and this competition strengthened their nationalism and also their anti-semitism. In the Austrian and Russian portions, business remained overwhelmingly in Jewish hands, which preserved the old type of anti-semitism (among peasants and in the Catholic church) but did not give rise to much of the new type of anti-semitism of rival business classes.

In Poland at the end of the nineteenth century the rapid growth of industry, and consequent growth of the industrial labour force, brought the working class into politics. The Polish Socialist Party (PPS), founded in 1892, had the usual aims of European socialist parties, but its leaders also aimed at Polish independence and unity: only a small faction led by Roza Luksemburg rejected these aims.[2] In the PPS there was a long struggle between those who gave first priority to social revolution or to national independence. The latter view was expressed above all by Piłsudski, who eventually ceased, together with his closest comrades, to be a socialist at all, but continued to enjoy much sympathy in the Polish socialist movement until the late 1920s. In Hungary the role of the working class in the national movement was minimal. Budapest workers supported the 1848 Revolution, and a few socialist intellectuals, especially Jozsef Táncsics and the poet Petöffi, played prominent parts; but at that time industrial workers were very few. At the end of the nineteenth century the Hungarian social-democratic party was more important, but it was strongly opposed to the Dualist regime, and was forced to devote itself to attempts to reconcile or eliminate the national conflicts within its own ranks due to the membership of many non-Magyars. One must thus conclude that the working class was an important element in the Polish national struggle but negligible in the Hungarian.

The Polish peasantry was also drawn into the struggle. In 1863 Polish peasants had made little response to the Rising: many were inclined to see the Polish landowners as greater enemies than the Russian government. However, the calculation of the Russian government that by giving Polish peasants the lands of Polish landowners they would win peasant gratitude proved to be quite misplaced. Once the power over them of the Polish landowners had been removed, the peasants saw very clearly that it was the Russian government which was exploiting and misruling them. When the Russian government started to try Russifying them through the schools, they became more hostile. In Prussian Poland similar results followed the policy of Bismarck and Bülow, designed to transfer land from Polish to German hands in Pomerania and Poznania, which affected peasant small-holders as well as larger landowners. The peasant parties which developed in both Russian and Austrian Poland had, it is true, economic and social aims, but their leaders and members were also resolved to defend Polish national culture and, should the opportunity ever arise, they hoped for an independent united Poland. In Hungary the role of peasants was small. It is true that Hungarian peasants supported the Revolution in 1848, that they provided the soldiers of Kossuth's army, and that the revolutionary regime abolished the remaining feudal dues. However, the Dualist regime preserved large landed estates, and refused either the vote or a land reform for the peasants. They could rely to some extent on peasant support for policies directed, with suitable demagogy, against the non-Magyar nations of Hungary; but this was a dwindling asset, increasingly counteracted by the peasants' impatience for social reform.

Thus the social composition of the national movements in Poland and

Hungary, starting from very similar conditions, remained very similar until about the 1870s; after which, while Hungary obtained a measure of national independence under an oligarchic regime, the Polish movement continued to be repressed, and in the process attracted support from the great majority of the population.

## The language manipulators

If we consider the national movements of the smaller peoples of Central and Eastern Europe, we find in two cases some resemblance to the Polish and Hungarian cases, but in the others a substantially different pattern.

In Croatia a landed nobility existed, from which in the nineteenth century emerged an intellectual elite which provided the first nationalist leadership. The pattern was very similar to the Hungarian, and was indeed doubtless influenced by it. However, in the late nineteenth century changes took place which bear some resemblance to those in Poland. In Dalmatia emerged a bourgeoisie, in the Western sense, consisting of businessmen, members of intellectual professions and a few officials. It was from them that the leadership of the Yugoslav movement developed. In the rest of Croatia the peasants became involved in politics, under the leadership of intellectuals of non-noble origin, the able organisers Ante and Stepan Radić. Their peasant movement pursued radical social reforms, but it also supported the Yugoslav idea. During these years the Croatian nobility lost most of its political influence, and tended to remain loyal to the Habsburg Monarchy, whether under the existing Dualist system or on the assumption of its replacement by a Trialist policy which was never achieved.

In Moldavia and Wallachia, which became united as the kingdom of Romania, a nobility also existed. The aristocratic families were Greeks, who had grown rich by tax-farming on behalf of the Ottoman government; but after 1821 the nobility, including those of Greek descent, mostly adopted Romanian speech and habits, and consciously played the role of leaders of a Romanian nation, furnished with the necessary historical mythology by the Romanian-speaking intellectual elite of Transylvania, subjects of the Habsburgs. The brief national revolution in Bucharest in 1848 was led by French-educated intellectuals of noble landowning background. When a Romanian state emerged, in the aftermath of the Crimean War, the leaders in the process of making the new nation were a combination of landowners, bureaucrats and members of the intellectual professions. It is worth noting that sons of the Romanian nobility, in their admiration for West European, especially French, bourgeois society, overcame the aversion to commercial activities characteristic of landed nobilities. Many of them sought a career in business, and came up against the entrenched positions of Jewish capitalists, who had poured into Moldavia, and to some extent into Wallachia, since the Russo-Turkish treaty of 1829 had opened those lands to trade. Thus Romanian anti-semitism from a rather early date acquired an element of business rivalry. Meanwhile the Romanian peasants, living in great poverty at the mercy of the landowners, were virtually excluded from the nation; while a working class barely yet existed.

In the lands of Romanian speech in the Habsburg Monarchy—Transylvania, Banat and Bukovina—the situation was different. Here only a handful of Romanians belonged to the Hungarian nobility, and none were large landowners; the government officials were Hungarians; and most merchants or small businessmen were Jews. Leadership of the Romanian national movement therefore came from the intellectual profes-sions: lawyers, schoolteachers, journalists, writers and priests, both Or-thodox and Uniate. To these must also be added a growing, though small-scale, Romanian business class. The mass of the population were peasants, most of whom consciously and strongly supported the national movement against Hungary, at first hoping for protection from the Habsburg dynasty, and then, as these hopes receded, increasingly looking for union with the kingdom of Romania, which was brought about by war in 1918.

This social composition was fairly typical of the national movements of Central and Eastern Europe. The pattern can be briefly stated, and variant combinations of social groups can then be noted.

In these small peoples, the most important single factor determining their national consciousness was, I have argued, language. It is natural that the leaders of the incipient national movements should have been those whose expertise was the manipulation of language: members of the intellectual professions, and especially grammarians, writers and journal-ists. Czechs, Transylvanian Romanians, Slovaks, Serbs, Bulgarians, Greeks, Slovenes, Ukrainians, Lithuanians, Latvians, Estonians, Finns, Tatars, and Armenians either had no landed nobility of their own or the nobility of their country had become assimilated to the culture and nationality of the ruling nation. Leadership came from those who—inspired by intellectual curiosity resulting from their access to the official system of education; by sympathy for the humble people who shared their language but knew no other; and by enthusiasm for the ideas of the Enlightenment, which reached them directly or indirectly from Vienna, Paris or even St Petersburg—studied the structure of the vernacular tongues, and worked to develop them into modern literary languages. They needed material support, which they sought from richer compatriots, or from benevolent patrons among the ruling nation; and where neither of these existed, there emerged in time, in response to the need, a class of small businessmen capable of giving financial help. This association between intellectuals and small capitalists varied from case to case.

In the first stages of the Czech 'national revival' grammarians and professors played an outstanding role, but as the nineteenth century advanced the capitalist element grew in importance. Already before 1848 many Czech peasants were prosperous, and economic progress in Bohemia made it possible to concentrate the savings of thousands of small proprietors in banks, which grew bigger and wealthier. Small industrial enterprises in Czech ownership grew into big enterprises, small Czech capitalists into big capitalists. There were also large numbers of Czechs in the Habsburg bureaucracy. All three middle groups had large Czech components, and all three were welded together by a bourgeois ethos. The well-worn phrase 'bourgeois nationalism' accurately describes the Czech national movement, but it is important to add that in the early twentieth century a large part of the numerous Czech industrial working class also supported varying degrees of nationalism.

The development of the Slovenes was rather similar. The role of language experts was even more pronounced. The struggle for Slovene nationality in the south-eastern Alps was essentially a struggle for the Slovene against the German or Italian language in the schools and churches of hundreds of villages. Priests, schoolmasters and local journalists were the leaders, and the hard-won savings of an industrious but increasingly prosperous peasantry provided the financial means, and created small Slovene capitalists. Slovene nationalism, like Czech, was bourgeois, but followed perhaps half a century behind.

The Slovak national movement started from a tiny group of intellectuals, Catholic priests and Lutheran pastors who at first acted on parallel lines rather than in direct cooperation. From these small beginnings emerged a rather larger intellectual elite, including secular writers, journalists and lawyers, and the reading public extended to at least some thousands of people including peasants. In the second half of the nineteenth century Slovak small businessmen made their appearance, again as proprietors of savings banks. A similar trend can be seen with the Romanian national movement in Transylvania. The pioneers of Romanian nationalist doctrine (which also made itself felt across the mountains in the culturally and economically more backward Moldavia and Wallachia of the eighteenth century) were priests of the Uniate Church. Nationalist aims were then taken up by the Orthodox priesthood, and by the secular professions which developed within Dualist Hungary. Romanian savings banks and Romanian small capitalists arose. Enemies of Slovak and Romanian nationalism argued that they were created by capitalist cliques which did well out of them; yet it is equally true that if Slovak and Romanian peasants were to escape dependence on Jewish moneylenders who were exponents of Magyarisation, they had to have their own banks, even if these bankers did make money out of them. Arguments as to whether capitalism created nationalism, or nationalism created capitalism, in these conditions, do not get us much further.

In the Ottoman empire the leaders of the Greek national movement came from a rather wide range of social groups. Intellectuals and language reformers were of great importance, first among them being Adamantios Koraïs, but the most eminent operated from a distance—in Paris or Vienna. The richest merchants and the Orthodox hierarchy in Constantinople were understandably cautious. More active were small Greek businessmen from both the Ionian and the Aegean islands, whose seafaring brought them both profit and contagion with modern political ideas. The third element of importance were the local notables, especially in the Peloponnese, who belonged to neither of the categories of 'landowners' or 'officials', but had some elements of both roles. In Serbia the original rising was the work of similar notables, supported by the local priesthood and the local incipient capitalists in the form of pig-merchants. It was only after independence that intellectuals, coming from Habsburg lands of Serbian speech, especially from southern Hungary (Vojvodina), became important in shaping national consciousness.

In Bulgaria, which remained under Ottoman rule until the 1870s, intellectuals who had learned the latest European socialist doctrines were a leading element, but the national cause was promoted also by merchants, for example from the textile centre of Gabrovo, who had considerable funds available to help education and propaganda in a nationalist spirit.

In all these lands the mass support came from peasants. In all also the bureaucracy was in enemy—that is, Ottoman Muslim—hands. It was only after liberation that these nations acquired their own bureaucracy, and it was largely recruited from the intellectuals who had led the struggle. In power, these men soon found themselves repressing their unsatisfied compatriots. The revolutionaries had turned into pashas, and a new generation of intellectuals was forced into a struggle against them not unlike the struggle which they themselves had waged against the Ottomans. The careers of such men as Pašić and Stambulov, and the history of the socialist and communist parties of Serbia, Bulgaria and Greece, well illustrate this point.

In the Russian empire language experts were very prominent in the national movements of the non-Russian nations. The creation of a standardised Ukrainian language, with some literary works of really outstanding merit, transformed regional discontents, and legal and social diversity from Muscovy, into a positive Ukrainian national consciousness. The Ukrainian movement was based almost wholly on intellectual leadership and peasant following. There were of course landowners, bureaucrats and capitalists of Ukrainian origin, but virtually all considered themselves

Russians. In the working class Ukrainian nationalism made some progress before 1917, but it was a minority trend.

In the Baltic region, too, language reformers were outstanding. This is especially true of the creation of a Lithuanian national consciousness based on the Lithuanian language. Until the fourth quarter of the nineteenth century 'Lithuanian' was a geographical concept, with of course a long historical tradition. 'Lithuanians' included persons whose language was Polish—among them the poet Adam Mickiewicz and the nationalist Jozef Piłsudski. The identification of the Lithuanian nation with Lithuanian-speakers was largely the result of ideas spread by newspapers published in the city of Tilsit in Prussia and in the United States. Lithuanian nationalists had two enemies: the Poles who formed a large part of the educated classes in their country, and the Russians who were their political masters. The Latvian national movement had a similar predicament: the class enemies were Germans and the political enemies were Russians. An important difference between the Lithuanian and Latvian situations was that the Latvians had, by 1917, a large industrial working class, which was much influenced by Russian socialism, and conflicted with the peasants and the rural intelligentsia of schoolteachers and Lutheran pastors who aimed at national independence; whereas the lower social strata of Lithuanian-speakers consisted almost exclusively of peasants, who followed the nationalist intellectuals.

In Estonia also nationalism derived from the revival of the language—the work of pastors, teachers and writers—and the enemies were the same as in Latvia—German landowners and Russian bureaucrats. In the social basis of the movement, peasants were the main element: the urban working class was less important than in Latvia.

The Tatars of the Volga valley provide an interesting example of cooperation between a new intellectual elite and a business class. The efforts of Gaspirali to elaborate a modern common language for the Turkic peoples have been mentioned above. They failed, but the modern schools, created in competition with the *medrese* by the Tatar democrats and Muslim nationalists, produced a new Tatar intellectual elite which was the bearer of Tatar national consciousness. These schools were made possible, in the face of the hostile indifference of the Russian authorities, by the funds contributed by a substantial Tatar business class.

### Immigrant societies

The new nations of the Americas, and of the European settlements in the southern hemisphere, were entirely new as nations, but were derived from old and developed societies. The social structures of the peoples of

European stock in the American, Australasian and South African colonies were similar to those of England, France, Holland, Spain and Portugal of the period when the colonists left, though they afterwards developed on different lines. One difference was that there was in many of the new territories a labour force of slaves or helots—negroes in the southern states of British North America, the Caribbean, Venezuela and Brazil; Amerindians in New Spain, the Andean regions and Paraguay. Another difference was that the overseas social structure almost completely lacked the European upper stratum of noble landowners. However, in the course of two to three centuries new classes of great landowners, descended from military adventurers or successful farmers, emerged, and gave themselves aristocratic airs. The aristocracy of Virginia or the *hacenderos* of Chile were of course *parvenus*: the nearest thing to a genuine European nobility, partly of noble origin, were the *seigneurs* of the St Lawrence valley. In those overseas European societies which had a more egalitarian ethos, the aping of social graces was less frequent: Australian graziers and Boer big farmers were nevertheless a sort of landowning elite.

In the political movements which led the way to independence, and in the struggle itself, social classes were divided. There were landowners and merchants who fought for the king of England or the king of Spain, and others who followed Bolívar or Washington. Both George Washington and Thomas Jefferson were slave-owning landowners. Some creole merchants bitterly resented Spanish commercial policies, and others did well out of them: much the same may be said of Massachusetts and New York with regard to British commercial policies. Members of intellectual professions were certainly prominent in American resistance, and small farmers and working men fought against the redcoats; yet there were also such people among the Loyalists. In the Boer republics the struggle for independence was the work of an alliance of intellectual elite (Calvinist pastors, then secular professions too) with a people of farmers—a combination not unlike that in Scotland in the seventeenth century. Afrikaner nationalism within the Union of South Africa was also led by members of the professions: it is striking how many leading Afrikaners were lawyers and became politicians, and how many leading English-speakers were businessmen and ignored politics. Something of the same is to be found in Canada. A new stage in mid-twentieth century Quebec politics began with the enrolment of the growing working class in nationalism.

The American nation was new in one other important respect: in its absorption of a flood of immigrants of different languages and traditions. To a lesser extent this is true of Argentina, Chile and Brazil. Australia and Canada of course also had large numbers of immigrants, but these were, until very recent times, overwhelmingly of one language. English, Scots and Irish created in both countries great diversity, but it was not on the scale of the diversity between Poles, Italians, Germans, Irish, Lebanese, Armenians and others in Chicago and New York. Quebec received very few immigrants, since France was the only great European nation which sent no great flood of emigrants overseas in the nineteenth century: this partly accounts for the toughness and national solidarity of the *Québécois*.


## Anti-colonialist elites

Of the states which emerged from colonial rule in Asia, some (Vietnam, Cambodia and Burma) can hardly be called new, since they corresponded approximately to states which had existed before European conquest. India and Indonesia were new states, embracing greater territories than had ever previously formed a single unit in those lands; and a single state of the Philippines was a creation of the Spanish conquerors and their American successors. It is difficult to describe their peoples as 'new nations', for they had existed as religious and cultural communities longer than any European nation; yet national movements and nationalism in the modern sense were borrowed from Europe.

It is impossible to do better than make imprecise statements about the class composition of the Indian nationalist movement, for the class structure of India was and remained infinitely complicated by caste. Undoubtedly, persons influenced by British education played a leading part. Even the members of this comparatively small minority varied in social origin and status: Nehru was a rich Kashmiri Brahmin with financial means of his own; Gandhi trained as a barrister in London and practised in South Africa before embarking on his political career; and from the beginning of the Indian National Congress, Bengalis, of various castes and sometimes of humble origin, employed in various non-manual occupations from office clerks to highly educated professional men, provided a large part of the cadres of Indian nationalism. These were also increasingly supported by capitalists small and great, from Gujarat and Bengal and other provinces, extending from small businessmen to the great industrialists Tata and Birla. Of the rather small number of Indians in the higher civil service, most were rather deeply permeated by the ethos of loyalty to the British Raj, and this was still more true of Indian serving officers in the Indian Army; yet, as organised Indian nationalism grew stronger, a certain ambivalence inevitably developed in those whose duty was to serve and defend India, and there were some who supported the Congress. Thus, all three middle groups were involved, but the intellectual element was the most important of the three. Mass support came first in the cities, and grew slowly. It was Gandhi who, with his brilliant combination of religious appeal and political tactical sense, brought the urban and rural classes into politics and made Congress a mass movement.

In Indonesia nationalist leaders came from both the Javanese nobility and the urban business class, whose ideas derived both from Islamic modernism and from European socialism. In the first nationalist organisation, *Sarekat Islam*, in the early 1920s, the Muslim merchant element was predominant; the movement in fact derived from rivalry with Chinese merchants rather than from hostility to the Dutch rulers. Later, nationalism split into a number of groups. The most militant leaders were, like Ahmed Sukarno, European-educated intellectuals of noble origin, who had learned their socialism in Europe (Sukarno, like Nehru, had been influenced by the communist-controlled League against Imperialism). Each of the nationalist movements had its following among peasants and urban poor, though—as in India—there remained millions who were untouched by politics. In independent Indonesia Javanese nationalism soon split between the moderate Muslim democrats, the *Masjumi* party, in which Muslim businessmen were influential, and the Nationalists of Sukarno, based on an alliance between intellectuals and officials, which proclaimed socialist principles but also looked back to a paternalist concept of government: pre-capitalist elitism and post-capitalist socialism could be made to look easily compatible.

In Burma nationalist leadership came from the small European-educated group, while the non-European businessmen were not Burmese but Indian. In Malaya both the intellectual and the business elite were Chinese. In French Indochina a small, but more thoroughly European-educated group formed the leadership. Some of these accepted French culture whole-heartedly, and sought to associate their people with it. Others learned from French culture the radical doctrines which moved them to fight against France. The most radical of these in the 1920s and 1930s was communism, whose exponents were more successful than any previous radicals in freeing themselves from European, and thus from colonial, associations. One could be a communist and a Vietnamese, in the fullest sense, at the same time. Ho Chi Minh was of course the outstanding figure, but there were countless lesser examples.

The African states that emerged after the Second World War were certainly new, and their peoples were new nations, though they were not new as inhabitants of their homelands, and they were by no means 'without history'. Nationalism was an idea learned from the foreign rulers, and its first bearers were those who had received a European type of education. The essential point is not the absolute level of Western erudition acquired by the individual, but the relative level in regard to his people as a whole. The Senegalese leader Senghor, a classical scholar and a fine poet in French, would stand out in any cultured society in the world; the secondary school graduate clerk Patrice Lumumba was an intellectual giant among the Congolese. African traders also played their part in the national movement. Some African peoples, previously backward and held in low esteem, adapted themselves well to the needs of the colonial power, and from their midst emerged disproportionately large numbers of persons with the right kinds of business and intellectual skills. Such were the Ibos of Nigeria, who might be called the Bengalis of West Africa. Others, like the Yorubas, had a long tradition of commercial skill. Those who rose in the new professions were sometimes from African upper classes, such as Houphouet-Boigny; others were of humble origin.

In general the nationalist movements fought not only the colonial rulers but also the indigenous privileged classes, or chiefs, on whom the rulers relied, denouncing them as 'stooges'. In some regions, however, the princely families managed to keep power in their hands, first standing aside from nationalist activity, and then joining in when they saw that the nationalists were winning. In Ghana, the Ashanti ruler proved no match for Nkrumah. But the traditional rulers of northern Nigeria more than held their own for the first years of Nigerian independence. It is a strange irony of history that the two political protagonists of those first years—the northern emirs and the Ibo intelligentsia—were the two main casualties of the Nigerian civil war.

In the independent states, there was an inadequate government machine from colonial times, sufficiently staffed at the lower levels but with gaps higher up. These were filled by the nationalist politicians and intellectuals, who soon showed that the widespread belief that they were a Westernised intelligentsia, belonging to an alien culture and cut off from their own peoples, was only half true. They soon showed themselves capable of ruling in traditional African style, or if they were not so capable they were replaced by others who were. In this the development of politics and of social classes in the new states of Africa recalled that in the new states of the Balkans in the late nineteenth and early twentieth centuries. Intellectuals turned despots became the targets of a new generation of intellectuals; but Nkrumah and Obote had a tough way of dealing with students, not to mention the European-trained NCOs, promoted generals—Mobutu and Amin.

As for mass support, this was certainly forthcoming from the peasants and the urban workers. It is true that those who gave their support to nationalist leaders may have been moved by tribal or religious loyalties, by economic or regionalist motives, rather than by any firm national consciousness. Nevertheless, even if the nationalists came to power with the support only of minorities, these were bigger than rival minorities, and certainly bigger than those who consciously preferred the colonial rulers.

## Nationalist elites under communist rule

Soviet-type Marxist writers distinguish between 'feudal nations', 'bourgeois nations' and 'socialist nations'. The latter are formed in countries ruled by socialist governments (that is, by communist parties approved as such by the keepers of the Soviet ideological conscience). They may be created from unshaped human raw material, like the Uzbek, Tadjik and other Central Asian nations which did not exist before 1917; or they may be made by the social transformation of existing bourgeois nations, like the nations of the 'liberated' Baltic states, or those of the Socialist or People's republics of Eastern Europe. Feudal and bourgeois nations, ruled by other nations, have to fight for their national independence; but socialist nations have no such need, since they belong to the fraternal community of socialist nations which is the USSR.

This picture corresponds in part to reality. Many national movements have been led, as we have seen, by social groups which are described in Soviet terminology (though this is imprecise) as 'feudal' or 'bourgeois'; and both the new Central Asian nations and the older nations of Eastern Europe have had their social structures transformed by Soviet rule. What has not proved true is that these 'socialist' nations have been contented to live within the Soviet community of nations. In Czechoslovakia, Poland, Hungary and Eastern Germany there have been popular insurrections against Soviet rule; in Romania the communist leadership has openly and successfully resisted Soviet policies; and in the Ukraine, the Baltic, Caucasian and Central Asian republics there have been frequent individual or collective expressions of resistance, which Soviet official spokesmen have rather indiscriminately condemned as 'bourgeois nationalism'.

In reality, it is doubtful whether anything which could be called a bourgeoisie (in the sense defined above) existed in Central Asia, while the bourgeoisies which did exist in the Baltic republics, Armenia and the East European countries were deprived of any possibility of influence by many years of communist party rule. The national movements against Soviet Russian domination came in reality from two main social groups.

The first was from the intellectual professions. These could reasonably be described by the Soviet phrase 'toiling intelligentsia', for they consisted largely of young people of peasant or working class origin who had obtained their education under the communist party regime, together with a certain number of older persons whose social origin and past education might rather cause them to be regarded as a 'bourgeois intelligentsia', though most of them were members or supporters of the communist party. (Obviously, this latter group were less numerous in Czechoslovakia in 1968, twenty years after the communists had taken the whole country's education system into their hands, than in Hungary in 1956, only nine years after this had happened.) It is worth stressing that the young plebeian intellectuals, who owed their career opportunities to the communists, led the movement against them. They felt themselves to be the heirs of Petöffi and Táncsics, but saw in Rákosi the heir to the Habsburgs' General Haynau.

The second group which was most active was the working class, in theory the darling of the communist regimes. In Hungary in October 1956 the workers of the Csepel factories arrived with their arms to fight first Gerö's police and then the Soviet army in Budapest, and workers' militias defended their factories bitterly for days on end after the massive Soviet invasion of 4 November. In East Germany in June 1953 it was the workers who rebelled. In Poland in October 1956 it was the Warsaw workers whose determination to fight against Soviet counter-revolution decided Khrushchev to accept a compromise with Gomulka. Above all in Czechoslovakia the workers were united in defence of 'communism with a human face'; they elected their own delegates to the communist party congress; and held the congress illegally in a Prague factory under the shadow of the Soviet military occupation. In all these cases the workers' class struggle against a Soviet-sponsored exploiting class of party bureaucrats was inextricably fused with the national struggle against Soviet Russian imperial rule.

It is true that in all these cases the peasants appeared to be passive. Yet to conclude that the peasants were indifferent to the national struggle would be a mistake. The very small peasant participation proves only that there was no time—so swift, brutal and effective was the Soviet reaction—to organise them. It always takes longer for revolutionary leaders to involve the scattered rural population than to mobilise the people of the cities.

## National and class struggles

Almost all struggles for national independence have been inextricably connected with class struggles.

National movements have not been successful unless they have mobilised a significant section of the common people—peasants and workers; and this has usually been possible only when their direct personal feelings and material interests were concerned. Two partial reservations may be made. One is that deeply felt religious beliefs have often moved hundreds of thousands into support of a national movement; yet in these cases too it is usually arguable that the interests of social classes were also involved. The second reservation is that in some African colonies of both Britain and France, independence was granted before there had been any mass movement, and indeed before there was much sign that a nation existed at all.

The leadership of national movements has also come predominantly from certain social classes which, in addition to their conviction of the importance of their identity as religious or linguistic or cultural communities, were also impelled by class hostility to their existing rulers. Of this there are many combinations: for example, noble landowners against a foreign military and bureaucratic power (Poland 1863); noble landowners and intellectuals against a similar opponent (Hungary 1848); intellectuals of non-noble origin against foreign landowners (Slovakia 1848); intellectuals of plebeian and of local notable origin against a colonial foreign government (most of West Africa in the 1950s); intellectuals and capitalists against foreign bureaucrats and landowners (Czechs in the early nineteenth century, Volga Tatars in the late nineteenth); intellectuals, with some local capitalists and notables, against a colonial rule (Yorubaland in the 1950s); intellectuals and working class against a government dominated by politicians, capitalists and officials of different speech (Quebec in the 1960s and 1970s); intellectuals and workers against a foreign colonial regime operating in the name of socialist brotherhood (Hungary in 1956, Czechoslovakia in 1968).

Situations have inevitably arisen in which class interests and national interests have pulled in different directions. Sometimes the most prosperous or powerful class has felt a greater common interest with the foreign government than with the national movement. The Bohemian nobility was for the most part *kaisertreu*, and supported neither the German nationalist nor the Czech nationalist opposition to the Habsburg Monarchy (though some families, and some individuals, were to be found in each of these movements). Indian *zamindars*, North Nigerian *emirs* and other African chiefs may have disliked the British rulers as usurpers of their powers and alien to their tradition, yet feared them less than the new nationalist movements led by persons whose social status they despised. The reforms of General Kaufman in Russian Turkestan benefited the Asian peasants and damaged the Asian upper class, yet in the longer term they did not cause the peasants to love Russian rule. Czech and German workers might have a common interest in fighting the capitalist class of the First Czechoslovak Republic; yet such comradely cooperation as existed between them in the prosperous 1920s broke down in the economic depression of the 1930s and made of many German workers militant white-stocking-wearing, *Heil-Hitler*-shouting devotees of the Third Reich. In Latvia in 1918-19 the workers of Riga followed the socialist leaders, who were close in outlook to the Russian Bolsheviks, and wished to keep their country inside the Russian socialist republic; while most Latvian-speaking (though not German-speaking) members of the middle groups, and most Latvian peasants, preferred an independent Latvia. In China in the mid-1920s workers fought for their class interests, and peasants were interested in land reform, which placed the communist party in a difficult dilemma:

should it go all out for revolution, and thus break the united front against foreign exploiters of China, or devote all its energies to the national struggle and thereby strengthen the class enemies inside China?

To nationalist leaders, obstinate social revolutionaries appear as traitors to the national cause: to Soviet-type Marxists, nationalists who persist in their nationalism, after they themselves believe that the stage of social revolution has begun, appear as pernicious and reactionary diversionists, either misled by their inability to understand the 'scientific' laws of 'history', or conscious agents of 'the bourgeoisie' or 'the imperialists'. Marxists console themselves with the reflection that the national struggle is but a passing phase, to be followed sooner or later by the proletarian revolution. Yet recent history suggests that the problem is not so simple as that: victorious socialist (or self-styled socialist) dictatorships seem always themselves to become 'nationalised', and soon show this in their dealings both with persons of other nationality among their own subjects and with other states, whether these are 'socialist' or not.

# 12  Nationalism and Ideological Movements

## Nationalism and liberalism

In the first half of the nineteenth century, it was generally assumed that individual liberty and national independence or unity would go together: both were regarded as equally desirable by nationalists, equally objectionable by absolutist governments. Nationalism and liberalism were a single cause. Their champions were for the most part members of the educated elite, whether 'upper' or 'middle' class. They desired political freedom for themselves, and assumed that in demanding it they spoke for the whole nation except for reactionary rulers, indigenous or foreign. It may be argued that 'the liberal bourgeoisie' was pursuing its own aims, canalising popular discontent into channels which would further its own narrow interests. This is less than fair.

The eighteenth century concept of popular sovereignty was designed for the whole 'people', even though in the first instance it was assumed that the most educated and enlightened citizens would have to guide the people, and bring it gradually into political life. However, it is certainly true that the driving force came from the educated elite, and that first priority was given to issues which most directly interested that elite. In Western and Central Europe in the mid-nineteenth century that elite, I have argued, was a bourgeoisie; but when the process reached Eastern Europe, the Muslim lands, southern Asia and Africa, there was no bourgeoisie at hand—only intelligentsia and a few merchants—while the most powerful forces which opposed the new elite were often not so much a landowning class or capitalists, as a bureaucracy, indigenous or foreign.

The liberal phase of nationalism reached its climax in 1848, in the Assembly in the Paulskirche in Frankfurt and in the revolutions in Italy. In 1848 conflicts appeared between moderates and radicals, and these developed further in the second half of the century. Growing numbers of moderate liberals in Germany and Italy became content with such constitutional gains as had been made, and with the national unity which had been achieved by governments. Both they and the moderate republicans in

France became indifferent or hostile to demands on behalf of the masses of the people; while on their left appeared not only radical but also socialist movements. The bourgeoisie had got rid of foreign rule, and had its share in political power; it was now challenged from below by the rising working class.

Among those European nations which, unlike the Germans and Italians, had not yet achieved independence or unity, this differentiation was delayed, partly because the national cause retained first priority, and partly because, since these nations consisted in their majority of peasants, there was not yet much foundation for a strong socialist working class movement. Nevertheless, both the need to mobilise the masses in the national cause and the spread of socialist ideas influenced the nationalist leaders. Knowledge that they might soon face strong competition from incipient socialist movements on their left obliged them both to devote more thought to social problems and to propound political aims more immediately and generally attractive. Nationalist parties thus became more 'populist', and at the same time found themselves compelled to indulge in increasingly bitter polemics against socialist ideas. An outstanding example is the National Democratic Party in Poland, which certainly was socially radical in its early days, but whose bitter hostility to all nations bordering on the Poles—not only to Prussian and Russian conquerors but also to Ukrainian, Lithuanian, Byelorussian and Romanian fellow-victims, as well as to the large Jewish element in their midst—led it into violent hostility to all internationally minded groups, especially to socialists.

After the First World War the socialist movement split, on a world scale, into the two hostile camps of social democracy and communism. In Italy the fascist movement and regime appeared as a reply to the threat, real or imagined, from the socialists. Fascism was to some extent a model for Hitler's National Socialism, which in the 1930s not only became a mighty force in Germany, but exercised a powerful attraction in many European countries, as well as in Latin America, the Muslim world and the Far East. Parties arose which can loosely be termed 'fascist', and fascist ideas strongly influenced the leaders of many national independence movements in various parts of the world. The military successes of Germany in the first three years of the Second World War increased this influence. After the collapse of the Third Reich fascism ceased to be fashionable: instead the victories of the Soviet Union made 'socialism', as understood by the Soviet leaders, extremely attractive, especially to national movements in colonies of European powers.

I shall now briefly consider in turn the attitudes to nationalism of pre-1914 socialist leaders and movements, and the relationship of nationalists to both fascists and communists. In this chapter the emphasis is on political movements and political actions, not on doctrines (though points of doctrine will from time to time be mentioned). It is assumed that readers have some idea of what is meant by 'socialism', 'fascism', and 'communism': if they have not, there is a vast analytical literature at their disposal, which I do not propose to try to summarise here. I also see little point in trying to analyse nationalism itself as an ideology. It may even be doubted whether nationalism deserves to be called an ideology. Its essence, I have suggested, is very simple: it is the application to national communities of the Enlightenment doctrine of popular sovereignty. As to what constitutes, or is thought by its members to constitute, a national community, it is hoped that the readers who have read this far will have been able to form their own ideas. The rest of nationalist ideology is rhetoric.

**Socialism**

European socialists inherited the tradition, deriving from Louis XIV but reinforced by the French Revolution and Napoleon, that large centralised states were progressive and small regional autonomies reactionary. Thus, where a number of small territories were inhabited by people who wished to unite with each other, their aims were usually acceptable to socialists, but where small groups wished to secede from large states and form states of their own, they were viewed with suspicion: German, Italian and Polish nationalism in general appeared to the early socialists as respectable causes, but the nationalism of Czechs or Serbs or other small Central European peoples did not.

It is also important that some nations had a long tradition of liberal nationalism, in which the demands for political liberty and social justice were associated with the demand for national unity. This was especially true of the Poles, who had tried to implement a 'Jacobin' constitution and had been crushed by foreign invasion; and whose legions had then fought for liberty all over Europe. It was also true, to a smaller extent, of both Germans and Italians, among whom the Enlightenment and the French Revolution had won much support.

The contrast, in radical and socialist eyes, between progressive and reactionary nations was sharpened by the events of 1848-49. Socialists, no less than radicals and liberals, welcomed the German and Italian movements for unity and the Polish national movement in Prussia, though they naturally favoured the most extremist trends within these movements. For European socialists, radicals and liberals the main enemies were the Austrian and Russian autocracies. They therefore also strongly supported the Hungarian national struggle, within which radical elements were conspicuous. The other national movements however did not enjoy their approval. Czech nationalists disrupted plans for a democratic Greater

Germany, and were also suspect because of their Panslav sympathies, which caused them to be regarded as tools of the Russian tsar. It is true that Michael Bakunin was an exception, as he favoured some sort of revolutionary Slav solidarity with a strong anti-German flavour. This was one of the issues on which Karl Marx quarrelled with Bakunin, and in later years the international socialist and anarchist movements drifted even further apart. As for the small nations which resisted Hungarian nationalism, they were treated with contempt by Marx and Engels. Slovaks, Croats, Serbs and Transylvanian Romanians were mere fragmentary language groups doomed to extinction, destined to be absorbed into German or Hungarian or Italian culture. During the 1848 Revolution their leaders had chosen to support the Habsburgs, using their peoples as mere mercenaries of despotism.

The most formidable reactionary force in Europe now appeared to Marx and Engels to be Russian tsarism. Therefore national movements which were in any sense allied to Russia must be enemies of progress, while those which opposed the tsar's aims must deserve sympathy. To this latter group belonged not only the Poles but the Romanians of Bessarabia (though the Romanians of Transylvania had been denounced for helping the Habsburgs against the Hungarian revolutionaries). Marx himself later expressed his sympathy for the Bessarabian Romanians.

Hitherto socialist attitudes to the problems of national independence and unity had been essentially negative and opportunist. Oppression of one nation by another must be condemned. However, nationalism was a phenomenon of the bourgeois stage of social evolution, and would be overcome in the socialist stage. Class struggles were more fundamental than national struggles. In the socialist republics of the future, solidarity of the workers would overcome all national conflicts. Meanwhile, those national movements which furthered the movement towards socialism must be supported, and those which were useful to the cause of despotism must be opposed.

The country in which a more constructive and imaginative attitude to nationalism was devised by socialists was Austria-Hungary. The outstanding theorists were Karl Renner and Otto Bauer, whose books came out in the first decade of the century.[1] The essence of the policy was that, whereas the state administration and legislature should be centralised, culture should be decentralised and left to each component 'nationality'. Each should have its own cultural organisation, responsible especially for education, maintained by taxes levied on the members of the 'nationality', according to their own declaration of national adherence. Thus, for example, not only would cultural life in regions of compact Slovak population be in the hands of Slovak cultural authorities, but a Slovak living far from the Slovak homeland—say, in Dalmatia or Bukovina—

would be able to have his children educated in Slovak schools.

In the Russian empire a similar, though more limited, idea was put forward by the *Bund*, the organisation of Jewish Social Democrats.[2] It claimed to represent all Jewish workers, in whatever part of Russia they might live. Acceptance of this claim by the Russian Social Democrats (RSDRP) would have meant that a Jewish worker might have a dual loyalty, to the *Bund* and to the RSDRP. This was opposed by the Russian leaders, especially by the Bolshevik group led by Lenin, and the *Bund* therefore seceded from RSDRP at its second congress in 1903. Many Russian Jewish socialists remained members of RSDRP, both of its Menshevik and of its Bolshevik faction, and accepted their centralist discipline; others followed the *Bund*; and still others combined socialism with forms of Zionism.

An important conflict on the national problem emerged within the Polish socialist movement. The Polish Socialist Party (PPS), founded in 1892, desired the independence and reunification of Poland: the class struggle and the national struggle should go together.[3] There were however disagreements on relative priorities; and one group, led by Roza Luksemburg, broke away altogether in 1900, to form the Social Democracy of the Kingdom of Poland and Lithuania (SDKPL). Luksemburg maintained not only that an independent Poland could not be created in the foreseeable future, but that it was positively undesirable: the true interest of the Polish workers was that they should remain within the three great states in which they had been incorporated by the partitions, and which would in due course be transformed by revolution into the German, Austrian and Russian socialist republics. Within these republics Polish workers would live and work in proletarian solidarity beside German, Russian and other workers.[4]

Lenin strongly opposed the autonomous aspirations of the *Bund*, the extreme internationalism of Luksemburg and the proposed solutions of Renner and Bauer. It was Lenin who inspired Stalin's essay of 1913: though clearly written, it contains no original ideas.[5] Its essential point is the insistence that nationality is inseparable from territory: it therefore rejects any policy of personal national autonomy within a multinational state. Lenin, for whom Stalin was the mouthpiece, insisted that every nation should have the right, if it wished, to separate from a multinational socialist republic; but that if a nation decided to remain within the same state as another or several others, then its members must accept the centralised institutions of the republic. Centralisation applied even more strictly to the organisation of the party, which could not accept any sort of federalism or regional autonomy: the party organisation at each administrative level must be fully subordinated to the next level above it.

The doctrine of the Russian Bolsheviks, who finally formed themselves into a separate party in 1912, was national self-determination to the point of secession. This did not mean that a nation *must* secede, only that it was *entitled* to do so if it wished. There remained however a difficult problem. How was it to be decided what the nation wished? If a 'bourgeois nationalist' party obtained an electoral majority and wished to secede, but the working class, though a minority of the population, wished to remain within the multinational socialist republic, then which of these conflicting groups should be entitled to exercise or to renounce the right of self-determination? Precisely this situation arose in Riga and in Baku in 1918. The question never received a theoretical answer. In practice the issue was decided by force. Wherever the Bolsheviks were strong enough to maintain their rule over non-Russians by force, they did so: wherever other forces proved too strong for them, they failed, and for a time at least recognised the independence of the seceding nations. Thus the Poles, Latvians, Lithuanians, Estonians, Finns and Bessarabian Romanians seceded from Russia for twenty years; the Georgians, Azerbaidjanis and Armenians for two or three; while the Ukrainians, Tatars and Central Asian peoples were retained by force within the Russian empire, renamed Union of Soviet Socialist Republics.

### Fascism

In the first half of the nineteenth century, the demand for the involvement of the whole nation in politics was voiced by the liberals and men of 'the left'. It was assumed that if the masses played a part in politics, they would support the reforms proposed by the radicals, and would drive the old ruling elements out of politics. For this reason democracy—that is, government by the people, or at least by a much larger proportion of the people than hitherto—was preached by the left and opposed by the right.

After 1848 however it began to dawn on leading politicians of the upper social strata that the masses might act quite otherwise, might support traditional patriotism and traditional leaders, especially if these disguised their aims in a new style of rhetoric. The first large-scale example was Bonapartism in France: Napoleon III showed himself a skilful manipulator of the newly enfranchised poorer social groups. Disraeli in England believed that extension of the suffrage would give the Conservatives new opportunities: the immediate result of the 1867 Reform Bill did not confirm this view, but it was amply justified some years later. Bismarck made good use of universal suffrage in the Reichstag after 1871, and won support by a programme of social welfare in the 1880s, while keeping the suffrage in Prussia restricted. His success was largely due to his ability to exploit national pride in the new German empire of which he was the principal architect.

It was in France after 1871 that nationalism was most strikingly used as a means of mobilising the masses behind the traditional ruling strata. The humiliation of defeat by Prussia was widely and bitterly felt. Thé Commune of 1871 was not only a social revolution but also to some extent a patriotic movement. In the early stages of French socialism, nationalism and internationalism coexisted and conflicted with each other. The nationalist writer Maurice Barrès long considered himself to be a socialist. By the turn of the century, however, the internationalist trend had prevailed within French socialism, and its enemies increasingly emphasised, in their polemics against it, its treasonable disruption of national unity in the face of the triumphant German enemy. On the extreme right there developed the doctrine of *nationalisme intégral*, whose chief prophet was Charles Maurras. The nation was held up as the supreme value, side by side with God, and increasingly as a substitute for God. The main political task must be to remove from the nation all those forces which were corrupting it from within—the Protestants, the *métèques* (offspring of mixed marriages between Frenchmen and foreign immigrants) and, above all, the Jews.

I have argued that France and England had no need for, and did not historically develop, nationalism in the sense in which we understand 'nationalism' in this book—that is, a movement for national independence or national unity or a policy of creating national consciousness within a politically unconscious population. There was however, from the 1890s to the 1930s, something which is habitually described as 'French nationalism'. This was in fact something different from nationalism as hitherto discussed in this book, yet undoubtedly relevant to it. It was a political doctrine, whose aim was power within the nation. Its clearest formulation was the *nationalisme intégral* of Maurras, but it extended far beyond the limits of the rather small political group of *Action française*, the periodical and movement of which Maurras was the leader. In particular, this nationalism affected the syndicalist section of the labour movement, rather strong in the last years before 1914, which, partly under the influence of another prophet, Georges Sorel, advocated heroic and violent action, denouncing intellectualism, rationalism, parliamentary institutions and peaceful legal procedures as degenerate.

Similar tendencies were to be found in other countries. Germans can hardly be said to have suffered, like Frenchmen, national humiliation in 1870. Nevertheless, the most passionate German nationalists in Austria, especially those who lived in the Bohemian and Carinthian borderlands in proximity with Czechs and Slovenes, felt humiliated by being deprived of membership of a single German Reich, and endangered by the growing numbers and cultural pretensions of their 'sub-human' Slav neighbours. They too increasingly extolled violence, and hated rational and legal procedures. They too hated all forms of internationalism, and identified these with the Jews in their midst. For them too, the German *Volk* was growing into a substitute for God.

In Italy something of the sort was also to be seen. Nearly all Italians were united in one state; but there were still some unredeemed who were being threatened, while still subjected to the indolent and antiquated government of Vienna, by the rising flood of Slav Slovenes and Croats. Italy also suffered from being a latecomer to the company of European imperial powers. She must claim for herself a share of the colonial spoils which the older nations had divided among themselves. Irredentism kept nationalism a living force in Italy, and it had its support also in the labour movement, in which, as in France, syndicalism and the romantic cult of violence were a strong force. Nationalists welcomed the war for Libya in 1911. The poet Ugo Foscolo, in a famous speech, used the phrase '*la grande proletaria s'è mossa*'. As he saw it, Italy was a proletarian among the nations, now claiming her due. Similar sentiments emerged still more strongly in the First World War. The Italian socialist movement was split by the Libyan war, and further defections occurred in 1915. A socialist who had taken the internationalist view in 1911, Benito Mussolini, now came out as a militant patriot. The peace settlement of 1918-20 bitterly disappointed Italian nationalists, who saw most of the lands they had claimed go to the new Yugoslavia. Mussolini emerged as the leader of the militant nationalists, and the enemy of socialists, communists, liberals and internationalists. It was he who chose the word 'fascist' for his movement.[6]

This word, and the rhetoric associated with it, gave its name to a period of ten to twenty years in European and world history. Though it is a matter for argument whether there was ever a single phenomenon of fascism, there was certainly an Age of Fascism; and it is more enlightening than confusing to speak of certain governments and certain political movements of that age as 'fascist'.

After Mussolini's triumph in 1922 the Italian nation was extolled as a substitute for God, but as time passed it became more true to say that Mussolini, as the symbol of the nation, was himself raised almost to divine status. *Il Duce ha sempre ragione* (the leader is always right) was proclaimed in inscriptions all over Italy. The effectiveness of this apotheosis in Italy was, however, limited by the profound innate political scepticism of most Italians (including, it is fair to say, Mussolini himself) and by the necessity of coming to terms with the very powerful Catholic church, whose status was legalised by the concordat of 1929.

In Germany the national humiliation of 1918 was immensely deeper than that of France in 1871, let alone that of Italy in 1918. Determination to reverse the peace settlement of Versailles, and to reassert German national greatness, was widespread. It can be divided into two main trends. One was conservative, based on the old upper classes and industrialists, distrustful of the common people. The other was populist, hostile to the old rulers, socially radical and convinced that power could be achieved only by mobilising the masses in a vast movement. The second trend prevailed under the leadership of a politician of genius, Adolf Hitler. Hatred of internationalism, of socialism and above all of Jews were the main points of his programme, and, aided by the disastrous economic depression which began in 1929, they proved very popular. Once in power, the process of deification first of the *Volk* and then of its leader Hitler, knew no bounds. It is no exaggeration that for the most active members of the National Socialist Party Hitler was indeed a substitute for God.

Hatred of internationalism, socialism and liberalism, combined also to a varying extent with romantic idealisation of pre-industrial society and of the virtues of the noble peasantry (which was a feature of German National Socialism, though not of French *nationalisme intégral* or of Italian fascism) are, together with anti-semitism, the main characteristics of the most successful fascist movements in smaller European countries during the 1930s, especially in Romania, Hungary, Belgium and Spain. In all four countries the cult of the supreme leader was also important, but there were some significant differences. The Romanian and Hungarian movements had strong support from a large part of the most genuinely religious section of the population. It is therefore doubtful whether one should speak of the deification of the nation, or of the leader. Codreanu and Szálassi were pious believers: they perhaps considered themselves, and were considered by their followers, as prophets. Degrelle, the Belgian leader, was probably, like Mussolini, a sceptical manipulator rather than a prophet. As for the Spanish leader, José Antonio Primo de Rivera, he was killed at a very early stage of the movement. He, like Codreanu (who led the movement for more than a decade before being murdered) and the victims of the Dublin Easter Rebellion of 1916, became the object of a cult of the martyred comrades which gave a peculiar character to the Iron Guard, the Spanish *Falange* and the IRA.[7]

The worship of the Nation required that all morality should be subordinated to the interests of the Nation, as interpreted by the Leader. *Recht ist, was dem Volke nützt* was the guiding principle of the National Socialists. During the 'night of the long knives' of 30 June 1934, when the leaders of the SA and other prominent Germans were murdered by his orders, Hitler was, he claimed, the personification of the Justice of the German *Volk*. Against the enemies of the nation, and the traitors in its midst, all forms of repression were permitted, ranging from short terms of imprisonment or physical assault on individuals in the first years of the regime to mass extermination of whole categories of human beings in the years of climax in world war. Indeed, to take part in mass extermination was glorified as the heroic performance of a higher duty to the Nation. In a famous speech at

Poznán, in occupied Poland on 4 October 1943, Heinrich Himmler, Hitler's security police chief, said: 'Most of you will know what it means to have 100, 500 or 1,000 corpses lying there beside you. To have endured this, and at the same time—with a few exceptions due to human weakness—to have remained honest men, that is what has made us tough. This is a page of glory from our history such as has never been written, and will never be written again'.

In the rhetoric of nation-worship, Mussolini was the pace-maker. It was he who invented the resounding phrase *lo stato totalitario*. In reality, the grip of Mussolini's government over Italians was far less than total. It was in Hitler's Third Reich that reality came closest to the ideal of nation-worshipping totalitarianism. Many attempts have been made to define totalitarianism, none of which has been successful, not even the well-known six points of Friedrich and Brzezinski.[8] In so far as these attempts were associated, especially in the United States in the 1950s, with an anti-Soviet political attitude, the reaction against what was labelled 'cold war mentality' led to a widespread demand by academic political theorists that the whole concept should be discarded. This seems to me to be going too far, for in fact there was, and still in the mid-1970s continued to be, a significant political phenomenon, of which the word was intended to be a description. On the other hand, I do not believe that totalitarianism, any more than nation, class, democracy or socialism, can be precisely defined. I suggest that the phenomenon with which we are concerned is the *tendency* to concentrate all political, economic and spiritual power in the hands of an infallible leader with access to modern means of mass communication and mass mobilisation; and the *tendency* to deny any autonomy to the private life of the citizen, who must at all times and in all matters place the leader's wishes before anything else at all. In the case of nation-worshipping totalitarianism, the supreme value which the leader personified or symbolised was the Nation. In the three countries in which a form of nation-worshipping totalitarianism prevailed during the Age of Fascism—Italy, Germany and Japan—worship was directed towards a single person, not a group. In Italy and Germany, Mussolini and Hitler were the real holders of power (though, like all rulers in history, partly dependent on their advisers and subordinates); in Japan, no single individual held all the power at the top, but the emperor was made, against his will, into a semi-divine symbol, the essence of the national polity (*Kokutai*) to which all individuals and all values must be subjected.

In reality, the power of the leader, or of those who controlled the semi-divine emperor, was less than total. In Italy, Mussolini's orders were obeyed until military disaster overtook him; but the bureaucracy, the armed forces, the church and the industrial elite operated according to their pre-fascist habits and values. There was in fact a balance of power and of material advantages between the old elites and the new regime. Mussolini did not try to impose the ideology of his fanatics on those whose skills and whose organised hierarchies he needed. Forced national unity and national expansion were accepted as a common aim. Approximately the same was true in Japan. Here the balance was seriously modified in the 1930s: the industrial magnates became less powerful, the military chiefs more powerful. The military chiefs were pushed towards a more adventurous policy of foreign expansion by the fanatics within the armed forces who assassinated a number of politicians, generals and admirals; but the fanatics were not able to take over the government. Within the ruling elite, rivalries between army and navy chiefs, and between civilian politicians, were not eliminated. Cultural life and family life were not much affected. In Germany the regime made itself more profoundly felt in all fields than was the case in Italy or Japan. The armed forces were purged before war was started; industrialists were placed under very strict state control, though permitted to make vast profits for themselves; and the churches were subjected to far-reaching interference, which led to some compliance but also to some resistance, persecution and martyrdom. After the unsuccessful attempt to overthrow Hitler in July 1944, the determination to impose National Socialist doctrines and morality on every individual, and to destroy every autonomous organism in German society, was greatly intensified. But the needs of a war that was being lost prevented these plans from being carried out. Though the National Socialists maintained their grip over the German nation until the end, fighting on until only a tiny piece of territory was left in their hands, they were ultimately crushed.

The defeat of the Third Reich brought to an end the Age of Fascism, and discredited the word 'fascism', perhaps for ever. It seemed likely that the precise combination of doctrines and style, characteristic of the fascist movements and regimes of the 1930s, would never be repeated. This did not however mean that there would not be new varieties of nation-worshipping totalitarianism. The conditions for its revival remained, especially in countries whose people had recently escaped from foreign rule, or were humiliated by continuing indirect domination by foreigners. These conditions were seen in several countries of Latin America, Asia and Africa, after the Second World War. The regimes of Perón in Argentina from 1945 to 1955 and of Nkrumah in Ghana showed a family relationship to the regimes of the Age of Fascism: in both cases the tendency to nationalist totalitarianism and to leader-worship increased in the last period before the dictator's overthrow. Similarities of style rather than of content could be seen in the last period of the rule of Sukarno in Indonesia; and nation-worship, though without worship of a single infallible leader, characterised at times the regimes of the *Ba'ath* in Syria and Iraq.

## Communism

The word 'communism' can be made to cover a multitude of doctrines and of movements, aiming at the sharing of earthly goods between the members of a community; and examples can be traced back to very distant periods of history. In modern times however the word can be confined to doctrines and movements which claim to be derived from the teachings and the political example of Marx and Lenin.

All Leninists repudiated nationalism. They claimed to be proletarian internationalists, and maintained that the workers had no fatherland but the whole world. Every Leninist movement had the duty to work for a proletarian socialist revolution in its own country. When a Leninist movement obtained power in any country, it should regard itself as a vanguard of the world socialist revolution. From 7 November 1917 for nearly thirty years, only one Leninist movement in fact held power: the Bolshevik party in the greater part of the former lands of the Russian empire.[9] The basis of legitimacy of Bolshevik rule was not the support of the people of the former empire, or of the Russian nation; in fact, in the election to the Constituent Assembly in November 1917 a large majority both of the whole population and of the Russian nation voted against the Bolsheviks. The basis of legitimacy was the claim that the Bolshevik party stood for the immanent interest of the working class of the whole world. This claim was based on Lenin's profound conviction that the Bolshevik leadership—which he, a man without petty personal vanity, identified with himself—were the only persons who had a complete and 'correct' understanding of Marxist theory. After Lenin's death, there came into use the expressions 'Marxism-Leninism' and 'Marxist-Leninist science'. Official doctrine continued to be that his wisdom was exclusively embodied in the leadership of the CPSU, which in the 1930s came to mean in one man, Stalin.

The 'cult of personality',[10] of which Stalin was the object, raised him to the level of a substitute god. The apotheosis of Stalin began about the same time as the apotheosis of Hitler, and they developed on rather similar lines. At first however there was one clear difference between them: the ersatz-god Hitler symbolised the German nation, while the ersatz-god Stalin symbolised the international working class. The Germans were invited to worship the German nation in the form of the Führer, but the Russians were not invited to worship the Russian nation (and still less, the non-Russians to worship their nations). However, the difference became less sharp as the years passed. Stalin was held up to all communists as an object of worship, together with the Soviet socialist state. 'Socialism' was, by definition, what existed in the Soviet Union. The interests of the workers of the world were whatever Stalin said they were. Communists all over the world must always serve above all the interests of the Soviet state. Léon Blum's remark that the French Communist Party was *un parti nationaliste étranger* was not far from the truth, though it was not entirely accurate: the object of devotion of the leaders of the PCF was not a foreign nation but a foreign state. Yet as the process of neo-Russification (briefly discussed in an earlier chapter, pp. 313-319) made itself felt; and as a new form of Great Russian chauvinism (so sincerely and fiercely hated by Lenin in his lifetime) increasingly pervaded Soviet political and social life, the difference between the avowedly nationalist legitimacy of Hitlerism and the allegedly internationalist legitimacy of Stalinism dwindled. During the same year also the common totalitarian features of the two regimes became more prominent. In Soviet Russia no less than in the Third Reich was visible the *tendency* to concentrate all political, economic and spiritual power in the hands of an infallible leader, and to deny any autonomy to the private life of the citizen. In reality, the power of the Soviet regime approximated much more closely to the totalitarian aim than did that of the Third Reich. There were no institutional islands protected from the party in Russia, as there were in Germany; but in Russia, no less than in Germany, the attempt to abolish family loyalties and religious beliefs failed.

Enough has been said in earlier chapters of the reimposition of imperial rule in communist form on the non-Russian nations of the Soviet Union, of the new type of neo-Russification which emerged under Stalin, and of the evolution of Soviet neo-colonialism in Eastern Europe after 1945, culminating in the Brezhnev doctrine of limited sovereignty. We need now to consider the treatment by the Soviet leaders of conflicting nationalisms in countries not ruled by communists, and the relationship between communist and nationalist movements struggling against capitalist governments or against non-communist imperial or colonial regimes.

The Soviet leaders attempted, through the local communist parties, to exploit the national conflicts which kept Central and Eastern Europe in a condition of permanent unrest between the world wars: for example, conflicts between Poles and Ukrainians, Czechs and Germans, Hungarians and Romanians or Serbs and Bulgarians. They had little success: in the 1930s, when both national and social discontent rapidly grew throughout the whole region, it was the fascists rather than the communists who benefited from them.

The first major opportunity for the exploitation by communists of an anti-imperialist movement outside Europe came in China. The Bolshevik Revolution was soon seen by some Chinese intellectuals as the work of one of the great European nations, directed against European imperialism, in the name of the most advanced social doctrines yet devised by European thinkers. Hitherto the best Chinese minds had been frustrated by this cruel contradiction: the ideas which held out hope for the peoples of the world, including the Chinese people, came from Europe and North America, yet the might of European and North American government and business was being used to exploit China. A Chinese who promoted progressive Western ideas found himself working for Western domination of China; a Chinese who opposed Western ideas found himself holding China back in an antiquated world, under the sway of values and institutions doomed to perish. The Bolshevik Revolution changed this. Li Ta-chao and Chen Tu-hsiu welcomed communism because it enabled them to use Western ideas to fight Western power. In the 1920s numbers of young Chinese intellectuals joined the communist party. In 1926-27 the communists played a part in the northward march of the nationalists, but were then crushed, with great losses among their best men, by Chiang Kai-shek.

This disaster for the communists was a direct result of Soviet policy. Stalin, who controlled the Communist International (Comintern) which gave the directives to communist parties, was unable to resolve the contradiction between the interests of the Soviet state and the interests of the Chinese revolution. If he were to encourage the communists, who had a large following among Chinese workers and peasants, to fight it out with Chiang Kai-shek, this would break the precarious unity of the Chinese nationalist front, which was directed against the European power which was then considered to be Soviet Russia's main enemy—the British empire. Stalin therefore forced the Chinese communists to hold back the forces of social revolution, to refrain from attacking Chinese business and land-owners, and to maintain cooperation, first with Chiang Kai-shek and then with the left wing of the Kuomintang. The result was that Chiang was able to choose his own time to attack, and destroyed all but a remnant of the communists.

In the 1920s and 1930s the Comintern produced numerous directives and much rhetoric on the subject of anti-imperialist action, and made efforts to win support in Asian colonies. Some Indian and Indonesian leaders—notably Nehru and Sukarno—learnt much from communist anti-imperialist specialists during their visits to Europe. The relations of the Indian National Congress and of the Indonesian nationalist movements with the Indian and Indonesian communist parties were not, however, very friendly. The French communists were rather more successful in Indo-China. In Ho Chi Minh, who worked for some time in Paris, the communist cause won an outstanding personality. However, in the 1930s anti-colonial nationalists, like discontented European nationalists, looked rather to the Axis Powers, Germany and Italy, or to Japan. Pro-Axis Arab nationalists included Shakib Arslan, the mufti of Jerusalem and various Egyptian and Iraqi army officers. In India, Subhas Chandra Bose made contact with the Japanese and visited Nazi Germany. Aung San became commander of a Burmese National Army, and Sukarno of an Indonesian political administration, both under Japanese control. In Latin America, nationalism directed against foreign—first British and then American—capitalists was exploited more effectively by Nazi agents than by communist.

If communists had little success in capturing national discontents for their purposes in peace-time, the situation changed with foreign invasion and occupation. In 1937 and 1938 the Japanese defeated the regular armies of Chiang Kai-shek, and occupied the main cities and lines of communication. It was the communists, far more than Chiang, who mobilised the civil population, with patriotic anti-Japanese slogans, to resist the Japanese. Their successes were due, not to wise advice from the distant Stalin (who in fact made a treaty with Japan in 1941 at the expense of China to protect his own eastern frontier), but to the skill of the Chinese communist leader Mao Tse-tung and his colleagues. A second country in which communists successfully put themselves at the head of resistance to foreign occupation was Yugoslavia. Here, as we have seen, they eventually won support by their policy of national equality and common resistance of Serbs, Croats, Slovenes and Macedonians against the Germans and the rival nationalists whose quarrels the Germans were exploiting. A combination of appeals to patriotism and promises of social and political reform also won strong support for the communists in Albania and in Greece; and similar attitudes account for the success of both the Indochinese and the Malayan Chinese communists in resistance to the Japanese. The military organisation and mass support created by the communists in northern Vietnam enabled them after 1945 to resist the returning French, and later to extend guerrilla action to the south. Thirty years later they achieved their aims throughout the whole of Vietnam. In Malaya the Chinese communist guerrilla was directed from 1948 against the returning British, but it was defeated after many years of effort.

In Eastern Europe after 1945 the communists in some cases sought to solve national conflicts by conciliation, in others to manipulate them for the advantage of the Soviet state. The most important example of the first is Yugoslavia, discussed in an earlier chapter; of the second, the relationship of the Poles with Germany.

Poland acquired territories formerly inhabited by some nine million Germans; and the Czechoslovak government in 1945 (when communists were the main party in power but did not yet possess a complete monopoly) expelled three million Germans from the borderlands of Germany. It was the conscious aim of the Soviet leaders to create a deep gulf of hatred between the Germans and their eastern neighbours, and so to make Poles and Czechs absolutely dependent on Soviet Russian help against any revival of German power. For many years this was successful, and resentments remained bitter on both sides. However, in the 1960s a marked change appeared in both public opinion and government attitudes in Western Germany,[11] a desire for reconciliation with the Poles became very widespread, and many Germans even began to accept the new eastern frontiers of Germany as permanent. The new generation of Germans from territories incorporated in Poland found new homes and jobs in the Rhineland, Bavaria or Hesse, and the elder exiles who clamoured for return to their old homelands were dying off.

This new conciliatory mood in Germany was viewed with alarm by the Polish communists. During these years Poles were growing more and more exasperated by Soviet Russian domination—which the events of 1956 had mitigated but not removed—and the only means which the Polish leaders still had, if not to make themselves popular then at least to retard the growth of opposition, was to maximise fear and hatred of Germany. They needed the bogey of aggressive Western Germany to keep themselves in power, and their Soviet protectors had the same interest, if only to persuade the Poles that 'the Germans are even worse than the Russians'. Thus anti-German propaganda continued in Poland long after German hostility to Poland had diminished.

Then suddenly Soviet policy changed. The Soviet government decided that economic cooperation with Western Germany would be useful to them, and that this required the termination of anti-German propaganda. Immediately the Polish communists had to do likewise. The agreements of 1970, which included West German recognition of the Polish western border along the Oder and western Neisse rivers, were followed by reasonably polite official relations between the states. The whole story is one of manipulation of nationalist passions by the communists, in accordance with the state interests of the Soviet Union.

In the newly independent states of the Muslim world and Africa, communists were few, and were distrusted by the nationalist governments in power; but these governments sought, and increasingly received, Soviet political and economic support whenever they were in conflict with Western governments, or with other Asian or African states who had good relations with Western governments. Egypt was the outstanding case: Nasser disliked, and from time to time persecuted, Egyptian communists, yet this did not prevent the Soviet Union from giving him valuable and continuous aid. In Syria and Iraq the fortunes of the local communists varied from fierce persecution to strong influence, but these fluctuations could not be simply correlated with the rise and fall of Soviet aid to the governments of those countries. In India the communist movement was disunited: the most pro-Soviet faction supported the Congress governments, especially that of Mrs Indira Gandhi, who was glad to have their support and made full use of it when she decided to make herself dictator in June 1975. However, the influence and power of the Indian pro-Soviet communists remained limited. Genuine Indian revolutionaries were unwilling to act as agents of a new European imperial power, and, as has been shown, factions broke away on the left wing of the communist party.

In 1960 the Soviet ideological specialists propounded a new doctrine of 'national democracy'. This flattering description was given to a number of new states which showed themselves hostile to Western government and to Western capital, maintained dictatorships with social policies broadly acceptable to communist aims (land reform was especially stressed), and tended to move from a foreign policy of neutrality towards one of regular cooperation with the Soviet Union. The outstanding examples praised by Soviet spokesmen at this time were the regimes of Ben Bella in Algeria, of Nkrumah in Ghana, of Sukarno in Indonesia and of Sékou Touré in Guinea. In the following years, however, all but the last of these regimes were overthrown.

During the late 1960s the phrase 'national democracy' fell into disuse in the Soviet political vocabulary.[12] However, non-communist nationalist dictatorships favourable to the Soviet Union, or influenceable or exploitable by Soviet policy, increased. Though Sékou Touré at one point quarrelled with his Soviet advisers, the two governments were reconciled, and Guinea remained to some extent an outpost of Soviet influence on the west coast of Africa. Somalia on the east coast also offered favourable opportunities; but the revolution in Ethiopia placed the Soviet government in a dilemma not unlike those which had faced earlier imperial powers. Both the Somali and the Ethiopian revolutionaries mouthed quasi-Marxist slogans, but they were hostile to each other; and this hostility could hardly be reconciled as long as the Eritreans, whose leaders mouthed similar slogans, were in revolt against Ethiopia on the borders of Somalia. The victory of the Mozambique guerrilla movement and the Angolan MPLA further strengthened the Soviet position in Africa and increased the output of quasi-Marxist rhetoric. African revolutionaries and Soviet leaders joined in urging black Rhodesians to reject any settlement by negotiation between white and black Rhodesian politicians.

The most promising of the original 'national democracies' soon turned into something else. Fidel Castro was not originally a communist. His ideology was an individual combination of some sort of socialism with anti–North American nationalism. However, after he had been in power for some time he declared himself a Marxist-Leninist, proceeded to take over the leadership of the existing communist party in Cuba, and—to the astonishment and exasperation of the regular party leaders—received Moscow's approval for such action. Cuba thereby graduated to the status of 'people's democracy'. As such, it proved expensive as a recipient of

Soviet aid, but also proved valuable as an example of a successful amalgam of anti-Americanism and locally flavoured Marxism.

In 1976 Castro handsomely repaid his debt by transporting 12,000 Cuban troops, equipped and trained with Soviet bloc weapons, in Soviet aircraft, across the Southern Atlantic to Angola, where they ensured the victory of the MPLA over its internal rivals, while the American former masters of the Atlantic looked on unmoved.[13]

Hitherto I have been assuming that all communists followed Soviet directives, and that the world communist movement was 'monolithic'. Strictly speaking, this was not so even in the mid-1930s, since followers of Stalin's exiled enemy Trotsky existed in several countries. A more important breach came in 1948, when the Yugoslav communists were excommunicated by the Soviet leaders; after which they proceeded to develop both theory and practice on their own lines. But a still more important schism came in the 1960s, when China broke away from the Soviet camp. The Chinese communists, like the Yugoslav, had made their own revolution and won their own war of national liberation; both, for essentially similar reasons, resented the patronising attitude of Stalin, and both were for essentially similar reasons distrusted by him. But the breach between Soviet Russia and China was more important than the breach with Yugoslavia, because China was a potential world power.

In the 1960s Chinese-sponsored communist parties appeared in various countries; and one communist-ruled state—Albania—unreservedly supported China against the Soviet Union. Apart from this, communist factions in several countries declared themselves to be Trotskyists. In Europe and North America many intellectuals of the extreme left profoundly distrusted the Soviet Union, which seemed to them a bureaucratic state with imperialist ambitions. These people, of whom the student agegroup formed a high proportion, supported numerous Trotskyist or 'Maoist' sects (not all the latter being approved by responsible Chinese spokesmen). Their cumulative influence on public opinion in Western Europe, North America and Japan was not negligible.[14]

In the mid-1970s in the Soviet Union communism meant a semitotalitarian bureaucratic state, treating its subjects more mildly than in Stalin's time, pursuing a world-wide expansion in which traditional Great Russian nationalism and imperialism were reinforced by the selfrighteousness of residual revolutionary rhetoric, while the national aspirations of some 120 million non-Russians were denied expression. In its East European dependencies it meant a variety of more or less tolerable compromises between irremovable national consciousnesses and irresistible demands of the imperial power. In Yugoslavia the balance was internal, and very complex: no attempt was made to crush any nation by any other nation, yet the ability of at least six nations to coexist with each other remained precarious. In Albania communism meant a unique mixture of revolutionary fanaticism and xenophobia, made possible by isolation and by primitive needs and low expectations. In China communism meant a tremendous revival of the most numerous people and the oldest continuous civilisation in the world, inspired by a revolutionary zeal which seemed determined to deny the essence of that civilisation. It was difficult for a Western mind to comprehend the motivation of the rulers of any of these polities (except the Yugoslav) and still more difficult to judge how stable or precarious they might be. The difficulty did not however inhibit Western media-stars from making confident assertions or prophecies.

In the rest of the world in the 1970s an epidemic of violent rhetoric and small violent actions—kidnappings, piracy, urban and rural guerrilla— made it difficult to distinguish 'communism' from 'nationalism', or either of these from 'fascism', or indeed to give a precise meaning to any of those three words. There was a nationalisation of communism, a Marxisation of nationalism, and a predilection by the adepts of both to ape the style of Mussolini. Though the top cadres of established communist parties remained disciplined exponents of orthodox Soviet-type Marxism-Leninism; and though the leaders of nationalist parties or nationalist regimes neither considered themselves to be communists nor were accepted by true believers as being communists; yet below the highest level in both types of party it was increasingly difficult to say whether an activist was primarily a nationalist, a Marxist, or a pseudo-Marxist revolutionary.

# 13 Nations, States, and the Human Community

## Patterns of national movement

In the record of the formation of nations, of which numerous cases have been mentioned in the preceding pages, generosity and *hubris*, self-sacrifice and denial of others' rights, flowering and withering of culture are woven inextricably together.

The English and French nations came slowly to maturity. For a hundred years or so they displayed two variants of a combination of liberty, power, civility and vigour perhaps more admirable than any yet attained in human history. This age of greatness was preceded by many centuries of savagery and squalor. The road to glory was strewn with the bones of slaughtered serfs and rebels, and of the vainglorious tyrants who had once trampled on them. In the 1970s, half a century or so after their age of greatness was over, the English and French nations seemed to prefer the postures of two elderly aunts, quarrelling with each other about trivialities, and united only in the firm belief that their families, and everyone else's too, owed them a comfortable living for all time.

There were other nations which had come to the threshold of greatness; had fallen or had been pushed back into disunity or subjection to others; had reemerged to a new sense of a national mission, briefly achieved unity within vast territories, giving them dominion over others; overreached themselves, and been thrust back again into division or dependency or frustration. Such has been the modern fate of both Germans and Poles.

Another pattern is the great community held together by a splendid civilisation extending over a vast territory, which suffers eclipse (from social or cultural decay, internal discord, foreign invasion or several of these together), and then seeks to reappear in a new guise as a modern nation.

Hellas was transformed into Alexander's empire; reincarnated in the Byzantine; engulfed by the Turks; resuscitated by a new nationalism; inebriated with a Great Idea which proved to be but another form of classical *hubris*; and plunged back into a frenzy of self-destruction, from which its friends continued to hope that it would save itself and bring new gifts to humanity.

The Islamic empire brought not only destruction but spiritual and intellectual enrichment to the Mediterranean world; tore itself to pieces by its factions; stagnated for centuries; and gave birth to the idea of an Arab nation, whose pioneers started out with high hopes, but whose successors, meeting with closed doors and closed minds wherever they turned, seemed reduced to mass production of rhetoric and civil strife.

Iran, the first of the great territorial empires of the West, lost its conquests to other empires but preserved its basic homeland and its religion for nearly a thousand years; lost both of these but preserved its language, even though greatly modified, and the memory of its culture, even though greatly distorted; and reemerged as a modern nation with aims at first more modest than those of Greeks or Arabs, but increasing with astonishing speed as the first modest successes were achieved.

Alone of the great communities of civilisation, the Chinese survived for more than three thousand years; not always in the same territory; suffering for centuries at a time from alien conquerors wielding power through their own chains of command on Chinese soil, coexisting with Chinese civilisation; always tolerating variety of religions and languages within their realm; yet preserving in unbroken continuity their own essential and unique character (whether one calls it 'cultural' or 'social' or 'national' or all three); and reappearing, in the age of modern giant powers, as one of the giants.

Different again were the empires which expanded by military power far beyond their homelands, bringing peoples of utterly different culture under their dominion. Such were the Portuguese, Spanish, British, French and Russian, variously established across America, Asia and Africa. The first four, built by sea power, eventually abdicated, after varying processes in which decay, defeat and consent were variously combined. The first to be founded, the Portuguese, was also the last to be surrendered. The fifth of the empires showed no sign, in the mid-1970s, of imminent surrender. Two special features of the Russian empire may be noted. First, it was built by expansion overland, not by sea; and as land communications and inter-locking trade multiplied, the links between metropolis and periphery were strengthened. Secondly, the ruling elite, which was descended from those who had built, and which itself had added to the empire, was overthrown by a great convulsion, and replaced by a completely new elite with a consuming lust for power; whereas the elites of the other four imperial nations, though modified by some degree of social mobility during the last decades of their rule, remained basically the same, and were subject to a steady process of erosion of will to power. The will to power of the Russian elite, in its Soviet form, was reinforced by its claim to possess a monopoly of the sole completely scientific doctrine of the past, present and future of human society. How long the doctrine would survive, how long the will to power would resist erosion, and whether contiguity on land would always ensure more effective control than communication by sea, remained uncertain.

### The nation as object of worship

The nationalism of the twentieth century has usually been more bitter than the nationalism of the nineteenth. Nationalism has often inspired the fanaticism which in earlier periods was reserved for religious conflicts. There is indeed much to be said for the view that the increased fanaticism of nationalists is causally connected with the decline of religious belief. Nationalism has become an ersatz religion. The nation, as understood by the nationalist, is a substitute god; nationalism of this sort might be called *ethnolatry*. Much the same may be said, incidentally, of the attitude of many Marxist or quasi-Marxist social revolutionaries towards the idea of class. The Working Class, as interpreted by the Central Committee of the Communist Party of the Soviet Union, is also a substitute god; official Soviet communism might be called *taxolatry*. (Whether ethnolatry or taxolatry was the dominant element in the outlook of the leaders of the Soviet Russian empire in the 1970s was open to argument.)

Sometimes national and religious aims have been consciously identified. The Dutch in the sixteenth century were fighting for both the freedom of the Netherlands and their Protestant faith; the *Ikhwan al-Muslimin* were both Egyptian nationalists and Muslim fundamentalists; the Romanian Iron Guard believed themselves to be defending both the Romanian people and the Orthodox Church against Franco-Anglo-Judaic exploitation. Hitler and the elite of the National Socialist Party believed in no god but the German *Volk*, as symbolised by the Führer, though it is probably true that large numbers of National Socialists still held to the slogan of *Gott mit uns*; and it is known that at the end of his life Hitler bitterly confessed that the real German *Volk* had proved to be unworthy of his conception of it.

The perversion of nationalist doctrine, and the follies and crimes committed by nationalists, must appal any one who tries honestly to study human history. Unfortunately there are two traps for the intellectually unwary, into which it is all too easy to fall.

One is the belief that although past nationalist movements have sullied themselves with crimes, and other nations are burdened with sin, one's own nation is different. It is pure, noble, generous, incapable of injustice towards others. This form of nationalist utopianism has its counterpart in the social utopianism of those revolutionary intellectuals who are unshakably convinced that, though past revolutions have drenched humanity with blood and have been followed by merciless tyrannies, their own revolution will bring only universal benevolence and happiness. Such attitudes may seem ridiculous to a reader nurtured in the sheltered political climate of a Western democratic polity: to him, self-righteous complacency and Pharisaical professions of exclusive virtue appear comic. Unfortunately this too is an error. The persons of whom I am thinking are not comic but mortally dangerous, not Pharisees but devoted fanatics. No reasoning will deflect them. It is useless to argue with them that utopianism itself is the cause of subsequent bloodshed and tyranny. It is no good discussing the facts of a situation or the merits of a movement, because truth *is*, by definition, whatever the national or social revolutionary leader says it is; and the common good *is*, by definition, whatever the leader declares to be his aim at any particular moment. No agreement is possible with nationalist or Leninist or Trotskyist revolutionary fanatics except by total acceptance of their assertions and total subordination to their will.

The other intellectual trap is to dismiss all nationalist movements as utterly foolish and to denounce all nationalism as an unmitigated evil. There are perhaps some persons who have genuinely risen above all national prejudices, and whose loyalty is given solely to the human race as a whole. Perhaps the late Dag Hammerskjöld was such a man. Perhaps there are others among the permanent officials of the United Nations, or the exalted Olympians of some great scientific laboratories, or on the heights of abstract art and *avant-garde* music. Such people are scarce, and their capacity for leadership of real men and women is doubtful. If they refuse to look more closely at the nationalist passions and prejudices which animate so large a portion of humanity, if they will make no effort to distinguish the component elements of nationalism from each other, the truth from the fiction, the positive from the destructive, they cut themselves off from the real world. Much more numerous than these unworldly humanitarians are those who think themselves to be above nationalism but are in fact full of unconscious nationalist prejudice. They are especially numerous among successful 'satisfied' nations which have enjoyed independence, unity, prosperity and greatness for many generations past—the 'super-power' Americans and Russians and the old and still comfortable (though materially declining) nations like the English, French and Swedes. The unconscious, though obvious and unmistakable, arrogance with which they view those nations which they regard as tiresome upstarts, leaves an unpleasant Pecksniffian taste.

Newer smaller nations behave with less dignity, and often abuse temporary successes. Yet members of older nations are unimaginative and ungenerous if they cannot recognise the creative energies and the spiritually and materially productive forces which have been released by the independence of new nations. The disappearance of the Habsburg Monarchy in 1918 meant cultural impoverishment for Europe; but it is also true that the upsurge of cultural energies of the newly independent peoples whose states replaced the Monarchy enriched the culture of Europe. Poets and novelists and dramatists multiplied in the less-known languages, more rapidly than when these languages had been painfully emerging from the condition of peasant dialects in an empire with one great European language as the medium of high culture. These languages grew more complex and more beautiful, their literatures took their place in world literature, and the ideas which they expressed found their way through translation into other literatures. This infusion of new talents and energies extended from literature to the theatre and the cinema: the achievements of Czechs, Hungarians, Poles and Romanians in these fields need no comment. In the visual arts and music, and in all branches of natural science and learning, the same was to be seen.

It is of course arguable that these achievements could have occurred within the framework of large multinational states; that creative energies do not require independent sovereign states for their expression. It is easy for 'satisfied' nations to argue thus. They achieved their independence, and their creative energies burst forth, a long time earlier.

There is another side to the question. The refusal of national demands creates growing resentment, and this leads to an accumulation of explosive material. In short, excessive nationalism is dangerous because it can turn into aggression against other states, and repression of upsurging nationalism is dangerous because it can produce explosions, or fears of explosions, within a state, which in turn may threaten other states.

## Nationalism as a cause of war

It is often said that nationalism has been a major cause of war. Often those who assert this mean no more than that sovereign states, pursuing their own aims regardless of others, clash with each other. This is true, but hardly worth saying.

It makes more sense to ask whether nationalist activities, in the senses used in this work—movements for independence, movements for unity and efforts to create national consciousness by government action—have been frequent causes of war.

The Franco-Austrian war of 1859, the Prusso-Austrian war of 1866, the Franco-Prussian war of 1870 and the Russo-Turkish war of 1877 were not primarily wars for Italian, German and Bulgarian national unity: rather they were wars by three rulers—Napoleon III, Bismarck and Alexander II—who sought to make their states dominant on the European continent.

However, these three national causes provided a good deal of the public enthusiasm for the four wars, and the wars resulted in the unification of most of Italy and most of Germany, and in the independence of most of Bulgaria.

The First World War was also a war between great empires. Nevertheless, it was started by a conflict between Austria-Hungary and Serbia, which was directly caused by the unsatisfied movement of the South Slavs for national unity. There were also other unsatisfied nationalisms within the Habsburg Monarchy which threatened its survival. These nationalisms had been largely provoked by the policy of the Hungarian government which sought to create a single Magyar nation out of several other nations by a policy dictated from above. In Russia, the chief antagonist of Austria-Hungary, a similar policy of creating a Russian nation out of several nations, by a policy dictated from above, had provoked similar nationalisms which threatened the integrity of the Russian empire. Some of the Austrian generals were convinced that the only way to preserve the Habsburg Monarchy was to crush Serbia, which they saw as the source of unrest within the Habsburg dominions. Some of the German generals took the same view, and together they convinced the Austrian and German civilian politicians. In Russia it was felt that if Serbia were not supported, Germany and Austria would dominate all Eastern Europe, and this would further strengthen disruptive nationalism within the Russian empire. Therefore Russia too had to go to war. To sum up, the complex interplay of national conflicts within the Habsburg Monarchy, the Balkan states and the Russian empire formed the largest single group of causes which brought about the First World War.

In the case of the Second World War these same forces operated. It may be argued that Hitler was himself a nationalist, resolved to perfect the union of all Germans which had been left incomplete in 1870. He succeeded in annexing the great majority of 'unredeemed' Germans in 1938 without war (Austria and the Bohemian borderlands of Czechoslovakia), but he was unable to annex the million and a half Germans of Poland and the city of Danzig without going to war with the Poles, and this let loose a European war which in turn became a world war. It can also be argued that a series of conflicts, concerned with the status of unsatisfied nations (Croats and Slovaks) or of divided nations (Hungarians in Czechoslovakia, Yugoslavia and Romania; Bulgarians in Yugoslavia, Romania and Greece), created in Central Europe an atmosphere of mutual hatred between states which caused each in turn to succumb either to the blandishments or to the aggression of Hitler. Thus nationalism played an important part. Nevertheless, it is equally clear that Hitler's aims were not limited to anything which, even if the phrase be stretched to the utmost, can be described as German nationalism. His aim was to conquer all Europe and a good deal more besides. Mussolini aimed to create a new Roman empire in the Mediterranean, the Japanese a Greater East Asia Co-Prosperity Sphere embracing hundreds of millions who were not Japanese. In short, the role of nationalism in the origins of the Second World War was smaller than in the origins of the First.

The two most important wars since 1945, the Korean and the Vietnamese, may be thought to have been motivated by movements for national unity. At the same time the Korean and Vietnamese communists also had ideological aims (whether one thinks in terms of the perceived justice of their ideological cause, or of the imposition on others of an elite which considered itself to represent an ideology). It is difficult to disentangle the elements of nationalism and ideology. In the case of their main antagonist, the United States, nationalism played no part: American motivation was partly ideological (to resist communism) and partly strategic: to prevent the victory of political leaderships which were expected to be satellites of the main strategic rival of the United States—the Soviet Russian empire.

Thus, not only has nationalism undoubtedly been an important cause of wars in the twentieth century, but forcible repression of national aspirations has also been, and has still remained, a potential cause of regional and perhaps even global wars in the mid-1970s.

Wars however are started by governments, and are waged between states. National movements threaten to disrupt states; and states promote national movements in order to disrupt other states.

It has become a dogma of nationalists that the nation cannot be free, and cannot freely develop its culture, unless it is in possession of the apparatus of a sovereign state of its own. Rulers of sovereign states in which there is a national movement demanding independence usually regard such a movement as a threat to their security, and use varying methods, mild or harsh, to repress it.

It is only partly true that 'nationalism causes wars', or that 'the sovereign state is an obstacle to peace'. The truth is rather that conflicts between national movements and sovereign states are one of the main sources of wars. Peace would be best served if national movements could aim at something other than state sovereignty, and if rulers of sovereign states that are multinational would accept the reality of diverse national cultures.

## Sovereignty and national cultures

Somehow the aims of national movements have to be separated from the dogmas of state sovereignty; yet the need for a type of closer international cooperation overriding state boundaries must not be made an excuse for crushing national cultures or humiliating national consciousness. The last two hundred years have shown that, though states may be formed with enthusiasm, collapse with ignominy, and disappear altogether; yet national cultures are almost indestructible, and national consciousness denied or humiliated becomes an explosive force of deadly power.

A plan for the separation of national culture and state sovereignty was put forward, as we have seen, before 1914 by the Social Democrats of Austria-Hungary. Its essence was that members of each nation should enjoy cultural autonomy; and that the national cultural administrations should coexist with the centralised political and economic administration of the state.

Neither of the two rather different schemes, of Otto Bauer and of Karl Renner, was ever attempted in practice, because the Habsburg Monarchy remained under the control of unsympathetic political classes in Vienna and Budapest until it disintegrated. Unfortunately also, as we have seen, because the ideas of Bauer and Renner happened to incur the wrath of Lenin, the whole concept of cultural autonomy has been rejected ever since, as a matter of dogma, by all communists. Hostility to the ideas of the Austrians became part of the hotchpotch of conventional wisdom mouthed by *marxisants* in all five continents.

Of course the particular proposals of Bauer and Renner were out of date more than fifty years after the empire which they sought to invigorate had ceased to exist. Yet they pointed in a direction which many contemporary political leaders might do worse than explore. They seemed especially relevant to those many states in Asia and Africa in which there were numerous communities differing in language, social customs or religion from each other, but in which a definite national consciousness had not yet crystallised, or perhaps even was not likely to crystallise. If something similar to the Bauer or Renner schemes had been established in Nigeria, for example, one wonders whether the Ibo communities in the North and West would not have been better able to coexist with the majority peoples among whom they lived, and the Ibos in the East have become less desperately convinced of the need to break away. In cities like Addis Ababa, Ibadan, Khartoum and Kinshasa, swollen by the influx of thousands upon thousands of persons from different peoples with different cultures, there would seem to be a case for considering these ideas. Almost all African states were bedevilled by the contradiction between cultural diversity and state unity. Ritual denunciations of 'tribalism' were but a poor substitute for constructive policies. The Nilotic peoples, Eritreans and Somalis were not likely to give up their struggles for unity or for independence just because different dictators in Sudan or Ethiopia mouthed 'progressive' slogans. It did not appear in 1976 in Angola, either that 'progressive' slogans would create an Angolan nation, or that repression of hostile peoples, even with the help of 'socialist' allies, would put an end to their different cultural needs. Other

Eritreas and Angolas might well appear almost anywhere in western, central and southern no less than eastern Africa. Right across southern Asia, above all in India, similar problems threatened.

The policy of cultural autonomy seems less well suited to deal with movements of national discontent in communities where national consciousness has been crystallised, and where sovereign states exist which are allegedly based on nationality—that is, in Europe and in the Muslim Middle East. A case might be made for Kurdish cultural autonomy in Turkey, Iran, Syria and Iraq; but the first three governments were unwilling to consider it, while the promises made in Baghdad had been repeatedly violated. Israelis were understandably unattracted by any type of cultural autonomy within a wider Arab political system, whose practical operation would depend on the goodwill of persons who asserted their implacable determination to destroy 'Zionism', an aim which could not very easily be distinguished from that of extermination of Jews as such. In the Soviet empire, the existence of political units described as 'Soviet republics', 'autonomous regions' or 'autonomous provinces' had not in fact guaranteed respect for national cultures. In the East European area of Soviet neo-colonialism, the existence of nominally sovereign states, each based on one or two nations,[1] had not prevented Soviet policies designed to falsify the history of these nations and to deprive them of their national cultures. The only remedy for this state of affairs was a change of policy in Moscow, of which in the mid-1970s there was no sign. Only in Yugoslavia were sincere efforts made to combine national cultural diversity with a state system that was in one sense highly decentralised, yet in another sense held together by a single party that was intended to be (though it was not always in reality) highly centralised. In Yugoslavia both the conflict between Serbs and Croats and the discontents of an Albanian community numbering about a million and a half persons had remained dangerous.

In the West European regions of dissatisfied nationalism, cultural and economic and ideological-political discontents were variously mixed; yet in all cases the essential claim was recognition of the nation as such. This was true of the Catalans, who certainly derived economic advantages from living within a single Spanish state, and also had economic grievances against the government and privileged classes; yet would not be content with economic concessions unless Madrid would recognise the existence of a Catalan nation and create institutions for it within a federal or confederal Spain.

The Scots, it may be argued, already possessed the essence of cultural autonomy in the form of their own church, law and schools, though it is also true that not much money was available for encouraging literature in Lallans or Gaelic. Scots had derived economic advantage from the Union; their country had then become a 'distressed area' which received little aid from prosperous south-east England; and then they had seen the prospect of wealth from North Sea oil which they felt should be theirs. Yet the Scots were not just asking for financial aid to their industry or their literature: they were asking for institutions that would recognise their status as a nation. This need was probably felt to some extent by a majority of Scots, most of whom however did not wish to break the Union or to set up the ridiculous paraphernalia of a separate republic. Yet the obtuse inability of the English politicians of both main political parties to understand that national feeling cannot be quantified in pounds and pence, drove great numbers of Scots into support of crackpot fanatics.

In the case of both Scots and Catalans, the Bauer-Renner types of solution did not seem appropriate. A more promising direction would seem to be a confederal Spain or a confederal Britain; yet it appeared doubtful whether the rulers in either Madrid or London had sufficient political imagination to pursue such ideas further.

The growth of language groups into nations, and the consequent disintegration of multinational states, as it has been described in this book, especially in Central and Eastern Europe, is a pattern which could, but need not, be repeated in Asia and Africa. One essential aspect of what happened in Central and Eastern Europe is that, with the development of schools and industry and with the spread of Enlightenment ideas, there arose new elites of language manipulators who identified the language-group as the unit on behalf of which democratic rights must be claimed. This phenomenon was not unknown in Asia: Bengali and Tamil national-ism based on language were important forces within independent India. However, the predominant trend among Asian intelligentsias, applying both to ideological 'left' and 'right', was in favour of state unity. This was still more true in most of Africa. The new elites sought to create a new nation, based on the frontiers of the state, and denounced the trend towards the creation of national consciousnesses based on language as 'tribalism'. They hoped to develop mass loyalties not to individual indige-nous cultures but to a new social order founded on growing material welfare for the masses and on growing pride of the masses in their state. Paradoxically, in most of the new states the establishment of a non-'tribal' higher loyalty, binding on all the language groups and religious groups, required the retention at the higher administrative and educational level of the language of the former European imperial nation. The country in which a higher African loyalty was most passionately pursued by a black intelligentsia, at the accepted cost of adopting one or two white men's languages, was South Africa. The white South African government by contrast encouraged the development of individual African languages and cultures, with the undoubted aim of dividing the Africans in order better to rule them.

To some extent one may say that in Asia and Africa, as in Central and Eastern Europe in an earlier period, language manipulators predominated in the rising elites before independence. However, there is a difference. In both cases writers, journalists and lawyers were prominent, but one key element in the Central and East European case was lacking in the African case: the grammarians and philologists. There were no African counterparts of Dobrovský and Vuk Karadžić, no attempts to make Wolof or Kimbundu or any other local African language the basis of national identity. The African intelligentsia identified the nation with the whole population of the state, or (in the case of Nkrumah and other Panafricanists) with the whole non-white population of Africa.[2]

Yet it would be rash to assume that there was no future in Africa for linguistic nationalism of the Central or East European type. This was bound to depend very largely on the development of the social structures of the African states. There are other potential elites beside language manipulators; and in new states former language manipulators become professional soldiers, bureaucrats and politicians, and their outlooks change. Mass discontents can arise on the basis of an indigenous regionally defined culture, and these can create their intelligentsias. Eritrean and Somali nationalism seem already to have some of the features of earlier Danubian nationalism, and Ethiopia some of the features of the Habsburg Monarchy. It is unwise to prophesy, but prudent to be aware of possibilities, even if some of these are unpleasant.

### The sovereign state and the international order

In the twentieth century the number of sovereign states, whose relations make up world politics, has steadily increased, especially in the 1960s and 1970s. Yet it is obvious that some sovereign states are in reality more sovereign than others. There are a number of well-known developments of the last decades which have limited the reality of state sovereignty.

One is the immense discrepancy between the military and industrial strengths of states. In the mid-1970s the two super powers, the United States and the Soviet Union, stood far above all other states in the world. At least one other state, China, appeared capable of growing into a super power within a fairly short time span. Japan was a fourth potential candidate for super power status, though geographical vulnerability and lack of many vital raw materials were rather important obstacles. By contrast, three of the former European great powers—Britain, France and Germany—seemed destined permanently to occupy a second rank position, even though the first two possessed nuclear weapons. A genuinely united Western Europe could be a super power, but the degree of unity necessary for this purpose was not even remotely in sight in the mid-1970s.

A second limiting factor was the growth of so-called multinational corporations. These industrial giants, whose capital was provided from several countries, but in most of which United States capital predominated, possessed great power within a number of states, large and small; and the group of individuals who took decisions on their operation were not responsible to the government of any single sovereign state. The power of the multinationals caused genuine fears for the independence of states; while xenophobic demagogy by politicians in individual states hampered activities by the multinationals which were potentially of common economic advantage to all concerned.

Decolonisation from 1947 onwards caused a proliferation of new states, most of which were very small and many of which had frontiers which corresponded to no significant geographical or economic or cultural units. Each of these states claimed full sovereignty, and had an equal vote in the General Assembly of the United Nations. Equality between the United States and Kuwait appeared absurd. Yet the sovereignty of the small states was not entirely fictitious. Those at least which possessed some special asset—wealth in raw materials, or an important strategic position—were wooed by larger states, or by the super powers. Their governments had enough freedom of manoeuvre to be able to play off the super powers against each other, and they were thus an autonomous factor in the balance of regional or world-wide power. Excessive stupidity or greed on the part of governments of small states, no less than of large, or of super powers, could create dangerous international crises, and might even bring about large-scale wars.

This was true in the nineteenth and early twentieth century, when the new states in the Balkans played this part, no less than in the 1930s, when it was the turn of the new states in Central Europe, or in the 1960s, when this phenomenon was visible mainly in the Muslim world and tropical Africa.

The idea that the sovereign state is an anachronism, and that an excessive number of sovereignties constitutes a major cause of war, had been widespread since the 1920s. The League of Nations was created largely because it was felt that there should be a higher authority, raised above sovereign states, which should prevent conflicts between states from leading to war. The League did not fulfil this task, essentially because no government of a sovereign state—even less of a large state than of a small—would submit its interests to League decision. After 1945 the United Nations failed to fulfil the same role, for essentially similar reasons.

Less ambitious attempts on the basis of large regions, or of associations covering a large number of states and nations, sometimes achieved a measure of success.

The British Commonwealth, conceived as a free association of states which had emerged from the British empire, was at first based on some genuine common interests; but these grew weaker as the years passed, while bitter conflicts arose between members. Sympathy between the peoples of the 'Old Dominions' remained a fact even in the 1970s, but economic and strategic priorities pulled them in different directions.

A certain sympathy existed from the beginning between the Europe-derived nations of the Americas, and was first formulated in President Monroe's message to Congress of 2 December 1823. However, latent mutual distrust between peoples whose cultures were mainly of English or of Spanish origin, and the growing discrepancy between the material power of the United States and of its southern neighbours, limited the sense of solidarity between them. In the twentieth century the Monroe Doctrine came to mean United States hegemony. In both world wars several Latin American states intervened on the same side as the United States, but without much enthusiasm or military effect; while the sympathies of many Latin Americans were on the other side. After 1945 an Organization of American States was set up within the United Nations. A certain genuine community of strategic interests was largely counteracted by resentments of both economic and cultural origin, which increased as education spread and expectations grew. Reluctance in the 1930s to be committed to an anti-fascist stance (and widespread admiration, whether avowed or not, for fascism) had a parallel in the reluctance to denounce communism in the 1960s (and similar admiration for the communist government of Fidel Castro in Cuba). Spanish-American, and to a lesser extent Brazilian, atti-tudes were ambivalent. The United States was admired, and its cultural influence was immense even on those who thought themselves impervious to it; but few Latin American politicians could refrain from periodical defiant gestures or bouts of insulting rhetoric directed at the United States. Yet the attempt to replace inter-American by Latin American, or specifi-cally Spanish-American, solidarity had no more success. A rather abstract sympathy existed, and gave rise to floods of oratory; but in practice no large body of citizens of any Spanish-American nation genuinely placed the interests of all Spanish America (which were in any case hard to identify) above the interests of its own nation.

There was some talk of Asianism after 1945, but the bitterness of the conflicts between Pakistan and India and China showed it to be unreal. Asia has never been more than a geographical expression: the realities have been the great cultures of Islam, Hindu India, China and the Buddhist world, within each of which fluctuations of diversity or unity could be discerned. Afro-Asianism also proved to be a mirage. The only reality to which Asian and Afro-Asian slogans related, was the sense of solidarity between anti-colonial nationalists in both continents, which rapidly dimin-ished after independence was achieved.

Panafricanism was a more serious phenomenon. It is true that solidarity between northern Arabs and sub-Saharan blacks was a pious fiction, concealing the reality of the partnership between slave-driver and slave, as the case of south Sudan, discussed above, clearly shows; yet among the black Africans themselves, it must be recognised that the belief so strongly upheld by Kwame Nkrumah—that the first loyalty could and should be given to Africa, and that loyalty to each specific African people must come after that—survived Nkrumah's overthrow and death, and remained strong among the intelligentsias of black African states. It was easy to deride this belief by pointing to the history of Nigeria, Sudan, Burundi or Congo. Yet African solidarity was more than rhetoric. It was largely due to the Organisation for African Unity, founded in May 1963, that the supplies and training were made available to the nationalist armed forces in the Portuguese colonies, which enabled them to place so long and severe a strain on the military and economic resources of Portugal that the Portuguese government was overthrown in Lisbon, and independence was conceded to the colonies. The consequences were not so impressive: the OAU was first divided between the competing groups in Angola, but then decided to recognise MPLA, with a flourish of denunciation of South African intervention but not a murmur about the Cuban invasion. Even so, there remained Africans of all colours of skins whose goal was that one day there might arise an all-African organisation within which black and white African nations would cooperate.

The idea of a united Europe can be traced far back in the past. In the twentieth century it had its most eloquent champions in France and in Germany, the two countries whose governments perhaps did most to destroy such unity as (despite the series of wars between 1854 and 1870) was growing steadily between 1815 and 1914. Aristide Briand and Gustav Stresemann believed in the unity of Europe, though each was also much concerned to pursue the specific interests of his own nation. European solidarity had, in the first half of the century, overtones of racial superiority towards Asia and Africa, and of cultural superiority towards America; but when Hitler and Stalin had done their worst for Europe; when independence had been won by many peoples of Asia and Africa; and when North America had clearly emerged not only as the region of highest material civilisation but also as a centre of vigorous social thought and culture, the character of Europeanism radically changed.

Both the French and the Germans suffered defeat, conquest and foreign occupation; and both, with the help of their American protectors but also by their own persevering efforts, climbed painfully out of the abyss of destitution and humiliation into a new world, with new dangers and new opportunities, in which old quarrels and old vanities hardly seemed worth pursuing. To some of the most imaginative and articulate of their leaders the unity of Europe seemed to be the first aim. The same idea quickly appealed to Belgians, Dutchmen and Italians. It appealed also to other European nations—to Castilians and Catalans in the West and to Czechs, Poles, Hungarians, Romanians, South Slavs and Greeks in the East; but the former were cut off not so much by the Pyrenees as by the determination of West Europeans to isolate General Franco and of General Franco to isolate himself; while nations of the Danube valley and Carpathians were dragged backwards into the Soviet Russian empire. The idea also had its followers among thinking people across the Channel; but the leaders of British political parties, aware of their nation's prowess in the war that they had won, having no need to clamber out of an abyss which they had escaped, believing themselves still to have a mission as a great power in the world at large, and especially in the Commonwealth to which they attached an almost mystic quality, turned their backs on the enterprise of uniting Europe.

So there came into being a community in which the economic rather than the cultural aspect was stressed, and in which French and Germans shared the leading parts. It achieved great economic successes, and pressure grew from businessmen in Britain (not hitherto a group conspicuous for its devotion to, or even awareness of, European culture) for British entry into this profitable Common Market. British entry was long resisted by General de Gaulle, of whom it might be said, slightly amending his own famous words, that *il s'était fait une certaine idée de l'Europe*. Not for him to abandon old quarrels or old glories, or to forego satisfaction for old wrongs. After he was gone, Britain was admitted; but by this time, on both extreme flanks of the British political body bitter opposition to membership had arisen. The strange antics of the British Labour Party, in power and in opposition between 1964 and 1975, need not be recounted here. The referendum of June 1975 ensured British membership of the EEC; but it would be premature to assume that 'Europeanism' had prevailed over all its foes on either side of the Channel.

The European Idea was something broader and deeper than support for the EEC. It was a powerful force throughout the continent. If it had been possible to arrange free expression and careful analysis of public opinion, it is likely that this would have revealed stronger support for European unity and deeper concern for European culture between the Baltic and the Aegean than in the member states of the EEC. Yet the European Idea also evoked powerful counter-forces, ranging from doubt to outright hostility, not only from the champions *in partibus infidelium* of the Soviet Russian empire, but also among persons of moderate views and limited imaginations. In any case, it was clear that though the European Idea formed a challenge to conventional national loyalties, it could not be expected to replace them, but must rather be adapted to conciliate and incorporate them.

## Dissolution of national cultures

Contemporary controversies about the dangers of sovereignty, and the 'obsolescence' of the 'nation state', are usually based on the assumption that if national loyalties are to become weaker, they will be replaced by larger loyalties based on greater regional units or on ideas which claim to be universal. One should however also consider the opposite phenomenon— replacement by narrower loyalties.

A modern phenomenon that deserves attention is the break-up of a formerly homogeneous nation by separatist forces which are not territorial. If we imagine the nation as a pyramid, then this, like some forms of stratified rock, can be splintered either horizontally or vertically.

Horizontal fracture has long been familiar not only to historians but to newspaper readers of average intelligence. This is the class struggle: peasants against landowners, city merchants against agricultural magnates, factory workers against bosses. That these struggles have existed, and still exist, only the politically blind can deny. Disagreement among intelligent people begins when they argue whether the conflicts should and can be mitigated, or even eliminated, by mutual concessions in the interest of national unity; or whether they should be pushed to extremes, in order to smash the illusion of a nation and the reality of an incurably rotten society.

Those who take the latter view are in turn divided into many groups. Each has its own vision of the ideal future. However, the most numerous and powerful groups are those who claim that the immutable laws of history, discerned by Marxist-Leninist science as interpreted by the current exponents of the infallible Central Committee of the Communist Party of the Soviet Union, prove that class conflicts are irreconcilable, and should be consciously and systematically exacerbated until revolution destroys the old order and introduces the new and permanent social order, guaranteed for all time by the collective wisdom of the CPSU, expressed by its leaders who personify this infallibility—until such time as these persons are 'unmasked' as agents of foreign secret services, or objects of an all-devouring 'cult of personality' alien to Marxism, or simply incompetent demagogues enamoured of 'hare-brained schemes'. Those not gifted with this infallible wisdom, and not disposed to believe that any one really possesses it, are reduced to the more modest view that class struggles exist, but that the causes which intensify or diminish them remain rather mysterious, and that it simply is not possible to say *a priori* whether any given class conflict can or cannot be reconciled or mitigated by mutually tolerable compromises. In the most powerful capitalist state in the world, with the greatest contrast between wealth and poverty in the world, many forms of discontent existed and exist in the twentieth century, but of a massive class consciousness and class conflict between 'working class' and 'bourgeoisie' there was very little sign: rather, an increasing number of workers, as their material conditions improved, considered themselves 'middle class', and others aimed, by their own efforts and a bit of luck, to achieve that status. In Britain, by contrast, class hatred and obsessive envy of all who fared better than oneself, appeared much more widespread in the prosperous 1970s than in the desperate 1930s.

Vertical stratification has been much less studied, but it appeared in the 1970s to be increasing in the advanced industrial countries. Essentially it consists in the growth of a form of loyalty confined to one's own occupational group: Coventry automobile workers, or New York dustmen, or Breton farmers *contra mundum*. The most obvious examples involved trade unions, but this was by no means a solely 'working class' phenomenon, for employers and professional men would be at least as likely to take the side of the workers in their section of the pyramid as to prefer a wider national interest. It was arguable that vertical sectionalism was promoted by the spread of television, which encouraged families to stay at home and watch the box, where they had fewer contacts with the rest of the population. It could also be argued that the built-in professional deformation of mass media communicators, to seek always something new and exciting, led to the flooding of homes with a rapid succession of fashionable and ephemeral ideas which had in common only an intense dislike of established values, of which one of the most obvious was the notion of national solidarity, so often described by a name which became virtually a smear-word: 'patriotism'. These two arguments must be mentioned, because a certain *prima facie* case can be made for them; but neither of them can be considered proven, nor is indeed capable of proof.

Vertical stratification and splintering must be distinguished from local community solidarity. The idea that less should be done by the central government of large nations, and that more should be left to local authorities within the nation, was something different. Such local solidarity still existed in the 1970s in New England townships, on Hebridean islands, and no doubt in many other places remote from great cities. It was perhaps still most successfully institutionalised in Swiss cantons. Whether such local solidarity, initiative and participation was likely to grow, or was doomed to perish as vast centralised units absorbed everything, was a subject for a great deal of doctrinaire rhetoric; but by its very nature this question probably could not admit any single answer.

The vertical splintering which I am now considering was something different and something which could only be harmful. The sectional interests for the most part were not concentrated in small identifiable units, but were scattered over a whole country, being confined to an occupation and not to a home area. The concession of big material gains to one powerful sectional interest would inevitably bring poverty, unemployment and wastage of resources to other sectional interests. The victorious sectionalists were quite indifferent to the price paid by others: no old-fashioned class solidarity would hold them back from grabbing what they could get. Obviously every society and every nation has contained conflicts of sectional interest; but if they cannot be controlled, the society must slide into anarchy. The powers of the great sectional groups within twentieth century industrial nations recall the stereotype of the conflicts between feudal barons in the England of King Stephen (1135-54) or in fifteenth century Scotland. However, just because their powers were not, like those of individual barons, limited to specific regions, they were potentially more dangerous.

### National cultures and human civilisation

To mock the loyalty of members of a football club or trade union to each other is as foolish as it is unjust. The union deals with things that touch its members' lives on every working day of their lives, the club at least once a week for most of the year. What they read, in the rest of their newspapers beyond the sporting pages, of what are called national affairs, concerns them much less often, and perhaps—though not certainly—less deeply. But membership of a nation is something different from membership of a club or a union, and something which, despite popular fallacies, cannot be sloughed off at will.

Some would reply that national consciousness is a superstition, derived from the outworn and discredited past, and that it not only can but should be abandoned as quickly as possible. If it be true that in most parts of the world men still remain victims to nationalist passions, that is all the more reason why the peoples whose societies and cultures have progressed the farthest, should abjure their nationality, should reject 'patriotism', and should throw into 'the dustbin of history' the whole costly apparatus of 'national defence', whose many ramifications penetrate and poison society. Those who do this, these enthusiasts argue, will set an example of civilised behaviour which others will then emulate, until a peaceful and a better world is made.

Unfortunately, the incomplete evidence, both from past history and from the observation of the contemporary world, suggests that any government which did this would not in fact help to bring a peaceful and a better world to birth, but would only cause its own nation to be trampled upon by the rulers of other states, who could compel the obedience of their own nations for the task of grabbing the resources of those not willing to defend themselves.

Indifference to the national heritage, and refusal to defend the nation, are signs not of progress but of decay, not of the health of a body politic but of critical sickness. The disease attacks both the head and the limbs, both the leaders and the crowd. Unsure of their own right to lead, consumed by a sense of social-political guilt, too tired to exercise their imaginations, and at the same time cynically determined to enjoy the fruits of power, the leaders have nothing to offer but a crude hedonism, no other aim for their followers than immediate material gratification. Such leaders can inspire in the members of the crowd nothing but contempt. Unable to respect their rulers, they demand more and more for themselves. Unable to identify themselves with the government of the nation, encouraged to believe that the nation is a fiction, men cling the more passionately to the sectional loyalties which have precise meaning to them. The fissures in the society multiply and grow deeper. If the process goes too far, it can be reversed only when a power-hungry new elite, indigenous or foreign, imposes itself by force. No 'scientific' measurement has yet been, or is likely to be, devised, that will pinpoint the moment of no return for individual societies. It is always possible to try to avert disaster, up to the moment when disaster has occurred; though clumsy attempts may through failure accelerate the disaster itself.

Not only is rejection of national consciousness and national heritage a sign of political sickness rather than health: it is in itself an act against civilisation. Human beings have much in common with beasts; and twentieth century thinking, both of the 'right' and of the 'left', has largely favoured the 'liberation' of mankind by the reassertion of its simple beastlike loyalties and the removal of artificial constraints. Yet humans differ from beasts in two things: they reason and they remember. By reason and by memory numerous human communities have slowly built the treasure-house of varied national cultures to which mankind is heir.

National cultures were created through the history of nations. History is the collective memory of human communities. Beasts do not have history; primitive men have only oral traditions; civilised men have recorded history. Recorded history is full of uncertainties, of unanswered questions and of questions which have not yet even been put. It includes the teachings of prophets and saints, which they believed were revealed to them by God, which millions still accept as such (even though they often disregard them in their own lives); while other millions reject their divine origin but still accept their guidance in diluted form. History includes the achievements, crimes and sufferings of kings, soldiers and politicians; and the achievements, crimes and sufferings of unnamed millions whom they led or sacrificed. It has become fashionable to pay more attention to the unnamed millions than to the leaders, which is more difficult because there is less evidence, but is entirely admirable as an aim; yet this should and need not cause the leaders to be ignored, or the myths to be forgotten (even in the rare cases where the truth in the myth can be surgically separated from the fiction).

In some countries it has become a dogma that 'the people' were always virtuous and oppressed, the ruling classes always exploiting and wicked. For example, it is argued that Cortés and his men were no more than murderous aggressors, and all that was constructive in the formation of the modern Mexican nation came from the indigenous peoples. Or again, though Russian tsars invaded and conquered neighbouring lands, the Russian people, it is claimed by the tsars' successors, were always the best friend of neighbouring peoples (Poles, Romanians, Tatars and the rest). Such dogmas are legends fit for unbalanced adolescents.

Nations cannot escape their history, and individuals cannot opt out of their nations (though they can of course betray them to their enemies). Young Germans, appalled by the crimes of Hitler, wished to repudiate Germany's history—not only the Nazi era, but the Prussian past which was said to have been the source of Hitlerism. Yet this they could not do, though they were themselves innocent of the crimes. This was understood by an innocent German who by a great act showed himself a great man: Willy Brandt who, as German chancellor, knelt in public at the monument in Auschwitz[3] where Hitler's men had gassed Jews and Poles by the hundred thousand. Since Brandt's act the air has become purer in all Central Europe.

There are those who believe that history can be defused of all explosive content; that it should be rewritten so that no one may be offended; that all peoples can be vested with virtuous uniformity, a mish-mash of benevolent humanitarian verbiage. This mercifully is still only a nightmare.

Meanwhile we are still faced with two sets of truth, equally valid. The first is that nationalists, fanatically determined to set up their own independent state, usually with the aid of a government hostile to the government which they are fighting; and nationalists in possession of a sovereign independent state determined to impose their nationality on peoples within their jurisdiction who do not own it, or to seize territories under another government's rule which they claim should be theirs; are capable of terrible civil wars and interstate wars which, in the age of nuclear weapons, may threaten the whole human race with extinction. The second is that nations, created over longer or shorter periods of time, with their own speech and culture and beliefs and institutions, are virtually indestructible; persecution and massacre more often intensify than eliminate their national feeling; and continuous repression serves to keep them in an explosive condition which also threatens wars which treaten all humanity.

The survival of human civilisation depends on the recognition of both sets of truth: that neither absolute state sovereignty nor the abolition of national identities is possible; that there must be a balance between national cultures and interstate cooperation, no less than a balance between class interests and interclass cooperation within nations, if destructive civil wars and nuclear holocausts are to be avoided. It may be that the vast bulk of the human race care not for any of these things. That does not absolve those who do know and do care from making an effort to explain them.

# Notes

## Chapter 1

1. For example, Sylvia Haim, *Arab Nationalism* (University of California, 1962) and Elie Kedourie, *Nationalism in Asia and Africa* (1970).
2. See pp. 447-448.
3. *Nationalism* by Elie Kedourie (1960).
4. At Paris were *nationes* of France, Picardy, Normandy and Germany: the Norman included persons from various northern lands, the German at one time Englishmen. At Prague in the late fourteenth century were Bohemian, Bavarian, Saxon and Polish *nationes*, but their composition too was rather mixed.
5. The Székély were a people from the steppes, originally distinct from the Hungarians (or Magyars), but culturally assimilated towards them in the course of time. The Saxons were Germans established by the kings of Hungary in the thirteenth century.
6. An exception was Hungarian, in which the distinct words *nemzet* and *nép* were assiduously preserved: this was a result of the long continued maintenance of political power of the nobility. A systematic comparative study of the evolution of the use and meaning of these words in Europe has yet to be done: it would be invaluable to historians and even to social scientists.

## Chapter 2

1. In 1204 the Fourth Crusade, at Venetian instigation, captured Constantinople instead of fighting the Muslims, and installed Frankish dukes, whose descendants were ousted by the Greek dynasty of the Paleologi in 1261.
2. The choice of title for this section caused me a good deal of difficulty. 'Nations of Britain' would exclude the Irish. 'Nations of the British Isles' would imply that Ireland is a British island, which savours of imperialism. The title chosen is, I believe, satisfactory: English, Scots and Welsh are all

British nations—that is, nations living within the island of Britain. The use of the plural after 'British and Irish' leaves open the question whether there is or is not a British nation, and whether there are one or two Irish nations. Those who hold these different views can accept my title, though they may reject my opinions.

3. The older names used for the two forms are Goidelic ('P') and Brythonic ('Q'). From the second is derived the Latin name Britannia. In terms of language, the only 'Britons' surviving today are the Welsh. Galloway, the south-western corner of Scotland, had a distinct population, probably originating from Ireland, and speaking 'Q–' rather than 'P–Celtic'.

4. The Celtic language spoken thereafter in the Scottish Western Highlands and Islands, long known as Gaelic, developed differently from literary Irish. In modern times the word 'Gaelic' is often used for the Irish as well as for the Scottish variant: the context in which the word is used usually makes its meaning clear.

5. If modern doctrines of linguistic nationality had been current in those times, the border between England and Scotland would have been not the Tweed but perhaps the Pentlands and the Annan.

6. See pp. 67-68.

7. The lowest level (*rí tuaithe*) was a tribal chief ruling a small number; the next (*ruiri*) was an óverlord of these; the highest (*ruirech*), a king of overkings, was the ruler of a large province (Munster, Ulster, Connaught, Leinster). Even the lowest level chief had a sacred character, which makes the use of the word 'king' appropriate. Rivalries between provincial kings were frequent and bloody. The traditional view of the evolution of a 'high kingship' over all Ireland is critically examined by a recent scholar, Donncha O'Corrain, in *Ireland before the Normans* (Dublin, 1972), 28-42.

8. The use by historians and other writers of the words 'Angle', 'Saxon' and 'Anglo-Saxon' is confusing and inconsistent. We speak of Angles in south-east Scotland; of Pope Gregory's alleged remark about some Angle slaves as 'non Angli sed Angeli'; of the *Anglo-Saxon Chronicle* and Saxon church architecture. Should any specialist on these subjects chance to read these pages, I trust that he will pardon my uncertainties.

9. William I, infuriated by King Malcolm's repeated raids into Northumberland, invaded Scotland in 1072, and Malcolm met him at Abernethy and 'was his man'. The terms of this homage are not exactly known. In 1174 King William ('the Lion') of Scotland, captured at Alnwick and taken prisoner to King Henry II in Normandy, did him homage for Scotland as well as for his lands in England, by the Treaty of Falaise. However, Richard I on his accession released William from this obligation in November 1189. The whole question of homage, and also the history of the attempts by the kings of Scotland to obtain Northumberland, Cumberland and Westmorland, are explained in the most important recent work

on medieval Scotland—A. A. M. Duncan, *Scotland: The Making of the Kingdom* (Edinburgh, 1975), chapter 9.

10. G. W. S. Barrow, *Feudal Britain* (1956), 410. See also the same author's *Robert Bruce and the Community of the Realm of Scotland* (1965).

11. See Barrow, *Feudal Britain*, p. 350ff.

12. See pp. 175-178.

13. It is arguable that similar phenomena took place in the Muslim world, where Arabic words came to dominate the intellectual vocabulary, while the grammatical structure and material vocabulary remained Turkish, Malay, or post-Sanskrit. But the English and Romanian fusions were not marked by a clear-cut division between intellectual/religious or material/social vocabulary: the overlapping of the two word-funds was wider and richer. Perhaps the Persian case is somewhat nearer the English, as intellectual words of pre-Islamic Persian origin survived. See pp. 244-245.

14. From 1303 the popes were prisoners of the king of France in Avignon, and from 1378 to 1415 there were rival popes in Avignon and Rome, and for part of this time also a third claimant living in Spain.

15. I refer to my earlier argument that the English nation only came into existence in the fourteenth century: the struggles of Britons against Romans, of Romanised Celts against Saxons, and of Saxons against Normans should not be regarded as 'English' national independence movements.

16. I find it very hard to make up my mind as to whether a 'British nation' is a valid concept. 'Britain' is of course a much older word than 'England' or 'Scotland'; but if the word is used in its strictest historical sense, the only people entitled to call themselves 'British' are the Welsh. There has been at times a tendency for the English to interpret 'British' as English writ large, and to expect Scots and Welsh to become English if they are to be truly British. Yet it is also true that until recently the sense of belonging together to a British community, and pride in this community, have been extremely strong among the Scots and Welsh: indeed, one might argue that Scots and Welsh have been 'more British' then the English. Does this add up to a British national consciousness, or should some other word be found?

17. See pp. 147, 163.

18. F. S. L. Lyons, *Ireland Since the Famine* (1971), 632-633, quoting B. O. Cuiv, *Irish Dialects and Irish-Speaking Districts* (Dublin, 1951).

19. At this point the author must admit that there are limits to the detachment which is his usual aim. Descended from generations of Scots and Irish, but with a working life lived, like that of my parents, mostly in England, I cannot think that the break-up of Britain could be anything but a disaster.

20. See first page of Introduction.

21. The name is derived from Lotharingia, the share allotted by the Treaty of Verdun to Lothair, one of the three disputant grandsons of Charlemagne.

22. These terms refer to the word used for 'yes' at the time—*oïl* being later modified to *oui*. The word Occitania was in use in medieval texts, being derived from *oc* (not from *Occident* or West). Both 'Languedoc' and 'Occitania' were at times used to cover almost all France between the Loire, the Rhone and the Atlantic. Other words of variable geographical meaning are Gascogne (normally, the land between the Pyrenees and the Garonne, but sometimes larger or smaller regions) and Aquitaine (denoting varying extents of territory between the Loire and the Garonne). 'Languedoc' in more recent times has been confined to the region around Toulouse and Albi. Other regions which have at times been considered to belong to Occitania are the Limousin (region of Limoges) and Auvergne. There continued to be considerable differences of dialect between these many regions, but there was certainly a family relationship between them, extending also to the language of Provence, beyond the Rhone, and to a lesser extent to Catalan, spoken north of the Pyrenees in Roussillon. It is not fanciful to think of an Occitanian group of dialects, similar to each other and distinct from French. The history of these dialects is also complicated by the fact that different regions were under different sovereignties until the late Middle Ages—most of Aquitaine under the king of England, and Provence with the city of Arles under the Holy Roman Empire.

23. Occitanian nationalists would argue that it passed from the rule of one alien monarch, the king of England, to that of another alien monarch, the king of France.

24. To be more precise, the duchy of Burgundy, with its French-speaking population, came under the French monarchy; whereas the Dutch-speaking Low Countries passed to the Burgundian heiress and her husband, Arch-Duke Maximilian of Austria. See p. 61.

25. See below, p. 49.

26. In 1967, following General de Gaulle's melodramatic gesture in Montreal (see p. 228), an inscription could be seen in the small Pyrenean town of St Jean Pied de Port: *Vive le Québec libre! Vive le pays basque libre!* In the same summer, below the ruins of Montségur, there were leaflets proclaiming *Vive l'Occitanie libre! A bas l'impérialisme français!* In the summer of 1975 Breton extremists carried out sabotage, and Corsican extremists killed three French gendarmes in a pitched battle.

27. The monk Arius propounded a doctrine which denied the divinity of Christ. The missionary who converted the eastern Germanic tribes (often generally described as Goths) in the fourth century, Ulfilas, was a follower

of Arius, and therefore Visigoths, Ostrogoths, Vandals and Suevians became Arians.

28. See pp. 240-241.

29. See pp. 62-63.

30. For this interesting detail, I am obliged to my colleague Dr Isabel de Madariaga.

31. Fifth of his name as emperor, but first as king of Spain.

32. See the discussion of the well-known thesis of the great Dutch historian Peter Geyl by Charles Wilson in his *Queen Elizabeth and the Revolt of the Netherlands* (1970).

33. It is curious that the Celtic peoples of Scotland and Ireland, who possessed the same sort of indented western coastline, with splendid natural harbours and anchorages, as Norway, and an equally barren interior terrain, showed little aptitude for ocean travel. Is this because fish were more abundant in the inner Hebridean waters and mainland sea-lochs than in Norwegian, thus providing an expanding and reliable food supply close at hand? Or because there was no population pressure in Scotland and Ireland, although both countries were naturally as poor as Norway? Or is the explanation to be found in some innate lack of enterprise in Celtic peoples? One recalls the well-known Hebridean's prayer:

> *Oh that the peats would cut themselves,*
> *The fish leap on the shore,*
> *And I could lie upon my bed*
> *And sleep for evermore.*

We may also note at this point that the second Atlantic-dwelling people which later became a pioneer of ship design and of ocean travel, the Portuguese, had a coastline singularly deficient in natural harbours (the *rios* of Galicia were never under Portuguese sovereignty, though the language of the Galicians was closer to Portuguese than to Castilian). It is also noteworthy that the three other great 'Atlantic' nations of later times— the English, French and Castilians—only established themselves on the Atlantic littoral in rather recent times (north Devon and the coast between Nantes and Bordeaux being exceptions). Scots, Irish and Welsh served brilliantly in the English navy, Bretons in the French, and Basques and Galicians in the Spanish, but none of these original Atlantic littoral nations had been notable seafarers before they became part of the much larger neighbouring states founded by their non-Atlantic neighbours.

34. The capital city of Norway was named Christiania in 1624, in honour of King Christian IV of Denmark. It was renamed Oslo in 1929.

35. The exception is Denmark's dispute about the duchies of Schleswig and Holstein with Prussia in 1848 and with Prussia and Austria in 1864,

which led to war on both occasions.

36. See p. 44 and footnote 22, pp. 487-488.

37. See Christopher Hughes, *Switzerland* (1975), 148-153. This book is an up-to-date admirable survey of the extremely complicated problems of the Swiss past and present, by an author who is not only familiar with the sources but has long and intimate personal experience of Switzerland and the Swiss.

38. This phrase was invented by the contemporary Byzantinist Dimitri Obolensky, who made it the title of his comprehensive historical study *The Byzantine Commonwealth* (1970).

39. The phrase 'Little Russia' is found in Byzantine accounts of the fourteenth century, but came into general use in the seventeenth. At first it was used of themselves by the people of the south, but in the nineteenth century it was used only by those who argued that these people formed part of a single Russian nation. Those who believed that there were two distinct nations rejected the name 'Little Russians' and called themselves 'Ukrainians'. See pp. 186-187.

40. At one time several languages of this 'Baltic' group were spoken, but in modern times only two survived: Lithuanian and Latvian.

41. The situation of persons of Byelorussian and Ukrainian speech in the Grand Duchy of Lithuania, and the relations between Lithuania and Poland, are discussed in the next chapter, pp. 120-122.

42. A separate metropolitan of Kiev was appointed in Kiev under Lithuanian rule in 1458. Its first holder was Gregory the Bulgarian. Its authority was not recognised by the Metropolitan Iona of Moscow or his successors, who claimed authority over all the Orthodox of Russia. It was however upheld by the rulers of Lithuania and Poland until the Union of Brest-Litovsk of 1596 (see p. 122), and was respected by the Orthodox of Lithuania.

43. At the Council of Florence in that year the patriarch of Constantinople had agreed to a reunion of the churches, on terms which signified a victory for the Church of Rome.

44. See pp. 112, 114.

45. This word cannot be exactly translated. It does not, in this context, mean the abstract quality of nationality: rather, it suggests the possession of a state of mind, adhesion to the nation, not so much 'nationalism' as 'national-mindedness'.

46. See pp. 121-122.

47. The northernmost of the three provinces (Estland) was inhabited by Estonians, the southernmost (Kurland) by Latvians; while the third (Liefland, or Livonia) had a mainly Latvian population, with Estonians in its northern districts. Both Latvians and Estonians were Protestants. Their languages are far apart: Estonian is closely related to Finnish, while

Latvian and Lithuanian are closely related members of a distinct Baltic subdivision of the Indo-European languages. While Lithuanians were close to Latvians in language they differed in religion, being, like the Poles, Catholics.

48. See pp. 71-72.

## Chapter 3

1. Seven if one considers it completed by the annexation of the Sudeten-land after the Munich capitulation of 1938, five if the annexation of Western Poland and Alsace be thought decisive.

2. In 1806 Francis II gave up the title of Holy Roman Emperor. He had previously assumed a new title as Austrian emperor. As such he was Francis I.

3. Hanover became separated from England with the accession of Victoria in 1837. The conflict between Danish and German claims in Schleswig did not become acute until the late 1840s. There were murmurings of anti-German feeling by Russian bureaucrats in the Baltic provinces in the 1840s, but these did not become serious until later in the century.

4. See p. 153.

5. The events of 1848 in Italy, Bohemia, Hungary, Romania and the Yugoslav lands are mentioned elsewhere, pp. 104-106, 133, 153, 162-163, 178-179.

6. The Italian words *compromesso storico* were first used in this context in an article by the communist leader, Enrico Berlinguer, in *Rinascita* in October 1973.

7. The organisation of Christian peoples under Ottoman rule is briefly discussed in the following chapter.

8. The revolt of the Romanian Tudor Vladimirescu, and his relations with the Greeks, are discussed in the next chapter. Ypsilanti's force included a few Bulgarians and Albanians.

9. Jan Kollar, *Über die literarische Wechselseitigkeit* (Leipzig, 1842).

10. On the Lithuanian language, and its affinity to Latvian, see above chapter 2, notes 40 and 47, and p. 86.

11. The Order was founded by the pope in the thirteenth century for the forcible conversion of the pagans in the north-eastern borderlands of Christendom, and established itself in the land which became known as East Prussia.

12. Russia and Prussia took part in all three partitions, Austria only in the first and third.

13. Byelorussian is the Slav language spoken by most of the population in the central part of the old Lithuanian state. It differs from Russian

(Great Russian) and Ukrainian (Little Russian). It was used in official business and documents in earlier centuries, and in the nineteenth a modern literary language developed, followed by a national movement. This is not discussed in this book. The interested reader should consult N. P. Vakar, *Byelorussia: The Making of a Nation* (Cambridge, Mass., 1966).

14.  A brief account of the fluctuating relations of Alexander with the Poles between 1804 and 1815 can be found in my book *The Russian Empire 1801-1917* (1967), which also contains a bibliography with further references.

15.  It is often referred to as the fourth; but as I see it, the fourth partition took place in 1815.

16.  Joining the Soviet invasion army sent to suppress the Czechoslovak attempt at 'socialism with a human face'. See pp. 130-131.

17.  Austria only partly fits the pattern. Nevertheless, it is basically true that the rulers of the German and of the Russian nations between them held the Poles at their mercy. The single major exception, as regards generosity, was Alexander I; Alexander II's efforts were brief and half-hearted.

18.  See pp. 162-163.

19.  The Croatian *pravo*, like German *Recht*, and French *droit*, means both 'right' and 'law'.

20.  For the rise of Bulgarian and Albanian nationalism see pp. 145-146.


## Chapter 4

1.  The Arabic-Turkish word *millet* designated communities of this sort. In later Turkish usage, it was used to mean 'nation', being thought to be the nearest equivalent to that European concept.

2.  There was one partial exception: in 1557, probably as a result of the influence of the Bosnian-born Vizier Mehmet Sokollu, the Serbian patriarchate of Peć (set up as an autocephalous church by the Serbian tsar Dushan in 1346) was restored to its former title, and survived until 1755.

3.  It is widely believed, though it cannot be definitely established, that this was due to the presence of a large number of Bogomils, members of a dualist heresy similar to that of the Albigensians in south-west France. The Bogomils were persecuted by both the Catholic and the Orthodox churches, and it is thought that they welcomed the advent of Islam as a liberation.

4.  The disputes between the governments of Russia, Britain and Austria as to the size of this state in 1878, and as to the extent of its independence in 1885, well known to all students of European diplomatic history, cannot be summarised here.

5. In the Czech language the same word (*český*) stands for both

Bohemian and Czech. However, the lands of Czech speech include also Moravia, which was long a part of the same kingdom but remained geographically and administratively distinct; while until the nineteenth century the adjective Bohemian included persons of German as well as of Czech speech. In the German language there are two words: Bohemian is *böhmisch* and Czech is *tschechisch*. This use of two distinct words has been generally adopted in English usage.

6. The original periodicals were *Monatschrift der Gesellschaft des Vaterländischen Museums von Böhmen* and *Časopis vlasteneckeho muzea v Čechach*.

7. These words are quoted in Hans Kohn, *Panslavism: Its History and Ideology* (Notre Dame, Indiana, 1953), 27. For a recent appraisal of the work of Havliček, see article by T. I. V. Thomas, 'Karel Havliček and the Constitutional Question 1849-51' in *The Slavonic and East European Review*, 1974, no. 129.

8. See also p. 98.

9. In the Hungarian language the same word *Magyarország* means both Hungary and the land of the Magyars (those whose language is Hungarian). In German a distinction can be made between *ungarisch* (Hungarian) and *ungarländisch* (from the territory of Hungary). In English historical usage the Hungarian word 'Magyar' is sometimes used to describe the language, and the people who speak it, as opposed to 'Hungarian', which is reserved for the territory of the Hungarian state. However, the two words often get confused. In the following pages I shall normally use the word 'Hungarian' to denote the language and the people who speak it, and 'Hungary' to denote the whole territory of the Hungarian state at the relevant period. When ambiguity arises I shall sometimes use 'Magyar' if it can make my meaning clearer.

10. See article by G. F. Cushing, 'The birth of national literature in Hungary', in *Slavonic and East European Review*, vol. xxxviii, no. 91 (June 1960).

11. In German Kaschau, in Slovak Košice. This city had a mainly Hungarian-speaking population, but was set on the edge of a Slovak-speaking countryside.

12. See pp. 94-96, 104-106, 153.

13. The Croats had a special position within Hungary, recognised by the Hungarian-Croatian Compromise (*nagodba*) of 1868. See above, pp. 132, 137, 160.

14. The first half of this expression refers to the Dacians, the original inhabitants of Transylvania, conquered by the Roman emperor Trajan at the beginning of the second century AD.

15. Hungarian treatment of Jews is further discussed below, pp. 389-390.

16. Franz Josef was Austrian emperor, but also king of Hungary, and

within Hungary after 1867 only the second title was recognised.

17. The concept of 'Yugoslav nation' in force between the wars, which in essence was a form of Official Nationalism, has been discussed in the previous chapter; the concept of 'Czechoslovak nation', which is another example, is discussed in the next section of this chapter; and relations between Hungarians and Romanians in Transylvania in the subsequent section. Similarities of predicament and policy in India and in Ethiopia are mentioned below, pp. 298, 343.

18. See p. 119.

19. See above, p. 144.

20. For the original Uniate Church see p. 122.

21. See p. 113.

22. See above, p. 122.

23. The origins of the Cossacks are well discussed, on the basis of the original sources, by Günter Stökl, *Die Entstehung des Kosakentums* (München, 1953).

24. The word *Ukraina* means 'borderland'. It was used for a number of frontier regions, but eventually came to mean the Dnieper area, the south-eastern part of Poland and south-western part of Russia. Gradually also the phrase 'Ukrainian language' came into use, and later still 'Ukrainian nation'.

25. Kiev itself, and the area immediately behind it on the western bank of the Dnieper, were ceded by Poland to Russia in 1667.

26. The northern part of Moldavia, annexed from Ottoman sovereignty by Austria in 1775. The population of Bukovina was divided between Ukrainians in the north and Romanians in the south.

27. See the long essay on Makhno by D. J. Footman in *Saint Antony's Papers*, no. 6 (1959).

## Chapter 5

1. The territory of New Spain corresponded approximately to what has become known as Mexico. The name Mexico strictly speaking applied only to the Aztec kingdom centred on Tenochtitlan, on whose site the Spaniards built the city of Mexico, dominated by its vast sixteenth century baroque cathedral.

2. The southernmost Russian settlement, Fort Rossiya, was set up in 1812 only one hundred miles north of San Francisco Bay.

3. These matters are discussed at length in Bernard Bailyn, *The Ideological Origins of the American Revolution* (Cambridge, Mass., 1967).

4. Statistics from around 1800 show that in Venezuela negroes of various legal categories formed 60 per cent of the population, the most

numerous being free coloured (*pardos*), amounting to 45 per cent. Whites were about 20 per cent, and the Indians about the same. In New Granada whites formed about 35 per cent, and *mestizos* of either European-negro or European-Indian origin about 45 per cent. In Rio de la Plata whites were 38 per cent of the population and coloured of European-negro origin together with pure negroes 32. These statistics cannot of course be regarded as more than approximative. See John Lynch, *The Spanish-American Revolution 1808-1826* (1973), 38, 193, 227-228.

5. For the first two centuries there were only two viceroys, in New Spain (Mexico) and in Peru. In 1717 New Granada (Colombia) also became a vice royalty, with its capital at Santa Fe de Bogota; and in 1776 Rio de la Plata (Argentina) was promoted to the same dignity, and a portion of Upper Peru was transferred to it from the viceroyalty of Peru.

6. San Martín's forces landed in Peru in September 1820, and entered Lima in July 1821. San Martín met Bolívar at Guayaquil on 26 July 1822 to plan the last stages of liberation. The two men could not agree. San Martín returned to Chile, and then to voluntary exile in Europe; while the liberation of Peru and Bolivia was completed by Bolívar and his comrade-in-arms, Antonio José de Sucre, in 1823 and 1824. The last Spanish force surrendered, at the port of Callao, in January 1826.

7. These were: Mexico; the five Central American republics; Colombia; Venezuela; Ecuador; Peru; Chile; Bolivia (separated from Peru 1825); the United Provinces of Rio Plata (known from 1830 as the Argentine republic); Paraguay (separated from Rio Plata in 1811); and Uruguay (established by agreement between Rio Plata and Brazil in 1828).

8. North of the mouth of the St Lawrence was the great island of Newfoundland. South of the Gulf were the colony of Nova Scotia and two others which had separated from it—Prince Edward Island in 1768 and New Brunswick in 1784. To the north-west vast tracts of largely unexplored land were under the authority of the Hudson's Bay Company, established by royal charter at the end of the seventeenth century. On the north-west Pacific coast, first explored by Captain Cook in 1788 and Captain George Vancouver in 1793, there were also some British settlements. These were placed under the Hudson's Bay Company in 1848, but were formed into the Crown Colony of British Columbia in 1858. Vancouver Island was joined to British Columbia in 1866. The northern limit of the British Columbia coast was fixed at 54° 40' by a treaty of 1825 with Russia, which held sovereignty over Alaska.

9. Apart from Quebec and Ontario (as Lower and Upper Canada were now called), Nova Scotia and New Brunswick joined the Confederation in 1867. Other provinces became members in the following order. The territories ruled by the Hudson's Bay Company in the north and west entered as the Province of Manitoba in 1870. In 1871 they were followed by

British Columbia, which had included Vancouver Island since 1868. Prince Edward Island joined in 1873. In 1905 two further provinces, Alberta and Saskatchewan, were detached from Manitoba. Newfoundland remained a separate territory until 1949, when it too was incorporated.

10. For a more general discussion of European colonisation of Africa in the late nineteenth century, see pp. 324-331.

11. See above, p. 201

12. Their 'career from the cradle to the grave' was one of 'unbridled lust, of filthy amalgamation, of swaggering braggadocio, of haughty domination, of cowardly ruffianism, of boundless dissipation, of matchless insolence, of infinite self-conceit, of unequalled oppression, of more than savage cruelty'.

13. I have avoided using the expression 'national groups', because the quotas were based not on nationality but on state citizenship. The dissolution of old, and the formation of new, states in Europe in 1919 of course made necessary some recalculations.

14. Partial because it would certainly be wrong to deny that in these groups there are many who consider themselves to be true Americans and who are proud to be Americans.

15. Some examples are J. Cermak, mayor of Chicago 1930; Fiorello La Guardia, mayor of New York during the Second World War; Abraham Ribicoff, governor of Connecticut in the 1950s; and the rise to fame of Ralph Nader, the consumers' champion, in the late 1960s. More sensational were the first election of an Irish Catholic as president—J. F. Kennedy in 1960—and the appointment of a German-born Jew as secretary of state—Henry Kissinger in 1973.

16. Michael Novak, *The Rise of the Unmeltable Ethnics* (New York, 1973), Preface, xv. This book is both brilliant and perverse, both clinically analytical and passionate.

17. Sixteen eminent *québécois* intellectuals signed a statement urging capitulation. Among them were René Lévesque, leader of the *Parti québécois*, and the distinguished sociologist Marcel Rioux. The latter, in his book *Quebec in Question* (Toronto, 1971), concludes a brilliant analysis of the Quebec problem with a wild outburst of emotion about the events of October 1970. His rage against Trudeau's action causes him not even to mention the fact that the FLQ kidnappers had tortured Laporte before murdering him. The contradictions in M. Rioux's mind are a revealing example of the climate of opinion among *québécois* intellectuals.

18. George Grant, *Lament for a Nation: The Defeat of Canadian Nationalism* (Toronto/Montreal, 1965).

19. A considerable proportion of these were not originally of Dutch, but of French Huguenot or German stock.

20. The growth of national consciousness in the 1870s is sensitively and

clearly explained in F. A. von Jaarsveld, *The Awakening of Afrikaner Nationalism* (Capetown, 1961).

## Chapter 6

1. Before the First World War the more usual, and more accurate, expression was 'Near East'. The modern name 'Middle East' is used extremely vaguely, extending sometimes to the whole of North Africa, which is not 'East' at all, and sometimes to Pakistan, which is not 'Middle'. I might have used it in the title of this chapter; but it seemed to be better to give a more precise, even if clumsy, description.

2. This comparison I owe to the eminent Russian historian of religion, A. P. Fedotov, in his *Russian Religious Mind* (Cambridge, Mass., 1966), vol. I: 11. He is there concerned with the contrast between the forest-dwelling primitive Slavs and the pastoral peoples. He did not extend his comparison to the Greeks looking up to Mount Olympus or the Egyptians obsessed with the cats, kestrels, hippopotami and other beasts of the field and fowls of the air. The Zoroastrian religion of Iran, which was essentially dualist, with a god of good and a god of evil, does not fit the pattern: there were mountains and forests and deserts in Iran.

3. Muslim expansion into India (except for Sind, conquered in the eighth century), and into the Indonesian archipelago and sub-Saharan Africa, came later. These are briefly mentioned pp. 250-251.

4. Both the details of these quarrels within the inner circle of the Prophet, and the later doctrinal divisions between *Shia* and *Sunna*, and within the *Shia*, are complicated. Suffice it to say that they bore virtually no resemblance to the disputes between the Roman and Constantinopolitan churches, or later between Catholics and Protestants; yet that their effect on the Islamic world was analogous to the effect of Schism and Reformation on Christendom. As regards the words used, anyone who does not read Arabic must approach them with diffidence; but it seems that in scholarly usage *Shi'i* denotes the persons who follow the various branches of disciples of Ali, and that *Shia* is the community. It is in these senses that I shall use the words, adding at times the English plural 's' to the Arabic word *Shi'i*.

5. A fascinating study of this process, based on the documents of French bankers, is *Bankers and Pashas: International Finance and Economic Imperialism in Egypt*, by David Landes (New York, 1958).

6. See p. 292.

7. For an acute and melancholy analysis of the impact of these reforms in the Ottoman empire, both in Turkey and in Egypt, see 'Islam Today', the thirteenth chapter, by Elie Kedourie, of *The Civilization of Islam*, edited by

Bernard Lewis (1976).

8. Not all Armenians in Turkey disappeared: there remained Armenian merchants in Istanbul and other cities. See also pp. 315, 386-387.

9. See pp. 397-398.

10. *Wafd* means 'delegation', and refers to the request, refused by the British government, that Egypt be allowed to send a delegation to the Paris Peace Conference in 1919 to plead for Egyptian independence. For a penetrating study of Zaghlul, see the essay by Elie Kedourie in his collection of essays, *The Chatham House Version* (1970).

11. Bourguiba led a radical secession from the Constitutional Party (*Destour*) founded already in 1920.

12. The Jewish side of the Palestine problem is discussed in another chapter. The reader's indulgence is asked for the inconvenience which this unavoidable division may cause. If the two sections are read in succession, it is hoped that confusion may be avoided.

13. Arabic for 'the West', commonly used for the lands from Tunis westwards.

14. In one of these, the nationalists secured a great triumph by burning down the Turf Club in 1952, burning alive several elderly British civilian residents.

15. The British had effectively ruled Sudan since 1898. In the 1950s the British government was preparing to yield to the pressures of Sudanese independence movements; but Egyptian governments had long insisted that Sudan was legally part of Egypt: it had been conquered by the Egyptian ruler Muhammad Ali early in the nineteenth century, and since 1898 its government was officially known as an Anglo-Egyptian condominium. For further discussion of the Sudan, see pp. 325-327.

16. Hussein's father Abdullah, the brother of Feisal I of Iraq, had been murdered in 1950: this was widely regarded as punishment of one who had betrayed the Panarab cause by his friendship with the British. The kingdom of Jordan had been created by the combination of the old 'mandate' of Transjordan with those portions of the 'mandate' of Palestine which were not incorporated in Israel. See also pp. 397-410 and footnote 10, p. 503.

17. See p. 402.

18. This is broadly true, though of course the boundaries of modern Iraq do not coincide exactly with those of the ancient Chaldaean or Sumerian states, and even those of Egypt have changed a little since Pharaonic times.


## Chapter 7

1. Of the post-Muslim southern states the most important were those of

the Cholas in the tenth and eleventh centuries AD and Vijayanagara from 1336 to 1564.

2. It may be argued that Jewish civilisation is almost as old, being documented for at least three thousand years. However, there is the great difference that it was physically uprooted and forced to survive in small communities in diverse lands. This is the central tragedy of Jewish history. For discussion of the Jewish fate, and the Jews as a nation, see pp. 387-406.

3. The similarity between the balance of ruler and nobility in Japan to the feudal order in medieval Europe (see pp. 276, 287-288, 424) has often been noted and analysed by both European and Japanese historians, with differing conclusions. The parallels with the history of another island kingdom, England, are also interesting: the obvious difference is that in the Japanese case the equivalent of the Spanish Armada preceded the equivalant of the Wars of the Roses.

4. The word 'British' is used for the years after the Union of England and Scotland in 1707. Indeed thereafter many Scots played an important part in Indian affairs.

5. The southernmost islands resisted Spanish pressure until the late nineteenth century, and their people remained Muslim.

6. In 1826 further British settlements on the mainland were regrouped as the Straits Settlements, and other mainland Malay rulers accepted a British protectorate. In 1841 a British subject, James Brooke, made himself ruler of Sarawak, and in 1888 a British protectorate was created in North Borneo. The island was thus divided between British and Dutch rule.

7. It is only fair to note that some such officials—for example Sir Robert Hart, inspector general of customs from 1863 to 1908—considered themselves servants of China and gave generously of their talents.

8. The Chinese Eastern Railway, across Manchuria from west to east, beginning in 1896; and the South Manchurian Railway, from Harbin south to the sea, beginning in 1898. Both railway concessions involved cession of sovereignty over strips of land on both sides of the lines.

9. Babar's memoirs were originally written in Chagatay Turk.

10. For a discussion of this widespread fallacy, see Paul Brass, *Language, Religion and Politics in North India* (Cambridge, Mass., 1974), 119-182.

11. See pp. 248-249.

12. Judith M. Brown, *Gandhi's Rise to Power: Indian Politics 1915-1922* (Cambridge, 1972).

13. The lands mentioned in the book are: Punjab, Afghania, Kashmir, Iran, Sind, Tukharistan, Afghanistan and Baluchistan. The word is made up of the first letter of the first seven names, and the last letter of the eighth. 'Afghania' means the North-West Province of India as it then was. A more widespread version was that the name was made up only of Punjab,

Afghanistan, Kashmir and Sind together with the last syllable of Baluchistan. The word *pak* in Persian means 'pure'.

14. The census of 1951 showed a Hindi-speaking total of over 150 million. This included Urdu and Punjabi under the heading of Hindi. The 1961 census showed, for the same categories, a total of nearly 157 million, forming 35.7 per cent of the total population. However, in the 1961 census Urdu and Punjabi were listed separately, and the official total shown for Hindi-speakers was 133,436,360 or 30.4 per cent. Some people would argue that Bihari and Rajasthani are not separate languages, but are dialects of Hindi. If those who stated these to be their language, together with speakers of Urdu and Punjabi, were added, then the grand total for Hindi-speakers would be 188,621,866, or 42.9 per cent.

15. These were the states of Uttar Pradesh, Madhya Pradesh and Bihar; the state of Haryana, created in 1966 by dividing the state of Punjab on linguistic lines; the federal capital territory of Delhi; and the territory of Himachal Pradesh. All these territories together contained in 1961 42.4 per cent of the population of India.

16. This is convincingly argued in the detailed study by Paul Brass, *Language, Religion and Politics in North India* (1974).

17. For details, see Rounaq Jahan, *Pakistan: Failure in National Integration* (New York, 1972), chapters 4 and 5.

18. The word is the equivalent of the Urdu *sahib* ('lord' or 'master'), used by British officials of themselves. Its adoption was intended to indicate that the Burmese were equals of anyone.

19. See pp. 410-413.

20. The Ukrainian problem has been discussed separately in an earlier chapter.

21. In the case of the Volga Germans, to whose territory Hitler's armies never penetrated, the justification was that there was a danger that they might collaborate. There is perhaps a similarity between this case and the Japanese-Americans (Nisei) deported from the Pacific coast of the United States in 1941, though the latter were treated more humanely. It is perhaps worth noting that, though thousands of Burmese joined a Japanese-led army to fight the British, and the Burmese people did not prevent them from doing so, the British government did not deport the population of Burma to Arctic Canada. As far as I know, no British delegate to the United Nations has claimed credit for his country for this forbearance.

22. See above, pp. 83-84.

23. His case, and the historical and cultural background to it, are admirably described in Alexandre Bennigsen and Chantal Quelquejay, *Les mouvements nationaux chez les musulmans de Russie: le 'Sultangaliévisme au Tataristan'* (Paris and The Hague, 1960).

24. The proportion of urban to total population of the main Muslim

nations of the Soviet Union in 1970 was 55 per cent for Tatars, 40 per cent for Azerbaidjanis, 31 for Türkmen, 27 for Kazakhs, 26 for Tadjiks, 25 for Uzbeks and 15 for Kirgiz. Tatars, who were 2.4 per cent of the total population of the Soviet Union, had only 1.9 per cent of the students in higher education; Azerbaidjanis, with 1.8 per cent, had 1.9. The other Muslim peoples had approximately the same percentage of students in higher education as of total population.

25. See p. 249.

26. See pp. 147, 446.

27. After the annexation of Bessarabia in 1940, and its transformation into the Moldavian SSR, a similar policy was introduced of creating a 'Moldavian' 'people' (*norod*) distinct from the Romanian people (*popor*).

28. It also diminished in Azerbaidjan, as well as in Georgia and Armenia. In all the European republics the percentage of Russians increased, while the percentage of all the republican nations except the Lithuanians diminished.

29. Persons under twenty years old formed between 52 and 56 per cent of the population of the six Muslim republics, and between 29 and 38 per cent of that of the European republics. The discrepancy between the Muslim nations and the others must of course be much greater than this, since there are many Russians living in Muslim republics and considerable numbers of non-Russians in the Russian republic (RSFSR).

30. For further discussion of this term, see pp. 338-339.

31. See above, pp. 141-142.

32. See above, pp. 119, 151.


## Chapter 8

1. The legend that Ethiopian dynasties were descendants of King Solomon by the Queen of Sheba may be based on reality.

2. The Christian church in Alexandria was divided from the mid-fifth century AD by the controversy concerning the single or twofold nature of Christ (human and divine). At the time of the Arab conquest of Egypt in 641 the believers in the single nature (monophysites) were in the ascendant. Under Muslim rule the Egyptian church developed on its separate lines, and the church of Ethiopia was linked with it. The Coptic language was derived from the language of ancient Egypt, and continued to be used in religious ritual, though it fell into complete disuse as a spoken tongue by the eighteenth century.

3. The word Swahili is of Arabic origin, meaning 'of the coast'. The African peoples of this coast were largely converted to Islam, and their language (belonging to the Bantu group) received, like the languages of

many other peoples converted to Islam, a large infusion of Arabic words. It became a *lingua franca* between the coast and the Great Lakes, and its literature was written in the Arabic alphabet. The language is more correctly called Ki-Swahili.

4. See below, p. 361.

5. This former German colony was administered by the government of South Africa as a mandated territory between the world wars. In 1945 the South African government refused to have its status changed to a trust territory under the United Nations.

6. Relations between whites and blacks in South Africa are discussed in chapter nine.

7. This is an estimate. No precise statistics on language or religious denomination have been published.

8. These figures come from G. N. Trevaskis, *Eritrea: a colony in transition 1941-52.*

9. After the defeat of Italy, both Ethiopia and Eritrea were under British occupation. The British government agreed to the wish of its Ethiopian ally to recover Eritrea, which had been part of its territory until the 1880s.

10. See above, pp. 332-333.


## Chapter 9

1. This attitude of the poor to Jews essentially resembled that of East Europeans in the nineteenth century, discussed in chapter 10.

2. See chapter 10, pp. 406-409.

3. See chapter 10, pp. 383-384.

4. The abbreviation commonly used for South-Western Township, the agglomeration of nearly a million black inhabitants lying to the south-west of Johannesburg.

5. The 1970 census showed 792,000 Indians of whom nearly half were in four states (Oklahoma 98,468; Arizona 95,812; California 91,018; New Mexico 72,788).

6. In the 1960s rewriting of history in favour of the Indians became fashionable in the United States. An outstanding example is the best-selling *Bury My Heart at Wounded Knee* by Dee Brown (1971). The wrongs suffered by the Indians are movingly told, though it is perhaps worth noting that the Indian raiders and torturers who figure so prominently in the traditional American mythology of the Indian wars, and who are simply left out of this book, *did* exist in history. The Indians were victims, but they were not paragons of unsullied virtue.

7. The census of 1950 gave figures for persons over the age of five who spoke Indian languages. The provinces which had the highest proportion

were Yucatan (63.8 per cent, speaking Maya), Oaxaca (48 per cent, speaking Mixtec and Zapotec) and Quintana Roo (43.7 per cent, Maya).

## Chapter 10

1. This statement is true for the overwhelming majority of Jews during this period; but it must be qualified by the fact that a remnant of Jews remained in Palestine, and in Jerusalem, throughout the successive centuries.

2. I refer to those Chinese who traded in ships owned by individual Chinese, from Ming times onwards, and indeed earlier. There were also Indian traders who crossed the Indian Ocean to Africa from early times (see K. M. Panikkar, *India and the Indian Ocean* [1945]). Those Chinese and Indians who were transported in European ships, in semi-slave conditions, cannot of course be regarded as seafarers.

3. The European colonies of settlement, in which new nations of European origin arose, are of course a quite different phenomenon, already discussed in chapter 5. A possible marginal case were the Dutch in Indonesia, where families both of pure Dutch and of mixed Dutch-Javanese origin continued to live for generations on end and in substantial numbers.

4. 'Mobilised and proletarian diasporas', by John Armstrong, in *The American Political Science Review*, vol. 70, 393–408.

5. See above, pp. 121-122.

6. The date is 'Old Style'—that is, twelve days earlier than the date in usage in non-Orthodox Europe. A fifteenth province was added after 1812, in the form of Bessarabia (or eastern Moldavia), then annexed to Russia (see p. 177).

7. It should be noted that mass anti-semitism was much more widespread in the Ukrainian, Polish, Lithuanian, Latvian and Romanian borderlands than in the provinces of Russian population; the reason is that the Jewish populations in the empire lived among the former peoples and not among the Russians.

8. A Jewish workman, Mendel Beilis, was accused of ritual murder, and proceedings were dragged on by the Russian authorities in Kiev, though it was obvious that there was nó serious case against the accused.

9. Walter Laqueur, *A History of Zionism* (1972), 203.

10. The 'Mandate' was an institution created by the peace treaties of 1919. Various formerly German territories in Africa and formerly Ottoman territories in the Middle East were placed under the administration of victorious powers (Britain, France, Belgium, Australia, New Zealand). The 'mandatory' power held them on trust for the League of Nations, to which

it submitted regular reports, and was expected to prepare their peoples for ultimate independence.

11. Arab movements for independence from Turkey, and Arab nationalism, are discussed in chapter 7, pp. 261-262.

12. Report by the anti-Nazi mining engineer Kurt Gerstein, published in *Vierteljahreshefte für Zeitgeschichte*, vol. I, no. 2 (Stuttgart, 1953).

13. The great majority of the Jews of Hungary in 1944 lived in the northern and eastern periphery, in lands which until 1938 or 1940 had belonged to Czechoslovakia or Romania. There is a widespread, but incorrect, belief that the losses of Jews were greater in Romania than in Hungary. The reason is that the Jews of northern Transylvania were exterminated. This was Romanian from 1918 to 1940, and after 1945; but in 1944, when its Jews were deported to the death camps, it was part of Hungary, and the orders were given by Hungarians.

14. *Statistical Abstract of Israel* (Jerusalem, 1971), 21-23, 45-46, 126.

15. The fluctuations in population are due not only to natural increase, but also to the return of some of those who fled, and to the annexation of territory in 1967 in Jerusalem and in the Golan Heights. The great majority of the population of the lands occupied by the Israeli army in 1967 (the 'administered territories') is *not* included in these figures.

16. See chapter 6, pp. 269-270.

17. *Narodnoe khozyaistvo SSSR v 1970 g.* (Moscow, 1971), 15.

18. This section is predominantly, but not wholly, based on the study by Hugh Tinker, *A New System of Slavery* (1974).

19. In 1970 there were 182,000 persons of Indian origin in Kenya, 105,000 in Tanzania and 80,000 in Uganda. Of these about a third became citizens of the new states.

20. In Guyana in 1970 it was estimated that Indians formed 51 per cent of a population of more than 700,000 while 42 per cent were of African or mixed origin and 4 per cent were Amerindians. In Trinidad, in a population of slightly under one million, 36 per cent were Indians and 60 per cent were African or mixed. In Mauritius Indians formed two-thirds of the population (531,000 in 1967—of whom about a quarter were Muslim—to about 200,000 African or mixed descent, with much smaller minorities of Chinese and of French-speaking Europeans). In Fiji at the end of 1971 Indians were slightly more than half, with 272,000 to the 231,000 indigenous Fijians and with some further small European and other minorities.

21. Another variant, not discussed here, is British Honduras, with a mixed black and Amerindian population, threatened by territorial claims from Guatemala.

22. An acronym for Malaya, Philippines, Indonesia.

# Chapter 11

1. See above, p. 80.
2. See p. 447.


# Chapter 12

1. Karl Renner (pseudonym Rudolf Springer), *Grundlagen und Ent-wicklungsziele der österreichisch-ungarischen Monarchie* (Vienna, 1906); and Otto Bauer, *Die Nationalitätenfrage und die Sozialdemokratie* (Vienna, 1907).

2. Its full name was All-Jewish Workers' Union in Russia and Poland. It was founded in 1897, and was a constituent group at the founding first congress of the Russian Social Democratic Workers' Party (RSDRP) in 1898.

3. See above, p. 129.

4. See her short work, *Die industrielle Entwicklung Polens* (Berlin, 1898).

5. The title of the official translation into English is *Marxism and the National and Colonial Question*.

6. The word *fascio*, derived from the Roman *fasces* of the lictors, had been first used in modern Italy by a movement of the left, the socialist *Fascio della Democrazia* in 1883. See C. Seton-Watson, *Italy from Liberalism to Fascism* (London, 1967), 96.

7. The IRA retained their cult when they moved from the fascist into the pseudo-marxist camp.

8. The six points are stated in Carl Friedrich and Zbigniew Brzezinski, *Totalitarian Dictatorship and Democracy* (Harvard University Press, 2nd rev. ed., 1965), 22. They may be summarised as follows, using as far as possible the authors' own words (in quotation marks): (1) 'an elaborate ideology, consisting of an official body of doctrine covering all vital aspects of man's existence . . . '; (2) 'a single mass party typically led by one man'; (3) 'a system of terror . . . through party and secret-police control . . .'; a 'technologically conditioned . . . monopoly' of (4) means of mass communication; and (5) armed forces; (6) 'central control and direction of the entire economy. . . .' Only the features covered in the first two points seem to me to be specific to totalitarian governments. The features covered in the other four points are certainly present and necessary to totalitarian government, but they are not specific; they can be found in non-totalitarian dictatorial regimes, and even in non-dictatorial government of modern states. On the other hand the authors have left out two specific features of totalitarian government: (1) the claim to control the whole private as well as public life

of its citizens; (2) the claim to direct their spiritual life and to be the sole source of morality.

9. In 1917 the Bolshevik party was renamed Russian Communist Party (Bolshevik); after the state itself was renamed Union of Soviet Socialist Republics (in 1923), the party became the All-Union Communist Party (Bolshevik); at its nineteenth Congress in 1952 it took the name Communist Party of the Soviet Union (initials in English CPSU, in Russian KPSS).

10. This phrase was used, in a pejorative sense, in the Soviet Union in the years when Khrushchev had discredited Stalin: it was not used in Stalin's life-time.

11. The rulers of Eastern Germany from the beginning accepted the new frontier with Poland; but they did this only because their Soviet masters ordered them to do so, and few Poles either thanked or trusted them.

12. The evolution of Soviet doctrine and political tactics in this field during the 1960s and early 1970s is brilliantly analysed in Richard Lowenthal, *Model or Ally? The Communist Powers and the Developing Countries* (New York, 1977).

13. It seemed possible that the MPLA leader Agostinho Neto might follow Castro's example, and that Angola would become a Soviet satellite, administered by Cubans in the Soviet interest, strategically as useful as Cuba and economically still more expensive.

14. This book is no place to discuss these sects in detail. The best survey of them all that is known to me is Klaus Mehnert, *Jugend in Zeitbruch* (Stuttgart, 1976).

## Chapter 13

1. In Czechoslovakia, Czechs and Slovaks; in the five other states one nation only.

2. 'Non-white' rather than 'black', because many Panafricanists were willing to regard the people of the southern Mediterrean littoral, beyond the Sahara, as Africans.

3. The proper Polish name for this place is Oświęcim, but I use the name the Germans used, because it was as such that it earned world-wide notoriety.

# Bibliography

To prepare a systematic bibliography of this vast subject would be the work of a lifetime: even to list all the works which I have read which bear on the subject, would require not much less effort than it has taken to write the book. In any case, as explained in the Introduction, the printed word has not been my only source.

Instead, I have prepared a list of most of those books which have been most useful to me, and mainly of such as I have used within the last few years. I have not listed individual articles, nor names of periodicals. The latter have certainly been an important source, and fall into three categories: specialised learned journals, intellectual reviews of broader scope, and daily newspapers. Of the latter the most important have been those appearing in England, above all *The Times* and *The Economist*, which have been a regular part of my intellectual fodder for most of my adult life; but they include also papers in other languages, and in other countries, read mostly in those periods when I have been living in their lands but also quite often from afar.

This list includes very few documentary collections. I have read a good many 'primary sources' over the years, chiefly from Central Europe and Russia; but it has seemed to me most useful to give readers a selection of general interpretative studies and monographs. I tried at first to plan the bibliography so as to fit the subdivisions of my chapters, but this proved unsatisfactory; and I have chosen the more conventional method of grouping them by regions and by countries, which I believe will make it easier for the reader to find what he or she wants.

The place of publication for the books listed below is given only when the books were published outside London.

### The European historical background

The following are a few works which, read at different times of my life but mostly a good many years ago, have brought me illumination, intellectual pleasure and in some cases real joy. None is concerned primarily or immediately with the subject of this book, but it is largely to their authors that I owe whatever understanding I may have acquired of the European heritage. The fact that some are now out of date, or that there are new, and more convincing, interpretations of their subjects by others, in no way diminishes my gratitude. All but one are concerned mainly with the Middle Ages. The exception, Paul Hazard's study of the beginnings of the Enlightenment, is placed in this section because it does not fit into any of the regional sub-divisions which follow.

Bloch, Marc,    *La société féodale—I: la formation des liens de dépendance; II: les classes et le gouvernement des hommes*, 2 vols (Paris 1939 and 1940).

Cohn, Norman,    *The Pursuit of the Millennium* (1957).

Dawson, Christopher,    *The Making of Europe 400-1000 A.D.* (1932).

Diehl, Charles,    *Figures byzantines*, 2 vols (Paris 1906-08).

Diehl, Charles,    *Byzance: grandeur et décadance* (Paris 1919).

Fliche, Augustin,    *Histoire du moyen age: l'Europe occidentale de 888 à 1125* (Paris 1930).

Ganshof, François Louis,    *Feudalism* (1964).

Hazard, Paul,    *La crise de la conscience européenne 1680-1715* (Paris 1935).

Huizinga, J.,    *The Waning of the Middle Ages* (1924).

Moss, H. St L. B.,    *The Birth of the Middle Ages* (1935).

Obolensky, Dimitri,    *The Byzantine Commonwealth* (1971).

Pirenne, Henri,    *History of Europe from the Invasions to the Sixteenth Century* (1948).

Pirenne, Henri,    *Les villes du moyen âge* (Brussels 1927).

Runciman, Steven,    *Byzantine Civilisation* (1933).

Volpe, Steven,    *Il medio evo italiano* (Florence 1923).

**General**

A work which does not fit the pattern of this bibliography, must be inserted at this point:

Wittfogel, Karl August,  *Oriental Despotism* (New Haven, Conn. 1957).

This is a great pioneering achievement, opening new perspectives to the mind of any historian or social scientist who is willing to learn, towering above most contemporary works, however disputable it may be on many major and minor specific points.


## Nationalism—general and theoretical

The following deal with nationalist theory or nationalist movements on a broad comparative basis, though inevitably each tends to pay more attention to a particular part of the world than to the others. The works of Bauer and of 'Springer'-Renner were designed for the special needs of Austria-Hungary at the beginning of this century, but both have an almost universal potential application. The work by Hroch is an intelligent and illuminating analysis, from a Marxist point of view, of the nationalist elites of a number of small European nations. Lemberg's two volumes are the most enlightening work I know from the perspective of Central Europe.


Bauer, Otto,  *Die Nationalitätenfrage und die Sozialdemokratie* (Vienna 1907).

Deutsch, Karl,  *Nationalism and Social Communication* (Cambridge, Mass. 1953).

Emerson, Rupert,  *From Empire to Nation: The Rise to Self-assertion of Asian and African Peoples* (Cambridge, Mass. 1960).

Hayes, Carlton,  *The Historical Evolution of Modern Nationalism* (1948).

Hroch, Miroslav,  *Vorkämpfer der nationalen Bewegungen beidden kleinen Völkern Europas* (Prague 1968).

Kedourie, Elie,  *Nationalism* (1960).

Kedourie, Elie,  *Nationalism in Asia and Africa* (1970).

Kohn, Hans,  *The Idea of Nationalism: A Study in its Origins and Background* (New York 1946).

Lemberg, Eugen,  *Der Nationalismus*, 2 vols (Munich 1967 and 1968).

Smith, Antony,  *Theories of Nationalism* (1971).

Springer, Rudolf       *Grundlagen und Entwicklungsziele der*
(Karl Renner),         *österreichisch-ungarischen Monarchie* (Vi-
                       enna 1906).

Stalin, Joseph,        *Marxism and the National and Colonial
                       Question* (numerous editions in English
                       and in numerous other languages).

## The nations of Britain

These are only a few works which illuminate some of the stages of development of the English language and English national consciousness, as well as the history of the Scottish and Welsh nations. I would single out for special gratitude the books of May McKisack, Geoffrey Dickens, Geoffrey Barrow, T. C. Smout and Douglas Young.

Barrow, Geoffrey,      *Feudal Britain* (1956).

Barrow, Geoffrey,      *Robert Bruce and the Community of the
                       Realm of Scotland* (1965).

Baugh, Albert C.,      *A History of the English Language* (1935).

Dickens, Geoffrey,     *The English Reformation* (1964).

Duncan, A. A. M.,      *Scotland: The Making of the Kingdom*
                       (Edinburgh 1975).

Jacob, E. F.,          *The Fifteenth Century 1399-1485*, being
                       vol. 6 of the *Oxford History of England*
                       (Oxford 1961).

Lloyd, J. E.,          *Owen Glendower* (Oxford 1931).

McKisack, May,         *The Fourteenth Century 1307-1399*, being
                       vol. 5 of the *Oxford History of England*
                       (Oxford 1959).

Mackie, J. D.,         *A History of Scotland* (1964).

Madgwick, P. J.,       *The Politics of Modern Wales: A Study of
                       Cardiganshire* (1973).

Smout, T. C.,          *A History of the Scottish People 1560-1830*
                       (1969).

Strang, Barbara,       *A History of English* (1970).

Williams, David,       *A History of Modern Wales* (1969).

Young, Douglas,        *Scotland* (1971).

## Ireland

Outstanding in my memory is Lyons's fine survey. The classic short work by Curtis remains a valuable guide.

Curtis, Edmund,     *A History of Ireland* (1936).

Edwards, Owen Dudley,     'Ireland' in *Celtic Nationalism* (1968).

Hammond, J. L.,     *Gladstone and the Irish Nation* (1938).

Lyons, F. S. L.,     *Ireland since the Famine* (1971).

Mansergh, N. S.,     *The Government of Northern Ireland* (1936).

O'Corran, Donncha,     *Ireland before the Normans* (Dublin 1972).

Pakenham, Frank,     *Peace by Ordeal* (1935).

## France

This too is but a puny list of a few books from which I have learnt much, chiefly in very recent years. Such understanding as I have of French history and culture goes back much further, and I could not possibly enumerate the books which have contributed to it. Of the following, I would stress those of Belperron (though I do not share his basic attitude) and Perroy. Yardémi's recent study has, from my point of view, the merit of dealing with the questions which interest me—which are not necessarily those of specialists of the period.

Belperron, Pierre,     *La Croisade contre les albigeois* (Paris 1942).

Cohen, Marcel,     *Histoire d'une langue: le français* (Paris 1950).

Dupuy, André,     *Historique de l'Occitanie* (Rodez 1974).

Fawtier, Robert,     *The Capetian Kings of France* (1964).

Fowler, Kenneth (ed.),     *The Hundred Years' War* (1971).

Kendall, Paul M.,     *Louis XI* (1971).

Perroy, Jacques,     *La guerre de cent ans* (Paris 1945).

Sagnac, Philippe,     *La formation de la société française moderne*, 2 vols (Paris 1945, 1946).

Wallace-Hadrill, J. M.,    *The Barbarian West 400-1000* (1964).

Yardémi, Miriam,    *La conscience nationale en France pendant les guerres de religion* (Paris/Louvain 1971).

## The Low Countries

Geyl, Huizinga and Pirenne were great masters, whose fame no word of mine could increase. I must also record the intellectual pleasure which I had from reading the lectures of Charles Wilson, as well as any books by Boxer which have come my way.

Boxer, C. R.,    *The Dutch Seaborne Empire 1600-1800* (1965).

Destrée, Jules,    *Wallons et flamands* (Paris 1923).

Geyl, Pieter,    *The Revolt of the Netherlands 1555-1609* (1932).

Geyl, Pieter,    *The Netherlands in the 17th century*, 2 vols (1964).

Geyl, Pieter,    *History of the Low Countries*—Trevelyan lectures 1963 (1964).

Huizinga, J. H.,    'Aus der Vorgeschichte des niederländischen Nationalbewusstseins', in collection of essays entitled *Im Bann der Geschichte* (Basel 1943).

Huizinga, J. H.,    *Dutch Civilisation in the 17th Century* (1968).

Pirenne, Henri,    *Histoire de Belgique* (Brussels 1926).

Wedgwood, C. V.,    *William the Silent* (1944).

Wilson, Charles,    *Queen Elizabeth and the Revolt of the Netherlands* (1970).

## Switzerland

A most erudite and fascinating modern study of this unique country is:

Hughes, Christopher,    *Switzerland* (1975).

## Scandinavia

The following are useful sources of information. The two works which rise above the general competent level, by their power to evoke excitement at least in this reader, are both by women: the article by a heroine of the Bolshevik Revolution who marvellously survived to a ripe old age, Alexandra Kollontay, and the fine modern biography by Ragnhild Hatton of Charles XII.

Anderson, Ingvar,          *A History of Sweden* (1956).

Bain, Nisbet,              *Scandinavia* (1905).

Bronsted, Johannes,        *The Vikings* (1960).

Derry, T. K.,              *A Short History of Norway* (1957).

Hatton, Ragnhild,          *Charles XII of Sweden* (1968).

Kollontay, Alexandra,      section on Finland in vol. 4 of *Obshchest-vennoe dvizhenie v Rossii v nachale XX veka*, a symposium by Social Democratic writers (St Petersburg 1908-1911).

Schybergson, M. G.,        *Politische Geschichte Finnlands 1809-1919* (Gotha 1926).

von Törne, P. O.,          *Finland under etthundra trettio år 1809-1939* (Stockholm 1943).

Wuorinen, John,            *A History of Finland* (New York 1965).

## Germany

The following cover various aspects of the development of German national consciousness and of the movement for unity, in its liberal and its national-socialist phases. Carsten covers much of the medieval and early modern, Barraclough the medieval empire and Dickens the Reformation. The book by Molisch and the first of those listed by Wiskemann are useful for the transformation of 'greater German' thinking among Austrian Germans from a liberal to a national-socialist direction.

Barraclough, Geoffrey,     *The Origins of Modern Germany* (1946).

Bracher, Karl-Dietrich,    *Die deutsche Diktatur* (Cologne and Berlin 1969).

Bullock, Allen,                  *Hitler: A Study in Tyranny* (1952).

Carsten, F. L.,                  *The Origins of Prussia* (1954).

Dickens, Geoffrey,               *The German Nation and Martin Luther* (1974).

Friedjung, Heinrich,             *The Struggle for Supremacy in Germany* (1935).

Glum, Friedrich,                 *Der National-Sozialismus: Werden und Vergehen* (Munich 1962).

Holborn, Hajo,                   *A History of Modern Germany—1640-1840* (1965); *1840-1945* (1969).

Mann, Golo,                      *Deutsche Geschichte des 19. und 20. Jahrhunderts* (Frankfurt 1961).

Molisch, P.,                     *Geschichte der deutsch-nationalen Bewegung in Österreich* (Jena 1926).

Schieder, Theodor,               *Das deutsche Kaiserreich von 1871 als Nationalstaat* (Cologne 1960).

Schweitzer, Arthur,              *Big Business in the Third Reich* (Bloomington, Ind. 1964).

Wiskemann, Elizabeth,            *Czechs and Germans* (1938).

Wiskemann, Elizabeth,            *Germany's Eastern Neighbours* (1956).

Wiskemann, Elizabeth (ed.),      *The Anatomy of the SS State* (1968).

Ziekursch, Johann,               *Politische Geschichte des neuen deutschen Kaiserreiches*, 3 vols (Frankfurt 1925-30).

## Italy

Except perhaps for Candeloro's extremely useful synoptic work, these works are not primarily concerned with the attainment of Italian unity, though all bear on the formation or development of Italian national consciousness. Venturi's book covers a large portion of the Italian Enlightenment which was the background to the movement for unity. Seton-Watson's survey of the post-unity kingdom, and the works on fascism, are all relevant to sections in chapters three, eleven and twelve of this book.

Candeloro, Giorgio,               *Storia dell'Italia moderna,* 4 vols (Milano 1956-64).

Mack Smith, Denis,      *Cavour and Garibaldi* (Cambridge 1954).

Mack Smith, Denis,      *Italy: A Modern History* (Ann Arbor, Mich. 1959).

Roberts, J. M.,      'Italy 1793-1830', chapter XV in vol. IX of *The New Cambridge Modern History* (1965).

Rossi, A. (Angelo Tasca),      *The Rise of Italian Fascism* (1938).

Salamone, A. W.,      *Italian Democracy in the Making* (Philadelphia, Pa. 1945).

Salvatorelli, L. and Mira, G.,      *Storia del fascismo* (Rome 1952).

Salvemini, G.,      *The Fascist Dictatorship in Italy* (1928).

Seton-Watson, Christopher,      *Italy from Liberalism to Fascism* (1967).

Valeri, Nino,      *La lotta politica in Italia dall'unità al 1925* (Florence 1946).

Valiani, Leo,      *Dall'antifascismo alla resistenza* (Milano 1959).

Venturi, Franco,      *Settecento riformatore: da Muratori a Beccaria* (Torino 1969).

Vivarelli, Roberto,      *Il dopoguerra in Italia e l'avvento del fascismo (1918-1922)* (Napoli 1967).

## The Iberian nations

The solid work of Altamira is a rich mine of information. The two short books by Ganivet and Ortega are two famous interpretative essays. Americo Castro's is a much longer, provocative and stimulating interpretation. Lévi-Provençal and Menendez Pidal are fascinating studies of aspects of medieval Spain. Elliott's book on the Catalan revolt is an impressive achievement of recent scholarship. Of the three titles quoted by Vicens Vives, the first two are exciting interpretative essays, the third a more detailed study with the emphasis on economic and social aspects. Brennan's book on the early twentieth century is a masterpiece of sympathetic understanding by a resident foreigner, already a classic. Carr's book is the only large-scale modern survey of nineteenth-century Spain.

Altamira y Crevea, Rafael,      *Historia de España*, 4 vols (Barcelona 1928-29).

*Biografíes catalanes,*   vol. 2: *Panorama del pensament català contemporani* (Barcelona 1963).

Boxer, C. R.,   *The Portuguese Sea-borne Empire 1415-1825* (1969).

Brennan, Gerald,   *The Spanish Labyrinth* (Cambridge 1943).

Carr, Raymond,   *Spain 1808-1939* (Oxford 1966).

Castro, Americo,   *The Spaniards: An Introduction to their History* (Berkeley, Calif. 1971).

Crozier, Brian,   *Franco* (1967).

Elliott, J. H.,   *Imperial Spain 1469-1716* (1963).

Elliott, J. H.,   *The Revolt of the Catalans* (Cambridge 1963).

Ganivet, Angel,   *Idearium español* (Madrid 1896).

Jackson, Gabriel,   *The Making of Medieval Spain* (1972).

Lévi-Provençal, E.   *Histoire de l'Espagne musulmane*, 3 vols (Paris/Leyden 1953).

Livermore, H. V.,   *A New History of Portugal* (Cambridge 1966).

Lynch, J.,   *Spain under the Habsburgs—I: Empire and Absolutism 1516-1598* (1964).

Madariaga, Salvador de,   *Spain* (1942).

Menendez Pidal, Ramón,   *La España del Cid* (Buenos Aires 1943).

Ortega y Gasset, J.,   *España invertebrada* (4th ed., repr. Madrid 1948).

Thomas, Hugh,   *The Spanish Civil War* (1961).

Vives, J. Vicens,   *Approaches to Spanish History* (Berkeley and Los Angeles, Calif. 1970).

Vives, J. Vicens,   *Noticia de Cataluña* (Barcelona 1954).

Vives, J. Vicens,   'Els catalans en el segle XIX' (Barcelona 1950), being the larger part of vol. XI of *Biografíes Catalanes.*

## Poland

The best single survey in English of Polish history under the partitions is Wandycz. The collective history edited by Kieniewicz is useful, though there are some curious omissions. Dmowski's reflections and Perl's history are classics. So are Roza Luxemburg's essay and Feldman's survey of political opinions in the nineteenth century. Lednicki's work consists of some brilliant and sensitive essays on Polish-Russian intellectual relations. Leslie's monographs on the two nineteenth century risings are useful examples of the anti-romantic school of thought. Polonsky's book is a most useful survey of the two decades of Polish independence. Roos and Rhode are two very fair-minded surveys by German writers.

Dmowski, Roman, — *Myśli nowoczesnego Polaka* (Lwów 1904).

Feldman, J., — *Geschichte der politischen Ideen in Polen seit dessen Teilungen* (Munich 1917).

Kieniewicz, Stefan (editor-in-chief), — *History of Poland* (Warsaw 1968).

Lednicki, W., — *Russia, Poland and the West: Essays in Literary and Cultural History* (1954).

Leslie, R. F., — *Polish Politics and the Revolution of November 1830* (1956).

Leslie, R. F., — *Reform and Insurrection in Russian Poland* (1963).

Lord, R. H., — *The Second Partition of Poland* (Cambridge, Mass. 1915).

Luxemburg, Roza, — *Die industrielle Entwicklung Polens* (Berlin 1898).

Perl, Feliks, — *Dzieje ruchu socjalistycznego w zaborze rosyskim* (Warsaw 1910).

Polonsky, Antony, — *Politics in Independent Poland 1921-1939* (1972).

Rhode, Gotthold, — *Geschichte Polens* (Darmstadt 1966).

Roos, Hans, — *A History of Modern Poland* (1966).

Wandycz, Piotr, — *The Lands of Partitioned Poland 1795-1918* (Seattle, Wash. 1974).

## The Habsburg Monarchy

In this section I have listed works relating to the 'Nationalities Question' in the Habsburg lands in the nineteenth century, which are discussed in numerous sections of this book, especially in chapters six, seven and eight. I have separated into subsections those which cover the whole Monarchy, or its northern and western provinces (conveniently known as 'Austria'), and those which concentrate on the lands of the kingdom of Hungary. In the first subsection the classical works of Eisenmann, Jászi, Popovici and Steed were very influential in their day. The more recent studies of Kann, Macartney, Valiani and Zwitter are also major contributions. Namier's essay on 1848 is a small masterpiece. The *Austrian History Year Book* has published many excellent articles. In the second subsection, Seton-Watson's book also had some influence in its day. Jászi's book was a fine achievement, more valuable perhaps than his later *Dissolution*. . . . The essays by Szekfü are a selection from the work of a great historian. Baranyi's book is a fine recent work of scholarship. Kemény did a good job in collecting documents of 'Nationalities' problems in several languages.

(a) *General*

| | |
|---|---|
| *Austrian History Year Book*, | published by Rice University, Texas (1964-72). |
| Eisenmann, Louis, | *Le compromis austro-hongrois* (Paris 1904). |
| Hantsch, Hugo, | *Die Nationalitätenfrage im alten Österreich* (Vienna 1953). |
| Jászi, Oskár, | *The Dissolution of the Habsburg Monarchy* (Chicago, Ill. 1929). |
| Kann, Robert A., | *The Multi-national Empire*, 2 vols (New York 1950). |
| Macartney, C. A., | *The Habsburg Empire 1790-1918* (1968). |
| Namier, Sir Lewis, | *The Revolt of the Intellectuals* (1946). |
| Popovici, Aurel, | *Die vereinigten Staaten von Gross-Österreich* (Leipzig 1906). |
| Steed, H. Wickham, | *The Habsburg Monarchy* (1913). |
| Valiani, Leo, | *La dissoluzione dell'Austria-Ungheria* (Milano 1966). |

Zöllner, Erich,                 *Geschichte Österreichs* (Vienna 1966).

Zwitter, Fran,                  *Les problèmes nationaux dans la monarchie des Habsbourg* (Belgrade 1960).

(b) *Kingdom of Hungary*

Baranyi, George,               *Stephen Széchényi and the Awakening of Hungarian Nationalism 1791-1841* (Princeton, N.J. 1968).

Eötvös, Baron Joseph,          *Die Nationalitätenfrage* (Pest 1865).

Jászi, Oszkár,                  *A nemzeti államok kialakulása és a nemzetiségi kérdés* (Budapest 1912).

Kemény, Gábor (ed.),           *Iratok a nemzetiségi kérdés történetéhez Magyarországon a Dualizmus korában* vol. I 1867-92 (Budapest 1952).

Kosáry, Domokos,               *Kossuth Lajos a Reformkorban* (Budapest 1946).

Macartney, C. A.,              *Hungary* (1934).

Macartney, C. A.,              *Hungary and her Successors* (1935).

Molnar, E. (ed.),              *Magyarország Története*, 2 vols (Budapest 1967).

Seton-Watson, R. W.,           *Racial Problems in Hungary* (1908).

Szekfü, Jules,                 *Etat et Nation* (Paris 1946).

**Czechs and Slovaks**

The works by Seton-Watson and Harrison Thomson are still the best general surveys in English. Masaryk's war memoirs are an important source. The work by Pichlik is an admirable reconsideration of the process of the formation of Czechoslovakia, a fine achievement of Czech scholarship of the late 1960s, when scholarship was possible. The work of the Slovak historian Butvin, on a less controversial subject, is also of high quality. Brock's valuable study of the intellectual origins of the Slovak national movement did not appear until my section had been written.

Brock, Peter,                  *The Slovak National Awakening* (Toronto 1976).

Butvin, Jozef,            *Slovenské národno-zjednocovacie hnutie (1780-1848)* (Bratislava 1965).

Dějiny Československa,     vol. 3, covering the period 1781-1918, ed. Butvin, J., and Havranek, J. (Prague 1968).

Dějiny Slovenska,         vol. 2 (1848-1900), ed. L'udovit Holotík and Julius Mésároš (Bratislava 1968).

Janšak, Štefan,           *Život Dr. Pavla Blahu*, 2 vols (Trnava 1947).

Liptak, L'ubomir,         *Slovensko v 20. storočí* (Bratislava 1968).

Masaryk, T. G.,           *The Making of a State* (1927).

Pichlik, Karel,           *Zahraniční odboj 1914-1918 běz legend* (Prague 1968).

Seton-Watson, R. W.,      *A History of the Czechs and Slovaks* (1944).

Thomson, S. Harrison,     *Czechoslovakia in European History* (Princeton, N.J. 1944).

## Eastern Europe—general

The following works cover several countries of the whole region. Outstanding is the classical work by Sir Charles Eliot on the Balkans in the last stages of Ottoman rule. Sugar's work appeared after I had finished writing.

Djordjević, Dimitrije,    *Révolutions nationales des peuples balkaniques 1804-1914* (Belgrade 1965).

Eliot, Sir Charles ('Odysseus'), *Turkey in Europe* (1900).

Kolarz, Walter,           *Myths and Realities in Eastern Europe* (1946).

Rothschild, Joseph,       *East Central Europe between the Two World Wars* (Seattle, Wash. 1975).

Seton-Watson, Hugh,       *Eastern Europe between the Wars* (Cambridge 1945).

Sugar, Peter,             *Southeastern Europe under Ottoman Rule 1354-1804* (Seattle, Wash. 1977).

Weber, Eugen,             *Varieties of Fascism* (Princeton, N.J. 1964).

## Romania

Riker's study of the background, in great power diplomacy, to the formation of the Romanian state remains invaluable, and Seton-Watson's general survey has not yet been replaced in English. Henry Roberts's book covers a broad area of political and social development between the world wars. All the recent Romanian works cited here are useful contributions: outstanding among them is the book by Prodan. The curiously entitled work of Nagy-Talavera contains interesting information on fascist movements in both Romania and Hungary.

Bodea, Cornelia, — *The Romanian Struggle for Unification 1834-1849* (Bucarest 1970).

Constantinescu, Miron (ed.), — *Desăvîrsirea unificării statului național român* (Bucarest 1968).

Dragomir, Silviu, — *Avram Iancu* (Bucarest 1965).

Hitchins, Keith, — *The Rumanian National Movement in Transylvania, 1780-1849* (Cambridge, Mass. 1969).

*Istoria României,* — vol. 3, from seventeenth century to 1848, ed. A. Oțetea (Bucarest 1964).

*Istoria României,* — vol. 4, from 1848 to 1878, ed. P. Constantinescu-Iași (Bucarest 1964).

Nagy-Talavera, N. M., — *The Green Shirts and the Others* (Stanford, Calif. 1970).

Netea, Vasile, — *Lupta Românilor din Transilvania pentru libertatea națională 1848-1881* (Bucarest 1974).

Oțetea, Andrei, — *Tudor Vladimirescu* (rev. ed., Bucarest 1971).

Prodan, D., — *Supplex libellus valachorum* (Bucarest 1967).

Riker, T. W., — *The Making of Roumania* (Oxford 1931).

Roberts, Henry, L., — *Roumania: Political Problems of an Agrarian State* (New Haven, Conn. 1951).

Savu, G., — *Dictatura regală* (Bucarest 1970).

Seton-Watson, R. W., — *A History of the Roumanians* (Cambridge 1934).

## Greece

Dimaras's history of modern Greek literature (of which there is also an edition in French) is also a history of social and political ideas of Greeks, from the time of Ottoman domination up to the twentieth century. His second work listed here is a brief brilliant essay on the eighteenth century. The joint book by Campbell and Sherrard is a comprehensive and perceptive survey. Woodhouse's two books are essential reading, the second being a biography of one who was not only a Greek national leader but an international statesman.

Campbell, John, and
Sherrard, Philip,

*Modern Greece* (1968).

Dimaras, Konstantinos,

*Istoria tis neoellinikis logotekhnias* (Athens 1948).

Dimaras, Konstantinos,

*La Grèce au temps dea lumières* (Geneva 1969).

Skalieri, G. K.,

*Laoi kai phylai tis Mikras Asias* (Athens 1920).

Woodhouse, C. M.,

*The Greek War of Independence: Its Historical Setting* (1952).

Woodhouse, C. M.,

*Capodistria: The Founder of Greek Independence* (1973).


## Albania

There is one pioneering work in English which throws light on the formation of Albanian national consciousness:

Skendi, Stavro,

*The Albanian National Awakening 1878-1912* (Princeton, N.J. 1967).


## Yugoslav problems

This list mainly comprises works concerned with the twentieth century—dealing with the South Slav problem under the Habsburgs and the creation of Yugoslavia. An exception is Ćubrilović's survey of ideas in Serbia throughout the nineteenth century, and another is Duncan Wilson's study of the pioneer language reformer. The collection of Slobodan Jovanović's posthumous essays includes two brilliant pieces relating to the First World War (on Pašić and on Dimitrijević-Apis). For the modern Yugoslavia since 1945 I have included only two views by American writers—Shoup and Rusinow, of whom both are acute observers but the second is the better. Elizabeth Barker's small book is still unsurpassed as a brief survey of the Macedonian problem, though a vast specialised literature exists.

| | |
|---|---|
| Barker, Elizabeth, | *Macedonia: Its Place in Balkan Politics* (1950). |
| Boban, Ljubo, | *Maček i politika HSS 1928-1941*, 2 vols (Zagreb 1974). |
| Boban, Ljubo, | *Sporazum Cvetković-Maček* (Belgrade 1965). |
| Clissold, Stephen (ed.), | *A Short History of Yugoslavia* (Cambridge 1966). |
| Ćubrilović, Vasa, | *Politička misao u Srbiji XIX veka* (Belgrade 1958). |
| Djordjević, Dimitrije, | *Milovan Milovanović* (Belgrade 1962). |
| Gross, Mirjana, | *Vladavina hrvatsko-srpske koalicije 1906-1907* (Belgrade 1960). |
| Gross, Mirjana, | *Povijest pravaške ideologije* (Zagreb 1973). |
| Hadžijahić, Muhamed, | *Od tradicije do identiteta* (Sarajevo 1974). |
| Janković, D., | *Jugoslovensko pitanje i Krfska deklaracija* (Belgrade 1967). |
| Janković, D., | *Srbija i jugoslovensko pitanje 1914-1915* (Belgrade 1973). |
| Janković, D., and Krizman, B. (ed.), | *Gradje o stvaranju jugoslovenske države*, 2 vols (Belgrade 1964). |
| Jovanović, Slobodan, | *Moji savremenici* (Windsor, Ontario 1962). |
| Marković, Svetozar, | *Srbija na istoku* (first published in 1872) (Zagreb 1946). |
| Purivatra, Atif, | *Nacionalni i politički razvitak Muslimana* (Sarajevo 1969). |
| Rusinow, Denison, | *Titoism 1948-1974: The Yugoslav Experiment* (1977). |

| | |
|---|---|
| Šepić, Dragovan, | *Pisma i memorandumi Frana Supila (1914-1917)* (Belgrade 1967). |
| Šepić, Dragovan, | *Supilo Diplomat* (Zagreb 1961). |
| Šepić, Dragovan, | *Italija, Saveznici i jugoslavensko pitanje 1914-1918* (Zagreb 1970). |
| Seton-Watson, H. and C., Boban, L., Gross, M., Krizman, B., and Sěpić, D., | *R. W. Seton-Watson and the Yugoslavs: Correspondence 1906-1941*, 2 vols (Zagreb and London 1976). |
| Seton-Watson, R. W., | *The South Slav Question* (1911). |
| Shoup, Paul, | *Communism and the Yugoslav National Question* (New York 1968). |
| Šidak, J., Gross, M., Karaman, I., and Šepić, D., | *Povijest hrvatskog naroda g. 1860-1914* (Zagreb 1968). |
| Wilson, Sir Duncan, | *The Life and Times of Vuk Stefanović Karadžić 1787-1864* (Oxford 1970). |
| Zečević, Momčilo, | *Slovenska ljudska stranka i jugoslovensko ujedinjenje* (Belgrade 1973). |
| Zwitter, Fran, | 'Slovenski politični prerod XIX stoletja v okviru evropske nacionalne problematike', in *Zgodovinski časopis* (Ljubljana), vol. XVIII (1964), 75-153. |

## Russia

Most of the following works are either solely or overwhelmingly concerned with the period in which, in my view, Russian national consciousness was being formed, that is, up to the end of the eighteenth century. I have not attempted to make even a short list of works on nineteenth and twentieth century Russia.

| | |
|---|---|
| Cherepnin, L. V., | *Obrazovanie russkovo tsentralizovannovo gosudarstva v 14-15 vekakh* (Moscow 1960). |
| Fennell, J. L. I., | *Ivan the Great of Moscow* (1961). |
| Florinsky, Michael T., | *Russia: A History and an Interpretation*, 2 vols (New York 1953). |

| | |
|---|---|
| Keep, J. L. H., | 'Russia 1613-1645', chapter XIX (2) of *The New Cambridge Modern History*, vol. IV (1970). |
| Klyuchevsky, V. O., | Kurs russkoy istorii, 5 vols (1904-1921, reprinted Moscow 1937). |
| Klyuchevsky, V. O., | vol. 4, translated by Lilian Archibald (1958). |
| Philipp, Werner, | 'Russia: The Beginning of Westernisation', chapter XXV of *The New Cambridge Modern History*, vol. V (1969). |
| Philipp, Werner, | 'Die gedankliche Begründung der Moskauer Autokratie bei ihrer Entstehung 1458-1522' in *Forschungen zur osteuropäischen Geschichte*, vol. 15 (Berlin 1970). |
| Pipes, Richard (ed.), | *Karamzin's Mémoire on Ancient and Modern Russia* (Russian text and English translation, Harvard 1954). |
| Pipes, Richard, | *Russia under the Old Regime* (1974). |
| Raeff, Marc, | *Michael Speransky: Statesman of Imperial Russia 1772-1839* (Hague 1961). |
| Raeff, Marc, | *Origins of the Russian Intelligentsia* (New York 1966). |
| Riasanovsky, Nicholas, | *A History of Russia* (New York 1963). |
| Rogger, Hans, | *National Consciousness in Eighteenth Century Russia* (Cambridge, Mass. 1960). |
| Spuler, Bertold, | *Die goldene Horde* (Leipzig 1943). |
| Sumner, B. H., | *Survey of Russian History* (1944). |
| Vernadsky, George, | *The Mongols and Russia* (New Haven, Conn. 1953). |
| Vernadsky, George, | *Russia at the Dawn of the Modern Age* (New Haven, Conn. 1959). |
| Vernadsky, George, | *The Tsardom of Moscow 1547-1682*, 2 vols (New Haven, Conn. 1969). |

## Ukraine

The following books refer to various periods in the history of the Ukraine, from a Ukrainian rather than a Russian standpoint. Some of the works listed below under *European Empires* also treat Ukrainian problems at some length. There is also material on Galician Ukrainians in volumes of the *Austrian History Year Book* (see *Habsburg Monarchy*).

Armstrong, John A.,    *Ukrainian Nationalism 1939-1945* (New York 1955).

Dzyuba, Ivan,    *Internationalism or Russification?* (1968).

Hrushevsky, Michael,    *A History of Ukraine* (New Haven, Conn. 1941).

Hrushevsky, Michael,    *Abrégé de l'histoire de l'Ukraine* (Paris 1920).

Luckyj, George S. N.,    *Literary Politics in the Soviet Ukraine* (New York 1956).

Mazepa, I.,    *Ukraina v vogni i buri revolyutsii*, 3 vols, 'Prometheus' (?Augsburg 1950).

Reshetar, John S.,    *The Ukrainian Revolution* (Princeton, N.J. 1952).

Stökl, Günther,    *Die Entstehung des Kosakentums* (Munich 1953).


## United States

All the following have been sources of enlightenment to me; but I will stress in particular the works of Richard Hofstadter and David Potter, who were not only admired colleagues but personal friends. Returning to their writings from time to time I do not fail to find fresh wisdom, and to feel the bitter loss of the men who wrote them.

Bailyn, Bernard,    *The Ideological Origins of the American Revolution* (Cambridge, Mass. 1967).

Bailyn, Bernard,    *The Ordeal of Thomas Hutchinson* (Cambridge, Mass. 1974).

| | |
|---|---|
| Brown, Dee, | *Bury My Heart at Wounded Knee* (1971). |
| Cash, W. J., | *The Mind of the South* (New York 1956). |
| Coulter, E. Merton, | *The South during Reconstruction 1865-1877* (Louisiana State University 1947). |
| Craven, Avery, | *The Growth of Southern Nationalism 1848-1861* (Louisiana State University 1953). |
| Dollard, J., | *Caste and Class in a Southern Town* (New York 1957). |
| Dubois, W. E. B., | *The Souls of Black Folk* (Chicago, Ill. 1903). |
| Elkins, Stanley M., | *Slavery* (New York 1959). |
| Franklin, John Hope, | *Reconstruction after the Civil War* (Chicago, Ill. 1961). |
| Frazier, Franklin, | *From Slavery to Freedom: A History of Negro Americans* (3rd ed., New York 1969). |
| Genovese, Eugene D., | *The World the Slaveholders Made* (New York 1971). |
| Handlin, Oscar, | *The Uprooted* (New York 1951). |
| Hofstadter, Richard, | *The Age of Reform: From Bryan to F.D.R.* (New York 1955). |
| Hofstadter, Richard, | *The Progressive Historians: Turner, Beard, Parrington* (New York 1968). |
| Hofstadter, Richard, | *The Idea of a Party System* (Berkeley and Los Angeles, Calif. 1970). |
| Hofstadter, Richard, | *America at 1750: A Social Portrait* (1972). |
| Jones, Maldwyn Allen, | *American Immigration* (New York 1950). |
| Key, V. O., | *Southern Politics* (New York 1957). |
| Kohn, Hans, | *American Nationalism* (New York 1957). |
| Lincoln, G. Eric, | *The Black Muslims in America* (New York 1971). |
| Morison, S. E., and Commager, H. S., | *The Growth of the American Republic*, 2 vols (1942). |

| | |
|---|---|
| Morison, S. E., | *The Oxford History of America*, vols 1 and 2 (New York 1965). |
| Myrdal, Gunnar, | *An American Dilemma: The Negro Problem and Modern Democracy* (New York 1944). |
| Novak, Michael, | *The Rise of the Unmeltable Ethnics* (New York 1971). |
| Pole, J. R., | *Foundations of American Independence 1763-1815* (1972). |
| Potter, David, | *People of Plenty* (Chicago, Ill. 1954). |
| Potter, David, | *The South and the Sectional Conflict* (Louisiana State University 1968). |
| Potter, David, | *History and American Society* (New York 1973). |
| Potter, David, | *The Impending Crisis* (New York 1976). |
| Stampp, Kenneth M., | *The Peculiar Institution* (1964). |
| Stampp, Kenneth M., | *The Era of Reconstruction* (1965). |
| Washington, Booker T., | *Up from Slavery* (New York 1900). |
| Woodward, C. Van, | *Origins of the New South 1877-1913* (Louisiana State University 1951). |

## Spanish America

The works on this list are of uneven quality. Outstanding are the book by Lynch, an excellent picture of the independence struggle, based on sources old and new, and the two by Stephen Clissold, whose admirable clarity of style and wealth of knowledge offer the interested non-specialist so much of what he wishes to know. Andreski's book is a brilliantly provocative analysis, which unfortunately seemed to arouse among specialists more righteous indignation than willingness to discuss serious issues. Victor Alba's survey of Mexican social ideas is also a fine piece of historical and political explanation. Having been encouraged, by friends who are Latin American specialists, to supplement the uneven historical secondary literature by some works of imaginative literature, I not only found this worthwhile but feel that I should include some of these. Outstanding from the point of view of the subject of this book is *Los rios profundos*.

(a) *History, political and social studies*

| | |
|---|---|
| Alba, Victor, | *Las ideas sociales contemporaneas en Mexico* (Mexico City 1960). |
| Alexander, Robert J., | *The Perón Era* (New York 1951). |
| Alexander, Robert J., | *The Bolivian National Revolution* (Washington, D.C. 1965). |
| Andreski, Stanislav, | *Parasitism and Subversion* (1966). |
| Bourricaud, François, | *Pouvoir et société dans le Pérou contemporain* (Paris 1967). |
| Chang-Rodriguez, Eugenio, | *La literatura politica de González Prada, Mariátegui y Haya de la Torre* (Mexico City 1957). |
| Cline, Howard F., | *Mexico: Revolution to Evolution 1940-1960* (1962). |
| Clissold, Stephen, | *Latin America: A Cultural Outline* (1965) |
| Clissold, Stephen, | *Latin America: New World, Third World* (1972). |
| De Avila, F. B., | *Immigration into Latin America* (Secretariat General, O.A.S., Washington, D.C. 1964). |
| Di Tella, Torcuato, Germani, Gino, Graciarena, Jorge, | *Argentina, sociedad de masas* (Buenos Aires 1965). |
| Haya de la Torre, Victor Raul, | *Treinta años de Aprismo* (Mexico City 1956). |
| Humphreys, R. A., | *The Evolution of Modern Latin America* (1946). |
| Kantor, H., | *The Ideology and Program of the Peruvian APRA Movement* (Berkeley and Los Angeles, Calif. 1953). |
| Linke, Lilo, | *Ecuador, Country of Conquests* (1960). |
| Lynch, John, | *The Spanish American Revolutions 1808-1826* (1973). |
| Mariátegui, José Carlos, | *Siete ensayos de interpretación de la realidad Peruana* (Lima 1952). |

Pendle, George,                  *Argentina* (3rd ed. 1963).

Robertson, William               *The Rise of the Spanish-American Repub-*
Spence,                          *lics* (New York 1918).

Salazar Bondy, Sebastián,        *Lima, la horrible* (Mexico City 1964).

Sanchez, Luis-Alberto,           *El Peru: retrato de un país adolescente*
                                 (Buenos Aires 1958).

Silva Herzog, Jesus,             *Breve historia de la revolución mexicana,* 2
                                 vols (Mexico City 1960).

Wolff, Eric R.,                  *Sons of the Shaking Earth* (Chicago, Ill.
                                 1954).

(b) *Literature or literary history, relevant to national, racial and social problems*

Alegria, Ciro,                   *El mundo es ancho y ajeno* (Mexico City
                                 1957).

Arguedas, Alcides,               *Raza de bronce* (Buenos Aires 1945).

Arguedas, José Maria,            *Los rios profundos* (Buenos Aires 1958).

Arguedas, José Maria,            *Todas las sangres,* 2 vols (Buenos Aires
                                 1970).

Franco, Jean,                    *Introduction to Latin American Culture*
                                 (Cambridge 1969).

Fuentes, Carlos,                 *La muerte de Artemio Cruz* (Mexico City
                                 1962).

García Marquez, Gabriel,         *Cien años de soledad* (Buenos Aires 1971).

Spota, Luis,                     *Casi un paraíso* (Mexico City 1956).

Vargas Llosa, Mario,             *La ciudad y los perros* (Barcelona 1965).

## Canada

Approximately half of the following works are historical studies and half political polemics. In the first category one may most strongly recommend the works of Creighton and Wade; in the second, those of Cook, Grant and Rioux.

| | |
|---|---|
| Barbeau, Raymond, | *J'ai choisi l'indépendance* (Ottawa 1961). |
| Chaput, Marcel, | *Pourquoi je suis séparatiste* (Montreal 1961). |
| Cook, Ramsay, | *The Maple Leaf for Ever: Essays on Nationalism and Politics in Canada* (Toronto 1971). |
| Creighton, Donald, | *John A. Macdonald*, 2 vols (Toronto 1952 and 1955). |
| Creighton, Donald, | *Canada's First Century 1867-1967* (Toronto 1970). |
| Grant, George, | *Lament for a Nation: The Defeat of Canadian Nationalism* (Toronto/Montreal 1970). |
| Harvey, Jean Charles, | *Pourquoi je suis anti-séparatiste* (Montreal 1962). |
| Quinn, Herbert F., | *The Union Nationale: A Study in Quebec Nationalism* (Toronto 1963). |
| Rioux, Marcel, and Martin, Yves (eds.) | *French Canadian Society*, vol. 1 (Toronto/Montreal 1971). |
| Rioux, Marcel, | *Quebec in Question* (1971). |
| Wade, Mason, | *The French Canadians 1760-1967*, 2 vols (Toronto 1968). |
| Wrong, G. M., | *Canada and the American Revolution* (Toronto and New York 1935). |

## Australia

Of this short list, the outstanding historical works are the classic by Hancock and the later one of Manning Clark, who has since published more detailed volumes. As examples of intelligent contemporary journalism of their time, the books by Horne and Pringle are of high quality.

| | |
|---|---|
| Coleman, Peter (ed.), | *Australian Civilisation* (Melbourne 1962). |
| Clark, C. Manning H., | *A Short History of Australia* (1964). |
| Hancock, W. K., | *Australia* (3rd ed.) (Brisbane 1961). |
| Horne, Donald, | *The Lucky Country: Australia in the Sixties* (1964). |

Pringle, John Douglas     *Australian Accent* (1958).

Ward, Russell,            *The Australian Legend* (Melbourne 1958).

## The Jews, anti-semitism and Israel

These have been useful to me. Two are outstanding—the essay by Bíbó and
the memoirs of Weizmann. Laqueur's history is an accomplished survey of
a large subject, and Christopher Sykes's study is sensitive and fair-minded.
The others contain plenty of information, including the two anti-semitic
works of Schickert and Schuster. A very large part of my sources has
consisted of articles, whether informative or polemical, over the years,
which cannot be listed here.

Bíbó, István,             'A zsidókérdés Magyarországon', written
                          in 1948, published in *Harmadik út* (1960).

Elon, Amos,               *The Israelis: Founders and Şons* (1971).

Frumkin, Ya. G. (ed.),    *Russian Jewry 1860-1917* (New York
                          1966).

Greenberg, Louis,         *The Jews in Russia*, 2 vols (New Haven,
                          Conn. 1951-53).

Laqueur, Walter,          *A History of Zionism* (1972).

Pulzer, Peter,            *The Rise of Political Anti-Semitism in
                          Germany and Austria* (1964).

Schickert, K.,            *Die Judenfrage in Ungarn* (Berlin 1937).

Schuster, Hans,           *Die Judenfrage in Rumänien* (Leipzig
                          1939).

Segre, V. D.,             *Israel: A Society in Transition* (1971).

Sykes, Christopher,       *Crossroads to Israel* (1965).

Weizmann, Chaim,          *Trial and Error* (1949).

## The Muslim world

(a) *General history*

I remember with gratitude the two books of Brockelmann and Hitti, from
which I obtained my first elementary knowledge of Islamic history when
war took me for the first time to Muslim lands. They may now both be

outdated, but they were exciting and stimulating to a beginner. The two volumes of the Cambridge History embody more recent and deeper scholarship, though not all contributions are of equal quality.

Brockelmann, Karl,      *Geschichte der islamischen Völker und Staaten* (Leipzig 1939).

*Cambridge History of Islam*, 2 vols (Cambridge 1970).

Hitti, Philip,      *The Arabs: A Short History* (1948).

(b) *Modern Arab nationalism*

Antonius's book is a classic apology for Arab nationalism in its early, comparatively liberal phase. Hourani's book is a more recent and more scholarly work covering some of the same ground but also exploring more thoroughly the historical origins. The first book by Kedourie here listed is an original and irreverent study of two idols of Muslim anti-Westernism, the second a collection of brilliant essays, of which the most important from the point of view of my subject is the chapter on Zaghlul. Bernard Lewis's short book remains a brilliantly relevant interpretation. Sylvia Haim's anthology contains a fine selection of rhetoric with a penetrating introduction.

Antonius, George,      *The Arab Awakening* (1939).

Colombe, J.,      *L'évolution de l'Egypte* (Paris 1951).

Haim, Sylvia G. (ed.),      *Arab Nationalism: An Anthology* (Berkeley and Los Angeles, Calif. 1964).

Hourani, Albert,      *Arabic Thought in the Liberal Age 1789-1939* (1962).

Husaini, Ishak Musa,      *The Moslem Brotherhood* (Beirut 1956).

Issawi, Charles,      *Egypt at Mid-century* (1954).

Julien, Charles,      *L'Afrique du nord en marche* (Paris 1952).

Kedourie, Elie,      *Afghani and Abduh* (1966).

Kedourie, Elie,      *The Chatham House Version* (1970).

Khadduri, Majid,      *Independent Iraq* (1951).

Khadduri, Majid,      *Republican Iraq* (1969).

Khadduri, Majid,      *Political Trends in the Arab World* (Baltimore, Md. 1970).

Lewis, Bernard,                *The Arabs in History* (1950).

Nasser, Gamal Abdel,           *Egypt's Liberation* (Washington, D.C. 1955).

## Iran

The two volumes so far published of the *Cambridge History* contain the results of modern scholarship on the first centuries of Islamic Iran. Avery's book is a useful though slightly disorderly collection of information. Browne's study is an indispensible classic. Lambton's book is not directly concerned with nationalism, but throws light on the social realities from which it emerged. Kasravi's enormous work on the constitutional movement, of which I have read a large part but not all, has been very illuminating.

Avery, Peter,                  *Modern Iran* (1965).

Browne, E. G.,                 *The Persian Revolution* (Cambridge 1910).

*Cambridge History of Iran*,   vol. 4: *The period from the Arab invasion to the Saljuqs*, ed. R. N. Frye (1975).

*Cambridge History of Iran*,   vol. 5: *The Saljuq and Mongol periods*, ed. J. A. Boyle (1968).

Kasravi, A.,                   *Tarikh-i-mashrutiyat dar Iran* (Tehran 1961-62).

Lambton, Ann K. S.,            *Landlord and Peasant in Persia* (1953).

## The Turks

The most useful single book on this list is Bernard Lewis's history, covering the nineteenth and twentieth centuries. Inalcik's work on the golden age of the Ottomans is a fine product of modern Turkish scholarship. The books by Bennigsen and Quelquejay and by Zenkovsky might have been placed in the section on European empires, but seem to me rather to belong here, since they are relevant to the history of Turkish national consciousness: both are of high quality, the first the better of the two. The memoirs of Aydemir are a truly fascinating account of the hopes, sufferings, political education and evolution of a young Panturanian who became a Kemalist.

Aydemir, Şevket Süreyya,       *Suyu arayan adam* (Ankara 1959).

| | |
|---|---|
| Bennigsen, Alexandre, and Quelquejay, Chantal, | *Les mouvements nationaux chez les musulmans de Russie* (The Hague 1960). |
| Gökalp, Ziya (ed. Niyazi Berkes), | *Turkish Nationalism and Western Civilisation* (1959). |
| Heyd, Uriel, | *Foundations of Turkish Nationalism* (1950). |
| Inalcik, Halil, | *The Ottoman Empire: The Classical age: 1300-1600* (1972). |
| Karpat, Kemal, | *Turkey's Politics* (Princeton, N.J. 1959). |
| Kinross, Lord, | *Atatürk: The Rebirth of a Nation* (1964). |
| Lewis, Bernard, | *The Emergence of Modern Turkey* (1961) |
| Mango, Andrew, | *Turkey, A Delicately Poised Ally* (Washington, D.C. 1975). |
| Zenkovsky, S. A., | *Pan-Turkism and Islam in Russia* (Cambridge, Mass. 1960). |

## European empires

Of the following works, Lenin's has undoubtedly been the most influential, though as a diagnosis of the phenomenon it can hardly be regarded as sufficient in the fourth quarter of the twentieth century. It is perhaps worth singling out three of the others—Landes's fascinating case study of Egypt, the reconsideration of empire in Africa by Gann and Duignan, and Philip Mason's pioneering attempt to analyse the dominance of nation over nation on the broadest scale.

| | |
|---|---|
| Bennigsen, Alexandre, and Lemercier-Quelquejay, Chantal, | *Islam in the Soviet Union* (1967). |
| Brunschwig, Henri, | *La colonisation française* (Paris 1949). |
| Conquest, Robert, | *The Nation-killers* (1970). |
| Duffy, James, | *Portugal in Africa* (1962). |
| Gann, L. H., and Duignan, Peter, | *The Burden of Empire: An Appraisal of Western Colonisation in Africa South of the Sahara* (Stanford, Calif. 1971). |
| Kolarz, Walter, | *Russia and Her Colonies* (1952). |

Landes, David S.,    *Bankers and Pashas: International Finance and Economic Imperialism in Egypt* (New York 1958).

Lenin, V. I.,    *Imperialism* (written 1917, numerous editions in English).

Mason, Philip,    *Patterns of Dominance* (1970).

Miller, J. D. B.,    *The Commonwealth in the World* (1958).

Perham, Margery,    *Lugard*, 2 vols (1956 and 1960).

Pipes, Richard E.,    *The Formation of the Soviet Union* (Cambridge, Mass. 1954).

Robinson, Ronald, and Gallagher, John,    *Africa and the Victorians: The Official Mind of Imperialism* (1961).

Seton-Watson, Hugh,    'Nationalism and Imperialism' in *The Impact of the Russian Revolution*, ed. Arnold J. Toynbee (1967).

Thornton, A. P.,    *The Imperial Idea and its Enemies* (1959).

Wheeler, Geoffrey,    *The Modern History of Soviet Central Asia* (1964).

Williamson, James A.,    *A Short History of British Expansion* (1934).

## South-east Asia

The following contain plenty of information on the various, very different, countries of south-east Asia, to which I have devoted very little space in this book. I have found particularly illuminating Wang Gung-wu's short but admirably clear essay on the Chinese overseas, Hunter's survey of the whole region, and Bousquet's study of the earliest stages of Muslim nationalism in Java. Devillers's book gives a good account of the development of anti-colonial nationalism in Indochina and the rise of Vietminh and Vietnamese communism. None of the vast literature on the rights and wrongs of the Vietnam war, and of its echoes in United States politics (some of which in book form and in newspaper articles has, inevitably, come my way), has any place in this bibliography.

Bousquet, G.,    *La politique musulmane et coloniale des Pays-Bas* (Paris 1939).

Carlson, Sevinc,               *Malaysia: The Search for National Unity and Economic Growth* (Washington, D.C. 1975).

Coughlin, Richard J.,        *Double Identity: The Chinese in Modern Thailand* (Hongkong 1960).

Devillers, P.,                *Histoire du Vietnam de 1940 à 1952* (Paris 1952).

Feith, Herbert,             *The Decline of Constitutional Democracy in Indonesia* (Ithaca, N.Y. 1962).

Gulick, J. M.,              *Malaya* (1963).

Hall, D. G. E.,             *A History of South-East Asia* (3rd ed. 1968).

Hunter, Guy,               *South-East Asia: Race, Culture and Nation* (1966).

Kahin, G. McT.            *Nationalism and Revolution in Indonesia* (New York 1952).

Tinker, Hugh,              *The Union of Burma* (1957).

Wang Gung-wu,            *A Short History of The Nanyang Chinese* (Singapore 1959).

Wilson, Dick,              *The Future of Singapore* (1972).

**India and Pakistan**

From this list I would stress the works of Romila Thapar (a summary of pre-modern Indian history); Seal and Judith Brown on the national movement before independence; Nagar on language policy after independence; and Brass on nationalism in the 1960s, especially in the Punjab. Kautsky's book was a pioneering study not only of Indian communism but of the problems of communists in any country of 'underdeveloped' social structure and multilingual population. Tinker's is the first volume of a detailed study of overseas Indians.

Aziz, Ahmad,              *Islamic Modernism in India and Pakistan* (1967).

Brass, Paul,               *Language, Religion and Politics in North India* (1975).

Brown, Judith M.,              *Gandhi's Rise to Power: Indian Politics 1915-1922* (Cambridge 1972).

Fickett, Lewis P.,             'The politics of regionalism in India' in *Pacific Affairs* XLIV/2 (Summer 1971).

Franda, Marcus F.,             *Radical Politics in West Bengal* (Cambridge, Mass. 1971).

Kautsky, John H.,              *Moscow and the Communist Party of India* (New York 1956).

Misra, B. B.,                  *The Indian Middle Classes: Their Growth in Modern Times* (1961).

Nagar, Balder Raj,             *National Communication and Language Policy in India* (New York 1969).

Rawlinson, H. G.,              *India: A Short Cultural History* (1943).

Rounaq, Jahan,                 *Pakistan: Failure in National Integration* (New York 1972).

Seal, Anil,                    *The Emergence of Indian Nationalism* (Cambridge 1968).

Spear, Sir Percival,           *A History of India* (vol. 2—since 1526) (1966).

Thapar, Romila,                *A History of India* (vol. 1—to 1526) (1966).

Tinker, Hugh,                  *A New System of Slavery* (1974).

Watson, J. H. Adam,            *The War of the Goldsmith's Daughter* (1964).

Weiner, Myron T.,              *The Politics of Scarcity: Public Pressure and Political Response in India* (Chicago, Ill. 1962).

Weiner, Myron T.,              *Party-building in a New Nation: The Indian National Congress* (Chicago, Ill. 1967).

Zinkin, Taya,                  *India Changes* (1958).

### China

The joint work of Fairbank, Reischauer and Craig seems to an interested non-specialist to be an admirable combination of factual exposition and interpretation. Wittfogel has a place among the great Western scholars of Chinese civilisation. The books by Grieder, Huang, and Meisner place three leading Chinese thinkers of modern times in their historical setting. Mary Wright is an illuminating guide to post-Taiping conservatism, Chow Tse-tung to the young nationalist radicals of 1919, and Benjamin Schwartz to a decisive period in the emergence of Chinese communism. One cannot read the three short reflective volumes of Levenson without bitterly feeling the tragically premature loss of so promising a scholar.

Balazs, Etienne, — *Chinese Civilisation and Bureaucracy* (New Haven, Conn. 1964).

Ch'en, Jerome, — *Yuan Shih-kai 1859-1916* (Stanford, Calif. 1961).

Chow Tse-tung, — *The May Fourth Movement: Intellectual Revolution in Modern China* (Cambridge, Mass. 1960).

Chung Li-chang, — *The Chinese Gentry* (Seattle, Wash. 1955).

Fairbank, J. K., Reischauer, Edwin O., and Craig, Albert M., — *East Asia: Tradition and Transformation* (1973).

Fitzgerald, C. P., — *China: A Short Cultural History* (1942).

Grieder, Jerome B., — *Hu Shih and the Chinese Renaissance* (Cambridge, Mass. 1970).

Herrmann, Albert, — *An Historical Atlas of China* (Chicago, Ill. 1966).

Ho, Peng-ti, — *The Ladder of Success in Imperial China: Aspects of Social Mobility 1368-1911* (New York 1962).

Huang, Philip C., — *Liang Ch'i-ch'ao and Modern Chinese Liberalism* (Seattle, Wash. 1972).

Hu Shih, — *The Chinese Renaissance* (Chicago, Ill. 1934).

Levenson, Joseph R., — *Confucian China and its Modern Fate*, 3 vols (1958, 1963 and 1964).

Meisner, Maurice, — *Li Ta-Chao and the Origins of Chinese Marxism* (Cambridge, Mass. 1967).

Michael, Franz, — *The Taiping Rebellion, Volume One: History* (Seattle, Wash. 1966).

Schramm, Stuart R., — *Mao Tse-tung* (1967).

Schwartz, Benjamin I.,     *Chinese Communism and the Rise of Mao* (Cambridge, Mass. 1951).

Wittfogel, Karl August,     *The History of Chinese Society: Liao* (Transactions of the American Philosophical Society XXXVI, Philadelphia, Pa. 1949).

Wright, Mary Clabaugh,     *The Last Stand of Chinese Conservatism: The T'ung-Chih Restoration 1862-1874* (Stanford, Calif. 1957).

## Japan

Sir George Sansom's works place in their debt not only all outsiders interested in Japan, but even specialists on the subject. The remaining books listed here are concerned with the last period of the Tokugawa regime and the Meiji period. I would especially single out Beasley's recent comprehensive survey and Dore's illuminating study of the pre-revolutionary education system.

Beasley, W. G.,     *The Meiji Restoration* (1973).

Craig, Albert M.,     *Choshu in the Meiji Restoration* (Cambridge, Mass. 1961).

Dore, R. P.,     *Education in Tokugawa Japan* (1965).

Hamada, Kengi,     *Prince Ito* (Tokyo 1936).

Iwata, Masazaku,     *Okubo Toshimichi: the Bismarck of Japan* (Berkeley and Los Angeles, Calif. 1964).

Jansen, Marius B.,     *Sakamoto Ryoma and the Meiji Restoration* (Princeton, N.J. 1961).

Sansom, Sir George,     *Japan: A Short Cultural History* (1931).

Sansom, Sir George,     *The Western World and Japan* (1950).

Sansom, Sir George,     *A History of Japan*, in three volumes: to 1334 (1958); 1334-1615 (1961); and 1615-1867 (1963).

Sheldon, C. D.,     *The Rise of the Merchant Class in Tokugawa Japan* (New York 1958).

| | |
|---|---|
| Smith, Thomas C., | *Political Change and Industrial Development in Japan: Government Enterprise 1868-1880* (Stanford, Calif. 1955). |
| Smith, Thomas C., | *The Agrarian Origins of Modern Japan* (Stanford, Calif. 1959). |
| Storry, Richard, | *The Double Patriots: A Study of Japanese Nationalism* (1967). |

## Sub-Saharan Africa

All the following contain useful information. The works by Oliver and Fage and by Davidson provide clear and readable introductions to the subject. Kirk-Greene's collection of documents on the Nigerian civil war and its origins is an indispensable source. Austin on Ghana, and Levine and Markakis on Ethiopia show not only detailed knowledge but an impressive power of analysis. Andreski is both provocative and penetrating, facing the wrath of specialists who insist on contemplating their various emperors' clothing with ritual reverence. Lowenthal's study of Soviet and Chinese doctrine and practice is included here because it is very largely concerned with Africa.

| | |
|---|---|
| Albino, Oliver, | *The Sudan: A Southern Viewpoint* (1970). |
| Andreski, Stanislav, | *The African Predicament* (1968). |
| Austin, Dennis, | *Politics in Ghana 1946-1960* (1964). |
| Beshır, Mohammed, | *The Southern Sudan: From Conflict to Peace* (1975). |
| Blanchet, A., | *L'itinéraire des partis africains depuis Bamako* (Paris 1958). |
| Clapham, Christopher, | *Haile Selassie's Government* (1969). |
| Coleman, James S., | *Nigeria: Background to Nationalism* (Berkeley, Calif. 1958). |
| Davidson, Basil, | *A History of East and Central Africa* (1969). |
| Davidson, Basil, | *A History of West Africa to the 19th Century* (1966). |
| Hodgkin, T. L., | *Nationalism in Colonial Africa* (1956). |

Kirk-Greene, A. H. M.,    *Crisis and Conflict in Nigeria*, 2 vols (1971).

Legum, Colin,    *Pan-Africanism: A Short Political Guide* (1962).

Levine, Donald N.,    *Wax and Gold: Tradition and Innovation in Ethiopian Culture* (Chicago, Ill. 1965).

Lowenthal, Richard,    *Model or Ally? The Communist Powers and the Developing Countries* (New York, 1977).

Markakis, John,    *Ethiopia: Anatomy of a Traditional Polity* (1974).

Oduho, Joseph, and Deng, William,    *The Problem of the Southern Sudan* (1963).

Oliver, Roland, and Fage, J. D.,    *A Short History of Africa* (1962).

St Jorre, John de,    *The Nigerian Civil War* (1972).

Touval, Saadia,    *Somali Nationalism* (Cambridge, Mass. 1963).

Trevaskis, G. K. N.,    *Eritrea: A Colony in Transition 1941-1952* (1960).

Ullendorff, Edward,    *The Ethiopians: An Introduction to Country and People* (1960).

## South Africa

This enchanting but distressful country does not lack writers worthy of it. Besides the classical surveys by Marquard and de Kiewiet, and Hancock's biography of Smuts, must be placed the more recent Oxford History, Kuper's sociological study, van Jaarsveld's two revealing works on Afrikaner nationalism and the still more recent book by Moodie. The publications of the South African Institute on Race Relations are a mine of information meticulously assembled. One of these authors, M. L. Edelstein, perished at the hands of a black mob in Soweto: his sympathetic study of young Africans' attitudes remains illuminating.

Adam, Heribert,    *Modernising Racial Domination: South Africa's Political Dynamics* (Berkeley, Calif. 1971).

Edelstein, M. L.,     *What Do Young Africans Think?* (Johannesburg 1972).

Hancock, W. K.,     *Smuts*—vol. I: *The Sanguine Years 1870-1919*; vol. II: *The Fields of Force 1919-1950* (Cambridge 1962 and 1968).

Hellmann, Ellen,     *Soweto, Johnnesburg's African City* (Johannesburg 1971).

Horrell, Muriel,     *The African Homelands of South Africa* (1973).

Jaarsveld, F. A. van,     *The Afrikaner's Interpretation of South African History* (Capetown 1963).

Jaarsveld, F. A. van,     *The Awakening of Afrikaner Nationalism* (Capetown 1961).

Kiewiet, C. W. de,     *A History of South Africa, Social and Economic* (1941).

Kuper, Leo,     *An African Bourgeoisie: Race, Class and Politics in South Africa* (New Haven, Conn. 1965).

Marquard, Leo,     *The Peoples and Politics of South Africa* (1952).

Mayer, Philip,     *Urban Africans and the Bantustans* (Johannesburg 1972).

Moodie, T. Dunbar,     *The Rise of Afrikanerdom* (Berkeley and Los Angeles, Calif. 1974).

*Oxford History of South Africa*     (ed. Leonard Thompson and Monica Wilson), 2 vols (Oxford 1969 and 1971).

*Survey of Race Relations in South Africa 1974*     (Johannesburg 1975). (This was the latest available to me of the series published year by the South African Institute of Race Relations.)

Wilson, Francis,     *Labour in the South African Gold Mines 1911-1969* (Cambridge 1972).

**Brazil**

Of the following, Wagley's short book is outstanding in its clarity and objective approach.

Bello, José Maria,    *Historia da Republica* (Rio de Janeiro 1940).

Fernandes, Florestán,    *The Negro in Brazilian Society* (New York 1969).

Freyre, Gilberto,    *The Masters and the Slaves: a Study in the Development of Brazilian Civilization* (New York 1946).

Skidmore, T. E.,    *Politics in Brazil 1930-64* (New York 1967).

Wagley, Charles,    *An Introduction to Brazil* (New York 1963).

# Name Index

Aasen, Ivar, Norwegian language reformer 73

Abbas I, shah of Iran 246, 247

Abbasid dynasty 240, 244, 245

Abboud, General, prime minister of Sudan 346, 347

Abduh, Muhammad, Islamic moderniser in Egypt 250

Abdulhamid II, Ottoman sultan 249, 256, 257

Abdullah, king of Transjordan, later Hashemite kingdom of Jordan 263

Adams, Samuel, American independence propagandist 198

Afonso Henriques, king of Portugal 51

Aga Muhammad, shah of Persia 251

Aguinaldo, Emilio, Philippine nationalist leader 280

Akbar, Moghul emperor 290

Akchura, Yusuf, Turkish nationalist writer 257, 258

Akintola, Samuel, Yoruba political leader in Nigeria 349

Alexander, king of Yugoslavia 139

Alexander I, emperor of Russia 71, 113, 122, 125

Alexander II, emperor of Russia 72, 120, 127, 390, 467

Alexander III, emperor of Russia 85, 87, 148

Alexei, tsar of Muscovy, 82, 118, 186

Alfonso XII, king of Spain 56

Alfred, king of Wessex 23

Ali, Caliph, son-in-law of the Prophet Muhammad 240

Alvarado, General Velasco, Peruvian president 381

Amin, Idi, president of Uganda 342, 408, 437

Anna, empress of Russia 83

Arabi Pasha, Egyptian nationalist leader 248, 250, 325

Arafat, Yassir, Palestinian Arab nationalist leader 269

Arguedas, José Maria, Peruvian writer 381

Argyll, 8th Earl of 32

Arslan, Shakib, Syrian Arab nationalist writer 456

Asquith, Herbert, British prime minister 38, 39

Atatürk, Mustafa Kemal, Ottoman general, later Turkish nationalist leader and president of Turkish Republic 115, 253, 259, 260

Attlee, Clement, British prime minister 296, 331

Aung San, Burmese nationalist leader 457

Awolowo, Chief Obafemi, Yoruba political leader in Nigeria 333, 349, 351

Ayub Khan, Field Marshal, president of Pakistan 304

Azikiwe, Nnamdi, Ibo political leader in Nigeria 332, 348

Babar, founder of Moghul empire in India 274

Bakunin, Michael, Russian anarchist 96, 153, 446

Bălcescu, Nicolae, Romanian nationalist and democratic leader 179

Balfour, Arthur, British prime minister, supporter of Zionism 262, 397

# Subject Index